# Theatre Buildings: New Edition

In 2021, its Diamond Jubilee year, the Association of British Theatre Technicians (ABTT) undertook to revise *Theatre Buildings: A Design Guide* (Routledge, 2010). This new edition (Routledge, 2024) has substantially re-written text with fresh images and entirely new reference projects, providing essential guidance for all those engaged in the design of theatre buildings. Edited by Margaret Shewring (Emeritus Reader, University of Warwick, former Director of the Postgraduate Diploma and MA in Theatre Consultancy), this new publication is written by a team of international experts, architects, theatre consultants, acousticians, engineers and industry professionals led by Tim Foster (Foster Wilson Size) and Robin Townley (CEO of the ABTT).

It provides an invaluable resource for those looking to build, remodel or conserve theatre buildings, taking into account the significant changes which have taken place in the last twelve years in all aspects of theatre design and technical practice. It locates those changes in the wider context of the need for sustainability in the theatre industry in response to the climate emergency, inclusivity, diversity of access, placemaking and concerns for health and wellbeing.

This new edition provides guidance for anyone who seeks inspiration and encouragement to create or improve a place of entertainment or who seeks to understand what might be required to accommodate an audience for the presentation of live performance and the successful use, operation and organisation of such a venue.

Its generous format and the thirty-two new reference projects, more than 260 high-resolution colour images and 175 diagrams and specially commissioned plans make it accessible and informative both to the general reader and the professional specialist.

**Margaret Shewring** is Emeritus Reader in Theatre and Performance Studies at the University of Warwick and former Director of the Diploma and MA in Theatre Consultancy. Much of her research and publication is concerned with spaces for performance from the Renaissance to the present. She is a Fellow of the ABTT.

**Robin Townley** is Chief Executive of the Association of British Theatre Technicians, with over thirty years' experience in the arts and entertainment industry. He is a member of the Standing Committee for *Technical Standards for Places of Entertainment* and Chair of the national Theatre Safety Committee in the UK.

**Tim Foster** is the founding partner in Foster Wilson Architects, now Foster Wilson Size. He is currently chairman of the ABTT Theatre Planning Committee and the former chairman of the International Organisation of Scenographers, Theatre Architects and Technicians (OISTAT) Architecture Commission. He is Fellow of the ABTT and, from 2009–2015, was a trustee of the Theatres Trust.

**David Hamer**, a theatre architect working on the design of both new build and refurbished performing arts venues, works for Theatre Projects consultants. He created the drawings for the ABTT book *Modern Theatres 1950–2020*, published by Routledge in 2021.

# Theatre Buildings
# A Design Guide

**New Edition**

Association of British Theatre Technicians

Edited by Margaret Shewring
Drawings editor David Hamer

Designed cover image: Front cover © Alex Wardle. Back cover (left) © Philip Vile/Foster Wilson Size. Back cover (right) © Chris Dales.

New edition published 2024
by Routledge
4 Park Square, Milton Park, Abingdon, Oxon OX14 4RN

and by Routledge
605 Third Avenue, New York, NY 10158

*Routledge is an imprint of the Taylor & Francis Group, an informa business*



First edition published by Routledge 2010

*British Library Cataloguing-in-Publication Data*
A catalogue record for this book is available from the British Library

*Library of Congress Cataloging-in-Publication Data*
Names: Shewring, Margaret, editor. | Hamer, David (Architect), editor. | Association of British Theatre Technicians, issuing body.
Title: Theatre buildings : a design guide / Association of British Theatre Technicians ; edited by Margaret Shewring ; drawings editor, David Hamer.
Description: New edition. | Abingdon, Oxon : Routledge ; [London] : in association with the ABTT, 2024. | Includes bibliographical references and index.
Identifiers: LCCN 2023016366 (print) | LCCN 2023016367 (ebook) | ISBN 9781032355290 (hardback) | ISBN 9781003327295 (ebook)
Subjects: LCSH: Theater architecture. | Theaters—Designs and plans.
Classification: LCC NA6821 .T447 2024 (print) | LCC NA6821 (ebook) | DDC 725/.822—dc23/eng/20230810
LC record available at https://lccn.loc.gov/2023016366
LC ebook record available at https://lccn.loc.gov/2023016367

ISBN: 978-1-032-35529-0 (hbk)
ISBN: 978-1-003-32729-5 (ebk)

DOI: 10.4324/9781003327295

Typeset in Optima LT Std
by Apex CoVantage, LLC

Printed and bound in Great Britain by
TJ Books Limited, Padstow, Cornwall

# Contents

# Foreword by Nica Burns

To build a new theatre is an immense and rare privilege for everyone involved.

I was lucky enough to be chosen by FTSE 250 property giant Derwent London PLC as their theatre partner in the regeneration of a prime location in a rundown corner of London's West End bounded by Soho and the Charing Cross Road. A fantastic location but with enormous challenges sitting immediately above the Central, Northern and Elizabeth underground lines. The brief to the engineers was tough: no vibrations and no whisper of a train rumble in an auditorium with a target background Noise Rating of 25.

Derwent assembled a top design and build team and I hired my long-time mentor, Association of British Theatre Technicians (ABTT) Fellow Ian Albery, as my personal consultant to guide me through the process. Ian's technical experience is extraordinarily comprehensive: he has built and operated theatres as well as produced. We toured the United Kingdom visiting new-build or substantially refurbished theatres, asking the technical and executive directors two questions: 'What doesn't work?' and 'What would you have done differently?' The answers were information gold.

Capital projects for theatre buildings essentially have two clients: theatre makers and audiences. I asked some of our leading theatre makers, 'If we could dream up a new mid-twenty-first-century West End theatre, what would you like it to be?' and 'What additional facilities would you like it to have?' Surprisingly, there was consensus. They wanted a theatre that would offer new possibilities, so not with a proscenium stage. An intimate, flexible auditorium with perfect acoustics and sight lines and great technical facilities. They dreamed of a rehearsal room on site with a green room and a bar. So that is what we built.

As we own and run six other theatres, we have learnt what audiences want because they tell us. They also want unobstructed views, great acoustics, comfortable seats with good legroom, enough loos, speedy bars, high accessibility standards and, if possible, a restaurant. We built that too.

On 15 October 2022, configured in-the-round, we celebrated the opening night of the first new West End theatre in fifty years. It had taken twelve years. So, what key learning points can I share?

## To the theatre operators

1. Do your research: you could do no better than to start by reading *Theatre Buildings: a Design Guide*, which will give you a vocabulary and framework, an understanding of process and scope, and it will sharpen your appreciation of detail. It will help you frame those most critical first questions. Then, consult with theatre colleagues who have completed builds. You will save time and reduce mistakes.

2. Make sure you have enough people with the right expertise: it will save you money in the end. You need to have your theatre team in design and specialist consultant meetings. You need to be present.

3. There is never enough time, space or money. You will have to drill down and be ruthless with your list of priorities. It is tough. If you get the infrastructure right you will be able to develop, grow and add later. With infrastructure, always have the future in your mind.

4. Think carefully whether you need all your bells and whistles. They can be expensive to build and sometimes prohibitive to run. Assess how much you are going to use equipment and the space it will occupy. Would it be cheaper to hire it in when you need it?

5. Once you have agreed on the vision for the theatre, it is all about the detail. See point 2.

6. Be realistic about the timetable. Give yourself enough time for overruns. You don't want your opening story being one of cancellations and postponements. It was one of the best pieces of advice I received.

## To the design and build teams, consultants and specialists

1. It should be a standard practice for design, construction teams and all the specialist consultants to return to their buildings a year after they have opened and review them with the theatre operating team. It will help you develop and grow your skills to design and build better.

2. Banish the word 'assumption' from the design process. Replace it with 'Ask the operator'. It will be much harder to solve issues created by misunderstandings as to how the theatre will operate once it is up and running. Post-completion fixes will be tough and particularly challenging if the problem is in the auditorium box.

3. Don't be afraid to engage with theatre people. We are disciplined and serious and have great attention to detail. Have the theatre client in the room as much as possible. We are not there to judge or criticise; we are there to work and contribute our operating and theatre-making expertise. We earned our place on the team as a useful asset in building and technical workshops and both the process and the decisions were better. It took time, but we got there!

## To everyone

There is no such thing as too much collaboration between the design, specialist consultants, construction and theatre operating teams. It is impossible to get everything right particularly with new and constantly evolving technology. Theatres are uniquely complex buildings. They are expensive and complicated to build, requiring a great deal of expertise. It is hard. It is also wonderful, exciting and thrilling.

I love my new theatre, as do our audiences, our creative and performing teams, our staff and, thank goodness, the critics. A big thank you to everyone involved – all the care and attention to detail was worth it! We collectively overcame a huge number of challenges and, on the day of our first test performance, I could see the pride and pleasure on the faces of our design, specialist consultants and construction teams. It is a building that we can all be proud of, and when we show it to our children and grandchildren and say 'I helped build this', they will be dead impressed.

What a privilege.

Nica Burns OBE
Theatre Producer and Owner

Photo © Geraint Lewis

**Nica Burns** OBE is an Olivier and *Evening Standard* multi-award-winning producer of over a hundred shows. She is Chief Executive and co-owner of Nimax Theatres which owns six beautiful West End theatres. She is longstanding Director of the UK's most prestigious live comedy awards, the Edinburgh Comedy Awards. In 2013 she was awarded an OBE for Services to Theatre and won UK Private Businesswoman of the Year. In 2021 she was named Producer of the Year at the Stage Awards. In 2022 she was recognised three times: *Evening Standard* Special Award, Critics Circle Award for Exceptional Theatre Making During Lockdown, *WhatsOnStage* Services to Theatre Award. In 2023 she was placed number 3 in *The Stage's* 100. Nica is a Fellow of University College London and was President of the Society of London Theatre 2008–2010 and Vice President 2011–2013. Previous Boards: Donmar Warehouse, Sadler's Wells, Chair of King's Head Theatre. In October 2022 she opened @sohoplace, the first new West End theatre in 50 years, producing 5 shows in its first year.

# Foreword by Mark Dakin

As a theatre technician, production or technical manager and charity trustee, it has been one of the many privileges of my career so far to have worked in, and stood on, the stages of some of the greatest theatres and opera houses on the planet.

The experiences of theatres I've had: from threading hemp rope and dropping wooden pulley blocks into the slatted grid of Teatro Municipale, now Romolo Valli, in Reggio Emilia in the 1980s, to witnessing the transformation of the Royal Opera House Covent Garden in London from a manual to an automated flying house in the late 1990s, and the things I've seen: from watching a hole in the ground be transformed into the dynamic performance space of the Bridge Theatre over a mere fourteen months in 2016/17 or marvelling at the palpable confidence in the future of shared live experience manifest when seeing the MSG Sphere as it rises from the ground in Las Vegas, repeatedly reveal to me that as a 'species' of buildings, I love them all, for their beauty, complexity, diversity and eccentricity.

Theatres have the potential to be uniquely glamorous as social statements about culture, art, entertainment and live performance in the neighbourhood and community in which they are built, renovated or refurbished. They are buildings like no other; ask any facilities director newly arrived into our world and they will confirm it, and while theatres must sustain a whole microcosm of interconnected activities, it is the nature of the sweet spot on the stage, where the performer's relationship to the audience is at its most powerful, which cradles the individual magic of each building. Around that crucible of communication, revelation and empathy, these structures are required to perform diverse and multifarious duties.

They must be unforgivingly functional, on the one hand sustaining and nurturing a financially viable business, on the other managing to deliver a balance between the unbound imagination of the world's directors, choreographers, designers, performers and technicians and the expectations of audiences now often living in the comfort and immediacy of a high-definition, high-fidelity world.

If the first 'technological revolution' was the ropes and pulleys of the eighteenth century – hello Reggio Emilia – the second was the hydro-automation of the late-nineteenth century, and the third was the hydraulic and electronic revolution of the mid-twentieth century, then the new integrated digital technologies of the twenty-first century must be the fourth, driving the need to revisit the technical installations of thirty to fifty years ago and offering both daunting challenges and inspiring opportunities to think differently, build differently and renovate differently.

Post-2020, 'cutting and pasting' past solutions, replacing like for like in an attempt to meet future needs, will serve no one well. Theatre buildings are no different.

High performance, low-impact designs, nimble construction, efficient refurbishment methods, innovative solutions, fully integrated building-wide technologies and deeper consideration of the operational life cycle of theatres are non-negotiables in the shadow of the climate emergency. We must maintain an essential acceleration of the ongoing re-evaluation of priorities.

Provocations for those with the opportunity to design, renovate and refurbish theatre buildings might include some or all of the following list.

- Don't assume you have nothing to learn about what your needs will be, and don't assume anyone else knows what you do: read *Theatre Buildings: a Design Guide* yourself and give copies of it to everyone with whom you must collaborate. It distils the principles and reveals the details you will all need to understand.

- Don't think that if only you get the right lawyers, the commercial contracts you sign will allow you to manage a capital project successfully. Performance is a collaborative art form, and creating successful premises to accommodate it also needs to be collaborative. Clients, design and construction teams should enter into ongoing partnerships. Fixed-price commercialism never did fit a world where the moment the doors are open, the creative process will instantly start to push any envelope you have provided . . . and that is the whole idea, isn't it?

- Don't think you will know what you will want to do tomorrow. The speed of technological change, increasing creative technological literacy and audience technological expectation dictate the need for a rethink of the priorities for any permanent technological installations.

- Don't be seduced by technological flexibility, and always remember the operational advantages of low-fi adaptability.

Theatre buildings require a strong vision and clear business model, which in turn will deliver a robust and complementary technical strategy. That vision's priorities need to be built by people who produce shows.

While clients may feel the need to create new bespoke solutions to underpin their relationships with, and requests to, donors and funders, the pragmatic need to move quickly and efficiently through the building process to opening night and the imperatives of environmental sustainability will often be better served by less elaborate solutions.

As workplaces, theatres need to nurture and enhance the joy of collaborative practice: through the daylight in a green room or rehearsal space or through the adjacencies of offices reinforcing the natural connections and relationships between the roles undertaken by those who use them. They need to facilitate the artistic application of technical expertise through sympathetic, integrated digital networks, and they need to ensure systems which enhance and deliver the artistic vision of creatives are balanced so they also optimise the business imperatives of producers and operating organisations.

So, when designing, renovating or refurbishing a theatre building, always, always, always speak openly with, and listen carefully to, the people who will inhabit and use it.

Mark Dakin
Principal Placemaking, TAIT

Photo © TAIT

**Mark Dakin** is Principal Placemaking at TAIT, the global company of creative engineers, fabricators, producers and technologists who bring the *extraordinary* to life for artists, performing arts spaces and brands. He has over forty years of professional theatre experience working as a technician, manager and trustee for some of the United Kingdom's most prolific producing and performing arts organisations, including the Royal Opera House Covent Garden, the National Theatre, English National Opera, Theatre Royal Stratford East, the Young Vic, Cameron Macintosh, Really Useful, the Bush Theatre, Bristol Old Vic and the Yard. A dyslexic art school drop-out with a passion for building inclusive, equitable and psychologically safe places of work and an aptitude for the detailed work of culture change, Mark is also a proud ABTT Fellow, Stage Sight co-director and Tangle associate.

# Preface

In February 2019 the Association of British Theatre Technicians held a meeting in London to discuss the potential need for a new edition of *Theatre Buildings: A Design Guide*, edited by Judith Strong and published by Routledge in association with the ABTT in 2010, itself a successor to the ABTT's pioneering theatre planning publications of 1972 and 1986, edited by Roderick Ham.

A great deal had changed in attitudes to theatre buildings, their accessibility and working practices since the first edition of *Theatre Buildings*, and the ABTT wanted to take the opportunity of their sixtieth anniversary in 2021 to commission a new edition to reflect these changes and their importance in relation to the design of theatres and other performance venues going forward.

The meeting in February 2019 was attended by Judith Strong and by many of the section editors and contributors of the first edition as well as others who had helped to shape developments and changing attitudes in the years since its publication in 2010. Some of the section editors were interested in taking *Theatre Buildings* forward, alongside several new section editors and contributors. At that time none of us anticipated the huge disruption to the theatre industry and its audiences that would be caused by the COVID-19 pandemic and the subsequent national and international lockdowns. Individually and collectively, we had to contemplate the unthinkable: not just how, but whether, our theatres could survive and even thrive again.

The target audience for the first edition were those building owners, users, design teams and stakeholders who were embarking on the process of building a new theatre or converting or renovating an older building. It was written at a time of rapid expansion of new audiences and new technologies, drawing on the work of architects and theatre consultants with international reputations and the creative teams and theatre managements with whom they collaborated.

This new edition, edited by Margaret Shewring, alongside a board of experienced section editors chaired by Tim Foster and guided by Robin Townley, seeks to build on the legacy of the first edition while articulating changing attitudes to the ways in which theatre buildings are designed and operated, as they have evolved over the last twelve years, reflecting new thinking and new technology for the next generation. It has been created in the context of a growing awareness of the pressing threat of the health and climate emergencies not just to the theatre industry and those employed by it but to those for whom theatre buildings offer entertainment, wellbeing, community engagement, education and inclusivity.

More than fifty contributors have shared their knowledge and expertise to develop guidance on a sustainable way forward. It has been produced with a strong commitment to social responsibility and with attention to best practices across theatres and the creative industries, as well as the importance of a theatre's place in its community. As before, this new edition takes the reader through the whole process of planning, remodelling or restoring a performance venue. It gives specific guidance on sightlines, acoustics, ventilation, stage engineering, lighting, sound and video, auditorium and stage format, front of house spaces and the backstage creative environment, as well as the particular issues raised by historic buildings. All the sections draw on examples from the last twelve years of theatre and performance venue developments and seek to highlight a series of key themes: inclusivity, diversity, access and safety, as well as crucial responses to health and economic emergencies and to the critical climate crisis, with its need for us all to embrace more sustainable practices into the future.

The main sections are followed by thirty-two reference projects, all of which are new to this edition. These case studies, which are well illustrated and include each building's plan and section (drawn to the same scale throughout), have been selected to provide detailed examples of a wide range of performance spaces, many built with adaptability in mind. They include new buildings, renovations, conversions, temporary and found spaces in a wide variety of sizes and formats.

This edition also includes a list of acronyms and abbreviations, an extended glossary of theatre terminology and a list of suggested further reading and useful organisations, all created to help anyone who wants to become involved in the building, restoration or operation of a theatre, as well as more than 260 colour illustration and 175 diagrams and drawings.

Margaret Shewring, Tim Foster and Robin Townley
March 2023

# Acknowledgements

We should like to express our thanks to all the book's contributors, former and current, for their generous support and their willingness to engage in discussions to enable us to bring together this new edition, as well as to the numerous photographers who have allowed us to use their images. Thanks are due, too, to former and current chairs of the ABTT and their teams, to the former editors of *Sightline*, the ABTT's journal of theatre technology and design, to its current editor Rebecca Morland and to the team at the Theatres Trust.

Particular thanks go to our drawings editor, David Hamer, and to our photographic editor, Sarah Wells, as well as to our photo researcher, Susannah Jayes. Fran Ford, senior publisher in architecture with Taylor & Francis (Routledge imprint); her former editorial assistant Trudy Varcianna; and her current editorial assistant Hannah Studd and Sophie Dixon-Dash, production editor (books), have been enormously helpful in guiding us through the production process: as have Kate Fornadel, senior project manager at Apex CoVantage and her team. We are most grateful to all them, their copyeditor and their graphic design team for their enthusiasm and patience.

Margaret Shewring, Tim Foster and Robin Townley
March 2023

# Contributors

## Notes on the editorial team, principal section editors, key theme contributors and section contributors

**The Association of British Theatre Technicians** is a membership organisation which sets and upholds standards in technical excellence, safety and compliance for theatre and live performance. The ABTT is a resource to support members through the provision of information and advice on good practice, safe working and enforcement within the theatre industry. It seeks to continuously advance technical expertise in theatre and live performance, advising on safety, planning, good practice and enforcement and providing publications to support this knowledge. The ABTT works with a range of organisations that all seek to support and promote varying aspects of theatre and live performance. The ABTT is the copyright holder for both the first edition and this new edition of *Theatre Buildings: a Design Guide*.

## Editorial team

**Editor: Margaret Shewring**, BA (Hons), PhD (University of Birmingham), is Reader Emeritus in Theatre and Performance Studies, School of Creative Arts, Performance and Visual Cultures, and former Course Director of the Postgraduate Diploma and MA in Theatre Consultancy at the University of Warwick. Her research concerns the performance context for Shakespeare and his contemporaries in London, Renaissance and Early Modern European court and civic festivals and entertainments and the design of spaces for performance today. She was associate editor of the Manchester University Press Shakespeare in Performance series (for nineteen volumes). Her monograph *Richard II in Performance* was published in 1996. With Ronnie Mulryne, Margaret owned a small independent publishing company. Their books concerned developments in theatre: *This Golden Round: The Royal Shakespeare Company at the Swan* (1989: with Michael Reardon and in collaboration with the RSC); *Making Space for Theatre: British Architecture and Theatre since 1958* (1995: with Iain Mackintosh and in collaboration with the British Council); *Shakespeare's Globe Rebuilt* (1997: with Andrew Gurr and in association with Cambridge University Press; reprinted in paperback, 2009); and *The Cottesloe at the National: Infinite Riches in a Little Room* (1999: with Jason Barnes and Iain Mackintosh and in association with the National Theatre). Margaret was co-founder with J. R. (Ronnie) Mulryne and Margaret M. McGowan of the Society for European Festivals Research and is a co-general editor of the society's series of publications. She is a member of the Society for Theatre Research, the Malone Society, the Society for Renaissance Studies and the International Shakespeare Association. In 2023 she was made a Fellow of the ABTT. She is a friend of the Theatres Trust.

**ABTT: Robin Townley** is Chief Executive of the Association of British Theatre Technicians. He has over 30 years' experience in the arts and entertainment industry gained in organisations such as the English National Opera, Stoll Moss Theatres, Theatre Projects Services, the Junction, DanceEast and Rambert. Robin has worked as a stage electrician, lighting hire client contact, lecturer in performance technology, technical director, building director and theatre consultant. He has delivered three new-build capital projects for performing arts organisations: the Junction, Cambridge; the Jerwood DanceHouse, Ipswich; and Rambert on the South Bank in London. Robin served as a founding member of the ABTT Training and Education Committee, a trustee of the ABTT and its honorary secretary. He is a member of the Standing Committee for *Technical Standards for Places of Entertainment* and chair of the national Theatre Safety Committee in the UK.

**Editorial Board Chair: Tim Foster**, MA, Dip Arch (Cantab), RIBA, was the founding partner in Foster Wilson Architects (formerly Tim Foster Architects), now Foster Wilson Size. Before establishing the practice in 1979, he worked for Roderick Ham and Partners and as consultant architect to Theatre Projects Consultants. Tim has been responsible for many theatre projects carried out by the practice, including the Tricycle Theatre and Cinema; the Salisbury Playhouse Redevelopment; the Trafalgar Studios; the Broadway Theatre in Barking; the redevelopment of the Theatre Royal Norwich; the Yaa Centre in West London; the restoration of the Everyman Theatre in Cheltenham; and St James Theatre, London. Educational projects include the Parabola Arts Centre for Cheltenham Ladies' College, the Caryl Churchill Theatre at Royal Holloway University and The Quarry Theatre at St Luke's for Bedford School. Tim was chair of the editorial board and a contributor to Judith Strong (ed.), *Theatre Buildings: A Design Guide*, published by Routledge in 2010. He is chairman of the ABTT Theatre Planning Committee and the former chair of the Architecture Commission of the International Organisation of Scenographers, Theatre Architects and Technicians (OISTAT). In 2019 he was a member of the international jury at the Prague Quadrennial. He was elected Fellow of the ABTT in 2012. From 2009 to 2015 he was a trustee of the Theatres Trust, the national advisory body for theatres in the United Kingdom.

**Drawings Editor: David Hamer**, BA (Hons) Architecture (Oxford Brooks University); Dip Arch (Brighton University); RIBA Part 3, Practice and Management (Oxford Brooks University), is a theatre architect working on the design of both new-build and refurbished performing arts venues. Earlier in his career he worked on the scenery design of opera and theatre productions for many companies including Welsh National Opera, English National Opera and the Royal Shakespeare company. He currently works for Theatre Projects, where his background in both theatre and architecture gives him a valuable insight into how complex theatre spaces are designed around the needs of the users. David has a passion for all stages of the design process from the formation of the client brief through to detailed design and site inspection. Recent buildings he has worked on include the transformation of Greighallen in Bergen, the Shangyin Opera house and the LG Arts Centre, Seoul. David also created the drawings for the ABTT book *Modern Theatres 1950–2020* (ed. by David Staples), published by Routledge in 2021. These drawings serve as an accompaniment to the text in exploring the characteristics of some of the most significant theatres constructed since 1950.

## Section editors and key theme contributors (in alphabetical order)

**Nafeesah Butt** studied stage management at Rose Bruford College and worked for ten years as a stage and company manager in both the subsidised and commercial sectors before working at the National Theatre, where she was part of the team who reopened the Dorfman Theatre and Clore Learning Centre following major redevelopment works. She was then General Manager of Kiln Theatre's capital project and went on to support a number of organisations undertaking organisational change alongside capital projects. Creating safe and imaginative spaces is always at the heart of Nafeesah's practice. Since 2021 Nafeesah has worked at Arts Council England as a relationship manager in the London Theatre team. She has been a trustee at Company Three and the Gate Theatre Notting Hill, a steering group member of Freelancers Make Theatre Work (FMTW; an advocacy and support organisation) and on the advisory committee for Mulberry University Technical College's (UTC's) Performing Arts Group (Tower Hamlets, East London). She has a particular interest in the intersection of social justice and the work of the creative sectors.

**Paddy (Patrick) Dillon** is an award-winning theatre architect. He is Interim Chair of the United Kingdom's Theatres Trust and chairs the International Theatre Engineering and Architecture Conference. In May 2020, he began the *Theatre Green Book*, an initiative to help UK theatres move towards sustainability. The first volume, *Sustainable Productions*, is being used by theatre-makers across the United Kingdom, with interest from around the world. The remaining volumes, *Sustainable Buildings* and *Sustainable Operations*, address the challenge of moving theatre as a whole towards a sustainable future.

**Simon Erridge** is an architect and director of Bennetts Associates. His twenty-year experience in theatre architecture has included leading roles in major theatre and performing-arts projects for clients including the Royal Shakespeare Company, the Old Vic and Shaftesbury Theatre. Simon is interested in the changing role of theatres and cultural buildings in our towns and cities, and his projects include new buildings such as Hampstead Theatre, as well as projects which re-purpose existing historic theatre buildings for contemporary use. The Royal Shakespeare Theatre project, which opened in 2011, involved the creation of a brand-new 1000-seat thrust-stage auditorium within the shell of the existing historic building but also involved the opening up of the RSC's Stratford-upon-Avon theatres for all-day visitors. The project was shortlisted for the RIBA Stirling Prize in 2011. Innovative thinking has been central to many of Simon's other projects, which include Storyhouse in Chester, one of a new breed of cultural hubs which are helping to regenerate town and cities. The building, which is open all day seven days a week, contains a theatre, a public library and cinema. Storyhouse has proved that with the right approach, theatre buildings can offer their communities much more than just a venue for attending performances.

**Paul Gillieron**, BSc (Hons), Physics, MIOA, is the Founding Director of Paul Gillieron Acoustic Design, a consultancy specialising in the acoustics of performance spaces and sound system design, and Founder of Brixton Art House in 1999 – a not-for-profit mixed-use arts centre on Brixton Hill serving the local community with two dance studios, four recording studios, offices and ten apartments. His is also Co-Director of Gillieron Scott Acoustic Design with Tim Scott, BSc (Hons) Audio Technology, MIOA, Salford University, 2015. Gillieron Scott specialises in auditoria with adaptable natural acoustics for orchestral, choral and chamber performances; opera; lyric theatre; drama; conferences; and amplified music. Their projects include the Royal Court, Crystal Palace Concert Bowl, The Roundhouse, LAMDA, the Young Vic, the Bridge Theatre, Sam Wanamaker Playhouse, Hoxton Hall, Battersea Arts Centre and Woolwich Works – all in London. Outside London, their projects include The Quarry Theatre at St Luke's, Bedford; MAXXI museum, Rome; Afragola TAV station, Naples; Saffron Hall and Music Centre, Liverpool Everyman Theatre; the Tom Wheare Music School, Bryanston School; Chichester Festival Theatre; Eavis Hall, Wells Cathedral School; Sarah Abraham Hall, Brighton College; and the Nazrin Shah Centre, Oxford. Paul is a Celtic musician, jazz saxophonist, composer and music producer (www.gsacoustics.org).

**Paul Handley**, BA (Hons) in English Literature, is Production and Technical Director at the National Theatre. Previously he was Head of Production at the Royal Court Theatre. He has worked for over twenty years a production manager on many productions in both the subsidised and commercial sectors, including many premières such as *Ashes to Ashes* (1996) by Harold Pinter and *Jerusalem* (2009) by Jez Butterworth, both at the Royal Court Theatre, and *The Hard Problem* (2015) by Tom Stoppard at the National Theatre of Great Britain, Dorfman Theatre. He sits on the advisory committee of the Linbury Prize for Performance Design. The primary passion of his working life has been the delivery of new plays to the stage and the support of the writers, directors and designers who make them. He speaks regularly on the future environmental sustainability of theatre.

**Chris McDougall** has over twenty years' experience working in technical theatre management, having worked at four national performing arts organisations and various producing theatre companies. In these positions, he has taken part in several capital projects involving both renovations and new builds. He is currently employed as Technical and Building Manager for the Edinburgh Playhouse. Previously he was Head of Technical and Production at the Esplanade Theatres–Singapore, where he was part of the project team assisting in the development of the brief and concept designs for a new waterfront theatre within Singapore's iconic Marina Bay. He also worked for the National Theatre as Technical and Client Project Manager for the redevelopment of the Cottesloe Theatre, later known as the Dorfman Theatre. He was responsible for the construction and delivery of the Dorfman Theatre, its foyer and two flexible creative learning/event rooms and the construction and operation of an award-winning on-site temporary venue, the Shed. He spent many years working as a freelance technical advisor, assisting organisations through large-scale capital projects, including Dance House Helsinki, Finland's first dedicated dance venue, and commissioning the stage engineering systems on behalf of Charcoalblue for P&O's flagship cruise liner, *Iona*. He also regularly undertakes organisational reviews for performing arts organisations. He is a keen believer in lifelong learning and has worked with various organisations, assisting in curriculum and skills competency framework development for the technical arts industry as well as guest lecturing at the Royal Conservatoire of Scotland.

**Julian Middleton**, BA (Hons), Dip Arch, Head of Project Design at Delfont Mackintosh Theatres Ltd., formerly Executive Director of AEDAS Arts Team Architects, specialises in the design of buildings to support the performing arts. He has extensive experience in auditorium design and in the early stages of project development, including brief writing, feasibility and concept work. Julian has designed both imaginative new-build auditoria and restored some of the United Kingdom's most historic performance venues. He has over twenty-five years of experience working exclusively in the performing arts sector. Julian's first theatre project was the acclaimed Donmar Warehouse Theatre, working in collaboration with director Sam Mendes. This small, character-filled theatre space went on to gain an international reputation – and is where he learnt his craft. Early projects included work on Bridgewater Hall, Manchester's international concert hall, Sadler's Wells Theatre and the home of Chickenshed, the integrated youth theatre company. He went on to lead projects including the innovative re-working of Northern Stage with directors Alan Lyddiard and Erica Whyman. Alongside new-build projects, he also designed and led acclaimed refurbishments of nationally important historic venues, including the Theatre Royal in Waterford, working with director Ben Barnes. Julian has worked with the team at Delfont Mackintosh Theatres for over twenty-five years, including auditoria in Stuttgart and Duisburg to host productions of *Miss Saigon* and *Les Misérables*; the refurbishment of the art-deco Prince of Wales Theatre; the re-imagining of the Victoria Palace Theatre, London; and, most recently, the transformation of the Sondheim Theatre.

**Andrew Nicholson**, BEng, MSt (Cantab), CEng, MIFireE, is Founder and Director of the Fire Surgery Ltd, an independent fire engineering consultancy in London. He is a chartered fire engineer with over twenty-five years' experience with fire engineering design. He was part of the second year to graduate from the unique fire engineering degree from the Holdsworth School of Applied Science at the University of Leeds and also holds a master's degree from the School of Architecture at the University of Cambridge. He has been responsible for the development of fire strategies for some of the most high-profile buildings around the United Kingdom. He has a special interest in public and cultural buildings, including theatres, music venues, galleries and museums and particularly heritage buildings. He has a passion for innovation and creative design and driving industry standards forward. He was a principal author of BS 9999, the advanced approach to fire safety design in the United Kingdom, and sits on numerous British Standard committees for fire safety. He is a committee member of the Institution of Fire Engineers special interest group for heritage fire safety and lectures regularly on this subject. He is a member of the standing committee of the ABTT and contributes to the updates of the *Technical Standards for Places of Entertainment*. Andrew won Best Fire Strategy of the year from the Society of Fire Protection Engineers in 2015 for the Sam Wanamaker candle-lit theatre at Shakespeare's Globe and also in 2021 for the new fire strategy for the Royal Albert Hall.

**Barry Pritchard** was a principal director of RHWL architects. He co-founded Arts Team, the practice's specialist team that designed theatres, concert halls and arts centres. He 'got into theatre' as a member of the National Youth Theatre of Great Britain before qualifying as an architect and undertaking a master's degree in architectural conservation. Practical theatre experience, architecture and building conservation form the basis of his professional career. For over forty years, Barry has been involved with forty built arts projects, including lauded theatre refurbishments; award-winning new venues; the restoration of the historically important Brighton Dome and London Coliseum; and a new building for the Guildhall School of Music and Drama, Milton Court, at the Barbican. As well as many high-profile projects, Barry has been involved with significant smaller projects, numerous studies and design proposals for new and expanding performing arts facilities. Barry is currently bringing this extensive experience to bear on a range of international projects with global theatre consultants Theatreplan. In 2015 he was made an associate of the National Youth Theatre of Great Britain. He is a member of the ABTT's Theatre Planning Committee and was a council member and honorary secretary of the ABTT (1992–1998).

**John Riddell**, BA (Hons) in History and Drama (King Alfred's College, Winchester), MA in Theatre Consultancy with distinction (2012) and PhD in Theatre Studies (2022), both University of Warwick, joined Theatre Projects (TP) as a consultant in 2008 and is now Principal Consultant and project leader. John worked for many years as a technician, lighting designer and production manager. He lit shows for many of Ireland's leading theatre companies, including the Lyric Theatre, Belfast, where he was Lighting Designer in Residence from 1995–1999. In 2000–2001 he conducted Auditoria, a technical survey of more than one hundred venues jointly commissioned by the Arts Councils of Ireland and Northern Ireland. John also worked in Scotland as a construction manager and production manager for the Scottish Opera and the Royal Conservatoire of Scotland, among others. Since joining TP, John has led teams delivering the design of many new build and refurbishment projects for theatres in the United Kingdom. He also contributes extensively to the early briefing and planning information on TP projects across the globe. His doctoral thesis concentrated on theatre spaces in Northern Ireland. John is a professional member of the Association for Lighting Production and Design, a professional member of the Institute of Theatre Consultants, a member of UK Theatre and a member of the International Society for the Performing Arts.

**Michèle Taylor** is Director for Change for Ramps on the Moon, the Arts Council England–funded consortium working to enrich the stories we tell and how we tell them by normalising the visibility of disabled and deaf people across the theatre industry. This programme is achieving a step change in the employment and artistic opportunities for D/deaf and disabled performers and creative teams and a cultural change in the participating organisations and beyond to enable accessibility to become a central part of their thinking and aesthetics. Following a career in theatre, Michèle set up her business as an independent trainer and strategist in disability issues. She has been running her own business for over thirty years training and advising arts, cultural and heritage organisations on making their practices, policies and premises inclusive of disabled people. Clients have included strategic bodies such as arts councils and local authorities as well as the Royal Shakespeare Company; the Royal Opera House; universities including Nottingham, Gothenberg and the University of the Arts in London; the British Museum; and Cultural Heritage Without Borders. Michèle is a registered member of the Institute of Equality and Diversity Professionals. She is an accredited coach, one half of the comedy duo Bitter and Twisted and has an MA in fine art photography. Michèle was recognised for her work by being awarded an MBE in the 2022 New Year's Honours List.

**Steve Tompkins**, MBE, LLD (hon), BArch, RIBA, is a founding director of Haworth Tompkins architects (AJ100 UK Practice of the Year 2022 and 2020, BD UK Architect of the year 2019, Stirling Prize winner 2014), a trustee of the Young Vic theatre and an ABTT Fellow. For twenty-five years he has led the studio's performing arts team alongside co-director Roger Watts. His completed performance projects include the Royal Court, the Regent's Park Open Air Theatre, The Bath Egg, the Young Vic (Stirling Shortlisted), the Oxford North Wall, Snape Maltings, the Liverpool Everyman (Stirling winner), the NT Studio, the NT Future project, the NT Shed, Chichester Festival Theatre, Battersea Arts Centre, the Bush, the Den in Manchester, the Bridge Theatre in London, Bristol Old Vic, the Peter Hall Performing Arts Centre Cambridge, Theatre Royal Drury Lane, Punchdrunk and the @ sohoplace auditorium. Current Haworth Tompkins performance projects include Theatr Clywd; the Kings Cross Lightroom; a new performance centre for the American Repertory Theater and Harvard University; the new Olympia Theatre interior; a new theatre for The Court in Christchurch NZ; the Old Vic Annexe; a major refurbishment of the Malmo Staatsteater; and a new cultural centre in Bergen, Sweden. In 2019 Steve co-founded the environmental group Architects Declare in response to the planetary emergency, now over 5000 practices strong in twenty-eight countries around the world.

**Alex Wardle**, BSc, MA, is a theatre consultant and lighting designer for Charcoalblue, previously a theatre consultant for Arup 2005–2011 and production manager for Kneehigh Theatre 1999–2005. Time with Kneehigh included site-specific productions in Cornwall and tours to Australia, China, New Zealand, Scandinavia, Syria and the United States. Alex studied German and Electronics at Keele University, then Theatre Arts at the Freie Universität Berlin and at Goldsmiths' College, University of London. Whilst studying for an MA at Goldsmiths' he directed the UK stage premiere of Paul Hindemith's one-act expressionist opera *Sancta Susanna*. He plays violin in his local amateur orchestra. Alex has worked on a number of high-profile projects, including the award-winning Dorfman Theatre at the National Theatre and the new Sadler's Wells Theatre at London's Olympic Park. Refurbishment projects in which he has been involved include Chichester Festival Theatre; Perth Theatre, Scotland; Darlington Hippodrome and neighbouring Hullabaloo Theatre; Glasgow City Halls; and the Royal College of Music, London. New build projects include the Théâtre Elisabéthain au Château d'Hardelot in northern France; Mareel, Shetland; Grand Canal Theatre, Dublin; Royal Birmingham Conservatoire; Brixton House (formerly Ovalhouse), London; and @sohoplace, the new West End theatre for Nimax.

**Emma Wilson**, BA (Hons) University of Warwick, MSc Imperial College London and PhD Metropolitan University, is the Director of Technical, Production & Costume at the Royal Opera House and has specialist interest in the areas of sustainability, workforce inclusion and diversity and health and safety in theatre. She is a trustee director of the ABTT, sits on the ABTT Safety Committee and is a member of SAGE (Safety Advisory Group for Entertainment). Prior to moving to the Royal Opera House in 2020, Emma was Director of Technical and Production at Sadler's Wells for 11 years, where she had the additional duty of Director of Health and Safety. She also chaired the Sustainability Committee, responsible for devising and implementing the policy and action plan for the organisation; is on the *Theatre Green Book* Steering Committee; and the Steering Committee for Opera Europa (Technical Directors). Emma has an academic background in environmental studies, with a PhD in Cultural Theory and Environmental Politics.

**Andrew Wylie** is a partner at Buro Happold with responsibility for leading the portfolio of the UK Culture Sector projects. His specialism is in structural engineering, and he has experience of leading multi-disciplinary design teams on a range of complex new build and refurbishment projects with particular experience in theatre buildings. Andrew has completed a Masters' degree in inter-disciplinary design for the built environment at the University of Cambridge and is a chartered engineer; he is also a member of the Association of British Theatre Technicians (ABTT). Most recently Andrew led the Buro Happold team in creating the *Theatre Green Book* and is currently engaged in authoring the Arts Green book for the ACE and GLA. He has worked on a number of high-profile theatre projects, including The Marlowe theatre in Kent, the Royal Shakespeare Theatre at Stratford-upon-Avon, The Factory in Manchester, the Centre for Music in London and the Birmingham Hippodrome. Andrew is leading Buro Happold's response to the climate emergency focusing on low-carbon engineering.

## Section contributors

**Peter Angier** was Founder, with Martin Carr, of Carr & Angier Theatre Consultants in 1974. He is Principal of the practice.

**Claire Appleby** is an architect and is the Architectural Advisor at the Theatres Trust, where she manages the Trust's work with Theatres at Risk and coordinates Advisory Review panels. She also sits on the ABTT Committee that oversees technical standards.

**Dominic Bilkey** is Head of Sound and Video at the National Theatre; formerly Head of Sound at the Young Vic. He also works freelance as a sound designer and has been nominated for Olivier and Tony Awards.

**Sarah Brigham** is Artistic Director and Chief Executive at Derby Theatre. Sarah has worked as a director, performer and facilitator across the United Kingdom and Europe. She was Artistic Director at the Point in Eastleigh and Associate Director at Dundee Rep, where she led their thriving Creative Learning Team.

**Borneo Brown** was formerly Head of Sound and Video at the National Theatre and Audio Manager at the Royal Albert Hall. He is currently a freelance theatre consultant, sound designer and engineer.

**Giuseppe Cannas**, HNC and HND in make-up and hairdressing (University of Westminster), is a freelance hair and make-up designer, former Head of Wigs, Hair and Make-up at the National Theatre (2011–2020). Cannas worked on *The Lion King* in Sydney, Melbourne, Shanghai, Johannesburg, Taiwan and Singapore (2011) before joining the National Theatre, London.

**Hazel Clover** heads up strategic, business and operational planning services for Theatre Projects. She has an MA in Theatre Consultancy from the University of Warwick and was on the editorial board of the 2014 International Theatre Engineering and Architecture Conference.

**Feimatta Conteh** is the Environmental Sustainability Manager at Factory International. She has worked across sustainability, technology development, digital culture and the arts for over fifteen years for organisations including the LSE, Arcola Theatre, Arcola Energy and FutureEverything.

**Mike Cook** is a director of property advisers Avison Young, leading on the project management of capital/construction projects in performing arts venues. His projects include the refurbishment of the grade 1-listed Theatre Royal Drury Lane, Liverpool Everyman Theatre, York Theatre Royal and Shaftesbury Theatre.

**George Ellerington** was a theatre consultant at Arup 2004–20 and previously worked at Theatre Projects Consultants, designing technical systems for theatres and music venues around the globe. Prior to theatre consulting, he worked at the National Theatre's production office.

**Gary Faulkner** has been a partner at Gardiner & Theobald LLP since 1999 and has over thirty years' experience specialising in the cost management of construction works for the performing arts. Gary was a contributor to the previous edition of this book.

**Karin Gartzke** is an arts management consultant and executive coach with a comprehensive understanding of the performing arts industry, having worked for forty years in UK theatre and international performing arts, both subsidised and commercial, including for Ambassador Theatre Group, the South Bank Centre and Arts Council England.

**Musa Halimeh** is currently the programme manager for the renewal of the technical estate and stage automation systems at the Royal Opera House in London. He previously worked as automation engineer for Dubai Opera and with Flying by Foy.

**Rob Halliday** is a lighting designer and programmer for theatre, film and television and works as a lighting consultant, specifying equipment for projects including Leicester Curve and Chester Storyhouse. He writes regularly for entertainment industry publications, including *Light & Sound International* (PLASA).

**Simon Harper** is co-director of Harper Tackley Consultants, where he advises and supports arts organisations on capital projects or organisational change. He has been involved in many major capital projects, including the Royal Court Theatre and the Coliseum in London and the RST in Stratford-upon-Avon.

**Darren Joyce** is currently the Managing Director of Cardiff Theatrical Services. Previously he was Head of Construction at the National Theatre and a production manager for both Welsh National Opera and Scottish Opera. He is a trustee for English Touring Opera.

**Judith Kilvington** is Chief Executive of Rich Mix, a Shoreditch-based multi-arts venue and workspace which welcomes the diverse communities of East London to create, enjoy and share culture. Judith has held chief executive roles in theatres including Graeae and Glasgow's Citizens Theatre.

**Carol Lingwood** was Head of Costume at the National Theatre for over twenty-two years (1999–2022), managing a team of more than forty permanent staff to create costumes for over twenty new shows a year. Carol is now a freelance costume professional.

**Dave Ludlam** is an executive director at UK theatre consultancy practice Theatreplan, specialising in stage engineering and theatre planning. As a chartered engineer with a background in industrial systems, Dave spent fourteen years with the Royal Shakespeare Company at the Barbican Theatre, London, where he was responsible for the design and management of all types of building services and stage machinery.

**Andrew Miller**, MBE, has been transforming perceptions throughout his thirty-five years in the creative industries and is recognised as one of the UK's most influential disability advocates, with extensive experience of the arts, film and broadcast sectors.

**Anne Minors**, BA (Hons), Dip Arch, MA in Theatre Consultancy. After ten years at Theatre Projects Consultants and twenty years as Anne Minors Performance Consultants, Anne joined acoustician Bob Essert to found Sound Space Vision with a multi-modal design approach. Anne has influenced iconic international performance spaces, including Koerner Hall Toronto, Glyndebourne Opera House, Cerritos Center for the Performing Arts and Disney Concert Hall in California and the Esplanade Singapore. Collaborating with architects, notable UK projects include Royal Opera House, Covent Garden; Menuhin Hall, Surrey; Nevill Holt Opera; Hull Truck Theatre; and The Egg Theatre, Bath.

**Britannia Morton** is the co-CEO of Sadler's Wells, joining the theatre in 2010 after leading operational teams at the Southbank Centre, Barbican, Royal Albert Hall and ENO. She works with the Artistic Director and the board to deliver a long-term strategy for growth, including leading on the development of Sadler's Wells East, their new venue opening in London's Queen Elizabeth Olympic Park in 2024.

**Nigel Nicholls** is a structural engineer and an associate at Conisbee. He has worked on a wide range of theatres, cinemas and art centre projects, including the redevelopment of the Victoria Palace Theatre and the Theatre Royal Drury Lane.

**Lucy Osborne**, BA (Hons), is an award-winning set and costume designer and theatre consultant. Known for bold, innovative designs which fuse architecture, light and music, Lucy co-founded Studio Three Sixty in 2015 to design the world's first 'flatpack' theatre, Roundabout, for Paines Plough. The Studio works with performing arts venues to design and regenerate buildings that enrich people's lives.

**Mark Price** is a town planner and built heritage specialist working in local government and in the private sector. He is the Heritage Advisor to the Theatres Trust and is an acknowledged expert in theatre and cinema buildings.

**Jonathan Purcell**, BSc, MArchSt, CEng, MCIBSE, LCC, is a qualified chartered building services engineer and Managing Director of Waterman Building Services. He is a low carbon consultant and an expert in dynamic thermal and energy modelling of the built environment. With over thirty years' design experience in the performing arts sector, his projects include the Everyman Theatre in Liverpool, Derry Playhouse and the Royal and Derngate Theatres.

**Peter Ruthven-Hall** is a stage designer and a senior theatre consultant with Charcoalblue. He spent eighteen years as a successful set and costume designer before moving into theatre consultancy, specialising in auditorium design and theatre planning. He has an MA in Theatre Consultancy (University of Warwick). He is recognised for his extensive contribution to the Society of British Theatre Designers and his three books on theatre design. Consultancy work includes the Dorfman Theatre, Hudson Theatre on Broadway and Leeds Playhouse.

**Deborah Sawyerr** is the Deputy Executive Director at the Mercury, Colchester. Previously she was the Executive Director at the Theatre Royal Stratford East, General Manager at the Bush Theatre, Executive Director at Talawa Theatre Company and Production Manager at Nottingham Playhouse and Palace Theatre Watford. She has experience in leading organisational change, developing processes and procedures and HR management.

**Iain Shaw** is a building services engineer and partner at Max Fordham LLP, a consultancy offering sustainable design and low-carbon engineering. Iain's projects include the refurbishment of the Contact Theatre in Manchester and the restoration of the Stockton Globe.

**Gemma Tonge**, BA (Hons) in Stage Management and Technical Theatre (Guildhall School of Music and Drama, 1999–2002), is Head of Company Stage Management at the National Theatre. Her career has included working as Project Manager at the Manchester International Festival, Company Manager at the Kenneth Branagh Theatre Company, Stage Manager, BBC Young Dancer 2015 and Company Stage Manager with Fabulous Beast Dance Theatre.

**Nicola Walls** is an architect with Page \ Park. Her professional involvement in arts buildings mirrors her personal interests, and, as Head of the Arts and Culture team, Nicola is actively involved in producing memorable spaces, creatively adapting existing buildings and democratising access to our cultural spaces. Nicola has led performing arts projects including the Eden Court Highlands, Theatre Royal in Glasgow, Leeds Playhouse and the new foyer extension to Symphony Hall Birmingham.

**Roger Watts**, BSc, BArch, is a director at Haworth Tompkins director and co-designer on award-winning projects including the Royal Court; the temporary Almeida theatres at Gainsborough Studios and King's Cross; the Young Vic; The Egg Theatre at Bath; the Liverpool Everyman; and The Bridge Theatre, London.

**Stuart West**, Stu Arts Consulting, has extensive international touring experience and has held managerial roles in mid- to large-scale touring and producing venues around the United Kingdom, including Sheffield Theatres, CAST in Doncaster, Royal and Derngate Northampton and Milton Keynes Theatre. He has been involved with the opening of several arts buildings and complexes, both new builds and refurbishments.

**Hilary Williamson** is Technical Director at Hampstead Theatre in London; she was previously Senior Stage Technician at the Young Vic, Stage Manager at the Orange Tree Theatre and a technician at the Arcola Theatre.

**David Wilmore** is an historic theatres expert whose company, *Theatresearch*, has advised on many theatre restoration projects. He has a PhD in the development of nineteenth-century stage technology and is a past chairman of both the ABTT and the OISTAT Research Commission. He is a Fellow of the ABTT.

# Illustrations

**Photo Editor: Sarah Wells**
**Photo Researcher: Susannah Jayes**

**Front cover.** The auditorium @sohoplace which opened in 2022, the first London West End theatre since 1973.
Photo © Alex Wardle

Building credits
Client: Derwent London; Theatre Owner: Nica Burns; Theatre Operator: Nimax Theatres Limited; Architect: Simon Allford for Allford Hall Monaghan Morris; Engineering (structure, services, fire): Arup; Cost Consultant: AECOM; Project Manager: Gardiner & Theobald; Main Contractor: Laing O'Rourke

Auditorium credits
Architect: Roger Watts for Haworth Tompkins; Theatre consultant: Charcoalblue; Theatre consultant to Nica Burns: Ian Albery; Acoustic consultant: Arup; Acoustic consultant to Nimax: Gillieron Scott; Services contractor: Crown House Technologies; Stage engineering systems: TAIT; Stagelighting and Audiovisual systems: Stage Electrics; Auditorium seating: Kirwin & Simpson; Bespoke houselight fittings: GDS; Auditorium joinery: James Johnson & Co Ltd

**Back cover (left).** Looking down through the grid at The Quarry Theatre at St Luke's, Bedford, UK. See Reference Project 05.
Photo © Philip Vile/Foster Wilson Size

**Back cover (right).** Refurbished fly gallery at the Theatre Royal Drury Lane, London. See Reference Project 32.
Photo © Chris Dales

Figure 1.2.1. Derby Theatre.
Photo © Chris Sedden

Figure 1.2.2. Chester's Storyhouse.
Photo © Peter Cook/Bennetts Associates

Figure 1.2.3. Riverside Studios, London.
Photo © Paul Bavister/Flanagan Lawrence

Figure 1.2.4. HOME, Manchester.
Photo: Leon van der Velden/Wikimedia

Figure 1.2.5. The Metropolitan Arts Centre (MAC), Belfast.
Photo: Ardfern/Wikimedia

**Please note: the photographic credits for the figures included in the 32 Reference Projects can be found immediately below each figure.**

# Abbreviations and acronyms

| | |
|---|---|
| ABTT: | Association of British Theatre Technicians |
| ACE: | Arts Council England |
| ACNI: | Arts Council of Northern Ireland |
| ACW: | Arts Council of Wales |
| A0 | (plotter): large-format printer, to print drawings and the like up to A0 paper size |
| BREEAM: | Building Research Establishment Environmental Assessment Method (UK) |
| CCTV: | closed-circuit television |
| CFD: | computational fluid dynamic |
| CIBSE: | Chartered Institution of Building Services Engineers |
| CIEH: | Chartered Institute of Environmental Health |
| CIL: | Community Infrastructure Levy |
| CNC: | computer numerical control (router) |
| COSHH: | Control of Substances Hazardous to Health Regulations |
| Creative Scotland: | arts funding body for Scotland |
| DAS: | Design and Access Statement |
| dB: | decibel |
| DCMS: | Department for Digital, Culture, Media and Sport (UK government) |
| DMX: | digital multiplex |
| DSA: | District Surveyors Association |
| EA: | electronic architecture |
| EPOS: | electronic point of sale |
| FOH: | front of house |
| F&B: | food and beverage |
| FSC: | Forest Stewardship Council |
| GFA: | gross floor area |
| GIA: | gross internal area |
| HVAC: | heating, ventilation and cooling systems |
| IoTC: | Institute of Theatre Consultants |
| IP: | internet protocol |
| IPTV: | internet protocol television |
| ITEAC: | International Theatre Engineering and Architecture Conference |
| LBC: | living building challenge |
| LED: | light-emitting diode |
| LEED: | Leadership in Energy and Environmental Design (North America) |
| LETI: | London Energy Transformation Initiative |
| LEV: | local extract ventilation |
| MAC: | Metropolitan Arts Centre, Belfast |
| mac: | Midland Arts Centre, Edgbaston, Birmingham |
| MADI: | multichannel audio digital interface |

MIP: mobility-impaired people
NPO: National Portfolio Organisation
NPPF: National Planning Policy Framework
NR: noise rating
OB: outside broadcast
OISTAT: International Organisation of Scenographers, Theatre Architects and Technicians
OP: opposite prompt
PEEP: personal emergency evacuation plan
PEFC: Programme for the Endorsement of Forest Certification
PPD: percentage of people dissatisfied
PS: prompt side
PYO: print your own
RCD: residual current device
RDM: remote device management
RfP: request for proposal
RIBA: Royal Institute of British Architects
RICS: Royal Institute of Chartered Surveyors
RT: reverberation time
S106: Section 106 of the Town and Country Planning Act 1990
SBTD: Society of British Theatre Designers
SiPA: Sustainability in Productions Alliance
SMA: Stage Management Association
TT: The Theatres Trust
TWG: tension wire grid
UKGBC: United Kingdom Green Building Council
48.3mm OD CHS: 48.3 outer-diameter circular hollow section of steel tube (standard scaffold tube)

## Note

### Four publications are referred to in abbreviated form throughout this edition of *Theatre Buildings: a Design Guide*

ABTT, *Technical Standards*: ABTT *et al.*, *Technical Standards for Places of Entertainment* (London: ABTT, 2015; updated 2020)

*Sightline*: *Sightline. Journal of Theatre Technology and Design* (Cambridge: ABTT in collaboration with Entertainment Technology Press)

*Theatre Green Book*: https://theatregreenbook.com, 3 vols, *Sustainable Productions*, *Sustainable Buildings*, *Sustainable Operations*

Strong (ed.), *Theatre Buildings* (2010): Judith Strong (ed.), *Theatre Buildings: A Design Guide* (London: Routledge in collaboration with the ABTT, 2010)

# Glossary of theatre terminology

## A

**Access (people)**
Generally describes a building which is inviting and open to all. More specifically used to describe equal access and provision for people with visible and invisible disabilities.

**Access (backstage)**
Generally refers to ease of moving scenery and equipment from delivery vehicles to the stage.

**Acoustic**
Describes all issues relating to achieving good hearing conditions and the suppression of unwanted noise.

**Acoustic separation**
Means of preventing unwanted noise travelling between spaces or breaking into or out of a building.

**Acting area**
Those portions of the stage in which any action of a performance takes place.

**Amphitheatre**
Stepped banks of seating surrounding an arena. Also describes the curved uppermost level of seating in a large theatre.

**Apron**
The extension of a stage projecting outwards into the auditorium. May be permanent or demountable.

**Auditorium**
The part of a building occupied by an audience for a performance.

**Automation**
Precise control of scenic elements by means of computer-controlled winches and motors.

## B

**Backstage**
Areas for production and performance to which the public are not normally permitted access. Sometimes referred to incorrectly as back of house (which refers to the entirety of the non-public estate of a theatre). See front of house and pass door.

**Band room**
Musicians' changing room. May also be a temporary structure located behind the scenery on the stage for a large musical production.

**Band shell**
Movable sound reflector placed behind (sometimes extending above) a group of musicians on the stage or in the open air to improve the acoustics.

**Bar/barrel/pipe/tube**
Length of metal pipe (usually 48mm outer diameter) suspended on a set of lines to which scenery or lighting may be attached. See truss.

**Barre**
Horizontal rail, usually of wood, used by ballet dancers when warming up and for class.

**Bastard prompt**
When the stage manager's control position is not on prompt side (PS) or stage left but instead is situated opposite prompt (OP) or stage right. Note: archaic and rarely used.

**Batten**
Length of (usually) wood used in scenery construction or used for hanging scenery cloths and the like.

**Border**
Abbreviated cloth hanging or semi-solid pelmet used to mask the top of suspended scenery or technical equipment from the audience's line of sight.

**Box(es)**
Separate seating compartments in an auditorium, typically found on side walls near the stage. In a classical Italian-style opera house, all seating at upper levels is in boxes.

**Brail line**
Generally a length of rope used to pull a piece of hanging scenery away from its normal vertical position in order to make room for a moving scenic piece.

**Bridge**
1. A gallery bridging across the stage or auditorium used for lighting and sound equipment.
2. A lift in the stage floor extending across the stage floor, usually to the proscenium width.

**Bridle**
A short length of certified lifting cable or sling used to distribute the load of a hoisted pipe or truss across two hanging points.

**Brief**
A document setting out the design requirements for a building project.

## C

**Call**
Warning to be ready for part of a performance. Usually given via a backstage-only public address system.

**Carbon emissions**
The carbon dioxide emitted into the earth's atmosphere when fossil fuels are burned, for example, to heat buildings, manufacture food and products and transport goods and people. See operational carbon and embodied carbon. The density of carbon in the atmosphere contributes to climate change, and international protocols attempt to control global emissions.

**Carbon footprint**
See carbon emissions.

**Carbon offset**
Compensating for carbon emissions by funding an accredited off-site carbon reduction or removal programme.

**Carpet cut**
Series of flaps in the stage floor, generally on the proscenium line, by which a stage cloth can be held in position.

**Catwalk(s)**
Overhead walkways in an auditorium providing access to lighting and rigging positions. Also see lighting bridges.

**Centre line**
The imaginary line running up and down stage, bisecting the setting line at right angles, used as a reference point from which permanent stage rigging and subsequent scenery are positioned.

**Changing places**
Toilets that are completely accessible and provide sufficient space and equipment for people who are not able to use the toilet independently.

**Circular economy**
A model of production and consumption that involves sharing, leasing, reusing, repairing, refurbishing and recycling materials and products in their existing state for as long as possible, rather than a linear economy which produces waste as an inevitable outcome.

**Cleat**
Wooden or metal fitment round which a line may be turned and/or made fast. See pin rail.

**Cloths**
A hanging painted cloth; may sometimes be cut to reveal part of another cloth behind, or a floor cloth, usually a painted canvas which might represent paving, floorboards, and so on.

**Control room**
Room(s) housing lighting and sound desks with a good view of the stage as a whole. Require soundproofing and preferably openable windows into the auditorium. Can also house audio describers, surtitle operators and other technical control or production staff.

**Co-production**
A production created by the collaboration of two or more theatres.

**Counterweight system**
A mechanical system for flying scenery in which the weight of the pieces of scenery are counterbalanced by the addition of metal weights in the counterweight cradle. The cradles move in guides via a loop of rope known as the hauling line.

**Crew**
Collective description of the technical staff working on a production; in a large theatre may refer specifically to the stage-based staff.

**Crossover**
A passageway behind or under the stage for actors or technicians to cross from one side of the stage to the other out of sight of the audience.

**Cue**
A signal for action during the performance by an actor or technician. Cues may be given verbally via headsets or via a cue light.

**Curtain line**
Imaginary line drawn just upstage of the proscenium (if fitted) marking the position of the house tabs when closed. Also known as the setting line.

**Cut**
Any long opening in the stage, generally across. See dip traps.

**Cyclorama**
Plain, curved, stretched cloth or rigid structure used as a background to a setting to give an illusion of great depth or to provide a surface, usually the width of the stage, for projection or lighting.

## D

**Dark time**
Periods when there are no performances in a theatre, such as for maintenance or construction work to take place.

**Dead**
A predetermined position to which a scenic piece is raised or lowered or brought on or off stage.

**Dip traps**
Covered shallow troughs generally running up and down stage at the edges, providing spaces for cables to prevent tripping hazards at stage level. May contain outlets for lighting and sound equipment.

**Displacement systems**
Ventilation systems where fresh air is introduced at a low level and rises to the top of a space through convection.

**Diversity**
The inclusion of all people regardless of their race, gender, sexuality or disability.

**Dock**
A storage area next to the stage. Scenery is unloaded and taken through the 'dock door' to the stage. Also see scene dock.

**Dock leveller**
A mechanical lift or ramp that brings the tailgate of a goods vehicle level with the floor in a loading bay or dock.

**Double purchase**
A system of pulley blocks and suspension ropes which gears the movement of the counterweights to half of that of the associated scenery load. See counterweight system.

**Doughnut economy**
See circular economy.

**Downstage (taken from the viewpoint of an actor facing the audience)**
Towards the audience. See also stage directions.

**Drapes**
Any non-flammable fabric hanging in folds as a scene or part of a scene, especially curtaining fabrics such as wool, velvet, and so on.

**Drencher**
A perforated sparge pipe that will, in the event of a fire, spray water on the upstage face of the safety curtain to stop deformation.

**Drinks python**
A bundle of small plastic supply pipes around a cooling pipe to maintain the temperature of a beverage between the cooler and the point at which it is dispensed.

## E

**Embodied carbon**
The carbon emissions resulting from construction and maintenance of a building, such as the energy used to make building materials, transport them to site and assemble them. See carbon emissions and operational carbon.

**End stage**
A stage which is located at one end of an auditorium with the audience facing it on one side.

**Environmental control**
Means of controlling the temperature and air quality in a building.

## F

**False proscenium**
Also known as a show portal or opera bridge. A structure placed immediately upstage of the proscenium opening. May be structural in order to place lights and sound equipment or purely scenic.

**Fire curtain**
See safety curtain and iron.

**Fireproofed**
Treatment of scenic elements with flame-retardant chemicals in order to slow the spread of fire. Fireproofing does not necessarily render the treated item noncombustible.

**Flight cases**
Rugged, rigid, wheeled enclosures usually specially constructed required for the transport of technical equipment such as speakers, luminaires and cables. Have the disadvantage of taking up as much space when empty as when full (but can be stacked to minimise footprint for storage).

**Floats (footlights)**
A trough at the very front of the stage for placing of lights and other equipment so as not to obscure the audience's view of actors' feet, and so on.

**Flown**
Suspended on lines, as distinct from standing on the stage floor, hanging from fixed rails and so on.

**Fly**
Lift above the level of the stage floor by means of sets of lines run from the stage grid. The term 'flys' or 'flies' is also used as an abbreviation for a fly gallery or the fly operators.

**Fly gallery**
A gallery extending along the sidewall of the stage, some distance above the stage floor, from which the machinery used in flying scenery is operated. This machinery may be manually operated or automated. Also known as the fly floor.

**Fly rail**
Heavy rail along the on-stage side of the fly gallery fitted with cleats to which scenery suspensions may be made fast.

**Flys operator**
A technician with skilled ability in the suspension, rigging and operation of flying scenic elements.

**Flytower**
The volume above the stage into which scenic pieces can be hoisted out of view and stored by means of the flying system, ideally high enough to raise scenery completely out of sight; this differs between theatres with viable proscenium performance heights and sightlines from the auditorium. May be 1.5 to potentially 3 times the height of the built (or 'hard') proscenium. Contains galleries such as the fly gallery.

**Follow spot**
A manually operated high-intensity spotlight used to follow lead performers during a production. Formerly known as 'limes' from the historic use of limelight.

**Forestage**
Portion of the stage floor in front of the curtain line. Generally forms the upstage edge of the orchestra pit.

**Found space**
Generic description of a space in an existing building not commonly used for performance but repurposed 'as found' with a minimum of alteration.

**Front of house (FOH)**
The public areas of a theatre with audience support facilities, which increasingly are open throughout the day and where performers in costume or in character are not normally seen, except for foyer performances. See also backstage.

**Foyer**
That part of front of house specifically given over to the gathering of audiences associated with a performance and where any bars and other services are also located.

# G

**Gallery/galleries**
Term to describe upper levels or balconies in an auditorium. May also include dedicated spaces for front of house exhibitions.

**Get-in/out**
The process of placing a production in the theatre and removing it when finished to leave a bare stage. Also refers to the related access doors, parking area, lifts, and so on.

**Grave trap**
An oblong trap, usually downstage centre (DSC), used for making actors appear and disappear during the course of the performance.

**Green room**
A communal room, generally close to the stage, where performers and others involved in the performance may prepare and wait before being required on stage. A relaxation area after the performance or rehearsals.

**Grid**
Framework of steel or timber beams at a high level over the stage used to support sets of lines used for flying scenery.

**Ground coupling heat exchange**
An underground heat exchanger which can capture heat from and/or dissipate heat to the ground, using the earth's steady subterranean temperature to warm or cool air.

**Ground plan**
Scale plan of the stage on which is marked the position of scenery and technical equipment such as lighting, sound, projection, and so on.

# H

**Hauling line**
Used by the flys operator in a counterweighted system to move the counterweight cradle to position a piece of flown scenery.

**Head block**
Device comprising three or more sheaves set together in a line or parallel on a common shaft and attached to the grid or flytower soffit directly above the fly gallery. The suspension lines of rope or steel are passed over to the fly gallery.

**Hemps**
The term usually employed to signify lines used for flying scenery made from vegetable fibre or even synthetic materials as distinct from steel wire ropes used in a counterweight flying system. A hemp house is a theatre equipped only with a direct lift flying system, as opposed to a counterweighted or automated system.

**House**
The audience for a performance (e.g., a full house).

**House border**
Adjustable-height (sometimes decorative) pelmet suspended immediately in front of the house tabs.

**House tabs**
The main curtains in a theatre, usually decorative and heavy. May be drawn (opened horizontally), swagged (opened to form bunches at the high-level corners of the proscenium) or guillotined (opened vertically). Derived from tableau curtain. Often lit with specific luminaires known as 'tab warmers'.

# I

**Inclusive design**
A design which is free of barriers for people with disabilities.

**Internet protocol television (IPTV)**
The delivery of television content over internet protocol (IP) networks.

**In-the-round**
A staging format where the audience surrounds the stage on all sides.

**Invacuation**
An emergency situation where people are directed to and held inside a building in response to an external threat.

**Iron**
See safety curtain or fire curtain.

# L

**Lantern**
1. Stage lantern or haystack lantern is the term for the automatic smoke ventilation opening located in the roof of the flytower. May also be manually operated.
2. Term for a stage lighting instrument. See luminaire.

**Legs**
Vertical length of fabric hung to mask the view into the wings, often used in conjunction with 'borders'.

**Lift**
Section of the stage that can be raised and lowered, sometimes also tilted to enable changes of setting to be made and provide a changeable acting area. See bridge.

**Lighting bridge(s)**
See catwalks.

**Lines**
Ropes used for suspension or repositioning of scenic elements. May be fibre, steel or synthetic composites. See set of lines.

**Loading gallery**
Narrow gallery above the fly gallery used for storing and loading the weights used in counterweight flying systems.

**Locking rail**
Rail on fly gallery or floor used to attach rope locks that hold the hauling lines stationary and so keep the flown scenic piece in position.

**Loft block or grid pulley**
Sheave in a metal frame bolted to the grid or flytower soffit and used to pass a suspension line, one block for each line in a set.

**Luminaire**
A stage lighting instrument. Also known as a lantern or a fixture.

## M

### Masking

A piece of scenery used to cut off the view of parts of the stage.

### Model box

A physical model of the stage into which designers can insert models of their set designs, traditionally at 1:25 scale.

## N

### Net-zero carbon

Having no net carbon emissions. A net-zero theatre is one where the carbon emissions of construction, maintenance and operation are minimised through the choice of materials, efficient design and good management. The balance of any remaining carbon emissions is then offset through an accredited carbon offsetting programme.

### Noise rating (NR)

A measure of ambient background noise levels inside or outside a building.

## O

### Offstage (taken from the viewpoint of an actor facing the audience)

That part of the stage house invisible to the audience, blocked by scenery, drapes or sightlines. See also stage directions.

### Onstage (taken from the viewpoint of an actor facing the audience)

In view of at least some members of the audience. See also stage directions.

### Operational carbon

The carbon emissions resulting from using a building, such as energy consumption for heating, lighting and cooling. See carbon emissions and embodied carbon.

### Opposite prompt

Traditionally stage (actors') right, regardless of the actual position of the prompter. Known as OP. See prompt side (PS) and bastard prompt.

### Orchestra pit

Lowered area to accommodate musicians between the audience and the stage. The floor is usually adjustable in height to suit different forms of performance. May become the apron or forestage.

### Orchestra stalls

The audience tier (or private boxes) separate from and surrounding the central stalls area, sometimes called the orchestra circle.

## P

### Packing rail

A 'stacking rail', usually a horizontal steel tube projecting from the stage wall used for tying to, or stacking against, large (flat) pieces of scenery.

### Paint frame

A frame to which backcloths, flats, and so on may be vertically attached for scenic painting. Vertical access is often provided by a paint bridge which may be suspended or mechanically lifted to give comfortable working access to the full width and height of the frame.

### Pass door

A fire-rated door linking the stage or backstage area to the foyers, for the use of staff only.

### Passivhaus design

The leading international low-energy design standard in construction, Passivhaus adopts a whole-building approach to design championing energy efficiency and thermal performance, along with the comfort of those using the buildings.

### Pin or cleat rail

Used in direct-hauled flying systems. The flying scenery suspension lines are taken over loft blocks and head blocks and brought straight down to the pin or fly rail for paying out and tying off. There are no counterweights or other means of sustaining the load of the scenery when the lines are free of the cleats.

### Placemaking

A multi-faceted approach to the planning, design and management of public spaces. Placemaking capitalizes on a local community's assets, inspiration and potential, with the intention of creating public spaces that promote people's health, happiness and well-being.

### Plenum

A space from which ventilation air is distributed under pressure, usually under the floor or above a ceiling.

**Point hoist**
A single line-powered winch for flying scenic elements. Generally used in groups. The suspension point on the grid is via a relocatable spot block (pulley).

**Portal**
A unit of semi-permanent masking which can be used to frame the stage and usually comprises both legs and a border constructed to look like one scenic unit. Can be arranged in a sequence from downstage to upstage in an array to create perspective and multiple stage entrances. Upstage of the proscenium and false proscenium.

**Powered flying**
System of scenery flying utilising motors only. Manual operation is usually only possible in an emergency.

**Presenting theatre**
A theatre which presents touring productions, sometimes known as a receiving house.

**Press night**
Performance to which the newspaper and media critics are invited for the purpose of reviewing the performance and after which they can publish their reviews.

**Producing theatre**
A theatre which originates its own productions, usually requiring additional space for set building, rehearsal and production staff.

**Promenade performance**
A performance where the audience follow the action, standing and walking with the performers (who may also be amongst the audience) rather than sitting in one place. Often used in site-specific rather than traditional theatre settings.

**Prompt box**
The traditional position for the prompter in opera is a box let into the front of the stage extending into the orchestra pit.

**Prompt corner**
The stage manager's control point and prompt position, which is usually located downstage left but can be on either side of the stage. See bastard prompt.

**Prompt side**
Traditionally stage (actors') left, regardless of the actual position of the prompter. Known as PS. See opposite prompt (OP) and bastard prompt.

**Properties or props**
Objects such as furniture, pictures, carpets, ornaments, weapons and so on used in a production.

**Proscenium or pros**
The theoretical fourth wall of a stage comprising the proscenium opening and its surrounding treatments. See also false proscenium.

**Proscenium opening**
The opening through which the audience views the stage.

**Purple pound**
The spending power of disabled households (i.e., where at least one person has a disability).

## R

**Rake**
Sloped floor of an auditorium or stage.

**Receiving house**
See presenting theatre.

**Regeneration**
Urban renewal of run-down inner-city areas through restoration and construction of buildings to restore economic viability through private and public investment, attracting new residents and businesses. Cultural buildings often play an important role in this process.

**Relaxed performance**
The presentation of a performance where the production and/or the audience environment have been adapted to suit people who might require a more relaxed experience when going to the theatre. These may include adults or children with dementia, anxiety, bowel and bladder conditions, learning difficulties, autism spectrum conditions or sensory communication disorders.

**Rester rail(s)**
Rails at minimum height in front of auditorium seating, on which the audience can lean to better view the stage.

**Reverberation time (RT)**
A measure of the amount of echo or reverberation in an auditorium, which should be matched to the performance type (e.g., speech or unamplified music).

**Rig**
To set up scenery on stage, usually referring to those elements suspended overhead. 'Rigging' is a collective term for the suspension equipment.

**Riser**
1. Vertical front of a raised stage where it faces the audience; also referred to as stage riser.
2. Vertical enclosed compartment stretching over many floors containing building services such as plumbing, electrical mains, air handling ducts, and so on.
3. The raised staging set out on concert platforms for orchestras.

**Roller**
Where there is no flying space over the stage, a backdrop can be rolled, known as a roller or a roll drop. Also known as 'tumbling'.

**Rope lock**
See locking rail.

**Rostra**
A modular system for creating flexible stages and seating tiers.

**Running wardrobe**
Wardrobe room where running repairs and maintenance of costumes for the current production(s) are carried out. Also known as a maintenance wardrobe.

## S

**Safety curtain**
Fireproof screen or shutter comprising a framework of steel or iron faced with sheet steel and fireproof heat-absorbing fabric. Mounted immediately behind the proscenium in guides, the shutter quickly creates a fire barrier between the auditorium and the stage house by means of an automatic closing system. See drencher.

**Scene dock**
An area close to the stage where scenery and equipment are stored. Also see dock.

**Seatway**
The clear space between seat rows when seats are unoccupied. The width of the seatway will determine the maximum number of seats permitted in a row.

**Secondary spending**
Spending by patrons other than the purchase of tickets, including programmes, show merchandise, food and drink.

**Set**
Arrangement of scenery units that together represent a single location. The term is also used as a verb to mean to put up or assemble scenery for use (e.g., to set a stage).

**Set of lines**
Unit group of suspension lines hanging from the grid or the flytower soffit for the attachment and flying of scenery; there are usually three or four lines in a set. See counterweight system and pin or cleat rail.

**Setting line**
The imaginary line across the stage, in front of which scenery cannot be hidden by the house tabs and a reference point from which permanent stage rigging and subsequent scenery are positioned. See curtain line.

**Sheave**
Grooved wheel or pulley over which a suspension line may be passed.

**Show merchandising**
Products being sold related to the performance being presented in the theatre.

**Show relay**
A system which broadcasts in real time the activity on stage to backstage areas such as dressing rooms, allowing actors to monitor the performance.

**Single purchase**
A suspension system where there is no gearing of pulleys. The counterweight and its travel will be the same as that of the object that is being suspended.

**Social model of disability**
The social model says that people are disabled by their environment, by barriers in society, not by their impairment or difference. Those barriers may also be caused by people's attitudes to difference, such as assuming disabled people can't do certain things.

**Social value**
The value placed on the changes people experience in their lives resulting from an investment or intervention.

**Sprung floor**
A non-solid floor designed to provide some flexibility when used for movement and dance and to prevent injury to performers.

**Stack effect**
The stack (or chimney) effect utilises hot air rising and exiting the building in the upper levels, or cooler air from outside moving into the lower floors and rising in temperature, to create air movement, which when controlled may increase energy efficiency.

**Stage directions**
These are taken from the viewpoint of an actor facing the audience.

**Downstage (DS) and downstage centre (DSC)**
Towards the audience.

**Upstage (US)**
Away from the audience. Historically stages were usually raked (gently sloped) towards the audience. Hence the part of the stage away from the audience was at a slightly higher level than that closest to it.

**Stage left (SL)**
To the actor's left (the audience's right). Usually where the prompt corner is located.

**Stage right (SR)**
To the actor's right.

**Offstage**
That part of the stage house invisible to the audience, blocked by scenery, drapes or sightlines.

**Onstage**
In view of at least some members of the audience.

**Stage door**
The access door to the backstage areas of a theatre used by performers, technicians and other staff. Usually where all postal deliveries are made.

**Stage engineering**
Mechanical systems installed in the stage area for the movement and suspension of scenery, lighting and other equipment.

**Stage house**
That part of a theatre housing the stage, wings and flytower. See back of house.

**Stage left (SL) (taken from the viewpoint of an actor facing the audience)**
To the actor's left (the audience right). Usually where the prompt corner is located. See also stage directions.

**Stage right (SR) (taken from the viewpoint of an actor facing the audience)**
To the actor's right. See also stage directions.

**Stalls**
The lowest level of audience seating in a multi-level auditorium.

**Swag**
Looped up curtain, border or leg.

## T

**Threshold**
The entry point to a building or room, as in threshold fear – nervousness about entering an unfamiliar space.

**Thrust stage**
A staging format where the audience are arranged on three sides of the stage.

**Tormentor**
Substantial wing, often semi-solid wooden or metal frame construction (not just a soft cloth), placed immediately behind the proscenium opening to mask the off-stage edges of the setting. Can be used to vary the width of the proscenium opening by moving both stage right and stage left tormentors in or out.

**Trap**
An opening in the stage floor, generally with a mechanism to raise and lower actors. The trap cover slides over to form a continuous floor when not in use.

**Trap room**
The area under the stage from where entrances or exits can be made (of people or scenery) through the stage floor via a trap. Originally a traditional trapdoor, a trap now means more generally an opening in the stage floor.

**Traverse**
A staging format where the audience is arranged on two opposite sides of the stage, facing each other across the stage.

**Truck**
Low trolley, either running in tracks or free moving, on which scenery and the like may be mounted for horizontal linear movements of settings. See wagon (1).

**Truss**
A latticed girder of steel or aluminium welded construction of square or triangular sections used for supporting

temporary lighting or scenic elements. Stronger and more rigid than a bar/barrel/pipe.

## U

**Under croft cooling**
Where the thermal mass is decoupled from the occupied space by creating a high thermal mass concrete under croft, with a large surface area constructed labyrinth through which air flows from the outside (either hot or cold, depending on external air temperatures). Contact with the earth and steady subterranean temperatures allows the outside air to reach equilibrium, providing free cooling in the summer and pre-heating of air in the winter.

**Upstage (taken from the viewpoint of an actor facing the audience)**
Away from the audience. Historically stages were usually raked (gently sloped) towards the audience. Hence the part of the stage away from the audience was at a slightly higher level than that closest to it. See also stage directions.

## V

**Ventilation**
The process, either natural or mechanical, by which air is changed and circulated through a space.

**Vomitory**
An entrance through a block of seating, as distinct from through the surrounding wall.

## W

**Wagon**
1. A large truck, usually guided, on which sets are assembled and moved on and off stage when required.
2. Vehicle in which scenery is transported between venues.

**Winch**
A rope-winding mechanism for moving scenic or other elements such as curtains, acoustic panels, and so on. May be powered or manually operated.

**Wings**
Offstage spaces to left and right of the acting area.

# Section 1

# Design principles

## 1.1 Starting points

Theatre brings people together to share the experience of live performance; it has an energy which invites us to challenge our ideas and assumptions about the world. Successful theatre buildings amplify this energy on the stage, focus it in the auditorium and channel it into public spaces and surrounding communities, creating identity and a sense of place.

Theatre buildings can be complex, with many functional and operational requirements that designers need to be aware of, but they are also significant public buildings, and it is important for designers to make the most of the opportunities that good theatre design can offer to both people and places.

This section describes the broad principles of theatre design and signposts later chapters where each aspect will be covered in more detail. It considers the opportunities offered by a theatre's location and different types of theatres; it introduces the functional parts of a theatre building and the different people who come together to make it work.

## 1.2 Theatre, place and people

The early twenty-first century has seen significant challenges for urban centres in the United Kingdom and the rest of the world, with structural changes in shopping and working patterns leading to a slow decline, which was accelerated by the 2019 COVID pandemic. Theatres and other cultural and community spaces have a vital role to play, cultivating the local economy and creating the sense of pride and engagement that is important to the identity and confidence of towns and cities.

### Theatre's role in the life of towns and cities

The role of a theatre in a town, city or rural community can be much more than simply a provider of culture in the traditional sense or a means to anchor urban regeneration plans. A well-located theatre with a design and programme that encourages engagement not only enables people to experience live performance but also generates social value. Theatres are part of our social and cultural infrastructure, and the facilities and experiences they offer have the power to regenerate neighbourhoods and to improve people's lives. A theatre can be a place where people can participate, learn, meet and socialise, reducing isolation and increasing wellbeing.

### Why location is important

A theatre's location might be determined by land ownership or town planning strategy, or even by the desire to re-use a suitable existing building. But, regardless of the size or business model, choosing the right site is a fundamental consideration. Clients, designers and architects need to be aware of the importance of this decision and the potential impact a well-located theatre can have on a town or city.

Evidence often points to successful theatres having an economic impact on a place, bringing visitors and encouraging secondary spend, but equally important is the positive impact a successful venue can have on the lives of the people who live there.

***Theatre's role in the life of towns and cities: Derby Theatre***

> In Derby the relationship between the public and our theatre building is not just confined to the auditorium. We understand our civic duty to our community goes far beyond putting excellent plays on our stages (although of course this is important too). Derby Theatre is a focal point for our community throughout the day. (See Figure 1.2.1.) From an all-day café where customers, who may never enter our auditorium, gather for a coffee to the weekly bingo session held in our upstairs foyer for the over 60s; we understand that our building needs to present an opening and welcoming atmosphere throughout the day. Large spaces for schools to workshop ideas and safe smaller spaces for groups of vulnerable participants to work in are all required as the building opens its doors at 9 am and doesn't close until after the show comes down. We sit at the heart of our community and whether it's an arts therapy class, a playwrighting course or a friendly cuppa we need our space to be flexible to encompass all of that. A

DOI: 10.4324/9781003327295-1

theatre for us is a town hall, a community centre, a place to dance, a place to eat, a place to heal, a place to celebrate and so much more and the architecture of that space can really help us to imagine what could be possible in our next interactions with our community.
Sarah Brigham, CEO, Derby Theatre

Figure 1.2.1 Derby Theatre is an example of an established venue which has become a focal point for its city and community through professional live performance, civic and community engagement and degree-level learning facilities.

## Synergies with other uses

A theatre is best located where the positive impacts on people and place will make the most difference, a place that is accessible all day to the broadest range of people and a place that will benefit from the footfall and activity that a theatre will bring.

The physical clustering of cultural, community and educational facilities amplifies the positive impacts described previously and has the potential to encourage creative collaborations between different organisations, which blur the distinction between different artforms, media, audiences and age groups.

There are benefits in locating a theatre close to other cultural and community facilities or even co-locating complementary facilities in the same building. For this reason, some theatres successfully accommodate other uses such as cinema, library, education, cafés and community spaces and as a result have far higher visitor numbers and longer operating hours than pure theatre buildings. Theatres can also make positive use of open spaces for visitors to assemble and disperse, for all-day catering facilities and for the programming of outdoor events and festivals (see Figures 1.2.2 and 1.2.3).

***Chester's Storyhouse and Riverside Studios, London***

Figure 1.2.2 The public spaces of Chester's Storyhouse were created from the shell of a former Odeon cinema. A new theatre, city library, cinema and café are clustered into a single building managed by one organisation. This means the building is open and busy into the evening seven days a week. See Reference Project 06.

Figure 1.2.3 The flexible venues which have been created at Riverside Studios in London can be configured for live performance, rehearsal or even TV broadcast. The building also includes cinemas, co-working office space, a café, gallery and production space. See Reference Project 21.

## Theatres and urban regeneration

The value brought by theatre buildings and their operation to a neighbourhood means that it is not unusual for theatres to be conceived as part of a wider urban regeneration proposal or even integrated into or co-funded

Figure 1.2.4 Situated on a new public square, HOME in Manchester is a multi-arts cultural hub. It was among the first buildings to be completed in First Street, an urban regeneration project which has created a new neighbourhood of offices, homes and shops. See Reference Project 23.

Figure 1.2.5 In Belfast's Cathedral Quarter, the Metropolitan Arts Centre (MAC) is an important element in an urban regeneration plan that includes a new city square enclosed by shops and apartments. See Section 4, Figure 4.9.3 and Reference Project 22.

by commercial property development. Theatres and other cultural buildings are strategically important to the future plans of towns and cities and are often given a prominent site where their day-long activity and footfall can bring vitality and focus to a new district (see Figures 1.2.4 and 1.2.5).

## Working with a place and its people

Designing a theatre that will provide these benefits requires an understanding of the cultural network of a place and the buy-in of the communities that might use it (not just those that currently do). Clients and designers need to engage with these communities from the early planning stage of a project in a two-way conversation that creates confidence, support and a sense of ownership.

By careful planning of an engagement programme, and by listening and feeding back to both individuals and groups during the development phase of a theatre project, a venue's facilities can be honed to suit the needs of potential users and its reach can be maximised.

## Audiences and travel

One of the key aims of most theatre developments is to build or grow audiences, and the theatre's business plan will include research which analyses any existing audience data and forecasts the likely 'catchment area' from which audiences will be drawn and the likely attendance patterns of individuals. Comparisons will be made to other venues in the area, and a brief will be developed which complements existing offerings.

Travel time for visitors to the theatre will be a factor which determines the potential audience size for any site, and available modes of travel will need to be co-ordinated with strategic plans for public transport, cycling, walking and parking in the area. The streets in the immediate context of the theatre also need to be considered carefully, as visitors who complete the last part of their journey on foot are more likely to contribute to the local economy through the footfall created in the immediate neighbourhood.

## Logistics and location

Theatre buildings have significant operational requirements for access, and this is often an early determining factor in the choice of location. The logistics of the theatre industry involve moving entire shows in and out of theatres in very large vehicles with minimal closure time, often late at night. Good road access direct to the stage for articulated vehicles is required for all but the smallest venues.

### Theatres as neighbours

Successful theatres are busy buildings which are active late into the night. In determining the location and orientation of the building, it is important to consider potential impacts on residential neighbours, so designing the building to prevent noise break-out during performances and the enclosure of loading bays to limit late-night disturbance are common design considerations. It is important to consider how people will be managed as they arrive and leave the building and this can be captured in an audience management plan.

Theatres can also be sensitive to noise and vibration coming from their surroundings which, if allowed to penetrate the building's structure, will be audible in the building during performances. Mitigating nearby noise and vibration sources such as rail lines can lead to costly acoustic solutions having to be adopted in the building.

## 1.3 Inclusive design

At every stage of planning, designing, constructing and fitting out, the designers of theatre buildings make decisions which will determine who can use that space comfortably and who feels at home there. Inclusive design considers the needs of disabled people on equal terms with everyone else and should be applied throughout the design process.

### Inclusive design as an opportunity

Inclusive design represents more than simple compliance with legislation. Disabled people actively participate in theatre as visitors, employees and artists. A successful theatre building will make the most of the creative opportunities offered by designing with inclusivity in mind, providing spaces that disabled people can use along with others.

The term 'disabled people' is used to refer to a wide range of people, including those with mobility impairments; hidden impairments; sensory impairments; mental health issues; and people who are deaf, neurodivergent or learning disabled.

Section 3 of this book covers the theme of inclusive design in detail. It describes approaches to inclusive design, as well as current legislation. By setting out principles, with examples, it offers creative solutions to inclusive design in theatre buildings which avoid specific instruction or proscription.

## 1.4 Theatre and the climate emergency

Growing levels of carbon dioxide in the atmosphere have caused a steady increase in global temperatures which has resulted in extreme weather events, rising sea levels and a catastrophic loss of biodiversity. To tackle climate change, society must cut carbon emissions to zero by the transition from fossil fuels including oil and gas to renewable or other net-zero carbon energy sources to power everything we do.

### The carbon impact of theatres

Theatre has a part to play in this transition, and, while its impacts are relatively small compared to other sectors of the economy, its influence is powerful and wide reaching. The amount of net-zero energy that can be made available in the coming decades is limited, so the available resources need to be shared, resulting in the need for significant reductions in energy use across all of society, including the energy used in the construction and operation of theatres.

The UK's Climate Change Act commits to eliminating all greenhouse gas emissions to zero by 2050. The route to achieve this requires buildings to set out on a rapid path of decarbonisation, with all new buildings operating at net zero carbon by 2030.

To calculate the total carbon impact of a theatre building, two types of carbon emissions are measured, operational carbon from the day-to-day running of the venue and embodied carbon emitted to construct and maintain the building.

- Operational carbon: carbon emissions resulting from operating a theatre include heating, lighting and cooling as well as creating the performances themselves. Carbon is emitted by everything from the power required to run electrical systems to the fuel used in transporting equipment and supplies and the carbon and waste associated with the materials placed on stage.
- Embodied carbon: the construction of a new theatre or the physical adaptation of an existing theatre requires the consumption of materials. These materials contain embodied carbon emissions associated with their extraction, production and transport to the theatre.

### Net-zero theatres

Clear definitions of net-zero are emerging, and, whilst it is ultimately for governments to create a unified strategy which aligns with national energy policy, organisations like the UK Green Building Council and networks such as the London Energy Transformation Initiative (LETI) have been at the forefront of establishing definitions and targets for net-zero which have achieved widespread acceptance.

To achieve net zero, a theatre will have to meet targets both for operational carbon and embodied carbon emissions. A theatre with net zero operational carbon does not burn fossil fuels, is powered by renewable energy and achieves a level of energy performance in use in line with national climate change targets. Best practice targets for embodied carbon also need to be met, and the building's design will need to incorporate re-used materials or low-carbon materials like timber in sufficient quantities to reduce overall embodied carbon.

### The theatre brief and carbon emissions

The design brief for any new venue needs to embed net-zero thinking in all aspects of the design and operation. This means establishing targets for both operational and embodied carbon at the very early stages of the project. The theatre building's performance requirements will be set out in the client's brief, and every aspect of the building, from acoustic performance to space planning and technical load requirements, will contribute to the carbon consumption of the project. Agreeing on realistic loading capacities and environmental performance targets in the brief will have the single greatest impact on the carbon emissions of the project before the design process even starts.

### Theatre as an advocate of climate action

The theatre industry can demonstrate its credibility by setting carbon targets, constructing sustainable theatre buildings and developing sustainable productions and operations. But theatre also has the power to advocate for change through shaping stories which can influence people's attitudes and behaviours.

For designers, the adoption of the new materials, tools and methods that will be required to achieve net-zero theatres provides an opportunity to explore fresh ideas and processes. Moving towards more sustainable ways to design theatre buildings and to make theatre offers an important creative challenge for the sector.

Further information about how theatre buildings can be designed to respond to the climate emergency is contained in Section 3 of this book, and a detailed methodology for reducing operational carbon in both buildings and performances can be found in the ABTT's *Theatre Green Book* series of publications.

## 1.5 Types of theatre

All theatre buildings share a series of common spaces for audiences and performers. However, there are many different sizes and types of theatre building, each tailored to specific types of performance, audience capacity or operating model. Before a theatre is designed, it is important to understand the range of performances to be accommodated and the intended operating model. This information should be captured and agreed in the design brief.

### Space for different types of performance

The breadth of performance types that are presented in a theatre can include drama, dance, musical theatre and opera. Each type has a different set of functional requirements depending on the scale and complexity of the performance and the size of the company. While the design of some theatres is specifically optimised for one type of performance, it is also possible for theatres to be adaptable to suit a range of performance types. Before the design process starts, the client and the design team need to have decided on the range of performance types that are to be accommodated in the theatre so that the emerging design can take these into consideration. See Figure 1.5.1, a diagram comparing the relative space requirements and company sizes for different types of performance.

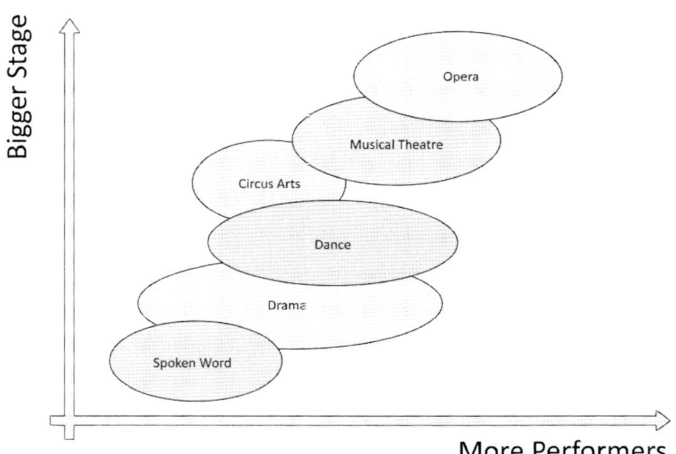


Figure 1.5.1 This diagram shows that a wide range of performance types can be accommodated in theatre spaces. Opera and musical theatre typically require the largest stage and backstage areas and have a large company, including musicians, whereas drama and spoken word can take place in much smaller venues.

## Audience capacity

Theatres for drama probably show the widest variation in seating capacity. Drama theatres can range from a 100-seat studio to over 1000 seats. Above this capacity, it is difficult for actors to communicate effectively with their audience, amplification may be required and those seated farther back in the auditorium may have difficulty seeing the actors' facial expressions.

Mid-scale venues for drama accommodate an audience of 400–600, with theatres designed for larger touring productions generally having a capacity of 800–1000. Some large drama houses have capacities of around 1,200 to 1,400, which is the preferred size for many of the commercial theatre operators in the UK.

Theatres for opera and ballet are configured with a large well-equipped stage and a large orchestra pit for musicians, accommodating an audience of between 1,200 and 2,200, depending on the artistic programme.

## Operational models

Theatres can operate in several different ways, and the brief for the principal spaces in the building, including the audience capacity and size of stage, will be dependent on the operational model. The main consideration for the design team is the extent to which the theatre will create its own productions in-house (a producing theatre) or whether it will mainly be presenting productions that have been created elsewhere (a presenting theatre). The client's brief and business plan should clearly set out the anticipated operational model before the design commences (see Figures 1.5.2 and 1.5.3).

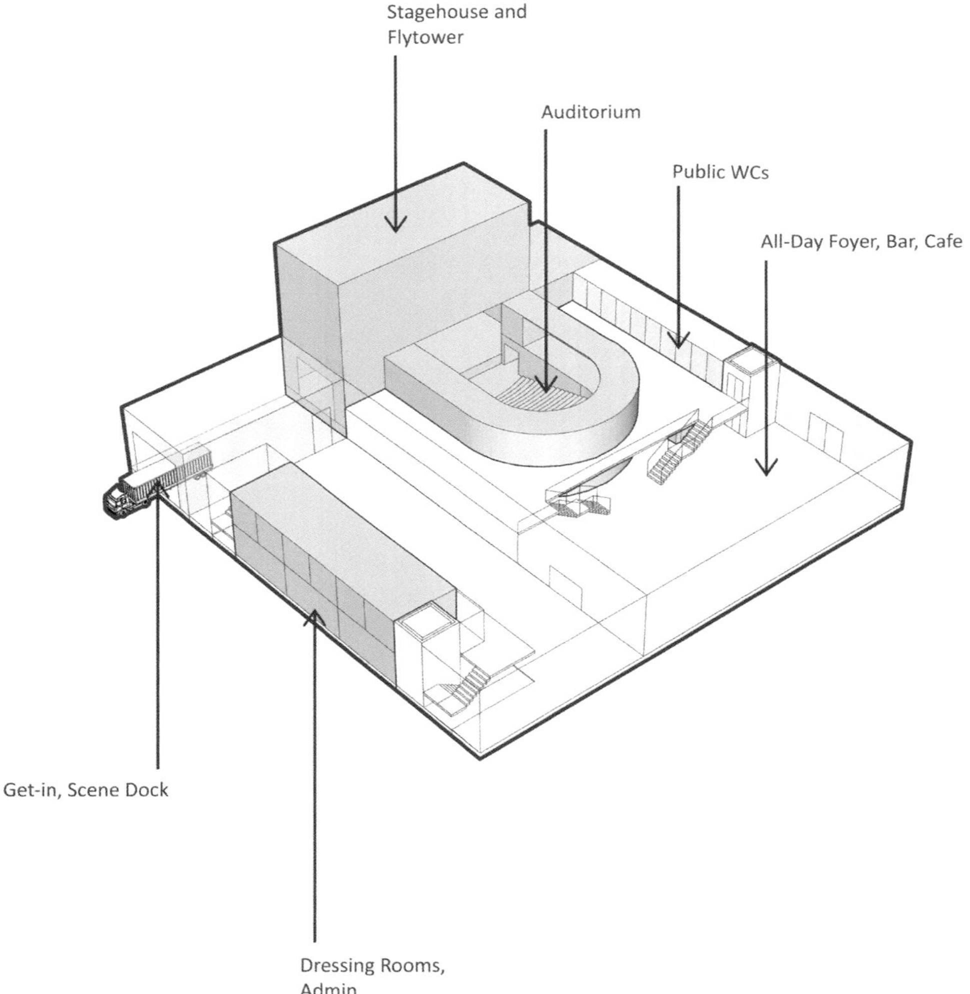


Figure 1.5.2 The layout of a typical presenting theatre. The main auditorium is the heart of the building, with public areas including foyers, bars and WCs on one side and backstage facilities adjoining the stagehouse on the other.

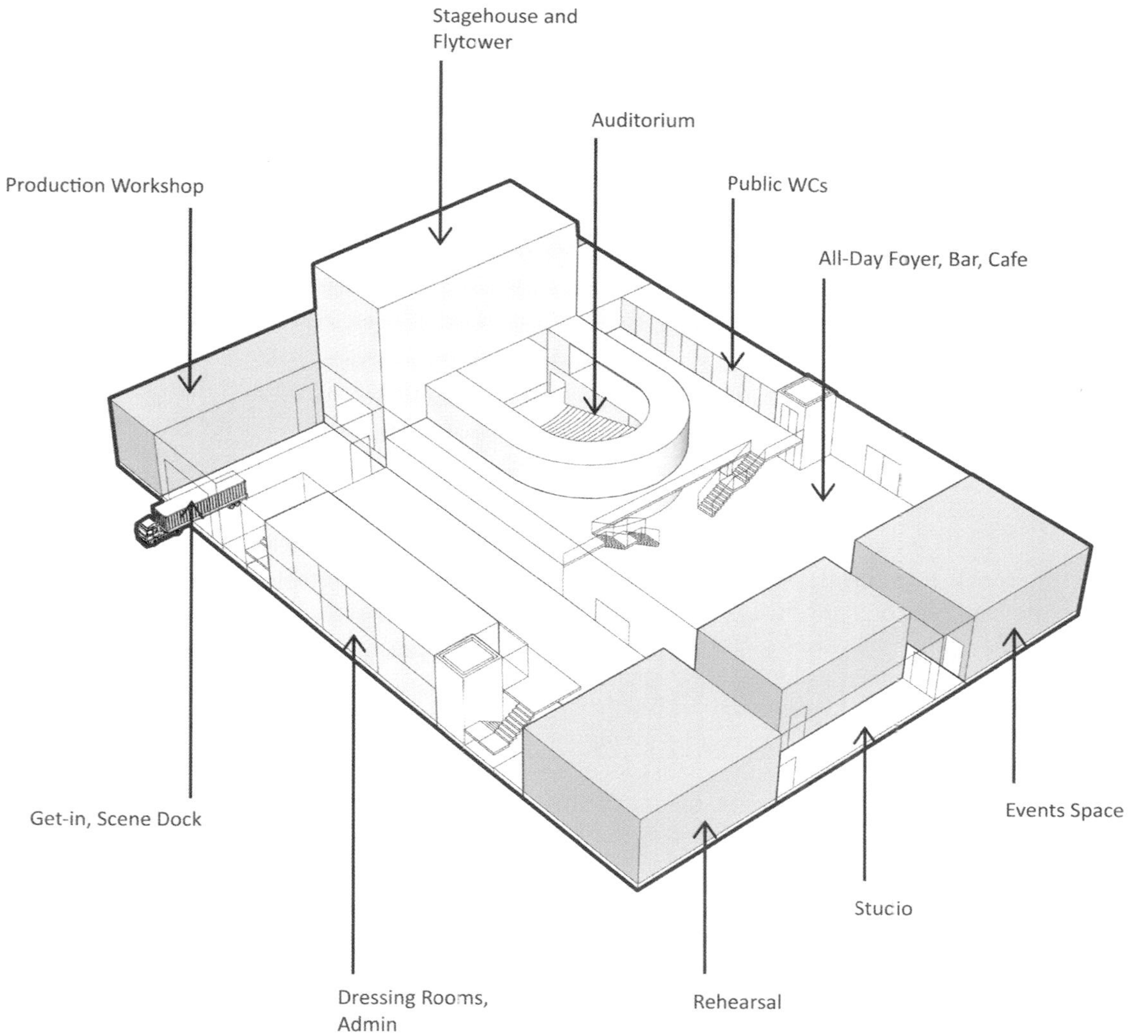

Figure 1.5.3 The layout of a typical producing theatre. The core of the building is similar to a presenting theatre, but additional facilities are provided like production workshops and rehearsal spaces where new productions are created. Smaller studio theatres or events spaces are also common in this type of theatre.

## Producing theatres

A producing theatre creates its own productions, choosing or commissioning scripts, hiring actors, rehearsing and designing and building sets, as well as all the other activities associated with the mounting of new productions. These theatres need a larger artistic and administrative team, rehearsal rooms and scenery, props and costume workshops, although these activities may take place off-site.

Producing theatres can also operate on a repertory basis. This means that they present a season of three or four different productions which alternate from one night to the next. Some repertory theatres present up to three different productions within a week to attract a maximum number of ticket sales to a visiting audience. This type of operation requires significant off-stage scenery storage. Sometimes an opera and ballet company share a theatre, with productions from each company running on alternate evenings.

## Presenting theatres

A presenting theatre, sometimes called a receiving theatre or touring theatre, predominantly presents a season of shows or events that tour multiple venues and which have been created elsewhere. The shows may only spend one night at each venue on a tour, so this type of building needs efficient, rapid changeovers between productions, where one show will get-out and the next show get-in within a twelve- to twenty-four-hour period. It will generally have a smaller administrative team and no, or minimal, production facilities.

Most presenting theatres have an auditorium in end-on configuration with the audience seated together, facing the performers on the stage, which may be separated from the auditorium by a traditional proscenium arch. This is because touring productions are mostly produced in this format and require a reasonably consistent stage size and technical set-up at all the venues in the tour.

In major cities around the world, some theatres will run shows for as long as they are commercially successful, for months or even several years. In London's West End these types of presenting theatres often have quite simple technical facilities, with the equipment being brought in specifically for each production. Frequently these theatres are refurbished, or radically remodelled, to accommodate a particular show.

### Hybrid models

Not all theatres fit strictly into the narrow definitions of producing and presenting, and, for many theatre operators, a hybrid model is desirable – presenting touring productions for some of a season and producing or co-producing home-grown productions for the rest of the year. Co-productions pool the resources of a number of theatres by jointly commissioning productions for in-house presentation and subsequent tours. In the UK the Christmas show or pantomime is one of the biggest and most financially important shows of the year and is often an in-house production or is outsourced.

### Future-proofing the design

Theatres should be designed to have a long and sustainable life, and to help make this possible, designers need to consider the future flexibility and adaptability of the design beyond the immediate requirements of the client's brief.

Artistic ambition, audience expectations and business models all evolve more quickly than theatres are rebuilt. Many theatres in the UK have successfully been in operation for well over one-hundred years, and this is because their design has been able to adapt to changes in audience and business needs. So, while the considerations of the brief and business plan may appear to be fixed at the outset of the project, it is important that the design team consider how future generations of artists, audiences and theatre managers may want the flexibility to do things differently in the short, medium and long term.

Short-term flexibility: could mean a range of possible stage and auditorium formats created quickly and cheaply to suit different types of production.

Medium-term flexibility: larger changes to the auditorium format for a season or longer period requiring several days to create.

Long-term adaptability: designing the building structure to allow more significant changes to the auditorium or other areas to suit new artforms or business models.

### Earning additional income from the building

Theatre buildings need to be worked hard to support the financial resilience of the organisations that run them. With the right design approach, theatre buildings can generate additional income from activities other than the sale of tickets. The secondary commercial income – from bars, catering, venue hire, meetings, conferences and other events – is usually built into the business plan from an early stage (see Sections 2 and 4) and needs to be considered alongside the programming of ticketed performances.

Venue hire can range from the renting out of simple meeting space to the hire of performance spaces for events. Opportunities for more specialist hires requiring TV or other live recording are on the increase, and getting the infrastructure in place to support these potential hires is an early design consideration.

Catering is a specialist activity, and making the most of it requires specialist input into the design of the offer and the space and fit-out requirements for the bars/cafés and for the support spaces. The design of these spaces is covered in detail in Section 4 of this book.

## 1.6 The working theatre

Before a theatre building can be designed, it is important to understand the people and processes that make up a successful theatre operation. The brief for a theatre project should capture the anticipated operational model of the theatre, and it should also outline the structure of the organisation that will run it.

### People and processes in a theatre

A theatre organisation is divided into teams with responsibility for different processes and aspects of the business. The size of the team can vary considerably from a handful of individuals with multiple roles in a small theatre to tens or even hundreds of people in a large producing theatre, but the scope of a theatre's activities remains broadly the same regardless of size.

The **Senior Leadership Team** is usually made up of the artistic director, chief executive, finance director, marketing director, producer, technical director and head of operations. This team can be bigger or smaller depending on the size and type of the organisation. This team is the group who are responsible for creating and delivering a programme of work and events which meets the strategic artistic and financial aims of the business and leading the other teams which run the day-to-day operation of the building and its productions.

The **Creative Team** is made up of directors, writers, set designers, costume designers, sound designers and lighting designers. Depending on the size and type of theatre organisation, these can be full time or freelance posts. However, most theatre organisations will want to engage with this team during the project.

In producing organisations, the **Production Team** work to deliver the physical production such as scenery, props and costume. This team often includes the production manager, stage management, heads of wardrobe, props and scenery construction, although these functions are increasingly outsourced in smaller organisations.

The **Company** includes the actors, musicians and dancers who perform in the theatre for the duration of a production run. They may be resident for a season as part of a resident company or for a very short time as part of a visiting company on tour.

The **Technical Team and Crew** operate and maintain the technical infrastructure of the auditorium and stage and are responsible for the running of shows and events. In some smaller organisations they may also have overall responsibility for managing the building's systems and maintenance.

**Marketing, Sales and Box-Office teams** are responsible for ticket sales, publicity and managing the theatre's relationship with its audiences.

**Operations/Front of House or Theatre Management/ Customer Service** teams are responsible for the visitor experience, managing catering and bars, greeting, directing and managing audiences and daytime visitors. This group may also encompass Facilities Management, depending on the size and operation of the organisation.

The **Learning Team is** responsible for the co-ordination of the organisation's learning and outreach programme, schools' engagement and other community work.

The **Development Team** is responsible for fund-raising to supplement the theatre's income and to provide funding for any capital project.

For a theatre to operate successfully, several different types and sizes of spaces are required, many of which have very specific requirements. Theatre designers find it helpful to categorise these spaces into three main areas of activity, as indicated in Figure 1.6.1.

- Auditorium and Stage: the heart of a theatre building, where the primary activity of experiencing and presenting performances takes place.
- Front of House: the public spaces used by visitors during the day and the spaces where audiences assemble before a show, during intervals and afterwards.
- Backstage: the spaces that facilitate the performance itself, with a wide range of accommodation for management, actors, musicians and technical staff and the facilities to handle scenery, costumes and equipment.

## 1.7 Auditorium and stage

In a theatre building the auditorium can range from a simple studio space with fewer than one-hundred seats to a multi-level room with several thousand seats and a large, mechanised stage house. In all cases, audience seating is arranged to view the stage, and the stage is a platform or area from which the actors perform to the audience. A crucial factor in the design of any auditorium is the complex physical and geometrical relationship between stage and every seat in the room that allows performers and audience to interact.

### Auditorium fundamentals

Live performance is a collective experience; audience members make a two-way connection with the performers on stage, but there is also a strong sense of shared experience within the audience itself, with reactions of emotion or applause spontaneously breaking out and transmitting around the space. A successful auditorium design will amplify the atmosphere of a performance by achieving the best relative positions and closest proximity of stage and audience and the best distribution of the audience around the room.

Earlier in this section we described the different types of performance that may be accommodated in theatre auditoria. Depending on the requirements of the business plan, these can range from intimate drama productions where the audience connect with the smallest details in the performance, to large-scale opera and musical theatre where scenic spectacle and amplified sound create epic events requiring large numbers of performers, musicians, and scenic changes. A theatre auditorium is often required to accommodate more than one of these types of performance, making the development of the auditorium's form and scale one of the most important principles in the design of a theatre building. Figures 1.7.1a–f show examples of different auditorium formats.

### Auditorium formats and flexibility

To accommodate the largest range of performance types, and to help with the transfer of shows between different venues, many theatres adopt a conventional end-on

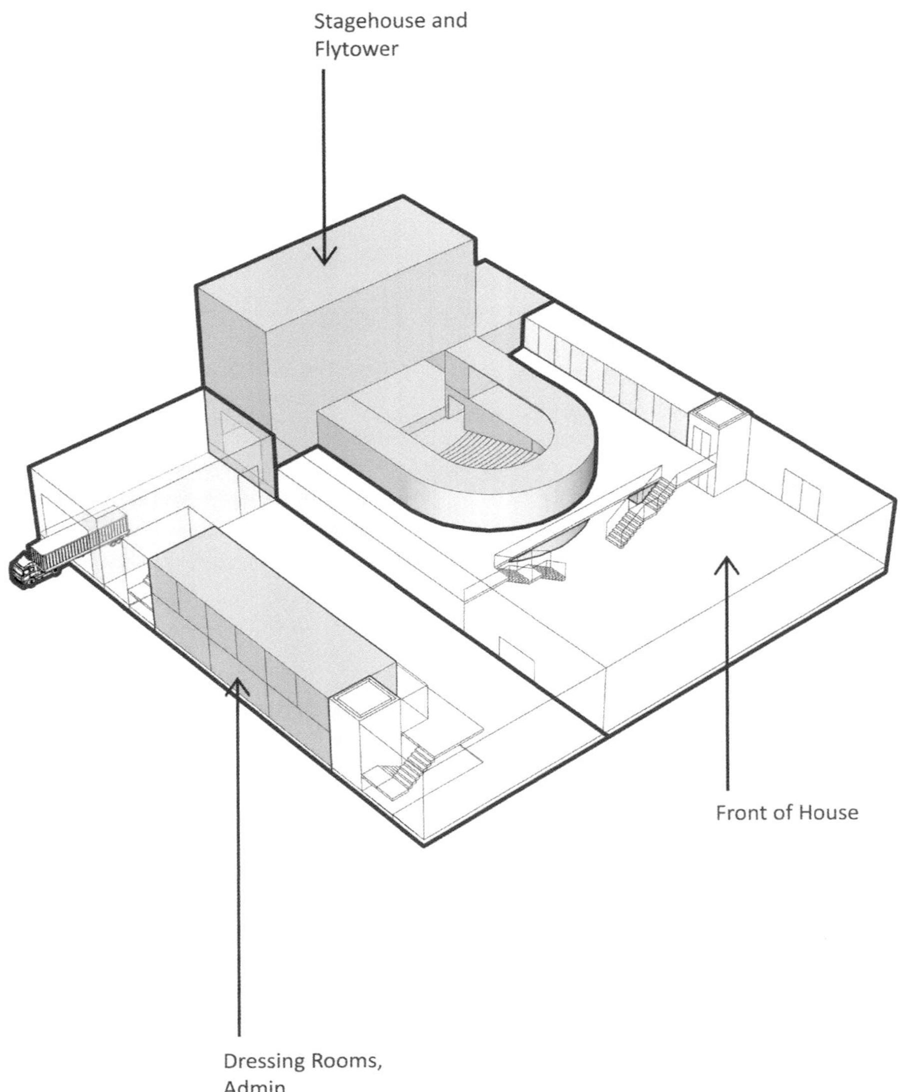


Figure 1.6.1 Diagram showing spaces in a theatre are categorised into the three main areas of activity. The auditorium and stage are where the performance happens, the front of house is where the audience gather and backstage is where the performers and technicians are based.

configuration where seating in fixed tiers faces a rectangular stage-house framed by a proscenium. The stage is equipped with a flytower to accommodate scenery and lighting.

However, the end-on format does not always result in the best audience experience, and many directors and designers look for ways of providing new audience points of view and more dynamic ways of presenting theatre. The configuration of the audience has an impact on the shared experience of the performance, and in some productions an audience might be seated or standing, in conventional tiered rows or facing each other across or on all sides of the stage. These formats give more flexibility in the position of the stage and audience and offer a range of different artistic possibilities.

To sustain a theatre business for the long term, auditoria need to be hard-working spaces which can present a reasonable range of performance types with minimal 'dark-time' between shows. They also need to be able to adapt to evolutionary changes in theatre practice, with an increasing diversity of media and performance styles which cross over traditional genres.

To find a balance between the practicality of the end-stage theatre and the artistic potential of different formats, many theatres are designed with a degree of flexibility, allowing changes between two or three fixed formats, which might mean changes to the position of the stage edge and positions of banks of seating in the auditorium.

Figure 1.7.1a End stage: Theatre 1 at HOME Manchester is an example of a typical end-stage auditorium with seating on three levels, stalls, circle and balcony. The stage is experienced as a separate space viewed through a proscenium arch. See Reference Project 23.

Figure 1.7.1b Thrust stage: the stage of the Royal Shakespeare Theatre in Stratford-upon-Avon projects into the auditorium and is surrounded by audience on three sides. The audience occupies a stalls level and two upper galleries. See Reference Project 27.

Figure 1.7.1c Orchestra pit: opera houses such as Nevill Holt Opera have a large orchestra pit for musicians in a sunken area in front of the stalls seating and below the stage. See Reference Project 08.

Figure 1.7.1d In-the-round: for some types of performance, the audience surrounds the stage area on all sides. The flexible Boulevard Theatre in Soho, London, can be configured in this format. See Reference Project 13.

The design of auditoria is covered in more detail in Sections 5 and 6 of this book.

## Found spaces

Theatre has a tradition of colonising existing spaces that were built for other uses and creating performance spaces out of them; think of the Roundhouse in Camden, a former engine shed (see Judith Strong (ed.), *Theatre Buildings: A Design Guide* (1st edition, 2010), pp. 258–61); Glasgow's Tramway carved out of industrial buildings; or the St Ann's Warehouse, a former tobacco warehouse in Brooklyn (see Section 12, Reference Project 04). Found spaces offer the scale and flat-floor flexibility for artists to create environments for performance that could not be conceived within traditional auditorium forms.

These spaces do away with the conventions of a raised stage and flytower altogether, creating large studio-like environments with the potential to place the stage and seating in any configuration. The atmosphere of these highly flexible spaces is very different from a conventional theatre auditorium, but their long-term flexibility and adaptability promise a long and sustainable future and the ability to present multiple artforms.

Figure 1.7.1e Studio: for smaller audiences below 200, the stage and seating can occupy the same flat-floor space in a variety of formats. Studio 3 at Riverside Studios is shown here in end-stage format. See Reference Project 21.

## Technology supporting the performance

Whatever the size of the theatre, the performance is often supported by a considerable array of technology in the form of lighting, scenery handling equipment and sound systems, all of which need to be integrated with the architecture of the auditorium. Advice on these installations is normally provided by a specialist theatre consultant who, as part of the design team, will consult the client and advise the designers on the technical installation and its operation, as indicated in the bullet points here.

- Stage engineering: in larger theatres, stage engineering installations are needed to handle the scenery and to make changes to the stage configuration, this includes items such as flying systems, wagons, bridges and elevators. Electrical power is usually required to operate this machinery, and control systems are located in separate equipment racks which emit heat and sound and need to be carefully located or isolated.
- Production lighting: lighting for the performance is installed on a show-by-show basis on lighting bars both in the stage and into the auditorium. The electrical services to these positions are also extensive and require careful planning. Safe access to these positions, to hang and focus lanterns, is also a requirement, which may involve the provision of walkways, ladder rails and fall arrest systems. Noisy equipment, such as the racks of dimmers which control the lighting, is usually housed outside the auditorium.
- Sound and communications: these encompass all the equipment used to provide both live amplified and recorded sound for a performance, public address systems in the front of house and backstage areas and video links and communications between staff and performers. In the auditorium, it will be necessary to integrate positions for loudspeakers and a range of positions for live sound mixing desks, located where operators can see and hear well. Amplifiers can be noisy and are often located outside the auditorium in a separate room.

Figure 1.7.1f 'Found' Space: for St Ann's Warehouse in Brooklyn, a new highly flexible auditorium has been created within the existing walls of a former warehouse. See Reference Project 04.

- Data: like most modern buildings, theatres rely heavily on data wiring to allow a wide range of equipment around the building to be controlled and to communicate with other systems. This includes office computer networks, wireless systems, video links, display screens, production lighting and sound control systems, stage equipment installations and control systems for mechanical and electrical services.

Further information on the stage, stage machinery, lighting, sound and video can be found in Sections 8 and 9.

## 1.8 Front of house spaces

The quality of the visitor journey from a theatre's entrance to a seat in the auditorium helps shape expectations and anticipation of the performance itself. But it is also in these spaces that practical issues such as ticketing to performances will be managed, where food and drink will be served and where toilets will be located.

### Welcome, legibility and flow

Designers need to understand that it is in the foyer and gathering spaces of a theatre that the audience first coalesces, and these spaces need to be consciously shaped to support the social activity that takes place around performance times by offering a variety of spaces to meet, socialise, observe and interact with others. The architect of the National Theatre, Denys Lasdun, described this as the 'theatre of the foyer', and, just as the design of auditoria are honed to create the best audience experience, so the other public spaces in a theatre should be carefully scaled and configured to help create a sense of togetherness amongst a diverse group of people.

The main public areas of a theatre need to be able to accommodate big changes in occupancy successfully. The foyers need to feel comfortable and welcoming during quieter daytime use as well as during very busy times before a performance or during an interval. (See Figure 1.8.1.)

Figure 1.8.1 The foyer at the Bristol Old Vic is easy to navigate; there are open views between entrance and the main functions such as the main stairs and bar. It has been designed to provide a variety of spaces for people to occupy during the day as well as in the evening. See Section 4, Figure 4.4.1 and Reference Project 31.

People may be visiting the theatre for the first time, so it is essential that the building be clearly laid out and legible, with the facilities arranged in such a way that the flow of people going to their seats is not impeded by people gathering at bars or queueing for lifts or WCs. In larger theatres it is helpful to disperse the bars and toilets around the building, near the different seating areas, to avoid contra-flows and the congestion this creates.

A theatre foyer will require clear way-finding signage to enable the audience to find their seats and the other facilities around the building. However, a legibly designed front-of-house where the position of elements like auditorium, stairs and lifts is clearly visible will be much easier to navigate without the need for excessive signage.

A more detailed analysis of front of house requirements is given in Section 4 of this book.

## Encouraging all-day activity

The public areas of a theatre building are a valuable resource; outside performance times they can accommodate ancillary uses which bring people into the building and facilitate the social and community engagement which is an important part of a theatre's purpose. The footfall which comes from this daytime use helps support the all-day opening of catering facilities which in turn helps to attract visitors and generate revenue. Typical daytime uses might be accommodating community groups, after-school activities and education programmes as well as offering co-working space, but some theatres offer a broader range of co-located functions, including a cinema, a public library or gallery spaces. The notion of a theatre as a 'cultural hub' offering a range of public and community activities alongside a core theatre space allows opportunities for programming across multiple artforms and has the potential to mix audiences of all ages and backgrounds. See Figures 1.8.2a and 1.8.2b.

Figure 1.8.2a Storyhouse in Chester incorporates library shelving throughout its main public area; library users mingle with remote workers, families, students, cinemagoers and theatre audiences throughout the day. See Section 11, Figure 11.1 and Reference Project 06.

Figure 1.8.2b The all-day spaces in Storyhouse have been created within an old cinema. A screen in the foyer is a focus for informal screenings and performances. See Reference Project 06.

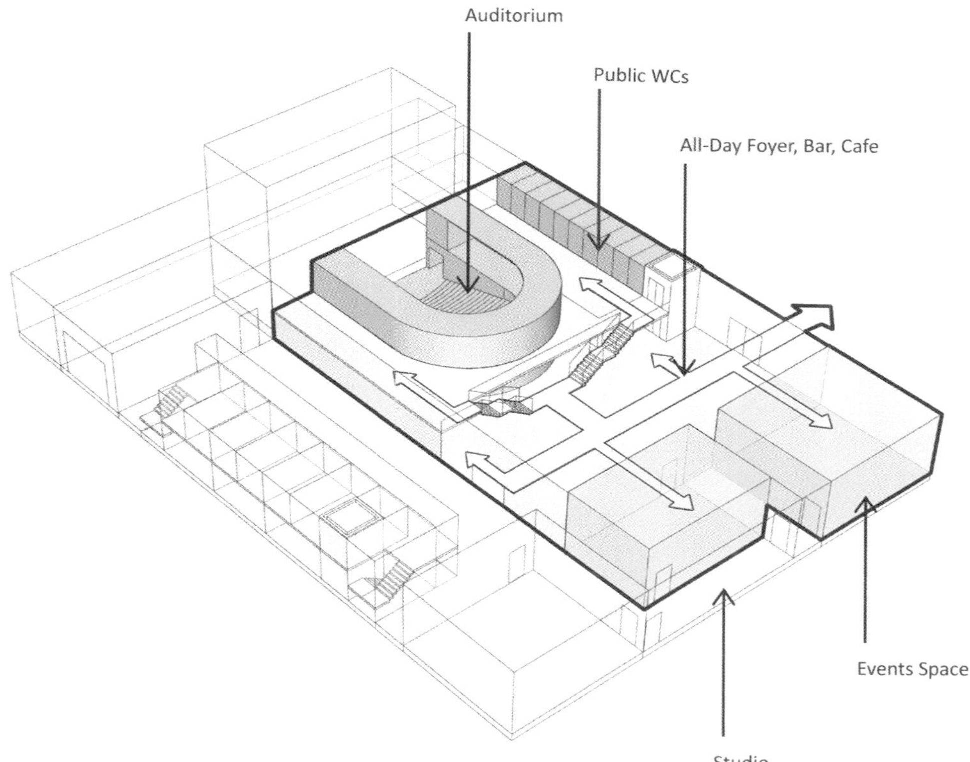


Figure 1.8.3 Front of house circulation: diagram showing the layout of a typical producing theatre showing open and legible circulation routes between the main front of house spaces.

### Front of house circulation

Theatre buildings should feel welcoming and familiar to visitors, which suggests legible planning that is easy to understand and routes which are, as far as possible, visible, logical and direct with a line of sight to the destination. For this reason, auditoria and other key public spaces are ideally placed directly adjacent to the main foyer. Most theatre buildings are on multiple levels, which means that stairs and lifts are ideally placed in clear view of the entrance or main foyer space. These features act as physical markers and help direct people to their destination. See Figure 1.8.3.

The best circulation spaces in theatres work in two ways, both as direct routes from street to seat and as places to wait, watch and socialise. Achieving both requires generous widths and edges which create places to dwell without blocking the flow of people at show times.

## 1.9 Backstage

For the staff and creative teams, the theatre's backstage is a place in which they will spend the majority of their working lives. A well-designed backstage can promote wellbeing for those who work there.

To encourage collaboration and creativity, designers need to apply the same rigour to the working spaces in a theatre as they do to the more high-profile public areas. This has not always been the case, and historically back-of-house spaces have often been heavily compromised by a lack of adequate space and even daylight.

### Backstage fundamentals

A well-designed backstage can reinforce the sense of teamwork and collaboration that is important in creating theatre. Circulation routes and informal break-out spaces strategically positioned to encourage interaction and communal spaces like green rooms with kitchen facilities often become focal points. Allowing the staff to use foyer spaces for refreshments and informal meetings adds to the atmosphere at otherwise quieter times of day.

The stage door is the traditional entry point to the working areas of a theatre, and it acts as a reception and security point for artists, visitors and deliveries. However, some theatres prefer the main staffed reception point to be in the public area of the building, adding to daytime activity front of house.

Traditionally a theatre's backstage is hidden from view, and visitors are not exposed to the inner workings of the theatre that supports the work on stage, but careful

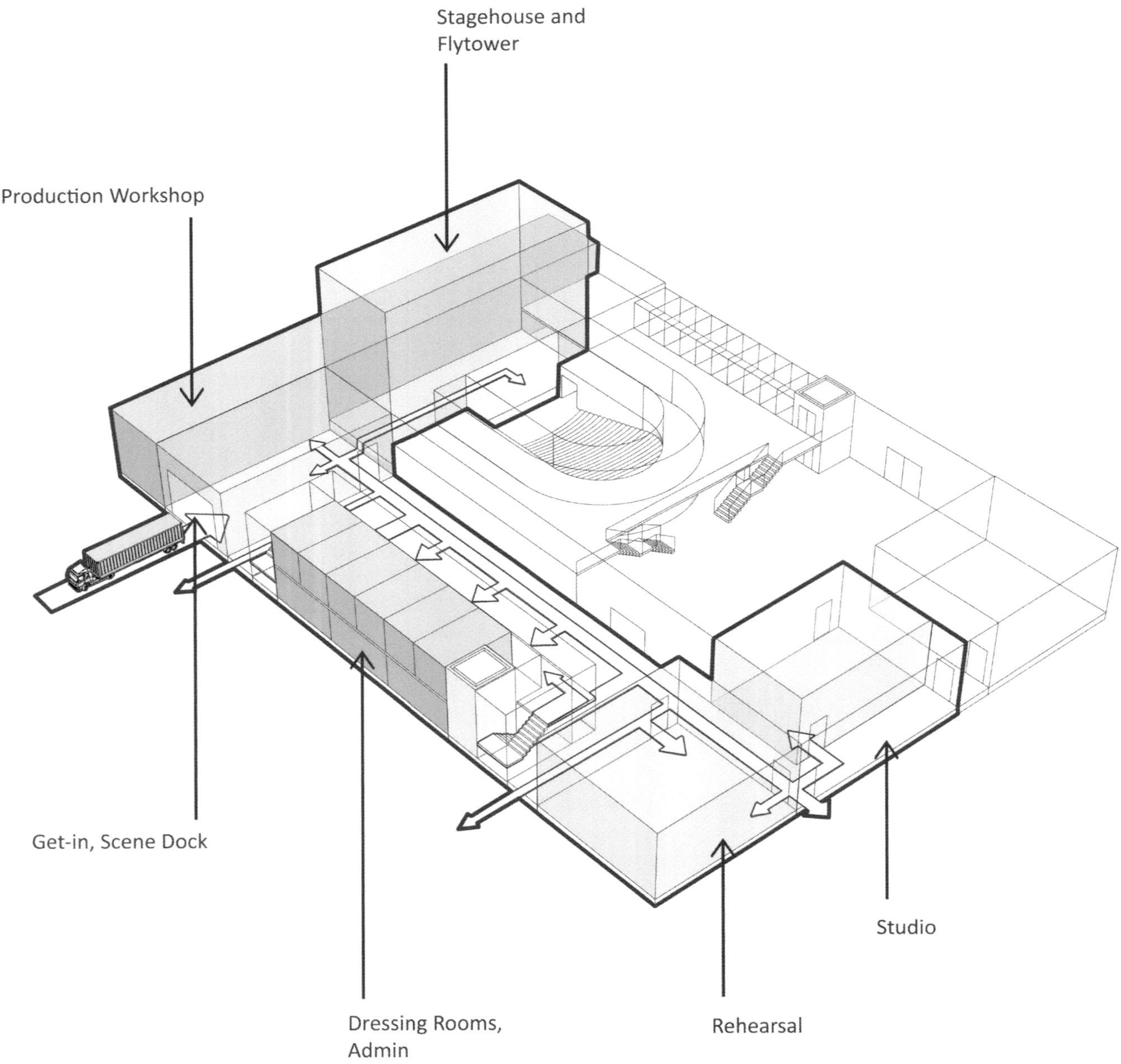


Figure 1.9.1 Diagram showing the layout of a typical producing theatre, the arrangement of backstage spaces and the generous circulation routes between them which do not cross over into public areas.

planning can create opportunities for appropriate glimpses backstage, and backstage tours and experiences are a way of engaging audiences and creating a deeper understanding of how theatres work.

## Functional requirements

For backstage areas designers need to consider the comfort and wellbeing of building users but also the operational needs of the theatre. Functional requirements should be discussed at the briefing stage so that designers can plan how the people and objects that need to find their way to stages and rehearsal rooms can be offloaded from vehicles or moved around the building with minimum reliance on labour or mechanical assistance.

Large and heavy objects like pianos, rostra, flight cases of equipment and laden costume rails need to be moved quickly and efficiently down corridors, through doors and into lifts, and the surfaces of circulation areas need to be protected from damage.

Likewise, actors have to get between dressing rooms and stage in costumes which may be large or cumbersome without delay or difficulty.

Ease and speed of delivery of large items of scenery and equipment to and from the stage are essential, particularly in presenting theatres where shows change frequently. For this reason, it is highly desirable for the delivery doors, or 'get-in', to be at the same level as the stage. Where this is not possible, it will be necessary to provide a very large elevator to move scenery and equipment from delivery level to stage level. This is expensive, adds considerably to the time and labour required to double handle large items and poses the risk of performances being cancelled if the lift breaks down. The reputation of a presenting theatre with touring companies can depend as much on the quality of the get-in as any other factor.

Designers need to allow for sufficient scene dock space between the get-in and the stage for the off-loading, handling and storage of sets and equipment. The scale of this will depend on the size and type of theatre and on whether more than one show needs to be stored within the building at a time. Significant amounts of storage are also required for stock items that are used regularly, such as access equipment, rostra, seats, lights, drapes, and musical instruments. Producing theatres may also require workshops for the manufacture of sets, props and costumes and for the maintenance of equipment, although the cost of providing these facilities on a city centre site means that they are sometimes located off-site, or the work is outsourced to specialist contractors with their own facilities.

Further detail on backstage activities and the backstage community can be found in Section 7 of this book.

## Dressing rooms and green rooms

Located as close as possible to the stage, the dressing rooms are the acting company's home away from home. More than just a functional changing space, it is a place to prepare mentally for the performance as well as a place to relax, even sleep between shows. Actors need secure dedicated space backstage to prepare for the performance and to shower and change afterwards. During the run of a show, the company will be performing daily, with two performances on some days. Designers should consider adding practical features like dressing tables and mirrors which can allow for personalisation with cards and flowers and the safe storage of personal items; daylight and view should be incorporated if possible, and furniture should offer a place to relax.

The scale of dressing room facilities will vary enormously depending on the size and type of theatre and may range from a single dressing room to accommodation for up to 200 performers. Dressing rooms must be provided with adequate toilets and showers. They will require additional support facilities nearby, such as a running wardrobe, for the maintenance of costumes and wigs, and a green room, where actors and other staff can relax, eat or wait, away from their dressing rooms or offices. Dressing facilities should generally be as close to the stage as possible but with sufficient separation to prevent noise from reaching the stage.

The catering and social space backstage is known as the 'green room' and is often provided for the use of the whole company and crew. Green rooms can range from a simple kitchenette and lounge spaces in smaller theatres to kitchen and dining spaces in larger theatres with resident companies. They can double up as spaces for company meetings and often become the social heart of the backstage area.

A more detailed analysis of the 'backstage creative environment' is given in Section 7 of this book.

## Technical spaces

The stage and auditorium are highly technical spaces which support the complex process of presenting a performance. Stage managers and technicians control the show from dedicated positions in in the wings and in a control room located at the back of the auditorium which is usually out of sight and acoustically isolated from the audience. Dedicated communications systems relay their cues and calls and broadcast the show audio and sometimes video relay around the building.

The technical infrastructure of a theatre – the rigging, lighting, amplifiers and dimmers – needs specialist space for operation and storage, and theatre technicians need ready access to equipment as well as conveniently located workshops to carry out maintenance.

The backstage areas of a theatre must meet the needs of both the performers (rehearsal, dressing, preparation and relaxation) and of the production and technical staff responsible for the delivery and preparation of sets, costumes and technical equipment.

Theatre stages are potentially dangerous places, and, as a result, theatre buildings are run with a rigorous culture of safety management. Designers must wherever possible engage with end users early in the design process to develop a building which is safe to use and operate.

## Administration spaces

A theatre will require office space for the staff who work in the building. The size of this will be determined by the staff structure of the organisation concerned, and it is important to gain an understanding of this structure at the briefing stage. It is often desirable to group all the offices together in one location, but in some cases, such as front-of-house management, technical or catering staff, the offices may need to be located close to their respective areas of responsibility. The ideal location for the offices is mid-way between the backstage and front of house zones so that easy access to both areas is possible.

### Space for creating productions

Producing theatres create their own productions and require specific space for these activities to take place. Turning a script into a production is a highly collaborative process involving directors, designers, artists and technicians, and this process is most tangible during rehearsals, which may run for a few weeks or months prior to the first public performance. The rehearsal process involves the company and creatives in intensive work during which the final form of the production emerges, and it often requires focused time isolated from the day-to-day running of the theatre and insulated from intrusive noise. Rehearsal spaces need to be designed for long hours of intense use, with good daylight as well as the ability to achieve a black out if required, robust neutral finishes, good access for scenic elements and nearby welfare facilities and break-out spaces. During rehearsals the room becomes a virtual stage, replicating the footprint of the theatre stage. The room needs the height to build simple mock-ups of scenery and multi-level staging and the space to allow a director to stand back and observe from a distance.

### Space for services

Service installations such as mechanical and electrical systems are required to keep people comfortable and safe in the building and during a performance. Making sure that the building can be run efficiently and sustainably means that mechanical, electrical and audio-visual installations need to be carefully designed and co-ordinated with the structure and architecture of the theatre. Developing a servicing strategy is an early design activity, and space needs to be captured in the building for the services routes, risers and plantrooms that will be required to run the building and control the environment inside it.

### Backstage circulation

Backstage, the efficient operation of the building requires close links to all the stages from the get-in and from dressing rooms. Levels are important, and placing the get-in and some of the backstage accommodation, including at least one dressing room at stage level, is recommended so that lifts do not need to be relied on during performance times and get-ins. Other dressing rooms and backstage spaces are often stacked up on multiple floors around the stages connected by dedicated backstage stairs and lifts. See Figure 1.9.1.

## 1.10 Environmental control

Much of the operational carbon emissions from theatre buildings come from the mechanical and electrical services which are required to create a comfortable environment for building users. To reduce carbon emissions, designers need to consider strategies for environmental control which achieve the best balance of comfort conditions in the theatre building with minimum energy use. Once the most energy-efficient strategies for achieving comfort have been established, then the lowest-carbon sources of heating and cooling can be considered.

### Defining comfort

A large amount of energy can be consumed trying to maintain set temperatures in a building, and, in many circumstances, this is unnecessary and wasteful. Comfort is not simply achieved by maintaining a set temperature or ventilation rate in a space; people's perception of comfort will also depend on their circumstances. A seated audience paying high ticket prices for a performance will have a different expectation to a standing audience in a live music gig or comedy show.

The concept of adaptive thermal comfort allows the comfort level to be set based on percentage of people dissatisfied (PPD) and considers factors including local climate, recent weather conditions and level of clothing, allowing a tailored solution to be arrived for each type of event. BS EN ISO 7730 'Ergonomics of the Thermal Environment' and ASHRAE 55 'Thermal Environmental Conditions for Human Occupancy' are good guides to applying this method of provision of comfort and can be applied to both mechanical and natural ventilation systems.

### Layers of environmental control

In a theatre building, people's expectations of comfort vary depending on the type of space they are in, and this means that environmental control is less critical in transient spaces like foyers and circulation than it is in highly controlled spaces like auditoria and stages. It is helpful for designers to think about these different spaces as a series of layers containing foyers and ancillary spaces wrapping the most closely controlled space, the auditorium. See Figure 1.10.1.

The outermost layer contains the entrance doors and unheated draught lobbies which provide the transition from outdoors to indoors. These act as airlocks – particularly in winter to prevent cold winds from the street entering the building.

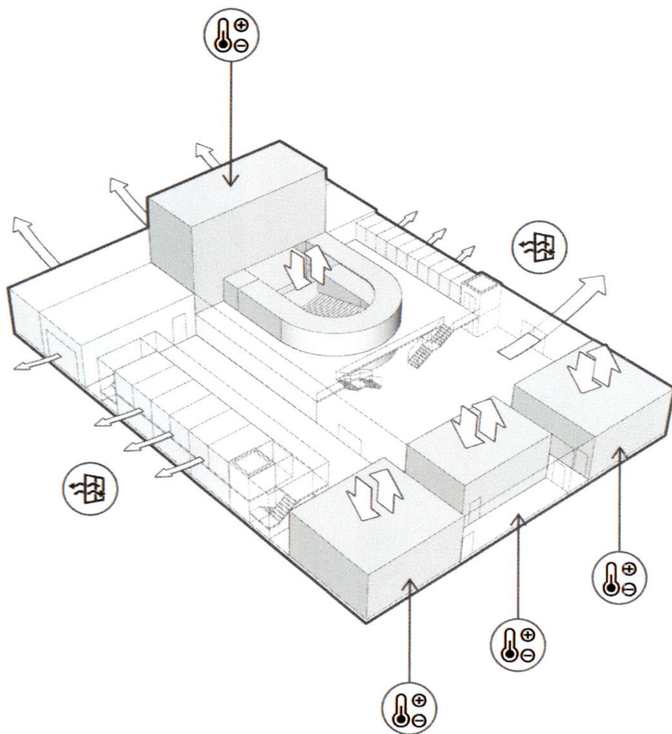

Figure 1.10.1 Diagram showing different levels of environmental control required by different spaces in a theatre. Performance spaces usually require the most control in order to maintain audience comfort whilst accommodating additional heating loads from the show lighting and equipment. Backstage spaces such as dressing rooms and offices are more domestic in scale and can be controlled using more traditional means such as radiators for heating and opening windows or fresh air supply for ventilation. Circulation areas are more transiently occupied by people who may be dressed for the outside and can therefore be managed within a wider temperature range.

The next layer might be an entrance space where people collect tickets or gather. Like other circulation spaces, this space requires basic temperature control as occupancy is transitional, although consideration should be given to the comfort of any staff that may work here for longer periods. Draught prevention from external weather is a high priority.

The entrance lobby provides a layer of protection to spaces like bars which may have high occupancy for short periods of time before and after shows and during intervals. These should be more closely controlled and designed for a general occupancy level rather than the short-term spike during an intermission, for example.

The auditorium sits at the centre of these layers and is protected from external conditions by the surrounding spaces. The auditorium will have a much more closely controlled set of criteria designed to create comfortable conditions even in the most intensive occupancy scenarios.

## Types of auditorium ventilation

The auditorium ventilation system is likely to be one of the largest single energy consumers in the building due to the high occupancy level and associated ventilation, heating and cooling requirements. Moving air in and out of the auditorium also creates noise, and the system needs to be designed to meet the desired acoustic criteria for the space. The ventilation system creates comfortable conditions for the auditorium in three ways:

- providing adequate fresh air and removal of contaminants
- heating the space for thermal comfort (usually before a performance)
- removing heat from occupants and theatre equipment during a performance.

There are two methods of providing air to the auditorium, either a mixing system which supplies air at ceiling level via mechanical means or a displacement system where fresh air is supplied at floor level by either mechanical or naturally driven systems.

## Displacement ventilation system

In a displacement system, air is provided at floor level at low velocity and treated to meet the heating and cooling loads of the low-level occupied zone only. Stratification means the polluted air rises and is extracted at a high level, with the fresh air continuously and slowly displacing stale air. For energy efficiency, a displacement system is the preferred strategy, providing fresh air via a plenum below the seating. For this to work effectively, a supply outlet is required for almost every seat in order to keep air velocity and regenerated noise low. Displacement systems work well for both mechanical and natural ventilation strategies.

## Mixing system

Where the theatre is an existing building or may be used as a standing auditorium where the seats are removed or reconfigured, a displacement system with grilles at floor level may not be possible. In these situations, a mixing system is the preferred alternative. In a mixing system, air is provided at a high level or from the sides and mixes with the air in the space so the whole space is homogeneous. Outlets such as nozzles and drum jet diffusers can provide high volumes of air, but they will need to be carefully selected to avoid creating excessive noise and draughts which will disrupt the comfort of the audience.

### Natural ventilation system

The most energy-efficient method of achieving comfort in an auditorium is to dispense with fans and use natural means to drive airflow through the space. Airflow is driven by the buoyancy of air inside the space being heated, then rising up and out, pulling fresh air in at a low level. At roof level, air terminals allow the air to escape and need to be designed so that airflow is maintained in a range of wind conditions. Incoming air can be naturally cooled by creating masonry-lined intake ducts or chambers below the auditorium floor, but the overall cooling capacity available is less than mechanical chillers could provide. For this reason, natural ventilation systems create a wider range of comfort conditions, and occupants will need to adapt their expectations to suit. The large open-air paths in and out of the auditorium that are required to achieve a natural ventilation strategy can allow unwanted sound transmission. Designers will need to consider adding acoustic attenuation to prevent break-in and break-out of noise. See Figures 1.10.2a and 1.10.2b.

Figures 1.10.2a and 2b. These images show two inventive designs that incorporate air terminals into the architecture of the roof lines to improve the ventilation of the buildings.

**Requirements of a naturally ventilated auditorium include**

- low-level inlets protected from the wind consisting of large underseat plenums and sound-attenuated air passages to prevent noise break-out and break-in
- underseat heating with low-level grilles
- large high-level outlets with attenuators
- a sophisticated control system to allow night cooling of the thermal mass in summer and prevent over-ventilation in winter by demand-led ventilation
- a theatre company and audience that engage with how the building works and accept that natural ventilation instead of a mechanical system means the auditorium will not be controlled to a 'perfect' 21°C all year round.

For further detailed discussion of auditorium ventilation, see Section 6.

Figures 1.10.2a and 2b In some theatres, the air terminals which drive natural ventilation systems are used to create striking features on the skyline. Examples include the newly refurbished Contact Theatre in Manchester (left) and the Liverpool Everyman Theatre (right).

## 1.11 Acoustics

Acoustic design is an over-arching consideration in the design of theatre buildings. Acoustic design principles are used to control the sound quality in auditoria and performance spaces and are also applied throughout a theatre building to make sure intrusive noise is kept under control.

### The acoustic environment

Consideration of the acoustic environment is important when selecting a site for a new theatre, as it can have a significant impact on the cost of the building.

The ability to create a quiet environment within an auditorium is essential, and this is made much more difficult if the building is located close to external noise sources such as railway lines, airports or major roads. While there are

Figures 1.10.2a and 2b (Continued)

construction techniques available to exclude high external noise levels, they are generally expensive and can be avoided if a quieter site is chosen, although this may conflict with the need for a city centre location. Noise break-out from the theatre is also an important consideration, particularly for venues that may wish to present shows with loud amplified music. Proximity to housing may provoke complaints from residents, which can lead to restriction of the operating hours of the theatre by the local environmental health authority or, in extreme cases, to enforced closure. It is possible to solve these problems using heavy construction and separated structures to prevent air-borne and structure-borne noise from leaving the building, but this can prove expensive.

High standards of acoustic separation can mean high levels of thermal insulation, with a consequent reduction in emissions. The involvement of an acoustic consultant to advise on these matters at an early stage of the project is recommended.

## Auditorium acoustics

It is important to understand at the briefing stage that the acoustic requirements of a particular auditorium will have a significant effect on its volume and form. Put at its simplest, there is a direct relationship between the volume of a room and its reverberation time. This means that a concert hall for un-amplified (e.g. classical) music will require a much higher volume per seat than a drama theatre, which needs a good acoustic for speech and mainly amplified music. An opera house will require a volume that lies somewhere between the two. These issues are examined in more detail in Sections 5 and 6, but it is worth noting here that establishing the approximate volume (e.g. height) of an auditorium, relative to its use, is critical at the initial planning stage, as it will have a significant impact on the overall massing of the building and on its cost.

### Acoustic separation

Acoustic separation between spaces is also an important consideration in the early planning of the building. If noise-generating areas can be kept away from quiet areas, it will avoid the need to employ expensive acoustic isolation techniques. If there is to be more than one auditorium, each needs to be separated from the other(s), with no shared walls or floors, to prevent noise crossover. See Figure 1.11.1.

- Rehearsal rooms and workshop areas should be well separated from stages and from each other.
- Auditoria and stages should be provided with acoustic lobbies at all entry points to prevent noise from foyers, bars and backstage areas from entering the performance spaces.
- Plant rooms, lifts and other noise-generating equipment should be located well away from performance spaces and other quiet areas to prevent plant noise and vibration from transferring to them.

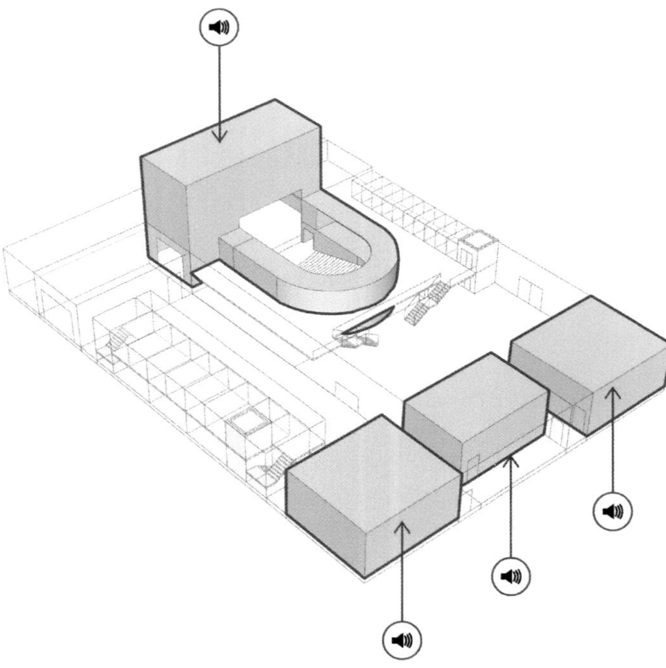

Figure 1.11.1 Creating acoustically controlled environments for performance and rehearsal spaces within a theatre building is most efficiently done by making sure that noisy and noise-sensitive spaces are physically separated both by distance if this is possible and also by acoustically isolating construction, such as multiple walls or floors. The degree of separation required will depend on the acoustic criteria and the level of noise anticipated, all of which can be advised upon by an acoustician.

If a building is to be used to its full potential, it is essential that all areas can be used simultaneously without causing acoustic disturbance. An acoustic consultant should be involved in the early stages of design to advise on appropriate separation techniques.

## 1.12 Fire safety and security

In the nineteenth century theatre fires were relatively common, and lessons from this period still form the basis of current fire-safety advice. The culture of fire safety in theatres has been improved greatly through legislation, advances in technology and better training and management, alongside recognised, structured guidance.

### The challenge of fire safety design in theatres

Theatre fire safety still provides designers and approvers with many challenges. Theatres often accommodate large numbers of people who are unfamiliar with the building, and there may be combustible materials on stage and potential ignition sources present. Older theatres may also have heritage listed status, providing unique challenges for upgrades and improvements. It is these challenges along with the innovative aspirations of theatre production teams and architects that have necessitated a more innovative approach to fire safety design.

In the UK it is possible to apply statutory guidance documents such as BS 9999 or the ABTT *et al.*, *Technical Standards for Places of Entertainment* (London: ABTT, 2015; updated 2020), but better strategies can sometimes be provided using a fire engineering approach. This is the application of knowledge in fire science and human behaviour, technology and performance of materials and systems to develop alternative solutions from the prescriptive guidance. The fire safety designs and strategies are developed specifically for the building or project under consideration and hence can be better tailored to its needs.

### Designing for other threats to safety

Fire is only one of several safety threats that now need to be considered in the design of theatre buildings, and those with responsibility for buildings accommodating larger numbers of people are advised to consider the threat from a broad range of non-fire threats resulting from terrorist activity. Such threats may include the use of a vehicle as a weapon, attacks with either bladed weapons or firearms and improvised explosive devices. This will depend on a security threat and risk assessment undertaken by a competent security consultant. See Figure 1.12.1.

Planning an emergency response, should such an incident occur, will require a range of emergency responses, including a consideration of emergency evacuation, invacuation (inward evacuation) lockdown procedures and the use of protected spaces. (See Section 3.)

Further detail on some of the common challenges faced by modern theatre fire safety design, existing guidance and fire engineering solutions that provide practical ways forward can be found in Section 3.

## 1.13 From principles to project

This section of the book has outlined the broad principles behind the design of theatre buildings. It has introduced the people and processes to be considered when designing a theatre and outlined the positive impact well-designed theatres can have on our towns and cities. It serves as an

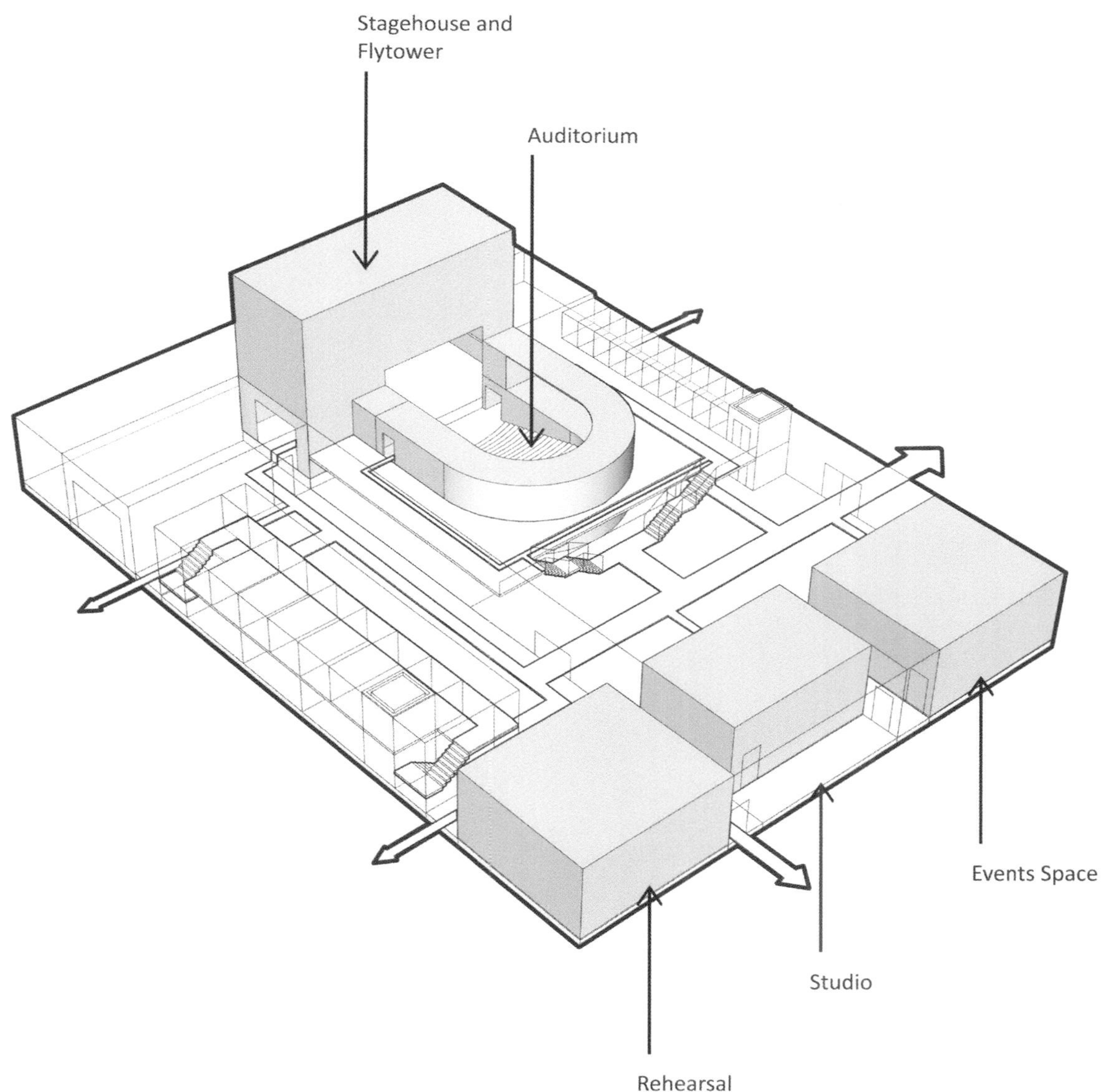


Figure 1.12.1 Diagram showing the circulation routes in a theatre that are designed to provide means of escape for large numbers of people to a place of safety. Front of house and backstage are usually treated separately so that audiences do not cross over into backstage areas. For most theatre buildings this means that multiple staircases are required. For large and complex theatres, the detailed design of means of escape will be part of each building's individual fire engineering strategy.

introduction to the many aspects of the design of theatres, and it has pointed to subsequent sections of the book, where each element of the building is covered in greater detail.

Much of this section has been concerned with the theory behind theatre buildings. It has outlined some broad design principles, identified common practice and described some typical building types. The next section of the book will look at the early steps needed to turn the vision into a reality.

## Section editor

Simon Erridge, Director, Bennetts Associates

## Contributors (in alphabetical order)

Sarah Brigham, CEO, Derby Theatre

Mike Cook, Director, Avison Young

Paul Gillieron, Director, Gillieron Scott

Simon Harper, Consultant, Harper Tackley

Judith Kilvington, CEO, Rich Mix

Andrew Nicholson, Director of The Fire Surgery

Iain Shaw, Partner, Max Fordham

Michèle Taylor, Director, Ramps on the Moon

Andrew Wylie, Partner, Buro Happold

# Section 2
# Developing the brief

## 2.1 So, you want to build a theatre?

> It's so important in this early phase of a development to be really clear about what the theatre's for and why it's needed. That's the only way to give the architect's team a clear steer on how to design it.
>
> Dame Rosemary Squire: co-founder, Trafalgar Entertainment

This section focuses on preliminary planning for a new or refurbished theatre, a temporary theatre or a building being redeveloped into a theatre from another use. It is aimed at the client, possibly a developer, theatre operator or local authority, and to assist architects, engineers and professional designers. It covers details of which each may have extensive experience; however, we hope there is new information of value to all. It aims to help the reader decide if embarking on such a project is the right thing to do and, if so, to move forward with a good understanding of how to get it off the ground and bring the right people together to steer the process. It describes how to create a vision and a strategic brief for the project and how to test its feasibility, and it considers how to build a professional team of architects and consultants to develop the brief and the design and the process of procuring a sustainable building that functions well for the anticipated use.

A theatre is a complex building, and the process of delivering it is long, with many risks that can affect cost, timeframe and the functionality of the venue. Theatres need audiences and performers, so the project must be rooted in a community with a proven need and the ability to secure funding for design, construction and sustainable operation throughout its life. Building and operating a theatre must be based on joined-up thinking on funding strategy, business planning and programming, as well as realistic estimates on capital costs and construction time.

Our aim is to ensure that by the end of the process described here, the reader will be able to decide whether to proceed, confident that they have thoroughly explored and tested the options available.

### A sustainable approach

The climate emergency, the most serious issue facing the world today, has accelerated recently – with the built environment contributing significantly to the problem. For any building project it is essential to mitigate and avoid negative effects on the climate and the environment.

The question 'Why build?' should be uppermost in the client's mind throughout the early stages of the process, and we examine alternative approaches to new build; opportunities to refurbish, reuse or repurpose existing buildings are preferable. If new build is the chosen route, the design must minimise the carbon impact of the building, the trend being towards zero carbon or net positive.

To be truly sustainable, a theatre needs to consider its social, economic and cultural sustainability. Economic sustainability will be considered in the feasibility study section subsequently, and Section 1 has addressed how theatres can contribute effectively to social sustainability and community. Theatres excel at cultural sustainability, through the work they present and their greatest assets – people and spaces – serving the community in which they sit.

## 2.2 Who starts off a project?

If you have picked up this book, then you may already be considering building or redeveloping a theatre and will have a vision, however simple, of what it will be like. You may already have started to gather people around you to help you and might have an architect developing the vision. It is a complex business with many choices, and this section will help you put the best people and practices in place at an early stage.

### The client body and the end user

In the whole life of the building, the most important people are the client – the individual or group that commissions the scheme and ensures it is paid for – and the end user – the operator that will manage the building, implement its artistic policy, organise its daily programme and determine how it engages with its community. Sometimes the client and user will be the same organisation. For example, a college that is building a theatre for its academic programmes will be both client and user. This has the advantage of easing decision making and ensuring that the building fulfils the requirements of the user exactly.

DOI: 10.4324/9781003327295-2

Frequently, however, the legal client for the project will be a different organisation from the end user. For example, a local authority/municipality may decide to build a new theatre as a home for the local theatre or dance company. Some theatres are built by non-theatrical private enterprises including developers, often where local authority planners want a social return on the commercial gain the developer will make. The developer may be responsible for constructing the shell and core of the building only, with the operator responsible for the internal fitout. The division of responsibility brings advantages and challenges, and communication between the relevant bodies must be extremely good to ensure the project is fit for purpose.

Typical client bodies include the following.

*An arts group*
An arts organisation, for example, a professional or amateur drama or dance company, becomes both user client and legal client for the construction project.

*A local authority or government department*
A local authority or government department, through its architects or public works department, could be the legal client for the project.

*A private trust or benefactor*
Sometimes a non-profit or charitable organisation may be established as the client for the design, construction and delivery of the project.

*A commercial organisation*
These may include developers, ideally working with an operator who informs the brief.

*An educational organisation*
Theatres constructed by and for schools, colleges or universities.

### Management of the design and construction project

Most schemes benefit from having the following.

*A sponsor or senior responsible owner*
Where public finance is involved, this role may be a requirement of the funding framework.

*A project champion*
A theatre construction or renovation project can fail at any point before construction begins. Projects which make it successfully to opening night often have a determined individual, with a clear vision, leading throughout.

*A project board*
Made up of individuals with relevant skills from architecture and construction, government, fundraising and finance, law and, of course, theatre and the arts. The project board typically gives their time free and is distinct from the professional team that will be appointed in due course. They can help guide the decisions made in the early stages and help with fundraising.

### Support

A key role of the founding advocates is to generate support for the project – this might include local politicians, residents, the professional and amateur artistic community, and the local print, broadcast and online media. Equally important is support that can be turned into funding for the project. In the short term there is a need for modest funding, which may come from a mix of sources. A funding strategy, explained in 'Where Will the Funding Come From?' in 2.7, is vital from the outset. As the project develops and moves into the more detailed planning stages, more significant funding will be required to undertake studies and engage the professional team.

In planning a new or refurbished theatre, it is essential to remember the needs of the audiences and the public. There will be many articulate arts organisations and lobby groups, statutory consultees and local groups who want to have their say in the development of the theatre or in its future life once completed. There will also be pressures from other stakeholders and funding bodies. All can exert influence over the planning of an arts building; however, a theatre is built primarily for the practitioners and audiences of the future, therefore it must be inclusive and ensure equality of access throughout.

## 2.3 How long will it take?

Creating a theatre building, whether through new build, refurbishment or as a temporary pop-up, is a project, and a project requires project management. This is distinct from the routine management activities of everyday operation.

This section is specifically about preliminary planning, but the stages between inception and opening night will happen over three consecutive phases, with success dependent upon the robust and suitable completion of the preceding phase (see Figure 2.3.1).

It is sometimes suggested that each of these steps takes about two years – a ⅓, ⅓, ⅓ model often being

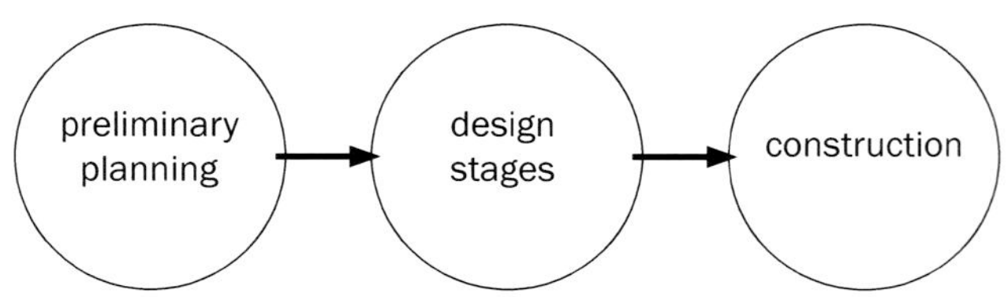


Figure 2.3.1 Diagram showing essential phases and steps.

suggested. A realistic generalisation is at least two years for preliminary planning, 18 to 24 months for detailed design and construction taking 18 to 36 months. To minimise risk and disruptive change later in the process, sufficient time must be allowed for each stage.

These phases sub-divide further and this section uses the Royal Institute of British Architects (RIBA)'s Plan of Work Stages 0–7 as its basis, as most countries adopt a process that is broadly similar (see Figure 2.3.2).

### *Preliminary planning (RIBA Stages 0 and 1)*

The duration of preliminary planning is influenced by many factors: stakeholder constraints including availability or suitability of a site and availability of funding; how it will be operated and by whom; how artistic content is produced or sourced; and how the building will be designed, built and funded and by whom. Answering these questions will enable a design brief to be developed.

### *Design stages (RIBA Stages 2–4)*

The project timetable for the design stages may also be driven by stakeholder constraints, including funding and site availability, amongst a wide range of other project constraints. The model traditionally used is set out in Figure 2.3.3.

### *Construction and handover (RIBA Stages 5–6)*

The period required for construction carries risks of unforeseen discoveries which can often cause delays. Once the building is complete, the end users will need time to familiarise themselves with its operation and train staff before opening.

It is essential that sufficient time be allowed for this process – projects sometimes find themselves short of time because the duration to completion was underestimated in the early stages. It is increasingly recognised that:

- the client should consider when to seek local authority town planning consent and whether to continue design during this period
- a strategy for procurement of the construction works should be agreed upon
- design should not continue during this procurement process
- parts of the design are often undertaken by the contractor and their sub-contractors, meaning that technical design is not complete until after the construction contract is awarded
- a pre-construction mobilisation period is required by the contractor to develop their health and safety and logistical arrangements, to start their design work and, if necessary, to commence offsite fabrication
- a period of several weeks or months, depending on scale and design, must be allowed for commissioning and fit-out after completion of construction.

See Figure 2.3.4.

### *Concept design (RIBA Stage 2)*

The architect creates initial concepts which may include several options or alternative designs for discussion with the client and stakeholders, options which will be evaluated before a preferred concept emerges. The concept design illustrates a broad direction for the building, its positioning on the site and the general placement of the major elements.

As the stage progresses, the design is developed with more detail on the planning of the rooms in the building. The overall parameters of the building will be fixed, sections and elevations drawn and preliminary input received from consultants and engineers.

| | **Preliminary Planning** | | **Design Stages** | | | **Construction** | | **In Use** |
|---|---|---|---|---|---|---|---|---|
| **RIBA Stage** | 0 Strategic Definition | 1 Preparation and Briefing | 2 Concept Design | 3 Spatial Coordination | 4 Technical Design | 5 Manufacturing & Construction | 6 Handover | 7 Use |

Figure 2.3.2 RIBA Plan of Work Stages 0–7.

Figure 2.3.3 RIBA work Stages 2–5.

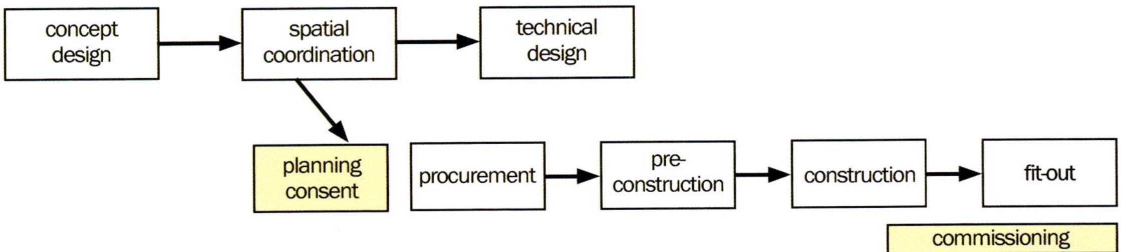


Figure 2.3.4 Procurement strategy.

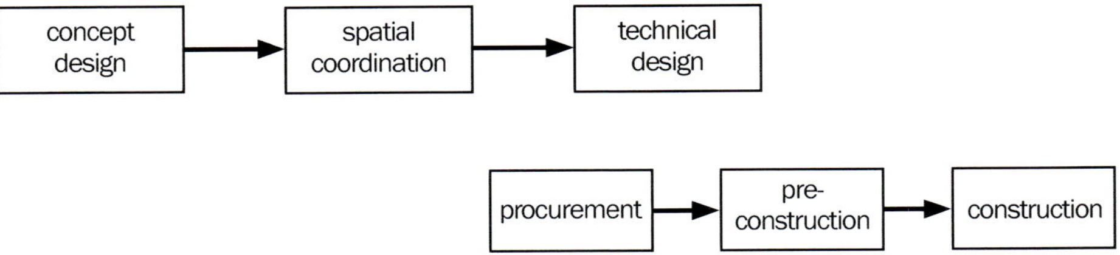


Figure 2.3.5 Works procurement and construction.

Concept design includes outline structural and building services design, associated project strategies, preliminary cost information, sustainability targets and the final project brief.

## *Spatial coordination/schematic design and planning consent (RIBA Stage 3)*

At this stage, the plans for the building are developed to a greater level of detail. All external materials will be selected, and architectural drawings and 3D visualisations will illustrate how the building will look within the context of its environment. The design of the auditorium and stage will be developed by the architect in conjunction with the theatre consultant. The interior plans of the building will be refined. Engineers will develop their designs to ensure that the correct area is allowed for the structure and building services and that sustainability targets are being achieved. Although some projects are still drawn in 2D, it is increasingly common for consultants to design using a 3D building model which will be progressively developed through to completion.

Typically, an application for planning consent will be submitted during or at the completion of this phase and the budget fixed with more confidence. The planning process involves discussions with the local authority and the community so – as mentioned in 'The Client Body' and 'The End User,' previously – good relations with community groups from inception will help to support the case.

## *Technical design, works procurement and construction (RIBA Stages 4 and 5)*

RIBA Stages 4 and 5 will overlap, as dictated by the project programme and the procurement strategy. A period of several weeks or months, depending on scale, should be allowed for procuring the contractor who will build the project (see Figure 2.3.5).

## *Construction*

There are many options as to when the contractor comes into the process, each with its own problems and benefits, and the method chosen will have a bearing on later design stages. Therefore, to avoid problems, the project team is strongly advised to consider options for procurement of the works during preliminary planning and early design stages. New methods of construction have led to some modular theatre buildings either as semi-permanent pop-ups including the Shed at London's National Theatre (see Reference Project 02) or The Bridge (see Reference Project 20), the auditorium and stage of which were made and tested offsite before being erected as fully coordinated, finished components within the building shell.

The traditional procurement model sees the design fully completed before being issued to several contractors to tender a fixed price sum. This method does not allow for early contractor engagement, contributing their buildability expertise, nor does it transfer responsibility for design to the contractor. This method was used successfully for the Liverpool Everyman Theatre. Retaining control of the design using this method has the potential to create the finest product; however, this also means retaining liability for the costs and delays. For information on the Liverpool Everyman, see Reference Project 17 in this book.

Other procurement options exist which may enable earlier commencement of works on site, such as construction management or two-stage tendering of a traditional contract. These allow a high degree of control over contractor selection and design completion, but each has its challenges and, if not well managed, can leave the client retaining significant cost and programme risk.

Whichever route is followed, the quality and clarity of the tender documentation is integral to the reliability of the tendered construction costs and ultimately to the successful outcome of the project.

## *Design and build*

Under design and build (D&B), the contractor designs and constructs the building based on the employer's requirements, a set of information, schedules and drawings prepared by the architect and consultant team. The client for Chester Storyhouse, Cheshire West and Chester Council, engaged a D&B contractor through the local construction framework. The client team found this created a collaborative environment where the contractor was part of the team from the end of RIBA Stage 2, helping to resolve site-specific issues of construction access, archaeology, utility services diversion and minimising neighbour disturbance, all prior to submittal for planning. Besides a high degree of cost certainty from an early stage, this helped the client secure planning consent free of pre-development conditions that enabled a quick start on site and gave the client the early completion and programme certainty they wanted. For information on Chester Storyhouse, see Reference Project 06.

## *Two-stage design and build*

A two-stage D&B strategy selects one contractor from several bidders, based on competitive initial offers of programme and management costs prior to completion of design. The contractor is given an interim engagement under a pre-construction services agreement to contribute their expertise to the completion of the design process, tendering to sub-contractors on an open-book basis. This leads to a full offer, taking on a singular design and build responsibility which can be contracted with the highest level of cost certainty and design and programme responsibility transfer. However, there can be a significant increase between initial competitive offer and the non-competitive second stage offer. The initial offer is typically invited at the end of RIBA Stage 3 but can be invited at end of Stage 2 or Stage 4. This method is often avoided for theatre construction, but if it is chosen, the employer's requirements must be detailed to at least RIBA Stage 3+, in order to reduce risks to quality, programme and costs.

## *Construction (RIBA Stage 5)*

Works on site begin at a relatively slow pace, sometimes with archaeology and demolition preceding structural works. Structural works are followed by the first-fix of electrical and mechanical services, after which internal walls and ceilings are installed. Theatres have intensive services requirements, and these installations often dictate the programme. Once first-fix is completed and walls and ceilings closed-up, the decorative finishes and services second-fix proceeds. Following this, there will be a period of several weeks or months, depending on scale, during which snags are rectified and the services are commissioned and put to work.

Fit-out may or may not be part of the construction contract, but there are typically some information and communications technology (ICT) and furniture and fixtures and loose equipment installations to complete before the operator occupies and begins staff training. The operator should contribute their operational expertise throughout to ensure the building meets their needs, particularly in relation to the schedule of accommodation, the fitting out, loose furniture and fittings and ICT requirements.

## *Planning for opening night (RIBA Stage 6)*

Throughout the design and construction period the theatre operator, in conjunction with the client, will have developed a business plan detailing artistic programme, organisational structure, marketing, community engagement and operational policies for the theatre. Programming and recruiting staff may take more than a year to put in place. A period of staff familiarisation with the venue is scheduled, including training in use of equipment, maintenance requirements, safety and fire procedures. A 'soft opening' should be considered involving local amateur or professional organisations to test operational readiness. From a programming perspective, the opening night is often a high-profile event and requires detailed planning and rehearsals to ensure its artistic and operational success.

## *Post-contract (RIBA Stage 7)*

There is normally a one-year period after completion in which defects, not visible before completion, must be rectified and while the final payments under the construction contract are made.

## 2.4 We have a founding team, what now?

The previous section shows that developing and or building a building is a lengthy process and not to be entered into lightly. The first stages of preliminary planning are crucial to ensuring the theatre is built on the correct assumptions (see Figure 2.4.1).

The preliminary thinking and planning process can follow many tracks, but before design can begin in earnest, there are three steps which must be undertaken in sequence, as each is dependent on the previous work having been carried out. They are:

- inception (RIBA Stage 0) – Why do we need a theatre?
- development (RIBA Stage 1) – What kind of theatre do we need, and how do we assess the need?
- design procurement – What specialist advice do we need?

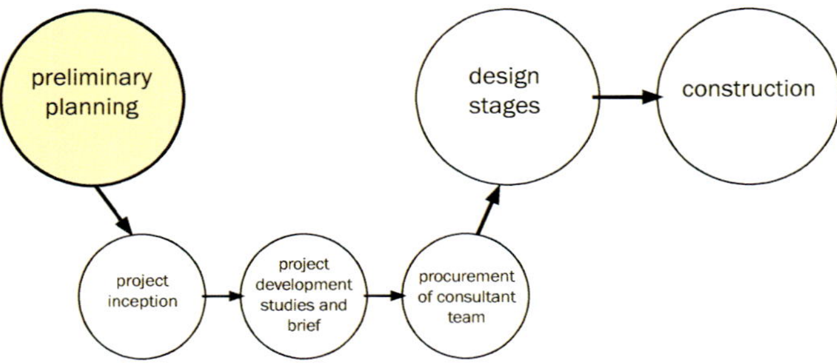


Figure 2.4.1 Diagram showing preliminary planning – the process.

### *Step 1: Project inception (RIBA Stage 0)*

The emergence of an initial vision for a new or revamped building involves initial discussions, building of support and the establishment of an informal organisation or lobby group, as well as deciding what the goals of the project are, what is required and why. The key question at the end of this stage is 'Do we need a theatre, and is it a good idea?'

### *Step 2: Project development, studies and brief (RIBA Stage 1)*

Further development and testing of the viability of the project follows, with the organisation becoming more formalised. Funding is sought for a more detailed appraisal of the project when several studies may be undertaken to test its feasibility and financial viability. The key question at the end of this stage is 'Do we have a viable project?'

If the answer is yes, the output from this stage will be the brief. The brief is the single most important document in the life of the project. It defines what the architect and other professional advisers are to design and needs careful preparation and consideration.

### *Step 3: Professional consultant team procurement*

The selection of an architect and design team is crucial to the success of the project. The client group also needs to grow into an effective organisation able to manage a significant design and construction project – a project board should be established at this stage, if not done already. Before proceeding with procurement of the design, the key question is 'Do we have the funding, site, organisation, team and business plan to undertake a capital project and achieve a successful outcome?'

### Why do we need a theatre?

The initial action is to create a preliminary business case setting out the needs and a justification for the investment required by the potential development. Stage 0 is about determining the best means of achieving the client's requirements *because a building might not be the most appropriate solution*. The stage should be strategic in nature, defining the statement of need, strategic brief, preliminary business case and client requirements (see Figure 2.4.2).

Preliminary planning should include business planning which identifies the market demand and the potential income and operating costs. Design and construction risks and commercial operating risks should be robustly considered. Ideally the operator is involved, providing definition and briefing inputs, from the start of this phase and throughout the project. Where the operator is not in

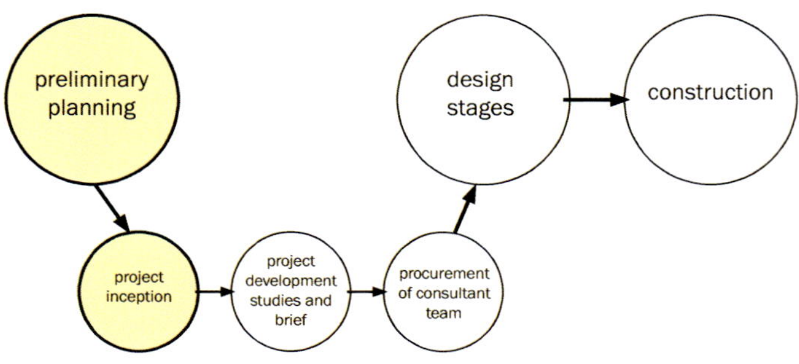


Figure 2.4.2 Diagram showing project inception.

place, a suitably experienced expert must stand in to the role. This input and advice could come from a combination of arts business planners and theatre consultants, but the project should not proceed without these operational considerations having a voice.

The team at project inception may be different in composition to the team for later stages, and, if architectural input is needed, it is recommended by RIBA to appoint a client design adviser on a short-term commission rather than an appointment for the whole project. When property development companies are involved, they may have in-house expertise with the capability to prepare a preliminary business case for a commercial development; however, this is unlikely to be the case for a theatre, and they should recognise that they will require specialist expertise. In such cases the appointment of a team of independent client advisers is necessary.

There are many ways in which the need for a new theatre can be perceived. An existing older venue may no longer serve the purposes of the operating organisation's artistic ambition or service expectations; similarly, a drama or dance company may need a new or adapted home to develop its productions and audience facilities. A commercial company or developer may decide to build a new theatre as a commercial profit-making venture. A local authority or other government agency may want to include performing arts provision within a wider cultural and placemaking strategy where provision of arts and cultural facilities are part of broader economic and town planning priorities. Or the local authority may decide that running or refurbishing what was a civic theatre is no longer a core service and it should facilitate the theatre's independence. Increasingly, theatres are being realised through partnerships with several bodies, which may include arts groups, local authorities and private investors or operators to achieve several community- or economy-driven aims for a town or city. A commercial developer may decide independently to include a theatre in their scheme to increase its attraction or be obliged to do so to satisfy a local planning policy.

## A vision or shared vision

A project can also be initiated by an individual or individuals who share a vision for a new building. These people may be artists (professional or amateur), community leaders, politicians, educators or businesspeople, and any one of them may become the project champion. Invariably it is the project champion or champions who will drive the project's vision, ambitions and delivery.

What is the vision for the new theatre? What are its goals? What benefits will it bring to the community, its users, audiences and the local economy? Projects without a clearly defined vision rarely succeed. Sometimes the vision and goals will be clear cut. For example, an educational institution requires a new performance space to support its programmes, or an orchestra needs a new concert hall to replace an acoustically inadequate space. More generally, the reasons for building a new theatre are complex, with several differing, and occasionally conflicting, requirements having to be met. These may include an artistic need; a wider cultural provision; an educational need; placemaking; and cultural strategy, diversity and wellbeing.

*An artistic need*

An existing arts organisation may benefit from a new, adapted or improved building in which to sustain and develop its artistic vision and customer service offerings.

*A wider cultural provision*

Including performing arts provision as part of wider cultural and leisure development projects, to provide for and engage communities and contribute to the overall creative and visitor economy.

*An educational need*

A school, college or university may need a theatre to support its arts education programmes. Or a community may determine that its young people should have greater opportunities and involvement in the performing arts.

*Placemaking*

Theatres can bring people, life and animation to an area. Many communities use theatre buildings as an integral part of their urban renewal, placemaking and regeneration strategies. In some cases, these may be 'landmark' buildings that contribute to a town, city or region's identity or the preservation, conversion, restoration or refurbishment of an existing historically important building, which may already be or have been a theatre or performance venue. Section 1 explored the role of theatres in such developments.

*Cultural strategy, diversity and wellbeing*

Wider cultural master-planning, the creation of arts districts or creative enterprise hubs may warrant a performance venue as part of the scheme.

## How do we assess the need?

A useful test for the proponents of a scheme is to ask, 'If we meet five years after the project has opened how will we judge its success?' Some of this assessment may be quantitative – including information such as size of audiences, number of performances being presented, breadth and quality of creative learning programmes, evidence of local community and business involvement. Other goals and achievements may be less tangible – has the perception of the community been positively changed by the theatre? Has the theatre contributed to the economic and or physical health of the vicinity through additionality – secondary income and attracting visitors? Has the artistic quality of the programme developed? If publicly funded through grants or subsidies, does the theatre represent value for money to residents? (See Figure 2.4.3.)

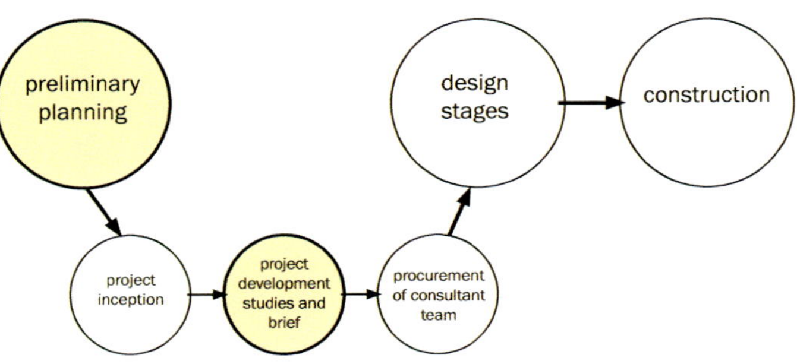


Figure 2.4.3 Assessing the need.

## Investment decision

After a period of deliberation, examination and review, and an assessment of likely funding sources, the client group may decide to proceed with the project. At this point a more structured and professional client body is needed and more significant funding will be required. The challenge in Step 2 is to develop a strong case for the project sufficient to generate the support and further funding needed to bring it to fruition.

## Feasibility study

A feasibility study is crucial to any theatre project to assess the physical and financial viability and achievability of the project and is important early work for the client group to commission.

During this stage, one or more studies may be undertaken to assess the physical and financial viability and achievability of the project. Some clients commission a comprehensive feasibility study to address all the key elements, for example, market analysis, needs assessment, business planning, capital cost estimating and a funding plan. Alternatively, studies or explorations can be separately commissioned to cover each specific area. An essential component is a site analysis to test the 'fit' of the brief on the site or sites. This may entail design work and visual material to help the client communicate the project vision to potential funders or stakeholders. Invariably a multi-disciplined team approach will be necessary to include the required expertise. These may include a theatre consultant, architect, engineers, quantity surveyors and business planners. The scope and contents of the study elements include the following topics.

*Needs assessment*

An objective, clear-sighted assessment to validate and provide evidence for the need for a new performance venue. What is the current provision in the near vicinity? Is there a demand for the user and programme make up? Who will benefit from a new venue – arts organisation, communities, visitors, touring productions?

*Market and competitor analysis*

Is there an audience for a new theatre? If so, what is the size and potential value? There is little reason to build a new or refurbish an old theatre if there is not a significant audience to support the completed project. The market for a new venue can be assessed in several ways – through population segmentation and profiling, qualitative and quantitative analysis, consultation, competition and benchmarking measured against the economic environment.

*Consultation*

A consultation process may be beneficial at this stage to gauge users, community, potential audience, funders and other stakeholder response. This may include soft testing of external operators (if relevant) and external professional programme providers (including producers and/or promoters).

*Governance model*

This controls who is responsible and accountable for running the building and its ongoing operations. More than one company, organisation or body may be responsible for the different components – artistic and educational activities (which may be a charity), commercial activities (catering, private rentals, conferencing) and building and asset management (owner, landlord). Theatres are generally governed by one of several models, including an education body such as a school, college or conservatoire, or a not-for-profit group – a trust or community interest company that is also a charity serving public benefit. Some are local authority operated or a partnership between a local authority and trust or commercial operator. Others are commercially run by a sole operator or in a commercially led joint venture between developers and a theatre operator, for example, theatres located in shopping centres or other retail or leisure park.

*Operating model*

The operating model informs how the theatre will be operated and what the programme and activities presented in the theatre will look like. The operating body may not be known at the feasibility stage; however, it should be known whether the client will be the operating body or whether operations and management will be outsourced or transferred to an alternative body (for example, a trust or commercial operator). The programme may in part be determined by the original vision, for example, a home for a theatre group or a concert hall for a city. The needs assessment and market analysis will ascertain further programming need and opportunity and how the theatre should be designed to serve this need. The feasibility study will consider a typical calendar year, anticipated occupancy levels across the spaces, pricing, the number of performances and distinction between artistic and ancillary commercial activity (private hires, conferencing etc.). Key to the operating model is how the programme content will be sourced – produced in-house or presenting visiting productions or a combination of both.

*Site analysis*

The location of a new performing arts building is critical to its success. In many cases, where an existing building is being remodelled or developed, the location is already determined, but in the case of a new building, it will be necessary to ensure that a suitable site has been secured before commencing the design process. Criteria for suitability of a site for the building of a new theatre will include structural integrity of land and existing structures, transportation and car parking, service utilities infrastructure, environmental, conservation and planning considerations, access, residential impact and cost.

Physical issues related to a preferred site need to be identified, criteria established and the potential site critically evaluated to ensure it fulfils the stated needs. Invariably this process will require consultation with stakeholders, residents and others impacted or affected by the building of a new theatre.

Where there is more than one site to choose from, it is common to carry out an options appraisal, using a rational methodology and scoring system to help ensure the best possible site is chosen. Site requirements were discussed further in Section 1.

*Project costs*

At the inception of the project there is often only a vague brief or ambition for the project, but some idea of capital costs will be required. At this stage it should be based on benchmarking against appropriate comparable projects and the experience of the advisers. See 'What Will It All Cost?' under heading 2.7.

*Business plan construction and operation*

The business plan is crucial in the preliminary planning of the project. It sets out the operational and financial objectives of the theatre and how the operating organisation may achieve them.

Central to a performing arts venue business plan is trying to ascertain whether income achieved through its artistic programme and ancillary income streams (such as catering and rentals) can be realised to justify either capital expenditure, revenue expenditure or both and setting out the resource necessities against realistic timescales. There are two parts to creating a successful new theatre building – its design and construction and its operation.

The business plan should include:

*construction*

- preliminary design brief – what kind of building is required?
- budget and funding plan (see 'Where Will the Funding Come From?' under the first subheading in 2.7)
- action plan and timescales
- key performance indicators (KPIs)
- risk register

*operation*

- governance and operating model
- artistic programme model (professional and amateur)
- management and staffing structure
- marketing plan
- role of resident organisations, if any
- financial plan, including realistic estimates of all incomes and expenditures, profit and loss
- maintenance and building investment plan
- standard operating procedures (health and safety, risk management, licensing requirements, emergency planning).

Both parts of the plan inform one another and are essential if the architect is to design the right building. This also needs to take account of the social issues raised in Section 3 in this book.

## 2.5 We have a feasible project, what now?

Having determined that there is a need for a project, the next step is to prepare a brief for the architectural teams that will bid for the design contract. The design team is not generally appointed until RIBA Stage 2 when design work commences; however, it is worth considering employing an architect and/or other specialist consultants experienced in theatre buildings on a fixed contract, to help write a meaningful brief.

## Writing the brief

**The brief is the single most important set of documents for the project and is only as good as the studies that precede it and should, if possible, accompany it. The brief contains significant information about the proposed building and conveys the rationale behind it, the client's goals and aspirations and how they will operate it. The brief is what the architect and consultant team will refer to when planning and designing the building, its systems and equipment. It should provide sufficient information to ensure the consultant team fully understands the requirements but not be so prescriptive that it inhibits their creativity. In the UK, the brief will effectively encompass the requirements of RIBA Stage 1.**

A good brief will include three types of information:

- narrative description
- schedules
- drawings.

These three different strands complement each other giving the consultant team a thorough description and minimising misunderstanding. Some parts of the brief will be more detailed than others and will be dependent on the makeup of the professional team appointed to assist.

## Narrative description

This document describes the building as the project team sees it, setting out:

- goals and aims for the project, *what* it is for
- rationale for the building, *why* it is needed
- background and context, *why now* is the right time
- project organisation – *how* the building will be procured and how, and by whom, it will be operated
- description of the type of building required
- the architectural vision for the building.

A useful approach is to describe the journey through the building for audience, performers, staff and crew. Audience arrival should address transport issues, how many visitors arrive by car, public transport or other means, also describing how the visitor will experience the building's exterior and landscaping and how the project team sees it contributing to its context in the public realm. The public journey through the building should describe the number and type of entrances, the look and feel of the public spaces, accessibility, signs, box office, information and cloakroom, if present, the food and beverage offer and the anticipated hours of use. A similar description should consider back-of-house arrival for staff, crew and performers, for theatre production deliveries and everyday deliveries for catering, administration and removal of waste. The auditoria and stages will be the central focus of the building and deserve detailed description. However, to allow the architect and consultant team to explore and develop the concept design, it should avoid being too specific. In other words, it should define the activities to be housed and their relationships but not how to house them: to paraphrase visionary modernist architect Mies van der Rohe, describe what the client does, not what they want. See Section 1, where similar issues are discussed.

## Schedules

The schedules are spreadsheets of information. The schedule of areas need not break down every room type into individual spaces; for example, it might describe the number of performers to be accommodated in dressing rooms and give a target area in $m^2$, leaving the architect and consultants to interpret this in the design. At this early stage, the cost plan is closely linked with the schedule of areas, using $m^2$ rates to estimate the cost of the building. As discussed in 'What Will It Cost?' (2.7), it is critical that the schedule of areas have a suitably high grossing factor applied to allow for circulation and plant space, or the cost allowance will be insufficient. When this figure is too low, it will result in an underestimate of the cost, which causes problems for later stages of the project and may result in abortive work, increased costs from the consultant team and delays to the programme.

- Schedule of areas or room programme – a listing of all the types of rooms in the building, how big they need to be and other key requirements including adjacencies, daylight/blackout and additional height.
- Initial cost plan – the budget for the project as developed in the previous stage.
- Risk register – a record of known and possible project risks and initial plans on how they might be mitigated.

## Acoustic performance

Acoustic performance must be built into all aspects of the brief, as it affects decisions about the design. If an acoustic consultant is part of the team that prepared the feasibility study, they can assist. If not, the project team should describe in their own words how the building should perform in terms of:

- room acoustics
- noise isolation between spaces and from neighbouring properties
- how much noise is acceptable from building services such as heating and ventilation plant.

## Sustainability targets

Sustainability targets should be clearly identified. Some will be statutory requirements, so the project team should be aware of local, regional and national guidance. The team may also aspire to meet non-statutory classifications in environmental design, which should be clearly established in the brief. Irrespective of this, the project team is required to consider the whole life of the building from design to demolition.

## Drawings

- Site – plans, description, opportunities and constraints.
- Diagrams of building functions by area or zone – for example, auditorium, stage, public areas and backstage areas – indicating their adjacency to one other.

If a site has been identified, or if several sites are being considered, the drawings should indicate their urban context. It will be helpful to the consultant team to be as clear as possible about any constraints, for example, restrictions on building height, heritage considerations, transport restrictions and known environmental concerns such as flood risk or geological limitations.

## Scope of information required

The following list summarizes the range of information required for each part of the building. The other sections of this book provide more detailed analyses of these.

*Auditorium*
Form, seating capacity, adaptability, design guidance, room acoustics, accessibility, sightlines, lighting (Section 5 and 6).

*Stage*
Size, capabilities, flexibility, stage machinery, grid height, substage trap rooms and orchestra pit (Sections 8).

*Lighting, sound and video*
Infrastructure, operator positions, rigging positions, technical communications (Section 9).

*Public areas*
Foyers, box office, cloakrooms, catering, retail, visual art spaces, informal performance spaces, other uses (Section 4).

*Backstage areas*
Rehearsal space, dressing rooms, band room, green room and related provision (Section 7).

*Production spaces*
Get-in, scene dock, workshops, wardrobe (Section 7).

*Exterior*
Appearance, lighting, signage and advertising, accessibility, servicing, parking (Sections 1 and 4).

*Ancillary accommodation*
Office space, creative learning and community areas, conference facilities and storage (Sections 4 and 7).

*Restoration or conversion*
The specific challenges and needs of working with existing buildings (Section 10).

# 2.6 How do we appoint a professional consultant team?

Having completed the feasibility studies and written the brief, Stage 1 is complete. Stage 2 can commence once the professional team is in place.

## Procuring professional appointments

After preliminary planning has been completed, a larger range of consultants will need to be appointed before design commences. (See Figure 2.6.1.) Projects with significant

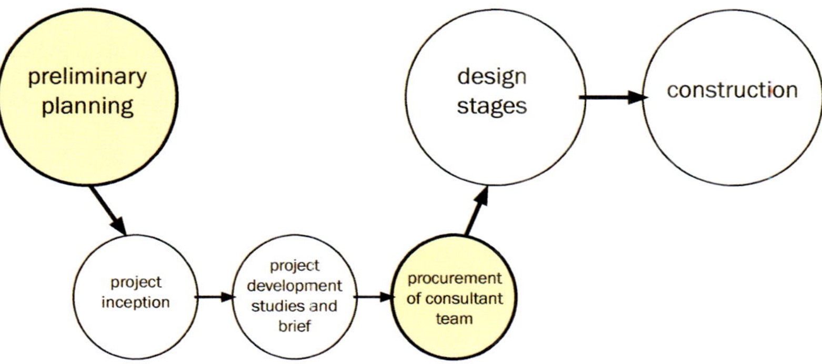


Figure 2.6.1 Procuring a consultant team.

public funding will have obligations for open and fair competition – private sector clients will be free to choose, although many would follow similar procedures.

Whilst procuring the architect may be the primary focus, on all but the smallest projects other design consultants will be essential including, structural engineers and building services engineers designing mechanical, electrical and plumbing (MEP), theatre and acoustic consultants and other specialists such as fire consultants, heritage advisers and lighting consultants, who may be required.

On some projects, there may be early engagement of the contractor and the design appointments may be made by the design and build contractor (such as on Storyhouse, Chester).

A consultant may be appointed at this stage to assist the client in choosing an appropriate procurement route and managing the design team appointment process.

## Challenges of team procurement for theatre

The client for a new or refurbished theatre building may only undertake one such project in their career and consequently do not have an established relationship with a professional team already used to working together. Teams are typically assembled *ad hoc*, which may result in a team of people who do not work well with each other. A commercial client who develops multiple building projects would select the best companies and individuals for the job, people who regularly work together and are already used to performing as a team. While this gives the client the opportunity to negotiate fees on the promise of potential future work, they have the experience to know whether the proposed fee is good value and will be willing to pay more for the right service, knowing that competitive fees always lead to shortcuts.

Few theatre clients can offer the incentive of repeat business and, as they often rely on public funding, are required to be accountable to funders. This leads to cumbersome reporting procedures, checkpoints and gateways that must be successfully negotiated for the project to progress and a team be appointed. While these are in place to ensure the public spending is transparent and free of corruption and offers value, it adds another layer of complexity to an already multi-layered project.

Projects receiving significant public funding may be backed by local or national government, who may express a preference for a contractor-led design, where a main contractor runs the process from feasibility through to completion of the building. The contractor employs the professional team and, like the commercial client, will often elect to work with the same teams; however, as theatre buildings are not as common as residential or commercial projects, the team may lack the experience needed. This approach is effective for projects with a clear unchanging brief from the start – theatre design is more fluid, and the client needs the flexibility to make valid changes throughout. Main contractors are in business to maximise their profit and, with the professional team under their employment, may influence the design accordingly, which can affect the quality and functionality of the building.

Similarly, some local authorities and large organisations, including universities, operate a framework agreement of approved designers, consultants and contractors, from which all project teams are selected. Again, these team members may lack the expertise needed for a theatre building.

Operating within these environments, the challenge for theatre clients and their advisors is to deliver a high-quality team that performs from the outset. The client team can help by getting involved with the selection process and ensuring the companies and individuals proposed have the appropriate experience for their project. The client team should feel comfortable that the people they are appointing can work well together and are enthusiastic about what may be a challenging process. In short, the client must feel that the professional team is a right fit for this project.

## Requesting fee proposals

Typically, the client appoints an architectural design team, but frequently a quantity surveyor and project manager join the team, and, as these professionals are not designers, consultant or professional team is a more accurate description. Other design consultants may be appointed at the same time or later, and there are many specialisms, including theatre consultant, acoustic consultant, fire engineer, principal designer (formerly health and safety co-ordinator), inclusive design, sustainability, transport, landscape, catering and more. Some may have given input into the planning stages; however, if their initial involvement was only for planning, the client has options to extend their role or appoint new team members.

For a small project, or for an initial appointment for planning stages or for a small role on a medium or large project, the simplest method of engaging a consultant is to issue a Request for Proposal (RfP) to a practice that is recommended or known from experience. The client, or their agent, should issue an RfP for each consultant role needed. The RfP should set out the details of the project, the services required and the terms and conditions the consultants will be required to agree.

## Competition without design (competitive selection process)

The client may decide to launch a competition to see value for money; in some cases, this will be an obligation from the funders. Accordingly, several potential consultancies for each role may be approached – RfPs are sought including from several architects, engineers and theatre consultants. There is no limit to the number in each discipline from which a proposal is sought; however, where more than four alternatives are sought by a client, the bidders are likely to perceive their chance of success as statistically lower and invest less time in preparing their bid.

*Multi-disciplinary team*
One option, suited to smaller projects, is to procure a multi-disciplinary team under the leadership of one discipline, typically the architect. The client issues an RfP to a selected group of architects, each of which selects the sub-consultants they want for each specialism and submits a joint bid. This reduces the analysis of options the client needs to make, although some architects are reluctant to take on responsibility for the payment and performance of their sub-consultants. The client may prefer more involvement in the choice of individual team members and the alternative of separate direct appointments give clients an easier mechanism for terminating parts of the team if it is found these are not performing. Project manager and quantity surveyor are often appointed directly to the client to give greater independence to challenge other designers where necessary.

*Direct appointment*
Another option is to procure one consultant first, possibly the architect or project manager, and use their experience to assist in procuring the rest of the professional team, each on a direct client appointment. This approach introduces competition and choice for the client while also helping to assemble a cohesive team with the appropriate experience.

*Open route*
Besides the requirement for competition, many funders require the professional procurement to follow an open route where the opportunity is openly advertised with clear criteria which are assessed fairly and, after the decision, the unsuccessful bidders are offered feedback on the evaluation. Unrestricted open procurement can lead to large numbers of offers for the client to evaluate and can lead to the situation where many bidders perceive their chance of success as statistically lower, and it is possible that the best candidates may elect not to tender, leaving the client in the unwanted situation of receiving offers from less qualified candidates.

*Two-stage restricted*
A way of addressing this is with a two-stage restricted process where the opportunity is openly advertised with clearly stated selection criteria and how these will be scored, allowing unlimited bidders to enter the initial or selection stage. The selection stage involves submission of business credentials such as practice experience and team qualifications, health, safety and environmental procedures in response to a pre-qualification questionnaire. The client evaluates the submittals, and a small number are shortlisted and invited to take part in an award stage with a more involved bid against further criteria, with fees typically paid for these.

In the EU, specific procedures exist for procurement of professional services and works, and in the UK, similar procedures are required under the Public Contracts Regulations 2015.

## Design competition

An alternative method of architect selection is a design competition, a major undertaking in terms of time, cost and effort required from the client. Open design competitions typically involve a publicly advertised open stage, resulting in a shortlist of teams that then complete more extensive design work. Often an honorarium is paid to the unsuccessful shortlisted bidders.

Design competitions should set out qualifications for entry, the marking criteria and process and generally require a specialist organiser or contest secretary and a jury or design panel.

An exhibition of the designs, often public, and procedures including discussion forums, interviews, site visits and resource and fee submissions, form part of the evaluation process. The identity of the bidders is often withheld, and scoring of designs by the jury is undertaken blind, without sight of the fee proposal.

A winner can be chosen at the first stage, or, in two-stage competitions, the jury selects several participants based on the announced selection criteria and shortlisted contestants are then asked to develop their proposals further.

## Advantages and disadvantages

The advantage of a competitive selection process is it allows the client to select an architect whom they feel they can work with and with whom they can collaborate to develop a design through an open dialogue. A design competition tends to freeze the design at an early stage before a dialogue has been established, and while it may produce a striking landmark building, it is less likely to fully meet the client's functional needs. The most famous example is the Sydney

Opera House, which is one of the most iconic buildings in the world, containing two very unsatisfactory performance spaces.

### Managing the professional procurement process

Professional procurement is demanding, time consuming and protracted – open advertisement is subject to minimum periods, which means the process can take six months or more. A client may choose to engage a construction project management consultancy to manage the process of procuring the professional team on their behalf.

## 2.7 What will it all cost?

The capital costs of refurbishing an existing building or creating a new building need to be realistically assessed. These capital costs will be estimated and recalculated many times during the development of the project. The estimation of costs requires skilled input from both the cost consultant or quantity surveyor and the theatre consultant. It is outside the scope of this book to describe the costing process in detail, but the following paragraphs give a sense of the processes involved.

Before looking at cost estimating at the different stages in the process, it is useful to introduce some terms: net area, gross area, construction cost, specialist theatre equipment cost, soft costs, contingencies, inflation, project cost and benchmarking.

### *Net area*

The net area of the building is the usable area within all the individual rooms in the building. The net area excludes circulation – corridors, stairs, elevators and so on. It also excludes mechanical spaces, ducts, voids and wall thicknesses.

### *Gross area*

This is the actual built area of the building including circulation, plant rooms and so on. In the early stages of planning the gross area is calculated by applying a grossing factor or multiplier to the net area. Compared with more conventional buildings, theatres are inherently inefficient in their use of space due to the generous circulation spaces required, as well as escape routes and mechanical systems. It is typical for the net area to be multiplied by 1.45 to 1.65 or more to calculate the gross area, but this is often contested as excessive by those experienced with other building types. It is essential that a grossing factor of this scale be applied if the theatre is to function well. See the specimen schedule of areas subsequently.

### *Construction cost*

This is the total cost of building the new or refurbished theatre, including all specialist equipment, fit-out and finishes. This is typically described as what would *not* fall out of the building if it were picked up and shaken. These costs are typically measured by a cost consultant or quantity surveyor.

### *Specialist theatre equipment cost*

The construction costs include all the specialist theatre equipment, including:

- production lighting systems
- stage equipment – flying systems, stage elevators, and so on
- sound, communications and audio-visual (AV) systems
- movable acoustic devices
- seats and movable seating systems.

Budgets for the specialist theatre equipment are normally developed by the theatre consultant and vary from around 5 to 15% of the total construction cost. Higher costs may be associated with the desired adaptability of the theatre and the sophistication of the equipment required. The amount and frequency of format change needed must be adequately explored in the business plan for the theatre; that flexibility may be delivered by manual rather than automated systems; therefore it is essential to balance the high capital cost of installed equipment against the high operational cost of doing the changeover by hand.

### *Soft costs*

Any project will incur a series of costs outside of the actual construction costs. These are often referred to as soft costs and include:

- fees for architect, consultants and engineers – typically the largest cost
- permits and licences
- site investigations and surveys
- client costs – project office and staffing
- site acquisition
- fundraising costs
- business planning
- taxes (including VAT where relevant)
- legal, accounting and audit costs

- architect and consultant team selection costs
- loose furniture and equipment
- it and box office systems
- removal costs/temporary accommodation
- administration, staff recruitment and training
- opening costs.

Typically, fees, licences and surveys can be 20% or more of the overall project costs, and on top of this, there are client costs such as project staffing, site acquisition, fundraising costs, non-recoverable taxes, loose equipment, ICT and box office systems, operating staff recruitment and launch/ opening costs. In total this can amount to 50% of the project cost.

### *Contingencies*

Every project should include reasonable contingencies to cover unknown or unexpected events and design development and client changes. It is common for a percentage to be allowed for contingencies and for that percentage to vary and be reduced as the project proceeds. At an early stage when there are considerable unknowns, a contingency of 25 or even 30% may be allowed. As the project becomes more clearly defined, with a firm brief and concept drawings, the contingency can be reduced, a portion being released at the end of each work stage with a reduced balance identified. Some projects allow separate contingencies for the design and construction periods. The design contingency is available to cover changes that occur during the design stages. The construction contingency is to cover unforeseen situations and circumstances that may arise during the construction period including contractor claims for delays caused by changes, incomplete or uncoordinated information.

### *Inflation*

Every project is subject to the effects of inflation on design fees, construction costs and so on. This can be a significant factor in the overall project cost.

### *Project cost*

The overall cost of the project including all the costs – construction, equipment, soft costs and contingencies.

### *Benchmarking*

As mentioned in the subsection 'How do we assess the need?' under 2.4.2, early cost estimates will be based on benchmarking against comparable projects and the experience of the advisers. There are hundreds of new office buildings, housing, schools and so on completed each year which provide a good database of comparative costs. By contrast there are few new or refurbished theatres completed around the world. Each project is often unique and significantly different from others, so there is a lack of reliable cost information on comparable projects, and the use of inappropriate or incomparable benchmarks can be misleading. International comparisons are even more difficult given differences in construction costs and exchange rates.

However, it is possible to benchmark costs even at this stage if the factors that generate cost differentials, such as location, quality, acoustic performance, flexibility and accommodation mix, are recognised in the benchmarking analysis. Costs based on overall area are always more reliable than costs based on seat count. As the project concept is developed and a firm brief is prepared, a clearer cost plan can be drawn up. This will usually be based on a schedule of areas for the building, developed as part of the brief (see 2.5), giving a total area for the building in square metres. Applying a rate per $m^2$ for the project will give a more accurate indication of the construction cost, as it has been found that there is a degree of consistency between the costs per unit area for similar building types. This can be refined by breaking the building down according to the types of space to be provided – auditoria, rehearsal rooms, stage areas, administration, storage, circulation and so on. Such an approach also allows comparative assessments for alternative proposals. (See Figure 2.7.1.)

With any of these proposals, one needs to be mindful of costs that are not specifically area related, like the specialist stage equipment, and ensure that the allowances made reflect the technical vision. Sometimes a cost model will be developed to illustrate qualitative assumptions and test options such as site selection.

When the design team starts work, then drawings of the building will be developed. These can be used by the cost consultant to calculate more accurate cost estimates. The theatre consultant will produce lists and budgets for the specialist theatre equipment. It is important that any variance from the figures assumed in the initial viability study be addressed at this stage.

As the design process proceeds, more detailed estimates of the costs will be prepared. The costs will be analysed by element and quantity (for example, excavation – number of cubic metres to be excavated; structural frame – such as quantity of steel or concrete required).

Almost every building project experiences cost overruns or budget difficulties at some stage, which may be due to outside influences, changes of the brief or an

| | SUMMARY OF TOTAL AREAS | Notes | Area (m²) | Occ. |
|---|---|---|---|---|
| A | Total Public Areas | | 1,080 | 1,200 |
| B | Total Theatre Auditorium, Stage & Support | | 1,654 | 900 |
| C | Total Performer Areas | | 374 | |
| D | Total Theatre School | | 1,343 | |
| E | Total Staff Rooms and Administration | | 164 | |
| F | Total Production Training | | 451 | |
| | | | | |
| | Total NET Usable Area | | 5,066 | |
| | | | | |
| | Grossing rate (50%): | 35% circulation | 1,773 | |
| | | 10% plant | 507 | |
| | | 5% technical areas | 253 | |
| | | | | |
| | | | | |
| | TOTAL GROSS AREA | | 7,599 | m² |
| | | | | |

Figure 2.7.1 Specimen summary page from a schedule of areas for a large theatre.

accelerated programme. The costs need to be constantly checked and reconciled against the budget. Almost inevitably there will be a need to reduce or rationalise costs. This is done by the client and design team through an ongoing process of cost cutting or 'value engineering'. The earlier this is addressed, the less disruptive the process and the more likely the savings will be realised. The most effective way to cut costs is to reduce the building size, but too great a reduction will adversely affect building function and staff, performer and audience experience.

## Where will the funding come from?

**The funding plan is another critical client action. It is a work in progress that will need updating as the project progresses.**

## Funding plan

Once the anticipated 'hard' and 'soft' project costs are known, a funding strategy is required that identifies from where capital costs for the project will be met. It is likely that funding will be required from a mix of sources; these may include local authority capital grants, public grants, development agency grants, private investors, trusts and foundations and public fundraising and donations.

The funding strategy will need to consider capital, soft and operational readiness cost planning across the project timetable and when revenue income can be realised to offset these. The extent of feasibility work required at the beginning of a project will be different for each theatre depending on the client's access to resources, size and type of theatre, new or adapted, stakeholder involvement, site knowledge and availability of funding and investment.

Public funding routes, including those from the Arts Councils and Heritage Lottery Funds in the UK, operate a two-stage award process, one funding award for design development and the second for project delivery.

All these studies may not be required, equally some projects may require more detailed assessment or analysis. For example, a funding body may require more evidence to test available markets and how the theatre will be inclusive and serve diverse audiences; in the case of urban renewal or regeneration projects, more detailed economic impact assessments may be required to demonstrate the role the theatre can play in the overall development; colleges may wish to explore how the theatre may be more viable if it operates with a professional programme for the public as well as an in-house academic learning resource. These change periodically as the awarding bodies reprioritise their funding criteria in response to changes in practice.

## 2.8 Getting ready to design

At the completion of the preliminary planning phase, the client should have:

- a defined or documented vision for the project
- a detailed written brief for the building design
- a site, selected against appropriate criteria
- a detailed view of the capital costs and sources of funding for the project
- a realistic delivery programme
- a robust programming, operational, business and financial plan for the sustained operation of the building
- selected and appointed an architect and specialist consultants.

The key question at the end of this process is 'Do we have the funding, operating model, site, delivery team and business plan to undertake a capital project and achieve a successful outcome?' If the answer is yes, design stages can proceed with confidence.

Successful new and refurbished buildings are opened regularly, but you can see that success is not easy and may take many years. We hope, however, that we have conveyed the importance of attention to detail in preliminary planning.

As the founding team, it is your vision for the building that will inspire and guide the project.

### Section editor

John Riddell, Principal Theatre Consultant with Theatre Projects

### Contributors (in alphabetical order)

Hazel Clover, Strategic, Business and Operational Planning Consultant for Theatre Projects

Mike Cook, Director of property advisers Avison Young

Gary Faulkner, Partner at Gardiner & Theobald LLP and a contributor to the previous edition of this book

Karin Gartzke, Arts Management Consultant and Executive Coach

# Section 3
# Social principles for the twenty-first century

## 3.1 Critical considerations of the social and safety agenda

This section of the book addresses social principles, the overarching ethical and safety principles and moral imperatives that have become more prevalent in our discourse since the first edition of *Theatre Buildings: A Design Guide* in 2010.

All the themes explored in this section are broadly concerned with safety, health and inclusion and are interrelated in how we use theatres, as well as having significant implications for theatre design. Theatre design of course embraces physical safety, but we must also, now more than ever, embrace the long-term wellness and psychological safety of those who use our theatres, as well as the health of our global environment. We have a moral imperative to approach theatre design holistically and to address these themes at every step.

To this end, although we have explored these themes in some detail here, we have also interspersed observation and guidance from the authors throughout the book, recognising that these concepts do not exist in isolation; they underpin and inform all our decisions in the design and use of a theatre. The themes explored here are, we hope, useful for client and architect alike, for the designer and the user, for the student and the professional.

We open with a contribution from Steve Tompkins, **notes on regenerative practice in theatre architecture**, in which he explores this fundamental concept of the interconnectedness of social and environmental issues, exploring the themes of civility, adaptability and generosity in theatre design.

The section then moves on to address **climate emergency and sustainability**, perhaps the most pressing issues of our own and future generations. Andrew Wylie highlights the importance of sustainability as a fundamental design consideration and addresses the part we have to play, as both consumers and generators of carbon emissions, in the construction of new and the operation of existing theatres.

Our next contribution comes from Michèle Taylor, who writes about **disability inclusion** and the key principles for designing and building a space that reflects fundamental good practice. At every stage of planning, designing, constructing and fitting out a theatre space, decisions are made which will determine who can use that space comfortably and who feels at home there. Inclusive design can make a space more widely usable, bringing in opportunities for innovation, creativity and inclusion.

The section continues the theme of inclusivity by addressing **social belonging**, the need for inclusive design that acknowledges difference and diversity so that we make spaces which everyone is able to access and use. In conversation with Nafeesah Butt, we explore how theatres and their design should welcome and reflect the diversity of people who could or should use them and enable accessibility and participation.

We then address the ever more pressing issue of **designing for health** and the design imperatives arising from recent epidemics and pandemics. Learning from responses in different countries to SARS, MERS and COVID-19, in conversation with Chris McDougall and with contributions from Tim Foster, we look at design choices that impact the health of staff and patrons alike and mitigations in design and use to better protect the health of all theatre users.

Last, Andrew Nicholson considers **fire safety** and the requirement for both technical systems and the safe and thoughtful management of a building. The climate emergency and the role of the built environment is rapidly developing and changing as a greater understanding of the impact of construction emerges. The tension between fire safety and sustainability targets for carbon reduction with an increasing use of engineered timber is explored, along with the challenges raised by our heritage theatres and the activities involved in staging productions.

DOI: 10.4324/9781003327295-3

## 3.2 Notes on regenerative practice in theatre architecture

As we absorb the implications of the COVID-19 pandemic, which has so starkly exposed the fragility of our social and environmental ecosystem, cultural organisations and artists are re-examining their mission and naming new priorities: to confront racism, injustice and inequity; to be an agent of change for a healthier population in mind and body; and to face the facts of the planetary emergency. These issues have often been seen as separate and distinct, but there is a growing body of thought that each is part of the same complex system and cannot be properly addressed without considering the wider networks of cause and effect. Within this framing, poor public health, poverty, colonialism, inequality and racism are inseparable from ecological degradation and the unsupportable planetary burdens imposed by the pursuit of endless, exponential growth.

To explore this more complex interrelationship in the round, progressive thinkers are developing system-based strategies around the idea of regenerative practice, which moves beyond the 'less-bad-business-as-usual' mindset of current sustainability narratives to seek a more active, positive contribution to societal and planetary healing. Recognising that humanity and the natural environment are indivisible and mutually dependent, the aim of such practice is to achieve a state of dynamic equilibrium, whereby global society's needs are met without threatening the wider life support systems of biodiversity and climate stability. What that means is a transition from a degenerative and divisive society towards a regenerative and distributive society, equipped to flourish within the 'safe and just space' framework created by economist Kate Raworth, which embraces social as well as planetary boundaries.

At their best, arts organisations aspire to thought leadership, so how might theatres play a leading role in that transition, which is now both opportune and necessary? In her seminal essay 'Leverage Points', the great systems thinker Donella Meadows concluded that one of the most effective ways to intervene at a systemic level is not to battle with existing rules and metrics but to change the narrative: to tell a new story. If this is the case, theatre – and theatre architecture – should be one of the key public forums in which those crucial stories can be enacted and new relationships built.

But within an expanded field of theatre practice, where connectivity and overlap are essential drivers, the model of a cultural building as a stand-alone, bespoke, single-purpose 'trophy object' – exotic in form but frozen in time, space and genre – is no longer useful. By contrast, the provisional, open-ended qualities of many found spaces, repurposed buildings and community-led venues are more socially inclusive, less colonising of existing communal territory, more open to conversation, experimentation, multi-purposing and slow evolution over time. To be part of a paradigm shift towards regenerative practice, the next generation of theatre spaces – either upgraded existing venues, converted buildings or new build projects – will need to encapsulate those socially purposeful qualities whilst also meeting exemplary environmental standards.

So, what would a theatre built or adapted using regenerative principles look and feel like? How could it help organisations and artists to maximise their agency, respond to new hybrid ways of working and become part of a movement for necessary change? From our own studio's practice, three key qualities have emerged as a guide: civility, adaptability and generosity.

**Civility:** architecture not as a static edifice but as the host to a web of thriving relationships. A building that puts people at their ease and encourages communication, where strangers can meet in peace, share their common humanity, feel relaxed, be vulnerable, explore big ideas and offer hope. A space for debate, dissent and celebration. A building that lifts the heart, fires the imagination and feels welcoming to people of all backgrounds and cultural traditions. A building that engages with its physical and cultural context with no barriers to entry, either physically or psychologically. An inclusive, classless and un-rarefied architectural language, not requiring conformity of behaviour or prior knowledge. A building purpose-designed for partnerships, knowledge sharing, co-productions and collaborations. Clear navigation and natural desire lines, universal access without medicalised infrastructure, good visibility and orientation around and within the building to encourage exploration. Back-of-house processes on view, multi-tasking rooms with no single fixed uses or formats rather than single-purpose dedicated spaces.

**Adaptability:** a building that enables operational and commercial flexibility to withstand future shocks and abnormal circumstances. A space that avoids answering all the questions but leaves space for artists to frame multiple stories. Loose fit, upgradeable and adjustable without expensive specialist intervention, bolt-on, easily adjusted technical infrastructure receptive to emerging technologies and artistic practice. Simple form and rational structure, designed for ease of maintenance, repair and recycling to minimise use of precious resources in construction, operation and eventual upcycling. A building that takes up the minimum physical and environmental footprint while offering maximum density of options for different creative uses and multiple activities throughout the day and evening. A place that takes every opportunity to be humming with life and overflowing with creative energy.

**Generosity**: a building that gives back more than it takes, contributing positively to wider planetary life support systems across its lifetime. Frugal in use of resources and operational energy loads, specifically designed to be enjoyed and densely used throughout the year with minimal energy use. A building made of carbon-capturing materials and built to robust, low energy construction standards combined with healthy, intuitive systems like natural ventilation, good daylight, intelligent orientation, optimal shading and maximum use of living plants. Fully or partially retrofitted existing buildings wherever possible rather than newly built from scratch. A building that not only targets zero whole life carbon in construction, operation and upcycling but delivers the equivalent biodiversity support, water harvesting and energy generating capacity of its own virgin, undeveloped land footprint.

## 3.3 Climate emergency and sustainability

Having recognised that the construction and operation of theatres make a significant contribution to atmospheric carbon emissions and environmental degradation, this section explores practical approaches to reducing this impact.

Through consideration in the design brief, design response, material selection and all building systems (heating, cooling, performance technology, etc.) it is possible to significantly reduce environmental damage when constructing a new building, indeed it is even possible through real focus and prioritisation to design and operate a building that is, as the introduction to this section makes clear, regenerative; giving back more than it takes from our natural environment. We are rapidly transitioning to a point where any new build or refurbishment project should deliver a regenerative contribution to the environment, simply doing less harm will soon become socially and environmentally unacceptable.

The *Theatre Green Book*, derived from a collaboration of theatre makers, venues, designers, technicians and architects brought together by the Theatres Trust and the Association of British Theatre Technicians (ABTT), was published in three parts in 2021–2022 and separately addressed productions, buildings and operations. While the users of theatres are so engaged with minimising their carbon use and are facing the challenges of working sustainably and collaboratively, it is crucial that the initial build or the refurbishment of any theatre also enables them to positively engage with the climate crisis and make operational choices that reduce environmental impact.

### Briefing

In any project, once the decision to build, refurbish or adapt has been made, the greatest impact on reducing environmental damage happens in the early decision making around the design brief and specification of the theatre. It is critical that in establishing a brief for a design team, any theatre organisation or commissioning client consider future practices and operational models rather than relying on historic precedent. Consideration must increasingly be given as to how the theatre might operate with less environmental impact over the decades to come. This must include future potential changes in behaviour that come about as a result of our adapting to cope with climate change.

The early stage of any design process should challenge the design team to consider the current brief and how it might be developed if the project is to minimise its environmental impact. Key issues that will have significant impact on material and energy consumption of a theatre include:

- **technical loading**: the higher the loading, the more material is needed to support those loads
- **structural deflections**: the control of deflections can put a significant demand on a buildings structure, requiring an overall heavier structure
- **environmental comfort and temperature**: the lower the set temperature or the tighter the control of the temperature, the more energy the building will require
- **daylighting**: increasing the use of daylight in all areas of a theatre will reduce the need for artificial lighting and benefit user wellbeing
- **acoustic control**: significant quantities of material are used to control acoustic transmission within a theatre.

The climate emergency is upon us now; designing buildings for possible future uses or flexibility that require excess materials in construction is no longer appropriate or acceptable. We can of course only work with the tools and knowledge we have today, and it should be noted that specific and retrofit solutions may also be possible in the future when any changes to operational requirements are identified.

A good brief for a design team should contain a robust environmental vision that the project must deliver against. This should be clear and succinct without referencing solutions but be broad enough to challenge an experienced design team. A project vision is best authored in collaboration with key organisational stakeholders, including funders, patrons, staff and leadership teams. It should inspire a creative design team to engage widely, think creatively and respond responsibly. It should contain targets for embodied and operational carbon emissions or provide a basis for the design team to establish targets and measurement systems early in their commission.

## Measurement

Measurement of a project's environmental performance is now commonplace, and the reasons for undertaking a measured approach to a project's environmental performance can be numerous. It is important to establish why you will be undertaking this assessment, as it will guide you to the selection of an appropriate measurement system. Funder requirements, patron and audience expectations to help guide and direct a design team to a recognised level of environmental achievement or a deep-rooted mission to build with the minimum possible impact are all common reasons. Each of these reasons will lead to different measurement standards, some specified by funders, some that have a public awareness and hence provide a 'badge of achievement' and others that require a higher level of rigour and commitment. It is also important to note that not all measurement systems address all areas of sustainable design equally.

The Building Research Establishment Environmental Assessment Method (BREEAM) is the most used scheme in the UK, with its North American equivalent Leadership in Energy and Environmental Design (LEED). There are assessment standards that focus on energy use such as Passivhaus (the leading international low-energy design standard in construction) and others that focus on wellbeing such as the WELL Building Standard. However, the most rigorous system currently in existence is the Living Building Challenge (LBC), as illustrated in Figure 3.3.1. Where schemes such as BREEAM and LEED help users reduce the

Figure 3.3.1 The seven performance categories of the Living Building Challenge, arranged as petals of a flower, each of which represents a different category: place, water, energy, health + happiness, materials, equity and beauty and inspiration, shown here as a simplified diagram based on https://living-future.org/lbc/.

amount of damage from a project, the LBC leads its users to a regenerative approach. Whilst this might not be possible for all schemes, this is the social and environmental aspiration.

In addition to the measurement of whole project performance, it is essential to measure the emission of carbon that your project will create over its lifetime and not simply in construction. Carbon is a key component of the sustainability assessment tools referenced previously, but water consumption and use of polluting materials and processes must also be measured and consumption reduced.

Whole-life carbon assessment measures the carbon embodied in the construction materials as well as the operational carbon emissions from servicing the building over its lifetime. This approach must be used to make design decisions to take advantage of the opportunities to reduce carbon emissions through material selection and design. The industry standard for this is published by the Royal Institute of Chartered Surveyors (RICS), as professional standards and guidance UK, *Whole Life Carbon Assessment for the Built Environment* (1st edition, November 2017).

## It is all about carbon, operational carbon

There are two principal ways a building, new or refurbished, is responsible for the emission of carbon dioxide into the atmosphere. These are commonly known and broadly categorised as embodied and operational carbon emissions. The embodied carbon is accounted for in the production, transport and assembly of materials to create a building, and the following section on materials explores key principles in reducing these emissions. In the United Kingdom, as the electricity supply grid is decarbonising through greater use of renewable power generation (solar and wind) and operational emissions are reducing, embodied carbon emissions are becoming the dominant building lifetime cause of carbon emissions.

Operational carbon is emitted because of the energy that a building consumes to heat, cool and light it via gas and electricity consumption. Key strategic issues to address early in the design process include the ability for a new or existing theatre to participate in a local low carbon energy scheme, a heat network or utilising natural ventilation with no mechanically assisted ventilation and cooling systems.

Overheating is a major issue in many theatres, due in part to the activities and the higher temperatures needed in key specialist areas such as dance studios but also to the volume of people using the building at peak performance times. However, increasing the amount of carbon-intensive mechanical cooling to reduce temperatures is not the answer we need in a climate emergency. The use of thermal mass and natural ventilation can be key in retaining the quality of the environment without the use of mechanical plant. Pre-show, interval, post-show and night-time purging through passive solutions such as natural ventilation, ground coupling heat exchange or under croft cooling, and high-level openings should all be considered during periods when the acoustic performance can be maintained or reduced.

Pre-cooling allows temperatures to rise during the first act, purging or reducing temperatures during the interval; then temperatures rise again through the second act (within acceptable agreed-upon parameters). Passive solutions can therefore reduce theatres' reliance on carbon-intensive cooling plant, but theatres will need to be become more dynamic, changing how they work throughout the day, and reduce their reliance on mechanical systems to an absolute minimum.

Design for good building performance starts with a highly efficient (well insulated and airtight) building envelope; the principles established by the Passivhaus Institute are a good resource: maximum use of the sun to heat the building, better than building regulation levels of insulation, minimal thermal bridging and heat recovery on all extract air.

A significant benefit to any energy-efficient building is selection of plant (equipment used to heat, cool, power and ventilate the building) and control systems. The design of building systems now shows a progressive move away from natural gas (and other fossil fuels), so we must embrace the replacement of gas boilers with more efficient and sustainable solutions such as district heating, electric heating systems, heat pumps and new technologies such as hydrogen fuel cells. The use of electrical heating and heat pumps will increase the electricity demand of the building, and it is therefore important that the capacity of the grid connection be checked. This move to all-electric buildings exploits the carbon benefits of a future decarbonised electricity infrastructure.

Ensuring that systems can be carefully controlled to only provide heating and cooling in occupied areas will not only enable the environmental systems to operate at much higher efficiencies but will also enable theatres able to operate efficiently when used more intensively, with longer opening hours and more diverse uses.

## Natural ventilation of theatres

The use of a natural ventilation approach to managing ventilation and air quality in a theatre is a significant contribution to the reduction of operational carbon emissions and can be seen in practice in the Liverpool Everyman Theatre's naturally ventilated auditoria, illustrated in Figure 3.3.2. This approach takes external air at a low level and directs it through the building, removing exhaust air at high levels through chimneys or similar elements. This is achieved through the stack effect, using natural buoyancy to drive the movement of air. Natural ventilation within theatres can be challenging to achieve if it does not form an integral part of the overall building design and is integrated into all aspects of the architectural, structural and building services design solutions from the outset. Careful consideration must be given to air lets, passive air distribution routes and air exhaust locations. Filters maybe required to remove or reduce particulates, and the use of boost fans to increase airflow at specific times may be required to ensure comfort levels are maintained.

The approach should always be:

- Can this theatre be served via natural ventilation and passive solutions?
- How much of the theatre's needs can be served via natural ventilation and passive solutions?
- How little cooling and mechanical plant needs to be provided?

We must change how we prioritise our approach to what is an acceptable design and operational solution. We can no longer rely on generic and out-of-date carbon-intensive mechanical equipment-based solutions. We must always prioritise natural ventilation and passive solutions, only

Figure 3.3.2 Liverpool Everyman Theatre has naturally ventilated auditoria. The main auditorium walls are built from bricks reclaimed from the dismantled older building, adding a significant amount of thermal mass, critical to the auditorium's natural ventilation, and the thrust stage enclosed on three sides of the audience seating with the brick walls behind gives a warm ambiance to the space. See Reference Project 17.

utilising mechanical plant when all other options have been exhausted.

## Materials and embodied carbon

The calculation of embodied carbon emissions is a well-regulated process with standards defining the system boundaries and calculation process to ensure all buildings' embodied carbon can be compared in an equitable way. At its simplest, the weight of a material is multiplied by a factor for the amount of carbon emissions per unit weight; this is done for all materials and summed to calculate the embodied carbon of a building.

This simple calculation tells us that to reduce the embodied carbon of a building, we should use less material, design a lighter building and prioritise the use of materials with a lower carbon factor. These materials typically are recycled materials and natural materials such as timber, stone and earthen products that have a limited amount of industrial processing.

Designing with materials to be part of a circular economy is essential; all building components must be reused or reusable with a minimum of processing. Designers must consider how a building will be disassembled at its end of life and how all building components might be replaced throughout its life. As prominent civic facilities theatre buildings are cherished by communities, designing buildings to function for longer than the current typical sixty-year design life is significantly beneficial in reducing whole life carbon emissions.

All engineering frame materials should be considered and designers encouraged to select the most appropriate material for different building functions. It is likely that the most appropriate theatre structure will be a hybrid frame using the most appropriate lowest-impact materials in different scenarios.

A capable design team must be given time to explore the material options for all components of the building, carrying out whole-life carbon assessments on different design options exploring for the minimum impact scheme.

The source of all materials should be of specific concern to designers and building owners. The location from which a building's raw material are extracted and components are manufactured will have a bearing on its embodied carbon due to the transport carbon emissions. The sourcing of materials might guide the aesthetic response of a theatre design, too, if limits are put on the distance that materials and building components can travel. This is something that is becoming more frequent in many environmental measurement tools.

A client or building owner who has set a challenging sustainability vision for the theatre design must care about the source of the materials used. Requiring chain of custody certification for all building materials and components is a way to strive for responsibly sourced materials. Some materials such as timber have well established chain of custody schemes such as the Forest Stewardship Council (FSC) and the Programme for the Endorsement of Forest Certification (PEFC), ensuring that the products come from well-managed forests. Timber from a certified sustainable source is the lowest embodied carbon material, and when incorporated into a long-lasting building, the building itself becomes a carbon store, locking atmospheric carbon into the timber components for the life of the building. It is used to great effect in the Elizabethan Theatre in the grounds of the Château d'Hardelot in France, a round playhouse built largely of wood and bamboo, which mimics the design of the Globe Theatre (see Figure 3.3.3).

Timber might not be suitable in all locations within a theatre, particularly around the support of automation systems. This should not preclude it as a structural material used in the building, and hybridising timber with smaller quantities of high-carbon materials such as steel is an appropriate compromise to consider.

Figure 3.3.3 The Elizabethan Theatre in the grounds of the Château d'Hardelot in France mimics the design of the Globe Theatre, a round playhouse featuring tiered seating and a standing stalls area, built entirely of wood and bamboo to fit into its natural surroundings among the trees. See Reference Project 11.

## Adapting to future climate change

Consideration must be given to future changes in our climate. Predictive weather files and climate change forecasts should be used to help inform the brief. Efficient and sustainable design will reduce the theatre's impact on the world it inhabits. Ensuring that climate adaptive solutions are integrated into the brief and design at an early stage will ensure the quality of the internal environment will be maintained throughout the life of the building.

As a society, we must accept that as our external environment changes and temperatures rise the internal environments of our theatres will need to adapt accordingly. We cannot allow our aspiration for the level of internal comfort to stay static as the world around us changes. Acceptable internal temperatures will need to increase to allow a more passive and sustainable approach to be achievable; even a one- or two-degree increase in allowable internal temperature will have an impact on the required cooling, be that passive or mechanical.

It is important, however, to get the right balance. It is inevitable that, as we move to a more sustainable model of theatre design and operation, we will need to increase our typical internal temperatures. However, we must be mindful of audience comfort levels. Allowing temperatures to rise, high volumes of fresh air and keeping $CO_2$ levels low (at around <800ppm) will help to balance the overall comfort level. But if our aspiration and requirements remain as they are, we are only increasing our reliance on mechanical cooling and carbon-intensive solutions.

## 3.4 Disability inclusion

Ensuring equality of access to theatre buildings and the activity that happens within them is vital for everyone involved: staff, managers, leaders, freelancers, audiences and participants. According to Arts Council England's (ACE's) research from 2017 ('Making a Shift', Arts Council England, 2017) in which disabled people report the barriers they experience to working in the arts, recurring themes include barriers to physical and communication access, attitudes to disabled people, working culture and lack of role models.

> The total percentage of disabled workers across the National Portfolio is 6%. Disabled representation at board level is 7%; with 9% Chief Executives, 8% Artistic Directors and 5% Chairs.
>
> (p. 6)

In its report 'Equality, Diversity and the Creative Case Report' for 2018–19, published in 2020, Arts Council England's research identifies that disabled people make up 12% of National Portfolio Organisations' audiences. Data on the purple pound tells us that the annual spending power of households which include someone who is disabled is around £274bn and that three in four disabled people have left a UK business citing poor accessibility.

To provide context; the 'Family Resources Survey' in 2018/19 showed that 44% of state pension–age adults report as being disabled and 19% of people of working age.

Designing disabled people out of our theatre spaces impoverishes the working and artistic cultures of those theatres. Sir Iain Lobban was director of GCHQ when he made a speech in 2012 paying tribute to Alan Turing. He said:

> [An] agency requires the widest range of skills possible if it is to be successful, and to deny itself talent just because the person with the talent doesn't conform to a social stereotype is to starve itself of what it needs to thrive.

At the time of writing, the theatre industry is in the midst of change with regard to disabled people: professional theatre-makers who are disabled are taking their place onstage and backstage and are no longer working only in disability-specific contexts. The six founding consortium partners of Ramps on the Moon are casting, commissioning and employing disabled people across their programme, and, prior to the COVID-19 pandemic, huge progress had been made with disabled performers in roles at these and a number of other theatres including The National Theatre, The Royal Shakespeare Company and The Globe. Demand for buildings in which disabled performers can work independently is only going to increase.

The final issue to highlight here is one of representation. Theatres are places where stories are made, told and celebrated; which stories are told and who gets to tell them can perpetuate or question societal norms. Designing theatre spaces that are genuinely useable by disabled people means that stereotypes can be challenged, and authentic stories can be told that challenge the pervading ableism.

Taken together, these financial, cultural and other moral arguments make a compelling case for designing with disabled people in mind, especially when we consider the fact that design elements that can be barriers to disabled people are often barriers for other people too.

It is important to remember that we are complicated individuals and rarely does a person carry one single protected characteristic or experience one single identity. The concept of intersectionality is important to bear in mind when designing a welcoming and useable environment for all.

It can be overwhelming to take an approach to design which is led by thinking about individuals' medical conditions; there is too much new information to learn and too many variables. In addition, each capital project has its own idiosyncrasies and each commissioning client has a different agenda, so this section offers principles for decision-making, planning and action which will maximise the usability of new or refurbished buildings and spaces by disabled people and others.

### A framework for inclusive design: the social model of disability

The social model of disability is a very useful tool for planning and design which simplifies the processes of, as well as the conversations about, ensuring that disabled people can use a building alongside everyone else.

The social model asks us to focus not on the individual and their medical conditions but rather on the environment and the ways in which it makes it difficult for people to function. It is a reaction against individual models of disability, most notably the medical model which says that individuals are disabled by things like spina bifida or cerebral palsy, blindness or deafness, mental health issues or Down's Syndrome. In contrast the social model says that people are disabled by their surroundings, by heavy doors, cobbles, stairs, poor lighting, attitudes, complicated text, noise and crowds, the absence of parking or using the accessible toilet as a storage space.

Within the social model, it is their environment that disables people: they are not people *with* disabilities but are instead *disabled people*, since people *have* medical conditions which are not necessarily disabilities in every situation, but they *are* disabled by obstacles in the environment in which they are trying to function, be that a physical, sensory, digital, attitudinal, intellectual, financial or any other type of obstacle.

It follows that if disabled people are to play a full part in theatre, the way theatres are built and organised must change. Removing the barriers which exclude people who have conditions is important in bringing about this change.

The factors that cause disability within the medical model are completely outside the control of planners, designers, architects and people staffing theatres. The factors that disable people within the framework of the social model are aspects of the environment which those same planners, designers, architects and staff create and sustain. With thought, and with a willingness to rid ourselves of our assumptions, we can design theatre buildings with stages and technical areas that can be accessed by everyone.

## The seven inclusive principles for arts and culture organisations

A useful overarching framework is provided by the 'Seven Inclusive Principles for Arts & Cultural Organisations'. This was written by Andrew Miller (We Shall Not Be Removed) and Michèle Taylor (Ramps on the Moon), working with Paraorchestra, Attitude Is Everything and What Next, to ensure proper regard for disabled people's place in the cultural life of the four nations of the United Kingdom. These principles are more broadly relevant than the COVID-19 pandemic and aim to ensure that planning and design take good account of the conditions that must be maintained if disabled people are to be active in every aspect of cultural organisations. The principles (slightly adapted for this context) are:

1. ensure compliance with the Equality Act (2010)
2. use the social model of disability and aim to combat and eliminate ableism
3. consult disabled people and undertake equality impact assessments at every stage
4. ensure that building design incorporates an information infrastructure that takes account of disabled people's requirements
5. ensure that the customer journey for disabled audiences and visitors is thoroughly mapped and assessed for equality
6. disabled artists are an important cultural asset in the United Kingdom, and capital works should facilitate their engagement in all creative projects
7. capital works should celebrate diversity, embodying anti-ableist principles.

The seven principles interact with each other and work together to give a robust basis for approaching the planning, design and build of new spaces. The rest of this section offers more guidance on implementing the principles.

## The Equality Act (2010), approved documents and British Standards

Whilst the UK's Equality Act (2010) does not prescribe the detail of building design, it requires everyone involved in design and delivery, including capital works, to:

1. ensure they do not discriminate against anyone on the grounds of their being disabled or having any other protected characteristic(s)
2. make reasonable adjustments for disabled people so that they do not face disadvantage in relation to buildings and facilities and access to information.

It is important to remember that:

1. the duties under the Goods, Facilities and Services provisions are *anticipatory*
2. the duty to make reasonable adjustment is a continuing duty, in other words, policies, practices and procedures, need to be under regular review.

The Equality Act (2010) does not include detail with regard to building for access. Part M (Access to and Use of Buildings) of the Building Regulations provides this detail (volume 2 covers buildings other than dwellings) but note that disabled people are referenced in other Approved Documents, most significantly Part K (Protection from falling, collision and impact) and Part B (Fire Safety). Note that the Building

Regulations represent *minimum standards* and are not aspirational in terms of equity for disabled people.

The British Standards document BS8300 goes further than the Building Regulations and is a best practice guide giving more detailed guidance.

## Principles of universal design

At every planning and design stage, universal design can be very useful in supporting you to enact principles 4 and 5. They were developed in 1997 by a team at North Carolina State University. The Centre for Universal Design at the university says that they can be used

> to evaluate existing designs, guide the design process and educate both designers and consumers about the characteristics of more usable products and environments

and they can be applied to the design of buildings, digital environments and print, as well as to programming decisions and service delivery (for example, workshop design and delivery in participatory programmes). These principles apply more widely than just to disabled people; they relate, too, to other social and economic factors that can exclude people from theatre spaces.

Confusingly, there are also seven principles of Universal Design:

1. equitable use
2. flexibility in use
3. simple and intuitive use
4. perceptible information
5. high tolerance for error
6. low physical effort
7. size and space for approach and use.

These principles are largely self-explanatory; examples are given here to illustrate how they work in practice (this, of course, is not an exhaustive list). For ease, the word 'buildings' is used here to encompass all aspects of design relevant to this book.

Equitable design refers to making sure that buildings are useful to disabled people, make sense to them and can be 'read' by them. The building must provide a means of use that is identical for all users whenever possible or equivalent when it is not. No user must be segregated or stigmatised, and the design must be appealing to all users.

For example, a main entrance must be clearly visible, clearly signposting itself to a wide variety of people allowing for independent access into the building. It is not acceptable to have an 'alternative' entrance for wheelchair users. In this case, options might be to change the main entrance to the level or ramped entrance or to create two (or more) equally high-profile entrances, as can be seen at the Leeds Playhouse and the New Wolsey Theatre in Ipswich (Figures 3.4.1 and 3.4.2). The same is true of the stage door.

Flexibility in use requires that there be choice in how to use and navigate a space (where none of the choices is seen as the 'main' one, with others as 'alternative' versions). Users must have a range of ways of accessing information, making their way through a building and making themselves comfortable and must be able to do so at their own pace.

For example, plenty of seating must be provided throughout staff, backstage and public spaces, and flow through the spaces must not determine how long each individual can spend there. Furniture should offer variety, for instance, some chairs with arms and some without, some higher than others, tables at different heights.

There should be a dedicated area which can be used as a quiet area to get away from the possibility of emotional or sensory overload (and this must be clearly signposted).

This relates, too, to offers such as relaxed performances, dementia-friendly performances and services such as sign language interpretation, audio description and captioning. Future-proofed, flexible provision must be built in to allow these services to be delivered in as integrated and seamless a way as possible, and to be developed in exciting new directions.

Simple and intuitive use means that the user must not require any specialist knowledge or experience in order to be able to move about the building and use all it has to

Figure 3.4.1 Leeds Playhouse has several entrances to the building, all of which have step-free access. The space inside is light and bright; there are spacious lifts to all floors, low counters, Braille signs, family toilet cubicle and changing places. The theatre spaces have wheelchair access through the main auditorium doors, wheelchair spaces and transfer seats with removable arms available.

Figure 3.4.2 The foyers and auditorium for the New Wolsey Theatre, Ipswich, are accessible from the street without encountering any steps and with automated doors at the entrance. The box office inside the main entrance has a low-level service counter.

offer. This principle is interesting specifically because it has relevance to ways in which the physical space impacts the *culture* of the theatre.

For example, signs front and back of house must be designed to incorporate pictograms as well as text; foyers need to be welcoming to all and not intimidating or more easily usable to people familiar with theatre layout; new audiences may not know what a 'Box Office' is, so nomenclature is important; and access to staff must be straightforward. Security devices should not rely on having to memorise a sequence of numbers.

Perceptible information means that all individuals must be able to receive information, whatever the ambient conditions and whatever their specific sensory abilities. For example, announcements both backstage and front-of-house must not be delivered via one sensory channel only; calls to dressing rooms must be visual as well as auditory, as must be announcements into the auditorium. Sound and lighting levels throughout must be easily adjustable.

Menus and bar lists should be available in a range of formats as a matter of course, and cafés and restaurants must offer easy-grip cutlery and straws.

High tolerance for error means that users must not be required to have fine motor skills or particular intellectual or sensory aptitude in order to use the space independently. Potential hazards must be removed, or there must be clear warning of their presence and nature.

For example, website links must not require precise positioning of the cursor in order to activate them; hazard warnings must take good account of anyone using a cane who will pick up physical cues only at ground level and just above. Controls and handles should be operable with one hand in a closed fist. The colour palette of a building must have good visual contrast so as to offer clear visual cues to the different spaces as well as to the features within the spaces; for example, grab rails, bannisters and furniture must all be visually distinct from their surroundings.

Low physical effort means that users must be able to access the building and all its features using a neutral stance and with minimum force.

Doors, for example, should open automatically or be light enough to be useable by all. Furniture, if designed to be moveable, should not be so heavy as to make it impossible for many people to move it. Kitchen equipment must be as light and easy to use as possible, for instance, tipping kettles.

Size and space for approach and use mean that all features must be easy to use and available with a clear line of sight, without excessive reach being required, with space for assistive devices and accommodating variations in size and height.

For example, counters must be set at two different heights (and the lower sections must not become the area where point of sale materials are displayed or where dirty glasses or crockery are cleared to), and spaces must be designed to have sufficiently wide corridors and doorways to allow easy access for anyone using a wheelchair or walking aids. In a staff kitchen, if a microwave is provided, it must be within easy reach of all staff. Café counters must accommodate a range of people of different heights, and table service must be offered (and clearly signposted).

## Consulting disabled people

The mantra of the Disability Rights Movement is 'Nothing about us without us', and it is helpful to bear this in mind. Consulting disabled people is an important part of designing a building and planning both the internal and external environment it will provide. Setting up a disability advisory group will be very helpful at the planning phase. It is good practice to offer participants a fee, or it may be appropriate, in some cases, to offer complementary tickets or vouchers for the café, for example. Access requirements must be met, and any out-of-pocket costs covered.

In addition, an access consultant will need to be involved to advise and feed back at all RIBA stages, and it is good practice to ensure that this is a disabled person.

## Thinking beyond the immediate site

Whilst there will be provision which is outside the project proper (for example, parking and public transport), a good design will take account of these factors and how they impact disabled people, offering mitigation where possible and developing conversations with other relevant bodies to influence local decision-making.

### Training

In order to maximise the use of the new space by disabled people, it is important that it be staffed by a team that are informed and confident in disability issues and cognisant of the ways in which ableism can be enacted and perpetuated in theatre spaces. Anti-ableism training from a disabled person will equip staff teams, managers and boards to actualise ambitions for disabled people's place across the theatre ecology. It will enable risk assessments to take account of individuals' perceptions, requirements and preferences and to be based on real data rather than assumptions which are imposed on people.

### Inclusive design for full participation

This framework provides a lens through which problems can be anticipated before they are actualised or caught by the access consultant. More than that, since this framework works on the basis that disabling barriers can be designed out from the very beginnings of conceptualising a space or a building, it invites innovative and creative design that has ease of use and welcome at the heart of the fundamental aesthetic of the building.

The question that the design and build team must have in mind at all times is not what do we have to do or what can we get away with but rather what might real people need in order to do their best work, to participate fully, and to have the best experiences in this building?

## 3.5 Social belonging

> In theory it should be a simple action, stepping over the threshold from one public space: a street/pavement, to another public space: a theatre/arts venue/cultural building. Yet many of us know that in reality these lines in the sand have been layered with barriers and rules that only some people know how to pass through unscathed. This action, of taking yourself from one place to another can come at such a high cost for many of us, whilst for others, that threshold is merely a line to brush past at speed, without a second thought for why there may be another person hovering on the step outside, hesitating over their next steps or questioning their place on the other side of the threshold.
>
> Nafeesah Butt, 24 October 2019, 'Stepping Over the Threshold', Theatres Trust Conference 19

Inclusive design is about making places that everyone can use. It should remove barriers and enable everyone to participate equally, confidently and with dignity. We need to replace a hierarchy of accessibility with a level playing field of accessibility. We know that not all places will appeal to all people, not all activities and productions in theatres speak to everyone, but we should remove the barriers that are imposed by design in all its forms.

Theatres and their design should have the ambition to welcome the whole community through the design concept, to reflect the diversity of people who should or could use them and enable all forms of participation. It may be that there is a particular use required of a building, perhaps focused on young people or local communities, but the design can still lend itself to everyone even if the use then makes it more specific.

The Midlands Arts Centre in Birmingham offers a range of practical creative courses and classes, as well as its performance programme, and develops work with children, families and young people of all backgrounds. The building relates to and serves its community with workshop facilities and artist studios; a café with an emphasis on local, sustainable and seasonal produce; a cinema; and a gallery, set in parkland with an outdoor theatre and with inclusivity at the heart of its operations (see Figures 3.5.1 and 3.5.2).

Social belonging (or lack of belonging) is a fundamental human driver and also a potential barrier to participation. Our level of participation in designed spaces is driven by our sense of that social belonging, or indeed social rejection, and theatre design has a responsibility to address this.

Design can address emotional and intellectual access to a theatre and therefore the full range of visible and invisible ways we are and in which we identify: race, sex, gender, physical abilities and age, as well as beliefs,

Figure 3.5.1 Midlands Arts Centre (mac) is in parkland south of Birmingham city centre with a lake beside it. It comprises several buildings close to one another, their façades a mix of brick and walls of large, colourful squares.

Figure 3.5.2 KILN café at Midlands Arts Centre (mac), Birmingham, was redesigned and refurbished during COVID-19 and reopened in 2021 with a focus on creativity, comfort and accessibility. The café incorporates vibrant colours, large artistic lighting fixtures for good visibility and generous windows affording natural daylight. Its name links the firing of pizzas in the café with the three pottery firing kilns in the craft studios, available for public use.

socio-economic status, neurodiversity, parental status and disability. It should ensure people feel confident in entering a building, placing the theatre at the heart of the community and promoting social cohesion and well-being.

Approaching inclusive design as an integral part of the design process, to acknowledge diversity and difference, will ensure the created space meets the needs of as many people as possible, offering security, choice and flexibility and inspiring users at all levels and in all spaces. It should enable social interaction and allow users to make confident choices navigating the environment with a sense of belonging. To that end, there is merit in engagement with the communities the space should serve for the whole journey of a capital project and beyond. Consider where this engagement might begin, architects and project teams alone may not necessarily be the right people to lead, particularly if the journey requires public engagement well before appointment and possibly beyond the opening into the working life of a building. Collaboration with stakeholders and working with them, not deciding for them, will enable design issues that impact on inclusivity can be addressed along the way rather than presented as challenges later.

Theatres all have a unique contribution to make towards social inclusion, with the potential to challenge inequality and discrimination through their work and with public access to their spaces and their engagement with the social, cultural and civic life of their communities.

## The entrance and journey inside

If we consider those who linger at a threshold to a building, who do not feel as if they belong, we must first consider the external appearance and first impressions. Are there clear signs? Is it welcoming, or does it require prior knowledge or awareness of idiom to understand? Are the doors open in summer; does it look like a public space all are welcome to explore? And are those same glass doors locked or are shutters put up at night? Is the lighting inside welcoming? It may be too dimly lit inside, so looking in from the outside it's an unknown space, or it may be too bright and exposing. In winter with the doors closed, is it impenetrable from the outside, with no glass walls and no opportunity to assess before entry, or are those glass walls reflective so no one can see inside?

We need to consider spaces for staff to be posted near the entrance, not security staff who monitor who comes into a building, but spaces that allow for long-term occupation (properly heated and ventilated) so that staff may be placed near the entrance to welcome and assist. Reception desks at a remote stage door that require a journey in an unfamiliar space or box office desks at a far distance in an empty foyer serve only those who are confident in navigating that space, who have an innate sense of belonging.

Welcoming desks and box offices near doors are not always possible, so we need a range of other methods by which to draw people into theatres. Transactional spaces give a sense of the familiar; cafés and bars, bookshops or souvenir shops. With this comes the placing and design of these spaces, are they for those who work there or is anyone welcome? Are they at the front or can they have the ambition to draw people further inside a building? And how open are they: do they allow browsing without purchasing? If there are no people readily available to assist, then we need public signals to give people license to enter and participate.

Not everyone is comfortable with these transactional spaces; they may not be familiar, nor can everyone afford them, so we do need to find options that do not rely on purchasing, like information points or community spaces. The journey to these spaces and around a building is important, transitioning spaces to get to other spaces (where scale allows). A range of options will allow a wider community of people to confidently enter a space knowing they are welcome and that they belong.

## Naming

Our language should make space for people, take on board the principles around equality, diversity and inclusion, and be explicitly anti-racist. Naming spaces can bring up issues of ownership and privilege: of course we have clients and donors and people we wish to acknowledge or honour, and there is nothing wrong with naming at base level, but we do need to consider the impact of a history of colonialism and naming and the risk of excluding those for whom certain names are a barrier or for whom naming implies you are not in the right place, with the right people, and that you don't belong.

Similarly, if we want to begin with the principle that we want to make spaces that embrace openness and allow a full community of people to engage, then we also need to consider where in the design is it all right to have more specificity, to address certain needs, to accommodate certain activities that may exclude others. We may wish to specifically address youth engagement, for example, and there is no imperative to make all spaces all things to all people. There is no single solution, as every theatre will serve its patrons and artists, its staff and performers, to different ends, but thoughtful consideration must be given to what our intent is and what the implications might be when we design spaces that serve some and not others.

## Using the building

Creating space for people to work, interact, engage with one another, and contribute to the life of a theatre has huge benefits. Seating areas in the foyers with electrical outlets and good lighting can create space which is openly welcoming, and which encourages people to work and to gather; it can animate the public areas of a theatre and drive engagement (see Figure 3.5.3, which shows the Scratch Hub at Battersea Arts Centre). When reaching the latter stages of design, these elements which are not revenue generating or part of the core function of a theatre can be value-engineered out, but the social good enabled by the generosity of design should be fundamental to our approach.

Theatre design should also give staff enough opportunities for them to create space for other people, be that patrons or participants, artist or staff themselves. Do we allow the possibility in design for theatres to flex and grow

Figure 3.5.3 The Scratch Hub at Battersea Arts Centre in London is a flexible workspace with fixed and communal desks, a mixture of white and brick walls softened with plants and pictures and social spaces including kitchen facilities and soft furnishings. See Reference Project 25.

with the work and with the artistic ambition? Is the design so prescriptive that only one vision is possible or has flexibility been built in, and is there room for a new artistic director to do things differently without redesign?

Every theatre serves a different community, local and remote, in attendance and online, but ultimately are people going to engage with more than the show they have come to? Have we made a space without agenda? Have we addressed our civic responsibility?

## 3.6 Designing for health: infection prevention and control

The built environment must balance design aesthetics and user behaviours with human health and well-being, and with twenty-first-century coronaviruses (SARS, MERS, and COVID-19), the control imperatives raised by pandemic and epidemics should give us pause as to how we address infection prevention and control in future design decisions. We need to consider design strategies for infection prevention and control both for new buildings and for upgrading older venues which also address wellness more generally, with aspirations for spacious, clean, light-filled buildings.

### Social distancing

We should, wherever possible, design adequate spacing in waiting areas, corridors, hallways, stairs, bars, cafés and foyers that addresses the need to maintain distance, to have one-way routes around areas and to allow for sufficient waiting or static space without interrupting through traffic. When designing circulation spaces, we should not confine ourselves to the minimum space to pass another person, but the space to leave adequate space between people, including doors which should, wherever possible, be wide enough to allow for people to pass easily side by side.

First aid and occupation health facilities should allow for suitable isolation facilities for infection control and should also be particularly well ventilated with the potential for windows and fresh air. Larger facilities should consider separate entrances and exits; a two-door approach could help mitigate against cross-contamination. Storage for additional first aid supplies should also be considered, perhaps close to the stage door entrance to minimise building access during deliveries and to provide a logical point of contact and collection.

Dressing rooms should allow for adequate space for performers both for occupancy but also with layouts that reduce pinch points and narrow entrances, particularly when showers or other facilities are included.

Crew rooms, workshops, costume areas and offices should be similarly considered in their design, recognising that larger open spaces with flexible furniture give options to rearrange for physical distancing when required and allow for easier flow of movement around the workspace.

The spacing of seats in the auditorium will become more significant and contentious, with an ever-present tension between box office income and suitable spacing between patrons. This applies between rows (front to back), as well as between adjacent seats, where double arm rests should be the norm, as well as space to pass in front of one another (rather than the intimate action we currently practice, squeezing past people often face to face, awkwardly standing just centimetres away).

Meeting rooms and workshops may need to be larger to allow for staff spacing and circulation; while many may be working from home and the culture of presenteeism is being challenged, most theatre workers are present in the theatre delivering productions, and occupancy numbers for rooms can no longer be defined by existing and minimum measures.

Similarly, offices need to be spacious, with the option to move furniture (so no fixed power or data points in the floor) and install temporary screens around desks where needed and as occasion arises. This allows us to create hybrid solutions and open offices to maximise space and ventilation while creating accessible cubicles for personal reassurance and safety.

### Circulation and movement

Public spaces raise a particular challenge with fluctuating numbers of users and less control over their movements than backstage areas afford. Box office, stage door, security desks, concession stands, cafés and bars should all be designed with adequate space for staff and the public to circulate freely.

Toilets overall will need lower occupancy numbers, and where they can be so designed, a door in and a door out will help reduce the incidence of close contact between people as they enter and leave.

Similarly, a one-way system in and out of an auditorium is a serious consideration, allowing patrons to flow through the space with less contact.

Both back of house and in public areas, where space allows, favour lifts and escalators where possible, to reduce the incidence of people passing on stairs.

### Technical spaces

Control rooms are too often small, cramped and occupied by too many people. Consideration should be given to allowing sufficient room, spacious working surfaces and space for both technical staff and creative teams.

Receiving theatres have the added complication of visiting companies and technical staff bringing their own equipment; while separate control rooms that ensure separation of house and touring staff and equipment may be beyond the capacity of most venues, the provision of separate rest facilities including green rooms and crew rooms should be given serious consideration, particularly where overseas travel is concerned, and mixing may at times be inadvisable.

In all design, and in existing theatres, efforts should be made to separate the often convenient arrangement of foyer lighting controls and bar bells being located in production control rooms. Wherever possible, the focus should be on reducing interaction between staff, particularly staff working in different areas and with large numbers of people, in this case one group mixing with the company and another with patrons.

## Ventilation

Under UK building regulations, the general principle is that if something exists which achieves a lower standard than current regulations, you do not have to improve it to meet modern standards unless you are doing substantial work to the building. There are certain exceptions to this particularly relating to thermal performance (windows, walls and roofs) but not ventilation. We know that many older buildings have substandard ventilation which does not achieve the standard; in older systems there is often no recirculation, but this wastes a lot of heat, so modern systems tend to recirculate a proportion to save energy. This, however, is counterintuitive for infection control more generally. Distribution is also important, as we know older systems may achieve the air changes required but do not reach all parts of the auditorium, particularly areas under balconies. This means the removal of airborne viruses in these areas by ventilation will be less effective.

In existing buildings, we should now consider introducing UV irradiation in return-air ducts, increasing fresh air ventilation rates and reducing recirculated air, and bear in mind humidity levels and the (potential) need to dehumidify alongside surges in cooling and heating loads.

We should also consider upgrading or installing openable windows, particularly where cross ventilation can be achieved (which will provide a higher ventilation rate than mechanical ventilation).

In new buildings the natural circulation of air should be maximised wherever possible, with open-ended corridors for ventilation and consideration given to integrating courtyards and open spaces into the building design. Such moves also have the benefit of introducing more daylight and sunlight into a building, with the accompanying germicidal properties of UV light.

## Finishes and construction methods

A virus will behave differently and have different life spans on different material surfaces, and the more people touch surfaces, the more the risk of transmission, so all finishes should be considered with this in mind. This is particularly significant for frequently touched surfaces such as staircase handrails, balcony rails, arm rests and seat backs in the auditorium and door furniture.

Wall finishes with small pores in the plaster or textured finishes should be discouraged; wherever possible, design should enable deep cleaning regimes without damage to finishes. Similarly, materials and finishes throughout the theatre should be durable enough to withstand enhanced cleaning regimes, including bleach and alcohol cleaning agents, and take into account the life cycle of a virus on different finish types, for example porous vs non-porous.

Doors should be designed wherever possible with sensors for automatic opening to eliminate contact. Sinks, showers and toilet facilities should also be installed with motion sensors to reduce the incidence of contact in both public and back of house bathrooms.

Lights should be motion activated wherever possible in non-auditorium and stage areas, including offices, stairwells, circulation spaces, stores and workrooms. This of course has the added benefit of reducing energy use, too. Dressing rooms may be an exception here, allowing performers to have the level of light they require at any point in the day/evening.

Multiple entrances into public spaces may need to be limited to better monitor entrances and exits when necessary and facilitate one-way systems where appropriate. And it may be necessary to reduce the occurrence of flat surfaces used as ledges for the public (particularly) to lean against and/or place personal items while waiting.

## Cleaning regime

The design aesthetic should incorporate a coherent cleaning programme; this begins with proper attention paid to the staff and facilities required to maintain an efficient cleaning regime. Cleaner cupboards should not be the smallest, otherwise-unusable space; there should be clean and well-maintained facilities for these staff, and plenty of them (and that includes proper rest areas for these staff, with the ability to tend to their own safety and hygiene at work).

This approach facilitates regular cleaning, and as increased staff numbers may be necessary for more frequent and thorough cleaning of all spaces (both back and front-of-house), sufficient space and importance given to the welfare facilities of these staff is paramount.

Design should look to the detail and make surfaces uncomplicated to clean: ensuring bannisters can be easily and thoroughly cleaned without supports underneath (which can be missed); making light switches safe to clean using solvents; sinks and basins with smooth surfaces, minimal interruption, and no crevices.

Sanitary facilities for staff as opposed to patrons is often minimal, providing only that which is required, not that which is desirable. With social distancing requirements, the need to have more spacious facilities back of house becomes essential, and they should be sanitised frequently; as much as with the regimes for public areas, the design and use of a building should ensure there are enhanced facilities for cleaning staff back of house as much as front of house.

### A healthier workplace

The scope for an architect in an ideal world would be informed by how much gross floor area (GFA) you need for all your activities, rather than how we can squeeze everything we have ambition for into a pre-defined GFA and therefore, of necessity, constrained space. To design with the luxury of space is perhaps limited in urban spaces, and certainly in theatres being renovated, refurbished or redesigned. Of course, the financial imperative of the box office will always drive the design of the public spaces, from bars to auditoria. But to have healthier workspaces, auditoria where audiences feel comfortable and safe, and back-of-house spaces which allow performers and technical and production staff to work safely, must be at the forefront of our considerations as we move through a century that has uncertain challenges ahead but which can be addressed in part with careful planning and design.

## 3.7 Fire safety

### Approach to fire safety design

In the United Kingdom the principal objective of a fire strategy is to meet the functional requirements of Schedule 1, Part B of the Building Regulations 2010. This is concerned with the life safety of the occupants and fire fighters.

It is important to establish early in the project if there are any additional insurer's requirements for the scheme or whether the client wishes to protect the property or contents. This will be particularly relevant to heritage buildings.

The fire strategy will consider single accidental fires or those associated and most likely to occur in theatre buildings with ancillary accommodation. The likelihood of fire is predominantly from the stage area; kitchens; cafés; bars and restaurants; and back-of-house areas including storerooms, plant rooms, workshops, dressing rooms and green rooms. The auditorium itself is not considered a high fire risk area.

The main principles of the fire strategy are to demonstrate that building occupants on any fire floor can escape into a place of relative safety (the protected lobby and staircase) in a reasonable time and evacuate the building to an ultimate place of safety. It must also demonstrate that there are reasonable facilities provided to ensure that the fire service can access and commence firefighting operations within the building in the event of a fire incident.

Essentially, there are two basic approaches to fire safety design, although similar principles will apply in both cases. These are:

1. Code-based design – which satisfies the standards laid down in the guidance documents. This will be appropriate for many conventional buildings.
2. Fire-engineering design – which develops a project-specific fire safety strategy that may offer more flexible solutions for complex buildings.

#### 1. Code-based design

Building codes prescribe the key functions that must be satisfied in a building. In fire safety terms, most codes will require that a building must:

- be provided with a suitable means of early warning of fire
- be designed with internal escape routes which lead the occupants to safety outside the building
- contain internal surface linings which resist the spread of flames over the surfaces relevant to the location of the surfaces and the risks presented
- be designed so that in the event of fire, its stability will be maintained for a reasonable time
- to inhibit fire spread, be sub-divided with fire-resisting construction and fitted with automatic fire suppression systems appropriate to the size and use of the building
- have external walls and roofs which adequately resist the spread of fire from one building to another
- be designed and constructed to provide reasonable facilities to assist the fire fighters in protection of life.

By adopting the guidance contained in the building codes, a scheme should be approved by the relevant approving authorities. This represents a code-based approach to achieving a safe building.

#### 2. Fire-engineering design

A fire-engineering solution takes a more holistic approach. It develops a design from first principles and creates a framework for the design, construction and management of a building which more accurately reflects the bespoke nature of that building. This alternative approach may be the only practical way to achieve a satisfactory standard of fire safety in some large and complex buildings. The solution, which will be developed by a specialist fire-engineering consultant, will be a building-specific strategy to provide a flexible and unique design.

Fire engineering is the application of engineering techniques to define a total package of fire safety measures, which may include enhanced passive fire protection, active fire suppression, fire and smoke ventilation and automatic fire detection and alarms. Some advantages of a fire-engineering approach may be:

- increased travel distances
- reduction in widths of escape routes
- reduction in the number of exits from a building or more appropriately located exits
- reduction in the standards of applied fire protection
- large compartment sizes facilitating open, multi-storey and interconnected spaces
- specific smoke control designs for stage and auditoria
- creation of more flexible theatre space including removal of the traditional fire safety curtain,
- considerations for the inclusion of sprinklers to mitigate the risk of fire.

It must be remembered that it is possible for a design to be largely code based but with elements of fire engineering to justify certain non-compliances with guidance (see Figure 3.7.1 the Sam Wanamaker Playhouse and Figure 3.7.2 the Georgian Theatre Royal in Richmond).

Figure 3.7.1 The Sam Wanamaker Playhouse at Shakespeare's Globe in Southwark is modelled on candlelit theatres of Shakespeare's London, made of a frame of green oak within a brick shell, with painted panels and wooden features, and lit with over one hundred beeswax candles, some of which are seen here in chandeliers over the stage. See Reference Project 10.

## Fire detection and warning systems

To manage an emergency, management must first be aware that the emergency has occurred and then must be able to communicate instructions to their staff effectively. Automatic fire detection and warning systems and staff communication systems are therefore essential tools in the event of a fire.

It is usually recommended that a theatre building be protected with a comprehensive category L1 system detection system throughout the building to British Standard BS 5839 part 1 2015. Smaller buildings may well have a lesser standard.

It has been proven that a directive warning and evacuation system (a staff and public address announcement) is the most effective way to encourage people to leave a building. This is particularly important when fire could be part of a performance, as the audience may not be aware when there is a real fire risk. The design of the fire detection and warning system needs careful consideration to ensure that adequate and appropriate fire detection is provided at all times.

Evacuation will normally be under management direction and carried out in a controlled and orderly manner.

Automatic warning systems are usually silenced during performance mode. A double knock system provides a first stage notification at the main fire alarm panel or other managed area such as stage door. This allows staff to investigate in timeframes previously agreed with the approving authorities. This time will be subject to the staff resource and the size and complexity of the building.

On confirmed fire, the principal manager will stop a performance and make an announcement on stage. Stewards in the building will then escort members of the public to the

Figure 3.7.2 The Georgian Theatre Royal, Richmond, was built in 1788 and is Britain's oldest working theatre in its original form. The auditorium, shown here from the stage, has a capacity of 154 seats arranged in rectangular form, with a sunken pit for the stalls seats, boxes arranged on three sides at stage level and a small gallery on the level above these boxes. The 2003 refurbishment included a more authentic colour scheme of wood and pale green through the auditorium, with simulated candlelight fittings.

appropriate escape routes. For this to happen there must be effective emergency planning and well-trained staff.

## Means of escape for Mobility-Impaired People

The range and severity of mobility impairments must be considered in the strategy. There may be people using sticks and crutches or wheelchairs.

Some mobility-impaired people may well be able to use stairs, albeit at lower speeds, but certain mobility-impaired people such as wheelchair users might not be able to leave their chair, and therefore consideration of wheelchair users on the upper or sub-ground floors of a building is the worst-case design aspiration for most theatres.

Where access is provided for those in wheelchairs to upper or lower levels in a building, a suitable means of escape strategy should be provided. The design should be explicit regarding the provisions of means of escape for disabled people, and it is not acceptable to omit such detail and state simply that management procedures should/will be developed to cater to these occupants. This is particularly important in theatres.

The strategy should be able to describe how means of escape in the event of fire is to be achieved from all accessible locations in the premises, whether or not it is intended that disabled people have regular or frequent access to those locations.

The design for wheelchair user evacuation is therefore a balance between the active and passive systems provided and the resource and training of staff to support escape.

The preferred method of evacuation for disabled people from upper or sub-ground floors is by evacuation lift. If these are not available, then it might be necessary to carry a person with limited mobility up or down the escape stair, but this should be a last resort given the complexities involved. If this approach is adopted, it should be clearly understood by the management of the theatre at the design stage since it is the responsibility of the premises management to ensure that all people can make a safe evacuation, the evacuation plan should not rely on the assistance of the fire and rescue service. This is an important factor that must be considered in any building design.

It is possible to use existing lifts in buildings to evacuate wheelchair users if it can be shown to be safe through a suitable risk assessment. This is documented in BS 9999 and is a useful consideration for existing theatres.

## Refuge spaces and places of relative safety

Upon confirmed fire alarm, wheelchair users will need to make their way to a place of relative safety where they can wait for assistance. The refuge area should be protected from fire for a confirmed period of time sufficient to enable the evacuation sequence to be completed without placing the person(s) needing assistance, or those rendering that assistance, at unacceptable risk from a fire within the premises.

There is commonly a protected enclosure separated from the fire by a minimum 30-minute fire resistance and clear of the escape route of ambulant people. Ideally this will be in a lobby area of a staircase and ideally with direct access to an evacuation lift. The size of refuge area per wheelchair user will depend on the actual wheelchair, but guidance in BS 9999 recommends an allowance of 1400 × 900mm per chair. The manoeuvrability of the wheelchair user should be considered by the architect and inclusive design consultant.

Refuges should only ever be treated as temporary waiting areas, where disabled people can wait until they can complete their evacuation to a place of ultimate safety. Refuges should not be used as a place to leave disabled people to await rescue by the fire and rescue service.

An invacuation (inward evacuation usually in response to a threat outside the building) may also be the most appropriate course of action if an incident occurs that renders an evacuation unsafe, including terrorist action but also local fire or chemical release or onsite intruder(s). In the event of an invacuation, a suitable location should be included in management plans and, as in theatres this is usually the auditorium, some consideration should be given to this potential in the design process.

## Numbers of wheelchair users and refuge spaces

For auditoria, the number of wheelchair-user locations will be defined as part of the inclusive design strategy, and therefore the fire strategy should respond by providing refuge areas in a place of relative safety for the actual number of wheelchairs. Consideration should be given to exits which may be blocked.

It is common for the ancillary areas of the theatres such as bars, cafés and restaurants to operate independently of the main theatre. In this scenario, it is difficult to determine how many wheelchair users may be present at any one time. However, given the building's use as a public assembly building and the drive for inclusivity, it would be insufficient to consider a single wheelchair user refuge space in these areas. Therefore, careful consideration will be needed with the theatre and their management in the design stage to agree on a sensible number of wheelchair users who may be present and the staff resource that will be needed to facilitate their evacuation.

In other parts of the building, it is important to determine the number of wheelchair users on upper floors. In most premises it is considered reasonable to have refuges that can accommodate a single wheelchair user. Where it is reasonably foreseeable that the proportion of disabled users in a building will be relatively high, or where the use of the premises is likely to result in groups of wheelchair users being present, an assessment should be made as to whether the size and/or number of refuges needs to be increased.

## Use of personal emergency evacuation plans

Wherever possible, personal emergency evacuation plans (PEEPs) should be produced for all people requiring assistance to leave the building. Through the recording of PEEPs, the management team should be made aware of the amount of staff support required for each evacuation.

This can be difficult to undertake in a public assembly building. However, the staff of the building should identify any persons in wheelchairs and discuss the evacuation strategy in place and determine whether this is suitable for them. The principal should be to use the lift where possible. This should be acceptable to most wheelchair users.

## Safety curtains and smoke control

Safety curtains have been a feature in theatres for a number of years and are used in typical proscenium arch theatres in conjunction with controlled ventilation at the top of the flytower (usually 10% of the stage area) to enable audiences to be safely evacuated in case of fire. This represents a code-compliant solution. The design of safety curtains and stage ventilation is detailed in the ABTT's *Technical Standards for Places of Entertainment*.

It is possible to consider theatres without safety curtains and also ventilation areas of less than 10% of the stage area part of a fire-engineering solution, and this is common in modern theatre designs, particularly open and thrust stage and theatre-in-the-round.

The performance objective is to demonstrate that people in the auditorium can escape safely from a fire on the stage. This is particularly important for those people on balconies at higher level where the smoke layer will form.

The fire-engineering and smoke control strategy will need to consider the following:

- the location of the fire relevant to the open stage scenario
- the likely size of fire on the stage (this will need to be agreed with the theatre, as it requires ongoing management)
- the height of rise and reservoir area created by the flytower, as this affects the amount of smoke produced through air entrainment
- whether a proscenium arch is available, as this creates a downstand and smoke reservoir.

Smoke modelling will be undertaken to determine the amount of free area required for smoke ventilators so that the auditorium is kept relatively free of smoke during the evacuation. The temperature and visibility of the smoke will be determined in the models to show a safe escape.

Mechanical smoke extract systems can also be used, and computational fluid dynamic (CFD) modelling can be undertaken to gain greater confidence in the design. This is particularly relevant if there is an unusual geometry, but simple zone models can be used if the space is not complex. The environmental conditions in the auditorium should also be very carefully considered, as this will affect the flow of smoke in the early stages of as fire until any heating, ventilation and cooling (HVAC) systems are shut down.

Any fire-engineering solution will require early engagement with building control and the local fire authority to agree on the principles, input parameters and acceptance criteria and any sensitivity analysis.

## 3.8 Interrelated themes

Theatre design, how we use our theatres, how we make changes and updates to existing theatres, fundamentally impacts the physical and mental wellbeing of all users, patrons, staff and performers as well as having a profound impact on the environment. To remain purposeful and relevant it is essential that the design and uses of our theatres, address the concerns and challenges prevalent today and discussed in this section.

The ethical and safety principles discussed, the moral imperatives and social needs and challenges of our communities and the challenges of the climate crisis must be central to our discourse if our cultural institutions are to become and remain dynamic and inclusive, central to the cultural and civic life of their communities.

### Section editor

Emma Wilson, Director of Technical, Production and Costume at the Royal Opera House

### Contributors (in alphabetical order)

Nafeesah Butt, Theatre-Maker

Chris McDougall, Technical Manager, Edinburgh Playhouse

Tim Foster, Architect, Foster Wilson Size

Andrew Nicholson, Founder and Director of The Fire Surgery Ltd

Michèle Taylor, Director for Change for Ramps on the Moon

Steve Tompkins, Architect, Haworth Tompkins

Andrew Wylie, Partner at Buro Happold

# Section 4

# Front of house and other public spaces

## 4.1 Making the commitment

A visit to the theatre is influenced by the building's presence on the street, the convenience of its layout and the conviviality of its interior. The foyers express the identity of a venue, its artistic programme and its potential to engage with the community. Lyn Gardner, in her theatre blog for *The Guardian* in 2015, recognised the increasing importance of front of house spaces to their wider communities.

> That theatre buildings belong to their communities is still not as well understood as it should be by some venues. They appear to simply want audiences to buy a ticket for their shows, turn up in time to spend some money in the cafe or bar and leave as soon as possible afterwards. But you can't make long-term relationships that way; you can't have proper conversations with people and an equal relationship if you don't fling open your doors and let them know that the building is theirs to use as they desire.
>
> (Lyn Gardner, www.theguardian.com/stage/theatreblog/2015/may/26/home-manchestertheatre-cornerhouse-library)

The primary function of any foyer is to serve the audience attending a performance; however, increasingly the foyers of modern theatres take on other functions to support the cultural mission of the organisation. They can help build community cohesion and promote social inclusion; facilitate partnerships with other arts organisations; provide for education and training; and offer opportunities for business meetings, conferences and hospitality.

Foyers normally account for around a quarter of a theatre's built area and can be more extensive than the auditorium. They are perhaps the hardest-working part of a theatre and are no longer just pre-performance and interval spaces. Particularly in regional theatres, they offer public facilities from early morning until late evening. The design of the foyers needs to:

- attract people in and encourage them to discover more
- promote additional income generation
- provide space for alternative activities such as conferencing, exhibitions, engagement and community events.

A well-designed foyer improves public perception of the arts and, above all, helps to build audiences.

For the purpose of this book, front of house (FOH) is defined as the spaces occupied and used by the public and support facilities, excluding the auditorium. The scale and composition of any foyer space depends upon the audience capacity of the auditoria, the organisation's artistic programme and business model and the range of facilities it offers. To a greater or lesser extent foyer spaces comprise public areas, other public spaces and support areas.

### Public areas include:

- arrival and drop-off
- external display
- entrance doors, preferably with a draught lobby
- assembly space, including open-plan circulation and stairs
- reception and information counter
- box office and ticket collection
- kiosk sales – confectionery and programmes
- cloakroom and toilets
- refreshment bars.

### Other public spaces (depending on the scale and ambitions of the organisation) may include:

- merchandising
- catering and food service
- hospitality suites (meeting rooms and conference breakout spaces)
- education, performance, rehearsal and community rooms

DOI: 10.4324/9781003327295-4

- informal performance areas
- exhibition area(s)
- spaces for rental and hire.

### Support areas (depending on the size and type of the theatre) may include:

- duty manager's office and security office
- FOH equipment store
- first aid room
- attendants' changing rooms and briefing office
- telephone, internet and mail bookings office
- box office manager's and cash offices
- merchandising, programme, ice cream and confectionery stores
- local and central bar stores, chilled cellar, spirits and empties stores
- kitchens, cold and dry stores
- local and central cleaners' stores
- refuse store, compacting and recycling space.

A distinction also needs to be made between 'foyers' that usually contain the theatre bars and areas for those attending a performance and 'concourses' found in larger developments with free access to the general public, encouraging 'cultural tourism' and serving cinemas, galleries, libraries and education facilities, all supported with cafés, restaurants, shops and public toilets. Examples of the latter include the Esplanades in Singapore; The Lowry, Salford; and Storyhouse, Chester (see Reference Project 06).

## 4.2 Basic principles

These design principles apply to all venues, large or small.

### Accessibility and inclusivity

All public areas must be accessible – not just physically but also conceptually. Front of house design must be inviting for those with disabilities and inclusive to those who are new to, or have felt excluded from, attending cultural events, by providing:

- level approach, negating the need for separate entrances or complicated ramps and handrails
- wide automatic doors avoiding queues or obstructions – physical and psychological
- clear points of entry and unintimidating views of the activities within
- a perception as 'permissible space' with no obligations.

### Legibility and ease of circulation

The circulation needs to be simply laid out, creating a point of arrival where all the facilities are clearly set out:

- ticketing
- cloakroom
- sales points (confectionery and programmes)
- stairs and lifts
- toilets
- bars, cafés, restaurants and retail
- entrances into the auditoria and studios.

The facilities need to be designed to avoid creating bottlenecks or generating long queues or cross routes which could impede circulation, including at the end of a performance when some may want to leave promptly whilst others may want to linger.

### Loose fit

Increasingly, theatre foyers need to be able to accommodate a range of activities from special events related to the artistic programme, as well as generating income from sponsorship, merchandising and catering, to hosting community activities which may not be directly related to the core business. Foyers and their facilities need to be adaptable to meet different tastes and changes of use. Audiences' demographic varies with different types of performance. The behaviour and expectations of an audience for comedy gigs, for example, are different from that for drama and different again for opera.

Future changes in the way society operates, hastened by the pandemic, such as less travelling and staying local, increased working from home and the local production and participation in broader cultural activities, are all opportunities for theatre buildings and their public spaces to increase their presence at the heart of a community.

## 4.3 The journey through front of house

The following description is typical for a theatre operating in 'performance mode' – catering to an audience attending the performance. Venues that open parts of their front of house during the day, creating greater opportunities for community engagement and commercial activity, will use their spaces differently. Non-performance activities, described as 'all-day mode', are covered in Sections 4.9, 4.10 and 4.11.

The theatrical experience commences upon arrival. It is important that consideration be given to the relationship of the public realm and a theatre's main entrance and foyers.

Routes from public transport, car parks and pedestrian paths to the main entrance need to be obvious and create a sense of arrival while taking account of safety and security issues. A theatre may open directly off the street or be approached through a concourse or piazza conceived as part of the development.

Theatres in busy streets can cause overcrowding on pavements and danger with passing traffic. These can be avoided by providing forecourts or entrance foyers that allow audiences to enter quickly into the building and, after the show, leave safely. It is helpful to have a drop-off for taxis and less ambulant visitors close to the theatre's entrance, with a taxi rank nearby. Parking for disabled visitors and cycle racks is also required. Many theatres are reliant on group bookings, so effective set-down and pick-up points for coach parties should be considered.

At the entrance, protection from inclement weather is welcome. Popular shows can create queues for security checks and ticket collection, and managing these queues needs to be planned to avoid nuisance to neighbouring properties.

As an adjunct to foyers, open-air unheated spaces, loosely enclosed with screens and canopies, can create a transitional outdoor space for *ad hoc* performance and events, making the building engage with the public and feel more inclusive.

A clear sign displaying the name of the theatre helps patrons locate the building from a distance or a side street. For some theatres, it may be the name of the show or a logo that is more significant and therefore needs to be displayed prominently (see Figure 4.3.1).

Advertising performances is essential and should be considered at the briefing and design stages in order to be integrated into the overall design concept. The style, quality and dominance of 'show signs' is the province of the theatre owners, producers and their advertising agents. This can take many forms: video screens, linked to the box office media display, are becoming popular. Large poster panels, external banners, flags and so on are frequent additions. Signs may also be subject to specific development control regulations.

Figure 4.3.1 The theatrical experience commences upon arrival. Leeds Playhouse, Yorkshire, UK. The exterior lighting of this theatre emphasises a sense of welcome and anticipation of the performance to come. The well-lit and protected entrance attracts patrons – it is arranged to give a significantly enhanced level of lighting to the forecourt. Digital billboards along the façade and visible internally beneath the entrance canopy are of equal importance to promote current and future productions. See also Figure 3.4.1.

## 4.4 Foyer design and layout

All visitors should enter through the same main entrance, enjoying the facilities regardless of where they are sitting within the auditorium. Good management will ensure that they are greeted and welcomed. From this moment the theatregoers may need to collect their tickets, leave their coats, wait for friends, buy a drink or get something to eat, buy a programme and use the toilets. Those with particular requirements, such as borrowing headphones, must be considered. All these needs have to be met with minimum effort and without queues.

During the interval, a change of environment, bars and toilets are the basic needs of an audience before they return to their seats. It is beneficial to provide a variety of settings – a place to stand and look around, a quiet intimate corner to sit and chat or an open space to drink with a party of friends.

At the end of the evening some of the audience may want to stay to enjoy the facilities before leaving. Some venues offer late-night or foyer events after the main show.

All this activity represents around 30% of the audience's time in the theatre, and everything needs to run efficiently if the whole visit is to be a pleasant experience.

### Space requirements

The foyer is essentially the open-plan circulation area which leads to the auditorium, where the audience assembles before a performance and during intervals. All the public support facilities open onto the foyer. The ability to understand the overall layout of a space makes a big difference to perceptions of a venue (see Figure 4.4.1).

Consideration needs to be given to the movement of people around the foyers:

- drawing visitors into the building, avoiding logjams in the entrance lobby

Figure 4.4.1 The foyer is essentially the open-plan circulation area. Bristol Old Vic, UK. See Reference Project 31. The foyer is an open plan space which is warm and welcoming to all visitors, whether it is the audience arriving for a show or a passer-by dropping in to discover something new. The layout is instinctive and legible, easy to comprehend and to allay any anxieties.

- avoiding paths crossing
- queues obstructing circulation routes
- adequate space on landings, in front of lifts and around sales counters
- ensuring passageways and stair widths are sufficient.

The size of the FOH accommodation is normally determined by the maximum seating capacity of the venue. Excluding space for stairs and counters, foyers range from 0.6m$^2$ per person to 1.2m$^2$ per person, although smaller foyers exist in historic theatres and larger ones in grand civic statements. Post pandemic, it is possible that the recommended area per person should be increased.

Foyer space should relate to the configuration and occupancy of the various levels of the auditorium while consolidating the audience in a physically and visually connected space.

Toilets should be allocated to all levels of the foyer to ensure convenient access.

Secondary spending is an important part of a venue's income. Sales points need to be provided for:

- bar sales and catering
- programmes, ice creams and confectionery
- show merchandising.

## Other activities

To contribute to the social and economic sustainability of a venue, the foyer needs to be adaptable for other purposes, including:

- community and engagement activities (studio/workshop space, meeting rooms)
- informal performances
- sponsor's recognition and hospitality rooms
- specialist bars (champagne bar, bottle bar or confectionery points)
- hot desking or co-working space
- merchandising opportunities.

Depending on the proposed business model for the theatre, thought needs to be given to the inclusion and location of:

- reception rooms
- a public bar, café and/or restaurant
- conference registration and business facilities
- large-scale catering provision
- VIP reception areas.

Such spaces need to look open and available when in use but not detract from the visitor's experience when they are closed.

## Security

Where theatre foyers are open to the public at times other than performance times, the design needs to address security issues. It should be possible to open and close areas of the building to suit the ebb and flow of activities within.

Theatres may open only the box office during the day and therefore need to ensure customers are not able to roam unchecked around the rest of the building. Other theatres, offering a wider range of activities, are open from early in the morning until after the evening's performance has finished. Visitors should be encouraged to participate but still need to be prevented from entering the auditorium where a technical fit-up or rehearsals may be underway. To encourage engagement, some organisations provide viewing opportunities from the foyers into the auditorium and backstage workshops.

Other issues that, unfortunately, need to be considered include:

- providing space at the front doors for bag checks and airport-style body scanning
- monitored CCTV of internal public areas
- 'lockdown' arrangements in event of nearby accident, terrorist incident or similar emergency
- health (temperature) checks.

## Environmental design

The foyer provides a transition zone between the street and the events on stage, providing an environmental gradient between the outside noise and bustle and the controlled environment within the auditorium. While daylight is desirable, foyers should avoid stark contrasts of light (such as direct sunlight or glare) and excessive differences in temperature with the auditorium.

Foyers are good places to display an organisation's commitment to addressing the climate emergency with carbon target indicators, to demonstrate biodiversity and record achievements in reduction, reuse and recycling of resources.

## Acoustic design

The acoustic design of a foyer should be tailored to the uses to which the foyer will be put. The space may be used for impromptu presentations, small-scale performances, live music, receptions and possibly parties. It is always desirable to include sound absorption to create an acoustic suitable for speech (mid-frequency RT 0.8–1.2 seconds when unoccupied) and take measures to mitigate noise breakout.

A traditional foyer with a plush carpet and high ceiling with lots of ornamentation on the walls will sound radically different to a contemporary one with hard floors, lots of plain glazing and a plasterboard ceiling. The latter will have less absorption and so will be louder, noisier and less appropriate for informal uses. It is always desirable to include a significant quantity of sound absorption to assist in controlling noise levels and provide an environment suitable for a range of activities and informal events.

Natural ventilation should be considered for the foyer to reduce energy consumption. External noise levels might render the simple opening window solution impracticable; however, attenuated inlets and discharges are possible and should be considered. Conversely, noise emanating from the foyer through opening façades could disturb people in nearby buildings. Mixed-mode solutions could be considered, with daytime ventilation being provided through a natural system, while peak hours (pre-show and during the intervals) are mechanically ventilated.

## Foyer services noise

Foyer services noise should be controlled to allow conversation:

- bar equipment should be selected for quiet use and where possible dish and glass washing carried out in a separate room
- acoustic separation between FOH and auditorium is of great importance – at least 60dB is desirable
- lobbies leading into the auditorium should be fitted with high-performance, effectively sealed acoustic doors, which are also quiet in operation
- external noise should be mitigated by the fabric of the building to a level close to the services noise level.

## Lighting design

Lighting plays an important part in setting the mood and atmosphere and needs to help make the FOH areas feel warm, welcoming and atmospheric prior to a performance but light, airy and dynamic during the day.

Foyer lighting can aid navigation, helping to highlight the box office, bars and the auditorium entrance doors, and can be coordinated with wayfinding to highlight key signs.

It is important that some means of adjusting the light levels and general mood of the FOH lighting be incorporated. This could take the form of a programmable scene-setting control system that can dim or switch individual circuits, store pre-programmed lighting scenes and be linked to daylight levels.

## Finishes

Building finishes should be carefully selected and detailed to create the right impression, to avoid safety hazards and for their durability and ease of cleaning and maintenance. Floor surfaces need to be selected for slip resistance, especially at entrances and potentially wet areas, and junctions between floor finishes must avoid trip hazards. Balustrades must be designed to prevent drinks glasses and other objects being knocked over and dropping to floors below.

## Furniture

Thought needs to be given to the range of people who are likely to use the venue, with a choice of seating to suit all ages. Seating near entrances is useful. While younger audiences may be happy to stand during the interval, older people may expect to be able to sit down, so bars and foyers need to be furnished accordingly, including chairs with arms to assist people to stand up. Fixed seating can make the foyer inflexible, but individual seats can be moved into dangerous positions and become a hazard.

Family-friendly venues should have suitable furniture for children and space for parking prams and buggies.

Waste bins are required in the theatre foyers, and there is an expectation from customers that waste will be recycled. How these items are specified and located needs to be thought through, especially where there is a heightened security risk.

Good information display is critical for marketing purposes and needs to be designed to ensure that audiences can be made aware of future productions without the foyers being cluttered with assorted display units for leaflets and posters.

## 4.5 Facilities within the foyer

The facilities described in this section are usually delivered from separate locations within the foyers by different members of staff. Alternatively, the facilities can be combined in one location with a 'Welcome' desk combined with the ticketing extending into sales of programmes, merchandise, food and refreshments, employing multi-skilled customer-facing teams. Before adopting a particular approach, the implications on service delivery, movement of customers and the business and staffing plans must be understood. Smaller venues are often supported by volunteers acting as FOH attendants or conducting theatre tours for whom provision needs to be made.

### Welcome desk

The venue may choose to have a foyer reception and information point welcoming customers throughout the day. It could be staffed or could provide an electronic concierge facility so that customers can learn more about the building and performances. There is increasing use of mobile devices to enable staff to book and issue tickets, answer queries, take orders for interval refreshments, address needs, promote merchandise, engage with visitors, build audiences and generate income.

### Ticket sales

Ticketing services are often outsourced and increasingly serviced by websites, including 'print your own ticket' systems or tickets downloaded to mobile devices. Some customers may still need to purchase their ticket in person or collect pre-booked tickets. Therefore, a box office facility may be required, with sales positions that can be used for advance booking, allowing customers to book in person for future performances and for those collecting their tickets immediately prior to the performance (see Figure 4.5.1). 'Press Night' tickets or a special 'on the night deal' may also need separate counter space.

Ideally the sales counter should not have glass separating the customer from the staff, as glass restricts sound and information exchange. Eye-level contact with the customer is preferable for staff. Local acoustic treatment will help speech intelligibility.

Most customers will use debit or credit cards to purchase tickets, so positioning for easy use of chip and pin machines needs to be considered. Cash needs to be quickly transferred to a secure location.

If an open style of box office is adopted, care must be taken to ensure that staff are secure. The counters arranged so that customers are not able to intimidate the staff, positioned away from draughts and provided with local environmental controls.

Induction loops at counters will help those with hearing difficulties. Wheelchair users should be able to get up close to the counter at a comfortable level for both parties to conduct the transaction (see Figure 4.5.2).

Displays around the welcome desk and box office may include:

- poster panels and leaflet racks
- screens and monitors as a flexible method for displaying seating plans and promoting forthcoming events
- a wall-mounted, video screen to allow customers to browse future events from the venue's own website.

Figure 4.5.1 Reception, tickets and information point. HOME, Manchester, UK. See Reference Project 23. Located in a highly visible position, the open plan box office and information counter is the focus of activity within the foyer.

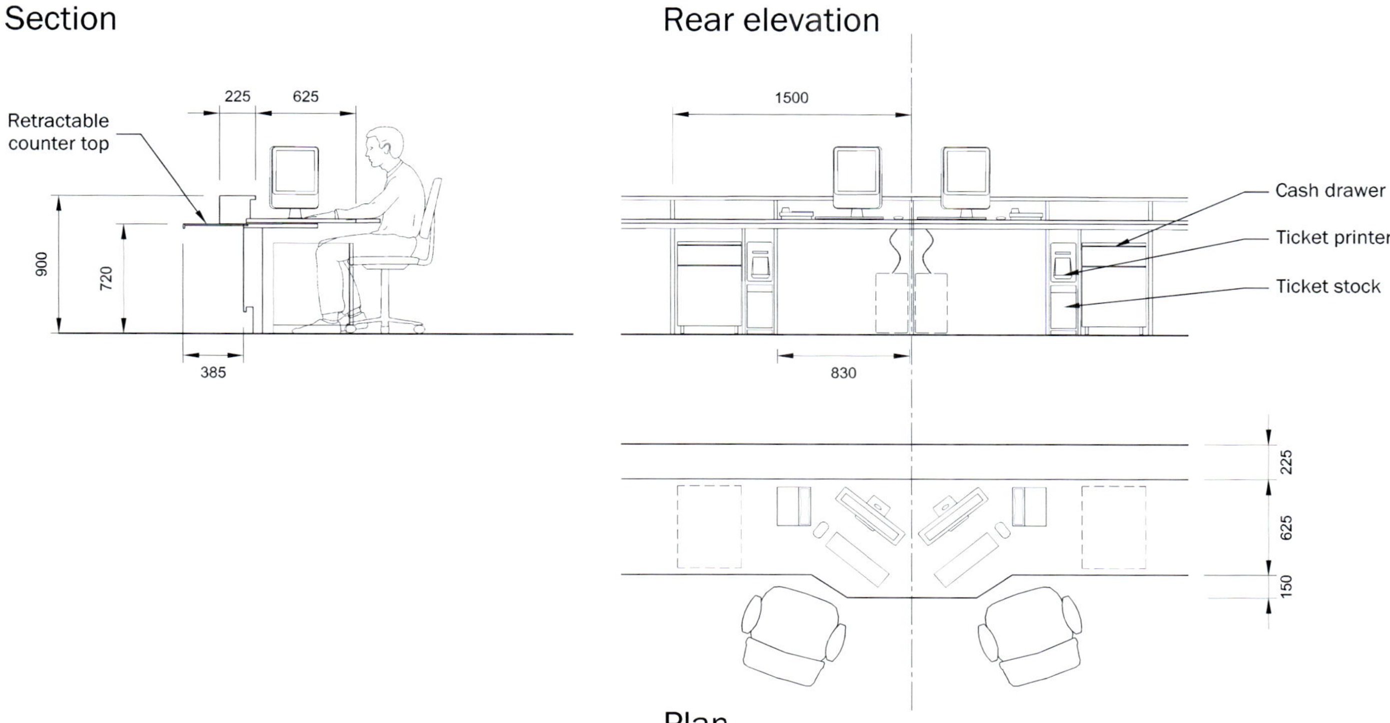


Figure 4.5.2 Plan and section of a box office counter.

## Telephone, internet and mail bookings

As noted previously, the manner in which tickets are booked, purchased and issued is changing rapidly. The continued growth of telephone and online sales means the function of a traditional box office is different, with many of the transactions taking place remotely. Where required on site, these support spaces are best located close to the box office and include the mail and telephone sales team, the manager's office, a safe (for cash sales), box office server and ticket stock.

## Cloakrooms

The need for, and capacity of, cloakrooms is much debated. Continental theatres often have one coat peg per seat, while in the United Kingdom, experience is that only 25–35% of the audience leave their coats, although a gala event, a day-long conference, or exceptionally bad weather will affect this. A guide is to allow 0.1m$^2$ per coat for storage. Additional space is required for folding bicycles, buggies and, when security is an issue, small bags that are not permitted into the auditorium. A cloakroom service is more important when an auditorium uses a displacement air delivery system, as coats stuffed under the seats can reduce the flow of fresh cool air (see Figure 4.5.3).

Cloak systems may be complimentary or charged for. Speed of service is important, particularly when leaving after a show. The choices are a manned cloakroom or a self-service system or a combination of the two.

Figure 4.5.3 Cloaks counter. Barbican Arts Centre, London, UK. Cloaks counters need to be low to pass over coats and bags with good circulation space on both sides and easily accessible hangers and shelves to enable items to be taken and returned quickly, avoiding long queues and frustrated patrons. Designed by Allford Hall Monaghan Morris Architects/Studio Myerscough/Cartlidge Levene.

An effective system depends upon a fast service and good space for circulation. A manned service requires a low counter over which staff can take and return coats using a numbering system that is easy to follow with easily accessible storage. A self-service system needs space for the audience to circulate and negotiate the locking system.

The cloakroom needs to be easy to secure once the 'house is in' and if unattended may need to be a separate fire compartment.

## Kiosk and confectionery store

For some, the confectionery kiosk is an important part of a theatre visit. Usually located in the entrance foyer, it needs a prominent position but without causing obstruction.

The kiosk needs to be highly adaptable. Confectionery may be very popular for one type of show, but the kiosk may be far better branded as a champagne bar or a coffee bar for another. The display system needs to be flexible and adaptable, able to stock and display a variety of merchandise.

The merchandise store needs to be secure and properly ventilated, located immediately behind the kiosk with space for a freezer and/or fridge.

## Programme sales points

Programmes and brochures are an integral part of front-of-house revenue streams; the selling of them needs to be highly visible and not block circulation, from fixed and mobile positions around the foyer and within the auditorium. Pre-show programme sales counters may be utilised as confectionary and ice cream sales during the interval.

## Merchandising

Some theatres see opportunities for retailing local artisan gift items, books and production scripts from past shows, and some merchandise is venue branded. This will require a retail unit with secure space for display in a prominent position, located in a part of the foyer that is open to the public at hours similar to the box office and café. It will also require a stock room close by.

A further retail opportunity is 'show'-related merchandising which will vary according to the performance type. If there is a long-running show, merchandise points are likely to be static. If the venue follows a rolling programme, the merchandise will change on a regular basis, as will the size and location of the sales points. There should be enough display and storage at each sales point to carry sufficient stock to last an entire show.

Venues with resident companies may operate their own shop, while in 'receiving houses', the production management may operate the merchandising service themselves or franchise the service out. Whichever system is adopted, theatre operators, who earn a percentage of the sales, will be keen to maximise the opportunity – resulting in highly visible locations outside the auditorium doors. Show merchandising can be an eyesore and a hazard if not well presented or thoughtfully positioned. Facilities should include:

- display space that does not inhibit wayfinding, circulation and escape routes
- each sales point will need electricity supplies for lighting and data-cabling for tills and credit card authorisations
- storage will be required (unless the franchisee brings in merchandise on each occasion), and displays will be set up prior to each show.

## Digital technology

Theatres are built with long lifespans, and technology that is unforeseen when the building is being planned will inevitably arrive. Wireless (Wi-Fi) coverage of the foyers, mobile device charging points and other informational systems need to be considered when trying to future-proof the facilities, particularly with the likely increase in security checks, access controls and health monitoring. Many of the larger venues already use digital displays (IPTV) and Bluetooth beacons for information and promotional material, digital ticketing, digital cloakroom tickets, digital ordering of drinks and meals and downloading digital programmes. The 'remote' ordering of interval drinks and snacks through an app and the trend of bringing food to patrons in their seats rather than having them all crowd into a small bar is likely to be amplified post pandemic.

High-bandwidth digital infrastructure, both wired and wireless, will continue to be essential to delivering customer experiences in FOH areas. Whilst the bandwidth needed to order drinks or buy a ticket is minimal, patrons now expect free high-speed internet connectivity to stream social media, and this requires more infrastructure, larger cable containment and careful planning to ensure digital security. With increasing dependence on digital technology, the use of translation devices and high availability communication networks and fault-tolerant digital services will become more important. To ensure compatibility with systems backstage specialist advice should be sought from the project's theatre consultant.

## 4.6 Bars and catering

### Options

Food and drink are increasingly seen as significant components of a theatre visit (and the organisation's business plan), and the provision needs to be considered early in the planning stage. Bar sales are usually far more profitable than food sales and can make a significant contribution to overall income. Whilst a theatre may forgo food service, it is unlikely to forgo 'wet sales'.

The theatre may choose to run the bar and catering services in-house or contract them out, though the latter rarely make the same level of financial contribution to the theatre as directly run operations. In some cases, the contractor will have a very clear view about the design and layout, and care is needed to ensure this does not conflict with the overall design and ethos of the theatre and its foyer space.

Theatre catering is a vital part of the all-day offer but has historically been regarded as risky, so it is advisable to seek professional advice from the early stages of a project. There is a wide range of options to be considered, from pre-theatre and interval bar snacks to a stand-alone restaurant, open to the general public. The user/client needs to decide if F&B sales are going to be a 'performance only' or an 'all day operation', as this will have ramifications on the FOH design. This decision is needed early in the briefing process. The choice of what is to be provided will impact the design and layout of the foyer area, the amount of space needed and the furniture and equipment to be installed. A catering consultant should be appointed during the briefing stage to advise at a strategic level on the market opportunities and the type of food service required. During the design stage, the catering consultant can assist with detail design and equipping of the catering provision.

### Bars and 'wet sales'

The location and scale of bars is important (see Figure 4.6.1). To maximise sales, audiences need to be confident that they will be served quickly and have time to enjoy their drinks. Theatres have very high peak/short-duration demand in the half-hour pre-show and during the interval. It is therefore usual to keep product choice narrow.

### Design considerations

The detail design of the bar front counter and back bar and local storage need to be adaptable. Opera and ballet audiences will provide higher sales of wines and spirits, while comedy gigs or rock concerts are likely to have higher beer sales; children's shows will sell mostly soft drinks, while matinees will see more tea and coffee sales.

The correct counter height is important for those working behind the bar and for wheelchair users. Lowered sections should be incorporated, and these should not be relegated to one end. Electronic point of sale (EPOS) systems are popular with customers using credit cards for bar purchases. Coffee service is a regular demand, high-profit service which can be delivered from a bar or from specific or mobile service points. Coffee must be served hot and speedily, so individual serving systems will be unsuitable for use during an interval.

Figure 4.6.1 Bar sales at the Bridge Theatre, London, UK. A busy bar with multiple serving stations arranged to serve everyone speedily during a short interval. See Reference Project 20.

### Location

The size and location of bars depends on the distribution of the audience within the auditorium. Bars need to be easily accessible and designed to aid quick and efficient service, allowing people to buy a drink and then withdraw to a less crowded space. Long bars with multiple cash tills produce quicker service, and segmented bars with specific serving positions encourage the customers to queue in front of each section (see Figure 4.6.2).

To reduce delays, audiences are frequently encouraged to pre-order their interval drinks requiring shelving where their drinks can be laid out away from the bar and out of busy circulation paths. Drink shelves need to be sufficiently long and marked up into clearly numbered sections to assist customers to find their drinks.

Plan

Cash till above bottle bin
Back counter shelves below
Optics display
Beer taps
2460
Front opening refridgerator
Chip and pin device
670
Cash till
Shelf for 'free pour' bottles
Sink and drainer
Coffee machine crockery trays below
900
1355
675

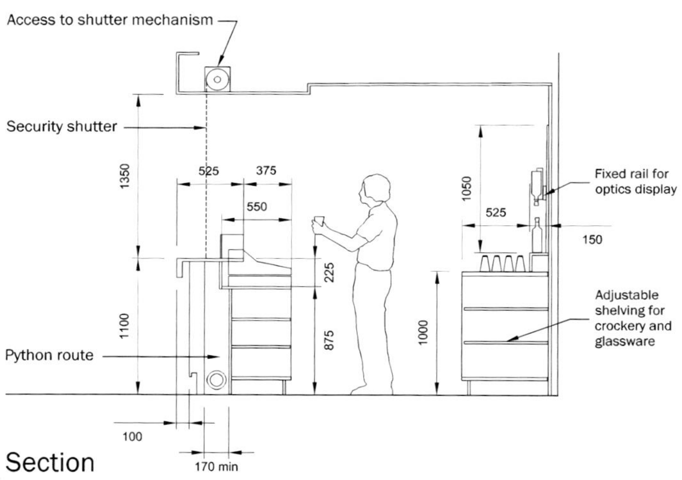


Figure 4.6.2 Plan and section of a typical theatre bar.

The design of bars should take account of cultural differences. In some countries alcohol consumption is not encouraged or not permitted. Those that can sell alcohol may need facilities that are discreetly located or within enclosed lounges.

Bars in the foyer should be located away from walls adjoining the auditorium. If this is not possible, additional independent walls need to be provided and all noisy and vibrating equipment efficiently isolated from the auditorium structure.

The bars should typically be divided into 1.5–1.8-m serving station modules, predicated by the width of equipment including bottle fridges, a range of spirits, soft drink dispensers, beer pumps, clean glasses and a till. For planning purposes, it is usually assumed that one service station can serve approximately one hundred people in a twenty-minute interval.

For the disposition of bars within the foyers, some interpretation is necessary, as in practice, spend will differ. For example, a theatre with 500 people sitting in the stalls, 250 in the circle and 250 in the gallery would expect to have three bars, one related to each level with a total of ten serving stations – five in the stalls, three in the circle and two in the gallery (because sales are likely to be higher in the circle than the gallery).

## Local and central bar stores, chilled cellar, spirits and empties stores

Each bar should have a local bar store with a wine fridge and an ice maker, possibly a glass washing machine and a coffee maker; if not provided within the bar counters, then a sink and separate hand-washing basin should be included here.

To facilitate the venue running at capacity a central store, which is easily accessible from all parts of FOH, will be needed for:

- a secure wine and spirit store
- a chilled cellar, where beer and soft drinks are stored
- an empties/recycling store.

Finishes to stores and delivery routes need to be durable and capable of being washed down.

Where draught beer and mixers are on offer, the location of the cellar is important. Kegs, gas cylinders and pumps will be kept in the cellar and connected to the individual bars by a python (a cluster of small plastic supply pipes with intertwined cooling pipes, usually supplied and installed by the contracted brewery). It requires a 225-mm-diameter conduit, with accessible large swept bends, linking the cellar and each sales point. The route should be thought about from an early stage and be as short and as direct as possible to minimise wastage.

Given the potential volume and weight of wet stocks, that is, kegs, cases of wine, spirits and so on, it is imperative that the point of delivery to the cellar be as short and obstruction free as possible. Manual handling risk assessments and careful planning need to be conducted before deciding on the location of cellars and bar stores.

## Food service options

Theatres need to decide why they want to serve food and should be conscious of the fact that catering is not the core function of the organisation. Theatres may well find it difficult to compete with surrounding restaurants, particularly if they are only offering a pre-show (single sitting) service, and theatres should establish a symbiotic relationship with neighbouring venues and eateries complementing rather than competing with them.

There may be a variety of reasons for including a food service:

- to generate additional income
- insufficient quality catering nearby
- to attract non-theatregoers during the day
- to offer in-house catering for functions
- a local caterer wants to be associated with the theatre.

Some venues choose to offer a food service pre- and post-show, which can be a stand-alone public offer or specifically for theatre customers. Service options are:

- table service, fine dining or casual
- assisted service (usually a buffet or counter service)
- food court (a series of autonomous counters where customers may either order or eat)
- pop-up kiosks (an outstation used to provide service for peak demand) either inside or outside.

## Location

The location of the restaurant/eating area needs careful consideration. If it is intended just for theatregoers and integrated into the main foyer, it needs to be in an area which is not disrupted by the movement of an incoming audience or by the draughts from doors (see Figure 4.6.3).

If the facility is intended to deliver catering for both theatre and non-theatre customers, it will need to be in a location where, for example, a schools' matinee audience will not cause disruption in the eating area. Conversely, if open to the public during performances, diners must not inhibit access to the bars, and the kitchen and noise and smells must not intrude upon the auditorium.

Anyone considering food service for a non-theatre audience must be aware that a successful café/restaurant needs to be available at regular times each day it is scheduled to be open. It is not practicable to run a café/restaurant which is intended to be open for non-theatregoers during the day but has to frequently close for theatre operational reasons.

Figure 4.6.3 Catering provision. Northern Stage, Newcastle upon Tyne, UK. Catering adds vitality to the foyers, particularly during the day, located so as not to intrude upon the functioning of the foyers at performance times. This figure shows the Northern Stage bar on the press night for *The Last Ship*.

To compete with other businesses in the high street, theatre cafés/restaurants need to remain 'fashionable', updating their ambience more frequently than other parts of the building. Consequently, these parts of the foyer may need to be treated as stylistically different.

## Kitchens, cold and dry stores

If the venue offers a catering service, then appropriately sized provision is essential. Not being the core business, the catering 'back of house' accommodation is usually considered secondary and can suffer from being undersized. Space of similar size to the eating area is required to accommodate:

- kitchen, preparation and cooking
- servery
- wash up
- dry stores
- cold stores
- crockery and cutlery store
- linen store
- wine store
- administration
- staff changing with separate toilets and a 'chef's shower'
- goods delivery
- waste disposal.

Hygiene regulations may require separate service routes for food and food waste.

## 4.7 Routes and signposting

### Auditorium entrance doors and lobbies

Entrances into the auditorium are a very important architectural element within the design of the foyers. Movement between the foyer and auditorium is an opportunity to build anticipation for the audience entering the auditorium and to reflect on the performance when leaving.

The aim should be to enable people to find the correct door without confusion. Each entrance has to be controlled by a member of staff to check tickets, so it is good practice to avoid numerous entrances.

Doors should be wide enough for people to get into the auditorium without queuing but manageable for checking tickets, with space nearby for selling programmes and, if drinks are allowed in the auditorium, space for changing from glass to plastic containers. With the advent of 'PYO' tickets or tickets on mobile devices, stewards increasingly use bar code readers to check tickets. Lighting levels near entrance doors need to be increased to enable tickets to be read easily.

Between the foyer and the auditorium there need to be lobbies to provide fire separation, reduce sound transference and avoid light spill into the auditorium. Ideally, they need to be planned so that one set of doors closes before the next set opens, and vision panels should be avoided. To aid circulation, doors should be on hold-open devices (as permitted by the licensing authority). Double swing doors are ideal for audience movement in and out of the auditorium but will require careful specification to meet fire and acoustic requirements. With so many requirements, doors should not be so large or heavy that they are difficult to open.

### Latecomers

Shows or performances may need to restrict the admission of latecomers to the auditorium, so thought needs to be given to accommodating them with either seats at the side or the rear of the auditorium or providing good audio/visual relay to a position in the foyer. If late entry is permitted, then latecomers' display monitors should be located near entrance doors for quick entry at the appropriate point in the performance. At other times the same monitors can be used for promotional purposes. To avoid vision panels, auditorium doors may have cue lights to enable attendants to usher latecomers quickly to their seats at a suitable moment in the performance.

### Escape routes

It is as important to plan escape routes from the foyer as it is from the auditorium. A practical way of achieving this is to position escape routes from the lobbies between the foyer and the auditorium. The maximum capacity of the public spaces needs to be considered. Whilst the capacity of the auditorium or auditoria usually dictates the required escape capacity, licensing authorities may argue that if the foyers are used for simultaneous events, then the escape capacity needs to be increased.

Within fire protected zones on upper levels and preferably close to a lift, refuge positions will be required, with space for each wheelchair user and additional space allowed for anyone who cannot manage stairs in an emergency evacuation.

### Wayfinding and signs

Clear, well-thought-out signposting is an issue for most public buildings; it is often left until late in the detail design process and does not take account of where people look – leading to an *ad-hoc* sign being added later. Clear planning will mean less reliance on signs and staff to give directions (see Figure 4.7.1 and Reference Project 29).

For those with sight impairments, signs, changes of level and obstructions need to be identifiable using colour contrasting and tactile surfaces, and the avoidance of glare. Braille and tactile signs can be helpful, as can the use of symbols and pictograms.

Signs need to be considered from the point of view of the theatregoer and be consistent in terminology and graphic style. A hierarchy of signs needs to be developed to suit the journey around the building (see Figure 4.7.2). The more complex the auditorium seating layout is and the more entrance doors there are, the more complex the signs are likely to become. The following information needs to be conveyed:

- auditorium (if not obvious or where there is more than one auditorium)
- seating level (stalls, circle or gallery)
- door or aisle (auditorium left or right)
- seating row (usually a letter)
- seat number.

The information given on signs within the foyers needs to correspond exactly with that shown on the tickets.

To ensure visual consistency, consideration also needs to be given to integrating ancillary signs – statutory signs, bar tariffs, and disclaimers and warnings regarding the performance including explicit scenes, strobe lighting or cast changes.

Other unsightly items can also quickly appear in the foyer (such as clocks, posters, donor recognition plaques, temporary signs and sponsors displays). Projection, digital signs and display screens are increasingly common and can help control this proliferation, but this requires early consideration.

Figure 4.7.1 Intuitive wayfinding at Theatre Royal, Glasgow, UK. The layout of the foyers provides a very intuitive flow towards the auditorium doors. The doorways are identified with colourful walls and large graphics, visible across the foyer above head level. See Reference Project 29.

## Lifts and escalators

Escalators or banks of lifts are only likely to be found in larger multi-venue buildings. In normal circumstances it will not be possible to have sufficient lifts for all the audience to use at the beginning or at the end of the performance, but adequate provision should be made for those who may need them such as wheelchair users, the elderly, infirm or families with young children. Lifts should be carefully positioned so that they can be easily located. Ideally lifts should be available for evacuation in event of an emergency. It is not acceptable to rely on evacuation chairs and carrying people with disabilities downstairs. Lift and escalator installations need:

- adequate space at landings to avoid pinch-points
- to run as silently as possible, isolated from the auditorium structure
- controls and floor numbers in Braille and/or in raised numerals

Figure 4.7.2 Integrated signs. CAST, Doncaster, UK. Signs are an integral part of the architectural concept and an important part of the interior design. Indicators need to instinctively lead visitors through the building from the point of arrival to their seat in the auditorium. See Reference Project 15.

- lift cars to be large enough for wheelchairs to turn around
- 'talking' level indicators which should be coordinated with the nomenclature used for parts of the auditorium
- lift cars to have easy-to-maintain walls and floors
- lift cars to be provided with protective wall coverings (for use when moving furniture and equipment around the building).

There should be more than one lift available in the event of servicing or breakdowns.

# 4.8 Toilets

Toilets have a marked impact on customer perceptions. Given the peaks of demand pre-show and at the interval, toilets need to be easy to maintain and service. For women, theatre toilets have long been synonymous with queuing. This is not only undesirable for audience members but also impacts bar and related sales. The ratio of male to female toilets needs to reflect audience composition, with some toilets capable of switching to women's use for certain performance types.

In theatres there is an increasing prevalence of unisex toilets in response to gender equality in society. They are far more inclusive for many LGBTQ+ people, disabled people and families.

Where a building type or form of entertainment is subject to license, the minimum scale of provision and the location and arrangement of the toilets has to be agreed with the licensing authority. In the United Kingdom, as a minimum, the design of sanitary facilities in assembly buildings should be in accordance with clause 6.8 and table 7 of BS 6465–1:2006 or the similar table 24 in section G1 of the *Technical Standards for Places of Entertainment*.

The location and planning of toilet accommodation should be clearly legible while avoiding direct views. Door-free access and one-way circulation maximise efficiency.

If the toilet provision is to achieve a reasonable level of user satisfaction, its design needs to consider key features from the user's perspective:

- surfaces that can be kept clean and dry
- hygienic and durable floor and wall finishes
- ample ventilation to avoid odours
- avoid views of urinals from adjacent areas
- easy-to-maintain lights, hand dryers and other electrical fittings
- cubicle doors that swing open when unoccupied
- cubicles wide enough to accommodate sanitary dispensers
- easy-to-maintain taps and WC flushing systems
- well-positioned mirrors, good-quality lighting and dry handbag shelves
- at least one full-length mirror
- easy to use taps, soap dispensers and hand dryers
- basins with wastes and overflows that cannot be maliciously blocked
- choice of paper towels or hand-dryers, which in operation need to be quiet and low energy
- tamper-proof toilet paper holders that contain a spare roll
- local storage for toilet paper, soap and towels.

Toilets should be located away from walls adjoining the auditorium or special measures taken to ensure that cisterns and hand-dryers do not cause intrusive noise.

Toilets for disabled people should be provided in accordance with BS 6465–1:2006 Clause 7. In addition to fulfilling these requirements, accessible toilets should:

- be close to where disabled patrons are seated and in sufficient number, at least two for smaller venues with six wheelchair positions and more for larger venues
- have a travel distance not exceeding 40m
- be unisex, enabling carers to assist if necessary
- where more than one facility is provided, offer WC pans with handed transfer positions
- a wider cubicle with outward-opening doors and grab rails should be provided in all male and female toilets to aid the less ambulant.

In the United Kingdom places of assembly, recreation and entertainment with a capacity for 350 or more people are required to install a 'changing places' facility when they are new builds or having a major refurbishment. These are larger rooms designed for people who need additional space, specific equipment, extra time and assistance to use the toilet safely and with dignity.

Baby-changing facilities should not be sited within the disabled persons' toilets. They should either have their own space or be in the principal female and male toilets (which must be large enough to accommodate the changing table in use without blocking circulation).

## 4.9 Provision for other activities

As outlined in Section 4.3, some venues will open up their FOH during the day, creating greater opportunities for community engagement and income generation. These non-performance activities are set out in this section with engagement and community activities discussed in Section 4.10 and potential for rentals and hires in Section 4.11.

### Informal performance spaces

Informal performances either during the day and before or after the show will enliven the foyers (see Figure 4.9.1 and Reference Project 06). They need:

- a focal point at which to perform with suitable sightlines
- space for standing and seated spectators
- possibly acoustic treatment to surrounding surfaces
- infrastructure for temporary sound and lighting rigs
- adjacent storage (say, for a piano).

Figure 4.9.1 Design that facilitates performances at Storyhouse, Chester, UK. Foyer space provides an excellent alternative with informal space for small-scale performances, talks, discussions and screenings. See Reference Project 06.

Performances may be acoustic or amplified. Providing a speech acoustic will help these spaces to work well.

## Sponsors' lounges, hospitality rooms and conference breakout space

Sponsors, VIPs and patrons are a necessary part of every theatre's life, and the provision of well-appointed reception rooms or at least one sponsors' lounge is desirable. Depending on the capacity and policy of the theatre, the type of hospitality will vary. Many events may only be entertaining 5–10 guests at a time or there could be two or three groups on the same evening. On other occasions, such as first or closing nights, larger parties may be held. Flexibility is essential, for example, one large space that can be divided into two or three smaller rooms. In smaller theatres a separate room may not be possible, so a discrete area that can be cordoned off for a special event should be incorporated.

Sponsors expect recognition. They will bring display boards, banners or images to project onto screens or display on monitors.

Sponsors and hospitality areas may need:

- ready access to kitchens or a food preparation space
- a suitable clearing area for dirty plates and glasses
- lounge furniture
- separate bar facilities
- easy access from the entrance lobby
- accessibility even when the auditorium is not open to the public
- quick direct access to the VIP seats.

Hospitality rooms will be used in different formats – including lecture, party or dining layouts, so it is essential to have adequate furniture storage adjacent.

If the theatre offers conferencing or banqueting facilities, room capacity will be determined by seating layouts and table sizes. To be successful in a competitive market, these rooms need to be able to accommodate Wi-Fi–enabled audio-visual presentations.

When education facilities are provided, they should, wherever possible, be in addition to the hospitality suites. (See Section 4.10.)

## Exhibition space

Theatre foyers may be used to stage exhibitions associated with the show or its sponsors or – in the case of conferences – a trade show. Exhibitions will need:

- sufficient floor to ceiling height
- higher floor loadings
- variable lighting
- power supplies.

Exhibitions must be positioned so as not to obstruct escape routes.

'Get-in'/'Get-out' of exhibitions may be more convenient if carried out through the front doors, in which case sufficient clear openings should be integrated into the design of the front entrance. For example, in a large foyer, a car or similar-sized object may need to be brought into the building.

The foyers may also provide gallery space for an additional cultural provision and for commercial income (see Figure 4.9.2). They will need additional requirements:

- an integrated hanging and display system should be considered in the overall design
- suitable lighting and environmental conditions
- additional security measures
- location that ensures fit-ups and dismantling do not to interfere with other activities
- high-level and floor-level power supplies
- plentiful IT and data outlets.

The exhibition space will also need adequate storage for display systems and exhibits awaiting display or collection.

Figure 4.9.2 Space that enables exhibitions. As a discrete part of the foyer, it allows audiences to view the exhibition whether attending a performance or not. This figure shows an exhibition at the National Theatre, London, UK.

## Public art installations

Public funding projects may require that work by artists and craftspeople be incorporated into the overall design (see Figure 4.9.3 and Reference Project 22). To be properly integrated, installations should be planned from an early stage. Clients may choose to select artists themselves, with their architect or use an art commissioning consultant to organise the process.

There is considerable scope for artists to be involved with design and fabrication of building elements in the foyers such as:

Figure 4.9.3 'Permanent Present', MAC, Belfast, UK. This is a major sculptural work by Irish artist Mark Garry commissioned by The Thomas Devlin Fund and the MAC, specifically for the foyer. It consists of 400 metal wires in the main foyer of the MAC, creating a spectrum of colour that travels through the space. See Reference Project 22.

- floor finishes
- balustrades and handrails
- doors and door furniture
- bars and counters
- lighting
- carpets and drapes
- furniture.

There are examples where artists have successfully integrated donor names into commissioned work – for example, an etched glazed screen, a tiled area, decorative brickwork and even a chandelier.

## 4.10 Engagement and community activities

For theatres, in common with many cultural organisations, engagement and community activities have grown significantly. In the United Kingdom, this work is often a condition of funding for publicly funded venues. Commercial theatre operators also appreciate the value of such work in relation to audience development, community relationships and their public image.

For a theatre to deliver a range of community-based activity, then the best scenario is to have the dedicated use of one or more studio spaces in which to work. This will provide flexibility and offer the best environment for the widest range of participants. Where space is limited, the studios may have to be multi-purpose and shared between education, rehearsals, corporate entertaining and even commercial hires. In such cases, it is important that the different uses be detailed and planned at the briefing stage.

Ideally these spaces should be visible from, or adjacent to, the foyers – an interactive zone can be a major contributor to the daytime liveliness of the FOH areas. When this is not possible, an identifiable meeting point should be provided for participants to gather before being led or directed to the studio/workshop.

Activities may include one or more groups of up to 30 people. The minimum space which is appropriate for community activities is in the region of 70–90m$^2$ before storage is considered (see Figure 4.10.1).

Figure 4.10.1 Community engagement. Polka Theatre, Wimbledon, UK. Purpose-designed, dedicated spaces will offer the best environment for users. See Section 10, Figures 10.9.1a and 10.9.1b.

### Community engagement and access

The spaces should be accessible to disabled visitors, with consideration being given to aspects other than simple access and egress. For example, a group of children with special educational needs must be able to enjoy a workshop experience comparable to that of non-disabled children. When relaxed and dementia-friendly performances are staged, a room close to the auditorium with a calming environment should be available.

Workshop activities may include 'making' or design-based work, which requires paint and other 'wet' materials. It is therefore useful to have a separate sink of a height which allows children to use it and to help keep the space clean and tidy.

Where workshops involve technical theatre activity, good provision of power sockets and rigging points will facilitate the introduction of specialist equipment into the space, such as sound desks, production lighting and computers.

Providing suitable flooring is important. Some work is better conducted on carpet – particularly that for young children, who will tend to sit on the floor and roll about – while other work is much better on wooden or laminate floors. Dance work needs to be conducted on specific types of floors (either sprung or with sufficient 'give' to soften the impact). Removeable dance mats and carpets over timber floors offer a solution (see Figure 4.10.2).

A balance of artificial and natural light is desirable. However, it is also worth considering whether some basic theatrical lighting will be beneficial, perhaps enabling a space to double as a studio theatre so long as blackout facilities are also installed.

Most theatre education departments will have a large collection of props and costumes, which needs to be easily accessible, either within the educational space itself or close by.

Figure 4.10.2 Community engagement. Sadler's Wells, Islington, London, UK. A foyer space known as the Dorfman Room in use for community engagement and outreach programmes.

Where possible, studio/workshops should have connection to the offices which the education department uses.

### Toilet requirements for these activities

Toilets and accessible toilets should be safe and easy to use by children and, in the interests of safeguarding, should not be open to the general public at the same time. For pre-school children and their parents, there should be adequate baby-changing facilities.

## 4.11 Rentals and hires

Many theatres hire out spaces within their buildings, and, increasingly, new theatres are designed to facilitate this. An example of such hires could be:

- play readings
- photo and film shoots
- corporate training sessions
- weddings, parties and social events
- student showcases
- award ceremonies
- charity fundraising events
- seminars, meetings and discussion groups
- book and product launches.

A theatre may be one of the few spaces available locally where large numbers of people can be accommodated. Many theatre auditoria work well for conferences and larger meetings, especially midscale venues with a flexible auditorium layout and the potential for an apron or forestage. Other areas within a theatre which have the potential to be hired out either commercially or for community activities include:

- meeting rooms if designed and located so that they can be used autonomously
- rehearsal space is generally in short supply and can be hired by other companies as well as by community groups and should be accessible from FOH and via the stage door
- a producing theatre might hire out its studio space to broaden its programme
- depending on the size, design, location and amenities, the foyer can be used for a variety of events by commercial and community organisations.

### Planning for rentals and hires

Where possible, these other areas should be designed so that they can be used independently, without impacting the theatre's performance or the audience's enjoyment of the bars and restaurants and other facilities.

Some issues to be considered are listed here.

- Noise: audiences entering and leaving the main auditorium could cause a distraction for events taking place elsewhere in the building.
- Provision of toilets: these need to be accessible for everyone; otherwise, additional facilities will be required.
- Safety: events and activities which coincide with the main performance will increase the number of people within the building at any given time. This could impact safety requirements.
- Economy: it should be possible to light and heat/ventilate individual areas so that small meetings do not incur large energy costs.
- Security: ancillary lettable spaces need to be designed so that those using them do not wander round other parts of the building.

### Conference use

Hiring the theatre out for conference use can prove lucrative; however, in all but the largest venues, a conference is likely to take over the whole of the FOH, the auditorium and ancillary spaces and be demanding in the technical resources required (see Figure 4.11.1). In addition to the auditorium, conference use will require:

- a reception area for the registration of delegates, which takes longer than checking theatre tickets
- rooms for break-out sessions; the delegates may need to divide into a series of working groups
- up to five breaks may need to be catered to, including a closing drinks party/reception
- technical support for use of video, projection and sound equipment
- an office or desk space with access to power and reliable Wi-Fi
- display space for promoting the organisation or 'branding' the venue.

Figure 4.11.1 A conference is likely to take over the whole of the FOH as shown here at The Lyric Theatre Hammersmith, London, UK. To accommodate the requirements of large conferences, additional catering provision may be required. Tea and coffee stations for breaks between sessions. Counters to rapidly serve a lunch to several hundred people and later drinks and canapes at the conference 'after party'.

## 4.12 Support areas

The following areas are not usually open to the public, and access needs to be controlled.

### Duty manager's and security office

This is the hub of the FOH activity. In larger buildings it usually has to accommodate two or three staff and many activities, including pre-performance briefings and the cashing-up of programme, ice cream and other sales money, requiring a safe that is separate from the one used for box-office takings.

The duty manager needs to maintain contact with other departments in the theatre throughout the evening. Radios are the usual means of communication between staff, but if a large amount of steel is used in construction, signals can be weak and thought needs to be given to how communications are maintained during show time. Most theatres still use a bell system to signal the start of a performance, and this is often accompanied by foyer announcements from the duty manager or from the stage manager. Dimming the foyer lights provides a visual signal to those with a hearing impairment.

The proliferation of CCTV has extended to include the foyers. CCTV monitoring may be carried out off- or on-site, in which case a control room or CCTV space may be needed.

Traditionally the stage door is the focus of security and fire control, but fire panels are a vital part of emergency equipment and need to be readily accessible to the duty manager and visible to the fire brigade upon their arrival. Small area zoning is appreciated by theatre staff who have to check areas and establish exit routes in an emergency.

To help manage energy consumption and minimise waste and disturbance, zoning parts of the building's lighting, heating and public address system should be incorporated and controllable from FOH.

### First aid room

A first aid room should be provided in larger venues, with a bed, a supplies cupboard and a screened space to store a wheelchair and stretcher/carrying chair. A washbasin, with drinking water, will be required and ideally an *en suite* WC. The room needs to be close to the point where ambulances arrive and positioned so that a full-length stretcher can be manoeuvred out.

## Staff briefing and changing rooms

Where staff are expected to wear a uniform, they should be provided with changing facilities and locker space. These areas should be close to a suitable briefing area for attendants, be equipped with notice boards and full-length mirrors and have vending machines for drinks or snacks and/or access to the green room.

## FOH equipment store

Storage is a real issue for theatres. The items that need a home in the front of house area are:

- radios and multiple recharge points
- translation devices
- hearing assistance headsets
- public health equipment
- tables and chairs not in use
- sponsors' materials
- VIP equipment; visitors' book, umbrellas, red carpet
- printer/photocopier for rotas, and so on
- cash bags for programme sellers
- boxes of programmes for the current show.

## Events equipment

Events, meetings, workshops and conferences all require a wide range of equipment, often including tables, chairs, flipcharts or electronic equivalent, projectors, screens and audio equipment. Suitable storage provision needs to be designated for such items. These items will be used regularly, so they need to be accessed easily and stored within the rooms or close to where they will be most used.

## Merchandising, programme, ice cream and confectionery deliveries

These goods are usually delivered via the stage door where they can be checked and kept secure, with the eventual storage located close to FOH, where the items will be sold. Printed material such as brochures, programmes, promotional leaflets and posters will be delivered in bulk and require a significant amount of storage space.

## Ice cream store

The sale of ice cream requires freezer space, sales trays and cash bags. The number of freezers will depend upon the size of the theatre and the frequency of delivery. Sales will vary between shows: for example, ice cream sales during the pantomime season frequently exceed alcohol sales. Freezers should be:

- centrally located in a well-ventilated dedicated space
- equipped with a suitable reliable power supply
- located near to the attendants' changing rooms.

When demand requires, additional freezers can be loaned from suppliers, requiring further space and a reliable power supply.

## Uniforms/stationery/disposables/glassware

Storage space for items such as uniform stock, stationery, disposables and so on will be needed and require frequent access.

## Housekeeping and cleaners' stores

All areas within the building need to be cleaned on a regular basis, with some requiring specialised equipment.

Consideration needs to be given to both the front-of-house and backstage areas and provision made which takes into account the likely number of cleaning staff operating at any one time.

Centrally located secured stores may be needed for larger items such as floor scrubbers, strippers, pressure washers and vacuums and cleaning materials subject to the control of substances hazardous to health (COSHH) regulations.

There should be cleaners' cupboards on each floor of the building containing a sink or bucket sink, storage space and shelving. They must be adequately ventilated to allow for the drying of equipment. Cleaning staff will need a locker room, and the housekeeper may need space for such tasks as administration, duty rotas and ordering.

To operate efficiently, cleaners need power services with an adequate number of well-located power points, good working lighting and access to sinks and water supplies.

## Refuse store, compacting and recycling space

These facilities should be located close to a rear entrance where the collection can be monitored and controlled and should be separate from stage waste, which will be bulky and produced mainly during 'fit-ups'. Rubbish needs to be sorted between recyclables and waste. Where breweries recycle bottles, space is needed for crates. To reduce volume and frequency of collection, compactors should be considered. Refuse stores need power, water supplies and drainage to wash down the area.

### Allowing for growth

Taking into consideration the size and scale of the operation, it should be possible to estimate a year-on-year growth projection to identify the amount of space to be provided for future storage provision.

## 4.13 Taking your seat

'Will the audience kindly take their seats, as the performance is about to begin', is the moment to drink up, buy a programme, find your ticket and head towards the auditorium.

The heart of any theatre building is the auditorium, so the foyers need to have been configured to provide easy and legible access and egress. The pathways and position of the doorways leading into and out of the auditorium are dictated by the number of seats and the sightlines within the auditorium, the escape distances, the height and rake of the seating balconies and the position of gangways. In both plan and section, the arrangement of the foyers is, by necessity, a response to the form of the auditorium.

### Section editor

Barry Pritchard, Architect

### Contributors (in alphabetical order)

Paddy Dillon, Architect

Dave Ludlam, Theatreplan Consultants Ltd

Deborah Sawyerr, Mercury Theatre

Nicola Walls, Page/Park Architects

### Contributors to the first edition (in alphabetical order)

David Blyth, formerly Ambassador Theatre Group

John Botteley, formerly Theatre Director

Colin Chester, formerly Ambassador Theatre Group

Stewart King, formerly Renton Howard Wood Levin Architects (RHWL) Arts Team

Ian Knowles, Arup Acoustic

Alan McKenzie, Project Design Manager, Building Design Partnership (BDP)

Jim Morse, formerly Lighting Design Associates

Howard Raynor, formerly World Class Service Ltd (d. 2011)

Ian Smith, formerly King Shaw Associates

Roger Spence, Theatre Consultant and Project Advisor

Nadia Stern, Arts Manager

# Section 5
# Auditorium design principles

## 5.1 Performers and audience

The auditorium is the most important part of any theatre. The design of this space holds the key to the scale, form and layout of the whole building. As the engine-room that drives the theatre machine, it simply has to be right.

This section explores the factors that need to be considered when designing a performance space. It looks at the crucial relationship between performers and audience – and how this is interpreted to serve different styles of production and different art forms. It also considers the practical issues of getting the audience to and from their seats, ensuring that they can see and hear what is being presented and that they are both comfortable and safe. Section 6 extends this commentary, looking in more detail at the quality of the sensory experience – and the practical imperatives – that combine to underpin successful auditorium design.

Performance practice evolves over time – and so does auditorium design. As a result, a range of auditorium formats and performance configurations have emerged, each suited to different art forms and differing presentational styles. A review of auditorium design during the latter half of the twentieth century can be seen as a quest to break free from the perceived restrictions imposed by the prevailing proscenium format – and the division between the world of the actor and that of the audience. This led to exploration of shared 'open space' and a preoccupation with the degree to which the audience encircled the stage. At the same time, changes in society encouraged theatre designers to create more egalitarian and democratic layouts. These developments were also allied to ideas such as 'the point of command' (the focal point of interaction between a performer and the audience) and the creation of spaces that could deal simultaneously with both epic and intimate theatre. In the twenty-first century the notion of physical adaptability, both in the short and longer term, builds upon these sensibilities. New spaces must nurture emerging artistic practice and support evolving performance imperatives to ensure the long-term relevance and suitability of the performance spaces we create.

Technological advances also have an influence, offering directors opportunities for experimentation and theatre designers' scope to extend the uses to which a single space can be put.

## 5.2 Factors influencing size and scale

### Seating capacity

The optimum number of seats in a performance space is not simply a case of the more, the better. Technology allows us to create spaces which can accommodate many thousands of people – although such spaces are only effective for large-scale, electronically enhanced productions. At the other end of the spectrum, theatres are still being created for audiences of fewer than one-hundred people – where a sense of inclusivity and theatrical intimacy is prized above all.

A range of factors influence the number of seats that should be provided, and which can be accommodated, within different types of theatre.

### Visual and aural limits

Historically, the size and layout of an auditorium was determined by the distance people can see and hear. For the natural spoken voice, the usual accepted maximum distance is for the audience to be within 20m of the setting line of the proscenium stage or the front of an open stage. This distance is also determined by the need to see the actors' expressions.

Contemporary standards of safety, comfort and access have reduced the number of seats which can be accommodated within these visual and aural limits, and a working norm now sets the maximum at around 1,000 seats for drama.

For musicals and opera, where the sound of the voice carries further, the maximum distance for communication can be up to thirty meters. In opera, as in epic theatre, sets are often more striking, and the costumes and gestures are enlarged. This helps performers communicate with the audience over a longer distance thus enabling greater numbers to be accommodated without losing a sense of engagement. For example, The Coliseum in London, home

DOI: 10.4324/9781003327295-5

to English National Opera, has a seating capacity of 2,358 over four levels.

With the advent of amplified sound, much larger audience capacities can be contemplated (with arena-style venues seating 20,000 or more), but aesthetic factors come into play when considering whether amplification is appropriate for any particular art form.

### Space for music and the sung word

Sung words carry further than spoken words, enabling a singer to fill a much larger volume of space. Musical instruments carry further than the voice by sustaining the sound for longer.

Spaces which are designed to house music need a certain amount of interior volume and carefully specified contours. Different styles of music require different volumes. For concert halls, the primary emphasis is on the quality of the sound while in an opera house a balance needs to be struck between designing for clarity in the spoken word and for the fullness of the musical sound.

### Intimacy, immediacy and audience cohesion

Theatrical intimacy, immediacy and audience cohesion are the essential tenets of good auditorium design. For the audience, the experience of live theatre involves a sense of participating in the 'event', of shared responses and of being part of a homogenous group. From the actors' point of view, a good space achieves the feeling of being embraced by the audience.

Theatrical intimacy is about enclosure and envelopment. One way it can be achieved is by the increasing the angle of the rake of the audience relative to the stage. Some directors find that a 'wall of people' in a steeply raked auditorium gives a perception of closeness as well as a clear view of the stage. Alternatively, 'painting' the walls with people in a series of shallow balconies can help achieve the desired effect – a technique demonstrated by the boxes in the traditional opera house and galleries in courtyard style theatres. A degree of 'closeness' in which each gesture and nuance of the actors' expression is clearly seen by every member of the audience requires a smaller auditorium and a format that wraps the audience around the production or even intermingles the action with the audience.

### Degree of adaptability

When considering the scale of a new auditorium space, set alongside the imperatives of being able to see and hear, there is the need to consider spatial flexibility and adaptability. A key discussion revolves around balancing performance formats with the density of an audience – and the imperatives of short-term and longer-term adaptability. While some spaces will be fairly fixed in terms of format others will be, and will need to be, more flexible in their configuration. Such 'loose-fit' spaces demand more area to deliver their variability. Some auditoria may alternate between two or three predetermined/known configurations, while others will be truly flexible spaces. Such spaces, through allowing a greater variety of use and varied performance activity over time, also address changing performance imperatives and shifts in attitude.

## 5.3 Auditorium formats and performance configurations

This section develops the discussion of different auditorium formats in Section 1. It guides you through the rich variety of performance configurations, indicating aspects of their historical development, typical use, opportunities – and limitations. The narrative starts with the proscenium theatre, as the most recognisable of theatre forms. It then works out from this, gradually eroding the influence of the proscenium opening and exploring the idea of the open-space theatre. The narrative also follows a course of gradually increasing the degree of audience encirclement and the preoccupation with achieving greater immediacy and theatrical intimacy.

The proscenium theatre format emerged in Italian opera houses of the seventeenth century and then dominated auditoria design for over 200 years, reaching its heyday in the latter part of the nineteenth and early-twentieth centuries. The defining characteristic of this particular format is that it separates the stage from the audience chamber. Since the middle of the twentieth century various different auditorium formats and performance configurations have emerged, gradually reducing the division of the proscenium and exploring ideas of the single room theatre. Responding to contemporary imperatives auditorium spaces have also become increasingly adaptable in terms of potential performance configurations – and aesthetic character.

### Proscenium theatre

In the proscenium theatre model the stagehouse and the audience chamber are separate, but interlinked volumes. The scenery and action are largely contained on the stage and the audience views the performance through the proscenium opening. Directors, designers and performers often refer to this opening as the 'fourth wall' of the stage. While in the ebullient theatres of the latter part of the nineteenth century, the proscenium surround was often treated as an elaborate picture frame, contemporary venues can choose to emphasise or downplay this zone. Above the stage is the stagehouse, or flytower, where scenic elements can be suspended or flown (see Section 8).

In this format, the audience is placed substantially 'end-on' within the auditorium to maximise their view through the proscenium opening onto the stage beyond. Spaces can also feature a small number of side seating positions and boxes. Proscenium auditoria tend to be multi-level, with a lower/stalls seating area and a single or series of tiers or galleries above. Initially, these upper galleries were fairly shallow, limited by structural capabilities. However, with the advent of the cantilever structure, the upper tiers got progressively deeper in an effort to maximise the proximity of the audience to the stage. The audience primarily sit facing the action, with shallower side galleries and boxes providing oblique views and linking the upper tier to the proscenium.

While performance practice and audience taste ebbs and flows, the proscenium format retains a key advantage which ensures its continued relevance: it remains the primary format for the presentation of large-scale and elaborate scenic effects. Contemporary theatre set design can play down the proscenium opening, when required, blurring the boundary between two spaces and reducing the sense of separation. In smaller venues, the full flytower may be replaced by simple suspension, whilst the proscenium itself can be a temporary construction of panels, pelmets and drapes.

## A designer's view

When an audience thinks of the theatre it is usually of the classic proscenium, which has framed the majority of [indoor] productions since the renaissance and is the backbone of our theatres. An inherent challenge of the format is that the audience are more disconnected from the actors – when compared to an in the round performance space for example. This is especially the case in musical theatre and opera which usually play with an orchestra pit at the front. However, combined with a fly tower, substage and decent wings the format gives the designer a huge flexibility to change the space quickly in a very controlled presentation. The proscenium opening, whilst the ultimate frame, can also be a barrier, doubly so when it's white or gilt and covered in lights and speakers. For sit-down shows like *Les Misérables* we have the ability to bring the set out into the auditorium, to blend the staging into the theatre, and to dress-over the technology. Whilst expensive and technically challenging to achieve in a proscenium environment, this helps release the show through the fourth wall and lets the audience feel at one with the world you have created for them.

Matt Kinley, Set Designer

**Example auditoria**

- Oslo Opera House, Norway
- Royal Opera House, London, UK
- Sondheim Theatre, London, UK
- Nevill Holt Opera, Market Harborough, UK (see Reference Project 08).

Figure 5.3.1 Victoria Palace Theatre, London. Contemporary reworking of an Edwardian proscenium theatre. See Reference Project 30.

## Forestage and apron stage

A forestage, or apron stage, is not a defined auditorium format. It is an adaptation or configuration within a proscenium theatre space.

In the proscenium theatre there is a limit to which scenic elements can be brought downstage towards the audience. This is normally about 1 meter back from the back face of the proscenium wall – and is known as the setting line. The zone between the setting line and the edge of the stage riser is termed the forestage. When this extends out into the auditorium this is known as an apron stage. In contemporary performance practice an apron stage helps to break down the perceptual barrier of the proscenium

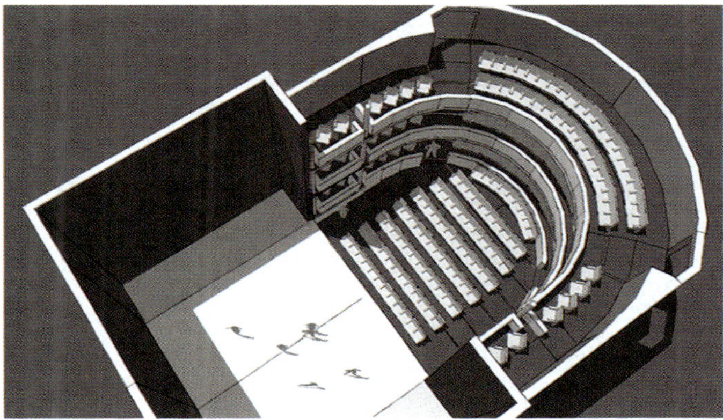

Figure 5.3.2 Proscenium format sketch. Audience and performers occupy interlinked but separate spaces.

and bring actor and audience closer together. It is a first step towards end-stage performance and the more open staging formats. In terms of performance style, a deep forestage within a proscenium format can allow directors and designers to combine epic scenic effects, with intimate scenes played well forward. The facility to do this is an essential part of modern proscenium theatre.

## End stage

The end-stage format is a modern abstraction of the proscenium theatre model. The audience is orientated end-on directly in front of the stage. With the audience set on one side of the acting area there is no encirclement. The layout means that an actor can address the audience as a group and hold their full attention as they are a unified single body. However, it is harder for an actor to make an aside or to be conspiratorial with just a part of the audience.

Figure 5.3.3 Stage 1, Northern Stage, Newcastle. Stripped down experimental space for an avant-garde theatre company.

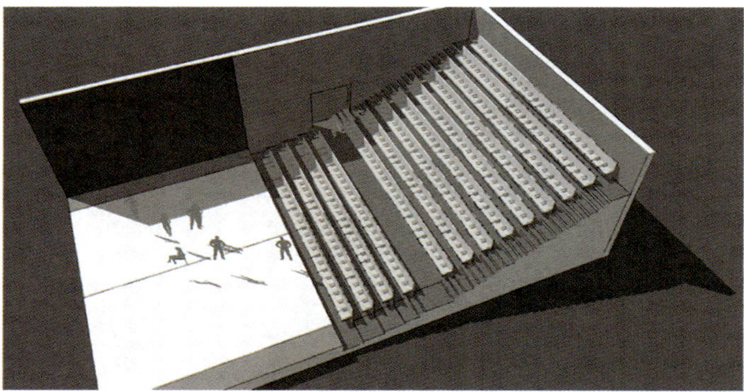

Figure 5.3.4 End stage format sketch. Audience set on one side of the stage, with no side seats.

A characteristic of this format is that all four corners of the acting area can be visible, which means that it is well suited to contemporary dance and some forms of physical theatre – particularly those that combine multimedia projection with live action.

End-stage spaces may, or may not, have a stage riser. Spaces without a riser tend to be single tier and fairly steeply raked. Spaces with a stage riser may have more than one tier, with a shallower rake at the lower level. Rows can be parallel to the stage edge or softened by being set out on a radius whilst still contained within the side walls. The stage end of the space may have a flytower or more modest suspension above the acting area.

Within the end-stage environment actors and audience effectively share the same physical space. So, while there are some similarities between the end-stage and the proscenium format, in this respect they are fundamentally different.

## A director's view

> Stage 1 at Northern Stage is unlike any space I'd met before. An intimate, direct and focussed auditorium on one level meets a stretched stage. Stage 1 is a playground for all theatre artists but directors and designers relish it most. It demands you bring your biggest and boldest self – Stage 1 can handle it, welcomes it. Because Stage 1 welds to confidence, impressionism and the epic – it's a political space because it communicates who gets to take up space in our imagination, in our consciousness, in the world. You're a changed artist once you've made a show on Stage 1 and we're always hoping audiences will be changed by it too.
>
> Natalie Ibu, Artistic Director and Joint CEO, Northern Stage

### Example auditoria

- Nederlands Dans Theater, Den Hague, Netherlands
- Laban Theatre, London, UK
- Stage 1, Northern Stage, Newcastle Upon Tyne, UK

## Corner stage

Setting the stage in a corner of the room creates, broadly speaking, a 90° arc arrangement with the audience set on two sides of the acting area. Philosophically, and geometrically, the layout is set between an end-stage and an amphitheatre. While there is an enhanced degree of encirclement with the audience embracing the front edge of the stage, the performance itself takes place against the stage walls or some form of scenic backdrop.

When supported by a flytower and appropriately planned upstage wing space, this arrangement retains a high degree of scenic potential. However, staging and set design are limited by the extreme side seats and their lateral sightlines. In contrast to proscenium and end stage layouts, performers can step forward of the scenic world and out into the audience zone. This can enable both epic and intimate staging – and a more clearly three-dimensional directorial composition. The form can be developed with or without an upper tier.

At larger capacities the format contains a number of inherent challenges. As the seating rows extend outward from the stage, row lengths increase rapidly and spaces can become excessively wide. Whilst an individual seat may not be physically distant from the stage, there can be a loss of aural inclusivity and intelligibility. For those on stage, playing to such a widely arrayed audience it can also prove difficult to establish a strong focus on stage, although the use of side boxes or raised tiers can help to address this shortcoming. The inherent scale in larger auditoria means they are more suited to epic theatre, while the most successful examples of the format tend to be fairly modest in scale – or when used for lecture theatres.

Figure 5.3.5 Olivier Theatre at the National Theatre, London. Large-scale multi-level auditorium with a corner stage and flytower.

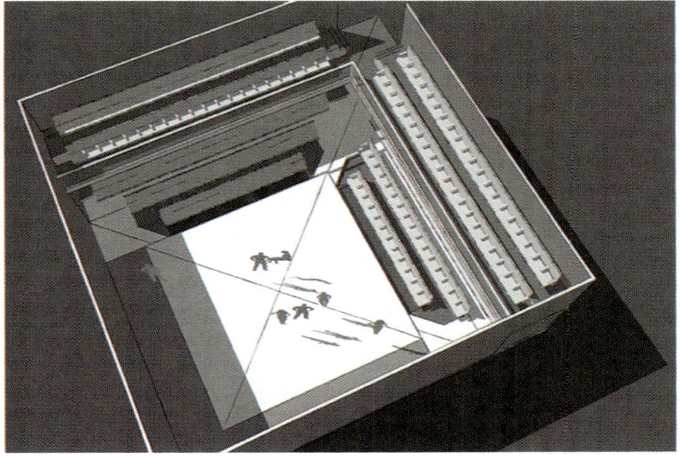

Figure 5.3.6 Corner stage format sketch. Audience contained within a 90° arc.

## A director's view

> The Olivier auditorium at the National Theatre is a singular room, unlike any other. In one sense it is Greek, an amphitheatre spanning around the circle of focus, but with a balcony and raised stalls left and right, resulting in a variety of different experiences for the audience. It has almost no wings, limited flying, and the massive drum below the stage, around which the whole of the National Theatre is constructed. As a consequence – and certainly more than any other space I've worked in – your sense of staging in the rehearsal room can be utterly unreliable. Everything must be remade when you get in there, and the consequent humiliation it can hand out is often brutal. But if you can accept and then tame it, it is a beautiful and very humane arena. Everyone can see the floor, so the actor is framed by both heaven and earth, and combined with the thrust, the whole creates a profound relationship between person and god – whatever that means. Conscience, aspiration, dreams and fears demand a confident hand in staging and framing, it eats story like no other theatre, and at its best is an electrically democratic playhouse.
>
> Rufus Norris, Artistic Director and Joint Chief Executive, National Theatre

**Example auditoria**

- The Olivier, National Theatre, London, UK
- Karolinska Institute, Stockholm, Sweden
- Live Theatre, Newcastle, UK

## The wide fan

Extending the encirclement of the stage by the audience to around 135° brings to the fore the idea of the actor's 'point of command'. This theory was strongly espoused by Sir Peter Hall and John Bury during the development of the Barbican Theatre in London in the late 1970s. It works on the principle that there should be a position, approximately 2.5m back from the leading edge of the stage, from which an actor can command the attention of the entire audience, without the need to turn the head.

Increasing the width of the seating plan and pushing the stage forward can increase the sense of visual immediacy – but does so at the potential expense of visual and aural intimacy. The width of the audience seating and stage can be daunting, whilst achieving a balance between a great battle scene and a more intimate moment can be problematic.

In practical terms the degree of wrap-around means that at any given time some actors are facing away from large sections of the audience. Allied to this, the extreme side sightlines limit the amount of stage setting that can be viewed by the audience as a whole.

**Example auditoria**

- Barbican Theatre, London, UK
- Theatre, Warwick Arts Centre, UK

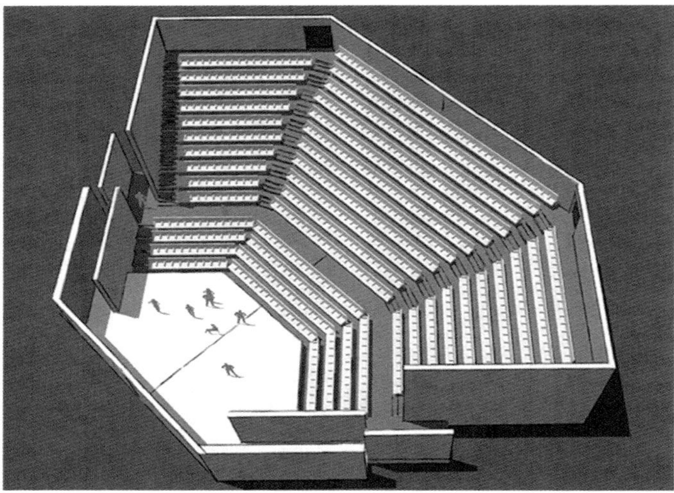

Figure 5.3.7 Wide fan format sketch. Audience wrapped around the stage to achieve 135° of enclosure.

## Amphitheatre

The Greek amphitheatre wrapped its audience around a central stage. The degree of encirclement extended to 220°. Carved into the landscape, these spaces were open to the sky.

Whilst Roman arenas fully encircled a central stage, their amphitheatres were also semi-circular in form, giving 180° encirclement. Here, whilst the seating block was geometrically focused on the semi-circular 'orchestra', the action took place on the 'proscenium' a linear strip running across the back of the semi-circle. A multi-storey architectural stone façade created a permanent backdrop.

The format is still in contemporary use in, for example, large-scale music venues and for external performance spaces – with 'amphitheatre' also used as a generic term for an outdoor venue.

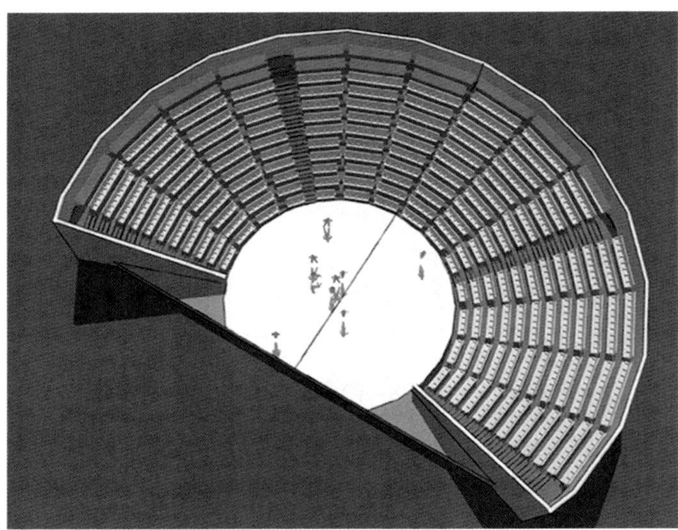

Figure 5.3.8 Amphitheatre format sketch. Audience wrapped around the stage to achieve 220° of enclosure.

**Example auditoria**

- Park Krasnodar Amphitheatre, Krasnodar, Russia
- Katara Cultural Village, Doha, Qatar
- 3Arena (formerly The $O_2$), Dublin, Ireland

## Thrust stage

The next step towards achieving enhanced theatrical intimacy is the thrust-stage – where the audience is positioned around three sides of the acting area. For a pure thrust-stage the audience members are equally distributed with the group on one side providing a backdrop to the action for those seated opposite. Large scenic elements are limited to the back wall.

Performers enter from the rear of the stage or through the body of the audience. The audience sees the performance from a range of differing perspectives. Performance style is three dimensional to ensure that no 'side' misses the action. The degree of envelopment around the stage edge ensures that a high degree of immediacy can be achieved for audiences of up to one-thousand seats.

The format is often associated with single, fairly steeply raked spaces – and audience disposition can be more irregularly balanced. Larger capacities have shallower rakes. There are also two-level auditoria, such as the Liverpool Everyman theatre – alongside galleried spaces like the Royal Shakespeare Theatre (see Reference Project 26).

The resurgence of interest in this format can largely be attributed to theatre director Tyrone Guthrie. His ground-breaking theatre in Minneapolis inspired a generation of theatre practitioners – and theatre builders.

## A director's view

A contemporary of Shakespeare's described watching an actor in the centre of a circle of ears – that's a great description of an audience gathered together experiencing live theatre. The thrust stages of the Swan and Royal Shakespeare Theatres in Stratford-upon-Avon are perfect for Shakespeare. Instead of pushing the audience back into the dark, they insist on them being part of the action. As an audience member you can't sit back and hide, or snooze, you are being addressed, included and involved. The course of the action depends on you.

The penny dropped for me when I worked with the then Artistic Director Terry Hands, rehearsing the scene in Juliet's bedchamber, when she is about to swallow the potion the Friar has given her. Rather than quietly ruminating to herself 'What if it be a poison, which the Friar,/ Subtly hath minister'd to have me dead?' Terry wanted the line opened to the occupants of the galleried space – 'your friends, your sounding board, your confidants. Ask them'. The actress tried it again, talking directly to us, with urgency, really asking the question. What if it's really deadly poison she's about to drink? And suddenly, it was edge of the seat stuff. Rather than passively observing, I felt part of her frightening dilemma, complicit perhaps, implicated even. That's what a thrust stage allows, immediate, unfiltered connection.

Gregory Doran, Artistic Director,
Royal Shakespeare Company

## A director's view

We never questioned the choice of a thrust-stage for the signature configuration of the new Everyman Theatre. It was the defining personality of the much-loved old theatre. However, we did interrogate improvement of sightlines, greater flexibility, fully integrated disabled access and inclusion of a circle. At 400 seats the Everyman has a magical ability to be both epic and intimate, essential for us as our programme ranges from fledgling plays for two actors to full-blown musicals and Shakespearean productions. Maintaining the grid close to the stage kept the space feeling snug and in scale. With the audience wrapped around stage this combined to create this fabulous allusion of epic intimacy. It really is a kind of magic.

Gemma Bodinetz, former Artistic Director,
Liverpool Everyman and Playhouse

Figure 5.3.9 Liverpool Everyman Theatre. Creating theatrical immediacy, the audience envelops the acting area.

**Example auditoria**

- Royal Shakespeare Theatre, Stratford Upon Avon, UK (see Reference Project 27)
- Everyman Theatre, Liverpool, UK (see Reference Project 17)
- Tara Theatre, London, UK (see Reference Project 12)

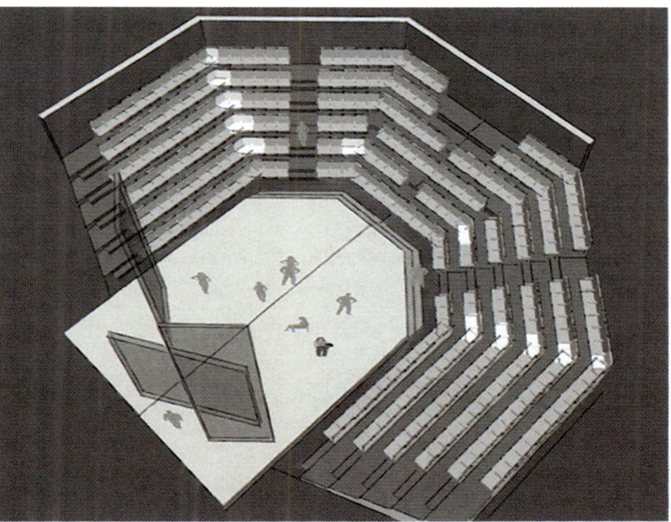

Figure 5.3.10 Thrust stage format sketch. Audience arranged equally on three sides of the stage.

## In-the-round

As the name implies, this format places the performance in the centre of the room with the audience encircling the action. The 360° wrapping of the audience around the stage is also occasionally referred to as an island stage (particularly when there is a stage riser), arena or centre stage format. There is no scenic backdrop and sets and props have to be fairly minimal to ensure the actors remain in view from any angle. Performers enter through the body of the audience, often sharing entry routes.

Historical precedent for the format can be found in spaces designed for activities not reliant on scenic backdrops such as circus. To a degree, a lineage can also be traced in the informal and impromptu use of galleried spaces such as the yards of the medieval inn.

At the smaller scale, in spaces such as the Orange Tree in Richmond upon Thames, the format can be astonishingly intense and demanding for both actors and audience. Spaces can be single-rake or multi-level, and volumes can vary considerably with the single-rake format tending to lead to a fairly large volume.

The Stephen Joseph Theatre in Scarborough is a good model of a single, steeply raked arrangement. The Royal Exchange Theatre in Manchester is a successful multi-level space, surprisingly compact for the format and providing a strong sense of focus.

## A director's view

The Module at the Royal Exchange is a metallic and glass, three-levelled, in-the-round, arena. It holds both the epic and the intimate, and when making work for this space, both have to be considered. Huge ideas, ambitious theatricality and bold production values can be achieved, but also the simple act of a human being standing on their own and bearing their soul to a gathered crowd, can make hearts beat faster. It's a space that you have to respect and listen to, but at the same time take on and grapple with fearlessly. It requires a degree of bravery for everyone involved, including the audience, as quite simply, there is nowhere to hide. Every muscle, every breath, every utterance is witnessed in a 360° perspective, and it is impossible to see a performance in there without simultaneously watching other people watch it! It is a truly communal and immersive experience and the exchange of energy, atmosphere and ideas is unique every night as a new community is assembled. You know when a production is flying in there by the collective lean-in that happens across the three levels when audiences instinctively pull themselves closer to the action.

While it can feel like a gladiatorial environment, it is also an absolute playground and the intimacy, liveness and sheer energy generated, keeps creative teams, actors and audiences on their toes. I have found that once you work in this space, you crave to do so again and to get closer to understanding the nuances, the sweet spots and the opportunities that this most unique of stages presents.

Bryony Shanahan, Artistic Director,
Manchester Royal Exchange Theatre

### Example auditoria

- Stephen Joseph Theatre, Scarborough, North Yorkshire, UK

Figure 5.3.11 Round Theatre, Steppenwolf. Stage in the centre of the room, audience provide the backdrop to the performance.

Figure 5.3.12 Theatre in-the-round format sketch. Audience arranged equally on all four sides of the stage.

- Royal Exchange Theatre, Manchester, UK
- Round Theatre, Steppenwolf, Chicago, USA

## Courtyard theatre

Alongside the exploration of differing degrees of encirclement, theatre directors and designers in the latter part of the twentieth century also looked to historical theatre formats which also engendered greater interaction and theatrical intimacy.

The theatre-model of the English Renaissance, the format that held the work of Shakespeare and his contemporaries, was compact, multi-levelled and open to the sky. The discovery of the Rose Theatre in London's Bankside greatly increased the knowledge and understanding of these buildings. The stage was thrust well out into the auditorium, with the two or three levels of shallow audience galleries providing a high degree of encirclement often in a broadly circular form. The stalls audience stood. The architectural form of the space extended behind the stage to provide a permanent setting. Audiences in such spaces were much closer to the action than in classical theatre forms and there would have been a strong sense of audience participation and involvement with the live event. Visitors to the reconstruction of Shakespeare's Globe in Southwark can gain a genuine sense of how exhilarating these original multi-levelled venues would have been.

The 'courtyard theatre' is a comparatively modern term. Whilst having strong parallels with the Elizabethan stage, the form also derives from the English late-seventeenth- and eighteenth-century playhouse. These spaces were multi-level and, as the modern name implies, often rectangular in form. The action of the play took place on what we would now describe as an extended forestage. Behind this was the scenic zone with suspension and stage machinery. Unlike the Elizabethan model the stage was directly flanked by the parallel side galleries and boxes. Side doors also gave actors access directly onto the acting area.

Performance spaces such as the Cottesloe (now known as the Dorfman Theatre) and the Tricycle Theatre in Kilburn, both in London, helped to re-establish interest in the courtyard format. While the Swan Theatre in Stratford-upon-Avon, which is strictly speaking a thrust-stage, is also a deceptively refined synthesis of the courtyard and Elizabethan models.

Contemporary courtyard theatre are often highly adaptable spaces and can host a range of different performance configurations. It is a favoured format for smaller-scale studio venues.

Figure 5.3.13 Courtyard Theatre, Hereford, UK. Rectilinear galleried auditorium.

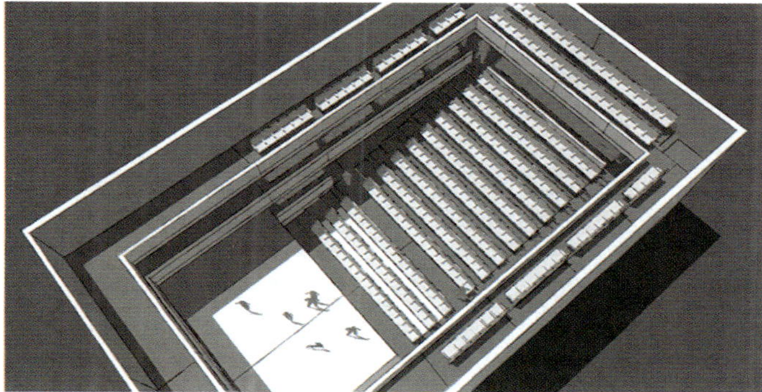

Figure 5.3.14 Courtyard theatre format sketch. Central body of seating supported by multi-level side galleries, lining the walls with people.

## A theatre designer's view

I was a thirty-year-old producer, and co-founder of the Prospect Theatre Company, when in 1963 we presented the first play for 100 years at the Georgian Theatre, Richmond – Vanbrugh's *The Provok'd Wife*. Eileen Atkins took the title role and, in her autobiography, she recalls that 'Restoration comedy is notoriously difficult, but once we were inside this beautiful little Georgian theatre we knew exactly how to play it'. We then transferred to the West End where it flopped in the dreary cinema-like, fully frontal auditorium. The place had turned out to be as much the thing as the play itself.

This Georgian experience was the prime influence in the design of the Cottesloe Theatre some ten years later, when working with Sir Peter Hall. The label courtyard which I attached to this format of theatre space stuck. For me, such spaces continue to ask the big questions: how does the designer of theatres interface with the makers of the live experience – the actors, directors, set-designers and audience? How does a space inform the work created? How do you address the paradox that good theatres have some seats with bad sightlines, while those with universally good sightlines are bad theatres? Can the lessons learnt by designers successfully reinvigorating our great old theatres be channeled into the creation of contemporary flexible spaces with capacities which, while making economic sense, also offer that fundamental quality of theatrical intimacy?

Iain Mackintosh, Producer and Designer of Theatre Space

### Example auditoria

- Dorfman, National Theatre, London, UK (see Reference Project 16)
- Channing School Theatre, Highgate, UK

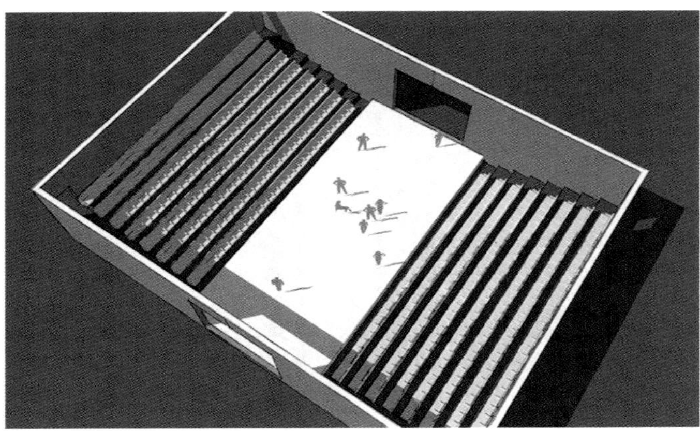

Figure 5.3.15 Traverse stage format sketch. Audience set on two sides of the action – facing one-another.

## Other configurations

A variety of other less routinely used formats draw inspiration from earlier public and theatrical events, where a performance might take the form of a street procession or were informally centred within the yard of an inn or market square.

### Traverse

The traverse format places the stage as a linear performance platform down the centre of the room with the audience arranged in equal blocks on either side. The audience watches the performance with other members of the audience as the backdrop. Scenic potential is minimal with larger elements restricted to either end of the space.

Although permanent traverse stage auditoria are rare, built examples do exist, the National Theatre in Mannheim being an example. The format is more generally associated with small to medium-scale adaptable venues, with the staging arrangement one of a range of potential formats. One of the more recent, and spectacular, productions in this format was York Theatre Royal's production of *The Railway Children*, which used a rail line and station platforms to create a temporary large-scale traverse stage – complete with a real steam engine.

### Promenade

In a promenade performance the choreography of the standing audience forms an inherent part of the work itself. The relationship between actor and audience is continually changing as the audience follows the performance around the space – the opposite of an audience sitting passively in its seats.

This style of production experienced a major revival in the 1970s with ground-breaking productions such as *The Mysteries* at the National Theatre in London and *The Ship*, a site-specific piece, at the McGovern shipyard in Glasgow. A new-generation of immersive theatre was founded in productions like those of De La Guarda, the Argentinian theatre-collective, in the late 1990s. This work and subsequent productions, such as *Fuerza Bruta*, which re-opened London's Roundhouse, and Nicholas Hytner's production of *A Midsummer Night's Dream* at the Bridge Theatre, reach out and engage younger audiences seeking immersive and participatory experiences.

## Adaptable space

Adaptable auditoria are a type of theatre space, rather than a prescribed performance format. These are spaces designed to operate in more than one performance configuration. Such spaces are split into two broad categories: those that allow a switch between several predetermined formats and those that support a much higher degree of flexibility and variability in use.

Some performance configurations sit comfortably alongside one another allowing a venue to switch between configurations. For example, it is a relatively easy task to create a space than can work between a thrust-stage, in-the-round and traverse-stage formats. However, creating a space that can adapt from a thrust-stage to a true proscenium-theatre format can be more challenging to achieve successfully. The primary issue in uniting these two particular formats is reorienting the focus of the audience.

The Bridge Theatre in London is a good example of a highly adaptable, multi-format, contemporary performance space – designed in part to complement the array of proscenium theatre spaces that characterise London's West End theatre district. It has a modular audience stalls and stage floor, adaptable structural elements and a high level of performance infrastructure flexibility to enable it to support end-stage, thrust-stage and promenade formats. It can also host proscenium productions – but there is a degree of compromise in this. Such a space illustrates the importance of a balanced performance hierarchy in defining what the space does best – and what other configuration it can support. The *circa* 1000 seat capacity of the Bridge Theatre is also an important factor in its success. The venue accommodates 1050 in promenade mode, 950 in end-stage configuration and 900 in thrust-stage layout (see Reference Projects).

This illustrates the importance of defining capacity at an early stage of design development, both artistically and economically, as not all formats can have an equal capacity. There are also practical limits in the scale of re-configuration in terms of suitability, visual ambience and acoustic performance. This is a balance between format, density and how the adaptability is achieved. Consideration needs to be given to the cost of adaptable infrastructure to maximise the return on the investment and the time, ease and resources required to turn a venue around between formats.

Other 'loose-fit' adaptable spaces can be more fully flexible in that they can host a wide variety of performance events and support different configurations. A good example of this in the Dorfman Theatre at the National Theatre in London (see Reference Projects). This space began life as the Cottesloe Theatre and gained an international reputation for its ability to be reinterpreted by different directors and designers – and for the work created as result. This deceptively simple space is a rectilinear galleried auditorium. The underlying geometry and proportions enable the space to work in end-stage, thrust-stage, in-the round, traverse and promenade formats. While the thrust-stage necessitates a degree of compromise – the space is able to support this format in an appropriate setting. At *circa* 400 seats the Dorfman Theatre illustrates that a greater degree of flexibility is easier to achieve in smaller scales. This is primarily as fewer people are being moved around, the component parts are smaller – and the acoustic challenges are less onerous.

For many contemporary theatre practitioners, the ideal theatre space would comprise two large sheds: one full of theatre parts – and an empty one into which different formats could be constructed and deconstructed over time – offering unending flexibility and creative freedom. Venues such as London's Bridge Theatre and Dorfman theatre, alongside St Ann's Warehouse in Brooklyn offer partial and imaginative realisations of this dream. In their physical and aesthetic adaptability these forward-looking spaces support long-term cultural and social sustainability in providing spaces that can vary their format and respond to changing performance imperatives.

An adaptable studio is often a second space within a performing arts complex, enabling a more experimental programme of work to be mounted, complementing the primary venue. This loose-fit format is also often used within the educational environment, where the variability and potential for experimentation are important.

#### Example auditoria

- The Bridge, London, UK (see Reference Project 20)
- Storyhouse, Chester, UK (see Reference Project 06)
- Dorfman, National Theatre, London (see Reference Project 16)
- St Ann's Warehouse, Brooklyn, USA (see Reference Project 04)

Figure 5.3.16 Bridge Theatre, London, UK. Multi-format adaptable performance venue.

## Found space

The idea of found space needs to be touched upon as a concluding part of this overall sequence. This is not as a prescribed configuration or auditorium format though the term will often surface in conversation as a 'type' of performance venue. Found space refers to a production taking place in a space not designed for the purpose. This can range from redundant buildings through to railway arches and churches – but any space can be used.

Found spaces are often temporary, to host a particular performance or season of work. Once 'found' some spaces can go on to become formalised performance venues. They can also be re-found, or rediscovered, theatres spaces – such as the much-loved Brooklyn Academy of Music's BAM Harvey Theatre (formerly The Majestic) in New York.

The appeal of such spaces is in part the ephemeral nature of their existence as theatres. They also allow a unique creative dialogue for the director and designer as they work with, and respond to, the unique quality and character of a particular building.

As a performance aesthetic and practice, the found-space movement has grown in influence and has had profound impact on the design of many new experimental spaces, both in terms of physical and philosophical adaptability – and also ideas of aesthetic neutrality.

#### Example auditoria

- Roundhouse Camden, London, UK
- Bouffes du Nord, Paris, France (see Strong (ed.), *Theatre Buildings* (2010), Reference Projects, pp. 198–201)
- Grand Hall, Battersea Arts Centre, London, UK (see Reference Project 25)

Figure 5.3.17 The Southwark Playhouse temporary venue, London, UK. Set within a vaulted brick railway viaduct.

## 5.4 Positioning the audience

### The experience

The sense of participating in a shared experience is one of the key factors in live theatre, where audience reaction impacts on the performance and there is a two-way transference of energy. From an actor's point of view the audience are a community of people so it is important that the audience is cohesive and does not appear overly segregated or dispersed. In larger auditoria side boxes, or galleries, can assist the performer in providing a direct link out and upward to seating tiers. From an audience perspective such devices can help lead the eye down to the scale of the stage. Side seating also serves to unite the levels of audience who otherwise may not be aware of one another, critically enhancing the sense of audience cohesion.

### Sectional considerations

The primary objective in the design of an auditorium is to bring as many people as close as possible to the performance area. This has to be done within optimum viewing and aural limitations. An understanding of historical precedent and development can be invaluable in knowing how best to arrange an audience.

As outlined in the discussion on formats, one way of increasing the numbers of people with proximity to the stage is to increase the degree of envelopment. An alternative strategy is to add levels or tiers enabling a greater number of seats to be accommodated without increasing the distance between the stage and those seated furthest away.

The different levels of an auditorium have held a profusion of names over time: at or below stage level the audience is referred to as the stalls, orchestra stalls, parterre or pit; one level above the stage they can be referred to as the first circle, dress circle, royal circle or grand tier; the audience located two levels and above from the stage can be referred to as upper circle, balcony, gallery or 'gods' and the shallow side rows as slips. These names have historically served to convey the cultural context, level of luxury and prestige – and the extent of social segregation.

The complexity involved in designing multi-level spaces comes in balancing sightline requirements to achieve good standards throughout the auditorium. The theoretical angle of rake in the stalls needs to be reduced to ensure that upper tiers are not pushed up too high or that their rakes become too steep. The rake of an upper tier is determined by visibility of the stage front and by regulations. The impact on upward sightlines from rear rows also needs to be considered. A qualitative balance needs to be sought as tiers set too close together can create the effect known as a 'letter-box' – where the stage is viewed through a narrow slot between two seating levels.

For some types of performance several shallower tiers can be more effective than one or two deeper ones. This is a defining characteristic of the traditional European opera house, where shallow tiers, in line with one another, wrap around a gently raked parterre. These tiers were generally subdivided into separate boxes (in part reflecting the way the buildings were funded), with divisions radiating from the centre of the stage. Generally, such boxes allowed two rows of seats. The small group of audience, particularly those in the sides could improve oblique views by leaning forward onto the balcony rail – without disrupting the view for others. With the removals of the box division an extra row or two could be added. However, restricted ceiling heights limit the degree of elevation of these rows.

The sale of individual boxes and loges, combined with structural limitations, had a significant effect on the development of the opera house form. Commercial imperatives also had a profound influence on the configuration of the nineteenth century theatre. In order to fit in as many paying customers as possible, tiers facing the stage became deeper. Structural developments (such as the cantilever) enabled upper tiers to be stepped back in order to maximise sightlines. Side boxes and slips remained as the oblique angles restricted the depth of any overhang.

In the early twentieth century auditoria design was also influenced by the emergence of cinema and the requirements of spaces that supported both variety performance and film presentation. In such spaces, oblique side views of the screen were unacceptable. Auditoria became simplified with a stalls and circle only – often almost as visually separate spaces within a single volume.

When in live performance mode, or when such ideas were transposed into theatres, many lacked the fundamental sense of theatrical intimacy and audience cohesion.

In contemporary auditoria the section is still largely determined by sightlines; however, the depth of overhang is heavily informed by acoustic parameters. Spaces reliant on a natural acoustic require shallower overhangs. A good rule of thumb is to limit the depth of the overhang to the vertical clear height between the tiers themselves. In spaces supported by amplified sound the overhang can be deeper.

Determining the geometry of the auditorium and critically the sectional composition must begin early in the design process. Sightline and acoustic parameters provide key criteria that cannot be easily adapted or adjusted. It should be the auditorium's sectional arrangement that determine audience entry points and the primary floor level in adjacent spaces in the public areas.

## Seating layout

The following commentary is in part based upon the *ABTT Technical Standards for Places of Entertainment* and British Standard BS 9999, *Code of practice for fire safety in the design, management and use of buildings*, Annex D. While non-UK authorities will adopt their own regulatory requirements, BS 9999 and the ABTT *Technical Standards* provide a robust basis upon which to plan international projects. However, while acknowledging that different regions will have their own particular standards, the following sets out good-practice guidance alongside the minimum requirements.

## Useful dimension data

- The minimum back-to-back dimension between rows of seats with backs is 760mm. Such spacing should only really be used when working within the constraints of historically important building fabric. In new-build spaces a good practice minimum for contemporary audiences is between 850-875mm.
- The minimum width of seats with arms is 500mm centre of arm to centre of arm. A good practice minimum for contemporary audiences is between 525–550mm.
- The minimum width of seats without arms (individual seats or benches) is 450mm. A good practice minimum is 500mm.
- The unobstructed vertical space between rows is known as the seatway or clearway. The minimum dimensions vary depending upon the length and access to the row. See detailed table at Figure 5.4.1.

| Number of seats in a row | | |
|---|---|---|
| Seatway width mm | Maximum number of seats in a row | |
| | Gangway on one side | Gangway on two sides |
| 300 to 324 | 7 | 14 |
| 325 to 349 | 8 | 16 |
| 350 to 374 | 9 | 18 |
| 375 to 399 | 10 | 20 |
| 400 to 424 | 11 | 22 |
| 425 to 449 | 12 | 24 |
| 450 to 474 | 12 | 26 |
| 475 to 499 | 12 | 28 |
| 500 and more | 12 | Limited by travel distance to place of safety |

Figure 5.4.1 Simplified table based on D1 from the *British Standard BS 9999* (2008). This illustrates the clear seatway required for the number of seats in a row.

- Distance from seat to gangway is now more normally associated with number of seats in row (assuming typical seat width in the order of 500–550mm).
- Row lengths exceeding 28 seats are sometimes referred to as 'continental' seating.
- In a UK setting the minimum unobstructed aisle width is 1,100mm. (Note, as with escape staircases the handrails can project into this minimum zone). Internationally, this minimum varies both from a regulatory perspective and culture preference.

## Seating and seatways

Achieving the right balance between comfort, safety and commercial imperatives requires careful consideration in both new build and refurbishment projects.

Seating should ensure the audience's comfort, while keeping them alert. The spacing of seats is key to enjoyment of the visit but must not be so generous that the cohesion of the audience is threatened. Large seats, popular in cinemas, are not appropriate because in theatre it is important to relate to fellow audience members as well as to the actors on stage. One way of doing this is to be aware of other people's presence by sharing an armrest, sitting close on a bench, or seeing them in the peripheral vision.

There are significant cultural and regional sensitivities. Each country has their preferred seat width relating to the anthropometric data of their population. Today, some historic theatres are re-configured so that, in a given floor area, they seat about half the capacity of the original theatre when built. This is not just because people have grown, but more that they require a certain level of personal space, and safety, compared to the crowds who attended variety and music halls a century ago.

## Seat module

Auditorium seating falls into three broad categories; benches (with and without backs), fixed seats, and tip-up seats. Each of these can be with or without arms.

The requirements outlined previously define the minimum. It is not uncommon to find 500-mm module tip-up seats with arms in the commercial theatres. However, subtle distinctions exist between what audiences will accept in an historic theatre environment and what is expected in a new cultural facility. As noted, a good practice module for preliminary planning is a 550-mm seat with a row depth of 900mm.

It is important to establish the seat module early in the design process, taking account of the need to balance individual comfort with the imperatives of keeping the audience compact to retain theatrical intimacy.

## Seatway

The seatway is the unobstructed distance between two rows of seats, with the seat in its closed position if a tip-up type. The previous table outlines how the width of the required seatway rises as the number of seats in the row increases. The clear seat way is primarily focused on means of escape but is equally important in terms of access. The longer the row the more people will have to pass one another within the row and the wider the seatway the easier this is. A seatway of 500mm clear, normally associated with continental seating, allows audience members to pass by without needing seated members to rise.

Seat design has evolved rapidly. Greater comfort can now be achieved in more compact seats, with flatter (less heavily profiled) backs. This can radically alter the dimension when closed, enhancing the seat way. Such seats are particularly useful when reseating existing tiers.

## Extended row length

The term continental seating is used in the United Kingdom for longer seating rows – exceeding 28 seats. In the longer rows, the seatway is set at 500 mm, with limiting factor for the number of seats defined by the travel distance to a place of safety. Consideration also needs to be given to the width of side aisles due to the greater concentration of people using each aisle.

Longer rows have pros and cons. None of the best viewing positions are lost by having a central aisle and, for the actor, the audience is undivided. As row depths need to be wider, audiences have increased leg room. Whilst seats are gained where there would have been aisles, some are lost due to wider row spacing. Continental seating is therefore not necessarily a method for achieving more seats. However, hybrid layouts mixing longer rows at the front of a stalls with traditional seating arrangements behind can be very helpful in creating a strong sense of focus.

## Accessible seating

Within an auditorium wheelchair users, and those with mobility or sensory impairment, may need to view or listen or see interpreters from a particular side. They should be provided with spaces into which they can manoeuvre easily, and which offer a clear view of an event, whilst ensuring they are not segregated. Wheelchair users and people who have difficulty in using seats with fixed arms should also have the choice of sitting next to a conventionally seated person or a companion to the wheelchair user. By having some removable seating at the front and back of seating blocks, or within a cross-over aisle location, a greater flexibility in location can be achieved above the minimum requirements. Wheelchair users often sit slightly higher than those seated in conventional auditorium chairs and this needs to be factored into layouts.

A wheelchair seating position should allow a 900 × 1400 mm zone for the user. As a minimum, the provision of permanent spaces should be 1% of the audience capacity in larger-scale venues. In smaller-scale venues, under a capacity of 600, 1% of the capacity needs to be composed of permanent positions, with additional flexible spaces to achieve a minimum of six spaces in total. Where possible seating options should be provided at all main levels – although in re-working historic venues provision may be limited by access and egress constraints.

## Means of escape

Individual regions will have their own regulatory requirements. UK guidance on the distance from a seat to a place of safety for means of escape is set out in BS 9999. A maximum travel distance of 15m in one direction is permissible, with 32m as a limit, when escape is possible in two directions (of which only 15m can be in any one direction).

A minimum of two escape routes is required for an audience or tier of up to 600, and three routes minimum for above this figure. The escape route needs to lead either directly to a final exit – or to an exit via a protected route/space. Escapes should be equally distributed around the edge of the space, ensuring that an audience member can turn their back on a fire.

The width of escape routes is dictated by the numbers of people exiting and as outlined in documents such as BS

9999. The clear width is measured at its minimum point – which is often the clear opening width of a door-set, not the corridor. Within the auditorium circulation should be designed to ensure the smooth flow of people, particularly if radial and traverse aisles intersect. Aisles should remain a constant width, with seat edges in line; however, they may get wider in the direction of escape.

### Balcony/tier front design

The height of the balcony front guarding in front of fixed seating should be a minimum of 790mm from the floor of the first row. This can be reduced to 750mm if the top profile has a minimum width of 230mm.

The detailed design of the balcony front needs to take account of a number of factors. The upper element is often referred to as a 'rester rail'. This is a slight misnomer, as the audience should not be encouraged to lean on or over the tier front – and it should not be used for placing items such as coats, programmes and drinks. Canting the top profile back towards the seat discourages incorrect use and reduces the likelihood of items falling on the audience below.

The higher, narrower guarding, say a 50mm diameter rail, pulled as close to the seated audience member as the seatway will allow, can negate the need to lean forward. Additional toe space should also be allowed for in the front row of tier.

A full guard rail must be provided at the end of a stepped gangway, for the full width of the gangway. This must be 1,100mm high. Consideration needs to be given to the impact of such rails on lateral sightlines.

### Wayfinding

Legibility of circulation needs to be supported by clear wayfinding signage. Enabling patrons to get to and from seat easily aids operational efficiency and the quality of the audience experience. Signage needs to be both legible in terms of scale and contrast – and work with the building aesthetic. Illuminated signage assists in larger-scale venues and denoting key routes. (See the discussion of front-of-house wayfinding and signage in Section 4.)

## 5.5 Sightlines

### Viewing requirements

Giving members of an audience a good view of the performance is an obvious starting point in the design of an auditorium. That said, sightline imperatives have evolved over time, so it is therefore important to understand what is meant by 'good' sightlines as part of the overall qualitative experience.

Throughout the seventeenth, eighteenth and nineteenth centuries attending a theatrical performance was, for many, as much about being seen as seeing. The side boxes of the proscenium theatres of the period offered a relatively inferior view of the stage. However, they enabled ample opportunity for public display. To some degree, the restricted view was offset by the proximity to performers delivering major speeches and arias downstage – in a time before amplification.

The development of sophisticated cantilevered structures in the nineteenth century brought new opportunities to auditorium design. Column free tiers reduced restricted lateral sightlines. Creating spaces for ever larger audiences, specialist theatre architects of the day responded by pushing sightline design to the limits. Auditorium tiers sometimes stacked four high, developed highly complex three-dimensional geometries.

With the advent of the Modern movement in architecture and design in the early twentieth century, technological advancement was mirrored with rapidly changing social conditions. Auditorium design broke away from the highly segregated and hierarchical forms of earlier centuries. In attempting to democratise the auditorium, sightlines became a key tool.

This pursuit of sightlines equality had the effect of gradually pushing the audiences further away from the stage. As a consequence, the auditorium models that emerged in the latter part of the twentieth century began to reconsider the importance of a sense of envelopment in live performance. The thrust-stage movement achieved this through a reduction in scenic demands, whilst the courtyard-format focused on compact three-dimensional intimacy and audience cohesion.

The viewing criteria up to the early part of the twentieth century were dictated by the sightlines required to see a performer standing on the stage. Auditoria were generally designed for a single use. A contemporary auditorium, by comparison, may host an opera one night, drama to the next and dance the following evening. Audience's expectations for viewing opera are less demanding than say for dance, where it is important to see a dancer's feet on the setting line on the stage floor – and all four corners of the stage space. In some auditoria variations in format may radically shift the focus, whilst more experiential and immersive performance has increased the importance of the vertical and upward sightline.

The sightline criteria need to be established by the auditorium designer, defining how much of the stage floor, back and sides of the acting area must be seen. From this starting point it is possible to develop the geometrical volume within which the required number of seats can be contained. The seating rakes, disposition of audience members, and integration of tiers or balconies are all determined by acceptable visual limits and the lateral and vertical parameters for viewing the performance.

The methodology set out subsequently is a 2D guide to the basic geometrical sightline criteria. It should provide a robust basis upon which to establish an initial design. 3D modelling and interactive modelling of sightlines can then explore more complex sightline issue and be invaluable in helping to explain and guide clients through the development of the viewing criteria.

## Establishing the stalls rake

To develop the vertical, downward sightline in a conventional theatre stalls a number of key points need to be established.

***P: Point of sight***

This is the lowest point to be clearly visible on the stage or acting area. Its position can vary both vertically and horizontally. The stage can be a flat floor or a riser varying from 300–1,100mm. Point P can be located on the leading edge or on the setting line (approx. 1.0m back from the proscenium).

Point P may also have to take account of a variable stage edge – or forestage. For dance, audiences need to see the performer's feet. Point P is therefore set at the stage floor – and normally on the setting line. (Added to the restrictions on lateral sightlines this factor contributes to giving dance the most onerous sightline criteria). For some drama configurations, P can be raised up to around +300mm from the stage datum, but this needs to be evaluated in the context of the scale of the space and size of the stage riser.

It is critical that the criteria for determining the position of point P are clearly defined by the auditorium designer and clearly understood by the user. See Figures 5.5.1 and 5.5.2.

***HD: Horizontal distance***

This is horizontal linear distance between the eye positions of the audience members in consecutive rows. The dimension normally equates to the row dimensions.

***O: Offset***

Whilst HD is determined by the back-to-back dimensions of the individual rows, it does not normally coincide with the tread or risers. In reality the degree of offset from the riser is determined by the design of the seat. For early planning, 100mm offset allows for an assumption of the eye position in relation to the riser.

When a seat is selected, the detail ergonomics should be refined – particularly in regard to tier front geometries.

***EH: Average eye height***

A theoretical working height of 1,120mm is normally assumed.

***TH: Top of head***

Distance taken from the centre line of eye to the top of the head – normally 100mm for the basis of the sightline calculation.

***D: Distance front row eye position to point P***

The closer this distance, the steeper the resultant rake will be.

Using this guidance, working from point P back through the auditorium establishes the theoretical rake of the stalls seating. This gives a parabolic curve to the seating profile, getting steeper as the distance from point P increases. Each member of the audience achieves a similar viewing condition.

Whilst licensing authorities do allow parabolic floor profiles with an incremental increase in the risers in stepped aisles, larger rakes are often reduced to a series of angled sections.

For theatrical formats and dance use, the theoretical rake as described can lead to a fairly steep profile. Whilst acceptable in smaller-scale and single-level spaces, this can be problematic in larger venues with bigger capacities and where upper tiers of seating are introduced.

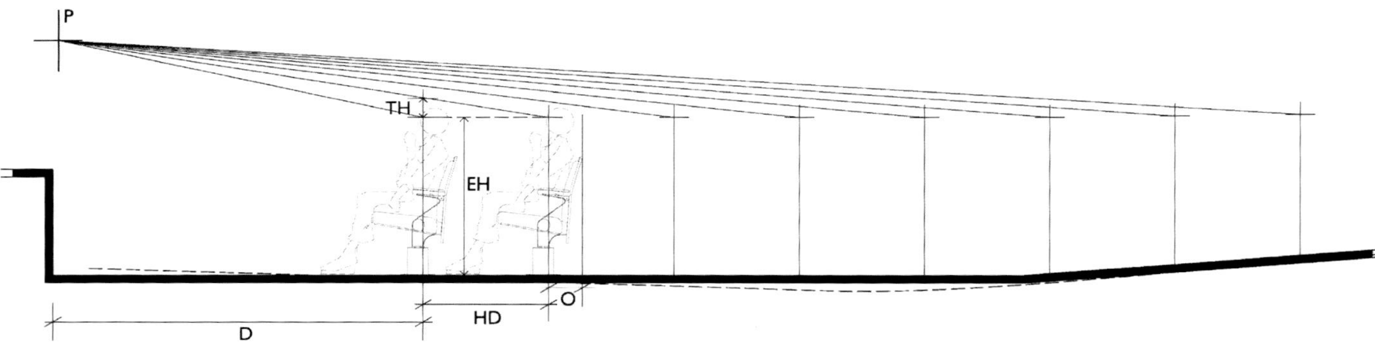


Figure 5.5.1 Vertical sightline with a high-level viewing point (P).

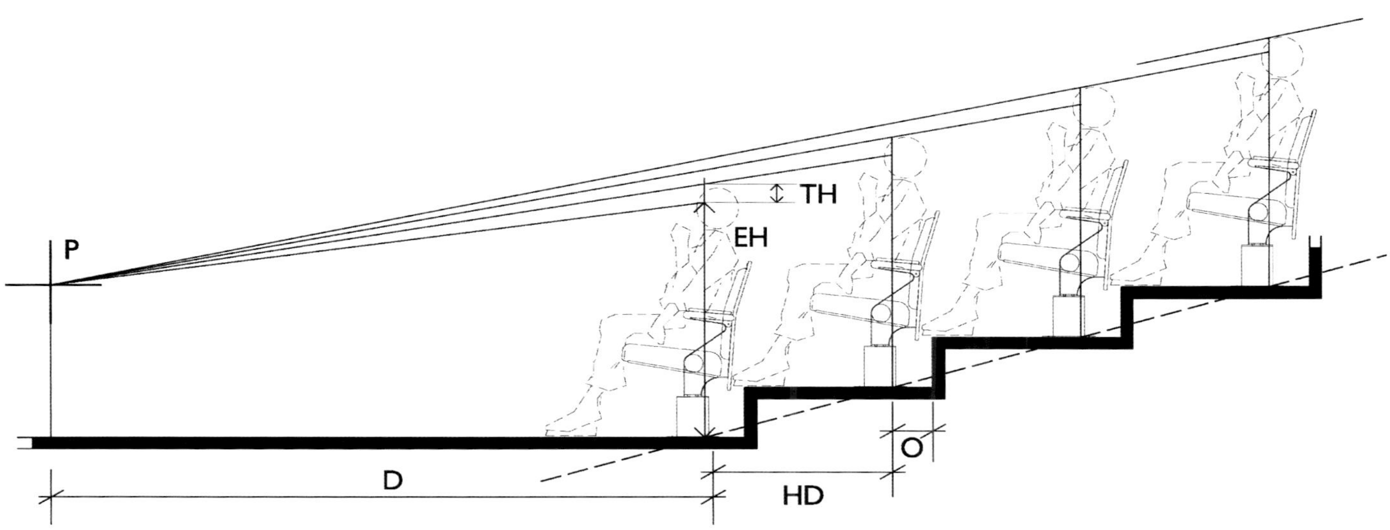


Figure 5.5.2 Vertical sightline with a low-level viewing point (P).

## The view between the heads

To reduce the degree of rake in the stalls the seating can be arranged in a staggered layout, with individual seats offset from the one immediately in front. Point P is effectively seen between heads. Sightlines on this basis can be developed graphically or with an assumption of distance between the eye line and the top of the head reduced to 65mm.

When working with between-heads sightline criteria it should be on a basis that the seating is set in a staggered/offset arrangement. (See Figure 5.5.3.) This is normally established on the auditorium centre line. As the rows extend to the side, particularly in curved auditoria, seats invariably come into line again; however, audiences to the side of the auditoria are more likely to be looking diagonally towards the stage.

Figure 5.5.3 The view between heads looking directly to the stage.

Refining the sightline in this manner illustrates the balancing of requirements necessary in the development of larger auditoria. Here visual and aural imperatives have to be considered alongside the degree of elevation of the audience in relation to the stage (from the actor's point of view) and average height and volume. Reduction in the height of the rake at lower levels leaves more room to accommodate upper balconies.

## Performer's perspective

In small auditoria, particularly where a limited number of rows encircle or embrace the stage, a steeper rake can be helpful in offering both a sense of enclosure and good sightlines. This should be balanced with the subjective view that it is preferable for a performer to have half the audience below their standing eye line.

## Upper tiers

The criteria for upper seating levels are fundamentally the same as in the stalls – with seated audiences needing to see the full three-dimensional performance. Allied to the vertical downward sightline is the upper sightline, which, for example, allows the rear row of the stalls to have an uninterrupted view of the top of the proscenium. (See Figure 5.5.4.)

### *P2: Point of sight*

As described, Point P2 is the lowest and nearest point that a balcony audience member needs be able to see. This can be the same as the position for the stalls' audience – on the

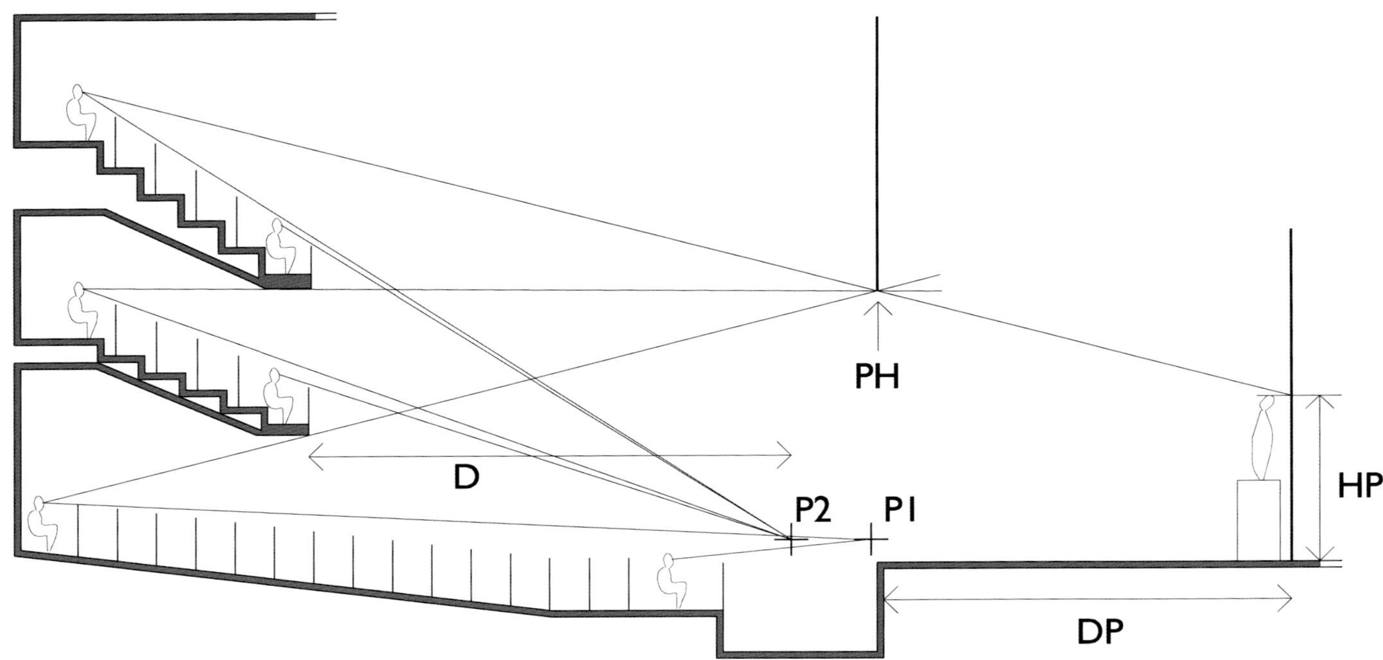


Figure 5.5.4 Section showing the vertical viewing parameters within a multi-level space.

leading edge of the stage or the setting line. It can also be different to the stalls, hence the suffix, and be out into the auditorium for a forestage extension, a view of the conductor in a pit or within the stalls seating, enabling upper levels to be aware of other audience members (contributing to a sense of audience cohesion).

***DP: Depth of the stage***
This is the working depth of the stage or normal acting area.

***HP: Clear visible height***
This is the clear height to be visible at the back wall of the stage or back of the performance area. This requirement can vary, and this height is a subjective one and needs to be developed with the client.

***PH: Proscenium height***
This is the height of the proscenium opening or the upper defined limit in an open stage space. Note: the panel above the proscenium may be used to provide surtitles.

***BF: Balcony front height***
For the sake of calculation 790mm should be assumed but take cognisance of any requirements for raised 1,100mm rails at aisles intersections.

***D: Distance to front row***
Distance from Point P2 to the front row.

## Sightlines across lateral gangways

Lateral gangways can be problematic for sightlines. It is good practice to ensure that the vertical rake continues uninterrupted, taking account of the wider width of the gangway aisle.

## Horizontal sightlines

Restrictions on horizontal sightlines primarily need to be considered in proscenium theatres, end-stage spaces and platforms for classical music. Given a particular performance area, defined by a proscenium opening, sightline requirements limit the width of the seating block. The view of the proscenium opening cannot be too oblique, or members of the audience will lose too much of the stage from view.

When considering horizontal or lateral sightlines, consideration should be given to reduced proscenium widths for touring shows. Audiences, in unrestricted view seats, should be able to see at least two thirds of the back wall of the acting area, unless the space is primarily for dance where all four corners of the performance area need to be clearly visible.

## Side seats

Side seats can be problematic in the early stages of a design – with the term 'restricted view' being a subjective one. While the seats offer an oblique view of the action, depending upon the format, it should always be remembered that they offer proximity to the performance, enhance theatrical intimacy, contribute to a sense of cohesion, and animate the side walls. The amount of side seats always needs to be balanced as part of the overall provision – with restricted view seats excluded from initial capacity calculations. In the early design stage, it is prudent to exclude side seats from initial seat counts for certain types of space.

## 5.6 Adaptability and flexibility in the auditorium

### Variability

Adaptability is often inherent in the brief for a new performing arts venue. As performance typologies evolved, auditoria became dedicated to single functions: opera house, musical theatre, concert hall and drama theatre. However, it is becoming less common to find new spaces that are designed exclusively for a single purpose. The costs associated with creating these highly serviced, and technically sophisticated, facilities necessitate that they host a wider range of performances. Even in larger arts complexes with complementary auditoria supporting different performance types and scale of event, each auditorium is likely to have its set of adaptable features. Adaptability can range from modest flexibility in one particular area to wholesale re-configuration of the space.

The usual areas where some form of adaptability is introduced are:

- orchestra pit and forestage zone
- adjustable proscenium width and height
- variable audience capacity
- adjustable acoustics
- format change and variable formats
- orchestra pit and forestage.

### Orchestra pit and forestage

The orchestra pit and forestage are perhaps the most common areas of adaptability in auditoria, and one of the most straightforward to achieve. It is associated with proscenium and end stage formats. See Section 6 for a detailed explanation.

### Variable audience capacity

This may be required, for aesthetic or management reasons, to close down the scale of a space for a particular piece of work. At its simplest this can involve closing off an upper tier, or part of a tier, through the use of drapes, screens or lighting. More complex solutions can require the movement of large-scale architectural elements, such as mobile ceilings, fully closing off the upper tier. Any variable capacity arrangement needs to be planned in advance, particularly with regard to entrance and egress routes.

### Adjustable proscenium

To accommodate smaller-scale productions some variability in the proscenium width and height may be required. These can be integral installations or production specific – and are normally located behind the house curtains. Tormentors and teasers, or a show portal, can also be used as a way of varying the proscenium opening. In developing an adjustable proscenium, it is important to consider the lateral sightline constraints of the smallest format.

### Adjustable acoustics

This kind of adaptability is required in spaces that change between music and drama use. For the performance of symphonic music in a natural acoustic setting the volume requirement for the space is in the order $10m^3$ per seat. This requirement drops for musical theatre, amplified music spaces and drama. Changes between music and drama also impact on the degree of diffusion, reflection and absorption required, as well as changes in ambience.

Such adaptability is relatively easy to achieve at the smaller scale of around 300 to 600 seats. The deployment of wool serge drapes can be highly effective in reducing reverberation time and changing the aesthetic tone of the interior. At large scale mobile ceiling elements can radically adjust the physical volume of the space to suit either classical music, lyric theatre or drama. The Sadler's Wells Theatre in London adjusts its reverberation time through the use of concealed absorbent banners.

In spaces primarily designed for drama, or where physical volume may not be attainable, assisted resonance systems can be integrated to create a longer reverberation time.

### Performance hierarchy

The key to creating a successful adaptable auditorium is to develop a clear hierarchy of uses of the space. This hierarchy needs to articulate both the qualitative and quantitative imperatives. When developed correctly it can establish a balance between what a space needs to do best in terms of quality – and what it needs to do best in terms of quantity.

### Components of the adaptable auditorium

Whilst many components (such as large mobile ceiling units) are highly bespoke, there are a number of 'standard components' that help to make up the adaptable venue.

### *Retractable seating unit*

This is a block of retractable raked seating, where each row folds back in on itself to create a compact linear unit when stored. The units can be a manual or electronically operated and turnaround time can be a matter of minutes. They are ideal in spaces where flat floor usage is required for alternative functions or as the basis of other formats. (See Figure 5.6.1.)

Figure 5.6.1a–c City of London School. Small, motorised, retractable seating unit in operation.

### *Rostra*

These are demountable components comprising frames, legs and floor units used to create raked seating or stages. Manufactured in steel or lightweight aluminium they are fairly labour intensive (in their simplest form) and used where a fast turnaround is less critical.

### *Seating wagons*

An alternative way of changing from a raked/stepped stalls, to a flat floor, is the use of seating wagons. These are mobile raked or stepped floor units, complete with seating. Wagons allow large seating blocks to be moved out of the auditorium, as a low-rise alternative to the retractable unit described previously. When not deployed within the auditorium, they are usually moved on the forestage elevator and stored below the front of stalls.

### *Mobile towers*

These multi-level units can contain seating and are moved on floor tracks or castors. Essentially these architectural components are particularly useful in radically remodelling the end stage zone of a space transforming between particular pre-defined configurations.

### *Floor lifts*

These are very similar in operation to the orchestra pit lifts. They can be as simple as a complete stalls floor plate on screw jacks, lowered to facilitate a standing area for pop and rock events. Alternatively, they can be modular panel sections in the form of scissor lifts to create a variety of profiles within the floor zone. One of the most memorable installations of this arrangement is The Schaubuhne in Berlin.

### *Tension wire grid*

A tension wire grid is a fine, open mesh working level, which is often use in adaptable studio venues. It allows production lighting to be rigged and focussed with ease of access. The performance is then lit through the tensioned wire itself. Such grids come into their own when used to match the flexibility at floor level within an auditorium – and where safety, for example in spaces for young people, is a priority.

### *Large acoustic door sets*

These allow the capability for interlinked spaces to be used either as two smaller venues, combined to make one larger one or connected to allow epic scenic opportunities. The Curve Theatre in Leicester demonstrates this to great effect.

### *Banners, blinds, drapes and reversible panels*

Changing the format or configuration often requires changes in the acoustic response of the room. Acoustic banners, blinds and drapes can be deployed at a high level or on wall surfaces. Reversible panels are also very effective in changing the acoustic response and aesthetic character of a room.

***Other specific elements***

In addition to the basic components described previously, there are many specialist interpretations from mobile lighting gantries to individual row lifts which can stow away their own seating to create a flat floor. In practice an adaptable auditorium will contain a combination of the different components to suit particular needs. It is also important to remember that substantial repositioning of the performance zone has a high degree of impact on the technical rigging and performance infrastructure.

## Aesthetic adaptability and ambience

Consideration should also be given to aesthetic adaptability. If the format change is from a thrust stage to an in-the-round scenario, then the adjustment in ambience is not too demanding. Where the change is from classical music venue to drama the aesthetic implications are more demanding. Concerts take place in an illuminated room, drama in a darker and more subdued setting. Spaces that play host to both activities need to establish an aesthetic treatment that supports both. A guiding rule should be to ensure that a space looks convincing and fully intended in each of its formats.

The following section explores the practical imperatives that underpin the detailed design of an auditorium – the integration of performance infrastructure and the delivery of an appropriate sensory environment for audiences.

## Section editor

Julian Middleton, Head of Project Design at Delfont Mackintosh Theatres Ltd., formerly Executive Director of AEDAS Arts Team Architects

## Contributors

Anne Minors, Co-Founding Director and Performance Consultant, Sound Space Vision

Lucy Osborne, Architect, Set Designer and Performance Consultant

Peter Ruthven-Hall, Performance Consultant, Charcoalblue

Roger Watts, Architect

# Section 6

# Auditorium: Sensory and practical imperatives

## 6.1 Audiences and theatre practitioners

Creating an auditorium involves the resolution of a wide array of complex design issues – which can often appear to have competing demands. An auditorium design must carefully balance the practical imperatives, for both the artists and the technical team, alongside ensuring that the audience is sitting within a comfortable environment – and that their sensory needs are met holistically. This section explores the detailed factors that need to be considered when designing a performance space. It looks at how to achieve a high-quality and comfortable environment for the audience, the technical imperatives for the performance – and at the less easily defined aesthetic qualities, which all combine to underpin a truly successful auditorium design.

The section builds upon the commentary in Section 5, which explores different auditorium formats and layouts, and discusses the underlying relationship between performers and audience.

## 6.2 Acoustic considerations

### Acoustic excellence

The design of auditoria must ensure acoustic excellence for performers and listeners. It should create a seamless chain of communication between the performer and listener, with an awareness of the psychoacoustics of performance and listening. For actors and singers, the acoustic impression of theatre should enhance the feeling of communication with other performers and with all the audience.

### Form and volume

Good auditorium acoustics start with the determination of form and volume. The construction, geometry and finish of an auditorium all impact on how audience hears the performance clearly without colouration – and ensure that performers can hear each other well to enable them to play as an ensemble. Many factors contribute. Close to the stage, the listener hears mostly direct sound, which dominates the weaker late reflections from the room surfaces. Further from the stage, listeners hear a combination of direct sound and reflected sound arriving as a series of discrete reflections, spaced in time. The reflected sound should arrive in an ordered way, maintaining the realism of the direct sound, reinforcing it and not containing strong long delayed reflections or echoes (see Figure 6.2.1).

The volume of any room has a direct relationship to its reverberation time (RT) in seconds and it is therefore important to establish the correct volume for a particular performance type, or range of types, at an early stage (see Figure 6.2.2). In found or previously built spaces, excessive volume may give rise to high RTs, which may be used by adding areas of absorption.

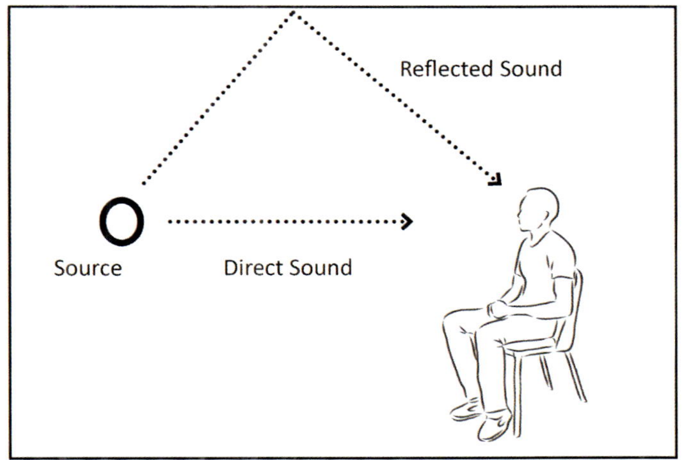


Figure 6.2.1 Direct and reflected sound paths.

### Speech

The reverberation time requirement for speech is relatively short, typically less than 1 second at mid frequencies, depending on room volume. This gives the optimum standard of speech intelligibility. The auditorium volume can be fairly low for drama, around 3–6m$^3$/person.

DOI: 10.4324/9781003327295-6

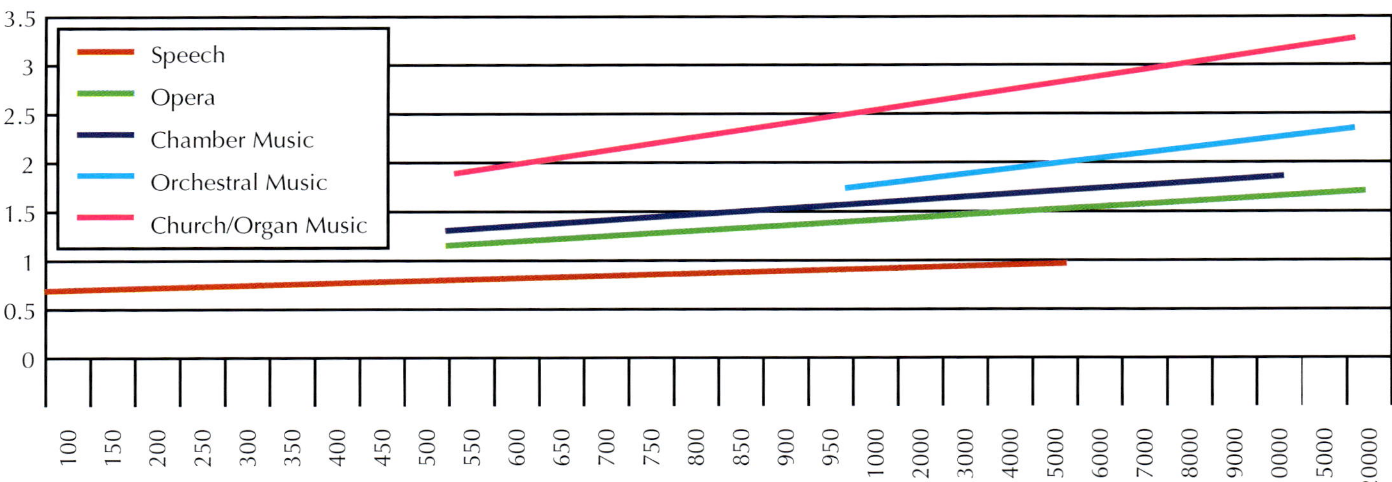


Figure 6.2.2 Chart showing volumes and reverberation time.

Direct, or early, sound arrives first at the listener. The elapsed time is dependent on distance from the source and this sound is unaffected by room reflections. The late energy arrives as a cascade of reflections after around 100ms and merges with the direct sound. Late strong single reflections, or echoes must be eliminated. The early to late energy ratio should be high – late energy arriving beyond 100ms at a high level affects intelligibility. Reverberation times should be appropriate to the use, around one second or less at mid-frequencies.

Subjectively, at an RT of 0.9 seconds at mid frequencies (500Hz), the listener is just aware of the room reflections. At 0.8 seconds or less, the late reflections are less apparent, and at 0.7 seconds, direct sound predominates.

To maximise direct sound, seating should be as close as possible to the stage. Good sightlines generally make for good acoustics, as what the eye can see the ear can hear. Theatres for natural speech work well up to around 800 seats. In larger theatres, speech reinforcement is used for opera and musicals, where orchestral balance is important, and there has been a trend in recent years for speech reinforcement to be used for drama, especially when recorded sound effects are used.

## Music

For music, the early to late sound energy ratio must be lower. Clarity is less significant and reverberance and envelopment are more important. To provide this, the reverberation time should be close to 2.0 seconds, with a rise in the bass. This means a volume of around 10m$^3$/person or more. The shoebox form, often a double cube, was used in many eighteenth-century concert halls and is still favoured by many acousticians. It guarantees high ratios of lateral energy, so important to instrument localisation and the listening experience. Audience size is optimum up to around 1800 seats, after which acoustic excellence becomes more difficult to achieve. Overhead reflectors with variable height can be used to provide early reflections to the audience and to improve communications between musicians.

Other auditorium forms have been and are successfully used for music, most significantly the vineyard layout, used by Hans Scharoun at the Berlin Philarmonie, completed in 1963. Here, the end stage format is subverted, with the orchestra placed in the centre and the audience in terraces with connecting walls to enhance lateral reflections. This provides a different experience acoustically and spatially and was informed by developments in the design of open stage theatres. In a music room the sound should be enveloping, unlike a speech acoustic, which is directional, to ensure high intelligibility.

## Developments in acoustic design

Until the middle of the twentieth century, auditorium design had evolved through experimentation and imitation. There were some spectacular failures. From the mid-twentieth century, acoustic scale models were built with sound absorption and sound sources scaled to around 1:20. As a result, acoustic prediction and guarantees of excellence improved dramatically. Physical scale-modelling is still used today but the advent of low-cost processing, computers are now used to predict performance using acoustic-modelling software. This is an extremely powerful and accurate tool, but its success depends on acousticians having an understanding of the acoustic parameters that they know will ensure excellence. After decades of research, listening and consultation with conductors, these parameters are now generally well understood.

## Multi-purpose spaces

In some larger auditoria, significant measures have to be taken to ensure a good acoustic for both speech and music. Specific measure can take something away from an ideal acoustic for one or the other of the uses – and conflicts of geometry will always impact on effectiveness. However, economic imperatives, and those of creating effectively programmed and sustainable venues, often dictate the demand for multi-purpose spaces, particularly those suitable for both amplified and unamplified music.

## Variable acoustics

To vary an acoustic, the room volume and/or the amount of absorption must be varied. A range of measures have been used, which include:

- concert halls with large reverberation chambers to increase reverberation times beyond 3 seconds
- concert halls with movable acoustic panels and curtains to vary reverberation time
- concert halls with movable ceilings to vary the free volume.

The full range of variability between a theatre and concert hall acoustic is, however, often difficult to achieve.

## Improving existing rooms

As we seek to maximise the sustainability and use of our existing built resources as part of the wider environmental agenda this is a growing area. Projects can range from refurbishment of Georgian and Victorian theatres to the repurposing of existing school halls, town halls and civic and industrial buildings. In established performance venues the need for change is often a result of the need to renew mechanical and electrical services or a desire to cater for a wider range of performance types. Increases in urban noise levels also mean that building envelopes need to be upgraded to exclude external noise. Whether refurbishing an existing performance space or creating a new role for a different building type, if the volume of the space is right, then much can be done to improve existing acoustics.

Many spaces can be reworked, for a range of purposes requiring different acoustic conditions. Traditionally, curtains and drapes would have been used to reduce reverberation, but this weakens reflections from the stage wall and the degree of change is small. More recently, other measures have come to the fore, changing the room volume with variable ceiling height and introducing moving panels or other structures to expose sound absorbing surfaces. Motorised banners are now commonly used.

Recently, variable acoustic structures have been designed which use narrow motorised reflective vertical slats in front of an efficient sound absorbing material. Here the room acoustic is optimised for its primary use, say orchestral music, with the slats closed. The RT may then be successively reduced by up to 30%, allowing for choral and operatic use.

Curtains may be then deployed for drama. The acoustic states for each performance style must all be convincing. In auditoria over 800 seats, the system can be used, but to achieve a convincing theatre acoustic, large areas of variable absorption are needed.

## Electronic architecture

Acousticians must create spaces for performers and audiences which are fit for their purpose, whether it is for public speaking, drama, musical or lyric theatre, or spaces for opera and music. It was realised early on that spaces that worked well for speech, with volumes of around 3–6m$^3$/person, were not good for musical performance. Speech needs a 'dry' acoustic, that is, one which is not reverberant, allowing each speech syllable to be heard separately.

Amplified music works well in theatres – the performance acoustic can be artificially set up within the sound system and imposed on the space. Orchestral music performed in such spaces, however, feels lifeless. There is poor communication between performers, and between musicians and audience, since direct sound predominates.

Other parameters are now known to be important and relate to the way and from which direction, reflected sound arrives at the listener. Since the 1950s, when manipulation of sound on a large scale using electronics became possible, acousticians have considered imposing acoustic conditions on theatres and halls to give more flexibility to their use and to correct acoustic faults. Experiments were carried out in Europe and in America. In the 1950s, the Royal Festival Hall in London was fitted with an early analogue 'assisted resonance' system to increase reverberance.

As systems became more sophisticated, other acoustic features were added, such as early and late reflection sequences and lateral energy. Systems have evolved from analogue to digital. The latest digital systems are extremely stable and are pre-set from a small control panel with about five settings. These systems, described as 'electronic architecture' (EA) systems, work extremely well, altering the reverberation time and reflection sequence of a space to simulate a range of geometries and acoustic environments.

They create strong lateral reflections, which are important in giving a sense of envelopment. Each system consists of an array of high-quality microphones connected to a large processor. This processor adds early and late delays, reverberation and lateral information, distributed by a number of small wall- and ceiling-mounted loudspeakers. They can be set over a range of values to suit different types of music.

In use, audiences are not aware of the system working, although the room acoustic is clearly altered. Properly tuned, the system will merge imperceptibly with the natural acoustic of a theatre. The installation of EA systems can extend the range of use considerably and give good listening conditions in all seats for chamber and orchestral concerts and all types of acoustic music performance.

## 6.3 Orchestra pit

An orchestra pit is the space in a theatre, located in a lowered area in front of the stage, in which musicians perform. Orchestral pits are utilised in forms of theatre that require music such as opera, musical theatre and ballet – or in cases when incidental music is required. Traditionally the pit is set partly within the auditorium and partly under the stage. The conductor is typically positioned at the front of the orchestral pit facing the stage. In many contemporary theatres the pit zone is a highly adaptable area to enable a number of different performance types.

### Pit size and modes of use

An orchestra pit for a large opera house may need to accommodate up to one hundred and twenty musicians. Pits in larger historic theatres may accommodate in the order of sixty to seventy players, while other auditoria, for example, those designed for musical theatre or contemporary dance, may accommodate no more than ten to twelve people. As general guidance, an allowance of 1.1m$^2$ should be made for musicians in open space, 1.5m$^2$ for those under the overhang, 5m$^2$ for a piano and around 6m$^2$ for the timpani.

To avoid extending the divide between stage and audience the pit can be partly under the stage. This is not normally an acoustic disadvantage, as it helps to balance the orchestral sound with that of the vocalists on the stage above. However, consideration needs to be given to the acoustic environment for the musicians and 'control of noise at work' regulations.

In an opera house the pit is a fixed feature. In other theatres, designed perhaps mainly for drama use, a permanent pit will act as a barrier that can damage the actor-to-audience relationship so there needs to be some adaptability in the pit zone. The area forward of the fixed stage edge defines the adaptable area.

In most such pits there are three key modes of operation (see Figure 6.3.1):

- forestage extension
- extended stalls
- orchestra pit.

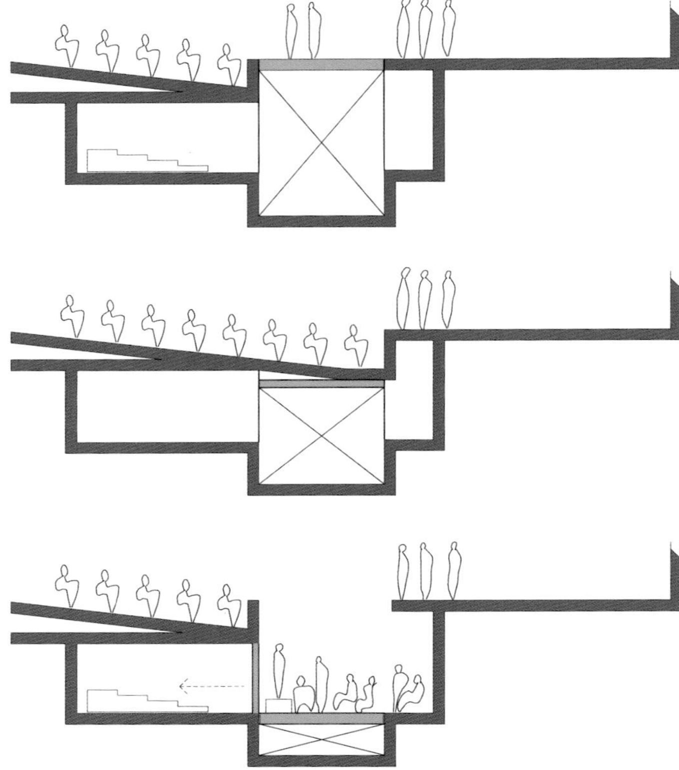

Figure 6.3.1 Three primary pit lift positions; forestage, extended stalls and orchestra pit.

### Acoustic imperatives of orchestra pits

Pit design should achieve the following:

- good communication between musicians
- good communication between musicians and to the conductor
- good communications between the pit and actors/singers
- a proper balance in the audience between musicians and actors/singers
- a safe acoustic working environment for musicians.

Acoustic treatment is required to control excessive sound levels, for example, acoustic/screening for amplified music in orchestra pits. In the United Kingdom adequate protection from long-term hearing loss for musicians and conductors is required.

In an operatic house with an orchestra in the pit, the layout of musicians will influence good communication.

Loud instruments tend to be at the rear. Some provision may be needed for screening, normally in the form of perspex screens between loud/quieter instruments. Finishes will normally be reflective, perhaps with some diffusive/absorptive elements. Noise at work requirements will normally ensure that musicians need to wear attenuators to mitigate the risk of hearing loss, with their hearing tested annually.

In a musical-theatre environment with amplified instruments, the local sound levels tend to be higher. There is usually a modern drum kit, electric guitars and brass/woodwind. Attenuators should be worn as necessary in such environments. With louder instruments, sound bleed into the microphone array tends to occur, making sound mixing difficult. Drums are usually heavily screened and sound absorption added to many surfaces. Other instruments are often screened.

## Sensitivity to sound

Like all the other senses, sensitivity to sound varies between individuals. Sensitivity to high frequencies of sound (1,000–5,000Hz) decreases with age.

In the United Kingdom the *Noise at Work Regulations* require employers to prevent or reduce the risks to safety from exposure to noise at work – including orchestra pits. Building management are responsible for monitoring levels on a continuous basis to ensure that musicians and staff are not affected by sound levels. (Audiences are unlikely to be affected by occasional exposure at the proposed maximum level.)

Employers are required to assess the risks to performers from noise at work, to take action to reduce the noise exposure, to provide hearing protection if the noise exposure cannot be reduced by other action and to ensure that the legal limits on noise exposure are not exceeded.

The regulatory guidance requires specific action to be taken at defined action values. The limits set out consider a musician's average exposure often referred to in dB(A) or 'A' weighting and maximum noise (peak sound pressure) in dB(C) or 'C' weighting which is a measure of peak, impact or explosive noises. After preventative steps have been taken to control the noise at source, hearing protection is often the only way to reduce musician's exposure, but it should not be used as an alternative to controlling noise at source.

The noise exposure action values are as set out in Figure 6.3.2.

## Pit operation

How this adaptability is achieved depends on the frequency of change-over from one configuration to another and on available funding. The change can be effected manually with panels installed over a demountable framework. This involves labour and time. Alternatively mechanical systems in the form of a pit lift, or lifts, can be used. Even in modest projects the initial investment in this piece of stage engineering can have a huge benefit in the flexibility and long-term sustainability of a venue. A pit elevator can also be useful in moving large and heavy items, such as pianos, between stage and basement/orchestra pit levels.

A single lift can be installed to create the three basic configurations noted. In larger pits, split lifts offer refinements in the size of pit or forestage and the degree of extra seating in an extended stalls area.

When the pit is in position a handrail, or pit rail, is required in front of the audience. This will need to retain appropriate seatway and leg room. It also needs to conform to the regulatory requirements in terms of loading and height. The rail needs to be demountable, usually achieved by dropping uprights into sockets along the pit edge.

Methods of pit lift operation include spiral lifts, screw jacks and hydraulic cylinders. Where deep construction is not feasible, a scissor lift mechanism is an alternative, although these are generally regarded as less rigid and more sensitive in operation. Side guides are generally needed. Any guide or elements which intrude into the pit itself need to be detailed so as to not impinge on the functionality of the pit.

## Detailed design

As with any area of adaptability, the geometrical configuration is only one aspect of the design. The front edge of the stage, the pit walls and orchestra pit rail zone all need to be carefully thought through for each of the

| Exposure Action Value | Lower | Upper | Not to be exceeded |
|---|---|---|---|
| | | | |
| Daily or weekly exposure of | 80dB(A) | 85dB(A) | 87dB(A) |
| Peak sound pressure of | 135dB | 137dB | 140dB |

Figure 6.3.2 Table of exposure limits. These exposure limit values take account of any reduction in exposure provided by hearing protection.

key positions. Electrical points, microphone outlets and traps need to be considered. Details need to be robust and durable, particularly on the audience side, where there may be interfaces with finer finishes.

### Safety

The pit operation diagram, previously, indicates the potential health and safety issues related to the operation of these large mechanical units. The requirement for safe edges, enclosing blinds, warning bells and dual operating controls is all part of the theatre equipment consultant's area of expertise.

Where fire separation between auditorium and stage is required, the pit is deemed to be a part of the auditorium. Continuity of fire separation means rear wall of the pit and overhang need to be fire resistant. Any opening between the stage and auditorium, outside of the proscenium with its safety curtain, needs to have protected lobby entrances with self-closing doors. This includes the pit access below stage level.

### Smaller types

Whilst the traditional pit described previously is the primary form, some smaller studio spaces have a pit that is more akin to a shallow recess in the floor zone. Usually for small numbers, the pit recess needs to be low enough for seated musicians not to interfere with the view of the acting area. Such pits are often accessed from the stage or audience side, and form part of an adaptable pit/forestage zone.

## 6.4 Ventilation and air handling

In the United Kingdom, during the theatre building boom of the Victorian and Edwardian eras, auditoria relied largely upon natural ventilation systems. Air was generally drawn in at a low level and extracted through the roof of the auditorium. Such systems were often erratic in performance. In some instances, the ventilation systems were manually opened during intervals and prior to performances starting. Distribution of fresh air was relatively uncontrolled with centrally located seats, or rear stalls and circle seats, receiving little to no fresh air, while some areas of the auditorium experienced over-ventilation leading to draughts and occupant discomfort.

After the tremendous breakthrough of electricity at the beginning of the 1900s, electrically-powered ventilation equipment began to be installed on a grand scale, especially in the United States, where it became commonplace in industrial plants, hotels, theatres and cinemas. It is said that a contributing factor to the rise of the American film industry was the fact that cinemas could offer a few hours of relaxation in a pleasantly cool venue.

Throughout the early years of the twentieth century, in all regions, a variety of building acts and codes gradually began to set systematic building standards. In 1965 the United Kingdom saw the introduction of regulatory requirements for fresh air supply through Building Regulations – augmented by subsequent British/European Standards. As regulatory frameworks became more prescriptive, reliance on natural ventilation systems became increasingly more complicated. By the middle of the twentieth century, mechanical systems had become the norm, as such systems were easier to design and substantiate – and were more reliable.

The advent of increased energy performance standards, the need to control energy use and the imperative to reduce carbon emissions, along with extensive advances in natural ventilation modelling and techniques, has led to this viewpoint being questioned. While naturally ventilated approaches do set considerable design challenges, such as balancing the large amounts of air required with the attendant acoustic issues arising from large openings in the external building fabric, it is now demonstrably feasible to ventilate smaller-scale auditoria by natural means in a temperate climate and in a quiet location. Venues such as the Auden Theatre in Holt, Norfolk, and the Contact Theatre in Manchester, led the way in demonstrating the viability of the natural approach. (See Figure 6.4.1.)

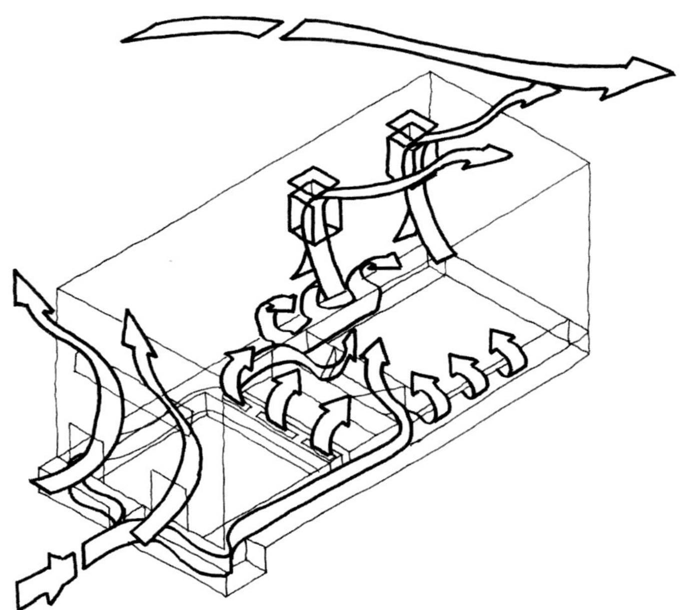

Figure 6.4.1 Auden Theatre at Gresham's School, Norfolk, UK. Natural ventilation schematic utilising the prevailing wind.

Larger projects in urban areas, on congested and noisy sites or in more demanding climatic conditions can remain reliant on mechanical ventilation. However, even this starting point is now in serious doubt following the design and development of theatres such as the Everyman Theatre, Liverpool (see Reference Project 17). The Everyman is located on a main arterial transport route into the heart of Liverpool, with poor air quality and high levels of noise pollution. Advances in modelling and ventilation control have meant even these challenging environments can be overcome in a sustainable, efficient way.

## Internal design criteria

Statutory regulations set high targets for air changes within the auditorium with minimum fresh air input normally set at 10 litres/per second/per person. The impact from the 2019 pandemic has also led to greater requirements for higher ventilation rates. These requirements can be designed-in to take account of comfort needs as well as the health and wellbeing of audience members, balanced alongside the imperatives of the climate emergency. Introductions to these issues can be found in Sections 1, 3 and 4. This section offers a more detailed analysis.

Acoustic requirements can be designed-in to take account of comfort needs, with greater control over the velocity of the air, the temperature and location at which the air is introduced into the volume. Low air velocities necessitate that supply and extract ducts have large cross-sectional areas to maintain air velocities within the auditorium to less than 1.5 and 2m/s directly adjacent to the auditorium. Threading these elements through an existing historic building, or planning into a new one, can be complex.

In temperate climates, deciding between a full air-conditioning system or a simpler heating and ventilation strategy can be marginal. In more extreme climates full air conditioning is a necessity.

Acceptable comfort conditions for audiences are very complex and need to consider air temperature, radiant temperatures, humidity, air velocity, activity, and clothing. A ventilation, heating and cooling strategy should avoid extremes in temperature and air quality whilst maintaining minimum energy expenditure. What are considered acceptable internal air temperatures depend on local climatic conditions. Traditionally, it has been widely considered that ideal internal air conditions for people living in in the United Kingdom, for example, is 22°C, with a relative humidity of 50%. In tropical climates audiences might find 30°C and 80% RH more acceptable.

Today, the principle of adaptive thermal comfort is widely accepted and using documents such as the Chartered Institution of Building Services Engineers (CIBSE) guidance, *TM54: The Limits of Thermal Comfort: Avoiding Overheating in European Buildings*, engineers are now able to offer greater internal comfort in naturally ventilated spaces by allowing the internal design criteria to 'float' in relation to outside temperatures. We allow internal environments to 'adapt' to their climate stimuli. There is no longer a defined internal temperature but an allowable differential temperature between the indoor and outdoor environments. Internal temperatures can now be allowed to rise, effectively tracking the external air temperature during peak seasonal months.

## Natural ventilation

Natural ventilation mechanisms, as the name suggests, work on naturally occurring phenomena such as wind driven, and buoyancy driven air flow. Such strategies reduce the reliance on heavy mechanical plant, assist in energy conservation and reduce associated running costs.

Design solutions for providing natural ventilation have very specific requirements. Successful solutions incorporate high-and low-level inlets and outlets that promote and encourage cross ventilation throughout the auditorium space. Many existing solutions incorporate architectural elements such as stack vents and inlet/outlet plenums. The inlet and outlet plenums offer the opportunity to apply attenuation for noise break in and break out. They can, as in the Everyman Theatre, also offer an opportunity to preheat or precool incoming air through the provision of thermal mass.

The main challenge with natural ventilation is the difficulty in controlling volume flow rates. Over-ventilation in winter can be as much as a problem as under-ventilation in summer. Internal air quality is difficult to maintain when low air volume flow rates are predominant. It may be appropriate therefore to provide a mixed-mode solution whereby mechanical ventilation solutions are employed to deal with significant extreme climate conditions, persistent poor indoor air quality, or high internal air temperatures. The use of controllable inlet and outlet dampers can provide methods for stabilising ventilation rates – and there are many examples of these technologies being successfully deployed.

Designs should look to provide air paths from inlet to outlet that have the least possible resistance to air movement. The more resistance to air flow the less air movement will be achieved. Air distribution through the volume of the space should also be considered with supply air being introduced as close to floor level as possible combined with high-level outlets. Micro air-movement analysis, using computational fluid dynamics or physical modelling, should be encouraged to determine flow patterns throughout these complex spaces.

With the advent of the low carbon economy, and governments around the world working towards the target of bringing all greenhouse gas emissions to net zero by 2050, more performance spaces will need to embrace natural ventilation techniques to provide for their internal environmental conditioning.

## Air-conditioning and mechanical ventilation

Air-conditioning as a terminology is often misused to describe simple mechanical ventilation systems with comfort cooling. Such systems provide temperature control, but no regulation of humidity. Full air-conditioning means that all aspects of the incoming air is conditioned, be it filtering to remove particles and odours or temperature and humidity (moisture control) to provide a tightly controlled internal environment. Such a system needs to be able to work in widely variable climatic conditions from freezing temperatures and very low moisture content to extremely high temperatures and near 100% humidity. This can necessitate cooling air via refrigeration to lower humidity in warm sticky summers and then having to reheat it before reintroducing into an auditorium. Conversely, low humidity in winter months may require air to be treated with humidifiers. The provision of cooling to any internal area comes at the cost of expended energy and increased carbon emissions. This is doubly true for full air-conditioning systems. Humidity control is extremely energy intensive and should be avoided wherever possible.

Specific attention should be given to humidity control in event spaces that are used exclusively or predominantly for stringed instruments (recital halls and chamber music halls), which are particularly susceptible to humidity changes, causing instruments to go out of tune. Humidity between green rooms and performances spaces can also cause significant changes to the tuning of instruments and should be assessed as part of the design process.

In hot weather, and warmer climates, it is also relative humidity that contributes significantly to audience discomfort. The body can tolerate higher temperatures and feel comfortable if its natural cooling mechanics (perspiration) can work. Warm moist air does not allow perspiration to evaporate and regulate comfort body temperature. In winter months and cooler climates, if warmed air is too dry, discomfort can occur, causing sore throats and dry irritable eyes as well as static electricity shocks.

Overcoming high humidity levels, without mechanically removing the moisture can be achieved through increased air flow across occupants' bodies. This goes against most concepts of comfort where low air velocities are considered highly important; however, air movement across the audience can vastly improve occupant comfort throughout. This is the same principle of a nice summer breeze causing comfort despite high external air temperatures. Mechanical-only ventilation systems can therefore be designed to offer variable flow conditions between summer and winter to maximise air entrainment in winter to allow maximum mixing to prevent draughts, but through providing more directed air flows in summer to increase air movement in the occupied zone. This can be achieved through variable flow pattern nozzle-diffusers, incorporating variable cores that can be automatically adjusted to change the air pattern through the auditorium depending on the season and where heating is being applied to the space.

## Air distribution

In temperate conditions, heating is generally only required for warming up the auditorium prior to audience arrival. The imperative during a performance is the supply of clean cool air. There are two main mechanisms for air distribution: mixed flow and displacement ventilation.

*Mixed flow* introduces air into the auditorium at a high level, entraining air with the room air and mixing fresh with existing air. The principle works on air changes of the entire room volume to maintain tenable internal air quality. Extract air can be at a high level or low level dependent on the auditorium design. Mixed-flow air-distribution can deliver both heating and cooling loads as well as fresh air and can be matched to meet the fresh air requirements of occupants only. These systems have a wider temperature delivery criterion; in cooling this can be as low as 14°C and in heating can be as high as 30°C. In heating mode, the air needs to be punched down into the occupied space to ensure the heated (more buoyant) air is delivered to the occupants. In cooling mode, the air needs to be entrained with the existing air in the space to ensure cold draughts are not created in the occupied zone. Both requirements lead to higher air velocity (more noise) and higher fan power (power energy).

*Displacement ventilation* on the other hand only ever delivers air at a low level and extracts at a high level. Air is delivered at a constant temperature throughout the year (usually 19°–20°C). The air is delivered into the occupied zone and is concentrated on being delivered adjacent to the audience who, through their own body heat, provide the locomotive energy for the air to rise through the space to the extract point at a high level, carrying with it heat, carbon dioxide and odours. This leaves the occupied zone an effective pool of fresh air, with exceptionally high levels of air quality.

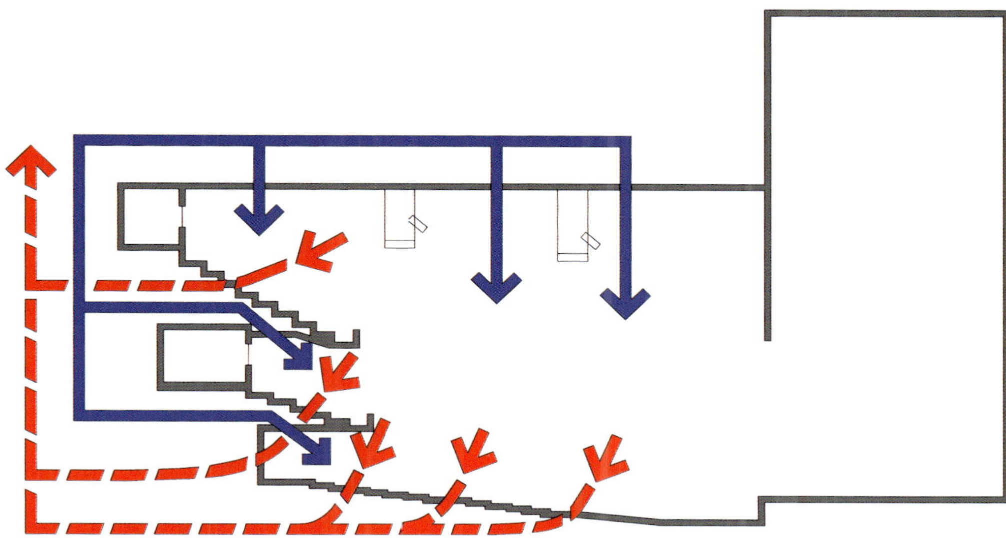

Figure 6.4.2 Diagrammatic illustrations with high- and low-level supply strategies.

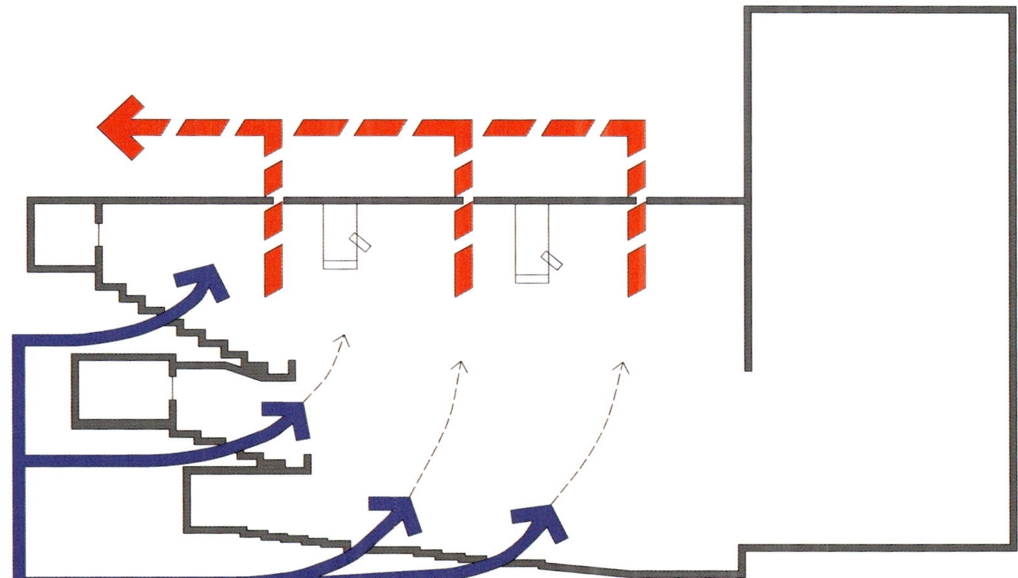

Figure 6.4.3 Diagrammatic illustrations with low-level supply displacement system.

## High-level supply (mixed flow)

High-level supply systems tend to be most suitable as a retrofit solution to older theatres undergoing refurbishment or remodelling. Most auditoria have large ceiling voids housing technical gantries. This quite often allows for the distribution of supply ductwork, allowing for connections to ceiling mounted diffusers. The air is supplied at reduced temperatures to offset the internal gains from equipment, lighting and occupants. Air can be exhausted, or returned, either at a low level under seating tiers or at a high level via the ceiling plenum, although careful consideration of air distribution is required to ensure short circuiting of air does not occur. Supply air can also be introduced to the rear of tiers in multi-level spaces with deep circle balconies.

In top-down systems, balancing air velocity with low noise levels can result in insufficient air distribution into some parts of the auditorium. Jet nozzle-type diffusers, located at a high level, can assist where a longer throw is required. Such systems give an increased sense of freshness as the air is being moved faster, but the increased supply velocity has the inherent danger of raising noise levels. The higher momentum air also has the advantage of being able to entrain deeper into parts of the auditorium, preventing 'dead spots' and areas of low air quality.

High-level supply systems often offer the cheapest and easiest solution for retrofitting ventilation systems into an existing theatre. Although they can use energy efficient heat recovery devices and provide a recirculation path to minimise fresh air loads, they are generally noisier distribution systems due to higher air velocities and less efficient than displacement systems, as they require higher fan powers and increased levels of cooling for reduced supply temperatures. Their ability to provide 'free' cooling is also reduced compared to displacement systems.

## Low-level supply (displacement)

Displacement ventilation is now the preferred air distribution method within most performance and lecture spaces, where fixed-raked seating is utilised. Displacement systems, as the name suggests, displace warm, vitiated air within the occupied zone with cool fresh air. Air is supplied at a low level, at around 19°–20°C under the seats, either in the riser or seat base. The air is supplied at extremely low velocities to ensure draughts are not created. Supply temperatures are also elevated compared with more conventional ventilation systems, at a temperature of only 2°C below the desired room set point. The principle is that the occupants effectively sit in an almost stationary pool of cool fresh air, and it is the occupants' own body heat that creates a plume of air that rises above their heads and away from the occupied zone. This upward movement of lighter, more buoyant warm air creates a differential pressure around the occupants, drawing cooler fresh air towards them, thus creating an air flow from a low level to high level. The beauty of displacement ventilation is that displaced air carries with it not just the people's body heat and moisture, but also exhaled breath, odours and particulates, which are transported into the vertical air stream.

Occupants are always seated within the freshest air within the auditorium, with the warm, moist air always moving upwards out of the occupied zone and towards the exhaust points at a high level. Fan power is much reduced, as air velocities and hence resistance to air movement are much reduced. The system uses natural buoyancy forces as an intrinsic part of the air movement pattern, again reducing the amount of power required by fans.

Displacement systems are generally the most efficient form of ventilation as they require far less cooling power (air is only ever cooled to 19°C instead of, say, 14°C) so chiller power is reduced, but also opportunity for free cooling is greatly increased in temperate climates where external air temperatures can spend as much as 80% of the year at or below 19°C, meaning there is no need for chiller plants to operate for 80% of the year. Displacement systems can use heat recovery devices also, but this is generally quite difficult, as often the supply and extract units are far apart from each other (supply air handling units being located at a low level and extract units at a high level). However, with careful planning devices such as run-around coils can be used that enable heat transfer to be undertaken from remotely located units.

Low-level supply can be more challenging to achieve in spaces that have variable configurations or offer a flat floor format. If prescribed layouts can be predetermined, then hybrid strategies can be deployed. In more adaptable spaces, the scale of the auditorium can be a key factor in balancing supply from the floor (where practicable) with perimeter positions.

## Pre-cooling, pre-heating and night-time cooling

The use of a pre-cooling strategy can assist in reducing plant size. As auditoria are not in constant use, there is an opportunity to pre-cool the auditorium volume prior to the arrival of the audience. The air is cooled several degrees below the required design temperature. The air temperature then gradually rises as the audience arrives and the performance takes place. Pre-cooling time is normally about an hour, although some theatres have facilities to provide larger amounts of cooler air during intervals to restart the process.

Pre-heating works in a similar way in the winter months. The auditorium is pre-warmed before the audience arrives. The heat given off by the audience, lighting and equipment then offsets the fabric and ventilation heat loss, allowing the mechanical plant to minimise requirements by only heating the fresh air.

A more useful strategy that is now becoming widely used is to incorporate night-time free cooling strategies which can be incredibly effective when combined with exposed thermal mass. The principle is simple, use cool night-time external air to flush out the internal heat gains from the day-to-day operations and performances of the theatre.

By having high thermal mass, heat gains within the space can be absorbed by walls, floors and roofing surfaces. This reduces peak internal temperatures and can push peak temperatures outside of the occupied times. Peak cooling loads where cooling is installed can also be reduced, saving further energy consumption.

Night-time ventilation strategies can effectively pre-ventilate and precool the space. The strategy can also over cool the space in summer to maximise the effects of the exposed thermal mass. By allowing the thermal mass to dissipate heat over night, the system effectively recharges the building's fabric, allowing the process to begin again the following day. This process is vital for naturally ventilated auditoria but can also be a very energy efficient solution for mechanically ventilated and cooled spaces, reducing overall energy usage and peak load conditions.

## Air distribution to the stage

Air distribution on stage is notoriously difficult to achieve, particularly in proscenium theatres, where the large volume of the flytower is generally empty, except for rigging and scenery, but is subject to over-heating or under-heating as the tower is generally unconditioned. Regular set changes, and a high levels of scenery movement within performance mode, mean that fixed ducting solutions are difficult to accommodate within the flytower.

Stage areas can also find scenery and props stacked against any available wall space or hanging from hastily erected wall storage. Most prompt corners and wings are covered with AV, lighting and stage panels requiring constant access and adjustments. This leaves wall real estate at a premium, often leaving no space left for ventilation or heating services.

Heating on stage is generally provided at a low level by recessed wall mounted radiators or convectors, or more often not at all, with heat losses being dealt with by air transfer from the auditorium. Radiant panel heaters may also be considered; however, all emitters and their location need to consider the detailed coordination with other services and overall use of the space. Ventilation ductwork and radiant panels can be hung at a high level in the wings under the fly gallery walkways, as this is usually the only 'dead' space with a stage area. There is usually very limited distribution of heat and fresh air from these positions.

Air movement on and around the stage needs to be carefully considered. Large air movement, even via buoyancy-driven pressure differentials in such large volumes, can create quite large air movement, leading to scenery and fire curtains being blown around. It is not desirable to have air movement between the auditorium and the stage, and as such they should have their own independent systems and be as close to pressure neutral as possible to prevent air transfer between the two volumes.

The stage floor plays a crucial role in performance, where vomitories and traps can be integral to the movement of performers, scenery and props. Supply grills or ducting are therefore not practicable on or under the stage. Equally, when there is a flytower, low-level extraction is unlikely to be able to compete with the considerable stack effect occurring in the flytower itself. Provision for return air should be made. This is best achieved at a high level, under the loading gallery, with a balanced, equal supply air volume supplied at lower level in the occupied zone.

In winter conditions and cooler climates, provision should be made to adequately heat the stage volume to avoid a column of cold air collecting in the flytower and flooding over the stalls' audience as an icy blast when the curtain is raised.

Where the staging is less formal, as a thrust or in the round facility, the stage effectively becomes part of the auditorium, and the overall ventilation system should take this into account, both in terms of its volume flow rate and its distribution. Careful briefing needs to be undertaken with a theatre's artistic director and facilities manager to understand all the potential performance modes that are being considered for these more flexible performance spaces.

## Other areas

There are a range of spaces coupled to the auditorium which require consideration within the ventilation strategy. The orchestra pit, for example, forms an integral part of the auditorium volume. However, it is generally tightly packed with musicians and equipment and can easily overheat. It requires its own dedicated fresh air supply, capable of providing cooled air to the entire pit volume.

Control rooms may be open (during technical rehearsals or in performance mode) or closed and fully sealed. They should be provided with an independent supply and extract system to avoid any crosstalk issues within the auditorium volume. Control rooms may also need independent cooling, as often they contain high levels of heat producing equipment, which will lead to overheating. Removal of heat build-up in other technical spaces, including dimmer and AV rooms, also need to be considered.

It is not generally advised to have these smaller independent rooms served from the general auditorium heating, cooling or ventilation systems, as these spaces tend to be used on a far more regular basis throughout the week, not just during performances. Having independent systems allow these smaller areas to be utilised without having to turn on larger systems that condition the entire auditorium.

## Noise levels

The target noise rating (NR) for theatre use should be NR 20, unless specifically required to be lower by the acoustic consultant. NR 25 can sometimes be acceptable, with NR 30 as an absolute maximum.

Achieving NR 20 level is onerous. It means noise levels generated by mechanical plant, alongside noise from adjacent areas or the external environment, cannot exceed NR 15. This can have a critical bearing on the basic planning of a building. It necessitates locating plant away from the auditorium or within an independent structure and the installation of large attenuators in the duct work systems. Vibration isolation needs to be considered at every stage of the design and installation. Service penetrations through the auditorium fabric need to be carefully considered, with attenuation measures being detailed at each position. Ventilation should have primary and secondary ventilation attenuation, with flexible connections, attenuators and anti-vibration measures being provided wherever a service passes through the auditorium envelope.

The design of auditoria must ensure acoustic excellence for performers and listeners. It should create a seamless chain of communication between the performer and listener, with an awareness of the psychoacoustics of performance and listening. For actors and singers, the acoustic impression of theatre should enhance the feeling of communication with other performers and the entirety of the audience.

The design process brings together many skills, reliant on collaborative working with architects and engineers to create, or modify, room geometry using models, choice of the correct internal finishes, keeping external noise to an absolute minimum and making sure that services noise levels are imperceptible.

## 6.5 Lighting and sound in the auditorium

### Requirements within the auditorium

The detailed requirements of production lighting, sound and video equipment are described in Sections 8 and 9. This sub-section focuses on the particular architectural considerations, and spatial requirements, of performance infrastructure within the auditorium. We look at the balance between permanent and show-specific installations – and the particular challenges when working within historic spaces. If auditorium designers do not integrate appropriate, practical and accessible positions for rigging lighting and sound equipment within a design, theatre practitioners have to make their own expedient adaptations.

Integration of technical equipment can be relatively straight forward in an open stage, or studio style venue – where the technology and the adaptability of the technical installation is an integrated part of the aesthetic treatment. In these spaces control positions are often open and set within the overall volume. The considerations and challenges become more complex within an aesthetic design that aims to conceal part of, or all, the production equipment. The following commentary has a focus on proscenium-format spaces.

### Key elements

Lighting requirements within the auditorium include booms, boxes and slots, all of which are primarily side lighting positions. The advance bar/bridge, lighting bridges, tension wire grids, side bridges and follow spot positions are all high-level lighting positions. Low-level front lighting is also often required and supported by circle fronts lighting bars, or bar located discretely under tiers. Rigging requirements for sound within the auditorium may include proscenium side booms, a central speaker cluster set above the proscenium and delay 'under balcony' speakers.

### Control positions

In smaller spaces the lighting and sound control can be within a shared space. In larger venues separate rooms are preferred. Control rooms for lighting and sound are ideally situated near the centreline and at the back of the auditorium. They should ideally be within acoustically separated volumes. The connecting window into the auditorium should be openable and non-reflective. The operator's sightline should give clear visibility of the stage with the downward sightline taking account of seeing over the audience members seated immediately in front – and ideally not be interrupted by someone standing in the rear rows. The upper sightline should give a clear view of the top of the proscenium.

The success of this space for mixing live sound will depend on the particular auditorium design and programme. It is often necessary to provide an additional sound mixing position within the auditorium volume, particularly for musical theatre and touring shows. Some theatres integrate such positions as permanent installations. Sound desks can be fairly sizeable, so aesthetic integration into say a rear stalls zone needs careful consideration. Access routes for heavy equipment and mobile kit needs to be thought through to avoid damage to seating – particularly with receiving venues.

Set centrally, or to either side at the back of an auditorium, follow spot luminaires are traditionally set in acoustically separated rooms outside the auditorium space, due to the noise of the equipment. In some contemporary auditoria they can also be set at a high level on bridges – where they are away from the audience. The introduction of improved LED follow spot lamps, with reduced operational noise, is, however, enabling the use of open follow spot positions closer to the audience, such as those in the Sondheim Theatre refurbishment in London's West End.

When working in historic theatres, a degree of flexibility in control locations is required. Locating the sound disk as centrally as possible is still an imperative, as are the imperatives of follow spot positions. However, there is more latitude in lighting control positions, and the recent refurbishment of the Victoria Palace Theatre in London exemplifies how appropriate control position can be thoughtfully integrated into period spaces (see Reference Project 30). Where possible, control position should be fully accessible.

### Lighting bridges in a proscenium space

Stage lighting must provide the ability to light any part of the stage from a wide range of angles. Some positions are fundamental, outlined subsequently, but there will be other production-specific requirements. As some stage lighting is required for the front of the stage, this is by necessity within the auditorium space.

Lighting the actors face at around 45° above the horizontal is essential to avoid unflattering shadows, whilst a lower angle may cause unwanted shadows on the set. Spotlights are rarely directed straight at the actor and are more normally crossed. This means that setting positions out on a cross section require an angle in the order of 55′ to achieve 45′ when crossed.

Lighting bridges require thoughtful integration into the ceiling design of an auditorium. While the basic diagram indicates linear position, installation can be curved in form or treated as sculptural objects within their own right, as part of the room aesthetic – exemplified by the installation at the Glyndebourne Opera House in Sussex.

In historic theatres the integration of high-level lighting positions to accommodate contemporary theatre practice with the auditorium can often be a challenge. In some spaces, a high-level bar position can be incorporated within the design, but these are often back from a central decorative zone. More radical approaches can involve having sections of a decorative ceiling opening up as the house lights dim to reveal the production lighting position, as illustrated at London's Royal Opera House. The degree of complexity depends on the importance of the aesthetic and the frequency of change over required.

See the commentary within key components of the adaptable auditorium for lighting bridges within non-proscenium auditoria (in Section 5).

### Tier fronts

Tier and box fronts primarily provide fall protection for the audience. In historical theatres they are highly decorative and also traditionally provide a location of house lighting. Both in period and contemporary spaces, tier fronts now also provide key position for lighting and audio-visual equipment. The integration of permanent cabling and production lighting boxes, and facilities for temporary cabling, is a balance based upon the performance programme of the venue. Consideration needs to be given to access arrangements and safety for installing, repairing and focusing lighting.

## 6.6 Materials, finishes and ambience

Figure 6.6.1 Tara Theatre, London, UK. Studied neutrality, and warmth, within a studio theatre environment. See Reference Project 12.

### Atmosphere

The primary concern of this and the preceding chapter has been to explore the physical, geometrical and technical parameters that underpin auditoria design. However, successful spaces are always a blend of both these practical imperatives and those that are less easily defined – aesthetic character and emotional response.

Reactions to theatre spaces can be highly subjective. Asking audience members, theatre directors, designers or theatre practitioners to consider their preferred performance spaces can often reveal a preference for historic theatres and atmospheric found spaces. While new auditoria will also feature, this perhaps indicates the importance of ambience in the setting of performance and the audience experience – and perhaps how difficult it can be to achieve.

Getting the balance right between the competing technical requirements and the aesthetic considerations can be what lifts a space beyond the underlying mechanics of engineering and architecture. These are the spaces that inspire and delight both practitioners and audiences – the ones that have that elusive and often indefinable quality – theatrical soul.

## Themes and approaches

The architectural character of the auditorium is critical in setting the scene and preparing the audience for the performance. The degree to which the architectural context remains apparent during the performance depends upon the type of space and the nature of the particular production.

Whatever the format of an auditorium, the materials, texture, colour and lighting are fundamental in defining its character. Different auditoria formats and types of performance require different architectural responses. An experimental studio, for example, has a very different aesthetic agenda from a large modern lyric theatre.

The open-stage space requires a degree of neutrality. The performance takes place within a space shared with the audience, and an overly dominant architectural treatment could conflict with the work on stage. Here architects and auditorium designers should resist the temptation to play the set-designer – these are spaces that should allow directors and designers the freedom to create their own worlds.

Over the last thirty years the starkness of the 'black box' aesthetic has gradually been eroded. A new sensibility, exemplified by venues such as London's Donmar Warehouse and Young Vic, exploits the tactile and sensory quality of the elements of their construction to define a studied neutrality. Such spaces also engage with the sustainability in both the sourcing and longevity of their construction materials. The architectural features of these spaces are both present and neutral – without the need for black paint. These spaces are also, and need to be, robust and durable – in response to their underlying adaptability. The Donmar Warehouse exemplifies a generous-spirited architecture that allows the focus of the space to gently fall to the work on stage.

This design sensibility, seen in venues such as Liverpool's award-winning Everyman Theatre, has strong parallels with the found-space movement. Found spaces allow directors and designers a unique freedom and creative opportunity to work with the individual character and atmosphere of a particular building. While found spaces can be used many times over, some host only a single production. There is an appeal to both practitioners and audiences in the sometimes-fleeting nature of their existence. Allied to this is the often unprecious, sometimes dilapidated, nature of the space themselves – which allows a subtle balance between the performance and the space. The provisional nature of such spaces can be liberating, with the character of the space informing the work but with an underlying neutrality that does not dominate.

A similar materiality and design sensibility can also be found in more conventional proscenium-theatre spaces. The Nevill Holt Opera House in the United Kingdom (see Figure 6.6.2) and the Oslo Opera House, Norway, both have auditoria where the tactile and sensory nature of the elements of their construction clearly define their character. Both spaces combine a restricted palette of materials with crafted geometries – blending a sense of austere neutrality with opulence. These unfussy, but appropriately civic, spaces provide a highly sympathetic setting for the contemporary performances they house.

Figure 6.6.2 Nevill Holt Opera, Market Harborough, UK, showing elegant use of a restrained material palette. See Reference Project 08.

## Learning from the past

The ebullience, and sheer exuberance, of late-nineteenth- and early-twentieth-century theatre interiors contributed hugely to generating a sense of excitement and anticipation in their audiences. Many were hedonistic palaces of entertainment and took liberties with the established architectural mores of the day. Though tastes and performance styles have moved on, there is much to be learnt from the sheer verve and glamour of these buildings in making the whole experience an event.

Architectural approaches to reworking historic performances spaces vary. Whilst it is sometimes appropriate to draw a visual distinction between the original interior and new elements – there is much to be said for retaining, and being guided by, the aesthetic completeness of a space. When considering decorative schemes, it is also important to remember that performance practice has evolved – and that contemporary lighting means we can light spaces in very different ways to that in which they would have originally been seen. The Victoria Palace and Sondheim Theatres in London are both exemplary in showing the creative reinterpretation of an original decorative scheme (see Figure 6.6.3), while the refurbishment of the Waterford

Figure 6.6.3 Sondheim Theatre, London, UK. Working within the context of, and reinforcing, the original design intent – to create a welcoming and coherent interior space.

Theatre Royal illustrates the overlay of a subdued colour palette in a period space to create a setting for avant-garde theatre work. For all their overt decorative qualities, durability and robustness of finishes are equally important in a hard-working period theatre. See Section 10 for a detailed discussion of the opportunities of the restoration and refurbishment of existing buildings.

While no one aesthetic approach fits all, the ambience of the auditorium must always be appropriate for the work on stage. The architecture of the room may need to be highly present clearly defining the atmosphere and architectural character – however, on some occasions it may also need to be capable of receding into the background when required to do so.

## Collaborative process

When creating a new theatre space, wherever possible, an auditorium-designer should work closely with the theatre company and their creative team in the design of the auditorium from the very outset. In many ways, mirroring the creation of a theatrical production, successful auditoria are the result of the creativity and collaboration of a cast of many players.

The following section explores the backstage areas of theatres. The design of these spaces shares some parallels with that of the auditorium. In supporting the collaborative venture of making theatre they must balance the integration of practical necessities, and ease of operation, with an aesthetic environment that enables performers and artists to be at their very best for that magical moment when they walk on stage – and meet their audience.

## Section editor

Julian Middleton, Head of Project Design at Delfont Mackintosh Theatres Ltd., formerly Executive Director of AEDAS Arts Team Architects

## Contributors

Paul Gillieron, Co-Director of Gillieron Scott Acoustic Design

Anne Minors, Co-Founding Director and Performance Consultant at Sound Space Vision

Jonathan Purcell, Services Engineer

Roger Watts, Architect

## Contributor to first edition

John Eames, Consultant Services Engineer

Section 7

# Backstage creative environment

## 7.1 The backstage community

> When you're a theatre practitioner, these areas are your manor. Where you live and earn your living. These areas bind us like glue to our colleagues, our fellow performers and the theatre staff who make it all possible. Back of house is where everything that happens to bring the show together occurs. It's the lab, the workshop, the alchemists' den . . . we exist in these areas to bring a show to the audience who have been waiting to see whatever it is we've come up with now. Somewhere for us to hide before we unleash whatever it is we've been doing. Hunkering places for an entire community to think and scheme and dream and create.
>
> Sir Lenny Henry

The backstage of a theatre is the engine that drives what is presented, on its stages and elsewhere, in any arts organisation. It is a home to the technicians and performers whether resident, freelance or touring. The type of work presented determines the scope of the facilities provided, but key principles underlie the space considerations for any scale of building: that the people working backstage are a community whose common purpose can be significantly aided by good design; that 'light' industrial-level activity in an often time-pressurised environment puts safety and risk assessment at the front of all considerations; that while historic stagecraft still has significant relevance to current practice, technology accelerates exponentially in its application to theatre; and that there is urgency in finding more sustainable models of production in which space plays a key role.

Accessibility and inclusivity are demanded legislatively and morally if the sector is to achieve its ambition of being for everyone. An increasingly diverse work force in the theatre has been professionalised in a way that has changed its outlook over the last decade. These workers demand welfare considerations, training and facilities in keeping with any other profession. The general public might attend the theatre for a couple of hours at a time: the individuals who produce the work that the audience sees will have been in that building for long hours on many continuous days. This environment needs to ensure that anyone can not just work safely but that they can thrive creatively.

Assessment of the likely type of programming in a ten-year period following the development of any theatre space is what will determine the extent of facilities provided. Excess space in the backstage of a theatre is rarely a problem, and expansion currently remains the trajectory of many organisations and artistic ambitions. Where space is limited by available footprint, budgets or scope of a company's work, then flexibility of space should be a primary consideration. This section lists many functions that in most building projects will not get their own dedicated space and therefore detailed analysis of the different infrastructural demands of each space is essential, whether that's ventilation, power supply, sound insulation, lighting or access.

Storage could be mentioned after every paragraph in this section. There is almost always never enough and building planners will often prioritise the needs of people over the 'stuff' of which productions are made and which can be hard to quantify in early design stages. This is an industry with a constant flow of materials and equipment and, as we develop more circular economies, storage will become even more important. Where it's not mentioned in this section is to limit repetition, but it should not be assumed it's not needed and should remain high on the list of interrogation in each area. In many projects this space often gets sacrificed to the later-stage practical thinking around services and containment. Earlier integrated thinking will save considerable frustration later.

Rigorous consultation with existing local technical staff is key to any successful redevelopment of an existing building. Theatres can be idiosyncratic spaces and, while attention can be brought to better practice elsewhere, local habits have often been established for very good reasons.

This section will sometimes give the impression that it is describing big organisation facilities, but it aims to draw back to the mid-scale and emphasise principal considerations rather than definitive and necessary

DOI: 10.4324/9781003327295-7

individual provision. While theatre spaces and companies vary enormously in their scale and the work they present, the greatest commonality is in the basic process of taking a production idea through from concept to delivery. In structuring this section through the key stages of that process, it is intended to provoke questions of a client that always come back to scrutiny of the workflow that in nearly all circumstances culminates in a performance.

## 7.2 Performance

Whether presenting or producing, a theatre building is designed with the principal aim of delivering live performances to an audience. The culmination of perhaps months of work, if not years of planning, the performance is the point at which a whole building is buzzing with life. The lights might have gone down in the auditorium with a hushed public focused on the stage, but the backstage will, in most circumstances, be full of urgent and precise activity (see Figure 7.1.1).

Show running staff may be a mixture of an organisation's permanent staff and those either specifically contracted to work on a show or touring crews. Performers may be part of a resident company or again contracted to a specific production or touring company. What is certain is that everyone backstage half-an-hour before performance has a critical role in the delivery of a carefully rehearsed

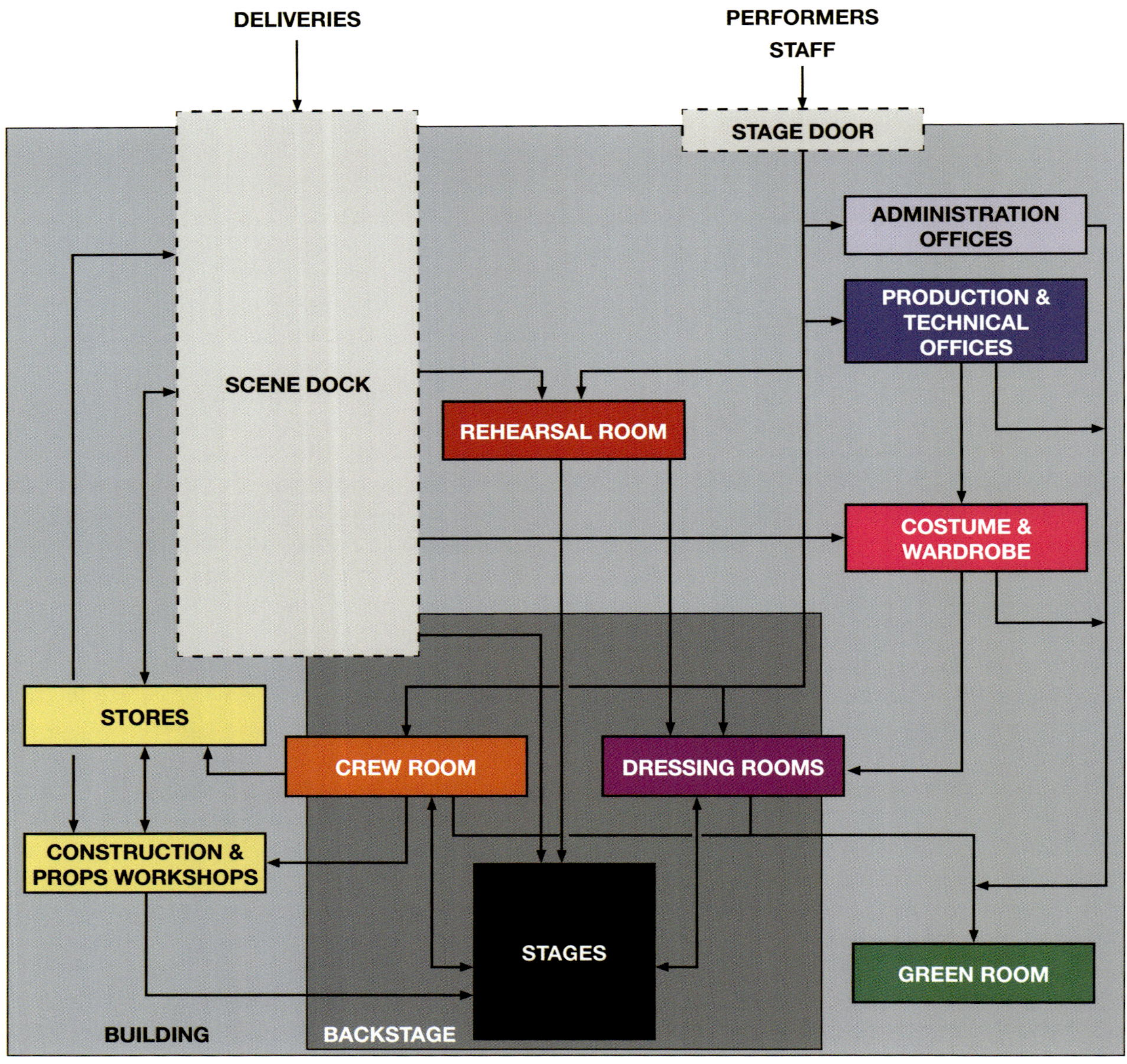


Figure 7.1.1 Diagram showing backstage adjacencies.

performance. They are a community more than at any other time in the creation of the work – reliant on each other, and equally valued.

## Stage door

Not all new theatre buildings will embrace a traditional stage door entrance on the back or side of a building, and may, instead, ask everyone to come through the front foyers where box office, visitor engagement services, security and reception might all be combined.

However, the traditional back of house stage door is an area that, in the public imagination, has historically glamorous connotations; the place where 'star' performers arrive and, post-performance, emerge to sign autographs and meet adoring fans. The reality of most buildings is that the stage door is the operating hub of the backstage world long before performance, where performers, creative teams and technical/production teams are first welcomed to the building. It should be warm and inviting as well as being functional; it is a reception area that at peak times must manage a considerable flow of people and anyone visiting back of house will have to pass through this area. It is also a security check point so there should be additional access-controlled doors to admit passage to the backstage area beyond the stage door reception area.

Reception desk space should be provided for visitors to sign in and out of the building, and to collect identification passes and access keys, as well as a working space for reception staff. This area will require space for a computer (monitor, keyboard and mouse), switchboard phone, paging system and visual display monitor space for other crucial systems such as CCTV and door access controls.

As well as human traffic, most deliveries including post will be processed through the stage door, so a storage room near the main reception area is useful. Productions will often see the delivery of numerous cardboard boxes of supplies, performers' post and parcels (as they are away from home for long periods of time personal correspondence comes to the theatre). For the opening and closing of productions mountains of flowers and gifts might appear. A 'pigeonhole' racking system may be useful to aid in the dissemination of post to performers and theatre departments.

Stage door is also often the access point to the theatre's administrative offices, so a waiting area for people arriving for meetings will be required. Most visitors require escorting through the backstage area, so at times this area can become busy. Space should be allowed to avoid 'bottlenecks' and security risks in the flow of people.

Stage door is also often the place to which security, fire protection and building management systems are routed, so real consideration as to the layout of all these services around the reception area is vital. Only one person may be on duty in this area, so the ergonomics and layout are essential to good workflow and responding quickly in cases of emergency.

Natural light is very welcome in this area, but consideration should be given to privacy as well. Once inside stage door, this area should offer performers a level of separation and safety from the outside world.

## Rehearsal rooms

While it is principally producing theatres that might need onsite rehearsal facilities, presenting venues might also see the income potential of rehearsal rooms. Rehearsal rooms are places of creative freedom where it is critical that performers and directors feel inspired and safe to explore the ambitions of a text or production idea (see Figure 7.2.1). The room must allow for a long list of collaborators, artists, technicians and other support staff, to participate in the project being made. Through a rehearsal process, the piece of work will be engineered, with input from many people, into something that can safely and securely be presented on stage.

Rehearsal rooms should be no smaller than the footprint of the biggest stage for which they will house rehearsals. The ceiling height should be no lower than 4.5m but could be much higher to allow complete scenery to be used in rehearsal. A grid or supporting structure for motors and trussing in the roof will improve flexibility and ability to mirror technical aspects of the realised production. The floor should be flat, level and, ideally, semi-sprung, with a loading capacity suitable for rehearsal sets, which could include structures and revolves. The finish should be equivalent to that of the stage, but an option for a removable dance floor should be considered.

Access is important for wheelchair users and the variety of equipment and physical production assets that may come into the room; extra wide or double doors are necessary, and a larger get-in door would be advantageous in bigger rehearsal spaces to allow for sets or structures to be assembled and removed. Surrounding corridors should allow for this traffic, and if the rehearsal room is not on the ground floor, a suitably sized goods elevator should be adjacent. Rehearsal rooms are ideally located close to the dressing rooms, green room and stage management offices. Proximity to wardrobe facilities will help minimise time out of rehearsals for necessary fittings. Provision for the care and welfare of the artistic team and acting company should be considered, as much as the technical support needed to manage the room. Stage management teams run these rooms and so should be consulted in the design phase.

Control of temperature, light and ventilation is important. Some plays may require actors to move very little, while musicals and dance performances will require vigorous activity, all of which impacts the ambient environment in the room. Natural light should be catered for where possible, but the light (both natural and artificial) in the rehearsal room should come from above and be evenly distributed. Windows and walls should have drapery to block out light and to soften the sound reflections in the room.

Acoustic separation is an essential consideration, both from within the room and external to the room. There needs to be zero to minimal distraction in the room from external sounds, and minimal sound emerging to cause distraction to other parts of the building.

The rehearsal room should have the ability to be technically equipped for small performances, with both lighting and sound. A good range of technical power sources and the ability to interconnect with other technical infrastructures around the building is important. Being able to set up a PA for rehearsal sound playback should be flexible and straightforward with minimum cable runs.

Screens are often used for reference films during rehearsals and wall space to easily fix reference images will be helpful. The space should be easy to clean and flexible storage solutions found for costume rails, chairs and tables.

Flexibility of the space to allow corporate hire among other uses will ensure maximum benefits to any size of organisation. Routes from the foyer and secondary escapes should be considered.

Figure 7.2.1 The Rehearsal Room above the Swan auditorium, with windows set into the base of the high sloping roof panels at the Royal Shakespeare Theatre, Stratford-upon-Avon.

## Dressing rooms

Rehearsals and performances are demanding; dressing rooms offer performers a place to rest, and to prepare both mentally and physically. It is therefore important that they are places of refuge giving comfort and safety away from the demands of a production. They have a practical element, of course, but they should not feel industrial or clinical. Where possible natural light should be available – enough of a performer's life is spent in a darkened theatre. There must, however, be control of natural light and privacy through adjustable window dressing, giving options dependant on the time of day and internal activity.

Dressing rooms should be similar to the profile and function of a hotel room, both in practical delivery and in the fixtures and fittings. Like a hotel room, dressing rooms should be hard wearing and easy to clean, the floor finish should be warm and soft under foot and suitable for mopping – a good vinyl works well. Dressing room doors should be clearly and uniquely identified and have the facility to display the performer's name, as well as the ability to identify if they do not wish to be disturbed. Doors should be wide enough, as throughout the building, for wheelchair access as well as wardrobe trundles and costume rails. The room layout must accommodate wheelchair turning circles.

Where possible keyless locks, with options for a key-pad code, means that rooms can be secured when not occupied, without the performer having to carry a key with them during a performance. A small notice board adjacent to the door is useful for messages, notices and mail. Consideration should be given for a visual doorbell system for performers or staff who have a hearing impairment.

In preparation for a performance there needs to be an area for applying make-up, styling hair or fitting wigs, headdresses or radio mics. This needs to be in the form of a countertop with mirror, face lighting and power outlets. There should be one station for each occupant, preferably with under-counter lockable storage with a mini-safe for personal possessions including electronic devices. In smaller dressing rooms (single or up to six occupants) these stations are generally fixed, but in larger chorus dressing rooms consideration may be given to making some of these mobile stations. This allows for greater flexibility in the layout of the room to meet the needs of both visiting and in-house productions (see Figure 7.2.2).

**Countertop:** this should be sturdy, hardwearing and easy to clean. It should project no further than 500mm from the mirror and give at least 700mm width per station. An adjustable height countertop would be an advantage, especially for occupants using a wheelchair or for child performers.

**Mirror:** this needs to be at least 500mm wide and 750mm tall offering the performer a clear view of their shoulders, head and any headwear while seated.

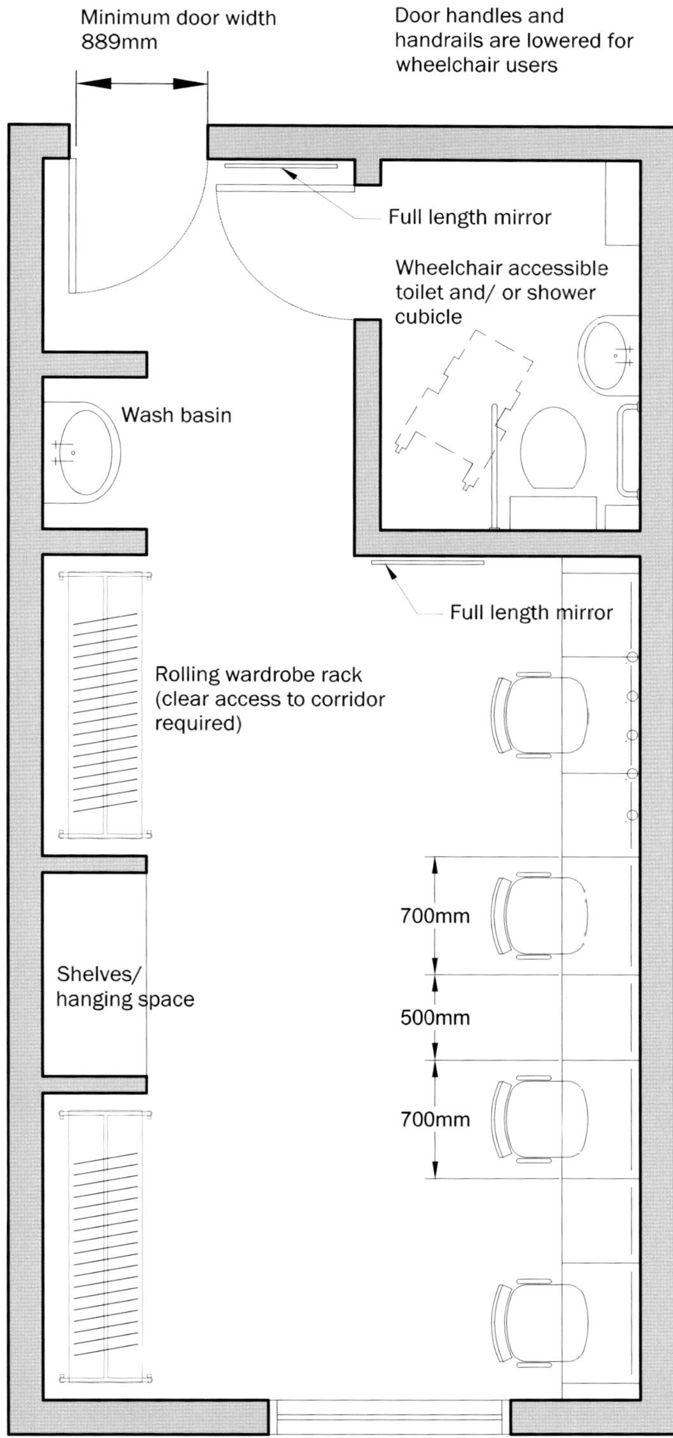


Figure 7.2.2 Dressing room layout diagram.

A full-length mirror should also be located somewhere near to the door to allow for last-minute checks before heading to the stage.

**Lighting:** dressing table lighting should come from left, right and above the mirror, giving soft, diffused and evenly distributed light across the face. The colour temperature should be equivalent to stage lighting (around 3,000–3,200k) and should be from an energy-efficient light source, such as LED. Mirror lighting control should be independent from other room lighting and be dimmable. Full length illumination should be provided for the full-length mirror, offering comparable quality of light to that of the dressing tables.

Room lighting should offer evenly distributed area lighting, preferably not cold or stark. It should be independently switched so that the mood of the room can be adjusted.

**Power:** at least one double power socket should be provided for each dressing table position and should incorporate USB outlets for electronic devices. A shaving power outlet should be provided between each pair of dressing table positions. There should also be general power sockets in the room for the use of cleaning equipment and any other toured or temporary equipment that may be brought in.

All power circuits should be protected by a residual current device (RCD).

**Furniture and Storage:** there should be an armless chair for each dressing table position, preferably upholstered, height adjustable and swivelling. A couch or daybed should also be considered, to allow principal performers to rest and sleep.

Each occupant will require a costume rail (this can be fixed or portable) at a minimum length of 700mm. On some productions, certainly where period dress is involved, more space is inevitably required. Another clothes rail for personal clothing is also advantageous to avoid mixing with show costumes. Space for hats or wig blocks will be required (this can be above the dressing table mirror) as well as a shoe rack to keep the floor space clear. A space for washing baskets will aid laundry collection at the end of a performance. Low-level hooks at around 1m above floor height, near to the costume rails are useful for hanging costume accessories such as canes/walking sticks, umbrellas and probably swords! Hooks outside the dressing room door are helpful for wardrobe staff to deliver laundered costumes without having to disturb the performer if relaxing.

**Bathroom facilities:** small dressing rooms (single or occupants up to three) should have an en-suite WC, sink and shower cubicle. This should be wheelchair accessible and provide all necessary access requirements. Larger dressing rooms (four to six occupants) should allow for separate toilets and washrooms, offering at least two sinks and two shower cubicles. Chorus dressing rooms (up to fifteen occupants) should have an en-suite washroom providing at least four sinks and four shower cubicles. Where space allows, an increase in numbers will improve performer turnaround time between and after performances. Chorus toilets should be separate from the washroom and can be accessed from the corridor outside, but nearby.

There should be toilet facilities located near to the entrances to the stage on either side. Additional facilities should be available on each dressing room level, especially as young performers work under strict safeguarding regulations and require dedicated bathroom facilities.

**Environmental controls:** there is no substitute for fresh air and, where possible, the ability to open windows to ventilate dressing rooms will be very welcomed by performers. However, it is still very important to have the right balance of temperature and humidity in dressing rooms – clean, fresh circulated air is essential for creating a comfortable environment. Performers may spend long periods of time barefoot, so making sure the floor isn't cold is all part of creating the right environment. This can be through good insulation and floor finish, or by underfloor heating. (See Figure 7.2.3.)

## Rest and treatment

Whether someone is temporarily unwell, injured or needing physiotherapy, a dedicated space big enough for a treatment bed with space around it will prove invaluable in venues programming large physical productions. Space for a wash basin, chairs and storage for first aid kits should be factored in.

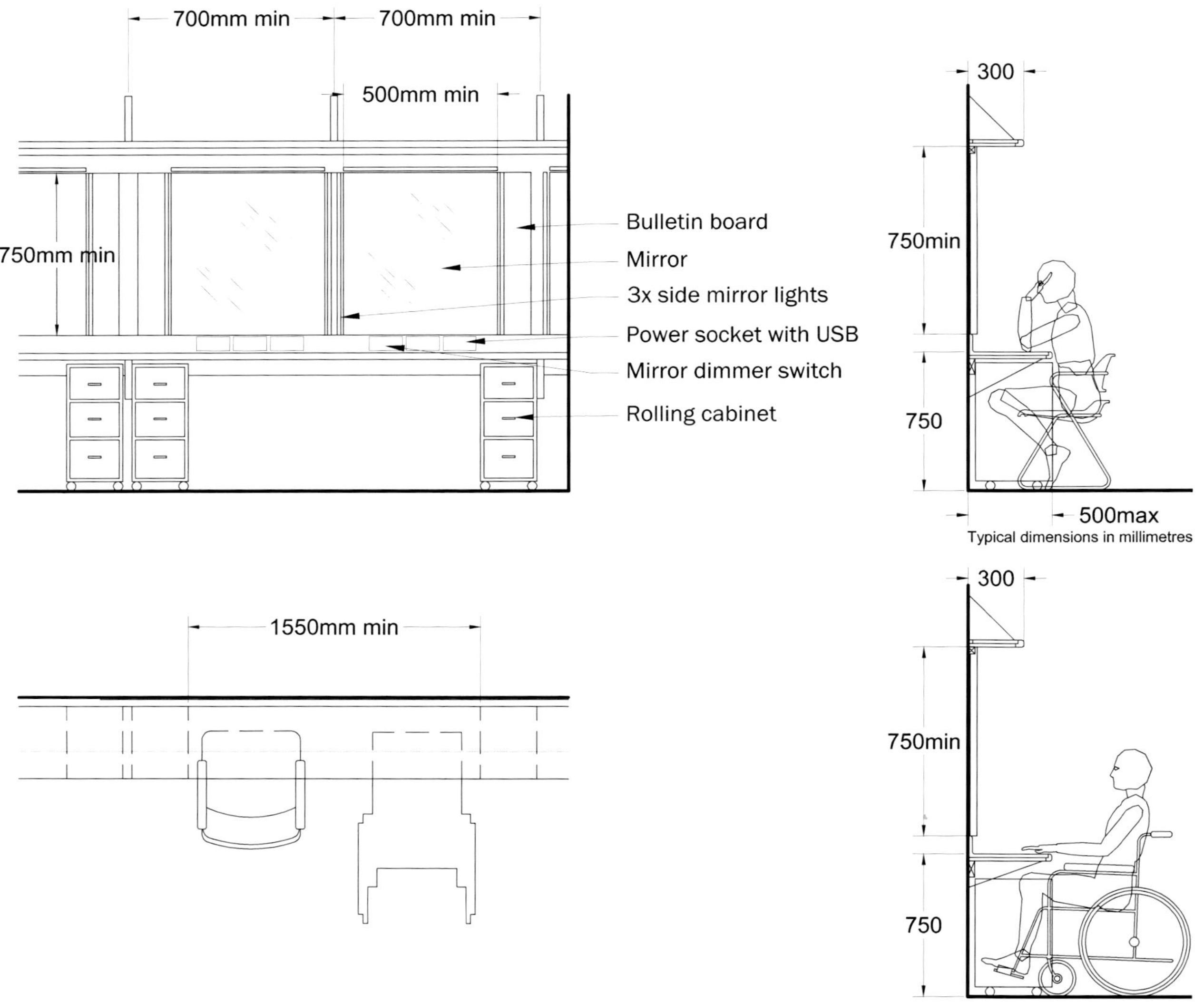


Figure 7.2.3 Table setting out a dressing room guide. The number of each type will vary as to type of theatre/size. Typically, a mid- to large-scale touring house requires accommodation for fifty to one hundred performers.

## Green room

Well-designed green rooms help to promote the sense of community within a theatre. There might be a fully serviced kitchenette/bar or just a kettle and fridge. Actors and technicians can relax here either before a performance or, most often, after. It can afford performers the privacy not available in a public space front of house. They might meet visitors escorted from the stage door post-show or talk to production staff on matters not directly related to work, permitting a social element to compensate for the late and long hours of theatre work.

No space is ever wasted in a theatre, and during the day this space might be invaluable for meetings.

The level of facilities provided will be determined by the scale of the organisation, but it should aim at an easy transition from a well-lit meeting or rest space during the day to a sophisticated and comfortable lounge at night.

For many theatres, green rooms become the equivalent of the home kitchen where food and drink preparation are focused around social interaction. Surfaces for food preparation, an area for heating food (there are never enough microwaves), an area for making hot and cold drinks and the ability to wash hands and dishes are all an essential part of fuelling the workforce. These can be as focused or as expansive as the available area allows; however, it is important to consider accessibility to these facilities, where the room layout, adjustable height countertops and considerations for wheelchairs and child performers are all important factors in making this room welcome to all in the backstage community.

# 7.3 Get in and out

Anecdotally amongst touring and freelance theatre technicians, theatres will often be defined by the ease, or more commonly the difficulty, of their 'get-in'. In that respect, it is one of the most important aspects of a theatre's design and layout and will very much determine both the ability to ensure safe working practice, and the efficiency with which productions can be taken in and out of the theatre.

Most productions travel in 45-ft articulated trucks, and the aspiration should always be that these trucks have enough space to reverse comfortably to the dock doors, allowing the contents to be directly rolled out onto stage level.

The reality is that many existing theatre sites or the tight footprints of new urban sites do not make this arrangement straightforward or possible. In many cases the stage itself will not be at street level.

Whatever the constraints of space there are critical considerations to be made through a risk assessment process:

- that vehicles of all sizes can turn safely to reverse to the dock doors
- that manual handling is reduced to a minimum
- that obstacles such as corners and unlevelled floors between the dock and stage are avoided
- that scenic items of every possible shape, size and weight that can fit within a high cube trailer can be handled into the stage space avoiding tight turns or fragile building services
- that vehicles can be loaded and unloaded in all weathers without damaging the contents or creating slippery surfaces
- that there is always enough light for safe working
- that noise issues in relation to adjacent residential buildings are considered
- that clear segregation of pedestrians and traffic can be achieved to avoid collisions
- that access to the building or evacuation routes aren't impeded by the positioning of an articulated trailer.

## A level through route

Scenery and the assets that make up a production come in all shapes, sizes and weight. Musculoskeletal disorders are common amongst theatre workers of current and previous generations. It is entirely possible to design the risk of such health conditions out of a production flow. It is also essential to the diversity of the workforce and accessibility to the profession that you don't need to be able to bench press 150kg to exist in this environment.

Even the smallest of theatres can accommodate tonnes of production materials and equipment which need to be moved on and off the stage at a frequency determined by the programming cycles of a venue. Considered design of the route from vehicle to stage can mitigate the hugely damaging potential of short-term accidents to long-term health consequences. It can also significantly aid the efficiency of production get ins by saving both time and the number of personnel required.

## Dock leveller

Consideration should be given to mechanical solutions that can assist in creating level access from the back of a vehicle into the venue without relying on ramps (see Figure 7.3.1).

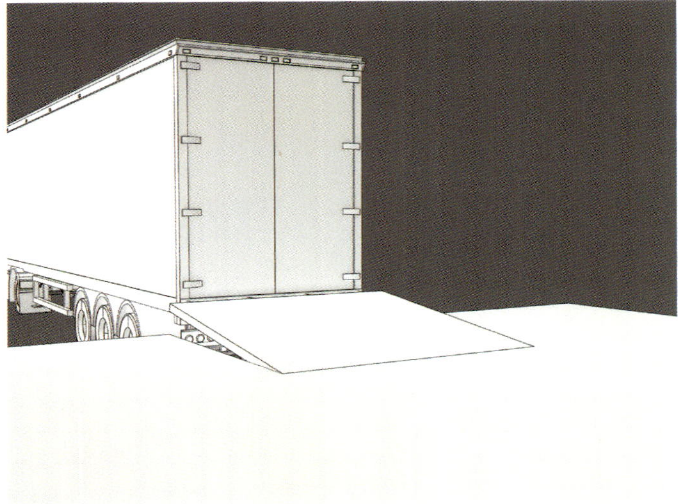

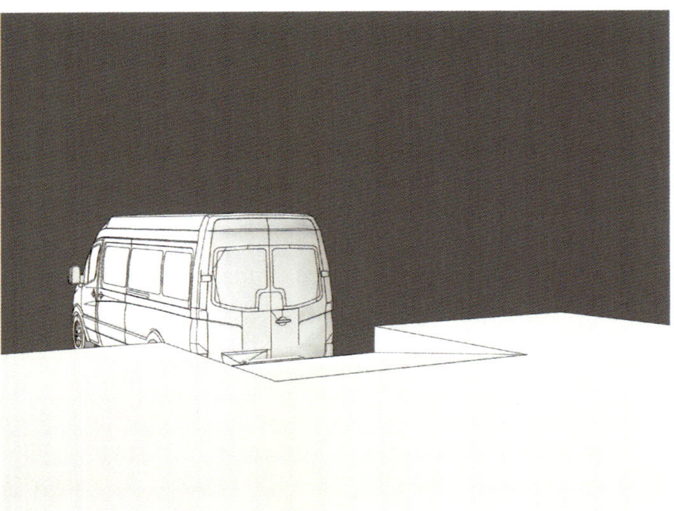

Figures 7.3.1a and 7.3.1b Dock leveller diagrams.

## Stages above or below street level

For a stage higher or lower than the street it will be necessary to provide an elevator to enable either the trailer or the scenery to get to stage level. The elevator can be located inside the building or outside. (See Figure 7.3.2.)

A trailer lift is preferable as this allows the contents to be unloaded directly to stage level, removing 'double-handling'. Such a lift can also be programmed to stop with the tailboard at floor level.

Warehouse-type rolling crane hoists above high-level doors have been used in the past, but these are an extremely slow method of operation and can be dangerous. They should not be used as the main means of get-in for a theatre.

Figure 7.3.2 Get-in lift at Chichester Festival Theatre.

## Dock doors

Construction efficiency and the speed of mounting a production can be compromised if the dock doors are not of a suitable size. A minimum of 3m wide and 4m high should be provided, but consultation with local staff will often reveal anecdotal evidence of the good reasons to be bigger than that.

Subject to further separation from the stage, acoustic performance will be a key determinant of what kind of door this is.

Consideration of heat loss through dock doors during winter months is critical. Energy-saving initiatives in an organisation can be wholly undermined if dock doors are open all day allowing all the carefully managed heat of a building to escape. Thermal curtains could be considered or a layout that allows a scene dock lobby to help reduce heat loss.

Putting a standard door sized access into the larger dock doors only operable from the inside also allows useful egress without creating heat loss or compromising security.

## Scene dock

Often between the stage and the dock doors there is a scene dock. This often becomes a critical production storage area, and at a time when the reuse of scenic elements in the pursuit of a low-carbon circular economy is so important, it needs careful consideration so that this essential storage doesn't block or interrupt productions getting in and out.

Height is important, and a common item to be kept on site will be masking flats that, as a minimum, might be the height of the proscenium. It is also important that this height can be fully utilised, so the ability to lift and hang items should be considered.

If adjacent to the stage this space can often be turned to creative use as an extension of the stage or an entrance.

## Outside broadcast

Modern theatre production has moved beyond allowing an audience to only see and experience the performance at the theatre. To reach more people in local communities, the wider country and internationally, theatre performances are being broadcast direct from the stage. To facilitate this requirement theatre buildings, need to be able to accommodate the temporary infrastructure that comes with outside broadcast (OB). Even a simple set-up may require at least a scanner and sound vehicle to be positioned outside the theatre. These vehicles will require easy access to temporary power as well as cable holes to distribute cables around the building – stage, auditorium, orchestra pit and rehearsal rooms. These routes are also useful for other types of events where a temporarily connected infrastructure is required.

Please refer to Sections 9.5 and 9.8 for further detail of infrastructural requirements.

## Waste

The reduction of waste must be the goal of all theatre practice, but for now it is inevitable that some waste is created in whatever type of theatre operation exists in the building. That waste will usually leave the building through the dock doors and so it is essential to plan the location of waste and recycling bins so that they don't inhibit activity through the dock.

Separation of waste materials on site has obvious benefits to the environment, so consultation with potential waste removal and recycling service providers about size of bins and level of separation is important.

# 7.4 Fit-up and technical rehearsals

The period that starts with the get out of one production to be replaced by another, either fabricated within the building or coming through the dock doors for the first time, is the most intensive part of the process where staffing numbers might easily quadruple and when schedules might demand 24-hour activity. (See Figure 7.4.1.) This is the time when the pressure on everyone is at its greatest. Will the set fit? Will the lighting rig be in the right place and not collide with the set? Will the sound rig sight line be compromised by the set? Is there enough space for costume and wig quick changes? Will it all be done on time for the first performance? A touring show may well have benefited from multiple assembly and disassembly, but it does not always negate the idiosyncrasies of a particular theatre even with the best ground plans.

Figure 7.4.1 Olivier Theatre at the National Theatre, London, fit up going 'into the round' (2020).

Compared with a building industry design and build schedule, the making of a production is very compressed. Even the most rigorous planning doesn't rule out problems. Technical rehearsals are a creative process, and though it remains a source of occasional friction, it is the artists' prerogative to adapt and have new ideas in this period within the resources of time and budget. All the skills that have been used in the making of sets, props, costumes, wigs and the delivery of equipment rigs will need to be readily available to adjust, fix and change things until the opening night.

## Crew rooms

Crew rooms can often be relegated to the remaining bit of left over space after all other demands and functions that have been catered for, meaning potentially lack of daylight, poor accessibility, limited facilities and tatty old furniture. Largely occupied by transient staff, whether freelance production technicians or show running stage crews, they rarely have a champion at the design stage of a building. Despite this, they have a key role in making staff who do physically hard, and often unnoticed jobs, feel valued.

While the production staff who run fit ups may be at the peak of their profession and should therefore be treated accordingly, the show running staff may be enthusiastic junior practitioners getting their first experience of theatre.

It is critical that they are treated no differently from other staff and are given a rest space that integrates them with the wider community of people working in the building.

Considerations should include:

- good natural daylight is preferred for all production staff
- lockers should be provided for both permanent and non-permanent staff
- basic kitchen facilities – fridge, microwave, kettle – may be elsewhere or located within the crew room
- show relay – audio and visual
- good Wi-Fi or networked workstation
- dedicated harness and safety equipment storage
- shelving for safety documentation and policy documents
- first aid kits
- comfortable furniture to accommodate largest anticipated show crews
- ideally located near stage management and dressing rooms to assist integration.

## Band rooms

Even theatres which are predominantly used for drama will often require facilities for musicians. Whether or not they are appearing on stage they may be required to change clothing before a performance. A reasonable provision might be for 15 musicians with the facility to provide separate accommodation for unequal numbers of men and women. Musicians are less likely to spend time in the band room other than to get changed, but they will require full-length mirrors, lockers for personal belongings and enough space for musical instrument cases. Broad shelves with resilient surfaces on which musical instruments can be placed are also required.

This room should be located near the entrance to the orchestra pit. Since it is likely to be used for occasional individual practice or tuning it should, where possible, have a good level of sound separation both from the auditorium and the dressing room area.

For large musical theatres or opera and ballet companies the room(s) may need to accommodate up to one hundred and twenty musicians.

## Musical instruments

Any intention to programme work with live music will mean consideration of where to store musical instruments with thought given to step free routes from the get in and to orchestra pits. Regular storage of instruments may require climate control.

## Running wardrobe

Although many venues might not have dedicated costume production areas, there will nearly always be a need for running wardrobe facilities, where repairs and alterations can be carried out to costumes on the current production. Even where the costume production facility is on the same site, the differences in the working patterns of production staff and show staff, and the need for maintenance facilities to be located close to the laundry, dressing rooms and the stage, make this space essential in all types of theatre.

These facilities require:

- a worktable and seating
- space for sewing machine/overlocker
- hanging space for costumes or space to house moveable rails
- racks for footwear, hats and accessories
- an ironing board
- space for storage drawers/boxes for haberdashery, spares, etc.
- access to water
- good lighting (either natural light or daylight bulb lighting)
- good ventilation or opening widows (due to steam/heat from irons)
- doors – large enough for rail movement
- show relay and monitors.

In a theatre which takes in touring productions, plenty of dry space with ambient temperature and good lighting is needed for unpacking and then for holding empty skips or mobile/touring wardrobe trucks is required.

## Laundry

The laundry should be alongside the running wardrobe and should include:

- standard industrial equipment
- dryer ventilation outlets
- deep double sink and drainer
- electrical points – two washers, two dryers, two hot boxes, twin tub, iron and steamer – which might all be used simultaneously
- ozone machine
- fixed costume rail as well as space for mobile rails
- good ventilation/extract
- table for sorting/folding laundry
- washable floor with drainage to take away water
- doors – large enough for rail movement
- show relay.

1 WASHERS
- Commercial grade or large-capacity domestic clothes washers
- Exact number varies with theatre size
- Provide power and plumbing

2 DRYERS
- Commercial grade or large-capacity domestic dryers (can be stacked)
- Exact number varies with theatre size
- Provide power, plumbing, and venting

3 SINK
- Large double-basin stainless steel sink with drying board
- Storage shelves or cabinets above
- Provide plumbing

4 WORK COUNTER
- Kitchen-style work counter with base cabinets below and wall cabinets above
- Provide utility outlets at counter height

5 FOLDING TABLE
- 3'x6' rolling table with locking casters and padded top

6 IRONING STATION
- Includes ironing board with gravity iron and vertical steamer
- Provide appropriate power

7 FLOOR
- Tiled floor with floor drain in center of the room

8 DOUBLE DOORS
- Shop floor should be at the same level as the hallway
- Double doors should have a flush threshold to accommodate rolling costume racks

9 ROLLING WARDROBE RACK
- Used to easily move costumes from dressing rooms to costume shop and laundry

10 COSHH CABINET
- For storage of chemicals and aerosols

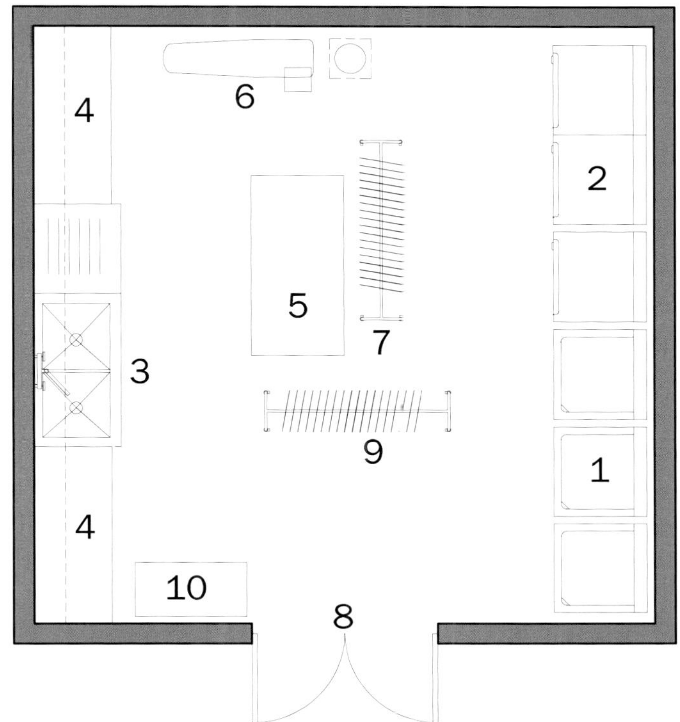


Figure 7.4.2 Example of a laundry room layout.

## Radio mic preparation area

Radio mics are no longer used just for large-scale productions and musicals. There are many reasons that they are now commonly used in smaller venues and for plays. Space very close to the stage where they can be prepped and stored is important.

## Prop preparation and storage

Most productions will need an area for the props to be prepared and stored. Large quantities of running props may need storage. These types of spaces often get sacrificed in later stage thinking about where to house services and containment. It is therefore advisable to 'ring fence' them.

Food may need preparing prior to each performance so consideration should be given to prevailing food and hygiene legislation when setting up a small kitchen area. Running water and space for large refrigerators should be factored in.

These spaces should be close to and ideally have easy step free access to the stage. Acoustic separation is important, however, to allow prep and clean up during performances.

# 7.5 Production planning

The work that goes into making a production successful, safe and financially well controlled is often intense and may be conducted over months before the production reaches the stage. The exact type of work, and the staff employed to do it, will vary from company to company and according to scale. A key theme of this book is to promote rigorous consultation with the staff likely to be using the facilities, and to fully understand the likely long-term plan for the type and scale of work to be produced. Nearly all companies expand as they achieve success, but without the ability to comfortably house the increase in staff.

Whether 'presenting' or 'producing', however, all buildings will have to house professional technicians who will need an environment which is comfortable to work in for many hours.

Whatever the scale and possibilities, or limitations of space, key principles should be acknowledged:

- good light and ventilation are essential, and preferably daylight to compensate for the long periods of time spent in daylight free performance spaces

- all offices, workshops and spaces should be accessible with clear signage to location in compliance with equality legislation
- good communication is central to any production process whether internally within a building or externally with the many suppliers and specialists who will contribute to making the work.

Alongside excellent IT and wi-fi, the infrastructure should allow for monitors – enabling staff in offices to stay keenly aware of what is happening on the stages at any time and especially during a performance.

Welfare space needs to include changing rooms, lockers, showers and break rooms that might also double as crew rooms to house performance staff as well as the production crew for the installation of each production.

### Technical offices

Traditional roles and their titles have evolved as the technical disciplines have become more specialised or at times integrated.

There may be a head of production who also functions as a production manager or a technical manager who focuses purely on technical delivery and infrastructure.

There will nearly always be a primary stage technician and lighting technician and increasingly someone specialising in sound.

The disciplines of production/technical management, stage, lighting, sound, costume and wigs/makeup will be represented as either permanent or freelance staff and need office space. As arts organisations develop their digital strategies new disciplines will require space.

Whether these staff share an office or have smaller individual spaces will depend on the philosophy of the organisation as much as available floor space. Despite specialism meaning a level of demarcation, collaboration remains central to any producing process and so these staff should be close to each other and to the stages. Room layouts that encourage staff and performers to pass each other *en route* to the stage help bolster the sense of community that defines the happiest and most productive producing houses.

Whether in separate or shared offices, there needs to be space for regular meetings and private conversations. As we move to paperless operations, a large screen in a meeting space to share technical drawings is important.

Drawing boards are largely a thing of the past and it is more important that everyone has access to a screen whether as a fixed workstation or as a portable device in a hot desking environment.

However, current practice still makes good use of an AO plotter to deliver construction drawings to workshops or layout drawings to staff working directly on stage and these require space if not their own room.

### Company and stage management

Company and stage management roles may be combined or separate and, in many places, be employed from production to production as freelance staff. An average team per production might consist of three members with or without a company manager.

A company manager will always need space for private conversations. Stage managers will always need space to cover the wide extent of their roles. In buildings with more than one performance space it is easy to underestimate how many stage managers might need a desk space, and in producing buildings it is equally easy to forget that there may be stage managers in rehearsal as well as in performance, with inevitable crossover.

As a minimum each team will need two workstations and good network connections. Their offices should be between the dressing rooms, the stage and the technical offices with which there will always need to be close collaboration.

### Artistic teams

Most artistic teams are made up of freelancers employed show by show. In a producing theatre the director, designers, choreographers, composers, fight directors, vocal coaches and many others will need to work extremely closely with resident producing staff to deliver the physical productions as they have conceived them, and within the resources made available to them.

It is often assumed that most freelancers have their own adequate studio space to work in but that is not always the case.

Such critical roles need integrating comprehensively into the life and work of the building and a space provided for them where possible. As a minimum, this requires a place to leave coats and bags and, as an ideal, a studio space with the same IT resources afforded to the technical offices.

## 7.6 Making and maintaining

In a producing theatre there are strong arguments for putting as much of the production process under one roof as possible: reducing transport-associated carbon, facilitating ease of communication, a greater sense of shared endeavour and, consequently, inclusivity, economic efficiencies, preservation of craft skills, local training and job opportunities.

Of course, far from every building project will have the space or business model to have room for such facilities.

However, whatever the scale of the theatre and whether it is a receiving or producing house, there will always need to be some provision for fabrication whether the making of masking flats; the repair of a complicated prop half an hour before a performance; the ongoing repair and maintenance of costumes and wigs; and the regular repair of lighting, sound and video equipment.

Some key principles apply to all these areas:

- consideration of adjacencies determined by production workflow and handling of items
- compliance with all current health and safety legislation but particularly with regard to extract ventilation for certain processes and the reduction of manual handling
- sound separation from performance, rehearsal and office spaces
- accessibility to all workshop spaces
- scale of fabrication spaces and access routes in alignment with size of performance spaces
- storage space for stock materials, fabricated and re-usable items
- good consistent lighting and temperature control
- adequate power supply
- flexibility of use where space is limited with compliance for multiple processes.

## Scenic workshops

There are several key considerations when designing a space dedicated to scenic construction, scenic art and prop making:

- the health, safety and wellbeing of the staff who will use the space
- the flow of materials from when they enter the space as raw materials through to their delivery on stage as a piece of scenery or out of the building as a waste product
- the storage of materials
- the scale of the scenery that will be created in the space
- the machinery/tools/equipment required for the creation of scenery.

If space is limited, then obviously there are many shared elements between any of the spaces described here, and it would be down to venue management to decided how integrated they want/need the spaces to be.

## Construction workshops

Construction of any sort relies on collaboration between all the technical disciplines but principally the designer, production manager, draughtsperson and construction staff will all need to work closely together. If there is a dedicated draughting team delivering construction drawings to the workshops, they will need a quiet ventilated office space in which to work. A meeting space that is not the workshop floor with a large enough screen to share and a big enough table for a 1:25 scale model is important for effective collaboration in an evolving design and build process.

If scale models remain an important communication tool, a suitable ventilated model-making area allowing for the use of spray paints and adhesives will be beneficial.

If possible, separate spaces should be created for carpentry and metalwork to take place, although this will be dictated by the scale of work imagined and the ambition and scale of the organisation. If the workshop is to be used to construct full sets for a single stage venue, then the workshop footprint should be at least ×1.5 that of the stage area. If more substantial construction is envisaged (either as a commercial supplier and/or for multiple stages) the footprint should be increased significantly. If the workshop is to be used as a support space for incoming pre-constructed productions, then less space will be required, although the end user will always end up filling the space. The same basic rules apply for scenic art studios. There should be enough floor space to paint an entire stage floor, and possibly to have a team of people working on a paint frame if there is enough space to fit one in. The paint frame should ideally be as big as the backwall of the stage, although it is possible to work with less space (but painting will take longer). It is not imperative that these spaces have the same height as the stage space, but it is useful to have somewhere where scenic elements can be stood up, and pre-assembled and/or painted, prior to going on stage.

Floors need to be flat and easily cleaned, ideally able to withstand being screwed into should the need arise to secure a piece of scenery or a machine to the floor. The loading on a floor should be appropriate for the machinery being installed. It is best to avoid wooden floors in metal fabrication spaces due to the fire risks of hot metal.

Workbenches need to be stable, and manoeuvrable. In larger spaces avoid fixed workbenches to enable flexible use of the floor space. Power sockets should be provided in convenient locations around the space. Check the local standard supply voltage for power tools in the country of the venue and provide accordingly. There should be a provision for both single and 3 phase power for larger machinery. There should be electrical isolator points in any workshop space, so that the power can be cut to all machinery and sockets in the event of an emergency.

Compressed air systems should be considered, as air tools are popular for certain tasks including nailing and stapling. Any fixed compressed system should have outlets mounted at an accessible height at various points around a workshop. Fixed hose reels can be considered if they are the preference of the end user. Variable pressure valves should be fitted at each outlet to enable the end user to set the pressure according to the equipment. The air compressor should be located away from the areas where people work, as they run frequently and can be excessively noisy.

Careful consideration should be given to the best location for any fixed machinery. Radial arm, and table saws in carpentry workshops are commonplace along with a combination of the following: wall saw, planer/thicknesser, morticer, tenoner, band saw.

Computer numerical control (CNC) routers are now common in commercial scenic workshops, so there should be some evaluation of whether this would be an appropriate investment for the type of work being carried out in the space. If the workshop is likely to operate full time, then the chances are there will be a return on that investment.

In a metal fabrication workshop/area there may be metal cutting saws, ironworkers for punching, notching, and shearing metal rolling machine to create curved metal bars, laser, plasma and water jet cutting machines.

Such lists are indicative of the machines required, but this will vary depending on individual requirements and the scale of intended use.

Material storage (location and type) must be carefully considered. Timber and metal remain the core structural components of scenery, but consideration must also be given to other materials such as: fabric – which can be delivered on rolls or in packs; plastics – with potential sheet sizes up to 2.1 × 6m.

As the world moves rapidly to reducing greenhouse gas emissions and more circular production, adaptation of existing sets and materials will be more widespread. Construction methodologies are changing, and systems of modular scenic components are starting to be developed. Just as skills will have to adapt to the green economy, so must space.

## Material storage questions

Poor storage choices can quickly clog up the flow of work in any workshop, and consideration should be given to the following questions.

- where do materials come into the space?
- where do materials go out of the space – either as waste, or as scenery?
- what machines commonly use which materials?
- how will materials be handled by the end users?
- how should each material be stored to keep it in the best condition?
- where should usable off cuts be stored?
- how are waste off-cuts managed?

It is important to ensure that any storage systems have clearly visible weight limits to prevent overloading. It is important to make a provision for how materials and built scenic elements will be handled and manoeuvred. Hoists (either at fixed points, or on rolling beams) on the ceiling should be considered along with storage space on the floor for any wheeled dollies/trolleys/forklift trucks.

All materials produce waste, and this needs to be carefully managed. Dust and vapours need to be extracted in a safe, and legally compliant manner. Consideration needs to be given to the location of any extraction unit as there will be filters that need changing, and containers that will need to be emptied on a regular basis.

Any workshop space will need storage for hand-held tools (both power and manually operated), and for hardware such as screws, staples, nails and specialist scenic fixings. These should be accessible from floor level, and lockable. Substances that can be hazardous to health must be stored appropriately, and it is worth checking the local requirements to determine the implications for storage. Improvements in battery technology mean that more tools can be powered by battery, so it is worth considering whether a dedicated battery charging station would be beneficial. Dedicated first aid stations should be provided in any workshop space, and there should be adequate storage for any PPE that will be required. There may also be a requirement for the temporary storage of scenic items whilst they are being worked on (see 'Assembly Area'). Again, the exact requirements will be very much dependent on the scale and volume of work being produced in the space.

## Scenic art studio

Contemporary scenic art studios use a wide variety of techniques and materials to achieve both two and three-dimensional scenic finishes. This may involve creating textures, carving, creating stencils, painted cloths, 'back projection' screens and gauzes. Painted cloths and gauzes may be more commonly found in opera and ballet but still have a significant role in contemporary drama. Huge advances have been made in large-scale printing, but the unique characteristics of hand painted cloths will be championed by directors, designers and lighting designers for a long time to come.

Scenic artists still often work from scale models and reference materials provided by the designer. Reference material is now commonly provided via digital media which can be used on the shop floor using tablets or mobile phones.

General requirements are:

- dimensions that allow for large floors and back cloths to be laid out for painting. Ideally the footprint is the size of the largest performance space
- height is also important as this allows for a static paint frame to be used for painting back cloths and large scenic elements to be constructed in the space. A paint frame will generally require appropriate mechanical platform lift access. Consideration must be given to the practical use and maintenance of any mechanical platforms
- consistent, good quality light is essential and direct sunlight best avoided. End user preferences should be understood and adhered to where possible
- consistent temperature aids drying times. Underfloor heating can be considered but needs to be controllable by the end user
- scenery is now commonly constructed before painting begins so access equipment is an important part of the kit needed to reach all textured/painted surfaces
- for considerations/requirements for the storage of materials and equipment please refer to the section on construction workshops (in 7.6)
- it is important to consider the environmental impact of the materials that are used in the process of achieving scenic finishes
- facilities including large sinks and paint traps should be provided for mixing paints and textures and for cleaning equipment. Taps should be lever operated, and mixer taps should be avoided
- a compressed air system should be available

Figure 7.6.1 Glyndebourne Production Hub 2.

- it is common for compressed air to be used to achieve some scenic finishes. This can be provided either from a central source or from individual compressors. When using spray equipment, the correct PPE should always be used. For any permanently installed system please refer to notes in the section on construction workshops (in 7.6).

## Assembly area

A pre-fit-up assembly area will, in many circumstances, be considered an extravagance, but the positive impacts gained in troubleshooting a fit up before that pressurised period on stage arrives extend from financial control to wellbeing.

If a set has been fully assembled before going onto the stage problems can be solved without costly overnight calls; designers can have given their most taxing notes; directors can have solved spatial and blocking issues before the pressure of a technical rehearsal.

Subject to the influx of other productions this might be perfectly achievable in the main construction area, but the benefits of being able to get on with other work while set dressing notes are finished elsewhere are obvious.

## Props workshop

A props workshop needs to be set up to accommodate a wide range of fabrication processes.

Local exhaust ventilation (LEV) and flexibility will be primary considerations.

In many theatres, receiving and producing, this smaller flexible workshop might be the only workshop that deals with both running set and props maintenance. It must be possible to carry out more traditional workshop tasks such as carpentry, metal work, sculpting and fibre glassing alongside tasks such as upholstery, printing, and general modifications to 'found' props. The props department may also be engaged in the evolution of additive manufacturing, and how this can be utilised for prop making so it is worth considering creating space for a 3D printing zone within the workshop.

Close access to the stage may be beneficial although acoustic separation will become a more significant factor. Many of the factors listed for the construction workshops (in 7.6) are relevant for props workshops.

## Armoury

A specific facility for looking after the manufacture and maintenance of swords, guns and other weapons will exist in only the largest companies. Grinding, welding, brazing and polishing will require adequate space and local exhaust ventilation.

Most theatres will just require secure storage that will need to comply with local legislation and police oversight.

## Costume production

What follows is a guide to the facilities required by the largest companies and in the largest theatres. Buildings designed for a smaller scale of presentation or those limited by considerations of space or finance may not be able, or need, to meet all these specifications. In these circumstances those skills will be found outside of their facilities – whether freelance makers or companies.

Costume production is distinct from the running wardrobe maintenance facilities which are described earlier in this section. Although, like the scenery workshop, it is not essential that this activity takes place in the main building, it is much better if it does. It will usually take up less space than that needed for scenery construction and there is a requirement for closer liaison with rehearsals, performers and the stage. If possible, it is helpful to put all costume production facilities together for ease of communication and use of shared facilities. It is also recommended to have the same lighting throughout the facility so that colour matching stays constant through all stages.

Costume production is a manufacturing process which must be carried out in a proper sequence if it is to be efficient. In addition to cutting, constructing and fitting costumes, facilities should be provided for dyeing and textile work; for millinery; for costume props /accessories and, in the larger companies, for making boots and shoes.

As a production process begins, the designer and supervisor will discuss concepts and ideas in the costume supervisor's office where a programme of work will be decided. The costume designer and supervisor will need a base to work from providing a desk/computer space, space to house rails and items of clothing/fabric/shopping as well as good lighting and space to meet with other collaborators. A place to lock things away (both personal and expensive show items) as well as access to a phone and mirror.

## Costume workshop

The actors' measurements are taken or checked, and patterns drafted. Fabric is then cut on the stand or at the cutting table. The construction stages include the use of stands (dressmakers' mannequins), sewing machine tables and access to ironing facilities. The following equipment needs to be accommodated:

- cutting table: 1,200 × 1,800–2,400 × 1,000mm high with all-round access and shelves for fabric storage. An allowance of 12–14m$^2$ per table should be made
- stands: both male and female in a range of sizes, mobile but requiring 3–4m$^2$ floor space
- sewing machines: each on its own table with a chair and a space around it; about 1,100 × 1,100mm with 13-amp socket outlets in a convenient position for each machine and individual lighting
- sewing tables: 750 × 1,200mm with a chair, requiring 5 or 6m$^2$ of floor space
- ironing boards: industrial irons with inbuilt water tank and power
- portable storage: a wheeled cabinet or trolley with shallow drawers for boxes of pins, needles, cotton reels and so on (for fittings)
- storage for haberdashery, books, fabric, personal belongings
- hanging rails: room for hanging rails for completed costumes and movable rails for things coming and going
- lighting: good overall illumination from both daylight and artificial daylight lighting with adjustable; lamps near each sewing machine
- access: costumes from the dressing rooms/running wardrobe as well as deliveries will regularly need to be brought into the department so level access and use of a lift (for upper floors) is essential
- there should be a sink and draining board with hot and cold-water supply
- a small kitchen/rest area (if space allows) is good for staff to take breaks away from their work and have social time together.

Figure 7.6.2 Costume workshop for the RSC. See Julian Middleton, 'RSC Waterside – the Costume Workshop', *Sightline*, Summer 2022, pp. 10–14.

## Storage/stock room

Supplies of fabric, haberdashery and other essential items for costume production will need storing away from (but nearby to) the main workshops. This could have a system of booking out of goods or could have a stock co-ordinator who controls and re-orders stock when required. Fabric rolls are between 1.2–1.5m long and shelf storage is also required for other items.

## Fitting rooms

In larger buildings, a flexible fitting room space is desirable. A large fitting room (approx. $20m^2$) could be divided into two $10m^2$ rooms (with separate entrances) for separate fittings or have a larger space when required. Fitting rooms need:

- good lighting (as in rest of department) and access to stage lighting
- controllable heating/cooling/ventilation
- vinyl flooring (pins catch in carpets)
- space for rails and mobile trolley/workstation
- table for goods
- chairs for actor to sit
- large wall mirror
- wall space/computer screen for designs
- blinds on windows
- ability to film fitting
- door large enough for rail access and turning space for rails
- near/off main costume workroom
- show relay
- phone.

## Textile studio

A separate area is needed for all textile techniques including dyeing, breaking down and printing of costumes.

One of the most important things to consider before designing a new textile treatment studio is the extract ventilation that will be required. This could well dictate the position within the building (extraction to outside air) as well as the position within the department. It is essential to ascertain what techniques will be needed and carry out a full risk assessment before consulting a local extract ventilation (LEV) specialist.

The layout of this room is also essential so consult the people that will be occupying it. A tiled floor is essential with drainage gully to take away excess water.

Basic equipment that will be required:

- a heated dye vat
- induction hob
- large industrial spinner
- a large sink with hot and cold water
- ironing facilities
- domestic washing machine (for sole use of dye shop)
- shelves and cupboards (lockable/chemical cupboards) for dyestuffs and acids chemicals
- bench for mixing dyes with extract
- large worktable with space all around
- access to computer and printer for digital work
- print table
- dark room for screen developing
- separate areas for clean and dirty working
- storage for personal goods/locker.

## Drying room

A drying room should adjoin the dye shop. This could be a tumble dryer but ideally access to a heated room. Also, a natural drying area is desirable allowing cloth to dry naturally while being draped over a drying rack. This could be made of steel tube, galvanised or plastic covered. The tubes of the rack should be fitted at about head height at about 0.5m intervals and each tube should be about 1.5m long As in the dye shop, the floor should be tiled with a drainage gully.

## Costume props

Although related to the work in the costume shop, this work should have its own separate area but be nearby. Costume prop skills are varied including sewing, sculpting and jewellery making, working with a large array of materials from fabric, wood, metal, leather, plastic, foam and so on. The work will usually be done seated at worktops worktables about 750mm wide and with about a 1m run for each person.

As for the textile studio, an assessment of the techniques/functions that will be carried out in the room will be needed and then a full risk assessment before consulting a LEV specialist to advice on what extract will be required. Some facilities could be shared with the Textile Studio, so positioning is key.

Other requirements may well include:

- storage for tools
- shelves for materials, storage, hat blocks, head blocks and so on
- sink – hot and cold water
- ironing facilities
- overhead lighting as well as task lighting
- power for small power tools
- access to computer and printer for digital work.

## Shoes

Boots and shoes are an important element in stage costumes, and some production organisations may include a separate shoemakers' workshop. Like other workrooms it requires a bench, a sink with hot and cold water, good light, both natural and artificial, power sockets, storage drawers and cupboards for tools and materials, and racks for the products.

Whether on site shoemaking is possible or not, space should be made for footwear storage as this is something that can be re-used many times, which can both save money and promote sustainability.

## Storage

Within the building, costumes are best hung on rails, either fixed or mobile. When they are taken out of the building (to go on tour, for example) they may be packed in skips or wardrobe trunks of average dimensions 900 × 650 × 650mm.

When considering a new costume facility, storage space should always be considered and always takes up more space than you would imagine. Often turnaround space is required when swapping from one show to another. Once a show has finished how will you either store or dispose of the costumes? For both financial and environmental reasons, it is good to be able to store past shows and this could be off site if necessary. Larger organisations might consider setting up a hire business to monetise the stock. Otherwise, everyone must consider how to sustainably dispose of the costumes not required.

## Wigs, hair and makeup

While only the largest organisations will make their own, wigs require daily maintenance. The use of hairspray and acetone and heat from wig ovens mean that this room needs careful thought. It will require:

- a room size of 3 × 4m minimum, with natural light if possible, to hold a maximum of two people
- running water to wash wigs and tools
- a wig oven (not to be confused with hot cabinet)
- high adjustable chairs (also for makeup and hair cuts)
- vinyl flooring is ideal
- room needs to be away from laundry or steam rooms (mostly to guarantee proper dressing of human hair wigs)
- wall mounted mirrors with top and side lighting and main sockets for electrical equipment close
- air extraction close to workbenches (essential due to use of chemicals such as acetone)
- shelving for wigs and wig blocks – 400mm deep
- if wigs are made and maintained in house, please provide a fixed table (desk like) with magnifying lighting and appropriate seating
- overhang worktop for attaching wig clamps or free-standing wig stand.
- electrical points for wig oven, heated rollers, tongs and dryers
- separate storage space for consumables and products
- control of substances hazardous to health (COSHH) cabinet to store chemicals and hairspray (please keep fluids separate from aerosols)
- when possible, the room should be close to the stage area.

## Lighting storage and workshop

Touring venues will mainly operate with hired equipment that comes in and out of the venue with each production. Most other venues will hold their own stock of lighting fixtures that will need storing and maintaining. There will need to be space whether for flight cases or steel frames to hold units that will be transported on trollies.

Shelving for lamps and bulbs will be essential in any venue as will wall space to hook coils of cable.

Sets increasingly have significant practical lighting installed and therefore a space to prepare this equipment prior to fitting becomes important. A good-sized workbench with consideration of local extract ventilation (LEV) will often be necessary.

## Sound storage and workshop

Like lighting, there will often be significant amounts of sound equipment that will need storing, maintaining and sometimes adapting. In larger venues much of this equipment will be moved around in-flight cases.

Video equipment will also tend to be held in the same area.

## Sound recording studio

Sound is as important a discipline as any other in the making of theatre. A room equipped for creating and editing digital sound effects and music is a requirement for most theatre companies.

It is often worth combining this with a facility for recording music and effects. The size will depend entirely on expected use but, in any event, it should have extremely good sound separation and the approach to it should be through sound lobbies with acoustic seals around doors and sound-absorbent material on the walls; ventilation should be as near silent as possible; and recording equipment should be in a control room separated from the studio by a double-sound-insulating window (note: double with air gap not double-glazed).

## Video editing studio

Video is used in many productions and on-site provision for either last minute edits or generation of content from earlier on in the process is important. Suitable hardware and software should be considered. Such provision could straightforwardly combine with a sound recording studio.

## Pre-visualisation studio

As further emphasis for the need of a digital studio in many producing venues, another function increasingly used is the ability to build 3D models of productions in which lighting and automation can be pre-programmed alleviating pressure on time compressed technical rehearsals. Such a facility can combine with many of the functions described previously in a single space but should be considered when assessing the workflow of any producing organisation.

The list of facilities in this section is not exhaustive and will vary significantly from building to building. At the time of writing the performance industry is undergoing great change as has been signalled in earlier sections. What will not change is the principal requirement of the backstage facilities to serve the work presented on the venue's stages. Sections 8 and 9 will go on to describe technical systems which need to be planned to support the artists and technical staff on stage.

## Section editor

Paul Handley, Production and Technical Director, National Theatre, London

## Contributors (in alphabetical order)

Nafeesah Butt, Theatre-Maker

Giuseppe Cannas, Freelance Hair and Make-Up Designer

Darren Joyce, Managing Director of Cardiff Theatrical Services

Carol Lingwood, former Head of Costume at the National Theatre (1999–2022), now Freelance Costume Professional

Gemma Tonge, Head of Company Stage Management at the National Theatre

Stuart West, Stu Arts Consulting

# Section 8

# The stage and stage machinery

## 8.1 Section overview

Since the first edition of *Theatre Buildings: A Design Guide* (edited by Judith Strong) was published in 2010, power flying systems and their controls have evolved rapidly and become more widely used, notably for performer flying; safety standards have responded to the way systems are being used; scenery has continued to become heavier; and we have become increasingly aware of the environmental cost of our work.

The fundamental requirement to provide rigging points above a well-proportioned stage and access below it has not changed for hundreds of years; thus, much content on systems such as counterweight flying is unchanged here from the 2010 edition. With an eye to simpler and non-endstage spaces in particular, this update considers the choices between automated and manual systems in more depth and discusses proactive maintenance and upgrades.

It is heartening that, despite continuing advancements, technical theatre remains a very personal craft. People are still more important than technology; and although theatres are essentially factories that create performances, they are factories with a particular atmosphere of creativity, collaboration, interaction and (mostly!) joy. It is a common misconception that theatre technicians love 'toys'. Many theatre technicians are happy to work with outmoded technology if their building is a pleasure to work in and a source of pride and inspiration to the resident team. The right space in which to do technical theatre work is more immediately important than filling a space with the latest technology.

It should go without saying that the following sub-sections are no substitute for proper professional advice: a set of guidelines followed do not alone a good theatre make.

## 8.2 Adaptability

Theatre buildings are sometimes designed to provide more than one auditorium format (as discussed in Sections 1 and 5), which introduces the need for moving components to provide this adaptability. The ultimate 'adaptable space' can be defined as a pair of large sheds, one with a hefty electrical power supply, rigging capacity in the overhead structure and circulation routes around, above and below the space at all levels, the other full of loose equipment such as chain hoists, rostra, truss and cable. Given sufficient time and crew, this would allow any theatrical space to be created within the shell of the shed.

Spaces equipped with multiple motorised platforms to set rows of seats at different heights at the push of a button, or equipped with dozens of stage elevators, can provide different arrangements of the space quickly – but only within the limitations of the machinery. Machinery saves labour cost: but maintaining the machinery costs money too.

Between these two extremes are spaces which thrive on there being no permanent stage, seats or machinery: walkways overhead provide easily accessible rigging points on rolling beams; and depth below stage level allows for entrances from trapdoors. Tiered seating may be constructed from rostra, with carpenters infilling odd corners as required: this blank canvas gives designers great flexibility to come up with staging arrangements to suit a particular production, rather than choosing a pre-determined seating layout. A well-established example of such a space is the Young Vic, London, where this transformation generally takes around one week with two skilled carpenters and six crew (see Strong (ed.), *Theatre Buildings* (2010), Reference Projects, pp. 278–79). Wall-sized doors through to the workshop allow a proscenium or large scene dock to be created.

When planning endstage theatres of a certain scale, forestage elevators will often be considered. These provide a quick turnaround from auditorium seating/forestage/orchestra pit and, if used regularly, are more cost effective in the long run than building a forestage from rostra.

When working within a limited volume, empty space is often more valuable to production teams than machinery. Many successful small theatres operate with 'pipe grids' overhead and a solid stage floor. Few of those would wish to sacrifice one metre of flying height for motorised overhead bars.

Rehearsal studios and areas of the foyer which may occasionally be used for performances can generally be

DOI: 10.4324/9781003327295-8

equipped with rigging points at little cost, allowing technical equipment to be rigged when required.

## 8.3 Sets and scenery

The role of the stage designer is to create an environment in which a theatrical performance can take place. The stage setting is more than decoration or illustration; it is an integral part of a production. It presents a visual stimulus to the imagination as well as emphasising the mood of the play. This subsection considers the facilities that set designers might hope to find in a theatre and what they might wish to avoid, as well as introducing some of the elements that are brought into play when working on the design.

Through discussion with the director, the designer will develop proposals, making sketches and rough models before producing working drawings and visual references to communicate the design to the workshops. The design may develop further through the rehearsal period and even while on stage.

### Designing for a producing theatre

In many theatres the format of the stage and its relationship with the auditorium is predetermined. The building itself may only be modified within narrow limits so sets have to be tailored to fit onto whatever stage exists.

When designing for a new producing theatre, where the scenery will be designed specifically for that stage, there is greater scope for the architect to determine an unusual theatrical space in collaboration with the theatre user. For example, particular formats such as the thrust stages at the RSC in Stratford-upon-Avon (see Section 1, Figure 1.7.1b and Reference Project 27) and the Crucible Theatre in Sheffield (see Figure 8.3.1 and Strong (ed), *Theatre Buildings* (2010), Reference Projects, pp. 216–19) or the in-the-round space at the Manchester Royal Exchange Theatre establish unique physical parameters for the designer.

Theatres such as these do not readily accommodate end-stage touring product.

### Touring scenery to receiving houses

Where a production is to be shown in a series of different venues, the designer might determine the spatial parameters by overlaying the footprint of each stage and the extreme sightlines onto a single composite drawing. This may result in a lowest-common-denominator approach to the set, or perhaps, as with large-scale opera productions, the need to tour 'large' and 'small' versions of the same set.

Figure 8.3.1 Model box by designer Lucy Osborne for *Rutherford & Son* at Sheffield Crucible, 2018.

Standardisation of touring houses – stage depth, width, height and space in the wings; position of suspension points; lighting positions and sightlines – would help immensely. Although this is not readily achievable in the United Kingdom given the wide range of theatre stock still in use, those planning new receiving venues need to be aware of the implications of straying too far from the norm. Later subsections, particularly 'Setting out the Stage House' (8.4), provide useful minimum design criteria and benchmarks for different types and scales of venue.

Since production financing is often tight, tours will play theatres of significantly differing size and format, relying on the ingenuity of the touring team to work out which bits of scenery are essential to make the show work – and which bits have to be left on the truck. To make a new theatre attractive to touring companies, key dimensions of appropriate benchmark theatres should be considered and matched or bettered.

### How might a set designer respond to a proscenium house?

The proscenium frames the human figure and places it in proportion to the scenic elements and to the frame itself. Whether two- or three-dimensional, these elements operate within the convention of a picture frame and create perspectives in which a foreground, mid-ground and background can be understood.

The provocative element is the line between stage and audience. Music hall and vaudeville traditions use it to tease and strut; architectural and domestic sets use it as the edge between different worlds. The frame – ornate or simple, historic or contemporary – presents the performance to the audience. So, choice over the shape, dimensions and style of the proscenium offers welcome opportunities for the set designer. Increasingly designers look for ways to connect the scenic world behind the proscenium to the auditorium. They may choose to utilise the area in front of the proscenium as an extension of the performance space, and build on the stage apron to bring the scenic elements of the production out into the auditorium. This can create a more immersive and intimate relationship between performer and audience.

Behind the proscenium, scenery and technical equipment is supported by a variety of mechanisms. Stage machinery can also create illusions and special effects in its own right. It may either be part of the permanent installation or installed specifically for a production. Later subsections discuss the methods for setting or changing scenery in greater detail.

## How might a designer respond to an open stage?

Flats and cloths cannot be used in the same way on the projecting portions of a thrust stage, nor upon a stage set in-the-round across which spectators need to have a virtually unobstructed view.

In such open-stage settings any scenery must be kept low or 'transparent'. Design elements may be restricted to a floor surface, furniture and props, costumes and lighting, perhaps with a 'picture' wall on one side only. As the most significant scenic surface, the floor should offer as much flexibility as possible: any depth below is useful, if only for cable routes; ultimately the entire stage floor should be removable over a substage level, with a modular lift-out panel design allowing traps to be formed at various locations without rebuilding the entire stage floor. Such scenic devices enable scene changes to be made and enhance the sculptural quality of the design by offering a changeable point of view from the otherwise fixed viewpoint of a theatre seat.

## Introduction to the scenic materials and effects that a designer might employ

### Drapery

Drapery is a significant part of any stage setting, from the lavish red plush front or 'house' curtain which conceals the scenery behind it, to the more austere 'black box' within. This latter neutral setting is created from side masking panels ('legs'), headers ('borders') and a backing ('tabs' or 'full blacks'). As fabric can be stretched, hung, seamed, folded and draped or painted to look three-dimensional, theatrical drapery may take on a sculptural quality.

### Cloths

The flying system which is installed may need to suit a range of different cloths, as the following five points suggest.

- The painted front-cloth or 'show drop', which might introduce a pantomime or vaudeville act and hide a scene-change taking place behind it.
- The backcloth, which may depict the sky or a distant view or be left plain (as a 'cyclorama') to take lighting or projection.
- A cut cloth – or series of them – typically representing trees or architecture can add perspective and depth.
- A gauze or 'scrim' offers a device for distancing the action or scenery or enables one picture (painted on it) to dissolve into another behind it simply by a change of lighting; striking effects can be achieved in this way.
- Black velvet/serge is used to imply infinite depth or may be peppered with numerous LEDs to represent a night-time sky (a 'star-cloth').

Painted cloths still predominate in traditional ballet and pantomime design because they take up least floor area and can be changed simply. They are seldom used in other forms of performance beyond an upstage cyclorama – painted or not. Cloths are light and can easily be folded or rolled when being stored and transported.

### The stage surface

Floors may be treated with a painted, heavy-duty canvas; a vinyl or sprung wooden flooring suitable for dancers; or a raised and sculpted surface. A raked stage is commonly used when a chorus or crowd need to see the conductor as much as to be visible to the full audience. A raised 'show floor', often required for musicals, may be a box of tricks accommodating travelators, traps, tracks and concealed lighting.

### Two-dimensional scenery

Behind a proscenium, three-dimensional effects can be represented by cleverly painted cloths or rigid panels, referred to as 'flats'. The lightest flats are made from canvas stretched over a timber frame much like a fine artist's canvas but at heights of up to 8.0m. Equally, skin plywood or a heavier construction, perhaps on a steel or aluminium frame, might be adopted. Relief applications such as timber or plastic mouldings can add architraves, bricks, foliage or texture, which help suggest three-dimensional qualities.

### Three-dimensional scenery

Sculptural scenery provides interest from all aspects, especially when lit. It tends to become heavier in construction as it contributes to a representation of a more substantial or robust setting. Structures include rostra, ramps or 'raked' stage decks; and elements such as stairs, balconies, rocks, columns and trees. (See Figure 8.3.2.)

Stage properties – or 'props' – are equally significant 3D objects which support the stage action and narrative. They might range from small hand-held items to furniture or rock formations, flown objects such as chandeliers, inanimate vehicles or practical machines. On an open stage, the costumes also assume a significant role in establishing locale as much as individual character.

Figure 8.3.2 In making Ramps on the Moon productions, consortium partners consider the access requirements of both company and audience. The working lift and the caption screen in Ti Green's set design for Birmingham Rep's *The Government Inspector* (2016) are examples of this approach.

#### Multi-dimensional scenery

Projected scenery can change, dissolve or even disappear. Technical developments now enable projection to track in line with moving scenic surfaces or for LED panels to operate in motion, opening up all sorts of opportunities for the designer.

The use and production of still images, moving images, multiple images and lighting effects are discussed further in Section 9.

#### Building fabric

For theatres which are converted from existing buildings, there are often architectural or construction features which make the building interesting. Structure such as columns or a brick wall can provide enormous opportunities and inspiration, even if at first glance they might appear to be a constraint or limit to scenic possibilities: existing constraints can lead to creativity.

There is no such thing as a neutral space. Instead it is important to carefully consider the form and aesthetic of the empty stage, and embrace the character and personality of any existing structure. Rich and interesting textures, colour and forms can be a gift to a designer and incorporated into the design of a performance, or covered over when they are not required.

## 8.4 Setting out the stage house

This section covers the planning of a proscenium stage with flytower and the variations in the layout which are needed for different types of use and size of auditorium.

When considering the need for a flytower, it is important to consider the performance needs of the theatre building and how it will respond to the needs of its community through its programming (see Figures 8.4.1 and 8.4.2). If there is a desire for the venue to accommodate large-scale touring productions then a flytower may be desirable to achieve parity with other venues. However if this is not an aspiration, then the space and money required for a flytower could be allocated instead to the provision of a smaller studio theatre or rehearsal space, depending on the needs of the building, its users and the type of work it intends to create or receive. It should never be assumed that a flytower will be necessary for a theatre production – a smaller fly loft may be sufficient and sometimes a series of flexible strong points overhead can be sufficient.

For many regional UK theatres, the annual pantomime generates a significant percentage of annual income and – as a spectacular show – places the greatest demands on the theatre. Panto requirements are likely to be a major factor in setting the parameters for flying height and stage size.

### Stage level – how wide are the wings?

Intrinsically, a proscenium stage needs to accommodate scenery. The stage arrangement must make the setting up and changing of scenery and lighting as easy and as flexible as possible. Scenery may be moved during a performance, or to make way for a new production. Movement can be horizontal into the wings on either side or into a rear stage. It can also be vertical up into the flytower or vertical down into a stage basement.

The easiest places to move scenery into are the wings so these areas are important. The wing spaces also need to accommodate prop tables (for the setting and running of props during a performance) and quick change areas (a temporary booth, constructed often on a show-by-show basis to facilitate a performer changing a costume with some degree of privacy when there is insufficient time to return to the dressing room). For certain productions the wings will also provide clear space to the side of the stage for dancers and other performers to run off the stage at

| Theatre type | Seating | Proscenium width (m) | Proscenium height (m) | Grid height (m) | Main stage depth (m) | Wing width (m) | Height under galleries (m) |
|---|---|---|---|---|---|---|---|
| Opera/dance | 1,200-2,000 | 12–18 | 8–10 | 24–30 | 15–20 | 6–8 | 8–12 |
| Large touring | 1,200-2,000 | 12–15 | 7–9 | 22–28 | 14–18 | 6–8 | 7–9 |
| Medium touring | 500-1,200 | 10–14 | 6–8 | 18–22 | 12–15 | 3–6 | 6–8 |
| Drama and small touring | 350-650 | 8–12 | 5–7 | 10–20 | 10–14 | 3–6 | 5–7 |
| Studio touring | 150-350 | n/a | n/a | 5-10 | 8-12 | 0-3 | 3-5 |
| Thrust (main house) | 800-1,200 | 10-12 | 6-7 | 8-10 | 15-18[1] | n/a | n/a |
| In-the-round (main house) | 400-600 | 6-9 | n/a | 5-8 | 7-10 | n/a | n/a |

[1] whole depth of the stage, including the thrust.

Figure 8.4.1 Table of indicative key statistics. Thrust and in-the-round formats represent upper limits and can be scaled down.

speed and decelerate out of sight without colliding with a wall or piece of equipment.

**Flying systems**

As well as issues of cost and available site area, the amount of wing space is influenced by the choice of flying system. An understanding of flying methods is therefore needed before the stage plan can be decided. Detailed information on flying system equipment is set out in the following. What follows here is a brief summary indicating how the choice of system impacts on the size and layout of the wing space. (See Figure 8.4.3.)

With traditional rope sets or winches operated by hand from a gallery well above stage level, the scenery load is directly suspended and there is no obstruction to the extent of the wings. With counterweight flying which has largely replaced ropes and hand winches, the load on a flying bar is counterbalanced by weights in a cradle running in guides on the side wall.

Counterweight sets can be either single purchase or double purchase. It is usual only to install counterweight cradles on one side of the stage. A full installation forms an unbroken row of equipment. If single-purchase sets are installed, their cradle travel comes down to stage level and limits the wing space to the flytower width. With double purchase, twice the weight of the equipment is carried in the counterweight cradle but travels only half the distance of the bar: hence the cradle travel is in the upper half of the flytower and does not necessarily limit the wing – which can then be as wide as necessary. (See Figure 8.4.4.) There are, however, disadvantages to this system (see Section 8.6).

For the past hundred years the flying system of choice has been single-purchase counterweights, which is why so many stages have an asymmetric plan with one wing much deeper than the other. The narrow wing results from a balance being struck between wing space and tower width. A very wide flytower is uneconomic and moves the operating position for the flying system a long way offstage. This restricts the flyman's view and limits other gallery uses such as sidelighting.

Like the original rope sets, motors for flying at a high level on galleries or the grid do not obstruct the wings. Without the intrusion of counterweights there is freedom to set flytower and wing widths to the ideal dimensions and cost is the only limiting factor.

## The proscenium and rear stage

Figure 8.4.4 relates wing width to proscenium opening. This is a good guide but regardless of proscenium width, the wing space from proscenium opening to a single-purchase wall frame should not be less than 4m.

The proscenium structural opening is the reference for setting out the wings, galleries and stage depth. The dimensions of the opening are closely linked to the size and

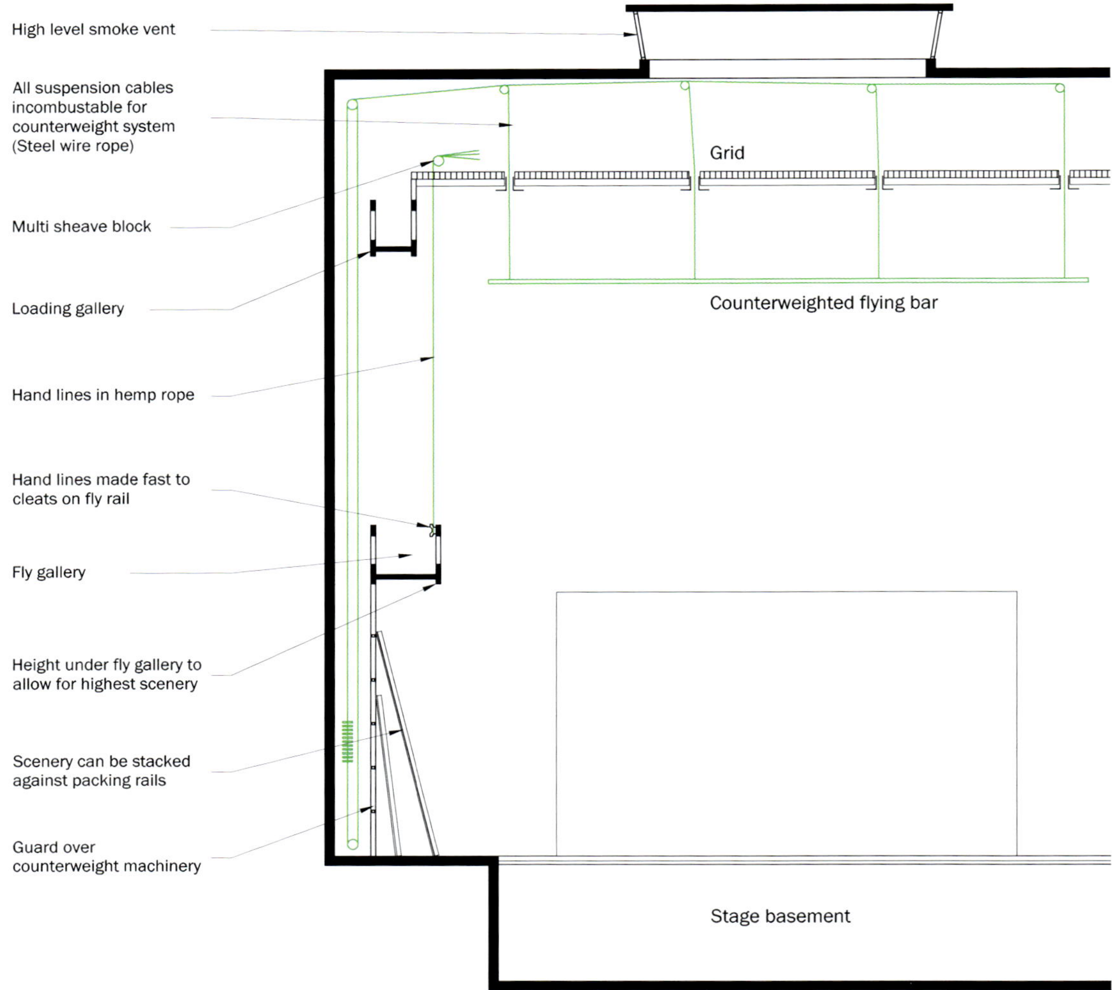


Figure 8.4.2 Drawing of section through stage house showing single-purchase counterweight flying system

general design of the auditorium. The width needs to give adequate sightlines for the audience to the full playing area while avoiding acute sightlines into the wings. The height must also be adequate for the view from upper seating tiers. Too large a proscenium results in a need for wider wings, higher grid and big events to fill the opening. Too small and the contact between player and audience is cramped or lost.

It is common to install a vertically moving safety curtain which can close the proscenium opening when released. Its historic purpose was to protect the audience from a stage fire. While it is not mandatory, it may be required as part of the fire strategy and can provide useful secondary roles in keeping the auditorium clean and warm during stage operations, providing a temporary stacking wall and masking a noisy interval change. There are various curtain types but the simplest should be the target, which is a flat, rigid, counterweighted, one-piece unit made of steel.

It should be noted that including a safety curtain is likely to have other implications for fire breaks above and below the proscenium. (More information on fire safety is given in Section 1.12 and Sections 3.6 and 3.7.)

Conventionally the proscenium opening can be reduced in width and height on the upstage side with variable black masking, sometimes called a 'tormentor'. It is desirable if this masking can be easily adjusted and quickly moved completely out of the way for those shows where it is not needed. In larger theatres a permanent adjustable proscenium system may be provided. Small platforms, offstage of the black masking forming proscenium wall

Figure 8.4.3 Flytower at Theatre Royal, Drury Lane (London), showing linesets and fly galleries. See also Reference Project 32.

perches, have a number of production uses. These should be detailed so as not to intrude into the working stage area and designed to move in tandem with any large adjustable proscenium system. (See Figure 8.4.6.)

A rear stage (without full flying height) is useful for storage and as an extension of the acting area (perhaps with a perspective set), but sightlines may limit its performance use. The opening width into the rear stage should not be less than the structural proscenium dimension and the clear height should not be less than the clearance under the lowest stage galleries to allow whole sets on wagons to move in and out. Extra height should be allowed over the rear stage to install hoists used for performance, assembly and storage.

## The flytower grid

The grid is the maintenance and access deck for the stage suspension systems (see Figure 8.4.7). It may also carry equipment loads.

Care needs to be taken over the height of the grid, as there is no substitute for grid height when it is needed and no remedy if it is lacking. While two-and-a-half times the structural proscenium height should be taken as a minimum if full-height flying is required, extra height is a production bonus, and three times the structural proscenium height should be the target. This additional height may also be necessary where an unusual stage/auditorium relationship creates awkward upward views into the flytower. It should be noted when checking sightlines into the stage that the end seats of front rows are usually the worst case.

Powered flying and control systems can now provide the sensitivity for in-show movement which was previously only possible by skilled operation of counterweight systems. Flying motors can easily be accommodated at grid level. They should be located at the sides to leave the central area clear for temporary rigging. Drive cabinets should be housed in a separate room – beyond or below the motors – since they make noise which may disturb a quiet performance.

Additional area at grid level, upstage of the stage back wall line, is useful for housing spotline hoists, leaving the central area of the grid clear for safe and easy access.

All permanent suspension lines over the grid should be mounted at a high level above head height, leaving the grid surface clear of pulleys. The grid structure should be sufficiently open to allow a chain hoist hook to pass through. It is desirable to form a suitably guarded opening section in the grid which can be used to hoist heavy production items to grid level. This may also be useful for powered flying hoist maintenance access if there is no personnel lift to grid level for heavy loads – though such a lift should be incorporated into the design where possible.

## Wheelchair access to technical walkways

It is considered impractical for a technician who uses a wheelchair to safely lift a 6kg lantern over a 1100mm rail, rig and focus it. This does not mean that we should not maximise wheelchair access to technical areas. Technicians who use wheelchairs can (and do) safely operate power flying, lighting, sound and video consoles. Where a wheelchair may go, so may a flightcase: providing wheelchair access to areas such as grids, galleries and walkways also improves access for moving lights and video projectors.

## The flytower galleries

Side galleries within the flytower have a number of uses apart from being the best operating position for the flying system (whether manual or powered). These include side lighting, 'breasting' and 'brailing' of fly bars (that is, the securing of flying bars in a lateral position up or down stage of their natural position), various special effects and (with counterweight systems) loading weights (see Figures 8.4.8a and 8.4.8b).

Conventionally the majority of stage lighting gallery outlets for spotbar connection are concentrated on the side away from the flying system. This leaves the flying operating area as free from trailing cables and sockets as possible. With powered flying, where the controls are likely to be small and portable, this separation is slightly less important but still valuable.

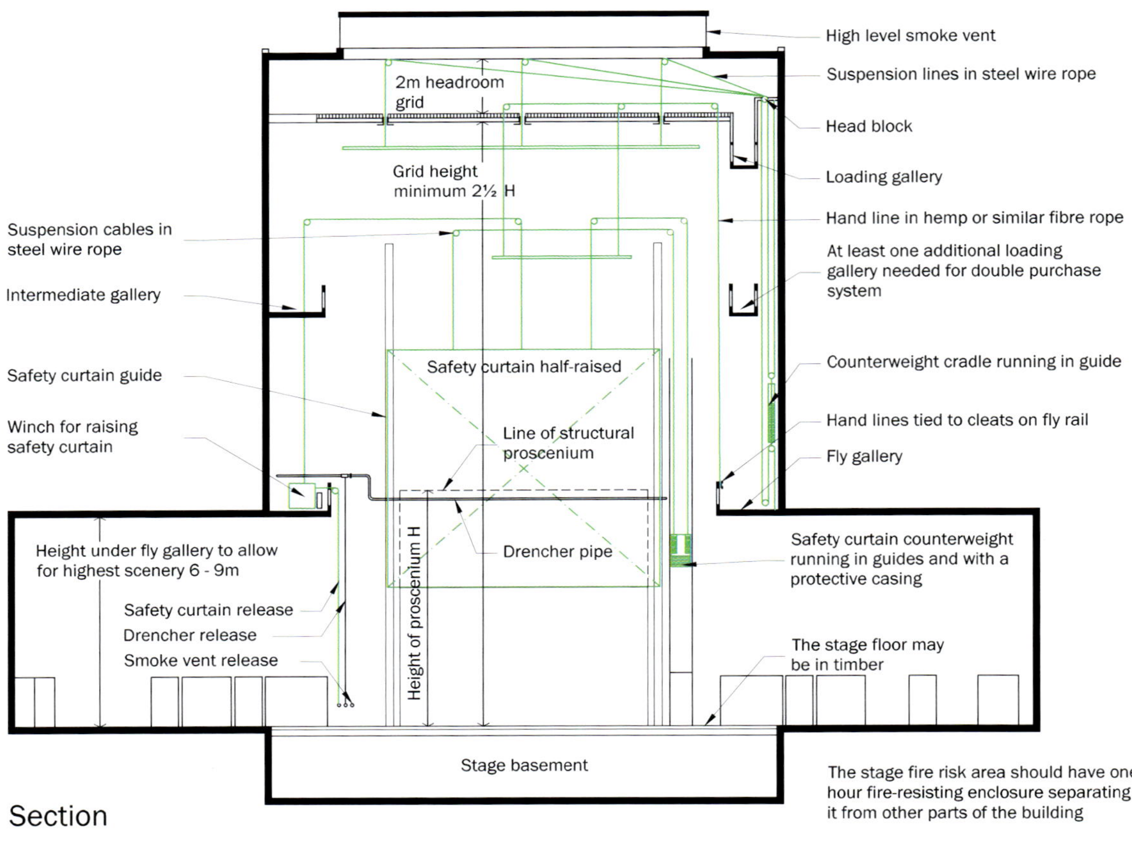


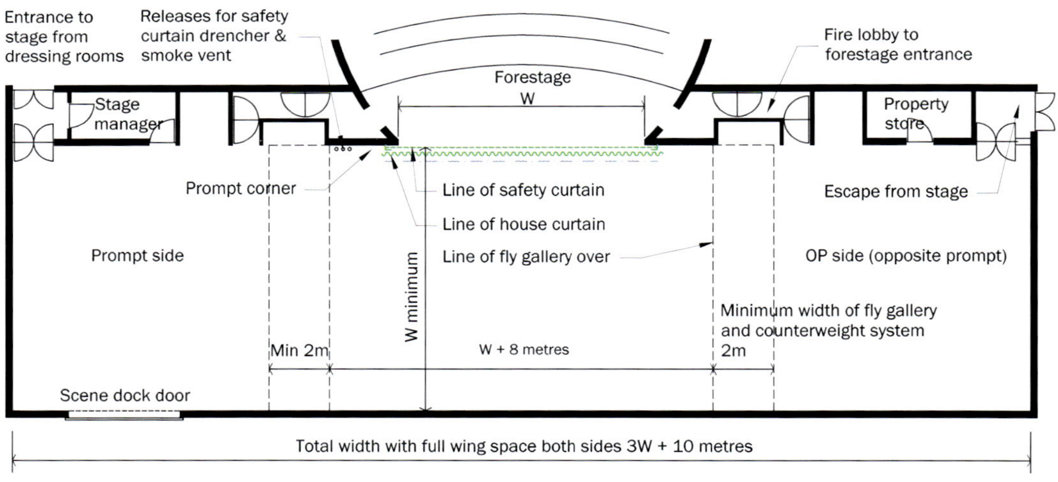


Figure 8.4.4 Plan and section drawings showing the layout of a stage equipped with a double-purchase flying system.

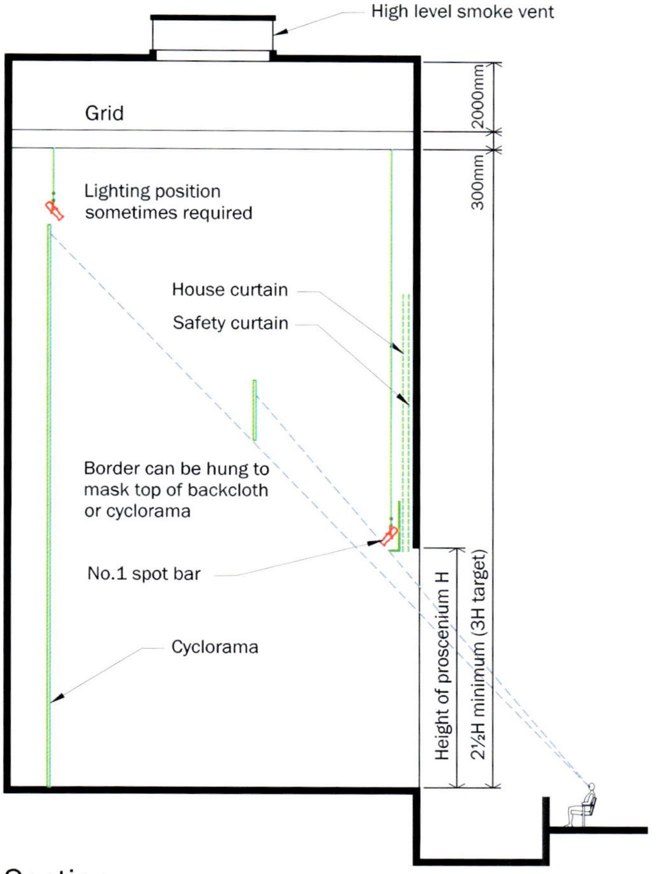

High level smoke vent
Grid
2000mm
300mm
Lighting position
sometimes required
House curtain
Safety curtain
Border can be hung to
mask top of backcloth
or cyclorama
No.1 spot bar
Cyclorama
Height of proscenium H
2½H minimum (3H target)

Section

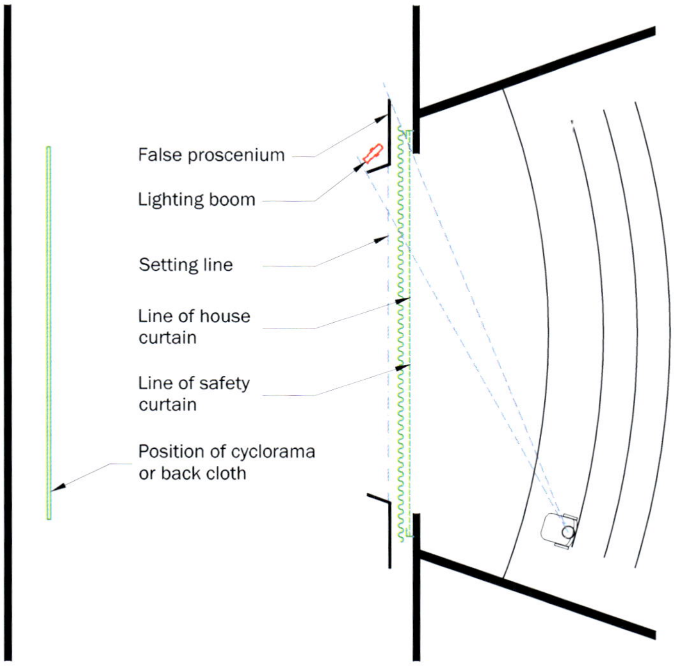

False proscenium
Lighting boom
Setting line
Line of house
curtain
Line of safety
curtain
Position of cyclorama
or back cloth

Plan

Figure 8.4.5 Plan and section showing front row sightlines.

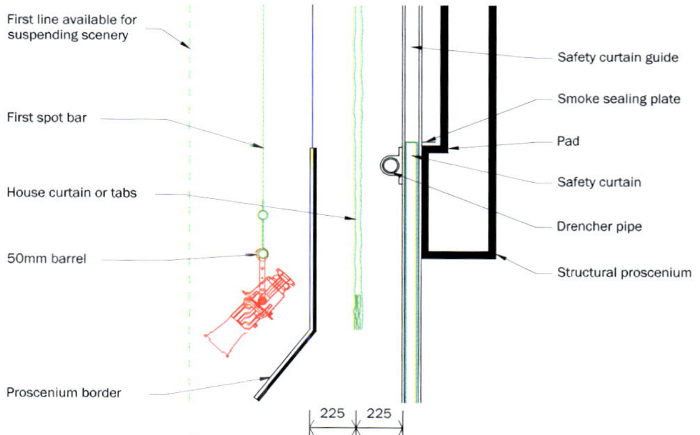

First line available for
suspending scenery
First spot bar
House curtain or tabs
50mm barrel
Proscenium border
Safety curtain guide
Smoke sealing plate
Pad
Safety curtain
Drencher pipe
Structural proscenium
225
225

Section

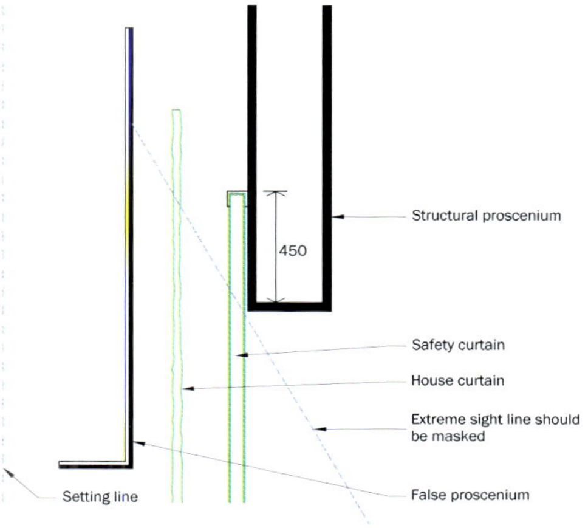

Structural proscenium
450
Safety curtain
House curtain
Extreme sight line should
be masked
Setting line
False proscenium

Plan

Figure 8.4.6 Typical plan and section of a proscenium arch.

Figure 8.4.7 Photograph of the grid at Stavanger Konserthus (Norway) showing chain hoists rigged from travelling beams, which run between suspension lines of the flying system.

Figure 8.4.8a Photograph of the fly gallery at the Theatre Royal Drury Lane (London). See also Reference Project 32.

High-level galleries for loading counterweights are only required on the counterweight side. Normally one is needed for single-purchase systems and two or three for double-purchase because of the longer cradles.

All other galleries should be in pairs, one on each side of the stage, with their onstage edges set back from the proscenium opening and lining up vertically. (See Figure 8.4.9.) The onstage edges should be symmetrically spaced about the proscenium centre line. The dimension from the proscenium structural opening to the onstage edge of galleries is important. It should be large enough to accommodate up/downstage flying bars beyond the cross-stage suspensions but not so large that all gallery activity is remote from the central stage area.

The lowest level of galleries is usually the best position for operating the flying system. With counterweights which are operated from the offstage side, the gallery should be relatively narrow to allow the operator a view down to the stage floor. A crossover, connecting galleries at this level, is highly desirable but should not take up valuable flying space. It is best placed behind the back wall of the stage and can often make use of a dressing room corridor.

Good vertical circulation for the flytower should be planned from the beginning, with at least one dedicated stair rising from stage to grid. Such stairs should be located outside the working rectangle of the flytower plan. For safety reasons cat ladders should not be used for primary access and should be avoided where possible. A grid lift for personnel and equipment will save much time and labour. The lift should have the principal gallery levels as intermediate stops.

## 8.5 The stage floor and substage

The stage floor should be level, without steps or ramps. Vertical movement of scenery below the floor on a large scale involves mechanisation using lifts. This sort of installation is often combined with horizontal movement of scenery on wagons. Wagons usually run into the wing and rear stage areas. Such extensive machinery generally only earns its keep in opera houses working in repertoire. In other types of theatre where it has been installed, it rarely remains in use. Mechanised methods for scene changing tend to impose a certain rigidity on methods of constructing and of operating scenery.

A more useful general purpose stage floor is supported on demountable modules over a stage basement. This allows the formation of traps or extended open areas to suit a particular production. The module size can be based on plywood sheet dimensions for ease of replacement. The modular area should be symmetrical to the proscenium centre line, equal to the proscenium opening as a minimum, and extend as far downstage as possible. The central module should straddle the centre line.

The clear basement depth should not be less than two-and-a-half metres. Although likely to be expensive, for a resident company a double-height basement extending down for 5m or more will be useful. If this is further divided into two levels by a demountable floor, it will significantly extend the range of production uses.

Demountable stage floors are most used in producing theatres where the designer can exploit the in-house facilities. In these buildings the area of removable floor should be a square, with sides the same dimension as the structural proscenium. Touring theatres make the least use of the floor because touring circuits rarely have a common floor module facility throughout the network. In these theatres a small area of demountable floor of about 18–20m$^2$ in a central and downstage position is usually adequate.

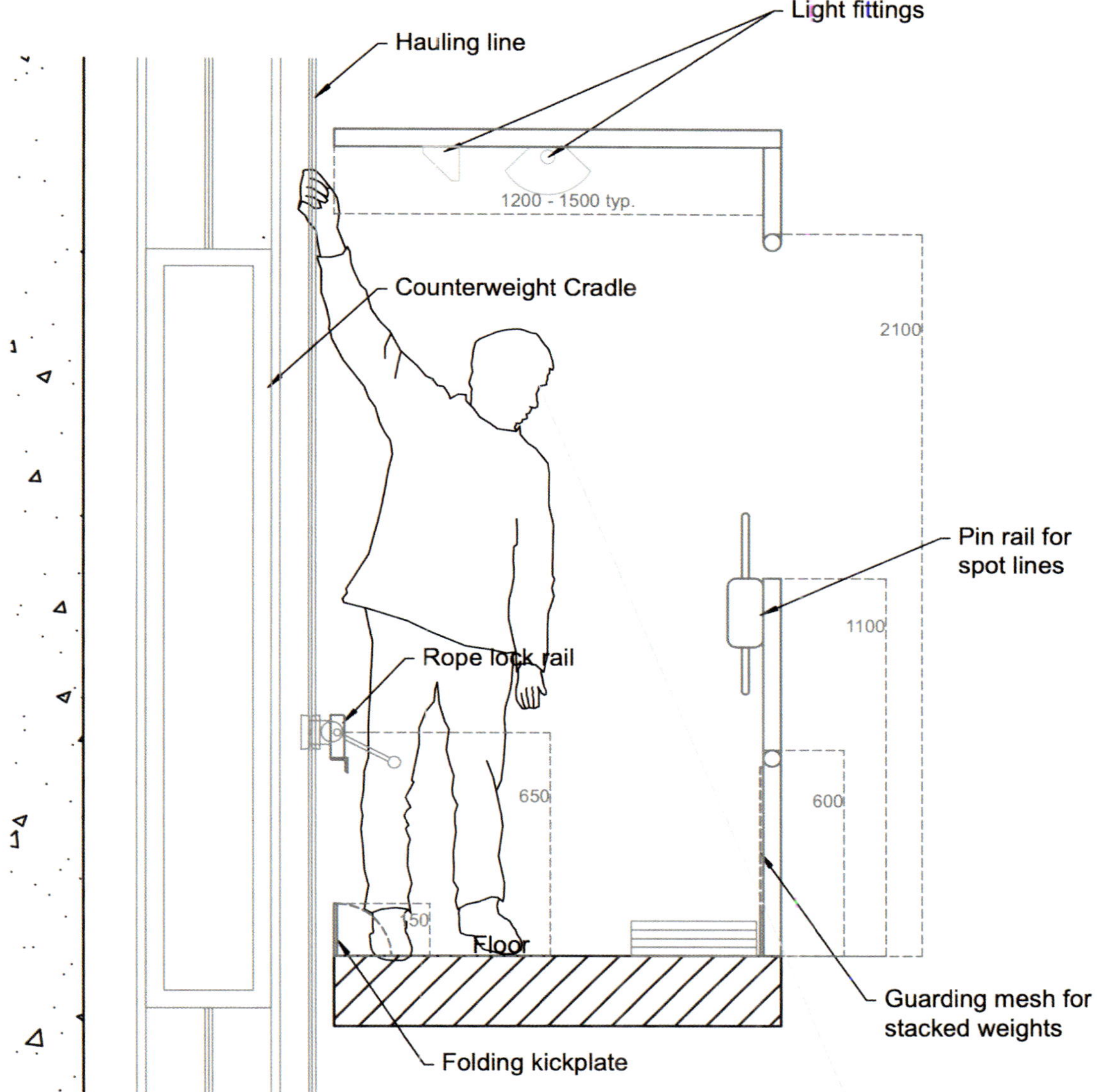


Figure 8.4.8b Drawing showing a typical setting out of a counterweight fly gallery. The measurements in the drawing are in millimetres.

## 8.6 Overstage machinery

Any equipment which suspends or moves loads overhead has to be extremely safe and must be designed, fabricated, installed and tested to the highest standard. Codes and regulations in most countries control what can be done and must be complied with. In addition to ensuring that the equipment is fit for purpose, it is vital that everyone using overhead equipment is thoroughly trained and that a comprehensive training regime continues for

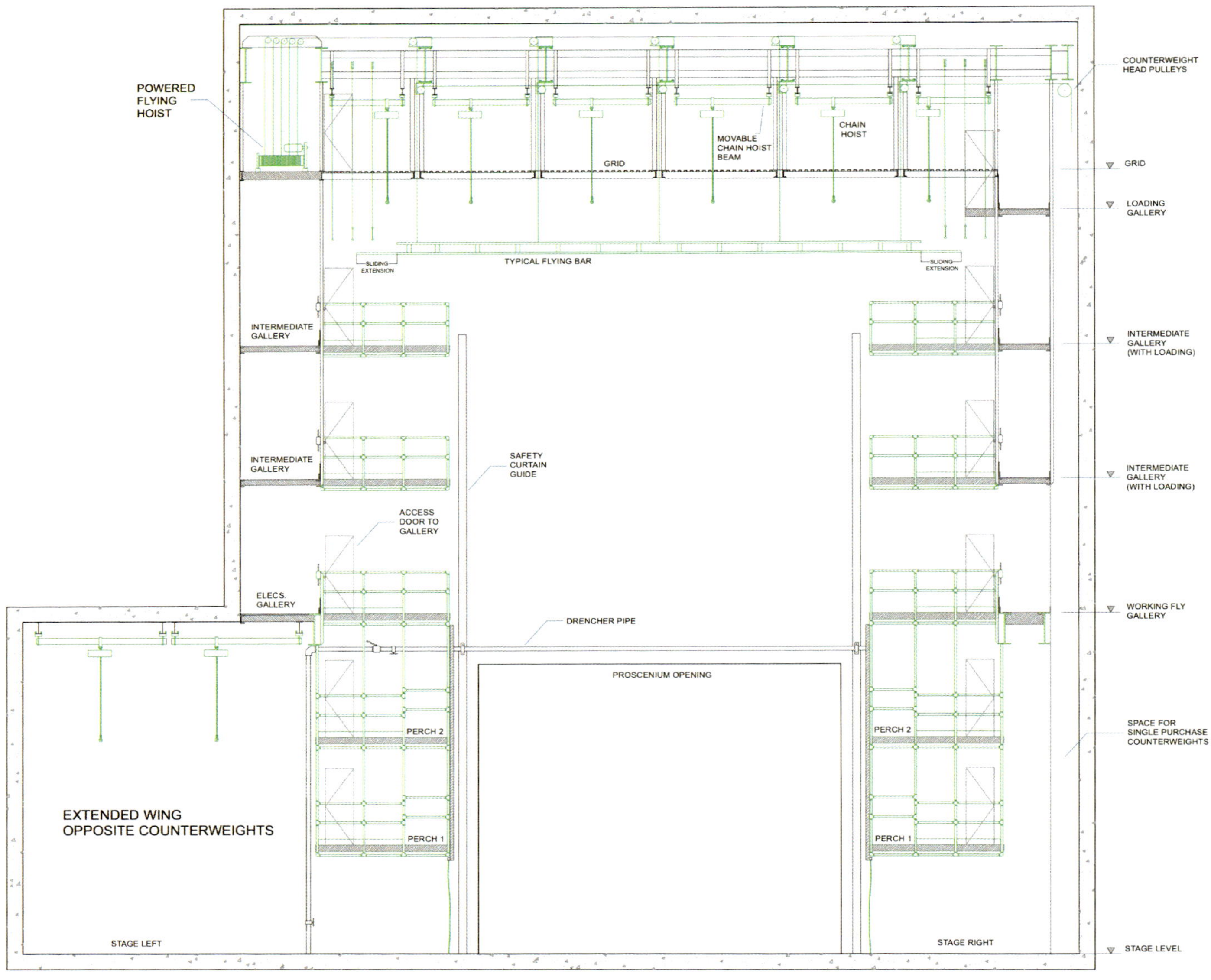


Figure 8.4.9 Section through stage house showing power flying and counterweight systems.

all new operators and for those involved in repairs and maintenance.

The operator of any moving overhead equipment must be able to see the loads that he or she is controlling, whether these are moved by hand or by machine.

## Manual flying

A large number of theatres are fitted with a form of manual flying, although many are moving towards powered systems as these become more economic and health and safety considerations become more important. The most basic form of suspension is to use ropes, which although historically referred to as 'hemp', should be Grade 1 Manilla or a quality polyester rope.

## Hemp

Direct haul theatre suspensions either have a single rope carrying a small piece of decoration, such as a chandelier, or a number of ropes, normally three or four, attached to an (aluminium) pipe to which the scenery is tied. The operator raises and lowers this scenery from a gallery at the side of the flytower. The ropes pass over pulleys on the grid and are tied off to cleats or pins fitted to a substantial rail on the onstage side of this gallery (see Figure 8.6.1), which must be

Figure 8.6.1 Photograph of a hemp fly gallery: Civic Theatre (now Hippodrome) in Darlington, prior to refurbishment.

Figure 8.6.2 Photograph of a rope lock at Theatre Royal Drury Lane (London). See also Reference Project 32.

wide enough to accommodate the many operators required for this form of flying and for all the loose rope when the scenery is raised.

## Single-purchase counterweights

Single-purchase counterweights are the most common form of scenery suspension. Wire ropes from each fly bar pass over drop and head pulleys before being attached to a counterweight cradle. The cradle is a steel frame which carries cast iron, lead or steel weights to balance the weight of the scenery. A hauling rope is attached to the counterweight cradle and reeved over pulleys at both top and bottom of its travel. It passes vertically through a rope lock device on the operating, or 'fly' gallery. (See Figure 8.6.2.) This rope makes the work of moving the scenery relatively easy, although considerable effort is required to load and unload the counterweights.

The counterweight cradle is guided on one wall of the flytower. The cradles pass behind the galleries on the 'working' side of the flytower where a space, usually about 800mm wide, needs to be available to accommodate the wall frame, counterweights and hauling ropes.

It is not good policy, either operationally or from an engineering viewpoint, to put counterweights on a rear wall or to distribute them on both sides of the stage. (See Section 8.4.)

## Double-purchase counterweights

The vertical movement of the counterweight cradles can be halved by doubling the weight in the cradle and double purchasing the wire ropes so that they pass over a pulley on the top of the counterweight cradle and are fixed to the head steels. This permits doorways, openings and sidestage access through the lower part of this wall and increases the available wing space.

The disadvantage is that twice as many weights have to be loaded and unloaded, and the reaction forces on the head steels are increased. The hauling rope is also double purchased but the cradles of double-purchase sets can be very long (over 4m on occasion), and the effort involved in accelerating and stopping a double-purchase set is increased by 50% over that for a single-purchase set, which adds strain to the operator's body.

Such a system should only be contemplated after considering other options, including a powered system.

## Powered flying

With the development of relatively economic AC inverter drives and control systems, powered systems for moving scenery have become practicable. These take two basic forms:

- powered assistance (counterweight cradles operated by an electrical motor)
- direct lift (the suspension wire ropes are wound directly onto a drum rotated by an electrical motor).

These systems must be designed to exacting standards by professionals, as the inherent risks cannot be understood without training in these disciplines. A number of proprietary systems are available, but these must be capable of complying with current safety standards, such as being designed to an appropriate safety integrity level.

## Powered assistance to counterweight systems

Powered assistance is only a solution where a suitable counterweight installation already exists: otherwise it is more economic to install a direct haul system. Powered assistance can be either electrical or hydraulic, and can raise or lower the scenery by moving the counterweight. Wire ropes attached to the counterweight wind on a suitable hoist which can be mounted in the basement, on the grid or on a gallery – wherever sufficient space can be found. It is also possible to drive the hauling line with a motor at fly gallery level, though this system is less commonly used.

## Direct lift hoists

Direct haul systems can use wire ropes or steel bands, and these hoists can employ either grooved or pile-winding drums. Where hoists need to be synchronised (as in most modern installations), pile-winding drums should not be used, as the winding diameter of two hoists at varying heights will be different and they will therefore be unable to lift at sufficiently identical speeds to maintain a level lift.

Most direct lift systems use a hoist with a grooved winding drum. (See Figure 8.6.3.) This can have a single or multiple wire ropes on it and can be made in many sizes with a range of performances. Typical units operate with loads up to 1,000kg at maximum speeds of up to 2m/sec. These hoists have a self-weight of between 50% and 75% of the load they are rated to lift.

Modern hoists are relatively quiet but should be enclosed or mounted outside the flytower if possible. Typically a winch room should be between 3 to 5m deep, and run the full depth of the stage. Often winch rooms will be located on both sides of the stage to achieve the close centres required, and to better distribute the structural forces across the building fabric. Occasionally a winch room may be situated above the grid, with a footprint in plan comparable to the grid, in a separate acoustic enclosure (for example, in the Copenhagen Opera House).

Figure 8.6.3 Photograph of power flying winches at Stavanger Konserthus (Norway).

Where quiet operation is not a particular requirement (where the hoist is being used for suspension rather than live flying), line shaft winches can be a lower-cost alternative.

Space near the hoists will be necessary for the variable speed drives as this allows cross-plugging in the event of a drive failure.

## Manual or automated?

To decide whether to opt for manual rather than motorised systems, it is vital to carefully consider a number of factors, including

- frequency of use
- manual handling viability
- capital + maintenance + replacement cost vs cost of labour
- flexibility vs speed: motorised systems tend to perform a small number of functions, quickly; but the machinery can get in the way (literally) of other possible functions
- space: manual systems typically consist of demountable components – where are they stored? Automated systems need motor and drive rack space.

The '40/20/10' rule helps to set long-term budgets for maintenance and planned replacement of components. Thus, a client planning a £5m power flying installation should plan to set aside 4% annually for servicing (£200,000) and a futher 4% annually to fund replacements of computer controls every ten years, drives after twenty years and the entire system after forty years. (See Figure 8.6.4.)

Manual systems can still be the right choice, even if budget is available for automation. For smaller receiving houses, the cost of an automated system plus its upkeep outweighs the cost of staffing a counterweight system. You can run a theatre without an automated flying system, but you cannot run a theatre without skilled technical staff. Figure 8.6.5 sets out some of the considerations to help make the right choice.

## Control systems

Modern flying control systems control a number of 'axes', each of which is the movement of one piece of equipment. As well as handling overstage hoists, the system can control stage elevators, stage wagons or revolving stages. Thus they are referred to as 'stage control systems' and will generally

| DEPRECIATION COSTS | | | |
|---|---|---|---|
| Item | % of cost | Lifespan | Cost |
| Mechanics | 60% | 40 | 1.5% |
| Drives | 30% | 20 | 1.5% |
| Computer Control | 10% | 10 | 1.0% |
| | | TOTAL: | 4.0% |
| | | | |
| **MAINTENANCE COSTS** | | | |
| Item | % of cost | % service | Cost |
| Mechanics | 60% | 2.5% | 1.5% |
| Drives / Electrics | 30% | 5.0% | 1.5% |
| Computer Control | 10% | 10.0% | 1.0% |
| | | TOTAL: | 4.0% |

Figure 8.6.4 Table showing depreciation costs and maintenance costs.

consist of a control centre, incorporating a server, and some control panels.

The hoists are connected to the control centre via an ethernet or other proprietary data network. Advanced systems enable the operation of the installation to be monitored and errors diagnosed remotely by the manufacturer over an internet connection. The control centre should be located outside the stage area but reasonably adjacent to the main control panel positions.

Emergency stop facilities will be required by regulations relating to rotating machinery. The emergency stop should be one system that stops all moving equipment: hoists, elevators, wagons or dividing shutters.

Creative aspiration from companies such as Cirque du Soleil – collaborating closely with automation specialist Stage Technologies (now part of Tait) – has pushed the boundaries of automation for live performance and driven the development of new technology. Synchronisation of performer flying axes with large moving scenic elements in close proximity to the audience would have been unthinkable twenty years ago. Responding to this development, safety standards have become more rigorous to safeguard performers, technical staff and the public. Control systems have become more sophisticated, particularly the user interfaces which now often include on-screen visualisation of all axes which move as the real machinery moves.

### Safety curtains, dividing shutters

Where a sound-reducing shutter is required to separate a side stage, rear stage, or scene dock from the stage, this may move vertically rather like a safety curtain that seals the opening between stage and auditorium in a proscenium theatre. Safety curtains are sometimes required to provide sound separation in addition to fire protection, in a similar way to most dividing shutters. To achieve these functions, sound-reducing shutters are heavy, up to 130kg/m$^2$ and, being counterweighted, require suitable structural support.

### Chain hoists

Chain hoists are thought of as noisy, clunky and slow fixed-speed lifting motors by riggers, but over the past ten to fifteen years, variable speed chain hoists with closed-loop control have become more common: features such as zero speeding help with brake noise control and smoother change in direction, load monitoring helps with safe load distribution and positional feedback allows operators to move to targets live in a show. Most touring rock and roll lighting and video rigs heavily depend on variable speed chain hoists for their effects.

Variable-speed chain hoists are driven by frequency inverters (drives) and can be controlled/programmed by automation consoles.

Chain hoists may be rigged on grid stands (see Figure 8.6.6), in which case the grid must be strong enough to take the load of the hoist plus its payload. An alternative is to hang these chain hoists overhead on fixed or rolling beams.

### Advance bars and other special rigging

Overstage rigging can extend into the auditorium when scenery, lighting or action is required above the audience. This will need load-tested attachment points on the roof structure, a facility required increasingly as touring shows with three-dimensional flying become more popular. Some coordinated openings in the auditorium ceiling are also necessary to accommodate chandeliers and lighting and sound equipment, or performers who might 'fly' through the ceiling or appear from above.

## 8.7 Understage machinery

### The stage structure

The stage has to be strong so that scenery and lights do not wobble when a vigorous dance routine or fight scene is staged. It may be required to support heavy scaffold structures, with several raised levels, stairs, ladders and walkways. It will also be subject to rolling loads from heavy moving scenery, grand pianos, cherry pickers, forklift trucks, tow trucks and other vehicles. It must be capable of adapting to varied production requirements and this means that most of it should be removable: it is much easier to loosen some

| AUTOMATED FLYING SYSTEMS COMPARED TO COUNTERWEIGHT | | |
|---|---|---|
| **ADVANTAGES** | | **DISADVANTAGES** |
| Generally considered safer, especially when the system is built from safety rated components (SIL rated) that are designed to fail safe. | | Machines can't always sense when they are catching/lifting other items, as a counterweight operator would. |
| More reliable and consistent for long running & rep shows: targets saved in a show file. Most systems are closed loop, with positional feedback: an automated cue will always hit the same target - essential when other technical departments rely on positional information to trigger their cues (SM, lighting, sound). | | Automated flying systems are not always as easy to change speed and direction as a counterweight system. Although consoles allow operator to slow down / speed up an axis mid-cue, this requires a skilled and experienced operator. |
| Wear and tear of mechanical components can be monitored and flagged to maintenance engineers, allowing for proactive maintenance rather than reactive troubleshooting. | | Troubleshooting and repairing automated systems during a live show can be extremely complex. If the safety network has failed, a show stop is almost certain. Contingencies must be in place for all failure scenarios. |
| Integration with other technical theatre systems. An advanced automated system can broadcast positional data to lighting, sound and video departments, allowing lighting to track scenery and triggering LX cues based on scenery positions. | | Automated systems require more space than counterweight systems (though not at stage level). Motors and control cabinets usually require a dedicated cooled room on each side of the flytower at 1 or 2 levels. |
| Upskilling staff: automation operators and technicians need complex skills, combining elements of electronics, telecommunications and networks, power, mechanics and rigging. | | The cost of installing an automated system is significantly more than a counterweight system. Once installed, the cost of maintenance, support and spares is significant. |
| Less physical strain on staff by reducing manual handling. Counterweight systems require loading and unloading of weights in and out of the cradle, which over time can have a physical impact on people. | | Overall life expectancy. Counterweight systems can run for 50+ years with little maintenance beyond replacing ropes. Automated systems can require components such as controls and electromagnetic brakes to be replaced every 10 years (depending on the environment, exposure to dust and frequency of emergency stopping during movement); the entire system is unlikely to last more than 40 years. |
| With automated systems you can set show deads both with soft limits 'software limits' and physical limits to ensure a piece of scenery doesn't overtravel and collide with any known surroundings (but the system only knows what has been programmed into it). With a counterweight system, the flyman depends on visual marks on the rope to stop. | | Component obsolescence. When upgrading controls, components can sometimes be replaced with a alternative products; but often a full control cabinet swap out is required. |
| Generally fewer operators required for shows with complex flying cues. | | A minor consideration which may become increasingly important: power required adds to electrical consumption of the theatre. |

Figure 8.6.5 Table showing automated vs manual systems.

Figure 8.6.6 Photograph of chain hoists mounted to grid stand at Guildhall School of Music and Drama, Milton Court (London).

bolts and dismantle a steel structure than it is to demolish reinforced concrete.

The understage structure must also provide stable support for actors, dancers, musicians, scenery, props, mechanical effects and technical equipment. It might also at times allow any of these things to appear or disappear through the floor into the void below. Wherever possible a cavernous space with generous headroom, sometimes several storeys deep, should be provided below the stage.

Historically many stage floors were raked to improve the sightlines, an effect enhanced by the perspective of scenes painted on flat scenery. The current preference is to build theatres with flat stage floors to reduce hazard in operation and provide dancers with their preferred surface. A raked floor can always be added on top when needed. Other special types of flooring may be built on top of the normal stage floor permanently of temporarily – a sprung floor for dance, for example (see Figure 8.7.2), or a raised show floor with tracks for scenic effects, but care must be taken to ensure these do not adversely affect audience sightlines.

Various useful technical features may be built into a stage floor including projection screen boxes; dip traps (for hiding cables); float troughs (for downstage lighting instruments); and carpet cuts (for fast removal of stage coverings). Many stages are constructed with removable timber floor modules which make it simple to open up large holes in the floor wherever needed (see Figure 8.8.3).

## Dip traps

These are panels in the stage floor that can be lifted up to allow temporary cable to be laid safely. (See Figure 8.7.1.) They often accommodate power and data outlets as well. There should also be a way to run cable from the stage to the auditorium out of sight and without interfering with the safety curtain. The troughs revealed when the traps are lifted should be deep and wide enough to accommodate the more commonly found connectors in theatre, such as 16A ceeform connectors, socapex and Harting-type muticore connectors typically used for stage lighting.

## Understage machinery

Understage machinery might be used to facilitate rapid scene changing and produce spectacular effects in front of an audience or to aid manual handling when changing over from one show to another. It may also be used to help reconfigure the auditorium for different types of event. These are important distinctions. Apparently similar items

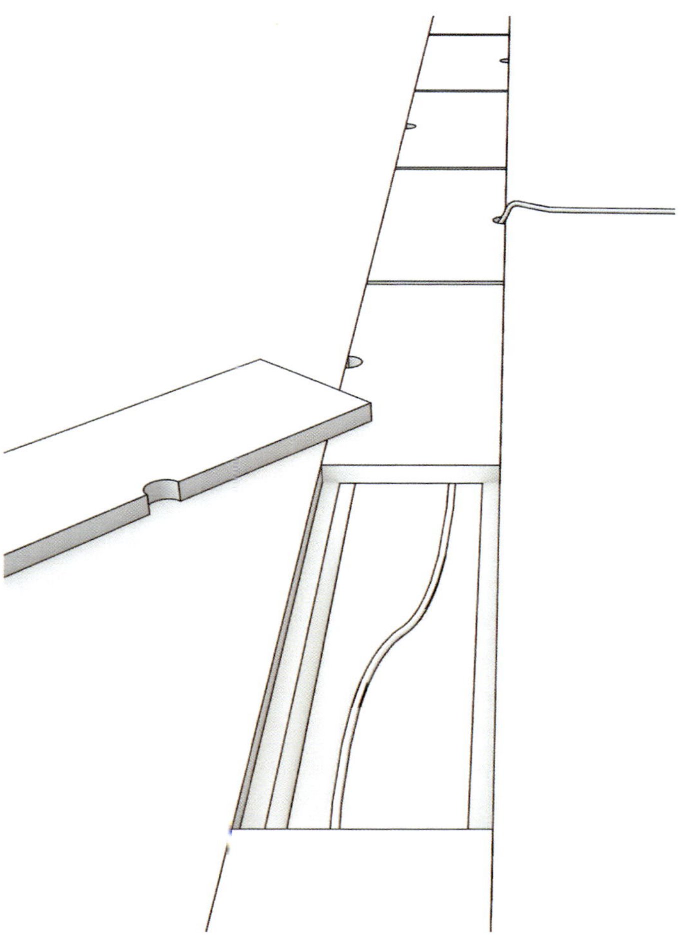

Figure 8.7.1 Sketch showing a 'dip trough' which typically runs in the wings upstage-downstage. Lids may be loose (as shown here) or hinged. Holes allow cables to pop in and out where required. A deeper trough would allow socket outlets to be incorporated.

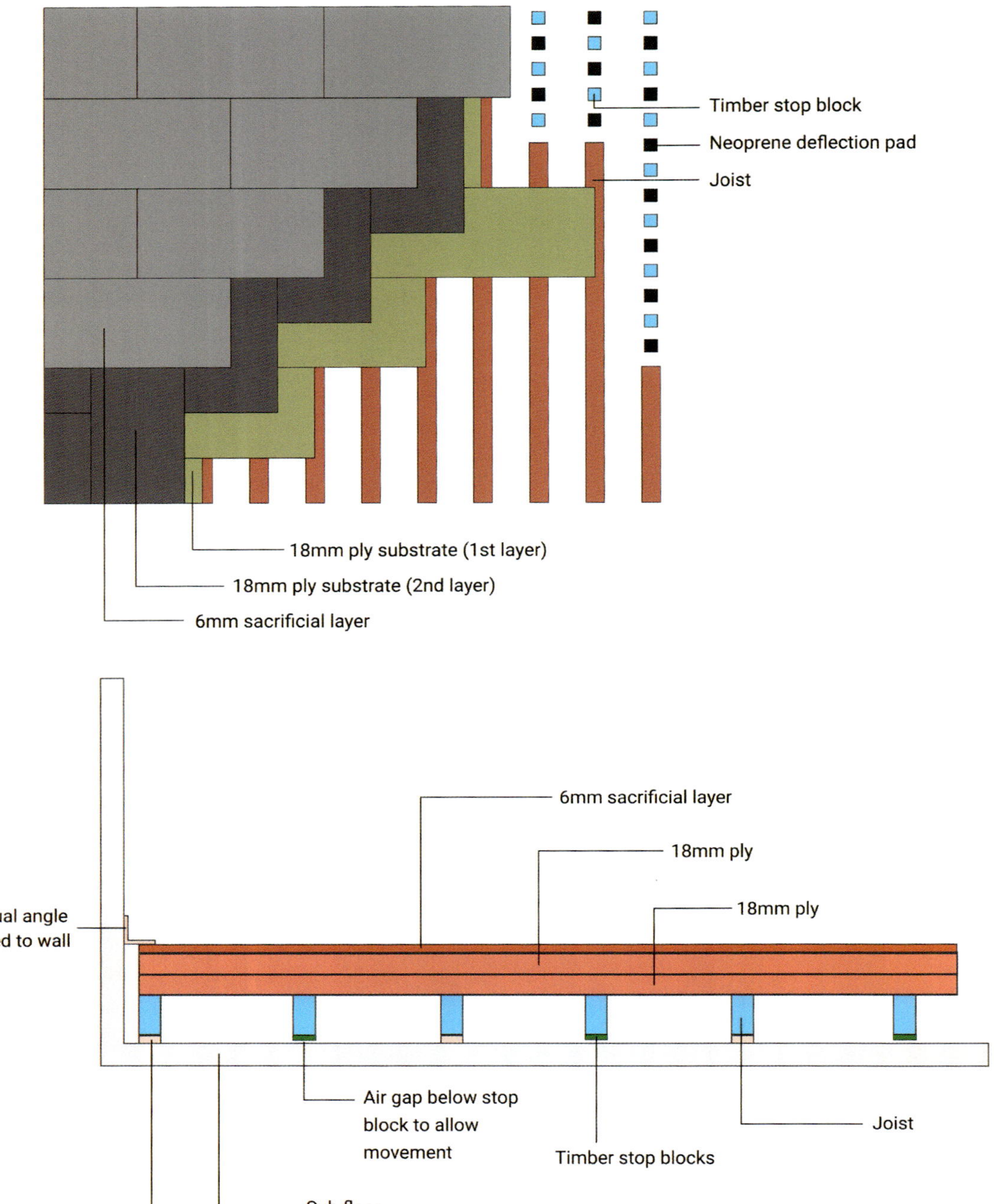


Figure 8.7.2a and 8.7.2b Plan and section showing build-up of a typical sprung floor.

of equipment may have very different noise or speed requirements, depending on how they are to be used.

Machinery may either be built in as a part of the infrastructure of the theatre building or it may be temporarily installed for a specific show or a season of shows. Big-budget musical productions employ much machinery that is often custom designed along with the scenery. In some cases this may require major structural alterations or in extreme cases an entirely new theatre to be built around a specific show.

At the other end of the scale, a repertory theatre producing its own shows may build up a collection of portable items of machinery or a kit of mechanical parts that can be adapted and reused for different roles in many shows.

Some examples of the different types of understage machinery that are commonly installed in theatres, traps, dip traps, stage lifts and revolves, are described in the following paragraphs.

## Traps

The simplest type of understage machine is the hinged or sliding trap door that may be opened to enable an actor to make an entrance from below or to exit down stairs into the understage area.

For rapid appearances, popular in pantomime, a fast trap device is installed below. This is a counterweighted rising platform that lifts a performer up to stage level and fills in the opening in the floor using a 'sloat' lid. Used in reverse, it enables a genie to disappear behind a puff of pyrotechnic smoke.

## Stage lifts

Stage lifts are used to raise and lower both larger items of scenery and groups of actors. Lifts are particularly good for growing forests of trees, for sinking ships and for elevating heavenly choirs. They vary enormously in size and style, but may cover the entire stage area and travel deep down into the basement. More powerful lifts are capable of shifting tens of tons of scenery and some will rise several metres above stage level to create instant raised acting platforms, often in modular form.

Lifts may have a double-deck construction. The lower deck services the main stage floor which can be equipped with trap doors and may support supplementary lifting equipment. The top level of a lift can be made to tilt to create a raking stage floor at whatever slope may be required – potentially changing the datum level and rake of the entire stage surface. Lifts within lifts are not uncommon.

To protect people on stage from falling into the hole left by a lift, various automatic rising barriers or folding safety nets may be incorporated into the system and doors below stage need to be interlocked. Shear edges must have protective devices to reduce the risk of injury and even of amputation. Generally though, safe operation depends on careful management, risk assessment and rehearsal.

## Revolves

Another popular scene-changing machine is the revolve. This can be a simple circular platform either built on top of, or recessed into, the stage floor. Two or more scenes can be built on a revolve and rotated into view as the show proceeds, often in full view of the audience. They are particularly good for chases or for switching from an exterior to an interior scene.

Revolves, like lifts, may be built with a second floor below, allowing entrances to be made while rotating. Larger revolves might incorporate smaller revolves or lifts within.

## Wagons

Scene changes can take place at stage level by rolling scenery on and off the stage from the side or rear. This may be done by building wheels into individual scenic elements or by constructing the scenery and props on top of big flat, wheeled platforms or wagons. The largest wagons may fill the stage and be capable of carrying an entire three-dimensional standing set in one piece. Wagons might incorporate a built-in revolve or may have trap doors that align with traps in the stage or lift floor below.

In some installations, wagons are designed to precisely match the size and shape of stage lifts and the lifts are used either to transport the wagons, loaded with scenery, to another level in the theatre or to sink the wagon into the stage floor. Adjacent compensating lifts can provide a sunken pathway so the wagons traverse with their top surface flush with the surrounding floor, thus avoiding awkward steps and enabling fluid scene changes to be made.

Traditionally wagons are guided by tracks in the floor and are hauled by motorised systems mounted under the floor. More recently automated vehicle technology has been employed to guide and position wagons remotely so they can wander freely around the stage area.

## Building for future use

Theatre buildings should be planned to support the unpredictable demands of show business and to anticipate future development, even if no machinery is to be installed initially. Allowances for suitable anticipated structural, electrical and mechanical loadings, as well as sensible acoustic protection, are essential elements of such pre-planning.

Where possible, it is sensible to use construction materials which may be adapted in the future with little waste and minimal effort: timber floors to technical walkways rather than poured concrete, for instance.

No theatre will ever have too much storage space. The more scenery which can be stored at the end of a run, the more can be re-used for another production.

## 8.8 Stage machinery for the open stage

Although the basic engineering concepts are the same for both the proscenium format and open stage, the particular constraints of the open stage format require innovative thinking when designing the stage machinery. The open stage in all its forms sets challenges for the stage machinery to solve as set out in the following.

- Scenery tends to be 'three-dimensional' rather than linear.
- Delivery of scenery and performers to the stage area occurs in full view of the audience.
- It is necessary to ensure that any machinery in view does not undermine the magic of the image; for example, the audience around an open stage is more likely to have a sightline to below stage when a trap is opened or elevator descends.
- Noise: systems tend to be much closer to the audience: actors waiting to enter and technicians operating the equipment will also be in close proximity.
- Suspension methods: ropes are much closer to the audience and thereby more attention must be paid to visible size, colour and reflectivity.
- Flying height and masking: stored scenery may be very visible to the audience and this can undermine the element of surprise in scene changes.
- Safety issues: flying over the audience and the creation of voids near to the audience may require consideration of barrier systems or other precautions.

### Setting out the overstage areas

Sufficient clear height above the stage is desirable to hide scenery beyond audience sightlines. This space may also be used to install temporary bridges and access platforms to enable performers to be hooked up, suspended and made ready to fly in on cue.

In some cases, where roof heights are restricted, it may be necessary to consider having no grid at all and suspending directly from the ceiling to achieve the maximum possible flying height. While this approach may improve flying capability, careful consideration must be paid to access methods used for rigging and maintenance. Preferably a permanent means of access should be provided, for example, technical walkways, mobile gantries and drawbridges, rather than relying on access equipment.

For overstage rigging, a traditional grating-type grid with high 'transparency' is desirable. As described in the following, the grid becomes the 'blank canvas' onto which the particular suspension layout to suit the production design is sketched. This may be achieved by diverting suspensions from high-level structure using travelling beam systems and such like or, by using the grid surface itself with appropriate diversion components, to route suspension ropes to the necessary drop point.

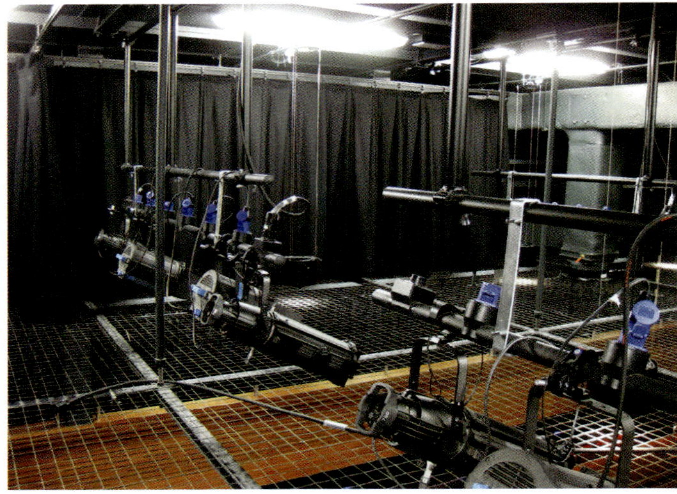

Figure 8.8.1 Photograph of tension wire grid (Berry Theatre, Hedge End, Nr Eastleigh, Hampshire). Lighting bars can be re-positioned as required. Noses of lanterns should be as close to the wire as pssible, while allowing space to focus.

A grating grid with a nominal cell size of 50 × 100mm (in order to achieve good porosity for chain hoist and winch hooks and suspension terminations) and floor load capacity of the order of 5kN/m$^2$ provides a 'systematic' surface to which standard diversion components may be mounted.

Tension wire grids (TWGs) may also be considered for flexible theatres with no fixed stage position or where technical work may be carried out by young people. (See Figure 8.8.1.) These are not particularly easy to work on if intensive rigging work has to take place. A TWG surface is made of narrow gauge steel wire and therefore impossible to fix pulleys or equipment to; and it is impossible to fly anything higher than the underside of the TWG. Beams of light from fixtures rigged above the TWG can catch the wires and be distracting to the audience.

'Egg-crate' grids of technical walkways may also be considered (see Figure 8.8.2). These are ideal for lighting positions and may be used to provide access at a high level for rigging purposes. Scenic elements (such as chandeliers) can be flown from openings between walkways. However, while bridges provide ideal access to lighting positions the stage engineering elements generally have to be rigged in the void areas with all the resulting 'working at height' safety concerns.

### Overstage machinery

Although there will be some requirement for regularly set-out 'linear' flying as in a conventional proscenium

Figure 8.8.2 Photograph of 'egg crate' grid above the thrust stage at Chester Storyhouse. Lanterns may be rigged to the rails, or by secondary rigging bars spanning the opening. See also Reference Project 06.

stage house (for example, masking borders and tracked systems), the majority of flying over an open stage will require a much more flexible method of suspension. Suspensions will vary to suit the scenography and therefore a 'sky hook' philosophy – the ability to rig a suspension point anywhere over the stage – is the required approach, to facilitate the suspension of an infinite variety of objects from trees to single light bulbs and everything in between. Many items commonly flown over thrust stages are small and lightweight – such as chandeliers or small props – for these, a manual hemp set is usually the best compromise of flexibility, speed, cost and operation. Diverting the line to practically anywhere for operation is very simple; it is more flexible in head-height so can run over/under/through other lines with more weight on, counterweight or extra travel can be added in a 'wing' if required, and the cost of making or changing the system is very low.

A manual or motorised 'point hoist' winch system should be considered a base requirement to allow for heavier scenic objects and for performer flying.

Point hoists come in several forms with the following characteristics:

- an electrically powered winch unit which may have one or two ropes
- a method of enabling the rope to be paid out and dropped at the correct position over the stage
- an electronic drive and control system to enable individual winches to be synchronised so that several hoists may safely suspend a single item of scenery
- wire rope as the means of suspension.

There are five basic spatial variants available which fulfil these criteria.

(1) Offstage mounted winch (mounted to the wall or in a frame with others – sometimes known as a 'winch farm') with rope paid out overhead or at grid level to the drop position via a series of modular diversion components which must be rigged for each specific use.
(2) Offstage mounted winch with double-purchase arrangement and crane jib-style track mounted trolley to allow variable positioning (along a linear path) of the suspension point over the stage without any requirement for re-rigging of diversion pulleys.
(3) Winch unit suspended on an overhead travelling beam system to enable direct pay-out from the winch at the drop point. This works reasonably for a few hoists; however, larger systems quickly lead to a congested grid and there can be manual handling problems in moving units about (i.e. transferring a winch from one position to another).
(4) Wheeled or trolley-mounted winch unit which can be transported across a grid to the point at which the rope drop is required. This is much more flexible than the overhead travelling beam-mounted system but requires greater grid floor load capacity.
(5) Multi-line winch where several rope drops can be realised by individually diverting multiple ropes from the same winch drum to different points, either via the grid surface or overhead. All drops are mechanically coupled and therefore place less reliance on the control system to ensure synchronisation.

Point hoist systems require high-end control systems to ensure synchronisation of suspensions.

With linear powered flying the flying-bar is suspended by a single multi-line winch which has the benefit of mechanical synchronisation whereby all the ropes go to the same drum.

With a point hoist system a single item of scenery or a performer may be suspended on two or more ropes each emanating from a different winch. Synchronisation is ensured by the electronics driving each winch and overall supervision and safety monitoring by the control system – as well as correct programming by the operator.

It is therefore vital that point hoist systems are:

- engineered to the highest level of safety as defined by appropriate standards
- have clear and intuitive operator interfaces – i.e. software that is easily learnt and operated
- have an infrastructure which permits operators to achieve high levels of vigilance – including

portable control desks, wireless systems and camera feeds to the console
- have features to allow complex programming – for example, the automatic recording of a series of manually developed moves for cue playback – often referred to as 'teach and learn'.

## Setting out the understage areas

The key requirements for below the open stage are common to those for the proscenium stage, that is, the need for a truly modular stage – a stage surface made up of a regular array of removable panels and modular riser panels to allow the insertion of trapdoors, staircases and other scenic elements. Ideally, the panelised floor should be supported on a demountable structure such as a 'drop-in bar' system where secondary horizontal members slot into a primary horizontal spanning structure to enable the formation of different sizes of void. These might vary from, for example, a small ladder trap, to a large elevator, to a swimming pool.

As deep a void as possible should be planned for the stage basement.

## Understage machinery

Even assuming a modular stage floor, it is unrealistic to conceive of a permanently installed simple elevator system which could meet all the reasonably foreseeable needs of an open stage show design. While large fixed elevators undoubtedly add an extra dimension, this type of system is more suited to a position upstage of a proscenium.

There are examples where the entire auditorium floor is made up of a series of modular elevating platforms which can provide a wide variety of different riser formats and seating tiers. However, this is an extremely costly approach and likely only to be considered as part of a prestigious new-build project. While appearing to be ultra-flexible, such a system constrains design by the imposition of a fixed geometry.

The most flexible and cost-effective approach is to combine a modular stage with stage machinery brought in for the particular show. The modular stage allows the creation of voids (of varying width, length and depth) to enable the incorporation of transportable elevator systems with or without automated doors and lids. (See Figure 8.8.3.) As with overstage systems, there is a requirement for comprehensive safety monitoring and control systems designed to meet the highest standards, applicable to life-critical systems.

Figure 8.8.3 Photgraph showing the modular stage at Theatre Royal Drury Lane (London). The beams and columns supporting the decks may also be removed, to create larger openings. See also Reference Project 32.

## Section editor

Alex Wardle, Senior Theatre Consultant at Charcoalblue

## Contributors (in alphabetical order)

Musa Halimeh, Renewal Programme Manager (Technical), Royal Opera House, London

Lucy Osborne, Set and Costume Designer

Hilary Williamson, Technical Director, Hampstead Theatre, London

## Contributors to first edition

Andy Hayles (as section editor), Senior Consultant at Charcoalblue

Peter Angier, Co-Founder of Carr & Angier, Theatre Consultants

Richard Brett, Stage Engineer and Theatre Consultant (d. 2014)

George Ellerington, Associate, Venue Consulting at Arup

Mark Priestley, Director and Head of Capital Projects at Unusual Rigging, London

Peter Ruthven-Hall, Senior Consultant at Charcoalblue

# Section 9
# Lighting, sound and video

## 9.1 Section overview

This section discusses the infrastructure required to support portable equipment – such as lanterns, loudspeakers and video projectors – which is generally repositioned from one production to another.

In most theatres, the layout and type of loose lighting, sound and video equipment changes for every production. One lighting design will require a lot of frontlight – perhaps because the set design features a ceiling which rules out the use of toplight – another will require none. Multiple rigging locations should be provided around the stage and auditorium to enable lighting, sound and video designers to position where required for each show.

There are some constants. Most theatres are built with rows of raked seating located to achieve the best sightlines relative to a fixed stage. Lighting bridges above the auditorium will therefore be useful in positions which relate to the location of the stage. In most theatres loudspeakers will be directed towards the audience, not the stage; and most seats in most theatres stay in the same position: so achieving optimum loudspeaker positions is a long-term gain (and not achieving suitable positions a long-term problem).

Video projectors need a surface to project onto, such as an upstage cyclorama or downstage screen: front- and back-projection locations for each should be considered. For video relay and capture, the most useful video camera angles should be anticipated and provided for.

The infrastructure must be planned to allow technical teams to rig and connect equipment where it is required for each production, with as much ease as possible, avoiding time-consuming and unsightly temporary cabling.

Safe access is imperative and thorough risk assessment of all rigging and focusing activities is required in both the design and the operation of the building. ABTT Codes of Practice provide useful guidance. Structural loading of lighting bars and access systems should be considered at the earliest stage. The ABTT's *Technical Standards for Places of Entertainment* provides useful advice.

### Procurement

Regardless of the size and status of the theatre in question, it is sensible to invest in an infrastructure of the best quality that can be afforded, as this will normally outlast the equipment threefold: a rewire might be expected every twenty-five to thirty years, while a lighting console is likely to have a useful lifespan of seven to ten years.

A typical theatre's technical equipment will cost between 10%–15% of the construction cost, including stage engineering. For producing theatres and opera houses this percentage may be considerably higher; for schools and community spaces it is likely to be lower.

Many of the elements discussed in this chapter are evolving rapidly as a result of developments in technology and sustainability. Where technology is evolving rapidly it is often a good idea to buy loose equipment separately from the infrastructure, or to structure the contract so that final choices of loose equipment can be made at the last possible moment. This should include equipment such as

- stage lighting fixtures
- control consoles for lighting, sound, video
- video projectors
- video monitors.

Managements should earmark a sum of money to help their technical team move into the building: to build storage racking, shelves and workbenches, appropriate to the equipment in use and the way it is used.

## 9.2 Rigging positions

### Lighting bridges

In a world of variables, let's start with one constant: it is useful to have a means of easily accessing equipment at a high level above the audience. Where possible, end-stage theatres generally have two or three lighting bridges spanning the width of the auditorium; in-the-round theatres have bridges around the perimeter of the room and a layout of walkways overhead, as do thrust stage theatres, but leaving

DOI: 10.4324/9781003327295-9

a space upstage for flying. (See Figures 9.2.1a and 9.2.1b.) The spacing of the bridges will vary according to the size of the stage and the auditorium, but all the bridges should be the full width of the auditorium to give the widest possible angles of view onto the stage. Where there is a series of bridges they must not restrict each other's view to the stage.

Although generally referred to as 'lighting' bridges, these walkways are frequently used as loudspeaker rigging positions, followspot positions, locations to rig show relay video cameras and microphones, a position for an assistant stage manager (ASM) to drop petals onto the audience or for

Figure 9.2.1a Lighting bridges for an endstage theatre: National Opera House, Wexford, Ireland. See also Strong (ed.), *Theatre Buildings* (2010), p. 93 and pp. 272–73.

Figure 9.2.1b Lighting bridges for a theatre in-the-round, New Vic, Newcastle-under-Lyme.

a performer to appear in a flying harness and descend from a point hoist – as required by the production.

Bridges consist of a floor, horizontal rigging rails and vertical supports, which may also be used to hang the bridge from the structure above. The floor can be lightweight timber, carpeted to deaden footfall; timber is easy to cut, so holes, small openings or even hatches may be added in the future for new equipment. If hatches are provided, suspension points should be provided directly above; and consideration given to size – small (less than 200 × 200mm) for spotlines and chain hooks only, or large enough for chain hoists, in which case guardrails should be considered. As a last resort, fall arrest PPE may be required and harness attachment points must be provided.

The horizontal rigging bars should be presented as 48.3mm outer diameter circular hollow section (48.3mm OD CHS), otherwise known as two-inch scaffold bar: this size accepts standard rigging clamps. The same size CHS can often be used for the hangers, which means they too will accept boom arms or scaffold clamps for temporary rigging.

A guardrail is required at 1,100mm above floor level; kickplate of 150mm; and, if fall-restraint harnesses are to be avoided, a mid-rail at 600mm. The rigging bar is generally positioned at around 900mm, outrigged from the handrail by around 250mm to allow space for the back end of a typical lantern: but this will depend on the type of lanterns in use and the angle to the stage.

Rigging points for hauling lines should be provided, to allow lanterns to be lifted to the bridge, rather than having to be lugged around the theatre and along the bridge.

Clamping rigging bars to supporting structure – rather than welding – allows them to be repositioned in the future, as the use of the theatre and typical equipment sizes change.

There is no one ideal design of lighting bridge (see Figures 9.2.2 and 9.2.3). Some need to have both sides 'riggable'. Some will have acoustic reflectors below them. Some will need to be wider, in order to be used as technical control or follow spot positions. An angled profile can be helpful to minimise the visual impact of the bridges from below, whilst retaining generous width at hip height, where it is most useful.

Location of electrical containment along lighting bridges needs careful consideration: it must not impede rigging operations or access, yet numerous services will be required. Working light is generally required at a high level (white) and low level (blue), which can be provided as LED tape along the kickplate.

Building a mock-up of the proposed lighting bridge design is invaluable (see Figure 9.2.4). It should be tested with appropriate equipment and the theatre's technicians – if

Figure 9.2.2 Lineset above thrust stage at Chester Storyhouse. See also Reference Project 06.

Figure 9.2.4 Mockup of lighting bridge for new Sadler's Wells theatre on the Olympic Park (London). Built from scaffolding and stock rostra in the studio theatre, complete with cardboard containment, various lanterns were rigged to test ergonomics.

Figure 9.2.3 Technical walkways at St Ann's Warehouse (Brooklyn). Floor width is minimal, walkway width increases above knee-height. Air supply nozzles (square tubes) line up with walkway hangars to minimise loss of rigging positions. (See Reference Project 04).

they are available at the time (difficult with new-build theatres) – to check that the design meets the actual requirements for this particular theatre, and to highlight potential manual handling issues.

Wheelchair access to lighting bridges is often discussed. It is certainly useful to have a lift to lighting bridge level, for transporting flightcases and other heavy equipment; if a lighting bridge is to be used as a control position, then a wheelchair user ought to be able to access it. It is generally deemed impractical and hazardous for a person in a wheelchair to lift a 6kg lantern over a rail at 1,100mm from floor level, the most common operation on lighting bridges.

## Lighting rigging positions

Every production has a unique lighting design. Lighting designers specify, usually on a scale drawing, where they require each lantern to be rigged (see Figure 9.2.5a and b). Once rigged, each luminaire or 'lantern' needs to be focused. 'Focusing' is pointing a lantern at the right place on stage, and adjusting parts of the lantern to adjust the beam's size, shape and 'sharpness' (i.e. the appearance of the beam edge). Each one is turned on individually. Automated luminaires ('moving lights') need to be rigged manually, but are focussed from the lighting console: removing the need to physically access each fixture, and allowing it to be re-focussed to different positions during a show.

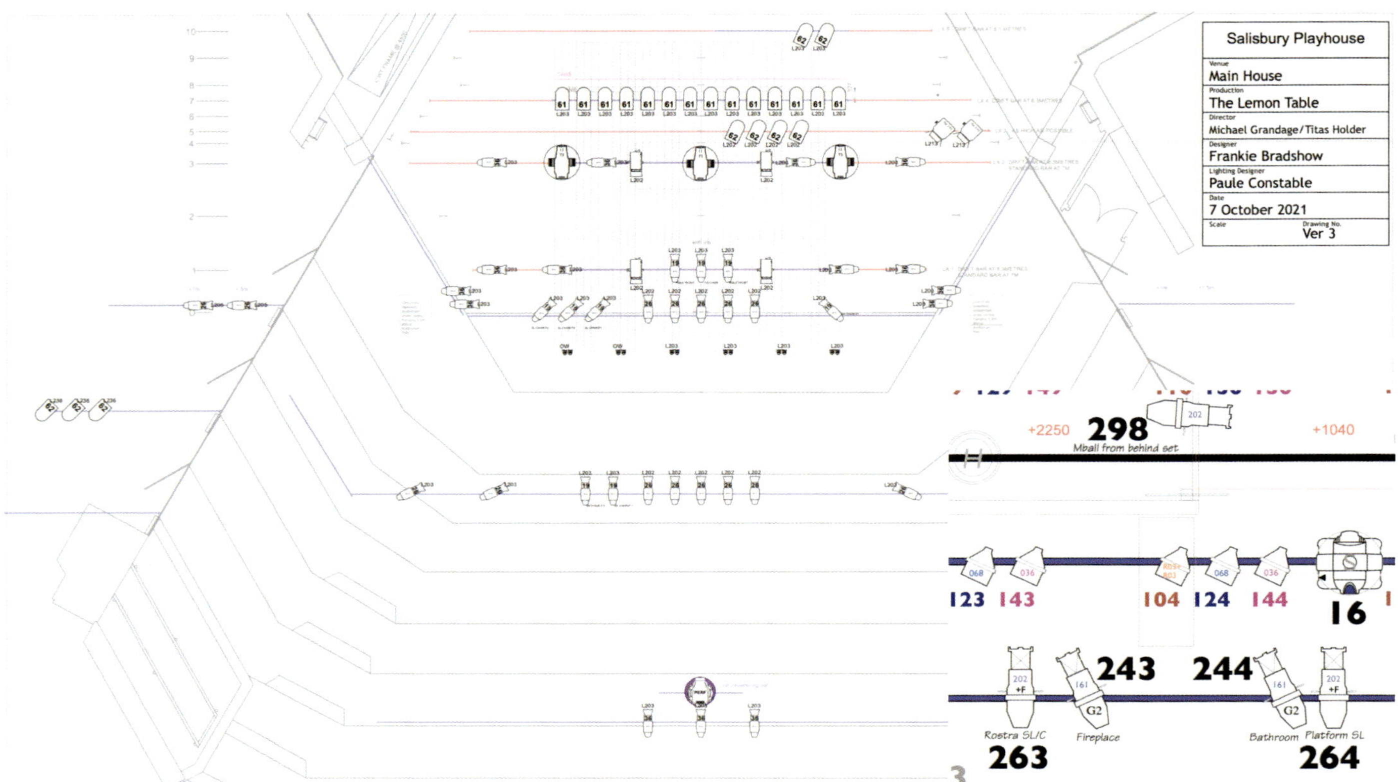


Figure 9.2.5a and 5b Lighting plans show location in plan view for each lantern. Each lantern is assigned a channel number. Tungsten lanterns may require a colour filter. Focus notes serve as an aide-memoir.

Lighting rigs can use from 50 to over 500 lanterns depending on the size of the theatre and the type of show. Lanterns are awkward and heavy, so moving them can be hard work, hazardous and time consuming, especially when working at height. A successful lighting position will make this process as safe, swift and comfortable as possible (see Figures 9.2.6a, 9.2.6b and 9.2.7). Trying to hide the lighting position from view is likely to render it impractical in use.

Safe access is imperative and thorough risk assessment of all lighting rigging and focusing activities is required in both the design and the operation of the building. ABTT Codes of Practice provide useful guidance (extract shown in Figure 9.2.8). Structural loading of lighting bars and access systems should be considered at the earliest stage. The increased weight of moving lights and LED fixtures requires ever greater loading capacity from rigging positions.

Figure 9.2.6a Balcony rigging bar at Bloomsbury Theatre, London. Loose cables run behind slats to facility panels.

## Overstage

Proscenium theatres have a series of overhead bars, normally part of a flying system, on which it is possible to hang lanterns. (See Section 8.6.) Bars are lowered to 'rigging height' (around 1m above stage level), lanterns are rigged onto the bar and the bar is flown out to the correct height (usually between 5 and 10m). Bars may be provided as 48.3mm CHS or a 'ladder bar' consisting of a pair of CHS joined by flat bars, which increases the load capacity.

Access to focus overhead bars needs to be considered. Large producing houses may use flown lighting bridges, with lanterns hung either side of catwalks which technicians

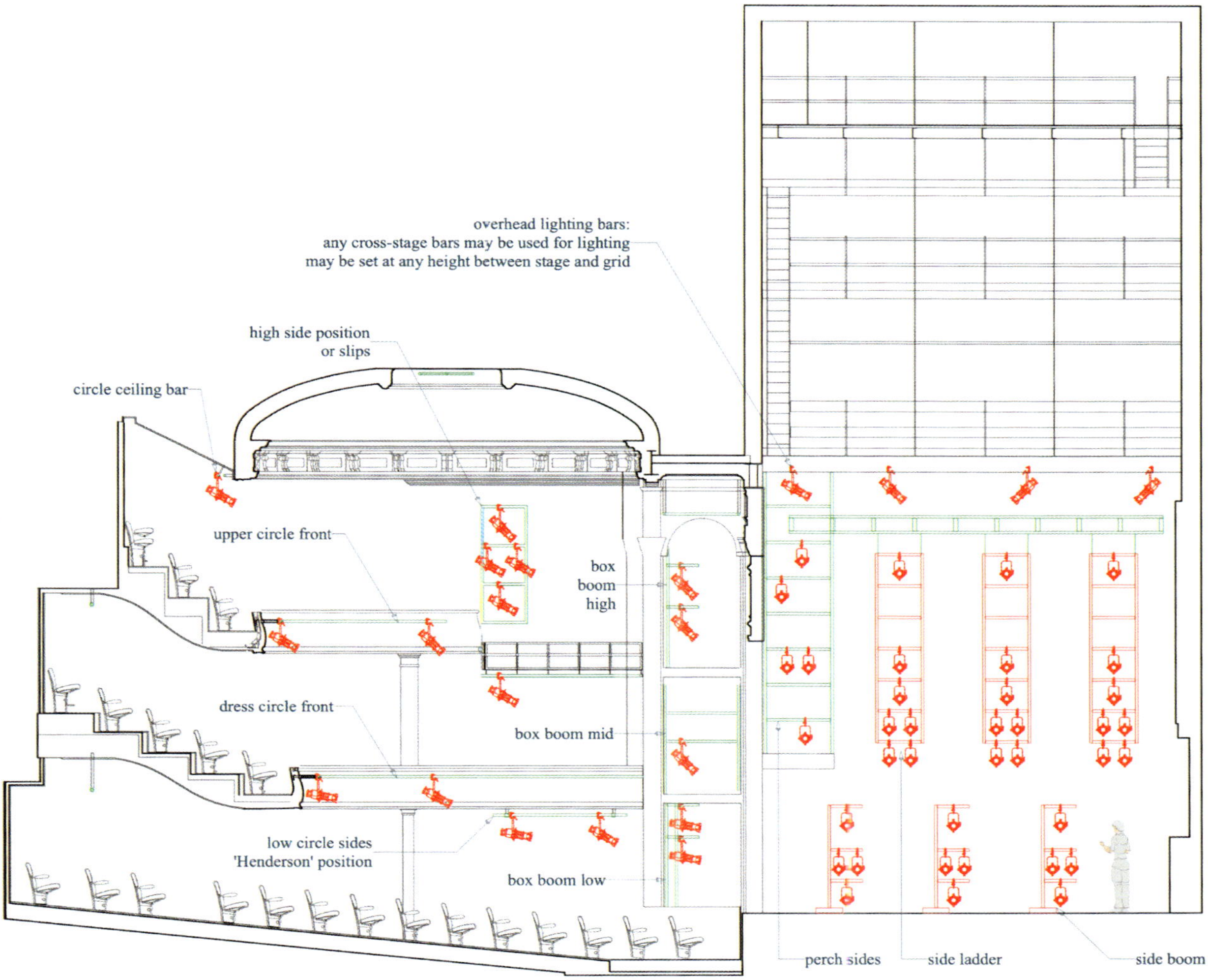

overhead lighting bars:
any cross-stage bars may be used for lighting
may be set at any height between stage and grid

high side position
or slips

circle ceiling bar

upper circle front

box
boom
high

dress circle front

box boom mid

low circle sides
'Henderson' position

box boom low

perch sides

side ladder

side boom

Figure 9.2.6b Section showing exemplar lighting positions, Royal Court Theatre, London.

Figure 9.2.7 Truss grid lowered for rigging at Brixton House Studio Theatre 2 (London). Tapered boxes collect cables as the truss is raised out. Unistrut between timber wall panels provide fixing points. (See Reference Project 26).

use to give them access to the rig: but these occupy space which might be needed for other equipment.

Most theatres will own at least one piece of access equipment such as a Tallescope or aerial work platform (AWP) which can either be pushed or motor-driven around the stage to focus lanterns. This operation is hazardous and needs careful management. Storage for the access equipment is necessary, close to the stage.

## Sides of the stage

### Ladders

Lighting designs often require side lights rigged at various heights on ladders hung at the sides of the stage, as shown in Figure 9.2.9. Their movable rungs start just above head height – so they do not obstruct performers' entrances and exits – and the top rung should be just below the fly floor.

Typical Front of House Lighting Bridge

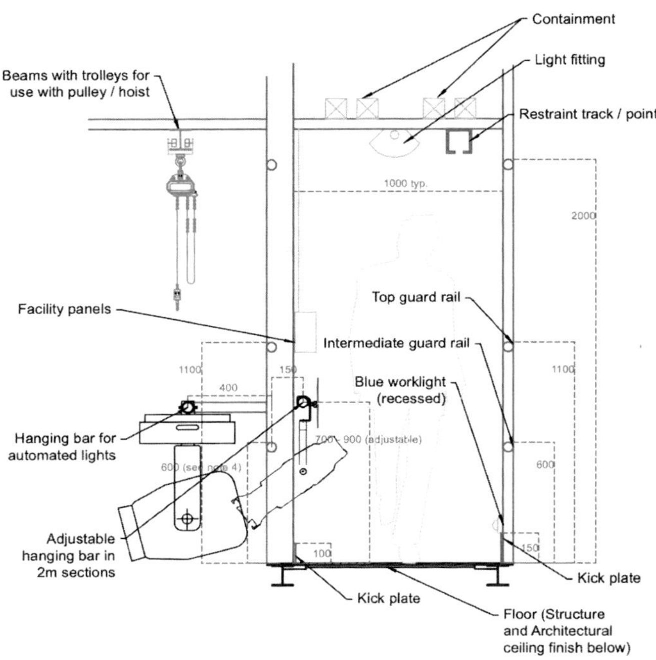


Notes
1. Minimum clear walkway behind luminaires 500mm.
2. Bridge width is typical and will vary with scale of theatre and bridge position.
3. Floor should be solid and non-slip for comfort and to retain loose items.
4. If intermediate rail is omitted, restraint track / points should be provided for use with harness.
5. Signage should be provided indicating maximum permissible loading on all lighting bars. Refer to Technical Standards for Places of Entertainment for typical ratings.

Typical Studio Lighting Bridge

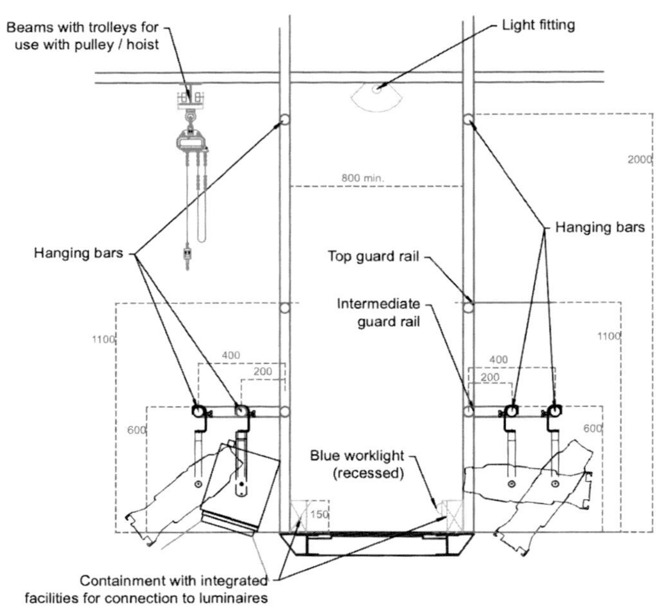


Notes
1. Bridge width is typical for two sided bridge.
2. Bridge edges should be minimised to allow luminaires to backlight under bridge.
3. Floor should be solid and non-slip for comfort and to retain loose items.
4. Signage should be provided indicating maximum permissible loading on all lighting bars. Refer to Technical Standards for Places of Entertainment for typical ratings.
5. 48.3mm diameter hangers / structure preferred to enable additional lighting positions, appropriately designed and with signage indicating associated load ratings.

Figure 9.2.8 ABTT code of practice drawings showing three arrangements for lighting bridges, including rigging bars, zones for containment, worklight and fall restraint. Measurements in the drawings are in millimetres.

They can be tracked or flown to varied positions to suit different productions and avoid conflict with scenery.

### Booms

Booms are vertical poles with lights attached, usually supported from the floor as in Figure 9.2.10. These allow lighting designers to use low angles of side light, much used in dance to light the performers without lighting the floor.

### Fly floor rail

Fly floors and bridges round the sides of the flytower should have one or more rails on which lights can be rigged, as shown in Figure 9.2.11.

### Perches

Another crucial lighting position is a vertical tower or 'perch' just upstage of the proscenium. These allow the rigging of lanterns at any height from floor level to just above the height of the proscenium. They should be accessed by a series of stairs/ladders and platforms.

If the theatre has an adjustable proscenium opening, these perch positions should track on- and offstage with it. A perch can also be provided in the auditorium, see Figure 9.2.12 and 'Box Booms'.

### Footlight positions

Footlights are sometimes used along the downstage edge of the stage. A channel with a removable lid along the very front edge of the stage should be installed to hide any cables and transformers that run to the footlights. If the theatre has an orchestra pit, it will also be helpful to provide a rigging position on the inside face of the orchestra pit wall. (See Section 6.3.) Unistrut along the underside of the stage edge can also be useful.

Typical Studio Lighting Bridge (alternate)

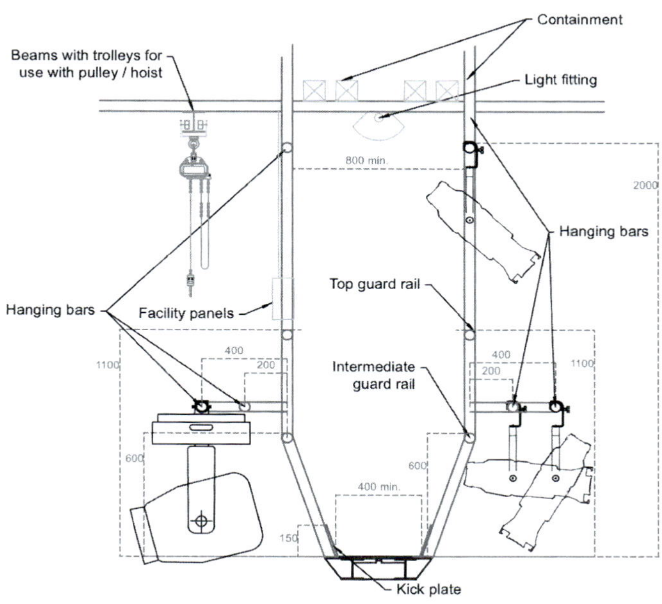


Notes

1. Bridge width is typical for two sided bridge
2. Bridge edges should be minimised to allow luminaires to backlight under bridge
3. Floor should be solid and non-slip for comfort and to retain loose items
4. Signage should be provided indicating maximum permissible loading on all lighting bars. Refer to Technical Standards for Places of Entertainment for typical ratings.
5. 48.3mm diameter hangers / structure preferred to enable additional lighting positions, appropriately designed and with signage indicating associated load ratings.

Figure 9.2.8 (Continued)

Figure 9.2.9 Lighting ladders hung from side bars running upstage-downstage. This use can cause the up-down bars to require a higher load capacity than the cross-stage bars.

## Lighting in the auditorium

### Box booms

Locations at the sides of the auditorium inside what may sometimes be audience boxes. It should be possible to rig lights at different heights from stage floor level to the top of the auditorium. Safe and easy access must be designed for these positions and they should be able to accommodate the rigging of large automated lanterns.

Consideration must be given to other uses of the boxes – sometimes they may be used for audience seating or performers may appear in them – and provide minimal infrastructure which supports the greatest number of potential uses. A vertical bar either side (48.3mm OD CHS or Unistrut) allows a single lantern to be hung from a boom arm, or several temporary bars to span between the two verticals and support numerous lanterns. When not in use for technical rigging, the verticals should be discreet.

### Slots

Many theatres have been designed with lighting 'slots' instead of boxes at the sides of the auditorium. These rigging positions are angled so the lights themselves are hidden from the audience. They must be wide enough to allow a lantern to see both sides of the stage.

### Advance bar

If the stage extends through the proscenium creating a forestage, it is usually necessary to provide a bar or a bridge, so that it can be lit from above. A bridge is preferable because access is possible for focusing and maintenance.

### High front light

An even front cover requires high frontlight positions, at an angle of about 45° from head height on stage. These can be provided as a series of bridges above the auditorium or

Figure 9.2.10 Lighting boom built from 48.3mm OD CHS and boom arms. Taller booms may require stage weights for stability, or restraint from above. This boom base has wheels to help move the boom into position.

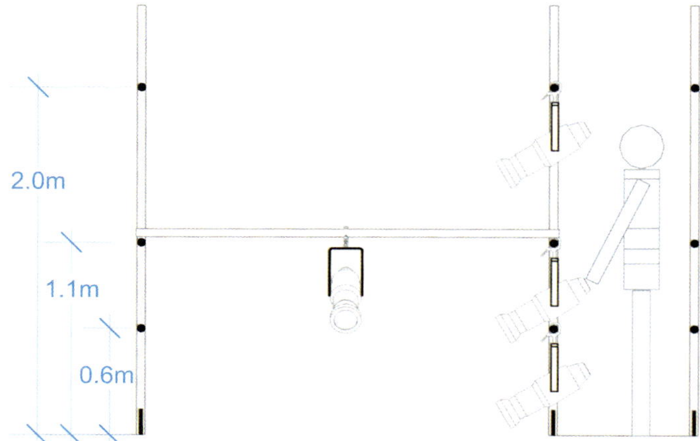


Figure 9.2.11 Diagram showing typical rail heights for lighting bridges, fly floors and egg-crate grids. The 1.1m guardrail is a building standards requirement, but may also be used for rigging. The 150mm kickplate prevents small objects being inadvertently kicked off the walkways. The 2.0m rail provides an alternative rigging height.

Figure 9.2.12 Auditorium perch lighting position adjacent to proscenium at Sadler's Wells Theatre, Islington. This is a popular location for rigging lighting and loudspeakers.

with rigging positions at the sides ('slips') and back of the auditorium.

### Circle fronts

Where the theatre has tiers or circles, lighting positions should be built into their fronts. These positions should follow all around the curve of the circle front, and allow a lantern to be rigged anywhere along it – especially on centre. Particular consideration needs to be given to how this area is to be safely accessed as rigging and focusing in this position can be both hazardous and ergonomically uncomfortable. The bar must be located so as to avoid the bar or equipment obstructing audience sightlines to the stage from both above and below (see Figure 9.2.13). In some cases, particularly in historic theatres, it is desirable for the bars to be removable when not in use.

Equipment here can be large and heavy: now that automated followspots exist, the circle front can be a useful location for moving lights which automatically track performers on stage. The circle front is a popular rigging position for video projectors, many of which have front to rear cooling and weigh around 50kg per unit (see Figure 9.2.14). Sound proofed 'hush' boxes can be installed around projectors

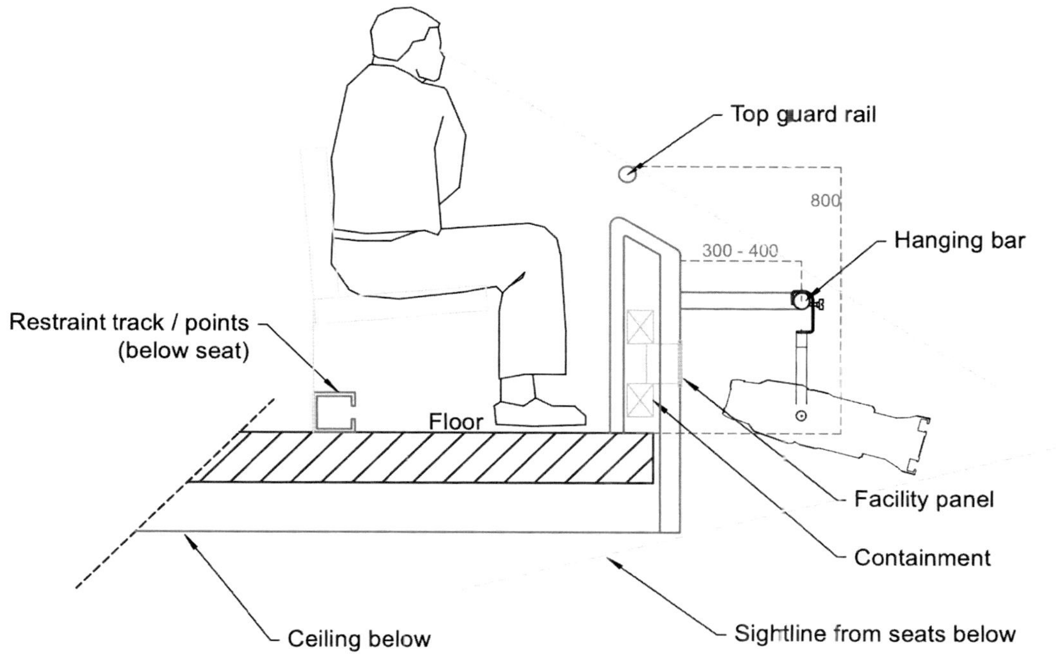

Notes

1. Refer to Technical Standards for Places of Entertainment for conditions where 800mm height guard rail applies, and when it does not.
2. Restraint system should be designed to prevent fall of technicians leaning over balcony front.
3. Luminaire hanging bar should be located for minimal impact on audience sightlines.
4. Where possible, points for hoist or pulley should be provided above to assist lifting heavy items to hanging bar.
5. Signage should be provided indicating maximum permissible loading on hanging bar. Refer to Technical Standards for Places of Entertainment for typical ratings.

Figure 9.2.13 Diagram showing challenges of designing successful balcony fronts. Where seats are fixed, the guard rail may be reduced from the normal 1100 to 800mm.

to limit their noise further: these reduce the emission of fan noise into the performance space but occupy more space and increase the weight of the installation.

A minimum clearance of 300mm (from the bar centre to the nearest obstruction – such as the circle front) is recommended. It is worth noting that this position is frequently an area where numerous video services congregate (such as video cameras), so providing multiple video tie lines is recommended.

### Bars in circle ceiling

This is another useful angle, but a safe system of access must be considered.

### Temporary cable routes

The most flexible auditoria will have a system built into the walls allowing lanterns to be hung in additional unusual places. There will also need to be a system for getting cable to them discretely via carefully planned temporary cable routes. These comprise a coordinated set of holes through walls and hooks over doorways and public thoroughfares that provide safe, fire-proofed and acoustically sealed openings for cables, when they are needed for a particular performance.

### Followspot positions

A room for followspots should be provided at the back of the auditorium. As followspot operators usually communicate through the show to coordinate with the stage manager and their fellow operatives, it is useful to place them in an acoustically protected booth away from the audience, though it is common practice for these to be 'open' positions. Followspot positions with a side view of the stage should also be provided.

Figure 9.2.14 A heavily rigged circle front rail at Theatre Royal, Drury Lane (London). This is a popular position for lighting, sound and video projection. Here, the facilities panels are built into the balcony front, accessed by lifting up the hinged velvet-clad panels. (See Reference Project 32 and Figure 9.5.2b.)

Figure 9.2.15 Studio theatres with little wing space benefit from vertical Unistrut/Halfen channel integrated into the wall finishes: this provides convenient fixing points for sidelight and other technical equipment. Photo: The Hullabaloo, Darlington. (See Reference Project 07)

## Lighting for the open stage

> Stage lighting for theatre in the round is a difficult subject *to write on* . . . there is a very wide range of possibilities, and there is plenty of scope for people to disagree.
>
> Stephen Joseph, *Theatre in the Round* (Barrie & Rockcliff, 1967), p. 74

In the open stage environment, particular care must be taken to provide adequate lighting rigging points to cover both an actor's 'looking-out' position (where the actor is standing at the edge of the stage facing the audience) and the 'looking-in' position (where the actor is standing at the edge of the stage facing inwards). Lighting the 'looking-in' position requires rigging positions in exactly the right places: making it possible to provide enough illumination to the performer's face without dazzling the front rows of audience behind them.

Top light, high side light and 'looking-in' lighting can only be provided from positions above the stage. Practical solutions to these positions are 'egg crate' grids of technical walkways, or tension wire grids.

## Sidelight in studio theatres

Where stage size is limited and wings may not be provided, booms can become visual and physical clutter. Steel support channels can be built into the walls so that lanterns or rigging bars can be bolted directly to the walls of the studio, avoiding floorstands (see Figure 9.2.15). A regular layout of vertical channels around the whole room can be neatly coordinated with panels which are decorative and/or serve as acoustic diffusion or absorption. Consideration should also be given to the appearance of the bare stage, since some productions (notably contemporary dance) will choose to use a space empty of masking and scenery: any permanent fixings or infrastructure to the walls should be neat and as free of visual clutter as possible. Consider also how cables can be run to unusual positions.

And finally . . .

If suitable positions are not provided, theatre designers and technicians tend to just create their own, as demonstrated in Figure 9.2.16. These will usually be more intrusive than the properly designed permanent position the building's design team avoided for fear of it being unattractive!

## Sound rigging positions

Imaging of the source of sound in theatre is of paramount importance. The listening audience should feel that the sound is coming from the performer and not from a large black box hanging from the proscenium arch. Optimum loudspeaker rigging positions will depend on the type of theatre and the requirements of each specific production; however, the necessity to cover every seat in the auditorium and ensure that each audience member has the best possible audio experience is always paramount.

Figure 9.2.16 Technicians will improvise to create lighting positions which have not been built in: this was a necessary addition for *Mary Poppins* at Birmingham Hippodrome.

## Proscenium positions

A position either side of the proscenium can be provided by a fixed upright ladder beam or 'proscenium boom' from which the speaker systems can be hung (see Figure 9.2.17). Access to rigging locations must be considered – if necessary, making provision for personal protection equipment (PPE) such as lanyard fixing points and fall arrest systems.

A great deal of negotiation is required between scenic, lighting and sound teams to share what is usually a very congested area of the theatre. The sound designer will want the speakers to go as close to the stage as possible while still allowing the speaker fronts to be 'seen' by as many members of the audience as possible; yet far enough to one side so as not to impede the audience's view of the stage. This is invariably the preferred location for the lighting as well; and the set designer may intend to clad the proscenium in a scenic way rather than leaving the building fabric exposed.

The sound designer's loudspeaker palette is constantly expanding with manufacturers offering many different options for speaker systems. When designing a sound system for a particular production this choice will be specific to that production, but often an installed sound system will need to be able to support many different genres and may need to include surround sound and overhead loudspeakers to create immersive audio.

The choice and size of loudspeakers will dictate how they are rigged: individual loudspeakers may be hung from trusses or lighting bars; but it is aesthetically cleaner to hang a single line-array from dedicated rigging

Figure 9.2.17 Proscenium boom formed from white-painted truss at His Majesty's Theatre, Aberdeen.

Figure 9.2.18 Delay loudspeakers rigged from circle bars at Theatre Royal Drury Lane (London). Other equipment rigged here includes video projectors, moving lights and video monitors for performers' view of the conductor. (See Reference Project 32)

points and remove the need for a truss. If the sound is part of the proscenium picture, then these points should be as close to the proscenium opening as possible, to ensure the sound from these loudspeakers seems part of the overall picture.

Speakers that are positioned below the acting area on/within the stage riser (front fills) help to pull the image to the stage rather than keep it high in the cluster, or wide on the proscenium booms. These will also help provide even coverage and intelligibility to the front rows of seating.

Modern loudspeaker systems try to achieve a balanced level throughout the listening space. If this were to be attempted using only the speakers at the stage opening, there would be a considerable loss of volume the further away from the source the listener is situated. This is usually overcome by the addition of loudspeakers rigged further into the auditorium under the balcony overhangs or from circle front bars (see Figure 9.2.18), ensuring that musical clarity and vocal intelligibility is consistent for the whole auditorium.

The size and positions for these speakers will depend very much on the production design and the area that they are required to cover. The audio content that passes through them is delayed appropriately, so that the sound picture stays on the stage: hence the generic term for these positions is 'delays', referred to in the United States as 'under-balconies'.

The amount of equipment required for a modern-day musical is growing every day and rigging positions that are complementary to the theatre architecture, if not thought about in the original design, can be difficult to achieve later in an aesthetically pleasing manner.

An open stage may require a particularly flexible sound system so that all sound reinforcement and effects sit properly in the overall sound picture and any music can be evenly distributed around the auditorium.

The necessity to be able to place loudspeakers in many positions both in the auditorium and on the stage is important on an open stage as localisation of the sound often explains certain aspects of a production.

## 9.3 Control positions

Control positions are required on stage, in the auditorium and in dedicated rooms. Dedicated consoles may be required for lighting, sound, video – each with a dedicated operator. A small-scale production may be run by a single technician or stage manager, but let us consider the norm for 'middle-scale' theatre.

Performances are 'run' by the deputy stage manager (DSM), who – in an end-stage theatre – usually sits to the side of the stage at the stage manager's console (see Figure 9.3.1) and calls lighting, stage management and flying cues over a ring intercom system (verbal cues: 'standby LX12', 'LX12 Go'); gives sound and other technical cues via cuelights (red = standby, green = go); warns actors and technical staff of upcoming cues using the backstage paging system ('Ladies and gentlemen of *The Cherry Orchard* company, this is your Act 2 beginners' call'); and announces to the audience, via the front of house paging system, that the performance is about to start ('Ladies and gentlemen, please take your seats').

Figure 9.3.1 Stage manager's console at Bloomsbury Theatre, London, positioned downstage right. The console may be detached from the wheeled stand, to allow the console to be used at production desks or in the control room.

The stage manager's console is the hub of this technical communication. It may include video relay screens integrated into the console for the DSM to have a front view of the stage and other necessary areas; generally from a colour camera and an infra-red camera to allow them to see stage activity during blackouts. It may be used from either side of the stage in a proscenium theatre, or from the control room. During technical rehearsals, it is useful to be able to operate the console from the auditorium so that the DSM is part of the production team and has a good view of the stage.

The lighting operator needs to be able to see the stage sufficiently to verify that the lighting state is correct, and sometimes to take visual cues – such as a snap blackout precisely co-ordinated to a performer's action. It is useful to be able to see lanterns rigged on an advance bar, to see what they are doing – such as pointing the wrong way and lighting the auditorium – but this is not always possible. Lighting cues are pre-programmed and it is not usually necessary for the lighting operator to 'live mix' lighting during the performance.

Sound for theatre comprises playback of music, effects, soundscapes and atmospheric backgrounds that set mood or establish location. Cueing, fading and routing is plotted and programmed during technical rehearsal by the operator so that sequences can be accurately reproduced for every show. Show control systems have enabled complex sound designs to be automated, and there are now many shows that can be operated by the DSM without the need for a sound operator.

However, when live performers or instruments are amplified, the role of the sound operator is especially important: to balance microphone sources, as well as to initiate playback of sound effects which will require operation from a central position in the auditorium. For a performance without microphones, the sound operator must ensure that unamplified performers' voices can be heard above pre-recorded sound and adjust the sound level as required. A high degree of artistic interpretation and sensitivity is required from the sound operator who will respond and adjust to the subtle variations of each night's performance.

Video design may require dedicated video operators or may be operated by the sound operator or DSM: some commonly-used sound playback software can also be used to play back video cues.

Since a single technician will sometimes operate lighting, sound and video, and provide backstage calls to the performers, control tielines for all of these functions are needed at all potential control locations.

## Control rooms

For a conventional proscenium arch theatre, control rooms for lighting, sound, video and audio description should ideally be at the centre-rear of the auditorium with an observation window giving a clear view of the stage, uninterrupted by pillars or by the heads of audience members and undistorted (by tinting or reflections). The rooms should be acoustically isolated from the auditorium but with a relay of the show audio. It should be possible to open the window for direct contact with the auditorium when required (especially during set-up and rehearsal); and the window should be angled by a few degrees to prevent operators from seeing their own reflection in the glass.

Effectiveness of the control room for sound mixing will depend on the area of the opening window and the depth of any balcony overhang in front: mixing from a control room is generally misguided. The control room will require both white 'worklight' lighting and localised performance lighting, adjustable for position and intensity (without flickering) and masked so as not to spill through the window. Many consoles have built-in touch screens: direct toplight often renders these illegible.

The control room will need flat working space for consoles and external monitors, and for a laptop or notepad (see Figures 9.3.2 and 9.3.3). Lighting operators should have sufficient space for an A3 copy of the lighting plan. Ergonomic, adjustable seating should be provided for the operator and at least one other person. Provision should be made for accommodating ancillary equipment in a rack beneath the main desk area.

Multiple mains outlets should be available both above and below the desk surface, and an uninterruptable power supply (UPS) should be provided for consoles and related show-critical equipment (some consoles have this built in). It can be helpful to provide worklight below the desk surface.

Figure 9.3.2 A modest lighting control position 2.0 × 0.9m provides sufficient space for an ETC Gio lighting console with two external monitors, keyboard, A4 file, desk lamp, cue light – and the inevitable coffee cup. A variable-height table is preferable.

Figure 9.3.3 Lighting control position at Curve, Leicester, showing ETC Eos lighting console with four external monitors and touch screen worklight control.

A concealed but accessible cable route from control room to stage enables visiting shows to use their own cabling and allows for future cable types; computer flooring is often used to manage cabling to installed patching and equipment racks.

Access to control rooms should be from outside the auditorium, the route preferably separate from public areas. The route should allow equipment to be carried or flightcases to be rolled easily in and out of the control room. (Flightcases are portable road boxes used by hire companies and touring productions and can be as large as 2500 × 800mm.)

The control room should be fully accessible for wheelchair users wherever such provision is reasonable. Where this is not possible, for example, in historic buildings, alternative operating positions should be provided.

## Shared or separate control rooms?

Control spaces can be shared by several personnel (including lighting, video, audio description) within a single room, but it is usually better to split control rooms according to function with separate rooms for lighting, sound and video projection equipment.

An audio describer watches the performance and describes the actions of the performers to audience members who are visually impaired, who wear headsets in the auditorium to hear the performance and the audio describer. If the audio describer is working from a control room, their voice is generally distracting to technicians in the same control room. Similarly, projection equipment can be noisy.

A suite of rooms with a range of control tielines in each can be set up according to the production requirements: one may need the DSM to run the show from the control room; the next production may have the DSM on stage but require a video operator. The director may want to watch the first few performances from a control room where they can make notes without distracting the audience; later in the run when the director has left, performances may be 'audio described' from that same control room

Particularly in flexible venues, other control positions may be required. The control infrastructure should reflect

Figure 9.3.4 A compact, open control position for lighting and sound (Bristol Old Vic Studio), including ETC Gio @5 lighting console with no external monitors and Yamaha TF1 audio mix console. Sound playback is from a Mac Mini (below the desk), the monitor and 'go' button fit within the control position.

Figure 9.3.5 Auditorium mix position at Kilden Konserthus (Kristiansand, Norway) with sufficient space for two operators and large lighting and sound consoles. For theatres, light spill from screens can be distracting to the audience.

this by making connection points available as widely as possible. For example, the Young Vic has no control room: lighting, sound, video and stage management all run from open positions around technical walkways at high level.

Purpose-built theatres in-the-round tend to have a steep stalls seating rake with a performers' run-round underneath: an alcove off this run-round is a useful location for the DSM.

## Auditorium mix position

The success of an amplified musical performance relies heavily on placing the operator at a prime location in the auditorium where they can hear and experience the show as if part of the audience. This is the reason mixing consoles are installed at visually prominent locations (see Figure 9.3.5), with the loss of numerous seats and consequent loss of ticket revenue. This loss can be mitigated by making the mix position variable in size, so that no more seats than necessary are removed. To minimise the labour involved in removing seats, it may be possible to incorporate a mixer lift storage garage into the auditorium design.

As a general rule, a sound control room at the back of the auditorium does not provide an effective operating space for live performance, and provision for an operating area within the auditorium, either temporary or permanent, is necessary.

Particularly in theatres that receive touring shows, there may be a need for the lighting operator to share this control position: so it should be possible to remove various numbers of seats, to suit the size of control position and keeping as many seats on sale as possible. Nearby storage for removed seats should be planned. Where possible, a motorised mix position elevator will reduce the time required to replace the mixing console wagon with a seating wagon.

The position should provide a flat floor with clear access for flight cases, and offer a cable route to the stage and control room and duplicates of the lighting control, power and communication system connection points (comms) and worklight and house light controls found in the control room.

Sound control equipment consists of a mixing console, audio processing and playback units. There is a considerable amount of cable and connections so clear access to the rear of equipment for set-up and troubleshooting should be made wherever possible. Digital mixing consoles have enabled space and wiring requirements for sound control to be significantly reduced.

Theatre playback software has replaced samplers, compact disc and mini disc players. A computer with sound card can be remotely located and triggered by the mixing console or from a remote pushbutton unit. Keyboard, monitor and mouse can be extended to the sound operator or to the designer's desk in the auditorium.

## Technical rehearsal control position: 'production desks'

Technical rehearsals are an intensive period of work for the whole team making the production. For lighting, sound and video designers, this is often where their work is integrated with the performers for the first time.

For a play, three days of technical rehearsals might be sufficient – stepping through the show with the performers in costume, building lighting, sound and video cues, firing pyrotechnics – and carefully recording each cue so that it can be reproduced. A musical or large show might be in tech for months. At the end of technical rehearsals a number of dress rehearsals take place, followed by previews and then opening night – the first occasion the press are expected to attend.

The lighting, sound and video designers will set up base from seats with the best view to the stage: in a proscenium theatre, this will generally be the middle of the stalls.

Lighting programmers often position the control desk next to the lighting designer, allowing direct communication with the designer and other collaborators and giving themselves the clearest view of the stage while focusing moving lights. In some cases, particularly in multi-level auditoria, the designer will sit in the stalls while the programmer will position themselves in the circle in order to get a clearer view of the stage floor.

Temporary desks and seating are often created from wooden boards laid over auditorium seating, but such ad-hoc arrangements are unsatisfactory ergonomically and cause damage to the theatre's seats. A more considered solution should be provided, such as the ability to remove theatre seats and replace them with ergonomic office chairs (see Figure 9.3.6): remember that for many designers and technicians, a significant portion for their working lives is spent at production desks. The production desk is their workplace: it should therefore be safe and meets legal ergonomic requirements. Research and guidance has recently been shared via the Association for Lighting Production and Design.

Connectivity (electrical, lighting control, comms) should be provided adjacent to this position to reduce set-up time and trip hazard risks. It is now an expectation for wireless internet access to be available to those working on a show. Wi-Fi networks should be properly designed to cope with the peak demand that will be placed on them, which will also involve provision of a good quality, reliable, high speed internet connection to the building as a whole.

Figure 9.3.6 Production desks at the Dorfman (National Theatre, London). Here, stalls seats fold into the floor and each row is mounted on an elevator: the technical staff have set two elevators at the same height and folded the seats away, creating a spacious area where ergonomic chairs can be used. (See also Reference Project 16.)

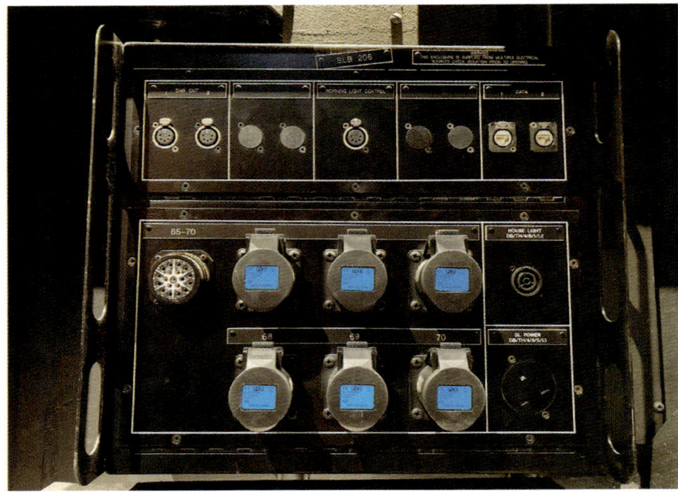

Figure 9.4.1 Stage lighting facilities panel (Soho Place, London). Dimmed power is provided on 16A Ceeform outlets, paralleled on Socapex multicore outlets. Houselight plug-in points use Neutrik True1. Extended side cheeks are provided instead of tiebars.

## 9.4 Lighting infrastructure

> In designing and planning your theatre and its lighting infrastructure think carefully about what you can't predict. Don't assume that every director will want to put the actors where you have put the stage.
>
> Mark Jonathan, lighting designer

### Stage lighting electrical system

The stage lighting infrastructure starts with the incoming power supply, usually in the basement, or for larger venues, at the electrical sub-station. The power then needs to be distributed from the electrical intake area to the dimmer room, thence to the dimmer racks, ideally using switch disconnect MCCB protection for each rack, providing individual dimmer rack isolation for service and maintenance.

The dimmer rack is a device for distributing dimmed and switched ('non-dim') power to lanterns. Load circuits are star-wired from the dimmer racks to numerous locations around the theatre, terminated within a facilities panel (see Figure 9.4.1): a local point concentrating facilities such as dimmer and non-dim outlets, general technical power and control data outlets. Technicians rig lanterns according to the requirements of the production, then run loose power and data cables from the lantern to the most convenient facilities panel.

Power outlets follow regional norms. In the United Kingdom, dimmed power is commonly provided by 15A roundpin or 16A Ceeform sockets: importantly, these use un-fused plugs, avoiding scenarios of searching for a blown fuse somewhere in a circuit.

No matter how comprehensive the infrastructure, a situation will arise in the future which requires an additional cable. This should be planned for in three ways:

1. by providing additional space in electrical containment – say, 25% – to allow for more cables to be added in the future
2. by providing temporary cable routes between key locations
3. by providing 'soft spots' in the walls of dimmer room/control room/etc to allow for more containment to be installed in the future.

### Dimming systems

The most common system in use today is a centralised system with one or more dimmer room at the heart of the installation (see Figures 9.4.2 and 9.4.3).

Large touring productions often bring their own dimmers to speed up the set-up time. For touring dimmers or productions requiring dimmers in unusual locations, large electrical supplies should be provided around the stage and auditorium for the connection of portable dimmer packs (sometimes known as 'distributed dimming').

Figure 9.4.2 Dimmer rack room at Bloomsbury Theatre (London), showing three ETC Sensor racks. The lighting data rack is to the right of the image.

TYPICAL SETTING OUT: 3 RACKS
Room 3.5m width x 2.8m depth

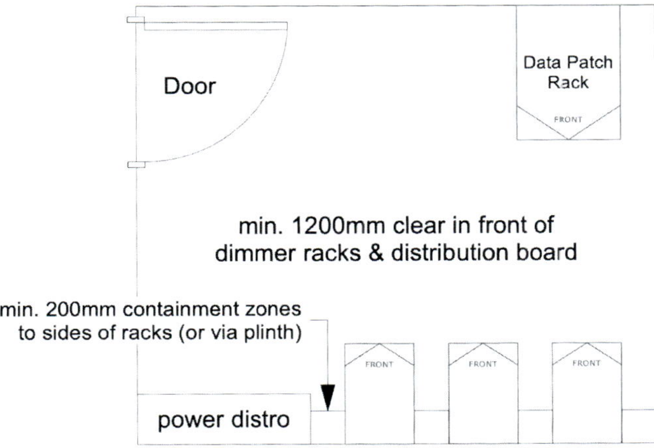


Figure 9.4.3 Diagram showing a possible dimmer room layout for three dimmer racks.

## Why do we still need dimmers? Everything is LED!

Most theatres today use a mixture of tungsten and LED lanterns. LED lanterns are much more expensive to purchase but use much less electrical power than tungsten. It is likely that theatres will continue to use their existing stocks of tungsten lanterns – perhaps until forced to change by legislation or unavailability of replacement lamps – and buy increasing quantities of LED to sit alongside them.

Tungsten lanterns require a dimmer channel per lantern to control brightness individually, but this is not necessary with LED lanterns, where brightness is set by the on-board driver, using a control channel. Despite the great difference in power required for LED vs tungsten, it is not possible simply to daisy-chain twenty-three 100w LED lanterns from a single 2.3kW non-dim channel: LEDs have a high inrush current, causing a spike in power draw when the light comes on – and this would cause the circuit to trip. In practice, it is usual to connect no more than four 150w LED lanterns to a single 2.3kW non-dim channel. So, we still need some form of power distribution. Circuits need to be protected by RCD (to conform with electrical regulations), and a centralised rack offers a convenient way of providing this. Lighting manufacturers produce dimming systems which offer modules which can be switched to act as dimmers or non-dims – to serve either tungsten or LED – at negligible cost difference.

Compared to dimmer installations of ten years ago, we now see a reduction in the overall quantity of dimmer channels, for two reasons:

- one channel can run several LED lanterns
- a variable-colour LED lantern can sometimes replace more than one tungsten lantern.

There is less demand for 5kW dimmer channels in small and medium-scale theatres: these were generally provided for cyclorama floodlighting – this purpose is served very well by LED lanterns – and for occasional very high powered fixtures, where it makes more sense to rent a portable 5kW dimmer pack.

## Dimmer room

The dimmer room should be in a position that best suits the lighting system. It should be big enough to house all the dimmers and associated switch gear and network/data distribution. The room should be well ventilated with the ability to maintain an ambient temperature within the guidelines of the dimmer manufacturer; this often requires a cooling unit.

It can be desirable in larger theatres to provide multiple dimmer rooms for shorter cable runs to ease cable size requirements and meet data run length limitations.

The room may benefit from a modular 'computer' floor to allow cable access to the base of the dimmers.

## Stage lighting control systems

A stage lighting console will control the dimmers and other devices via an ethernet-based control network. The lighting console stores information and cues for a production, which are recalled over pre-programmed crossfade times by the console operator. As well as controlling the lighting for a production, the operator will also need to control the working lights.

## Working lights, 'whites' and 'blues'

Low energy white-light fittings provide light to the stage areas when a performance is not taking place. Good working lighting of the stage area is important. Lights mounted at high level over the wings and under fly galleries will give good coverage of offstage areas. The central area of the stage can to some extent be lit from high-level side galleries but with large stages, worklights rigged on flying bars may be needed. Some side gallery fittings should be mounted to illuminate the underside of the grid.

During performances there should be good dim (often blue LED) lighting of all galleries and work areas, arranged so as not to spill onto the acting area or be visible from the auditorium. The fittings should be selected to minimise hard shadows and glare, to make working on stage comfortable.

## Worklight control systems

The working light control system can range from a simple bank of light switches above the prompt desk to a centralised processor system capable of recording and recalling states from the lighting console. It should control every lighting fixture visible from within the auditorium with any single door open: including the lighting within sound and light lobbies, control rooms and scene dock.

Most systems will consist of a central processor, contactors and/or dimmers to control the lights, together with wall-mounted touch screens and pushbutton panels around the theatre for local control of lighting circuits. Portable touch screens are useful for providing worklight control at auditorium control positions and production desks.

The part of the system that non-technical staff have to use should be simple and intuitive. Panels in public areas should be locked out during performances, to avoid an audience member inadvertently or maliciously turning on the houselights in the middle of the show.

A 'dead black-out' control is necessary to extinguish maintained lighting and exit signs for brief periods, subject to licensing requirements.

## Lanterns

The selection of the lanterns (variously called 'lights, 'luminaires, 'fixtures') is unique to the style and location of the theatre being built. It should not be assumed that the lighting equipment that works in a theatre in the United Kingdom will work for a theatre in Europe or the United States: although most consoles and LED lanterns are designed to operate on any voltage 100–240v, they are likely to need a different power cable.

It is important to involve the users of the venue, if they already exist, or lighting designers of similar venues. Their input is vital in conceiving a versatile lighting rig that will work for the range and style of productions that a particular venue will present.

Lanterns fall into four main categories.

1. Generic (or 'conventional') fixtures with a tungsten source that can have automated accessories added to it such as scrollers to change the colour of the light and gate accessories to rotate gobos and change the size of the iris.
2. LED fixtures: generic lanterns with LED sources, which often have built-in colour mixing and sometimes remote zoom focus under the control of the lighting console.
3. Automated fixtures ('moving lights') with motorised pan, tilt and zoom, variable colour and beam shape, under the control of the lighting console; most likely using an LED source. These are often used as a 're-focusable special' – highlighting a coffee table in Scene 1, a doorway in Scene 2, for example – rather than moving in a noticeable way. They are also useful in locations which are difficult to access for focus.
4. Follow spot: a generic lantern that is controlled during the show by a human being.

LED and automated fixtures require a power connection and a data connection, generally DMX512 rather than ethernet. Automated fixtures are more complex, expensive and maintenance-hungry than generic equipment but can perform many more tasks. They can contribute to safety when working at height as they can be focused remotely. It is important to note that while automated lighting fixtures allow for focusing to be carried out remotely, the rigging and 'plugging-up' is still a manual task that requires safe access.

Automated and LED fixtures are usually fan-cooled: a large quantity of these, especially if they are poor quality, can create an unacceptable level of background noise.

### Sustainability in stage lighting

Over the past ten years there has been tremendous development in the design of LED stage lighting lanterns, and there are excellent lanterns available from a number of manufacturers. The question of whether this is 'sustainable' is complex.

Although LED sources are generally reckoned to have a lamp life in the region of 50,000 hours, the colour calibration will vary and electronics may well fail before the LED source fails; and the entire lantern is likely to be redundant. Compared to tungsten, LED lanterns are much more complex and carbon-hungry to manufacture and to maintain. When a tungsten lantern fails, simply changing the lamp usually fixes it.

There are excellent uses for LED when they are expected to be used for considerable periods of time, such as

- houselighting – LED houselights can also serve as auditorium worklight, saving installation of copper cabling and duplicate fixtures
- cyclorama lighting – when a cyclorama or upstage cloth is part of the scenic design, it will often be lit (in various colours) throughout the whole performance
- front of house rig or in-the-round area cover – these fixtures will often form the backbone of the lighting rig and be used throughout the performance
- a superior alternative to 'scroller' colour changers for tasks such as an overhead wash, where multiple colours are used during the performance.

It is not all about LED. Switching should be designed such that equipment can be turned off properly at the end of the day, rather than leaving it drawing power on standby. The dimmer room should be located where a large proportion of circuits – on the fly floor, for instance – can be supplied with a short cable run: minimising not only the length of the cable, but the cross-sectional area.

Despite our desire for energy saving and minimising infrastructure, we should remember that energy consumption from stage lighting is relatively low when compared, for example, to the transport to get the audience to the theatre. It is important that we can light shows well: if we can't make the show look great, there is little point in doing it.

### Lighting control

Lighting control has changed dramatically through the years of electric light, from a crew directly manipulating dimmers side-stage to a single operator in a control room running a console remote from the dimmers. Lighting operators originally dealt with one parameter per light – intensity – everything else (position, colour, size, shape) was set manually at the light. With automated lighting, the programmer must deal with those other parameters at the console.

Since lighting controls and dimmers were separated there has been a need to connect the two: Digital Multiplex (DMX) is currently the standard lighting control protocol worldwide, each cable controlling up to 512 items. Lighting consoles offer multiple DMX outputs ('universes') catering for larger productions with thousands of channels, not only dimmers but also moving light controls, colour control and video media servers. Remote device management (RDM) adds bi-directional communications to the protocol, allowing operations such as remote addressing of LED fixtures.

Manufacturers have moved to ethernet to distribute lighting data – the cable and accessories are readily available, one ethernet cable can carry data for thousands of parameters – but many different, incompatible protocols were created, and no single protocol has been widely adopted.

While consoles can output data to ethernet, few lighting fixtures will yet receive any of the ethernet-based formats directly, instead requiring DMX data: so the chosen ethernet protocol must be converted back to DMX for final distribution to the fixtures using small converter boxes ('nodes').

A typical installation today will use ethernet cabling and routing equipment to distribute lighting data around the building (see 9.7), with nodes and DMX splitters installed at key locations. DMX should be wired using data cable to allow future conversion to ethernet. If the dimmers and console are both from the same manufacturer, there is benefit to using the manufacturer's ethernet protocol for this link, which allows for bi-directional communications such as error reporting.

Various forms of wireless DMX are used for control of lighting within scenic objects and for temporary installations, but this is to be avoided in permanent installations as it introduces an unnecessary element of complexity and potential unreliability.

## 9.5 Sound infrastructure

### Sound system infrastructure design

The sound equipment rack room is the heart of any sound system installation. It is not normally part of the main control area but may be sited next to it. The room houses the equipment racks which accommodate all of the patchbays and equipment for the various systems, with sufficient space to allow for future additions – a good rule of thumb is to allow 25 to 30% of unused space in any rack. The rack room

TYPICAL SETTING OUT: 4 RACKS
Room 3.5m width x 2.8m depth
power distro
Containment (to top of racks or via plinth)
min. 800mm clear to side
min. 800mm clear behind
Rack #1
Rack #2
Rack #3
Rack #4
Door
min. 1200mm clear in front

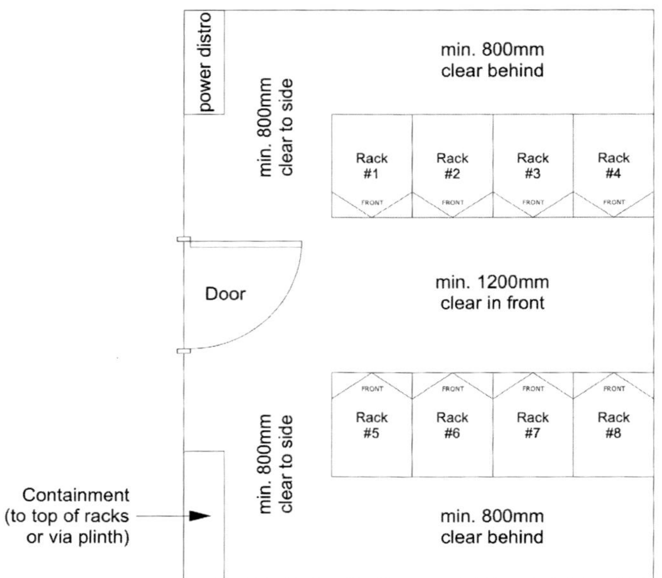


Figure 9.5.1 Diagrams showing four-rack and eight-rack AV rack room layouts.

should be located to minimise cable lengths to locations around the theatre; yet readily accessible by technical staff.

Each equipment rack requires a dedicated power supply (generally rated at 32A single phase) with internal power distribution provided in the rear of the rack. Dedicated cooling for the room is also normally required.

Racks should be as deep as possible – 800mm will accommodate most typical theatre AV equipment – and must have at least 1,200mm clear space in front and at least 800mm behind (see Figure 9.5.1). Racks should also be as high as reasonably practicable: 42U is a common height (one 'unit size' 1U = 44.45mm; a 42U rack provides 1,848mm height for rack-mounted equipment, the overall enclosure is around 2,053mm depending on construction), though taller racks are available. Allowance must be made for containment to be routed above the racks or alternatively in a plinth in the floor. Where racks cannot be mounted to provide for rear access, they will need to be installed in pairs with clear access to one side of each rack – but this is not an ideal solution.

## Audio, video and communications facilities in the theatre

### Mic/line analogue audio

Mic/line audio points provide a connection point for use with microphones or line-level audio source equipment. They are wired in screened twisted-pair cabling and are terminated with 3-pin XLR sockets, which may be parallel-terminated with 3-pin XLR plugs. Multiple ways may also be provided. These lines would normally be terminated at an audio patchbay in the rack room. It is no longer usual to install large quantities of analogue audio tielines: the widespread use of digital audio networks and availability of affordable digital audio mixing consoles and stage boxes has made analogue an expensive and cumbersome solution. A handful of analogue audio lines is still useful for occasions where a single microphone or active loudspeaker is required, without having to use a digital stagebox.

### Temporary cable routes

These comprise a coordinated set of holes through walls and hooks over doorways and public thoroughfares that provide safe, fire-proofed and acoustically sealed openings for cable, when put in the theatre for a particular performance (see Figure 9.5.2a and 2b). Notable important uses: touring productions' analogue multicore cables from auditorium control positions to stage and to the loading bay for outside broadcasts.

### Digital audio

Multichannel digital audio, along with other AV signals, are transmitted over industry-standard network cables, both ethernet cable and optic fibre. Tielines for other digital audio protocols such as multichannel audio digital interface (MADI) or Audio Engineering Society/European Broadcasting Union (AES/EBU) digital audio may also be provided where required.

Figure 9.5.2a Temporary cable routes often include hatches through fire-rated or acoustic walls. Proprietary hardware is available which allows large broadcast connectors to pass through and for the wall still to achieve fire and acoustic ratings. Hangers are useful for routes along corridors, as shown here at Scotland's Studio (Glasgow).

Ethernet cable runs are limited to 90m: runs beyond this need repeater boxes or the use of fibre optic instead. Installing a good quantity of fibre optic tielines is worthwhile, even if their use is not entirely clear. Most audio equipment manufacturers seem to have a solution to transmit data via fibre so it makes a robust, future-proof installation.

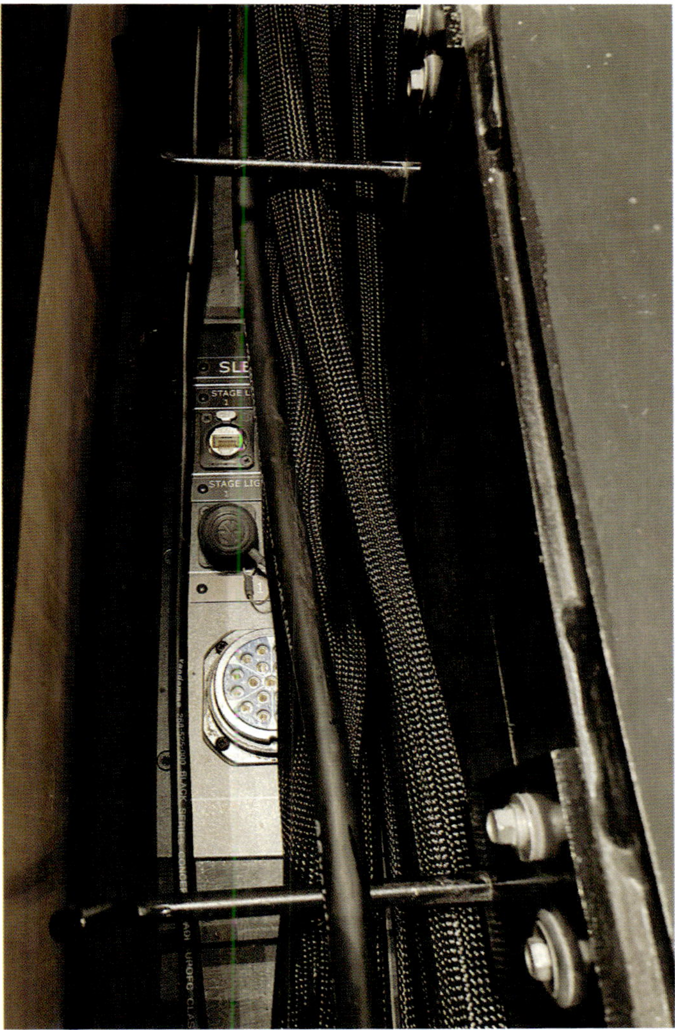

Figure 9.5.2b Facilities built into narrow slot within balcony front at Theatre Royal Drury Lane (London). Panels and space for temporary cables are accessed by lifting up the hinged velvet-clad panels.

**Cuelights**

Cuelight points provide a connection point for use with cuelight outstations fitted with red and green indicators. These are typically located in control rooms, stage technician locations such as fly floors; and at auditorium and stage entrances for performers. Cuelights are controlled from the stage manager's desk and often use the ethernet data network which avoids the need for separate dedicated cabling.

**Backstage communications**

Technical intercom points are for use with dedicated beltpacks and headsets with boom-arm microphones. The technical intercom system may also be interfaced with wireless belt-packs and headsets to allow operators to move freely around the stage.

A building-wide paging/show relay system distributes voice calls and show relay (the sound of the performance) throughout the building. Front of house calls are made to the audience. Backstage calls are made to the performers and backstage staff. Paging/show relay speakers are generally wired using multipair cabling carrying 100v line amplified audio. Paging microphone points allow the connection of paging microphones in key locations such as the stage door and the stage manager's desk.

Paging systems are generally a separate system to voice alarm – the zoning and local controls for paging is usually more specific; choice of fire-rated loudspeakers is limited and these tend to be more expensive.

### Video

Video signals are routed around the theatre to distribute production video (content delivery to projectors and video walls) and to provide video show relay to assist performers and technicians running the performance. This might include video monitors at the stage manager's desk and on the circle front carrying pictures from the conductor in the orchestra pit; and a feed from circle-front cameras showing the stage (see Section 9.8).

The video infrastructure may include camera inputs for broadcast and capture. 3G-SDI (a standard defined by the Society of Motion Picture and Television Engineers) video cabling is currently a good baseline standard and allows for high definition transmission. Fibre allows for high resolution to be carried over long distances, but requires additional hardware. Some video links – such as the DSM and performers' view of the conductor – are time-critical: low latency is important if using encoded video over a data network.

### Loudspeakers

Loudspeaker tielines carry amplified audio signals from amplifiers in the AV equipment room to the loudspeakers distributed around the stage and auditorium.

### Assisted listening

An assisted listening system is required for those with hearing impairments. Since the system needs to take audio feeds from stage and sound playback, it generally falls within the theatre technician's remit to run this system – unlike, say, local hearing loops at box office counters.

Hearing induction loop systems are generally preferable operationally – these systems operate directly with users' hearing aids, obviating the need for an external headset, and thus avoiding any visual indication of hearing impairment. The loop comprises a thin copper tape that can be installed under carpets – and is notoriously prone to damage. Care should be taken in multiple venue complexes to avoid cross-talk between induction loops. It is generally impractical to use hearing loops on retractable seating or seating fixed to rostra; making this solution less viable for flexible theatres.

Infra red and FM radio systems require audience members to wear a receiver – which is owned by the theatre and is distributed to the members of the audience who need it, and is collected at the end of show, cleaned and has the battery recharged. Infra red systems can offer two channels, selectable by the user (e.g. choice of audio description or assisted listening); FM systems in adjacent rooms can be set to different frequencies to avoid interference.

Connection points for infra red or FM systems need to be provided around the auditorium to allow transmitters to send the signal to the audience's receivers. Infra red requires a direct line of sight from transmitter to receiver; FM does not.

Wi-Fi solutions are available, where audience members use their own smartphone to listen to the audio feed. Although useful for relaying other content, at the time of writing these systems suffer from poor latency.

### AV system power

AV power is wired with standard electrical cabling and is generally terminated with unswitched power socket outlets. Some AV power outlets may be UPS-maintained, and AV power outlets may also be contactor-controlled to provide a method for switching off groups of AV equipment when not required.

Single-phase outlets may also be provided in key locations for use with large sound mixing consoles, large amplified loudspeaker systems and video projectors.

To minimise the risk of interference from mains-borne noise and voltage variation, AV power is distributed via a dedicated power distribution system which is used solely to supply AV equipment and is designed and installed to minimise the possibility of electromagnetic interference being induced in the AV signal cabling.

### Facilities panels

Designing an AV infrastructure involves selecting the locations and quantities of each of the facilities described previously (see Figure 9.5.3). Each panel is provided with facilities appropriate to its position. Schematic drawings show signal flow and set out the connectors on the facilities panels, and the equipment in the audiovisual equipment racks.

Figure 9.5.3 A small audiovisual facilities panel at Bloomsbury Theatre (London) with video and loudspeaker tielines, audio data and power. The tiebar provides a point to tie off cables, to stop the weight of cables pulling on delicate connectors.

**Containment**

Routing the wiring from each facilities panel back to the rack room requires careful coordination with the design team to find acceptable routes through the building, and to coordinate these routes with other wired services. It is usual to require a number of dedicated containment groups for the AV wiring, using fully enclosed metal trunking to provide protection from mechanical damage and electromagnetic interference, and maintain a minimum physical separation between sensitive signal wiring and mains power wiring.

## 9.6 Video scenography

Video has become a mainstay of the theatrical production process and now finds itself present throughout many stage productions. Format and presence can stem from scenic design elements, such as projected scenery, to projected textures enhancing scenic surfaces, to interpolated performance where the developments of technologies such as augmented reality establish the inclusion of video on the modern stage. Use of virtual reality and augmented reality has been seen in live theatre: with the audience wearing electronic glasses, for instance, which show objects on stage which are not there in reality; sometimes these are generated live via capture of real performers' motions on stage.

A video designer is generally responsible for developing the design concept of the video elements and often working with animators, editors and programmers to produce the content, editing it into cues and deciding placement of projectors. This is not new – artists such as Robert Lepage have been using video creatively since the 1990s; slide and film projection were in regular use on stage from the 1960s– but over the past decade it has been more widespread: and the projection and playback equipment has become more accessible.

Sometimes video cameras are used on stage to create live content; or handheld video projectors used to make virtual moving objects appear on real moving objects. Projectors have been integrated into moving light yokes with onboard cameras and media servers: they can be treated as a moving light that has digital gobos or as a conventional video source.

Video projection requires a surface to front-project or rear-project onto: typically this is a screen such as a cyclorama, cloth, a floor or a piece of scenery. These elements are normally designed into the production as part of the scenic designer's consultation with the video designer. Video walls and monitors can also form intrinsic parts of a video design and allow the video designer freedoms unafforded through projection.

Consideration should be given to the necessity for locating media servers, switchers, IP networking and media converters within the proximity of the stage.

A projection room may be useful for showing movies, but is unlikely to be in a useful location for scenic projection. Movie playback is typically a specialist application that requires a dedicated projection set-up incorporating a dedicated projector, screen and sound system allowing for cinematic performance. Projectors for this format are normally housed in dedicated projection booths at the rear of the auditorium, where the noise of the equipment is kept away from the audience. Nearly all movie projection is now digital and the 4k projection format is being widely adopted for this application.

A generous provision of rack space is advised for video and its affiliated systems, depending on the venues purpose this space might not only support projection for performance but also video capture for film and streaming applications. Some video servers tend to adopt a deeper form factor meaning middle and rear support rails are essential to support the equipment. Allowance should be made in video equipment rooms for the heat generated by this equipment as well as the noise generated by modern media servers due to the cooling processes involved internally. With the emergence of technologies such as AI and VR making their way into performance it is anticipated that the requirement from these systems will only increase.

**Video projectors**

Historically, projectors have been a source of fan noise within the auditorium and the size of lamped units have meant that their usage needed dedicated positions. Video

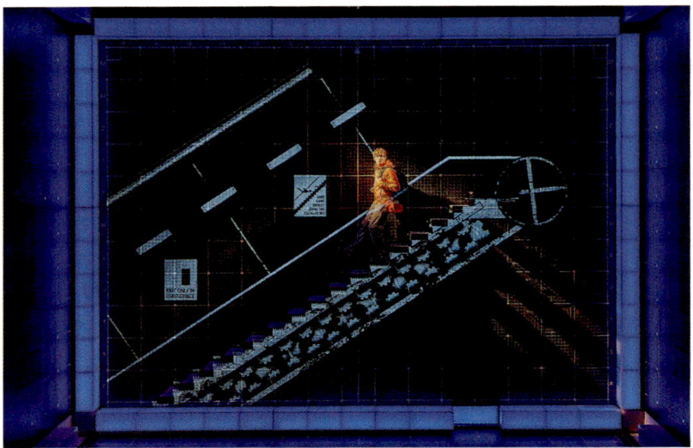

Figure 9.6.1 Luke Treadaway in the National Theatre production of *Curious Incident of the Dog in the Night Time* originally staged in-the-round in the Cottesloe, here in the production at the Apollo on Shaftesbury Avenue (2013). The escalator exists only in the video design (by Finn Ross). There are footholds designed into Bunny Christie's set. Paule Constable's lighting is carefully focused to avoid washing out the video, but still light the actor's face.

projectors are an area where an advancement in technology has driven a rapid change not only in the technology type but also the feasibility of units with sufficient output to compete with traditional stage luminaires.

LED and laser projectors have replaced most lamped units and offer better lumens (light output) against size/weight, quieter modes of operation and better options with regards to blackout and control throughout performance.

Due to the great variation in lens and unit requirement when used in performance it is frequently not economically viable for venues to own video projectors, so renting from a suitable company, when required, to suit the specific lumen, lens and size considerations is more common. HD (1920 × 1080) resolution is considered the base offering at the time of writing but 4K units are slowly starting to appear.

Where the projection is part of the story telling process (see Figure 9.6.1) or is the primary source of illumination then stacking of multiple projectors may be necessary: two projectors may sit one above the other increasing the coverage beyond the scope of a single unit.

Double or triple stacking units may be required for some scenic effects increasing luminosity and providing inherent redundancy to the projections.

## 9.7 Data networking

Over the past ten years, data networks have become one of the most essential components of technical infrastructure within theatres. Stage lighting networks carry much higher capacity than DMX and audio and video can be sent down ethernet or fibre optic with no perceptible loss of quality or time delay. Set-up times and infrastructure costs have reduced significantly as a result.

The move to digital formats for most audio and video infrastructure has reduced the amount of copper required by analogue tie lines.

It is sensible to provide DMX tielines as well as network, since most LED and automated lanterns still use DMX connections: providing DMX tielines avoids the need for numerous nodes, which are active equipment and relatively expensive. A few analogue audio tielines are useful for connecting an odd microphone or loudspeaker, without the need for a stage box to encode the audio ready to send over the network.

Video is an area where IP based networking is essential in the reliable and efficient operation of performance video systems. Projectors, media servers, switchers, control and content sharing nearly all utilise IP based technologies. When considering networking within the video environment, 10GB uplinks between locations should be considered the minimum specification if content and control is expected. Managed switches are highly recommended within this environment allowing the system to be configured optimally with all the different converging networks. Many media servers allow for integration with other departments in order to control and derive audio.

Production networks should be separate from building IT networks: technical departments need to be in control of this critical infrastructure, not least, so that they decide when updates to software are made, and control of permissions. When setting up a lighting network, specialists understanding the nature of production networks should be used. Data traffic on a production network is quite different from that in an office, often having long idle periods followed by spells of intense activity as a cue is run. Some ethernet routers assume this is rogue activity and suppress it, which can stop the show.

Generally lighting will run over one network with audio and video run over another one or more networks. IT data outlets should be provided at key locations (control room, dimmer/AV rack rooms) to allow links to the outside world to be patched into the production networks when required: for example for production specific equipment, remote diagnostics, software updates or streaming.

## 9.8 Video and audio relay and capture

Broadcasting and archival video has become a way of improving theatre's accessibility and delivering content to audiences when they are unable to visit theatres, either due to distance or global pandemics. Simultaneous live broadcasts are frequently distributed internationally to local cinemas and are available to stream from home, either free or by purchase of a virtual ticket.

Traditionally, the director of photography is looking for a shot where the lens height is fractionally above the eyeline of the performer. Extreme angles such as beneath the eyeline and steep angles from a balcony can look 'alien' and difficult to integrate into the mix of a multi-camera shoot. If a theatre anticipates that it will regularly broadcast performances, camera platforms or allocated spaces should be designed into the layout of the auditorium.

Wiring for visiting cameras is often particular to different camera manufacturers and formats. It may be worth installing some dedicated infrastructure if capture is likely to be frequent as this will reduce set-up time – in which case requirements from the chosen broadcast company must be precise to ensure that the installation is compatible with their equipment – otherwise a network of temporary cable routes should be considered.

Editing the content may happen live, within the theatre or outside broadcast truck, or after the show in a studio if the content is to be broadcast at a later date. Live content will need to be uploaded: in city centres, fast fibre links are taking over from satellite uplink dishes. Whether permanent or temporary, fibre links will be required within the building to connect camera positions and control rooms. These should, as a minimum, permit visiting TV companies to install temporary cabling from the OB truck parking bay (often the get-in), through any fire breaks to the rear of the auditorium, into the control rooms, to any in-house editing room and finally to the roof for a satellite dish or comms intake for a fibre uplink.

## Show relay cameras

Show relay cameras are typically mounted on the circle rail of a theatre and provide a fixed shot of the stage area to a number of services including the stage manager's desk, wings, green room, stage door and FOH latecomers monitors in the foyer. This is often via an IP encoder so that the video can be distributed via network.

Typically a minimum of two cameras will be located in this position: one designed for colour operation in optimal lighting conditions and the other optimised for operation under infrared illumination – essential for a view of the stage during blackouts and other low illumination situations. An infrared light source is often located on the circle front with these cameras to provide the light required for the low level light camera to operate. Cameras located in this position need to be appropriately chosen for their continuous duty cycle of usage as well as equipped with automatic irises, capable of adjusting to the vast range of illumination levels produced by stage lighting. Latency of such units should be minimised to ensure images received backstage are imperceptibly delayed compared to the live action and synchronised with audio show relay.

## Latecomers' monitors and digital signage

Latecomers' monitors are frequently integrated with digital signage provision in the foyer areas. This allows theatres to maximise advertising and audience engagement throughout the day, whilst allowing latecomers to the theatre the ability to view the performance whilst awaiting admittance at a suitable moment. Monitors chosen to fulfil this role should be chosen based on their brightness and resolution but particular attention should be given to their energy rating due to their long duty cycles in these locations.

## Section editor

Alex Wardle, Senior Theatre Consultant at Charcoalblue

## Contributors

Dominic Bilkey (video), Head of Sound and Video at the National Theatre

Borneo Brown (sound), Freelance Sound Consultant, Engineer and Operator

Rob Halliday (lighting), Lighting Designer and Programmer

## Contributors to first edition

Andy Hayles (as section editor), Senior Consultant at Charcoalblue

Mike Atkinson, Senior Project Manager at National Theatre, now with Theatreplan

Richard Borkum, Senior Consultant at Theatre Projects

Rob Halliday, Lighting Designer and Programmer

John Owens, Sound Designer

Bruno Poet, Lighting Designer

Jon Stevens, Senior Consultant at Charcoalblue

Flip Tanner, Project Coordinator at the Royal Shakespeare Company

# Section 10

# Restoration and conversion of existing buildings

## 10.1 Why work with existing buildings?

In a time of climate emergency, it is increasingly important to understand that the retention of existing buildings and the embodied carbon they contain is inherently more sustainable than demolishing and rebuilding them while at the same time preserving their heritage and the character of our towns and cities (see Figure 10.1.1). Retaining and giving new life to an existing building, compared with constructing a new one, will always be more sustainable and probably less expensive.

This section looks at the merits of the existing stock of older buildings and the arguments for conserving them. It outlines the planning and procedural issues and the particular problems that may be encountered when upgrading them to meet modern needs. It also considers how these lessons can be applied to re-purposing other types of buildings for theatre use, where the size and form of the original structure will dictate the scale and character of the facilities that can be created.

There is also an increasing desire by some theatre makers to work in the type of 'found space' which older buildings offer and to embrace the opportunities they often provide to create characterful venues at a relatively low cost. (See Figure 10.1.2.) The particular issues which arise when dealing with the repair, restoration and alteration of both existing theatre buildings and the re-purposing of other building types as theatres or cultural facilities are discussed here. Some projects will be major redevelopments, while others will be relatively modest additions or modifications. Theatre buildings have always been subject to change – to keep abreast of fashion, to meet the current needs and expectations of audiences, operators and artists; to introduce new technology; and to increase the operator's income. Almost invariably what is seen today reflects a gradual evolution over time.

In the days when theatres were lit by candle or gas they were not expected to last. Fire was the great enemy; the average life of a theatre building was less than twenty years. During the second half of the twentieth century, the increasing appreciation of theatre heritage, combined with the escalation in building costs and the scarcity of good city and town centre sites, has led us to consider how existing theatres can be adapted to meet modern needs. We have also come to understand that we have much to learn from the design of theatres from an earlier age when theatre was

Figure 10.1.1 The Theatre Royal Newcastle (1837): an example of a fine civic theatre which makes a major contribution to the streetscape.

Figure 10.1.2 A performance by Kneehigh Theatre in the ruins of Restormel Castle.

DOI: 10.4324/9781003327295-10

the primary from of popular entertainment. In many cases the buildings concerned will be historic or listed buildings, which enjoy some kind of statutory protection, and the challenges of adapting them to meet modern needs, while retaining their historic significance and special character, must be met with both imagination and an understanding of how they have evolved.

## 10.2 Existing stock of theatre buildings

Many countries have a rich heritage of historic theatres, ranging from the opulent, highly decorated theatres of the eighteenth and nineteenth centuries, to the streamlined, art deco theatres of the inter-war years and the modernist civic architecture of the post war years.

The majority of the UK's historic theatre buildings date from the theatre-boom years of the late nineteenth and early twentieth centuries, at a time when there were over 1,000 professional theatres operating throughout the country. Many were built by syndicates who created chains of touring houses. It was the age of theatre impresarios, such as Edward Moss and Oswald Stoll, and of the architects specialising in the complex design challenges associated with theatres – W. G. R. Sprague, Bertie Crewe and, the most prolific of all, Frank Matcham. At the peak of the theatre boom large towns would have had two or three theatres, while cities could have up to a dozen and London even more.

Theatre building entered a period of decline between the world wars, coinciding with the popularity of film and the emergence of the super-cinema. However there were also some significant new developments in theatre: the emergence of club theatres either side of World War I which showed specialist, political and experimental theatre, as well as showcasing the work of foreign writers; the rise of the Workers' Theatre Movement in the interwar years, using theatre to advocate social change and to educate the masses; and the start of repertory theatre, which evolved in the regions, introducing audiences to a wide variety of theatre at affordable prices. After World War II the mass medium of television emerged as the primary form of popular entertainment, contributing further to theatre's demise.

In the United Kingdom, the formation of the Arts Council in 1946 brought a new start to theatre building after the destruction of World War II, enabling public money to be used to support theatre in the regions, including the construction of new theatres. By then many older theatres were seen as old-fashioned and did not appeal to the modernist outlook of the post-war years. Falling audiences and increasing maintenance costs resulted in the demolition of many historic theatres, especially those situated in bomb-damaged town centres that were targeted for redevelopment. Others were fortuitously preserved by their conversion to alternative uses, such as cinemas, bingo halls, nightclubs and, more recently, churches. (See Figure 10.2.1.)

In the 1960s and 1970s, local councils were the main builders of new theatres, usually as part of their cultural and leisure programmes and often integrated into multi-purpose civic complexes. These new civic theatres were frequently designed for multi-purpose use and built in a more functional architectural style.

By the 1970s it was estimated that 85% of the historic theatres that had once formed the beating heart of the nation's entertainment industry had been destroyed or irretrievably altered, with under a tenth remaining in theatre use and a significant number lying empty, awaiting

Figure 10.2.1 The Tunbridge Wells Opera House, now a Wetherspoons pub.

a beneficial use and sufficient funds to repair them. The publication of *Curtains!!! – Or a New Life for Old Theatres* (Iain Mackintosh and Michael Sell) by the Theatres Trust in 1982, which for the first time recorded all of the UK's surviving pre-1914 theatres, represented a turning point in their appreciation.

## Protection for theatre buildings

Many of the UK's historic theatres are statutorily listed, marking their special architectural and historic interest. Buildings less than thirty years old are not normally considered for listing. Listing a building also brings it further under the consideration of the planning system, so that it can be protected for future generations (see Section 10.3).

Old theatres often occupy large, prime town centre locations, which are under increasing pressure of development for more profitable uses. Once lost, it is very challenging and costly to replace theatres due to the large parcels of land required to accommodate them. By the 1970s the demolition of theatre buildings was causing such levels of concern in the United Kingdom that additional protection was deemed necessary and was provided by the Theatres Trust Act: 1976. The Act founded a new organisation, the Theatres Trust, as the national advisory public body for theatres. The Trust is tasked with protecting theatres and theatre use and is a statutory consultee for all planning applications affecting land on which there is a theatre. While the United Kingdom is fortunate in the protection that is now afforded to theatre buildings, there are other territories offering little or no protection, where there has been even greater loss of the stock of historic theatres, which can never be recovered.

The Theatres Trust now holds a database of theatre buildings across the United Kingdom, which includes those buildings currently in theatre use, as well as theatre buildings that are in other uses, vacant or derelict. It also holds information on theatre buildings that have been demolished. In addition to the database, the Trust also holds a *Theatres at Risk* register that highlights those theatre buildings that are considered under threat and at greatest risk, which includes some unlisted theatre buildings.

Theatres in the United Kingdom have their own use class *sui generis* under the General Development Order 2006, which means that any change of use requires planning permission (see Section 10.3). This special status is an important form of protection. Once a theatre moves into another use class, there is a possibility of further changes being made, without the need for permission, which may lead to more harmful alterations. Theatre buildings are subject to changing fashions and financial circumstances, but these can change over time and the possibility of their return to theatre use in the future should be safeguarded, wherever possible.

Theatres are also offered some protection through the National Planning Policy Framework (NPPF), February 2019, which includes a requirement for positive planning for social, recreational and cultural facilities in communities and guarding against their unnecessary loss.

Existing theatres can also face external threats by changing circumstances in their immediate vicinity, for example the building of noise sensitive developments such as housing nearby. This has the potential to lead to complaints from new neighbours, particularly in relation to noise, and this can result in restrictions being placed on venues such as earlier closing times and a reduction in permitted sound levels. This in turn can severely impact a theatre by undermining the venue's operation and viability and, in the worst cases, can lead to closures. The 'Agent of Change' principle has recently been introduced as national policy in England and law within Scotland (and is expected to be extended across the United Kingdom) whereby consideration now needs to be given to the potential effects of locating new residential development close to existing businesses that cause noise. This states that the party introducing the change of use to a site is responsible for preventing harm to the operations of existing neighbouring uses and must take on any costs associated with making the new development acceptable. The recent changes to permitted development rules allowing offices to be converted to residential use without needing planning consent are now a particular concern in this respect.

There are also many instances of developers acquiring old theatres in the hope of redevelopment without appreciating the statutory protection they enjoy, or the costs associated with their renovation. For historic theatres in particular, the cost of the repair works required can exceed the increase in value of the restored property, resulting in a conservation deficit. This can lead to buildings lying empty for many years until a viable use can be found for them or, in the worst-case scenario, they deteriorate beyond repair.

Bringing old theatres back into use is often driven by the local community mounting a campaign centred on a shared passion for an historic building and a vision for its contribution to the local area. One of the earliest phases of work associated with bringing an old theatre back into use will be the development of a viable business model looking at the optimum use of the building consistent with its heritage significance. This may involve consideration of alternative uses, which provided that they do not fundamentally change the nature of the building, may be acceptable, such as nightclubs, music venues, cinemas and churches.

The value of theatre buildings to town centres is also increasingly appreciated as a part of the placemaking agenda to reinvent the high street as a social space and to offset the decline in retail. Theatres are now seen as key to increasing footfall and secondary spending in town centres and in supporting the night-time economy, with many being identified as heritage assets which provide a significant contribution to the local character and townscape of their area (see Figure 10.2.2).

Figure 10.2.2 Façade of the Theatre Royal Nottingham.

## 10.3 Planning and legal constraints in the United Kingdom

This section deals with some of the legal issues related to planning, listed buildings, conservation areas, locally listed theatre buildings and enforcement.

### Planning

Theatre buildings in theatre use are afforded the special protection of being *sui generis*. This means they are not in any specific use class and therefore any change of use requires planning permission. If you want to extend, demolish or make alterations to a theatre you will need planning permission from the local planning authority. In general terms, an application will always need to include: an application form (an application can be made online), a signed ownership certificate, a site plan and drawings of both the existing and proposed alterations, the correct fee and a design and access statement (DAS).

A design and access statement is a short report accompanying and supporting a planning application. It must explain the design principles and concepts that have been applied to the development and explain how relevant local plan policies have been taken into account, any consultation undertaken in relation to access issues, and how the outcome of this consultation has informed the proposed development. Other statements and reports that may be required will depend on the nature of the proposals and any heritage designation. It is always best to check on the local planning authority's validation requirements. These may include a heritage statement, viability studies and an options appraisal.

### Heritage statement

A heritage statement will be required if the theatre is listed as a heritage asset. A heritage statement is an assessment of the significance of heritage assets and/or their settings affected by a development, and of the impacts of that development upon them. In the case of theatres, these are usually best prepared by an historic theatre expert who will understand the particular characteristics of the building type. It is essential to start work on the statement at the beginning of a project, to understand the building's significance and how the proposals will impact it (see Section 10.4).

### Viability studies and options appraisal

There is no longer a requirement to assess viability for each individual site or development. However, a viability specialist may need to be commissioned to support and assess the financial viability of a scheme, especially where it may need to offset other planning policy requirements.

### Statutory consultees

Statutory consultees are those organisations and bodies, defined by statute, which local planning authorities are legally required to consult before reaching a decision on relevant planning applications. The main one for theatres is the Theatres Trust. It must be consulted on any planning application involving land where there is a theatre or that will have an impact on theatre use. The Theatres Trust Act 1976 and the Theatres Trust (Scotland) Act 1978 define a theatre as 'any building or part of a building constructed wholly or mainly for the public performance of plays'. In this context 'plays' has the same meaning as in the Theatres Act 1968 encompassing all forms of performance in a theatre, including drama, dance, ballet, opera, musicals, song, circus, acrobatics, physical theatre, puppetry, mime, comedy, variety, cabaret, magic and live art. Where a theatre is listed, a local planning authority may consult a range of heritage consultees depending on the nature of the application, including Historic England, Historic Scotland,

Cadw, the Victorian Society, the Twentieth Century Society, the Georgian Group, Cinema Theatre Association and the Ancient Monument Society. It may also consult local history interest groups.

## Section 106 Obligations and Community Infrastructure Levy

Planning obligations under Section 106 of the Town and Country Planning Act 1990 (Section 75 of the Town and Country Planning (Scotland) Act 1997), commonly known as S106 agreements, are a mechanism which make a development proposal – that would not otherwise be acceptable – acceptable in planning terms. They are focused on site-specific mitigation of the impact of development. S106 agreements are often referred to as 'developer contributions'. For example, they could include the fit-out of a new theatre or the gift of land. The Community Infrastructure Levy (CIL) is a cost that local authorities can choose to charge on new developments in their area. Existing theatres in theatre use are usually exempt from paying a CIL. However, CIL funds can be applied for theatre enhancements to a streetscape.

## Enforcement

Works undertaken without planning permission or listed building consent may incur enforcement from the local planning authority. Planning enforcement deals with breaches of planning controls, including where building work requiring planning permission or listed building consent is undertaken without such permission, where conditions attached to a planning condition are not complied with, or where the use of a building or site is changed without planning permission. A theatre may incur enforcement when, for example, signage or equipment has been installed without planning permission.

If a building is neglected, a local planning authority has powers to issue a Section 215 Notice. This type of notice is specifically served where the condition of the theatre building is considered to have a harmful effect on the amenity of the area. The theatre building can be of any age and does not need to be formally designated. In Scotland the notice is served under Section 179 of the Town and Country Planning (Scotland) Act 1997.

## Historic theatres

An historic theatre, no matter how modest, may be protected by statutory listing due to its special architectural or historic interest. There are additional considerations when owning a listed building or one that is within a conservation area. The current legislation in England and Wales is the Planning (Listed Buildings and Conservation Areas) Act 1990. The current Scottish legislation is the Planning (Listed Buildings and Conservation Areas) (Scotland) Act 1997.

Statutory listed buildings are known as heritage assets. These are buildings and structures which are considered to have special architectural or historic interest in a national context. When a building is listed it affects both the exterior and the interior, together with any outbuildings, walls or other structures that were built before 1948 within the curtilage or grounds of the listed building. Therefore it cannot be altered or extended without the express consent of the local planning authority, obtained through a listed building consent.

The following grades of listing are used to show the level of special interest of a building in England, Wales and Northern Ireland.

- Grade I buildings are of exceptional interest (just 2.5% of all listed buildings are Grade I listed).
- Grade II* buildings are particularly important buildings of more than special interest (just under 6% of listed buildings are Grade II*).
- Grade II buildings are of special interest (over 90% of listed buildings are Grade II listed and this is the most common grade for many theatres).

In Scotland buildings are put into one of three listing categories, similar to these, classified as Categories A, B or C.

## Listed building consent

In general terms listed building consent is required for all works of demolition, alteration or extension to a listed building that affect its character as a building of special architectural or historic interest. The requirement applies to all types of works and to all parts of those buildings covered by the listing protection (possibly including attached and curtilage buildings or other structures), if the works affect the character of the building as a building of special interest. It is a criminal offence not to seek consent when it is required. An application for listed building consent is made to, and determined by, the local planning authority, who are required to consult the national listing authority and the relevant statutory consultees (see previously) on certain applications.

If you plan to do work to a listed theatre, do not make any assumptions. For a highly graded theatre, even the smallest alteration may require listed building consent, such as redecoration or replacement of carpet and seats. The list description of a building provides a valuable indication of which areas of your building are considered significant, but just because a specific feature is not mentioned it does not mean it is not of interest – speak with your local authority conservation officer/heritage specialist and the Theatres Trust. Also remember a building can be listed for architectural and/or historic interest. For example, the specific interest may be to do with the design and layout, use of an innovative technology or because the building represents a good example of our national social/cultural history.

In England and Wales, a theatre may also be locally listed (non-designated heritage assets of special local interest). A local listing does not require any additional consent processes over and above those required for planning permission. The purpose of maintaining a list of historic assets is to ensure that the significance of local assets is taken into account in the planning process and there will be an accompanying council planning policy. In Scotland, where there is no local list, Category C listing applies.

### Conservation areas

A theatre may also be designated within a conservation area. Local planning authorities are obliged to designate as conservation areas any parts of their own area that are of special architectural or historic interest, the character and appearance of which it is desirable to preserve or enhance. Conservation area designation introduces a general control over demolition as well as control over alterations to exteriors. There will be accompanying council planning policy that will need to be taken into consideration when works to a theatre building are planned.

## 10.4 Conservation approach

When working with any historic building it is essential to follow good conservation practice, which in the first instance involves developing a thorough understanding of the heritage asset, its history and development over time, and the relative significance of its various parts. The idea that a listed building cannot be altered is a common misconception. Almost all buildings are altered over time to meet changing needs, but a case for change needs to be carefully argued against a background of historical understanding, which balances practical needs with a sensitivity to the value of what exists. To quote Historic England,

> listing is not a preservation order, preventing change. It does not freeze a building in time, it simply means that listed building consent must be applied for in order to make any changes to that building which might affect its special interest.

This does not exclude sympathetic modern interventions or extensions, which may be preferable to pastiche. (See Figure 10.4.1.) The acceptability of a proposal will depend on a balanced judgement of conservation losses and gains, the design quality of any new work and how the alterations will help to secure the building's beneficial use in the future. Early discussions with the conservation authorities to seek to agree a shared approach to these issues is recommended.

The preparation of a heritage statement is considered best practice before undertaking works to listed buildings and, in most cases, is mandatory. It should be prepared by a suitably qualified independent expert, who understands the building type, as theatres have special design and technical features, which need to be properly appreciated. Heritage statements involve research into the history and development of a building over time, the original architects and their other work and an assessment of significance. Historic drawings and photographs are particularly valuable to understand the original design and any changes which may have occurred. Where elements of the building have been lost, reference to other projects by the same architect may also provide clues on how to restore them. A sensitivity analysis will help identify those parts of the building with high significance, which should not be altered, and parts with lesser significance, which might be altered with appropriate justification. This is an invaluable tool when developing a design approach (see Figure 10.4.2).

Figure 10.4.1 The Royal Shakespeare Theatre, Stratford-upon-Avon: exterior showing a modern roof and side extension to the original 1930's listed building. Architect: Bennetts Associates. (See Reference Project 27.)

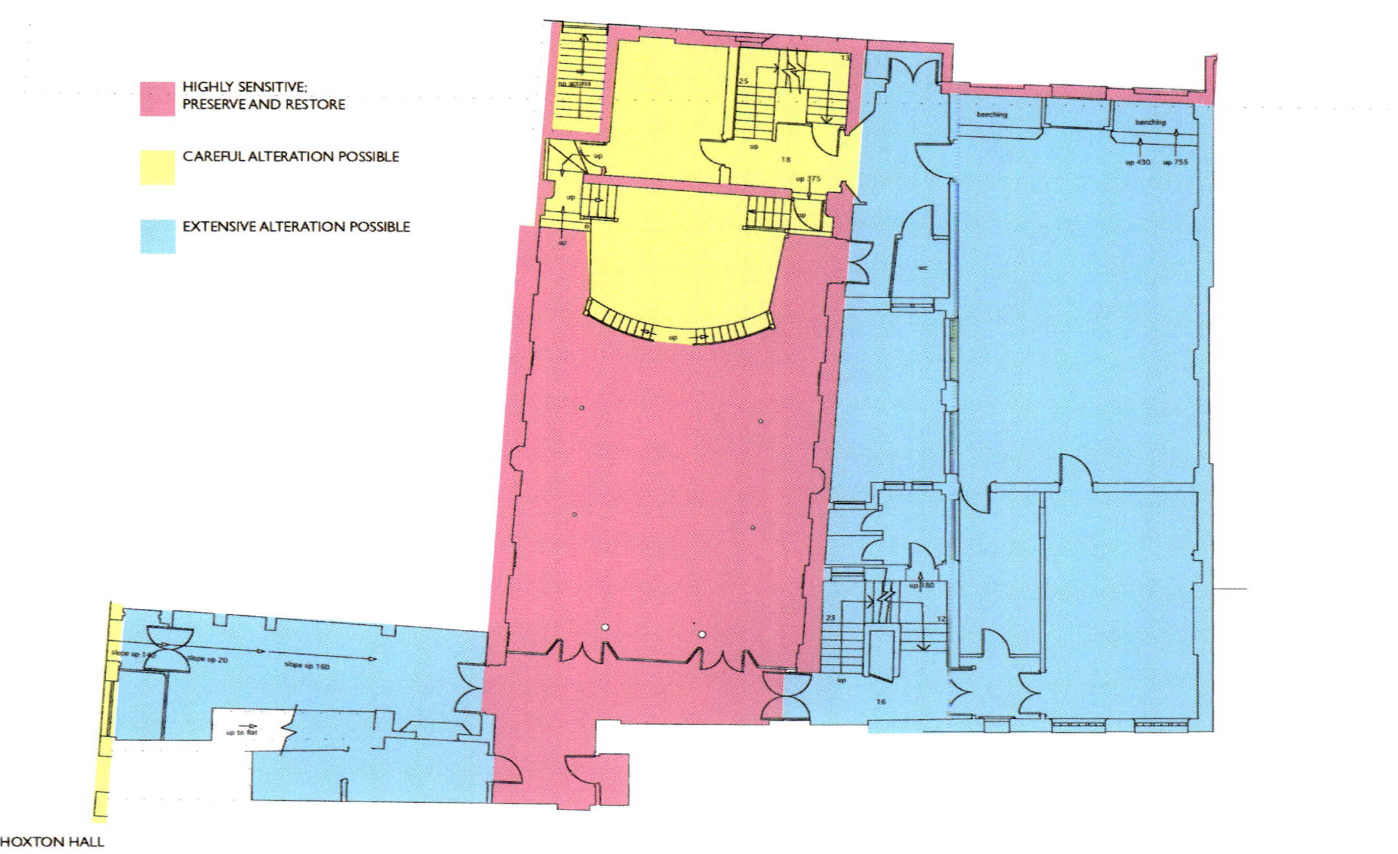


Figure 10.4.2 A sensitivity analysis drawing for Hoxton Hall, a listed Victorian music hall.

It will also be important in the early stages of a project to undertake measured and structural surveys, paint analysis and the careful recording of any elements which are to be removed.

Rigid application of modern building regulations and technical standards is not always helpful when dealing with historic buildings and waivers and alternative ways of achieving a particular goal can be negotiated. Modern fire engineering techniques can sometimes be used to show that an older building, which may not comply with current regulations, is nevertheless safe. This can sometimes help avoid the need for intrusive interventions to the historic fabric.

## 10.5 Common problems and opportunities

As a general rule, it is less expensive to remodel and restore buildings than to rebuild from scratch. An existing theatre building will already have the key ingredients of an auditorium, a stage and the means to access both, and probably has a good town centre location. It is also much more sustainable to reuse an existing building, in terms of the embodied energy it contains, compared to the energy required for a new construction. Old buildings often need sympathetic help and, sometimes, radical surgery to achieve worthwhile reductions in their carbon emissions, but it is possible to do.

There is another, less tangible, reason why many theatre practitioners may prefer to adapt an existing building rather than create a new one, which is that the building has a sense of history, which is impossible to create in a new building. Spaces like Wilton's Music Hall in London's East End (see Reference Project 28), the Majestic in New York's Brooklyn and the Bouffes du Nord in Paris possess an indefinable, almost haunted quality, as if the ghosts of past performers and audiences somehow live on and contribute to the atmosphere that makes theatregoing there such a special experience (see Figure 10.5.1).

In purely practical terms, however, it is often necessary to make some quite radical decisions when making an historic theatre fit for modern use. Most typical theatre buildings can be analysed on fairly predictable lines. One

Figure 10.5.1 Interior of the Bouffes du Nord theatre in Paris, a nineteenth-century theatre adapted for use by Peter Brook in 1974. An early example of 'arrested decay' although much of the distressed effect was created by scenic artists (see Strong (ed.) *Theatre Buildings* (2010), Reference projects, pp. 198–201).

overriding issue that must be considered right at the outset is whether there is scope to increase the floor area.

## Typical analysis of an existing building

The auditorium is often the most prominent and well-regarded feature of an existing theatre, and it may be feasible to adapt this, provided that the client is happy to maintain a version of what is likely to be a proscenium arch format. However, the front of house and circulation areas are more likely to need to be extensively remodelled and enlarged so that the whole audience can use the same entrance and have sufficient circulation space and proper facilities. Additional space may also be needed to increase backstage accommodation. This may include the construction of a new stage house with a larger and higher flytower. Provision for loading in with access for modern articulated vehicles and a new and larger get-in may also be needed. The remodelling of the old Empire Theatre in Edinburgh from its former use as a cinema, and later a bingo hall, to create the Festival Theatre represents a well-known example of this process, where front of house, stage and backstage were substantially re-built, and the auditorium was restored (see Figure 10.5.2).

Once the brief is established and it has been agreed which aspects of the existing building are worth retaining and what adaptations can be made, attention may then need to turn to securing additional space for expansion. The best solution will often entail the acquisition of an adjacent property or properties. Some theatre owners have to wait many years for such an opportunity to arise. If the chance

Figure 10.5.2 Festival Theatre Edinburgh: the modern foyer extension to the original 1928 theatre. Architect: Law & Dunbar Naismith.

does come it is essential to take it, even if this then means sitting on a vacant site until the time is right to build or subletting the space on a short-term basis.

Where expansion onto an adjacent site is not feasible, the first line of investigation is to consider whether any underused space can be reclaimed within the existing building. The initial research into its history should offer some clues. Careful thought should also be given to whether some activities such as offices, workshops and storage could be rehoused in less expensive accommodation off-site.

Building above an existing theatre may be an option, but this is likely to prove expensive. There is an added difficulty in introducing the structural supports that will be required and valuable space is also likely to be lost when the necessary lifts and staircases are installed. A further consideration is whether the extra accommodation provided will be at the level where it is most needed, namely for public or backstage use. A lightweight construction on an existing flat roof may be an option and help to release other space below. There may also be usable space within a roof void, though this may well have already been filled with ducts for ventilation and other services. There are also examples of overbuilding to create residential or office space, which on valuable city centre sites can generate surplus funds to restore the theatre. Planning consents may involve a Section 106 Agreement (see Section 10.3) requiring profits from commercial development to be reinvested in the restoration of the theatre itself.

Excavating below an existing building is another option but is also likely to be expensive. There are precedents, however, and this option is certainly worth investigating, particularly if there are no other opportunities to expand the building's footprint (see Figure 10.5.3).

Figure 10.5.3 Royal Court Theatre: model shot showing the cross section of the theatre with the new foyer extension excavated under the road and emerging into the square opposite. Architect: Haworth Tompkins.

### Why is more space needed?

Theatres today are used very differently from the time when older theatres were built, when the doors opened shortly before the performance and the audience was segregated by price and social status. Key differences now are:

- theatres are often open all day providing social space where people can meet
- audiences need to be treated equally, regardless of where they are sitting in the auditorium
- buildings must be accessible to all
- toilet provision needs to meet modern standards
- the sale of food and beverages is expected and provides important income
- seating comfort standards have changed
- modern technical equipment must be accommodated
- modern building services must be integrated
- larger stages are needed for certain types of production
- a producing theatre will need more space backstage for actors, staff and administration
- acoustic demands have changed with the increased use of amplification.

All these issues can result in the need for more space and how to achieve this must be resolved in the early planning stages.

## 10.6 Front of house

While the retention of a beautiful historic auditorium may be an over-riding factor in the desire to restore or re-use an existing theatre, there are many factors which make achieving modern standards of provision in front of house areas particularly problematic. These are dealt with in more detail in Section 4 but may include improved access, toilet provision, foyer space, food and beverage sales and other spaces which do not currently exist.

### Access

Providing level access for wheelchair users and the ambulant disabled in old theatres can be very challenging. Entrance doors are often up steps and level changes within the building are common. Creating a truly inclusive experience may require a major re-working of the entrance sequence and this is sometimes achieved by adding an entirely new foyer linked to the original building. Lifts may be needed to access upper levels or negotiate level changes. Wheelchair positions in the auditorium also need to be provided, preferably at every level of a multi-level theatre (see Figure

10.6.1). Generally, the social principles discussed in Section 3 should apply but achieving them seamlessly in an existing building requires considerable ingenuity.

Figure 10.6.1 A modern extension to the Theatre Royal, Glasgow, providing additional foyer space and new vertical circulation, including lift access to all levels of the theatre. (See Reference Project 29.) Architect: Page/Park.

## Toilet provision

One of the most common causes for complaint by audiences visiting old theatres, particularly in London's West End, is the inadequacy of the toilet provision, particularly for women. Any refurbishment should seek to provide modern standards of provision but finding new space for this can be difficult. See Section 4 for further details.

## Foyer space standards

These are discussed in detail in Section 4, but the space standards found in older theatres are often well below modern standards. This can best be addressed by some form of extension, but this may not always be possible. Sometimes there are opportunities to combine existing spaces to create additional floor area and improve audience flow.

## Food and beverages

Sales of F&B are an increasingly important income stream for theatres which will require sufficient service points and space for audiences to gather and be served in a short space of time. Appropriate kitchen facilities will be needed to match the proposed catering offer. In response to overcrowding in the bars of some older theatres and as a means of generating additional revenue, a recent development is the provision of 'in seat' service in the auditorium via a mobile phone app, so people do not have to leave their seats to buy refreshments. This requires provision of service points close to the auditorium.

## Other spaces

Today theatres often require a variety of other spaces to deliver their programme effectively, which may not exist in the original building. These can include studio theatres, rehearsal rooms, education spaces and hospitality rooms. These are discussed in more detail in Section 4; finding space for them in an existing building will always be a challenge, particularly if the footprint cannot be expanded (see Figure 10.6.2).

Figure 10.6.2 Exterior of the Belfast Grand Opera House showing the original Frank Matcham façade and a modern extension providing additional foyer space. Architect: Arts Team at RHWL with later modifications by Consarc Design Group.

# 10.7 Auditorium

The auditorium of an historic theatre is often the most atmospheric and highly decorated part of the building and authentic repair and restoration of its original interior is often desirable, although an 'arrested decay' approach which stabilises the existing time-scarred appearance can also be very effective (see Figure 10.7.1). Whichever approach is adopted there are some key issues which often need addressing.

Figure 10.7.1 Wilton's Music Hall: interior showing original finishes retained in the refurbished building. (See Reference Project 28.)

## Decoration

Careful consideration is needed when a major scheme of decorative renewal is anticipated within the auditorium. Much has changed since these theatres were built, not least the amount of reflected light that bounces off the stage during a performance. House-lighting levels were generally much lower in the gas-lit days of the nineteenth century. Even with the introduction of early electric lighting the levels were still lower than today, and the colour temperatures of both gas and the incandescent light bulb were markedly different from that of a modern LED light source.

Historic paint analysis is helpful, because it provides an indication of the various colour schemes that have existed in the past, as well as the chronological order in which they evolved. However, slavish copying of this analysis can often create problems, particularly where the original was seen under much lower lighting levels and will now appear too bright and garish under modern lighting.

The wholesale stripping of historic paint layers is to be avoided wherever practicable. When stripping must occur, because the substrate is inadequate, sample panels should be retained and locations recorded so that the generations who follow can carry out their own ever more sophisticated analyses. The retention of an 'as found' decorative scheme has much to commend it as opposed to a fully 'restored' reinstatement. However, there are situations where the original colour scheme is no longer appropriate and a new palette has to be developed. The key to making appropriate decisions will lie in the development of a comprehensive conservation plan, which addresses all these issues and in doing so develops a coherent and logically reasoned strategy.

## Seating

People have grown larger in the last century and the comfort of original seating is often unacceptable by modern standards. This is usually addressed by installing larger seats with improved row depths but this inevitably results in a reduced capacity, which has a commercial impact. It also poses some technical difficulties, particularly where the floor is stepped. If the floor is sloped, as is often the case in the stalls, it is relatively straightforward to re-space seating. Where the floor is stepped, as it will be in the balconies, this is more difficult. Re-tiering over the original floor to create greater row depth is sometimes possible but can adversely affect sightlines by reducing the rake angle or compromising the upward sightline, so great care is needed. Alternatively, it is often better and cheaper to retain existing steps and improve comfort through the use of higher more upright chairs, which can make a significant improvement to comfort and legroom, without loss of rows. In upper balconies where the original seating takes the form of benches on the steps with very small back-to-back dimensions, re-tiering is often more difficult and it may be better to retain the original steps with seats on every other row.

## Design

Just because an auditorium is historic does not necessarily mean the design works. There are sometimes fundamental design issues such as unsatisfactory sightlines or a poor relationship with the stage that may require more radical action. (See Figure 10.7.2 and *Sightline*, Winter 2017, pp. 7–13.) A careful review is needed at the outset to identify and understand these issues.

Over the period of an historic theatre's life it is likely to have experienced a number of interventions designed by both experienced and less experienced individuals. In general, interventions associated with seating usually opt for a revised seating layout built on top of the original one, which avoids disturbance of the underlying structure, which as discussed previously can sometimes lead to more problems than it solves and may need to be reversed.

It is also critical to understand the type of seating that was originally used, as the seats in historic theatres varied enormously and an understanding of what was there originally is important. The stalls were often split into two areas, with luxurious armchairs at the front (orchestra stalls) and timber benches behind (the pit). In the dress circle there would be tip-up seats, while the upper circle was often fitted with 'sit on the tier' seating, as was the case in the gallery where timber benches were

Figure 10.7.2a and 2b Darlington Theatre: proscenium boxes, before (top) and after (bottom) refurbishment, showing how an original design error can be corrected. Architect: Space Architects.

often the norm. (See Figure 10.7.3.) Attempts to install modern tip-up seats in these two upper tiers can have disastrous consequences.

Improvements to comfort and sightlines will usually result in a reduction in seating capacity, which theatre managements will often resist due to the loss of income this represents. However, it is worth bearing in mind that seating numbers are not always commensurate with seating yield. In other words, ten excellent seats, which are comfortable and have good sightlines, are usually worth more than fifteen poor seats.

## Removable seating

Some theatres may wish to have the ability to remove seating in the stalls to accommodate standing audiences, particularly for music events, or to introduce a cabaret-style layout with tables and chairs. The space required for a typical seat position is approximately 0.5m$^2$, whereas the space allowance for a standing audience member will typically be 0.3m$^2$ or as little as 0.25m$^2$. There is therefore the potential to increase the audience capacity in the stalls by up to 100%, which is commercially attractive, but before embarking on such a venture there are some important questions to consider. Can the existing escape routes support the increased capacity? What impact will the increased capacity have on other facilities such as toilets and bars? And how often will the seats be removed and at what cost in terms of time and labour?

In an historic theatre it may not be possible to increase the capacity of the escape routes but advice from a fire engineer may be able to demonstrate that the existing escapes are adequate for larger audiences by increasing the evacuation time, without the need for physical changes.

Toilet and bar provision may also be an issue, although for music events it may be argued that audiences are able to leave the auditorium at any time to use these facilities, thus reducing the usual interval peaks. It is important to discuss these issues at an early stage with licensing and fire authorities to secure their agreement.

The question of how to remove the seats, either manually or through mechanisation, will depend on the frequency this occurs, the speed at which it must be completed and the relative costs of labour and machinery. In either case, significant storage space will need to be found to accommodate the seats when not in use. This may be possible under the stage, using a forestage elevator to move them or, alternatively, it may be necessary to create

Figure 10.7.3 A modern facsimile of an historic theatre seat for Darlington Theatre, now Hippodrome. Seat by Kirwin & Simpson. Architect: Space Architects.

a separate storage facility elsewhere. For example, at the Eventim Apollo theatre in Hammersmith, one of London's largest venues for music and comedy, more than 1,000 seats are moved manually at least fifty times a year. (See Figure 10.7.4.) Chairs are stacked on trollies and then moved by fork-lift to a dedicated store at the back of the site.

Figure 10.7.4 Removable seating at The Eventim Apollo Theatre, Hammersmith. Seats by Audience Systems. Architect: Foster Wilson Size.

## Balcony fronts and safety rails

The design of balcony fronts and safety rails at gangway ends, to comply with modern regulations, can be a source of considerable problems, where these interfere with sightlines or are visually intrusive. Under UK regulations, a balcony guarding must be 800mm high where there is fixed seating, whereas at a gangway end, where there is no seating, they must be 1,100mm high. These rails can be very obtrusive, particularly for seats which have an oblique view of the stage with which they interfere. This problem can be mitigated, but not removed, by ensuring the rail is no longer than strictly necessary, is as slender as possible, and avoids the use of reflective materials which catch the light, such as chromed or polished metals. Knowing where the original safety rails were positioned, and their appearance, will be helpful.

Traditionally the fabric balcony rester in front of seats is re-covered time and time again during a theatre's life. Often the original safety ledge, no more than a large, raised timber quadrant, has been removed. Reinstating this small detail increases the safety as well the architectural elegance. Generally, rester rails should be designed with rounded or sloping tops to discourage the placing of drinks or other objects, which can fall on the audience below (see Figure 10.7.5).

Figure 10.7.5 View of the restored Trafalgar Theatre (formerly The Whitehall Theatre) showing new balcony front with lighting bars and inward sloping rester rail. Architect: Foster Wilson Size.

## Technical installations in the auditorium

Front of house lighting bars and loudspeaker positions are a necessary element in any modern theatre, and very few of the pre-1914 theatre stock made any provision for this kind of equipment. (Matcham began to provide a few FOH positions, for example, at the Theatre Royal Newcastle in 1901 and the Palladium in 1911.) Careful consideration is needed to design these in such a way that they can be safely accessed and detract from the historic interior as little as possible. The following points should be considered:

- lighting bars should be designed to be removable when not required
- balcony front lighting bars should be at a height where they do not interfere with both downward and upward sightlines
- electrical socket boxes should be recessed or mounted on internally wired bars
- provision of strong points to allow suspension of flown trusses (preferably these are above the ceiling, with guided steel tubes for chain hoists or winch cables to pass through) and their location needs to be carefully considered as if they are in the wrong place or are difficult to rig they will not be used
- safe access to focus lighting is needed which may require the provision of strong points to attach harnesses or the use of moveable access equipment such as towers or sliding bridges.

## Ceilings

Many historic theatres and cinemas have fibrous plaster ceilings, which deserve special mention. Fibrous plaster was first patented in 1856, although it was in use for several centuries before that. However, it was not until the theatre boom of the late nineteenth and early twentieth centuries that the material was used extensively in the construction of theatres, creating the highly decorative plaster interiors typical of the period. The material, which is lightweight, known for speed of production and installation and able to be moulded into complex forms, was often used for theatre ceilings and for box and balcony fronts as well as on proscenium arches and for cornices and columns (see Figure 10.7.7). The oldest surviving fibrous plaster in the United Kingdom was that within the proscenium arch and balcony fronts at the Royal Opera House in London (1858), and it was still in use in the cine-variety houses of the 1930s.

Figure 10.7.6 A good example of a front of house lighting position.

Figure 10.7.7 View of the restored fibrous plaster ceiling and balcony fronts at Frank Matcham's Everyman Theatre in Cheltenham (1891). Architect: Foster Wilson Size.

While theatre ceilings have always been required to be the subject of regular inspections and certification under the entertainment licensing system, there has been a significant raising of awareness and considerable new research into the material following the partial collapse of a fibrous plaster ceiling during a performance at The Apollo Theatre in London in 2013. This has shown the material's vulnerability to environmental conditions and other external factors, emphasising the need for regular surveys to inspect the condition and the necessity of regular maintenance and repair. In the United Kingdom, guidance is provided by the Association of British Theatre Technicians (ABTT), *Guidance Note 20: Advice to Theatre Owners and Managers regarding Suspended Fibrous Plaster Ceilings; Survey, Certification, Record Keeping etc.* (2015); and Historic England's *Guidance Note: Historic Fibrous Plaster in the UK: Guidance on its Care and Management*. Historic England is carrying out further research on the material and further publications are expected.

Factors affecting the safety of fibrous plaster include vulnerability to decay from environmental conditions, particularly moisture, defects in the structure to which it is fixed, physical damage made through alterations, excess loading caused by additional plant and accumulation of debris and the deterioration of fixing methods. The effect of these factors on the fibrous plaster and its method of suspension should be carefully assessed by a structural engineer or historic plaster specialist. There has been some suggestion that the failure of historic plaster ceilings may be caused by high noise levels which are part of a performance. However acoustic theory and testing suggests this is unlikely to be the case where a ceiling is maintained in good condition but may be a contributory factor where the structural support is already starting to fail.

It is vital that good access to the ceiling void is provided to allow ceilings to be thoroughly and regularly inspected from above, ensuring that walkways to enable this do not impose any additional loading which could directly affect the ceiling and its suspensions. It is also important to keep the back of the ceiling free from debris, both to allow visual inspection and to reduce excess loading (see Section 6.2).

## Balcony structures

The traditional balcony structure of a theatre from the mid-nineteenth century onwards usually consisted of a plate/box girder which spans from side to side across the full width of the auditorium. In some older venues there are intermediate column supports to the girder. The primary girder supports a series of raking beams that extend from the rear of the auditorium fixed to the girder and then cantilever to the balcony front. At the leading edge of the balcony there is typically a steel section that acts as a tie to the ends of the cantilevered beams and provides support to the balcony front upstand and balustrade. The tiering is typically formed in concrete or filler joist construction supported on secondary beams spanning between the raking beams.

Historic balcony structures were designed for static loads due to the self-weight of the structure and the imposed load from the seated audience. More recently some productions, mainly live music, have encouraged the audience to become active during the performance changing the static seated audience into a dynamic applied load due to synchronised movement. This change in the application of the imposed load has a major impact on how the structural elements behave, particularly long spanning members and cantilevers, as they are more susceptible to dynamic response. The movement caused by the dynamic loading may lead to the feeling of discomfort for some members of the audience, damage to the plaster finishes and the potential failure of structural elements.

The current requirement of D1.02 of the *ABTT Technical Standards for Places of Entertainment* stipulates that 'Dynamically sensitive structures should be designed to achieve a natural vertical frequency greater than 8.4Hz and a natural horizontal frequency greater than 4Hz as a way to maintain human comfort and prevent structural dynamic effects associated with the synchronised movement of an audience or performer/performance'.

Historic venues were not subject to this requirement and as a result the natural frequency of the existing members are unlikely to meet current standards. If discomfort is regularly being reported by members of the audience or the types of performance undertaken are to change from a mainly seated audience to music, it is strongly recommended an assessment of the existing structure be undertaken by a structural engineer. Consideration should be given to the event scenario, an example of which is given in Table 1 from *Dynamic Performance Requirements for Permanent Grandstands Subject to Crowd Action*, published by the Institution of Structural Engineers, 2008 (see Figure 10.7.8.).

## Soft architecture

The drapes, curtains and carpets in an auditorium, sometimes known as 'soft architecture', play an important role in creating the rich atmosphere of an historic auditorium. An integrated design approach for the soft architecture of the theatre is essential. Be aware that the original surface finishes of an old theatre were both decorative and functional. Frank Matcham's use of tiles in the rear stalls allowed both easy cleaning and a degree of acoustic reflectivity. Curtains also

**Table 1 Event Scenarios to be supplemented with a statement on agreed operational arrangements**

| Scenario | Exemplar event | Crowd behaviour | Management | | Acceptance criteria | |
|---|---|---|---|---|---|---|
| | | | Expected crowd make up | Stewarding | Crowd expectation | Natural frequency or design acceleration limit |
| 1 | Stand used for viewing of sporting and similar events with less than maximum attendance | Normally relaxed viewing public with spontaneous response to single events | Predominantly seated | Stewards require to be instructed as to the possible effects of motion of the structure resulting from coordinated crowd activity and, particularly for Scenarios 3 and 4, need to be provided with the means for instant communication with central control. | Comfort | Route 1 with 3.5 Hz min. or accepted at the discretion of a Listed Engineer |
| 2 | Classical concert and typical well attended sporting event | Audience seated with only few exceptions – minor excitation | Predominantly seated | | Comfort | Route 1 with 3.5 Hz min. Is normally adequate but otherwise Route 2 and 3%g max. RMS acceleration |
| 3 | Commonly occurring events including, inter alia, high profile sporting events and concerts with medium tempo music and revival pop-concerts with cross generation appeal | Potentially excitable crowd with crowd participation | All standing and participating during some part of the programme | | A few individuals may complain at lack of comfort but most will tolerate the motion | Route 1 with 6 Hz min. Otherwise Route 2, and 7½%g max. RMS acceleration |
| 4 | More extreme events including high energy concerts with periods of high intensity music | Excited crowd, mostly standing and bobbing with some jumping | Mainly young and active with vigorous participation | | Excitement and motion but with expectation of personal safety | Route 1 with 6 Hz min. Otherwise Route 2, and 20%g max. RMS acceleration |

Note
Appendix 1, Section A1.5 deals with Root Mean Square (RMS) accelerations and how these are defined and used in analysis.

Figure 10.7.8 Table 1 from *Dynamic Performance Requirements for Permanent Grandstands Subject to Crowd Action*, published by the Institution of Structural Engineers, 2008.

Figure 10.7.9 Typical 'soft architecture' at The Gaiety Theatre, Isle of Man.

perform a similar acoustic role whereby they modulate and absorb some of the acoustic reflections. It is therefore necessary to understand where the fabric was positioned and to a degree, how much 'fullness' was employed. In addition to the traditional decorative House curtain and pelmet, fabric was often used in the following areas: tier resters, surfaces below rear tier box fronts, proscenium box curtains and pelmets and door drapes and pelmets to prevent noise and light spill from foyers.

If available, the examination of historic drawings and photographs will often provide a useful indication of the surface finishes and design of the original drapes. (See Figure 10.7.9.)

## 10.8 Stage and backstage

### Raked stages

Most historic stage floors from the eighteenth to the early twentieth centuries were raked, and this played an important role in achieving good sightlines, particularly from a relatively flat stalls floor. Most modern productions are designed for flat stages, often with the use of scenic over-floors, containing mechanisation and lighting. For a producing theatre it will often be possible to continue to work with an existing raked stage, but for some presenting theatres, where incoming shows are designed for a flat floor, it may be necessary to consider levelling the stage.

The first flat stage in Great Britain was designed by Charles Phipps for Her Majesty's Theatre in London in 1897. Today we accept a flat stage as standard for modern theatres. However, the adaptation of a raked stage into a flat stage demands very careful consideration.

It is essential to understand that a raked stage cannot be flattened without commensurate alterations to the seating sightlines. The rake is designed for a specific set of sightlines that are carefully balanced in relation to it. Numerous issues need to be taken into account when undertaking this kind of assessment, which may include:

- access points and door datums onto the stage
- change in height of the stage riser

- impact on flying height (especially downstage)
- safety curtain implications
- impact on any historic sub-stage machinery
- significant changes to the sub-stage supporting structure
- potential loss of sub-stage headroom
- possible alterations to services distribution
- work required to alter seating sightlines
- potential loss of seats brought about by the changes.

Stages can be levelled either by retaining the height of the stage front and lowering the level at the rear or by retaining the height at the rear and raising the stage front, or a mid-way option which adjusts the heights at the back and front. Lowering at the back will involve replacing the existing stage structure and may produce problems with the headroom and any services under the stage, as well as the level of door thresholds. Raising at the front is simpler, as it means a new tapered floor can be laid over the existing stage – but it has the effect of increasing the height of the riser at the front of the stage, and this will have a greater impact on the stalls' sightlines. Solving this may involve raising the stalls floor, which in turn may have an impact on the levels of existing audience door thresholds or alternatively raising seat heights may be a less invasive option. Choosing the best option requires careful investigation of the wider implications for the sightlines, the existing building and the cost.

### Flytowers and grids

Historic theatres were mostly built with timber grids and hemp lines. Modern productions often impose much greater loads on the grid and require mechanised flying. When and how should a timber grid be replaced with a steel grid and counterweights or power flying to accommodate modern needs?

The first step is to analyse the capabilities and possibilities of the existing grid. To do this it is essential to engage a specialist structural engineer who has a clear understanding of the requirements of a theatre grid and the ability to correctly calculate the structural capacities of timber. If modifications are required for a specific production, it may be possible to introduce a temporary alteration which provides the necessary lifting capabilities. If, however, the changes are seen as an essential element to the continued use of the building as a theatre then a more radical solution may be required.

Analysis of the individual structural elements of a grid can prove to be extremely helpful. In some instances, the weakness may be contained within the grid slats rather than the timber trusses. Similarly, the timber trusses may be capable of greater lifting capacity if they can be relieved from supporting the whole of the roof load.

If in the final analysis the preferred option is wholesale replacement, then it is essential to undertake a scheme of accurate recording and, if appropriate, retention of any important historic elements. Schemes of this kind have been undertaken at both the Comedy Theatre in London and the Citizens' Theatre in Glasgow.

### Safety curtains

Under current UK fire codes, it is no longer mandatory to provide a safety curtain if other requirements such as adequate smoke extract and the use of fire-protected scenery are met. However, in an historic theatre it is important to understand that a safety curtain performs the function of protecting the built asset as well as the original primary function of audience safety. Both the Savoy Theatre and the Tyne Theatre & Opera House are historic theatres that would have been lost had a safety curtain not been in place when fires occurred.

### Historic stage machinery

Historic stage machinery and its preservation have not always received the attention they deserve. Most nineteenth- and early twentieth-century theatre equipment is inherently part of the structure of the stage house and cannot therefore be viewed as ephemeral. Whilst theatres need to evolve to meet the demands of modern technology, solutions can often be found whereby the old and the new can co-exist. Removal of sub-stage machinery is difficult to justify if it is to create new accommodation. For example, in the 1980s the whole of the original wrought iron 1878 sub-stage machinery (the first 'iron stage' in Great Britain) was removed from the Grand Theatre & Opera House in Leeds in order to create a staff canteen and rehearsal space for English National Opera North – activities which could have taken place anywhere. The loss of this machinery, and the loss of the future potential to introduce modern sub-stage machinery, are now deeply regretted.

Sensitive restoration of historic stage machinery can prove to be a positive element in a theatre restoration project. The key to delivering a balanced view is to understand the context and the significance at an early stage in any proposals to make alterations. The restoration of the stage house at the Tyne Theatre & Opera House (1867) after a disastrous fire in 1985 has proved to be a wise decision which has maintained the building's place in the highest, Grade I listed, category.

## 10.9 Re-purposing of non-theatre buildings

We have a rich heritage of old buildings which are not theatres but which no longer serve their original purpose and

Figure 10.8.1 Historic wooden stage machinery at the Tyne Theatre & Opera House (1867).

may lend themselves to conversion to provide characterful performance venues. Some of our best-loved cultural buildings, such as the legendary Roundhouse in London, have been created in reimagined existing buildings, which when carried out with skill and sensitivity have a richness and atmosphere which is hard to achieve in a new building. These are buildings which have often outlived their original purpose but which are worthy of retention, are often characterful and occupy prominent positions in towns and cities. Some may be protected, and some may not, but they all have the potential to be re-purposed, provided there is a good fit between the existing structure and the new use.

The restoration of an existing theatre building will generally be guided by the original structure with modifications to meet modern needs. However, there are many other types of existing buildings, particularly those with tall spaces and long spanning structures, which lend themselves to re-purposing as cultural facilities with performance spaces. These include town halls, churches, warehouses, industrial buildings and old cinemas. The best use for an historic building is usually its original use, but, where this is no longer viable, a new 'beneficial use' which secures the future use and upkeep of the asset will generally be supported by the conservation authorities.

These building types are unlikely to provide the facilities of a conventional theatre, particularly in the stage and backstage areas. The addition of a flytower may be necessary but often is not required. Theatre makers are increasingly interested in the opportunity to create work in non-theatre 'found spaces' where they can more easily explore alternative seating formats or promenade or immersive experiences. A large, flat-floored space with architectural character often lends itself better to this approach than a conventional theatre but will still require the discreet integration of building services, seating and technical facilities for lighting, rigging and sound systems. For example, old civic hall complexes with their range of different sized spaces, from large to small, often lend themselves well to arts centre use.

In some cases, where a conventional auditorium and stage is required, which cannot be accommodated within the existing structure, it may be possible to create them as a new extension, subject to land availability, allowing the existing building to provide foyers and other ancillary spaces. Good examples of this strategy are Storyhouse, Chester, where a new auditorium was added to an existing cinema, which was repurposed to provide foyers and a public library (see Reference Project 06) and, at a smaller scale, the Parabola Arts Centre, Cheltenham, where a new auditorium was added to a pair of listed Regency villas (see Figure 10.9.1).

Figure 10.9.1 Parabola Arts Centre, Cheltenham, showing the new auditorium linked to the existing Regency villas. Architect: Foster Wilson Size.

Polka Theatre in Wimbledon is a good example of a building built for another purpose, which has evolved over time into a modern theatre for children (see Figure 10.9.2 and *Sightline*, Winter 2021, pp. 21–25). Originally created from a 1920s church hall and an adjoining shop in 1979, it has recently been remodelled to provide two theatres, a rehearsal studio, a creative learning studio, a café and a shop, combining new construction with a re-working of the existing buildings.

When considering a re-purposing of this kind, an early feasibility study will be an important first step in analysing a building and assessing its ability to accommodate the needs of the design brief. A good fit between the two is essential to a successful outcome.

Some examples of different building types which have successfully been converted to theatre use are listed subsequently. These include fire stations, industrial buildings of all kinds, swimming pools, cinemas, churches, shops and a variety of civic buildings.

Figures 10.9.2a and 2b Views of the exterior and interior remodelled Polka Theatre. See Figure 4.10.1 for Polka's Adventure Theatre. Architect: Foster Wilson Size.

## Fire stations

- Hullabaloo Children's Theatre, Darlington (see Reference Project 07)
- Fire Station, Oxford

## Industrial buildings

- Canterbury Malthouse (King's School performing arts centre) (see Reference Project 09)
- Snape Maltings (concert hall)

- St Ann's Warehouse, Brooklyn (see Reference Project 04)
- Glasgow Tramway
- Leeds Carriageworks
- The Roundhouse, London (former railway engine shed) (see Figure 10.9.3 and Strong (ed.), *Theatre Buildings* (2010), Reference Projects, pp. 258–61)
- Woolwich Arsenal

Figure 10.9.3 Interior of The Roundhouse in performance.

## Swimming pools

- Bridewell Theatre, London
- North Wall Arts Centre at St Edward's School, Oxford

## Cinemas

- Storyhouse, Chester (see Reference Project 06)
- Stephen Joseph Theatre, Scarborough

## Churches

- Quarry Theatre at St Luke's, Bedford, Bedford School performing arts centre (see Reference Project 05)
- LSO St Luke's, London (LSO music centre); see Figure 10.9.4
- St George's Theatre, Great Yarmouth
- Tron Theatre, Glasgow

## Shopfront theatres

- Theatre Absolute, Coventry

Figure 10.9.4 Interior LSO St Luke's in performance. Architects: Levitt Bernstein

- Theatre Deli (use of old retail spaces in Sheffield; office buildings in Broadgate)

## Civic buildings

- Battersea Arts Centre, London (former town hall) (see Reference Project 25)
- Bush Theatre, London (former public library); see Figure 10.9.5.
- Royal Exchange Theatre, Manchester (former cotton exchange) (see Strong (ed.), *Theatre Buildings* (2010), Reference projects, pp. 264–65)
- Corn Exchange, King's Lynn (former corn exchange)

Figure 10.9.5 Exterior of the Bush Theatre. A public library re-purposed as a theatre. Architects: Haworth Tompkins.

## 10.10 Key points

In conclusion, there are some important key points to consider when working on the restoration or conversion of an existing building, particularly if it is an historic building.

The climate emergency is a compelling argument for the creative re-use of existing buildings, rather than their demolition. It is not only their heritage value which is important but also their embodied carbon and social value. Existing buildings, even comparatively modern ones, have a story to tell which a new building may not.

It is important to engage appropriate historic buildings experts at an early stage in the project as their research and analysis will help you to understand the form, history and development of the existing building. Discovery of historic drawings and photographs is particularly valuable, as these will often provide important knowledge about how a building has evolved and offer clues on how best to modify or restore it.

Try to work with the grain of an existing building rather than against it, allowing the form of the building to dictate design by matching new uses to existing spaces, with an understanding of the sensitivities of the existing building, based on a knowledge of what can be altered and what cannot.

Investigate the availability of adjacent land or property to allow the creation of new facilities, which the original building cannot easily accommodate. If this is possible it will allow the original to do what it was intended to do best and help to preserve its character, without unnecessary and expensive interventions.

Engage with the local planning authority, the Theatres Trust and other statutory consultees at the earliest opportunity to try to agree an acceptable design approach. These conservation authorities will generally want to support giving an existing building an appropriate and beneficial use and should be viewed as allies rather than adversaries.

Do not underestimate the cost of repairing and upgrading the building fabric, as this can often cost more than the proposed alterations to the building itself. Upgrading the thermal performance of an older structure to meet modern sustainability targets should also be a priority.

Investigate potential funding for your project. Heritage grants to address the conservation deficit of an historic building may be available but competition is often intense. The introduction of new uses which help to generate footfall and support the night-time economy may be eligible for funding aimed at the regeneration of high streets and town centres. Finally, and most importantly, funding to support energy efficiency measures which eliminate or reduce the carbon emissions of existing buildings will be, and should be, increasingly prevalent in the future.

### Section editor

Tim Foster, Architect and Founding Partner of Foster Wilson Size

### Contributors

Claire Appleby, Architectural Advisor at the Theatres Trust

Paul Gillieron, Co-Director of Gillieron Scott Acoustic Design

Nigel Nicholls, Structural Engineer, an associate at Conisbee

Mark Price, Built Heritage Specialist working in local government and in the private sector

David Wilmore, Historic Theatres Expert whose company Theatresearch has advised on many theatre restoration projects

### Contributors to first edition

Peter Longman (section editor), former Director of the Theatres Trust

John Earl, Theatre Historian and former Director of the Theatres Trust

# Section 11

# Moving forwards: a call to action

Environmental sustainability and climate change, the social agenda and engagement with communities and the digital stage and new technologies are all changing exponentially and must, as discussed in Section 3, be central to our discourse if we are to address moral imperatives and practical challenges as we design and refurbish our theatre spaces.

At the time of writing the International Theatre Engineering and Architecture Conference (ITEAC) is in planning for 2023 (itself postponed from 2022 due to the lockdowns and restrictions that were a consequence of the COVID pandemic). ITEAC is the leading international gathering for those involved in the planning, design, construction and operation of places of entertainment, and the 2023 gathering is based on the critical themes of community, sustainability and digital, very much echoing the sentiments that have been explored throughout this book. These themes are being widely discussed elsewhere, including Opera Europa (representing over 200 festivals and theatres in over forty countries), giving additional weight to our understanding that these are the most pressing of themes to pursue and to embed in our decision making. The urgency with which we must address these themes is matched by their interconnectedness, by a more holistic awareness that asks us to link environmental degradation with inequality and poverty and that connects the digital to greater inclusion.

Environmental sustainability should no longer be controversial, it is not a question of whether a drive towards sustainability should happen but one of when and how quickly. As Paddy Dillon (architect and *Theatre Green Book* coordinator) commented when discussing this section, we have a huge financial challenge in making our theatres zero (or even close to zero) carbon, and this will take theatre into difficult commercial waters: in the United Kingdom we have 700 theatres that are larger than 300 seats; this puts them beyond government support and philanthropic spending alone, and our ability to tackle the climate crisis is therefore compromised.

The connection between greater sustainability in theatre buildings and better psychological health speaks to the interconnectedness of our themes, including greater engagement with the communities that theatres serve. Britannia Morton (Co-CEO of Sadler's Wells Theatre) and lead for the client in the construction of a new theatre in London's Queen Elizabeth Olympic Park) highlights the importance of outdoor space; of openable windows, even in air conditioned spaces, as well as access to terrace spaces for all their new studios which allows for fresh air and (in a post-COVID world) easy access to the health benefits that engaging in an outdoor space can bring.

While not every theatre building can be redesigned to allow access to outdoor space, and while existing buildings are not always adaptable to a more sustainable model, we know that our productions and the stories we tell in the making of them are totemic, so our buildings do need to be more equipped for this; they need to allow us to view a production through a green prism that illuminates more than the artistic or financial benefits of a show and speaks to the leadership role that the arts plays in the life and health of our communities and our environment.

We are making headway in exploring the potential for sustainability in productions, in modular scenic designs being developed today by (among others) the Royal Opera House and the wider Opera Europa group, in how we reuse props and costumes, in how we make sets differently to make it easier to reuse materials and in how we share assets and have common stores. This narrative will increasingly inform the way we speak about how we make productions and how we should value and support creative people for being groundbreaking in terms of sustainability as well as artistic endeavour and process.

In this the *Theatre Green Book* (a volume each for Productions, Buildings and Operations) emphasises collaboration across the creative industries both in the sharing of resources and reusing materials but also in the gathering and sharing of data and best practice. There is progress in how we value and measure our productions to include more than carbon calculation and setting carbon budgets, a narrative change which enables us to tell stories about the ethical changes we have made, even about the decision not to do something or to do it differently. Feimatta Conteh (sustainability manager at Factory International)

DOI: 10.4324/9781003327295-11

says 'sustainability is a journey, a series of steps forwards, and should be inclusive, accessible, and address social justice'.

This speaks to the value of found spaces too, of work produced to be performed in unconventional and outdoor spaces, so that we join the threads of all aspects of theatre making; the performance space, the experience of the audience and the multiplicity of uses a building can have to serve the life of its communities. In using external and found spaces, however, we must be mindful of the need of many to access live performance with private transport or the unsuitability of some spaces for large sections of the population in terms of rest facilities, the impossibility of spending time in cold spaces or standing-only experiences. While such spaces are great for creative communities they do not allow for as wide a range of patrons as possible to engage independently (Robin Townley, CEO of ABTT). While 20% of the UK population is D/deaf, disabled or neurodiverse, we have a moral and commercial imperative to address the needs of all (Andrew Miller, cultural consultant and broadcaster, chair of the National Council's Disability Advisory Group), we should embed consultation in capital projects, and we should give the greatest number of people the best possible access to see live performance.

While live performance is worth preserving, and there are empathetic and synchronous effects in the experience of live audiences, the growth of the digital stage, by necessity accelerated during the COVID-19 pandemic, has allowed for more opportunities to break the line of the proscenium, to explore the immersive and to be more democratic in our offers to our audiences. While technology has allowed us to be more inclusive, to reach communities and individuals who may not have been able to access live theatre either physically or financially, the pandemic demonstrated that we crave the immersive, the communal, the live experience. Technology can be used to capture that sense of the live, to stream a sense of the moment without extensive post-production, and we should not revert to business as usual and lose the positive benefits and the sense of community that broadcasting into the home has brought to so many throughout the pandemic.

Our challenge with the growth of the digital stage and the technology we embed in our theatres must be how we harness technology to enhance the communal experience, how the digital is not merely a conduit of live performance but a valid experience in itself. 'Theatre is made, managed, and run by those who are used to going to the theatre' (Paddy Dillon), but COVID has turned the dial on the role that the digital stage can play in our lives. In an increasingly digital world it is not an either/or mentality that is needed but one which embraces a multiplicity of opportunities for a wider variety of communities. Those generations who have grown up in a digital and gaming world are more comfortable with complexity and want to be more engaged themselves. This is nothing new – the sense of sitting quietly in a dark space being passively entertained is not the only way, and is in fact a relatively modern way, of experiencing theatre.

Theatre is in an unsustainable place in terms of how it is funded, the age of its audience, and state of its buildings, but we can see these as opportunities and shift towards doing it differently. While regional theatre is in crisis with very small audiences, no support and funding and ageing buildings, theatres can be more multipurpose. This brings in new income streams but also gives us the opportunity to bring communities in throughout the day, instead of just at performance times, and to serve those communities more generously. (See Figures 11.1 and 11.2.)

In exploring other uses of our buildings we must also use the COVID pandemic as a wake-up call to seriously engage with all our audiences. Building in digital capacity at design stage to a highly sophisticated degree should be a given, not just a means to broadcast shows for another income stream. COVID has transformed the landscape of theatre particularly for the disabled, but the advantages to these groups afforded by distancing and face coverings have been overlooked, and we run the risk of the clinically vulnerable not returning to theatres (Andrew Miller). Buildings remain inaccessible, particularly backstage and administrative areas, and while the theatre sector has not historically responded well to the requirements of D/deaf, disabled and neurodiverse audiences, employees and artists, now is the time to go beyond guidance or regulations and take into account the needs of all.

Figure 11.1 Storyhouse in Chester is a cultural centre developed from a 1930s cinema that now incorporates two theatres, a cinema, restaurant and bars, and also a library with the longest opening hours of any UK library, open until 11pm every day. It also runs over 2,000 sessions a year for marginalised communities and allows the community to programme and create work wherever it can. (See Section 1, Figures 1.2.2, 1.8.2a and 1.8.2b, Section 4, Figure 4.9.1 and Reference Project 06.)

Figure 11.2 The Royal Opera House in Covent Garden, London, is open all day for tours and exhibitions, daytime performances, workshops, food and drink and a sustainably stocked shop. From 2015–2018 architects Stanton Williams opened up the foyer spaces and terraces with new bars, cafés and restaurants as well as refurbishing the Linbury Theatre as a sustainable 400-seat, walnut-panelled, intimate space with excellent acoustics much loved by directors, composers, choreographers, performers and audiences. The marble and wood foyer leading into the Linbury Theatre is often used for free lunchtime performances. Architects: Stanton Williams.

Theatre is 'an over stretched cottage industry making astonishing, complex and ambitious things for not many people' (Paddy Dillon). As we face a global climate crisis, address the long-term wellness and psychological safety of our communities and embrace the exponential growth of digital innovation, we know we must answer the call to action of this generation of architects, designers, technicians and engineers. There is nothing more important than the ethical considerations, safety principles and moral imperatives that must become the prevalent themes of our discourse around how we design, build, and use our places of entertainment. Only then can our theatres and the work that happens within (and without) them remain relevant, searching, challenging and life affirming.

The key themes and issues explored here are represented in aspects of some of the theatres in the following Reference Projects.

## Section editor

Emma Wilson, Director of Technical, Production and Costume at the Royal Opera House, London

## In conversation with (in alphabetical order)

Feimatta Conteh, Sustainability Manager at Manchester International Festival

Paddy Dillon, Architect and *Theatre Green Book* coordinator

Andrew Miller, Cultural Consultant and Broadcaster, chair of the National Council's Disability Advisory Group

Britannia Morton, Co-CEO of Sadler's Wells Theatre and client lead in the construction of their new theatre in London's Queen Elizabeth Olympic Park

Robin Townley, CEO of the ABTT

# Reference projects

## Project selection and process of documentation

The thirty-two reference projects that follow, all new to this edition of *Theatre Buildings: a Design Guide*, have been included as representative of the increasingly pressing challenges faced by those who have undertaken new build theatres or who have engaged in theatre renovations or restorations since 2010. The six categories of developments, and the theatres selected from them, are listed on the preceding page: arguably each category represents an emerging trend. Collectively they represent responses to the 'key themes' discussed in the previous sections, although few, if any, offer solutions to all aspects of the challenges presented by the need for theatres to play their part in the social, economic, cultural and environmental issues that many perceive to be so central not just to theatre and other performance venues but to wider developments in the built environment and the related needs of community and placemaking, inclusivity and diversity, access and wellbeing. These issues, which have been gaining traction since the millennium, have been highlighted further by the sense of loss and isolation that were the inevitable consequences of the restrictions and lockdowns imposed as a response to the COVID pandemic that has formed the backdrop to the preparation of this new edition.

The days of theatres in the United Kingdom and abroad opening to the public only for performances, and in the hours immediately preceding and following those performances, are numbered. Theatres are increasingly playing their part in both the daytime and night-time economies and experiences of their communities and visitors. They are part, too, of a wider cultural heritage and storytelling instinct. The very presence of theatres and other performance venues in capital cities, cities of culture and regional urban and rural centres increasingly provides focus and inspiration, inclusive creative and technical environments, educational spaces and shared resources for performance, wellbeing and social interaction.

## The selection

The editorial team consulted widely before settling on thirty-two projects to feature here. They include one or more theatres that opened in each year from 2010 to 2022, with the notable exception of 2020 (the year that felt much of the impact of COVID-19), with venues from each of the countries in the United Kingdom, alongside four located in the US, France and Taiwan, drawing audiences that are local, national and international from children and young people to students, families and life-long theatregoers.

They range from small, temporary, pop-up theatres, through existing buildings repurposed as theatres, new build theatres (small and medium) and arts centres, to historic theatres that have been remodelled or restored. Some include multiple adaptable venues, inside and outside their buildings: performance spaces in various formats, studios and rehearsal rooms, welcoming foyers, cafés, bars and restaurants, cinemas and galleries, conference and events spaces, libraries, book and gift shops, creative play areas and spaces for community arts, craft groups and accessible facilities for parent/carers and children. Increasingly their offerings include relaxed performances in welcoming spaces as well as consciously inclusive wayfinding and signs accessible to those with limited vision, hearing or mobility.

## The process

Once the reference project theatres had been identified, the process of gathering information about the buildings was undertaken to represent each in text, images, drawings and diagrams. Each project team was invited to send us details in response to the same points: a brief building description, the auditorium type(s), the design intent, specific features/strengths and users' verdicts. We also asked for detailed 'key facts' to allow readers to compare the projects and to understand the main characteristics of the different development initiatives, as well as a selection of images to enable us to illustrate each project as clearly as possible.

## Reference project drawings

Architectural drawings were sourced from the theatres' design teams and were received in a varying state of complexity and style. These drawings have been edited to give them consistency and enable the reader to make an accurate assessment of the unique characteristics of each building.

Each project is presented in a plan and section of the overall building showing the main areas of interest. For most theatres the main spaces for attention are the stage area, the areas that show the most intense backstage activity and the main concentration of public engagement. However, this is not the case for all the projects. In some examples, the most interesting aspects of design are connected to the supporting spaces found within the building and not the main auditorium. The third drawing included for each project is the site plan. This provides important context about the location of the building. Some theatres are set in a busy urban context; others, like the Cloud Gate Dance Theatre, are set in a green rural landscape. It is important that the reader get a feeling for the environment of each building. Some of the theatres among these reference projects are capable of a wide variety of performance formats and so, in some cases, additional diagrams are included that illustrate the flexibility of these spaces.

The scale of the drawings is an important factor. All buildings are shown at the same scale so that direct comparison can be made between them with respect to size and complexity. A common 1:500 scale (1 millimetre on the page equates to 500 millimetres of the full-size building) has been used for the plans and sections, with 1:2500 scale (1 millimetre on the site plan equates to 2500 millimetres on the full-size site) for the site plans. The format diagrams are not given at a particular scale; the important information is the layout of the stage and seating with the size having already been shown in the other drawings. The scale of the drawings is constrained by the page size of the book. The intense detail of the architectural drawings is not readable/legible in this format. It has therefore been necessary to remove much of the finer detail from the drawings. However, traces of the theatres' interior details have been retained to convey the unique characteristics of the spaces.

Finally, the style and annotation of the drawings remain consistent with line styles and line scales that allow sufficient detail. The drawings are mainly monochromatic to give a simple overall appearance with shading kept to a minimum and being used to focus attention on the important areas of the drawing. The tools that aid understanding of the drawings such as the north point and the scale bar are provided for every project and labelling of spaces is done by numbering areas that relate back to a key positioned to the side. The key attempts to follow a pattern whenever possible so that the main spaces of the theatre are easily identifiable.

## Captions and additional information

The photographs used in these projects each have their figure number and photographer's credit immediately below the image. The captions are gathered together at the end of the second 'Key Facts' column on the opening spread of each project, so as not to intrude into the main presentation of the project while allowing sufficient space for descriptive captions.

Where available, the same 'Key Facts' column includes details of articles on that project featured in *Sightline*, the ABTT's journal of theatre technology and design.

Margaret Shewring and David Hamer

# List of projects

Please note that the dates given after the name of each build or restoration project indicate the opening date of the project venue.

### Small/temporary/pop-up theatres

RP.01 **Garsington Opera**, Wormsley: 2011
RP.02 **The Shed at the National Theatre**, London: 2013–2017

### Existing buildings repurposed as theatres

RP.03 **Arcola Theatre**, London: 2012
RP.04 **St Ann's Warehouse**, Brooklyn, New York: 2015
RP.05 **The Quarry Theatre at St Luke's**, Bedford: 2015
RP.06 **Storyhouse**, Chester: 2017
RP.07 **Hullabaloo children's theatre**, Darlington: 2018
RP.08 **Nevill Holt Opera**: 2018
RP.09 **The Malthouse**, Canterbury: 2019

### New build theatres/small

RP.10 **Sam Wanamaker Playhouse**, London: 2014
RP.11 **Le Théâtre Elisabéthain du Château d'Hardelot**, Condette, France: 2016
RP.12 **Tara Theatre**, London: 2016
RP.13 **Boulevard Theatre**, Soho: 2019

### New build theatres/medium

RP.14 **Lyric Theatre**, Belfast: 2011
RP.15 **CAST**, Doncaster: 2013
RP.16 **The Dorfman Theatre and Max Rayne Centre**, NT, London: 2014
RP.17 **Liverpool Everyman Theatre**, Liverpool: 2014
RP.18 **Cloud Gate Dance Theatre (雲門劇場)**, Taipei: 2015
RP.19 **The Yard at Chicago Shakespeare Theater**: 2017
RP.20 **Bridge Theatre**, London: 2017
RP.21 **Riverside Studios**, London: 2019

### Arts centres

RP.22 **The MAC**, Belfast: 2012
RP.23 **HOME**, Manchester: 2015
RP.24 **Pontio Arts and Innovation Centre**, Bangor, Wales: 2016
RP.25 **Battersea Arts Centre**, London: 2018
RP.26 **Brixton House**, London: 2022

### Historic theatres remodelled/restored

RP.27 **Royal Shakespeare Theatre**, Stratford-upon-Avon: 2010
RP.28 **Wilton's Music Hall**: hall, 2013; houses, 2018
RP.29 **Theatre Royal, Glasgow**: foyer, 2014
RP.30 **Victoria Palace Theatre**, London: 2017
RP.31 **Bristol Old Vic**: 2018
RP.32 **Theatre Royal Drury Lane**, London: 2021

# Small/temporary/pop-up theatres

# Reference Project 01
# Garsington Opera Pavilion, Wormsley, UK

### Brief building description

The 600-seat summer Opera Pavilion at Wormsley is situated within a pastoral country estate, on a grand scale. It is conceived in the English tradition of a pavilion in the landscape (see Figure RP.01.01) and provides a new home for Garsington Opera, forty miles from their original site, enabling them to significantly upgrade their facilities in line with the expectations of twenty-first-century opera goers.

Figure RP.01.01 Photo © Richard Davies.

The new pavilion offers better acoustics, increased comfort and a perfect setting in which to experience opera performances of the very highest quality during the summer months. It was designed to be demountable, adaptable and experimental, a 'pop-up' rig for opera, and to leave no permanent trace once removed (see Figure RP.01.02).

Figure RP.01.02 Photo © Dennis Gilbert.

### Key facts

**Client**
Garsington Opera
Anthony Whitworth-Jones, former General Director
(from inception to completion of the Opera House)
Nicky Creed, Executive Director (Current)

**Site address/web reference**
Garsington Opera Pavilion,
Wormsley Estate,
Buckinghamshire,
HP14 3YG
www.garsingtonopera.org

**Opening date**
May 2011

**Auditorium type and seating capacity**
Auditorium: end stage
seating capacity: 628

**Stage/performance space size**
Stage size: 20.7m wide × 10.1m deep

**Other facilities:**
Not applicable. Some nearby buildings on the estate are used as dressing rooms and other back-up spaces.

**Overall area**
2,065m$^2$ (GIA)

**Design team**
**Architect:** Robin Snell and Partners
**Theatre consultant:** Iain Mackintosh
**Acoustic consultant:** Sound Space Vision
**Structural engineer:** Momentum
**Services engineer:** Buro Happold
**Cost consultant:** Gardiner & Theobald
**CDM co-ordinator:** Gardiner & Theobald
**Main contractor:** Unusual Rigging

**Construction cost at completion date (excluding fees and VAT)** £1.8 million (£872/m$^2$)

The Pavilion has won many national and international awards (eight in total), including three Royal Institute of British Architects Awards, Civic Trust and United States Institute for Theatre Technology Awards.

As part of winning the 2012 British Construction Industry Award for Best Building Under £3 million the client rated their satisfaction with the end product as 10/10.

See *Sightline*, Summer 2011, pp. 13–16.

**The five figures** show the Garsington Opera Pavilion's location in a country estate where it fits comfortably in its natural rural surroundings. **The first two images** (01, 02) show the opera pavilion across the lake and from Home Farm, while **the third** (03) shows the opera pavilion by night when it appears to 'float' over the landscape. This summer pavilion has equally impressive views from the auditorium out across the landscape, as in **the fourth image** (04) taken during a rehearsal in the auditorium, with a view across the stage. **The final image** (05) looks down on the innovative double-fabric roof.

### Auditorium type/types

The new auditorium was planned on similar lines to the company's previous auditorium at Garsington Manor, while providing 600 seats and six wheelchair positions. Both seat widths and leg room have been increased in the new house to improve audience comfort. Audience sightlines to the stage are very good. The width of the new auditorium is similar to old Garsington, and the rear wall is only two rows further back. The feeling and intimacy of the space have been retained, and the auditorium ceiling and walls have been specially designed to improve the room acoustic.

The ha-ha, separating the home farm buildings and main house from the park itself, follows the contours of the land and naturally creates the orchestra pit and under-stage trap room.

### Design intent

The Pavilion occupies a commanding yet intimate and sheltered position within Wormsley estate, with views over Home Farm and the lake. It is conceived as an elegant lightweight pavilion within a parkland setting, elevated above the ground and giving the appearance of 'floating' above the landscape (see Figure RP.01.03). It features covered verandas and terraces, which contain bars and places to linger and enjoy the views.

Figure RP.01.03 Photo Wiki/MikeHoban.

The auditorium design takes its cue from a traditional Japanese pavilion, such as the Katsura Palace west of Kyoto, in its relationship to its landscape setting and its use of sliding screens and verandas to link it to the landscape, both visually and physically.

### Specific features/strengths

Designed from first principles to be a totally flexible rig for artistic performance, entertainment and creativity, and able to change and adapt to future needs, the Pavilion was designed to be demountable, moved, reconfigured and re-erected either on the same site or potentially elsewhere. The innovative design of the building allows the audience to experience opera to a high standard in an intimate setting while also maintaining views out to the surrounding landscape (see Figure RP.01.04). The modular approach to design enables the theatre to be adapted to changing needs for different performance and artistic ambition but also allows systems such as electrical and lighting control equipment to be upgraded or replaced easily with no disruption or damage to the building fabric. A unique aspect of the design of the opera pavilion is that it is the first time that an auditorium has been created using a lightweight construction of steel and fabric to provide world class acoustic performance standards.

Figure RP.01.04 Photo © Dennis Gilbert.

Figure RP.01.05 Photo © Robin Snell and Partners.

**Users' verdicts**

First opened in 2011, the Pavilion is extremely popular with audiences and has been unanimously well received by the national and international arts press. Jonathan Glancey wrote in *The Guardian* that 'this pop-up opera house in the heart of the English countryside is one of the most thrilling venues in Britain', a sentiment extended by Rupert Christiansen in *The Daily Telegraph* who saw the Pavilion in its landscape as 'a new candidate for the accolade of Most Beautiful Opera House in the World' and awarded it 5 stars for its design.

A glassy, light-filled pavilion theatre which achieves an intimacy rarely possible at any other performance of such world-class calibre. *The Independent*

The enclosing clear fabric walls of the auditorium use stressed fabric sails, like windsurfer sails, shaped to enhance the room acoustic, and a double-layer fabric roof absorbs rain noise like the flysheet of a tent, reducing rain noise by 50% or 14dB. (See Figure RP.01.05.) Both these were subject to extensive research and development, mock-ups and acoustic testing to optimise the design before construction.

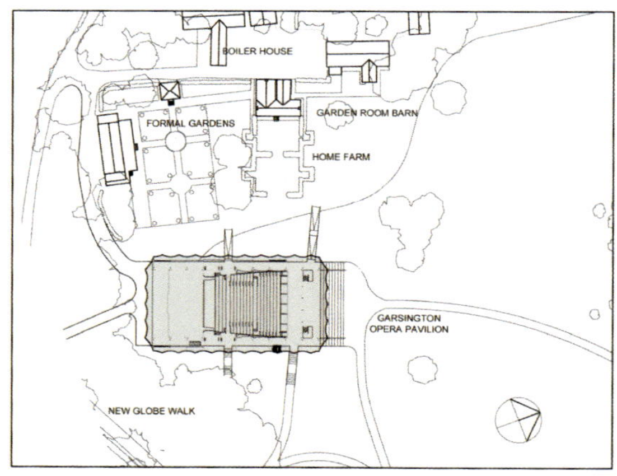


SITE PLAN - 1:2500

KEY
1 - STAGE
2 - AUDITORIUM
3 - FOYER - UPPER AND LOWER TERRACE
4 - CONTROL ROOM
5 - GET IN
6 - RAMP TO DRESSING ROOMS
7 - UNDERSTAGE
8 - ORCHESTRA PIT
9 - BACKSTAGE
10 - ENTRANCE STAIRCASE
11 - PICNIC STEPS
12 - VERANDA

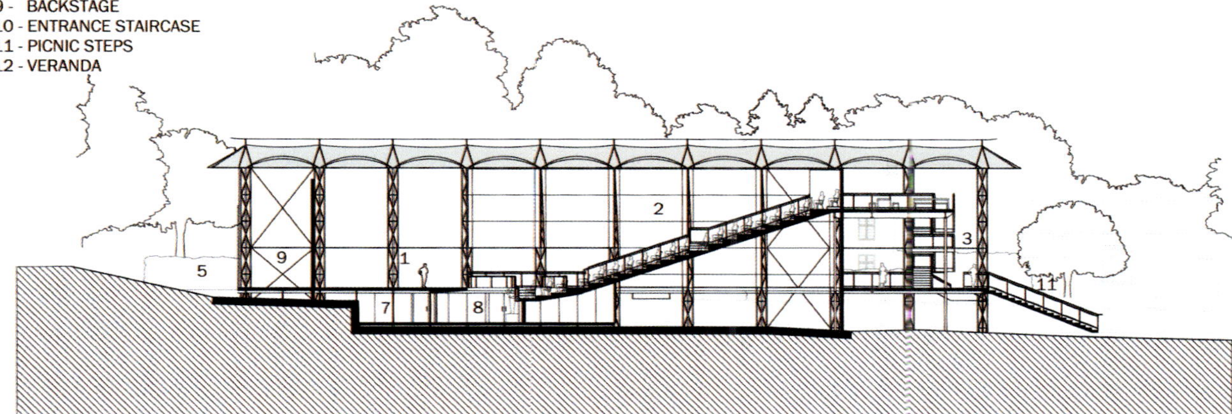

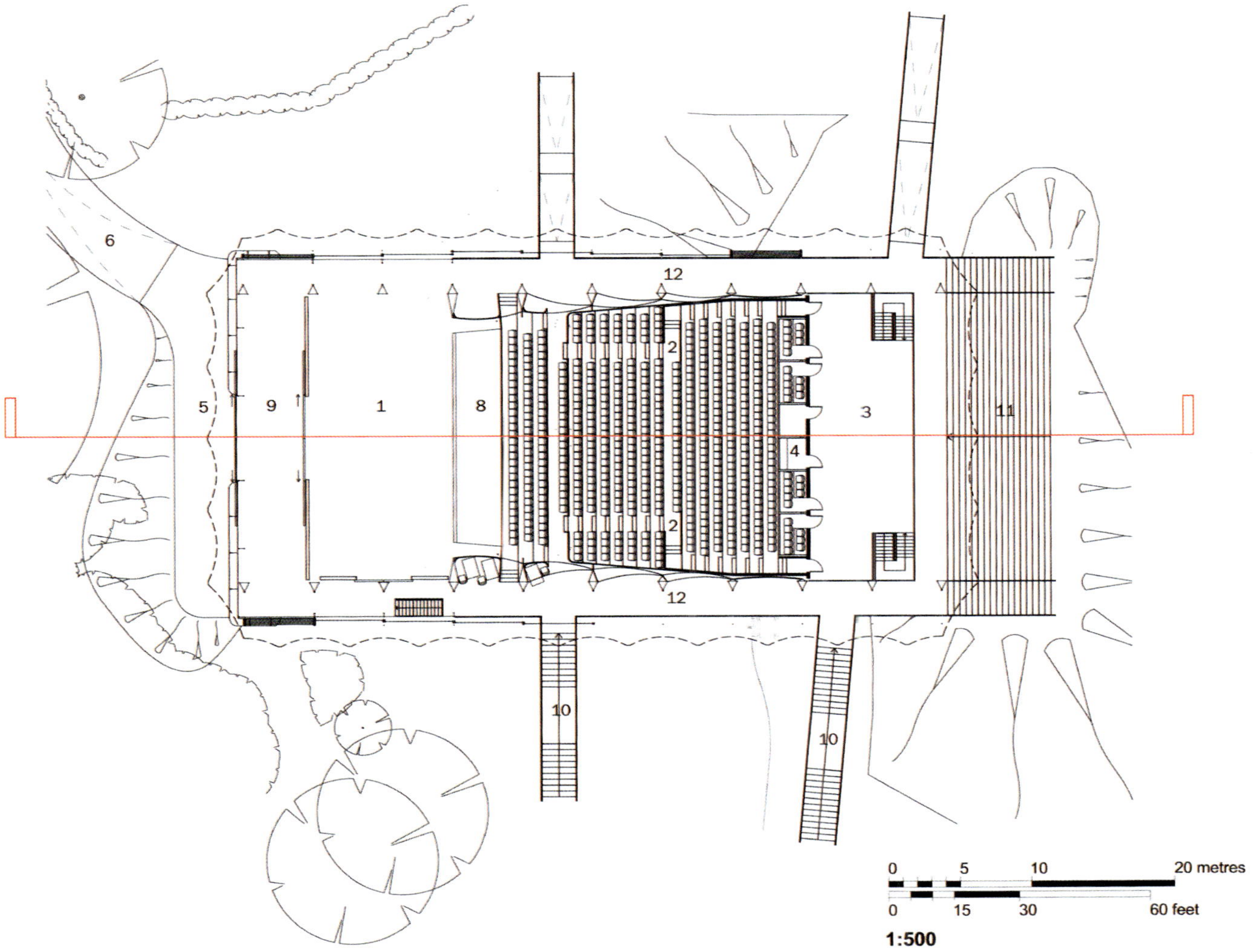

6
12
2
5
9
1
8
3
11
4
2
12
10
10

0 5 10 20 metres
0 15 30 60 feet
1:500

# Reference Project 02
# The Shed at the National Theatre, London, UK

### Brief building description

The Shed at the National Theatre was a temporary theatre building to provide a third auditorium while the Cottesloe theatre was being refurbished. It was formed of a new flexible auditorium structure and an associated foyer including its own bar and box office. (See Figures RP.02.01 and RP.02.02). The foyer was set below the existing terrace overhead with direct access from the South Bank as well as from the main Lyttelton foyer. The larger volume of the auditorium, clad in red painted timber boards, was designed to be a striking temporary installation for the South Bank area, viewable from Waterloo Bridge and the upper terraces of the NT.

### Auditorium type

The auditorium is a courtyard style flexible space allowing both thrust (see Figure RP.02.03) and in-the-round formats with a single gallery level.

### Design intent

As the Cottesloe Theatre was due to be closed for roughly a year for refurbishment as part of the NT Future works, The Shed allowed the National Theatre to keep the programme of its third auditorium running during the closure (for the Cottesloe see Strong (ed.), *Theatre Buildings* (2010), reference project pp. 210–11 and for the refurbished space, renamed The Dorfman, see Reference Project 16). In the end, The Shed was onsite from 2013–2017.

### Specific features/strengths

The auditorium seating was reclaimed from the Cottesloe Theatre.

**Key facts**

**Client**
The National Theatre

**Site address/web reference**
The National Theatre, South Bank, London. SE1 9PX
www.nationaltheatre.org.uk

**Opening date**
2013

**Auditorium type and seating capacity**
Thrust total:
217 (or 205 + 6 disabled) seats
In-the-round total:
277 (or 265 + 6 disabled) seats

**Stage/performance space size**
Thrust format:
6m wide × 9m deep
In-the-round format:
6m wide × 6m deep

**Other facilities**
Dressing room, foyer, bar and box office

Figure RP.02.01 Photo © Philip Vile/Haworth Tompkins.

**Overall area**
628m² (GIA)

**Design team**
**Architect:** Haworth Tompkins
**Theatre consultant:** Charcoalblue
**Acoustic consultant:** Arup Acoustic
**Services engineer:** Ingleton Wood
**Structural engineer:** Flint & Neill Ltd
**Fire engineers:** Lawrence Webster Forrest
**Quantity surveyors:** Gardiner & Theobald
**Access consultant:** All Clear Designs
**Main contractor:** Rise Contracts

**Construction cost at completion date (excluding fees and VAT):**
£1.2 million

See *Sightline*, Summer 2013, pp. 14–17.

**The five figures** capture the distinctive atmosphere of The Shed. **The first** (01) shows its red walls and towers outside the NT's foyer. **The second** (02) shows The Shed's foyer space with its rug and wooden furniture setting it apart from the main National Theatre foyer spaces. **The third** (03) shows The Shed in use for a performance with the audience seated on three sides. **The last two images** (04, 05) were taken at the final celebrations before The Shed was closed.

Figure RP.02.02 Photo © Philip Vile/Haworth Tompkins.

Figure RP.02.03 Photo © Philip Vile/Haworth Tompkins.

The auditorium was designed to be fully naturally ventilated. Chris McDougal has commented that 'the natural ventilation used the chimney stack effect and was wonderfully easy to operate (one dial), incredibly responsive, environmentally friendly and tremendously cost effective'.

The Shed was a lightweight temporary intervention within the existing Theatre Square. This allowed the dismantling of the building with minimal impact on the existing building at the end of its run.

**Users' verdicts**

This is a building that opens your heart before you get into the auditorium. It's a building that enables invention.

Susannah Clapp, *The Observer*.

The Shed is a technically flexible, efficient and immensely practical working theatre, but also one that has without doubt captivated all of those who have been lucky enough to work in and watch productions in it. On a technical level the de-mountable balcony rigging positions, the primary lighting/sound rig and the various other rated rigging positions offer lighting and sound designers a varied palette of creative choices while offering the technical staff multiple solutions to fulfil their ideas.

Chris McDougall, Technical Manager of The Shed Theatre, after its first ten months of operation (February 2014).

Figure RP.02.05 Photo © Andy Hayles.

Figure RP.02.04 Photo © Andy Hayles.

The Shed has been a lung grafted onto the side of the National Theatre. This scruffy, open-hearted, honest, space heralded a new start for the NT. It's meant that this scruffy, open-hearted, honest person could become the Artistic Director of the National Theatre.

Rufus Norris, first person to direct in The Shed, later Artistic Director of the NT, said this at the celebration for the space (May 2016)

KEY
1 - STAGE
2 - AUDITORIUM
3 - FOYER
4 - AUDITORIUM LOBBY
5 - EXISTING LITTLETON FOYER
6 - DRESSING ROOM
7 - MAIN ENTRANCE
8 - TOILET
9 - THEATRE SQUARE
10 - EXISTING CAFE
11 - BAR

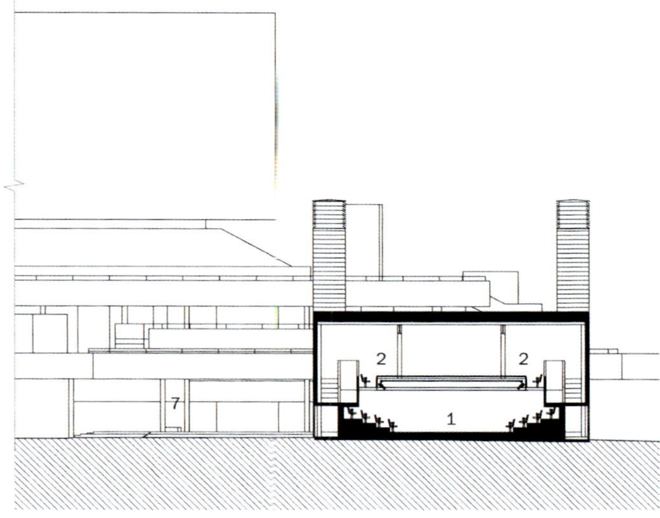


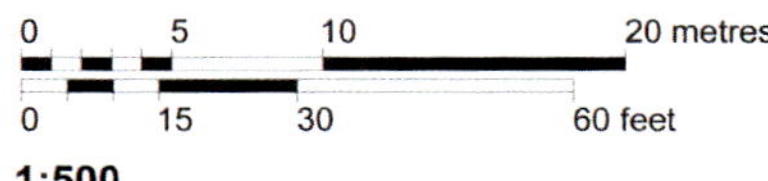


**1:500**

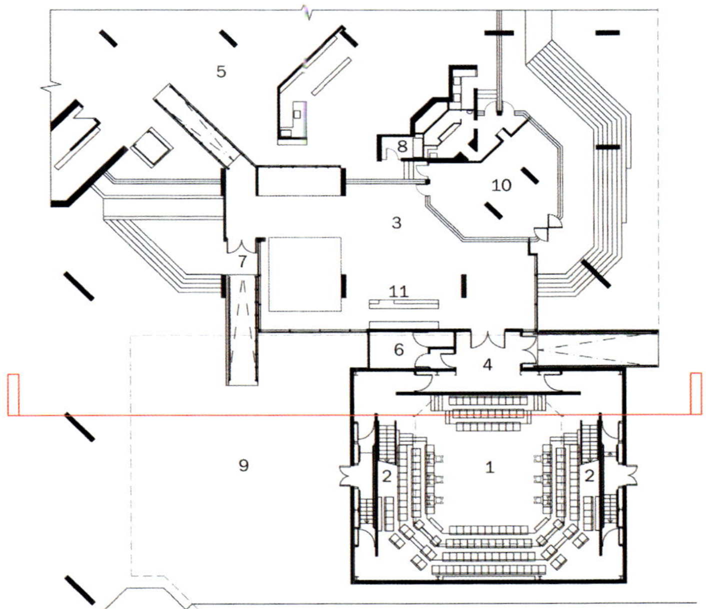


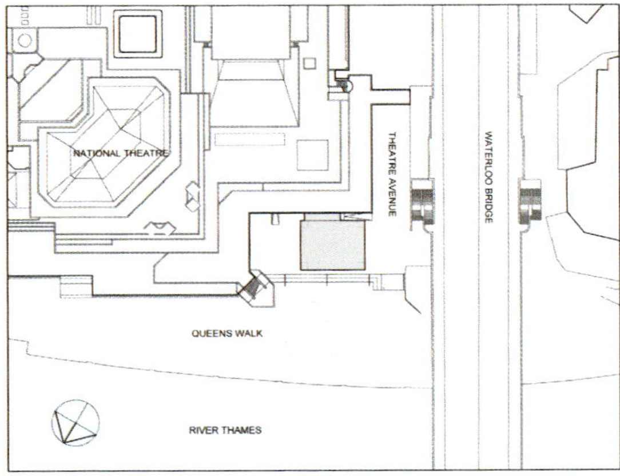


**SITE PLAN - 1:2500**

# Existing buildings repurposed as theatres

# Reference Project 03
# Arcola Theatre, London, UK

### Brief building description

Arcola Theatre is a producing and receiving theatre, in Dalston East London, with two studio performance spaces, rehearsal and meeting rooms and offices. It is located in the Colourworks, the former Reeves Watercolour paint factory, built around 1868.

In January 2011, Arcola Theatre marked its eleventh anniversary by moving from its original clothes-factory home on Arcola Street to the Colourworks. The basement, ground and first floors of the building were initially converted with the aid of many volunteers and the financial assistance of Arcola's loyal patrons, getting the building open in just a few weeks (including organising a parade of around one hundred supporters to carry furniture and small items to the new site). The unsatisfactory layout meant an obstacle course had to be negotiated to get to the toilets. There was no sound proofing for the studios and only space for about ten people to sit down in the bar. Performers had to change in a cubby hole in the basement. Buckets came out when it rained.

An Arts Council England capital grant of £1 million in 2012 enabled a more thorough refurbishment to make the building more suitable including the most urgently required works to improve function, comfort and accessibility. The Arcola team invited local volunteers on Open Saturdays, involving them in physical works and encouraging a sense of ownership of the building. Using local companies, volunteers and donations, the team's estimate is that they delivered at least £1.25 million worth of works.

### Auditorium type/types

2 studios:

- Studio 1 was created by removing a floor and reconfiguring access, including the installation of a permanent balcony, and incorporating original features from its former life as a paint factory (see Figure RP.03.01).
- Studio 2 was newly created through a process of excavation and demolition, underpinning of walls and better sound insulation.

Figure RP.03.01 Photo © Lidia Crisafulli.

### Key facts

**Client**
Arcola Theatre (Ben Todd)

**Site address/web reference**
24 Ashwin Street,
London, E8 3DL
www.arcolatheatre.com/

**Opening date**
3 October 2012

**Auditorium type and seating capacity**
Studio 1: Thrust stage with a balcony and a mezzanine; max capacity 197
Studio 2: Brick and concrete box, thrust seating layout; capacity: 100

**Stage/performance space size**
Studio 1 stage size: 5.9m × 6.3m plus balcony of 4.5m × 2.1m
Studio 1 in-the-round configuration: 5.9m × 4.0m
Studio 2 stage size: 7.5m × 4.9m

**Other facilities**
Two rehearsal rooms, three office areas
Two meeting rooms, foyer and bar

**Overall area**
Approximately 1,400m$^2$ over three floors

**Design team**
**Architect:** Arcola team supported by Cragg Management
**Theatre consultant:** Informal input from Neill Woodger and Alex Wardle
**Acoustic consultant:** Neill Woodger
**Fire strategy:** Andy Passingham, Buro Happold. Informal structural input from various Arup engineers
**Main contractor:** Arcola Theatre Production Company

**Construction cost at completion date**
(excluding fees and VAT): £1.2 million

### Design intent

The completed building is a visceral implementation of the principle 'we shape our buildings; thereafter they shape us'. The project was developed by the Arcola team with a self-design, self-build approach, based on the practical realisation that they were the best placed to create, then re-create the spaces they needed to thrive – making exceptional creative spaces at very low cost because they needed only to be 'good enough'. Flexibility in the design process led to decisions being discussed across the staff team in a collaborative and consultative process.

Arcola's message to audiences ahead of the 2012 refurbishments explained: 'we will be re-using, recycling and calling on the services of volunteers once more. But we promise that there will be nice toilets and a more spacious foyer!' (See Figure RP.03.02.)

### Specific features/strengths

The former paint factory was remodelled to ensure the two main performance spaces had acoustic separation, while sound proofing was also improved to the Bloomberg Arts Lab in Studios 3 and 4 to provide better space for rehearsals, youth theatre work, and other learning and community activities. More, and better, toilets were installed in a better location and level access was created throughout, as well as making the building less of a labyrinth to navigate. A new central staircase was created along with a new entrance on the west side of the building and a wheelchair accessible lift was installed serving all floors of the building.

Figure RP.03.02 Photo © Lidia Crisafulli.

Studio 2 was lowered one floor into the basement (see Figure RP.03.03), and all dressing rooms and back-of-house areas were expanded and refurbished.

A crucial aim of the project was to honour the history of the building. The appearance of the Watercolour paint factory with its double-height north-facing windows was maintained as were some specific original features including the old sprinkler system in the corner of Studio 3 and the barrel-vaulted concrete ceiling in Studio 2. The original Crittall steel windows were replaced with sympathetic double-glazing.

**The four figures** show the two studio spaces as well as foyer areas. **The first figure** (01) shows Studio 1 and **the third** (03) shows Studio 2. Each is a flexible performance space backed by reclaimed brick and panelled walls. **Figures two and four** (02, 04) show different areas within the foyers, each low-ceilinged and snug, with colourful decorations and a cosy, welcoming atmosphere.

Figure RP.03.03 Photo © Lidia Crisafulli.

Material reuse and a raw finish were important both as an aesthetic and a financial choice. This led to the reuse of over 10,000 bricks, so new walls matched the originals, as well as saving money and avoiding emissions from the manufacture and transport of new bricks. The brickwork across the building was cleaned to eliminate the need for painting and plastering saving weeks of work and significant cost. The factory's original timber joists were re-used in staircase supports and doorframes. (See Figure RP.03.04.) As part of the Olympic legacy and sustainability programme, Arcola received 450 sheets of used plywood from the Olympic Park. All of this resulted in raw finishes – bare brick, plywood, unpolished concrete – reducing the need for other high-spec finishes.

Figure RP.03.04 Photo © Lidia Crisafulli.

**Sustainability**

Long-term sustainability has been ensured with the installation of low-carbon heating, ventilation and lighting throughout and the integration of innovative low-carbon technology, including:

- waste wood-fired heating system
- solar heated domestic hot water system
- solar photo-voltaic panels; DC microgrids + battery storage: DC microgrids were connected to solar PV panels, enabling smarter energy management from hybrid sources, powering LED lights and laptops from DC-integrated desks
- assisted natural ventilation in Studio 1.

**Users' verdicts**

We succeeded in maintaining the ethos of the old Arcola whilst moving location and growing.

Abdulla Tercanli, Trustee and member of Arcola Ala Turka participation group

Last night saw a double celebration: the official gala reopening of the Arcola in its new, more central, and easily accessible location (opposite Dalston Junction overland), and the UK professional première of *Sweet Smell of Success* (book by John Guare, show based on the 1957 Hollywood film version). Venue and show are mentioned as one because, for this production, they inform each other so successfully; in this intimate 200-seat former paint factory with horseshoe shaped auditorium, exposed brick walls, tables with lights – and with a hard-working and talented live band on view in a little glass cubicle above the stage area – we could be in an off-Broadway jazz venue in the 1950s.

*British Theatre Guide* (Nov. 2012) review of *Sweet Smell of Success*

KEY
1 - STUDIO 1
2 - STUDIO 2
3 - FOYER
4 - CONTROL ROOM
5 - REHEARSAL ROOM
6 - DRESSING ROOMS
7 - BAR
8 - TOILETS
9 - STORE

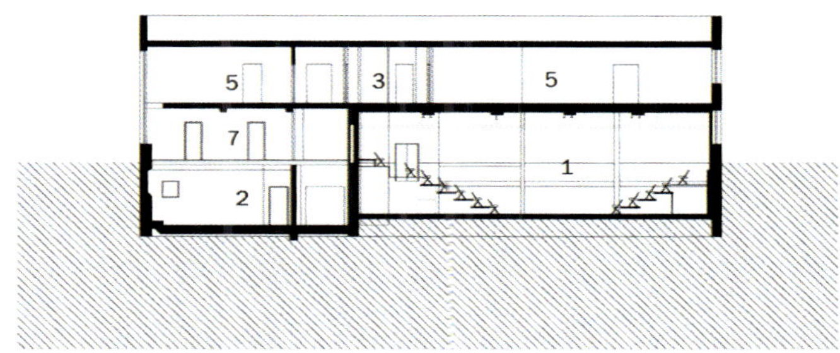


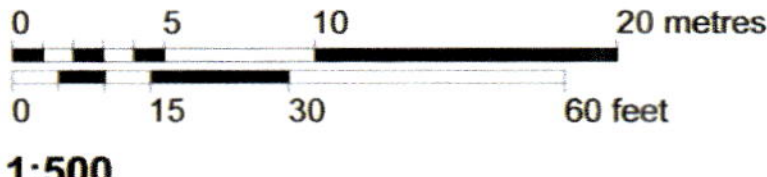


**1:500**

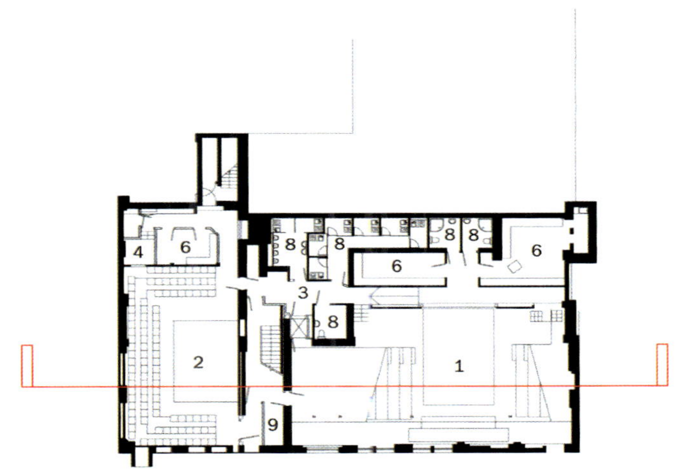


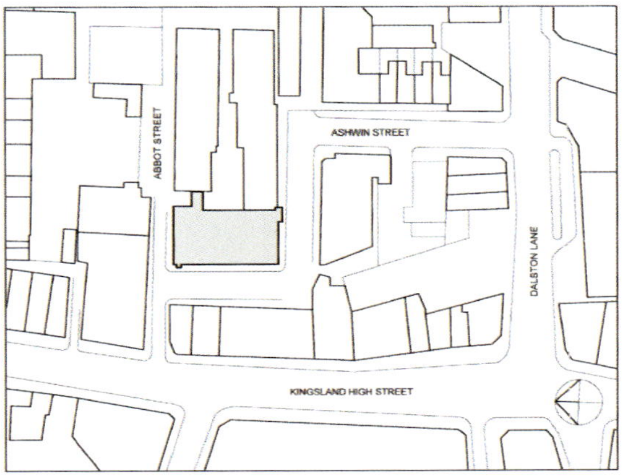


**SITE PLAN - 1:2500**

# Reference Project 04 St Ann's Warehouse, Brooklyn, New York, USA

### Brief building description

Located in a former tobacco factory near the waterfront in Brooklyn, St Ann's Warehouse (SAW) is at the heart of a thriving performance and gallery scene among cobblestone streets and converted warehouse buildings. It is the permanent home for a forty-year-old organisation, presenting and producing theatre and live music. A new steel frame has been inserted into the remaining historic walls to enclose the new building, allowing the existing arched openings to remain untouched. A portion of the existing walls enclose a public garden space that acts as a transitional entry from the adjacent Brooklyn Bridge Park to the new interior spaces (see site drawing).

### Auditorium type/types

SAW's open plan accommodates multiple formats including end stage at multiple capacities, in the round, traverse and thrust (see drawings of the various formats). The organisation of the building provides as much space and flexibility as possible for performances (see Figure RP.04.01). All support spaces, including dressing rooms, offices, community space, and restrooms are stacked into a two-storey zone along one side of the main space to allow the majority of the space to be used for performances.

Figure RP.04.01 Photo © Teddy Wolff.

### Design intent

The design of the new St Ann's Warehouse space pays homage to both the history of the Tobacco Warehouse and St Ann's Warehouse's past spaces, including the namesake church in which it started. Simple, rugged materials including glass brick, blackened steel, and plywood celebrate the tobacco warehouse's history and recall the qualities of SAW's past spaces. (See Figures RP.04.02 and RP.04.03.)

### Key facts

**Client**
St Ann's Warehouse
Susan Feldman, Artistic Director

**Site address/web reference**
45 Water Street, Brooklyn,
NY 11201, USA
www.stannswarehouse.org

**Building dates**
The new St Ann's Warehouse building is an adaptive reuse of a former tobacco warehouse.

**Opening date:** September 2015

**Auditorium type and seating capacity**
Flexible open plan theatre for end stage, thrust, in the round, traverse and boulevard/standing room presentations capacity adaptable from 325 to 1200.

**Stage/performance space size**
Flexible; up to 1,600ft$^2$ (150m$^2$)

**Other facilities**
Rehearsal studio/community space, dressing room/green room, administrative offices, production storage

**Overall area**
2,325m$^2$

**Design team**
**Architect:** Marvel
**Theatre consultant:** Charcoalblue
**Acoustic consultant:** Charcoalblue
**Building services:** Buro Happold
**Structural engineer:** Silman
**Main contractor**
Yorke Construction

**Construction cost at completion date (excluding fees and VAT)** USD 31 million

Figure RP.04.02 Photo © Alex Wardle.

Figure RP.04.03 Photo © Alex Wardle.

**The five figures** shown here capture the design and atmosphere of the new St Ann's Warehouse Theater, developed within the historic walls of a former tobacco factory and converted warehouse building (01, 02, 03). Its open plan, flexible format enables a range of performance configurations, with catwalks running throughout the building (04) and a newly inserted brick clerestory allowing light to come in by day and illuminated from within, like a beacon, by night. The final figure (05) shows St Ann's Warehouse nestled under Brooklyn Bridge, very much a part of a vibrant performance, café and gallery location for its community.

Additional height, above the top of the existing historic walls, was required for theatrical use. A new glass brick clerestory provides this additional height and acts as a beacon for the building, relating the new building's use to the existing masonry, and allowing natural daylight into the performance and foyer spaces (see Figure RP.04.04).

### Specific features/strengths

A catwalk system throughout allows for performances to take place anywhere, and the acoustic design protects the venue from a high level of external environmental noise while creating an internal acoustic suitable for a wide range of programming.

Figure RP.04.04 Photo © Teddy Wolff.

Figure RP.04.05 Photo © Pavel Antonev.

**Users' verdicts**

Transforming the pre-Civil-War Tobacco Warehouse into St Ann's Warehouse has delivered beyond our imagination and our dreams. The proof of this is in the joy and ease with which artists, technicians and audiences experience the place. The versatility of the open plan; the natural elements of brick, steel, wood, glass and concrete; the lack of intrusion and the harmony with the original building design make for a warm and welcoming performance space. The HVAC systems have performed brilliantly under the pandemic, allowing for robust filtration and air exchange, as well as adaptations to create a healthy and safe environment. The catwalks are of course a joy, allowing safe separations for multiple crews while providing the shared canopy we'd hoped for, conveying the feeling, yes, we are all in this together.

Susan Feldman, Founder and Artistic Director

My favourite theatres help the audience to feel they are in the same room with the actors, the same shared space. Simple as that. The acoustics must be good enough for the actor to speak without electronic interference and the physical relationship between actor and audience must be intimate, even in a large theatre. Oh, and finally the relationship with the outside world should be as direct and honest as possible. St Ann's Warehouse is a perfect example, a beautiful example. A joyous space to create and play in.

Mark Rylance, actor

They have created such a nimble, transformer-like building that can accommodate and welcome any kind of production and this, together with the love and creativity that must have been sprinkled into the materials (used), makes it an incredibly magical and wonderfully warm place to perform.

Ruth Negga, actor

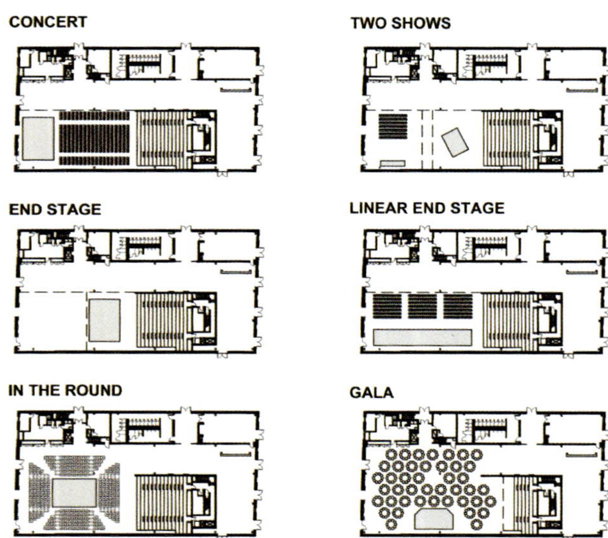


THEATRE FORMATS

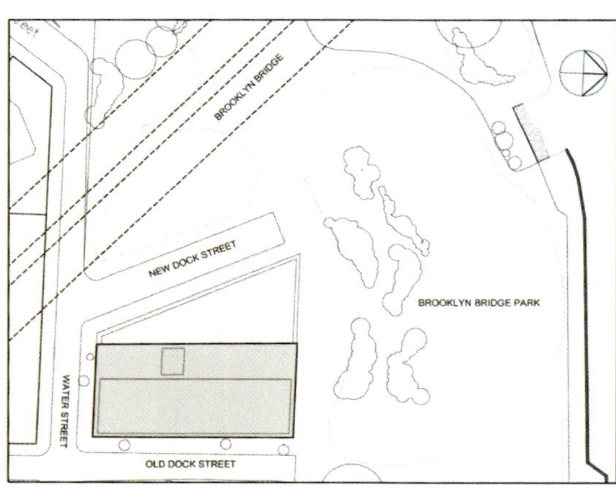


SITE PLAN - 1:2500

KEY
1 - FLEXIBLE STAGE
2 - FLEXIBLE AUDITORIUM
3 - ENTRANCE FOYER
4 - CONTROL ROOM
5 - RETRACTABLE SEATING
6 - DRESSING ROOMS
7 - PRODUCTION OFFICE
8 - TOILETS
9 - STUDIO
10 - GARDEN AREA

4
5
1
2
3

0 5 10 20 metres
0 15 30 60 feet
1:500
10
6
7
8
9
2
5
1
4
3
5
2

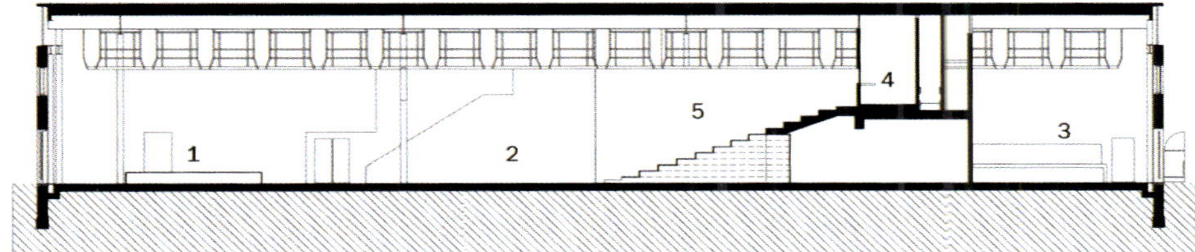

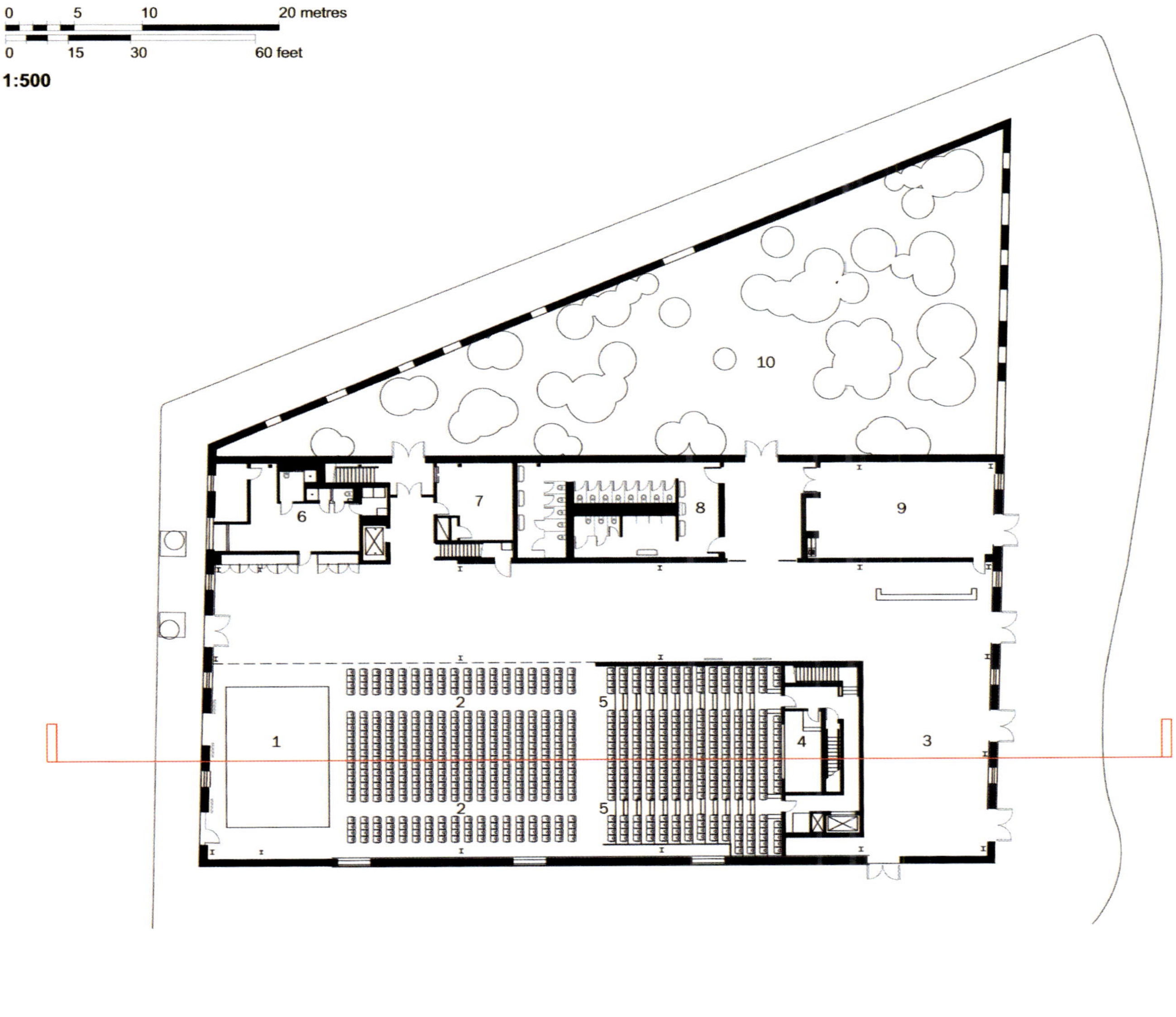

# Reference Project 05 The Quarry Theatre at St Luke's, Bedford, UK

### Brief building description

The Quarry Theatre at St Luke's has been created from a re-purposed, redundant nineteenth-century Moravian church and an eighteenth-century minister's house to make a new performing arts centre for Bedford School and the local community. The location, facing the town at the front and the school grounds at the rear, emphasises the link between the school and the community (see Figure RP.05.01). Historical research on the Moravian settlement in Bedford was followed by detailed discussions with conservation and planning officers to achieve consent for the remodelling of the Grade II listed building.

Figure RP.05.01 Photo © Philip Vile/Foster Wilson Size.

### Auditorium type/types

The theatre has been created by inserting a galleried structure into the church space, linked to the original church gallery. The theatre takes the form of a rectangular courtyard with galleries on three sides and a flat floor at ground level, which can be reconfigured using motorised retractable seating units. (See Figure RP.05.02.)

Figure RP.05.02 Photo © Philip Vile/Foster Wilson Size.

### Key facts

**Client:**
The Harpur Trust

**Site address/web reference**
26 St Peter's Street, Bedford.
MK40 2NN.
www.quarrytheatre.org.uk

**Opening date:** 2015

**Auditorium type and seating capacity**
200–300-seat theatre (see alternative layouts)
50-seat drama studio

**Stage/performance space size**
Main auditorium: 10 × 7m (subject to layout)

**Other facilities**
Staff offices and a small studio, created in the re-purposed congregation hall in the minister's house. A foyer in the old vestry and an extension containing backstage facilities, public toilets and a spacious bar opening onto the original church gardens.

**Overall area**
Gross internal area 1,355m$^2$

**Design team**
**Architect:** Foster Wilson Size
**Structural engineer:** Price & Myers
**Services consultant:** Ernest Griffiths
**Quantity surveyor:** Ainsley & Partners
**Theatre consultant:** Theatreplan
**Acoustic consultant:** Gillieron Scott Acoustic Design
**Landscape design:** The Landscape Partnership
**Main contractor:** SDC Builders Ltd

**Construction cost at completion date** (excluding fees and VAT): £4.3 million (2016 status).

**Project Awards**
Civic Trust Awards Regional Finalist, 2018
RIBA East Awards Winner, 2016
RICS East of England: Community Benefit Awards Winner, 2016

This allows a large area of flat floor for teaching and rehearsals, which can be changed to a performance layout quickly and easily. The lower gallery provides audience seating, while the upper gallery is a technical area.

### Design intent

This is a theatre for a school but was also intended as an important resource for the local community and needed to reinforce those links. It is used as a school facility during the day but presents a varied programme of professional work to the general public in the evenings. The auditorium was required to be flexible, offering a variety of seating formats, ranging from 200–300 seats, depending on layout. The theatre has a complete set of front of house and backstage facilities allowing it to operate independently outside school hours. (See Figure RP.05.03.)

Figure RP.05.03 Photo © Philip Vile/Foster Wilson Size.

See *Sightline*, Winter 2015, pp. 34–38.

**The four figures** here show the Quarry Theatre in its repurposed space. **The first figure** (01) is a view from the garden showing the new curved foyer extension and minister's house. **The second** (02) shows the courtyard-style main auditorium with galleries on three sides. **The third figure** (03) shows the new foyer and bar from the inside, overlooking the garden. **The final figure** (04) shows the flexible drama studio (which can take up to fifty seats).

### Specific features/strengths

In addition to the auditorium, the adjacent minister's house has been restored to provide front of house facilities, offices and a studio, with the addition of a new foyer and backstage extension at the rear. The new foyer wraps around the semi-circular wall to the original chancel and a curved wall of glass provides views over the secluded gardens of the old churchyard (see Figure RP.05.03). New interventions combined with sympathetic repair of the original fabric have created a warm and welcoming public space while giving new life to an important historic building.

Figure RP.05.04 Photo © Philip Vile/Foster Wilson Size.

LECTURE/ CINEMA

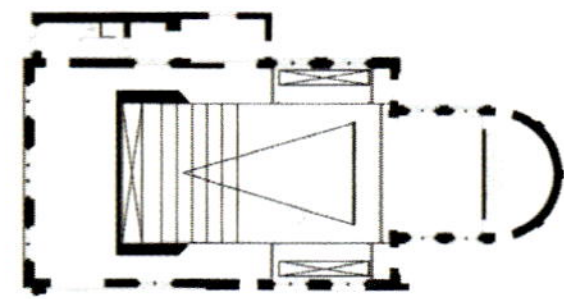

TRAVERSE STAGE

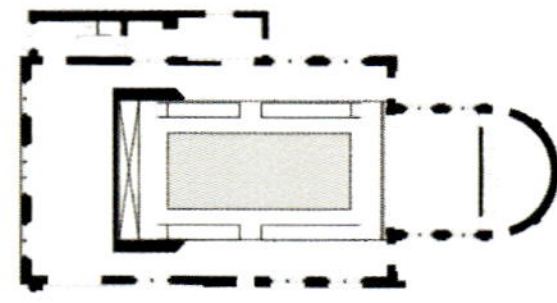

IN THE ROUND

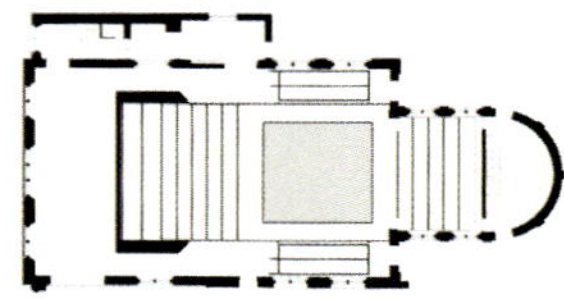

END STAGE

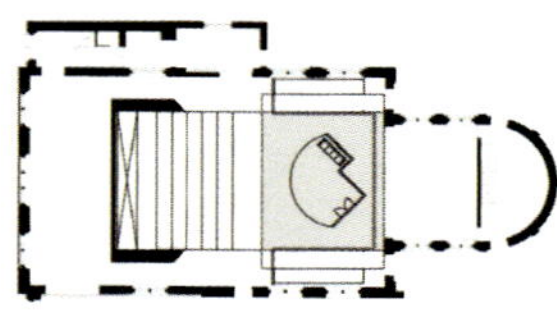

THRUST STAGE

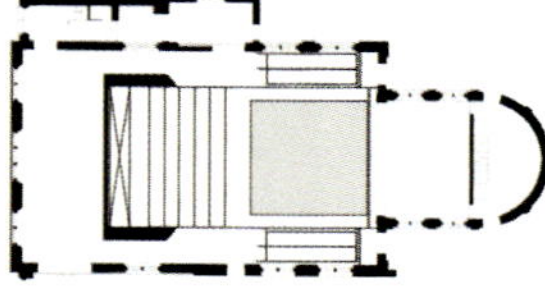

FLAT FLOOR

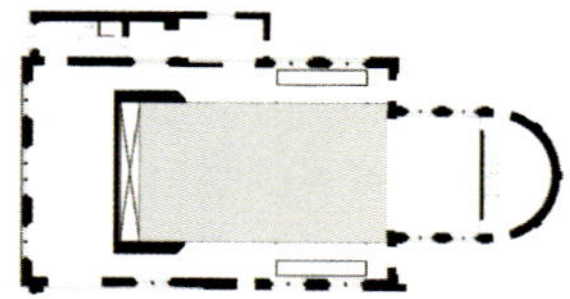

THEATRE FORMATS

**User's verdict**

Now in its sixth year, the Quarry Theatre continues to provide the school and surrounding community with a vibrant programme of events. Many people new to the venue comment on how beautiful the building is, especially during the summer months when they can spill out into the fabulous grounds of the Quarry Garden.

Since opening in 2015 we have expanded our technical assets making the venue even more flexible, and capable of hosting events, with little effort required to reconfigure due to its clever design. I am happy to report at time of writing [in 2021] that we have now passed the one thousandth event mark!

James Pharaoh, Director of Theatre, The Quarry Theatre at St Luke's

**KEY**

1 - FLEXIBLE STAGE
2 - REAR STAGE
3 - FOYER
4 - CONTROL ROOM
5 - RETRACTABLE SEATING
6 - DRESSING ROOMS
7 - OFFICE
8 - TOILETS
9 - BAR/ FOYER
10 - GARDEN AREA

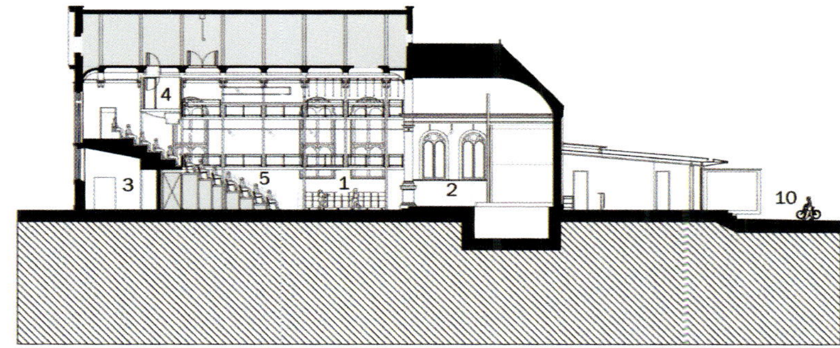


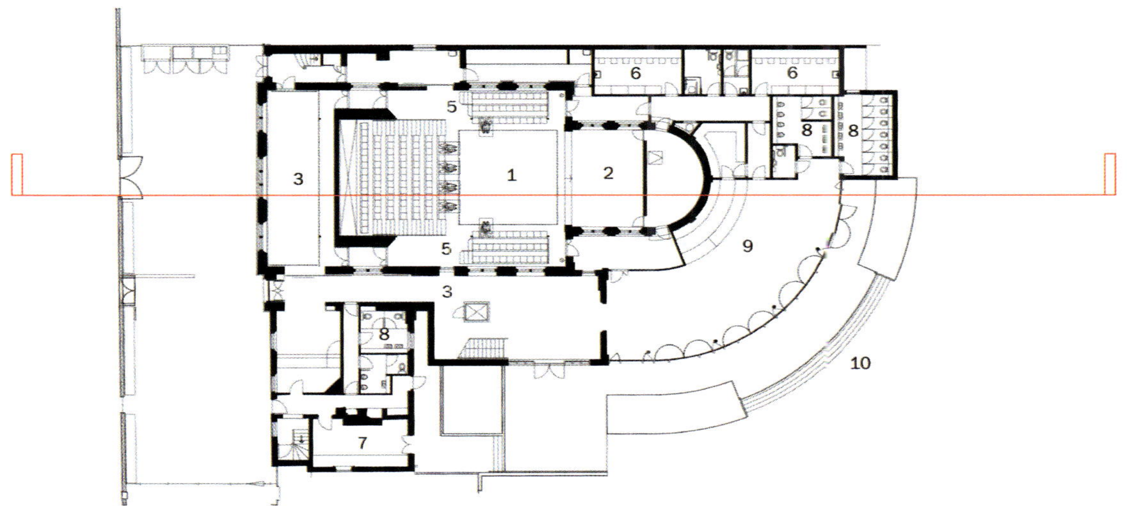


0 5 10 20 metres
0 15 30 60 feet
**1:500**

**SITE PLAN - 1:2500**

# Reference Project 06
# Storyhouse, Chester, UK

### Brief building description

Storyhouse is a multi-arts hub where theatre and cinema sit alongside a public library and an all-day café bar. The library and café occupy the open public areas which connect the main theatre and cinema spaces, and the building is open to everyone from early in the morning to late at night seven days a week.

Storyhouse presents its own theatre productions and also functions as a receiving house for touring work for some of the year.

### Auditorium type/types

The main theatre space accommodates an audience of 800 in end-stage format and is equipped with an orchestra pit and 20m-high flytower. The auditorium can be transformed by the addition of a modular thrust stage at circle level to create a more intimate 500-seat theatre space (see Figure RP.06.01).

Figure RP.06.01 Photo © Peter Cook/Bennetts Associates.

The smaller Garret Theatre, a flexible 150-seat studio space with a retractable seating unit, sits directly above the main auditorium and is acoustically isolated using a double floor structure.

### Design intent

Storyhouse is part of the regeneration of Chester's city centre. The cinema and library functions are housed in the shell of a Grade 2 listed former art deco Odeon cinema (see Figure RP.06.02), with the theatre and studio accommodated in a large new extension clad in glass, brick and copper.

### Key facts

**Client:** Cheshire West & Chester Council

**End User**: Storyhouse

**Site address/web reference**
Hunter Street, Chester CH1 2AR
www.storyhouse.com

**Opening date:** 17 May 2017

**Auditorium types and seating capacity**
**Main Theatre:**
Main Stage
End stage format, stalls and two balcony levels
Seating capacity: 800
Proscenium width: 11.2m
Width of stage and wings: 20m
Grid height: 20m
Stage depth 13.0m
Main Stage
Thrust format: modular thrust
Stage and pit seating built over stalls, one balcony
Seating capacity: 500
Modular thrust stage depth: 5.5m
Modular thrust stage width: 6.0m

**Garret Studio Theatre:**
Seating capacity 150 (retractable bench seating)
Flat floor area (seating retracted) 10.5m wide × 11.0m deep

**Other facilities**
Cinema screen: capacity 100 seats
Café/Bar: 150 covers
Public library shelving: 700m

**Overall area**
Total area with theatre in proscenium arch mode 7511.00m$^2$

**Design team**
**Architect:** Bennetts Associates
**Executive Architect:** Ellis Williams Architects
**Theatre consultant:** Charcoalblue

**Acoustic consultant:** Sandy Brown Associates
**Civil & structural engineers:** WSP
**Fire engineer:** WSP
**M&E engineering/sustainability/IT/ AV/**Foreman Roberts
**Lighting:** Pritchard Themis
**Heritage & conservation:** Tweed Nuttall Warburton
**Access consultant:** David Bonnett Associates
**Planning consultant:** WYG
**Catering:** Bentley Consulting Ltd
**Main contractor:** Kier North West

**Total project cost at completion date:** £37 million

**Major Awards:**
RIBA National Award and North West Regional Award 2018
Civic Trust Special Award for Community Impact and Engagement: 2017
The Guardian Public Service Awards 2018: Winner
UK Theatre Awards: UK's Most Welcoming Theatre 2019/20

See *Sightline*, Autumn 2017, pp. 34–37.

**The first figure** (01) shows the main theatre at Storyhouse in 500-seat format with the modular thrust stage and pit seating area deployed. **The second figure** (02) shows the main entrance to Storyhouse through the listed Odeon building which contains the library and cinema; the new extension containing the main theatre and studio can be seen in the background. **The third figure** (03) is from inside the foyer where the art-deco plasterwork of the listed Odeon cinema forms a natural arena for informal foyer performances. Open and highly visible stairs lead audiences to the main theatre and studio located in the new build extension.

Figure RP.06.02 Photo © Peter Cook/Bennetts Associates.

### Specific features/strengths

- Successful all-day multi-arts venue with theatre, cinema and library.
- Re-uses and extends a Grade 2 listed Odeon cinema dating from 1936.
- Flexible and adaptable auditorium transforms between 800-seat end-stage and 500-seat thrust formats.
- Shelving for 30,000 books in the public areas.
- Dedicated children's library.
- 100-seat cinema screen.
- 150-seat studio theatre.
- Study areas offer opportunities for learning and research.

### Upfront carbon emissions

Half of the accommodation at Storyhouse, including all the main theatre functions, is contained in a new extension to the existing Odeon. The new-build element of Storyhouse is typical of many theatres, with a steel and concrete frame, a concrete basement below the stage and cladding of brick and glass. Using Stage 3 design information and carbon intensities taken from the ICE (Inventory of Carbon and Energy) database the upfront carbon emissions of this new-build element is calculated to be 1,346kg$CO_2$ e/m$^2$.

Structurally, the frame and substructure combined account for 595kg$CO_2$ e/m$^2$ (around 50%) of the carbon emissions, with external walls at 185kg$CO_2$ e/m$^2$ and services at 163kg$CO_2$ e/m$^2$.

Upfront carbon emissions from the retained existing part of Storyhouse have not been calculated but from benchmark data these are likely to be around half those of the new build.

Figure RP.06.03

Photo © Peter Cook/Bennetts Associates.

**Users' verdicts**

- Over 1,000,000 visitors within the first year of opening.
- 125,000 tickets sold for events at Storyhouse within the first six months.
- Over 3,500 new library members and an increase of 145% library borrowing in the first 6 months of opening.
- Over 150 community groups using the building regularly.
- 52% of visitors said that Storyhouse was an important part in their decision to visit Chester.

This internationally acclaimed partnership between Storyhouse and Cheshire West and Chester Council is a model for cultural innovation. It's a new way to make, share and discover stories. Storyhouse unifies two theatres, a cinema and – uniquely – the city's library services. The project has garnered international attention as a blueprint for innovation.

Alex Clifton, Artistic Director, Storyhouse

The mix of public functions in the building ensures that Storyhouse is busy throughout the day and into the evening (see Figure RP.06.03), and the design has created an accessible and welcoming building which has become a focus for creative and community activity in the city.

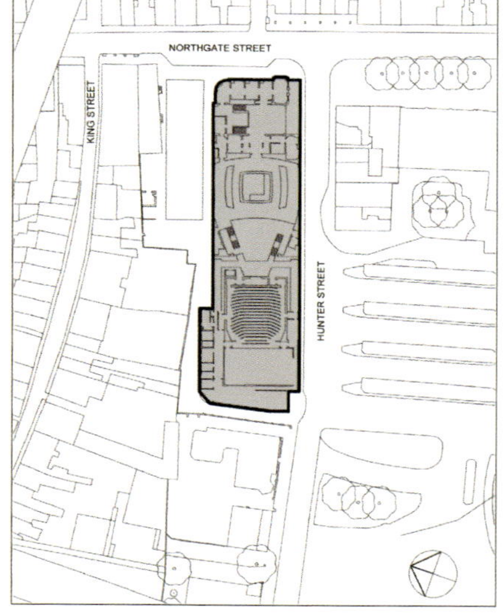

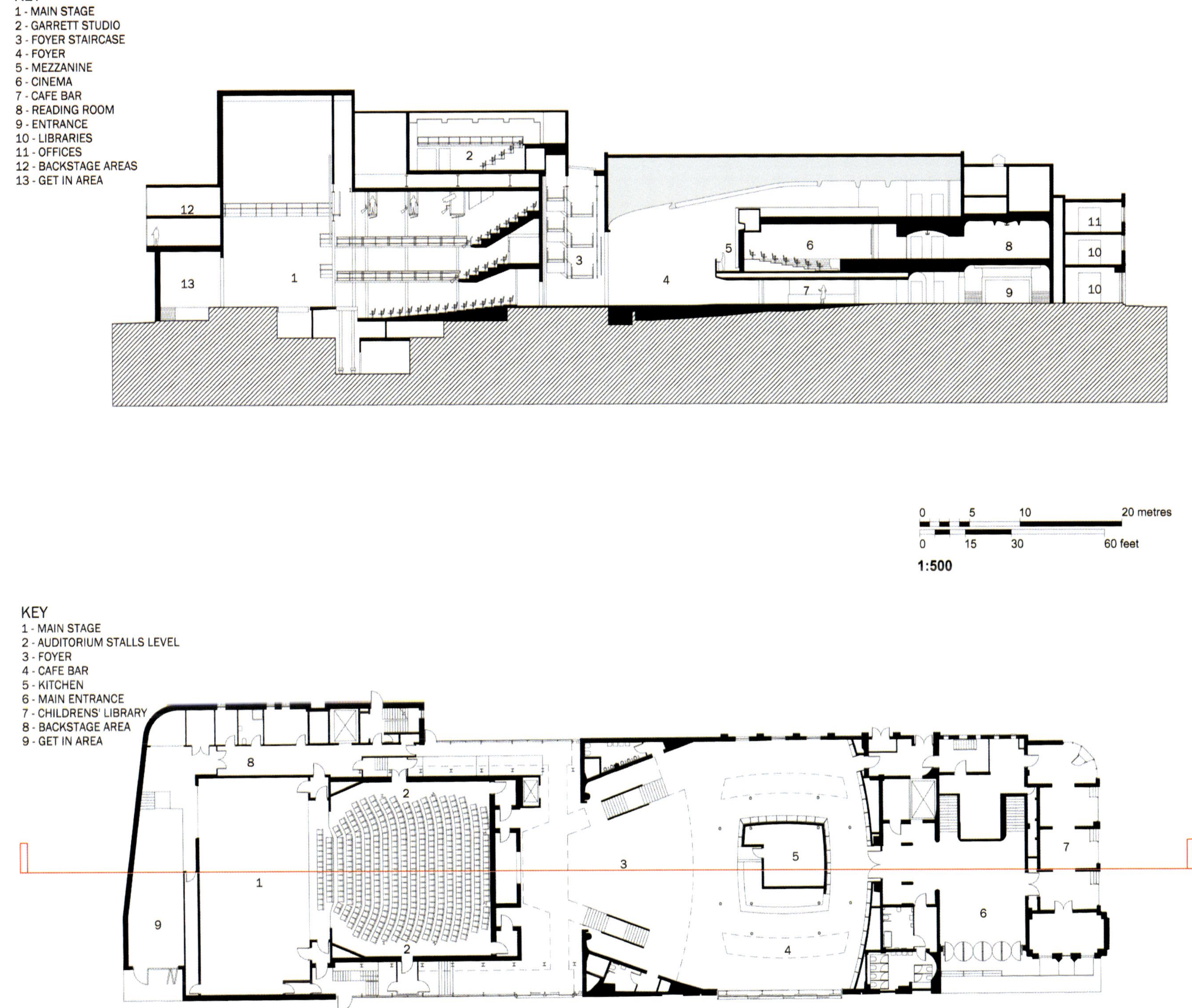
KEY
1 - MAIN STAGE
2 - GARRETT STUDIO
3 - FOYER STAIRCASE
4 - FOYER
5 - MEZZANINE
6 - CINEMA
7 - CAFE BAR
8 - READING ROOM
9 - ENTRANCE
10 - LIBRARIES
11 - OFFICES
12 - BACKSTAGE AREAS
13 - GET IN AREA
0 5 10 20 metres
0 15 30 60 feet
1:500
KEY
1 - MAIN STAGE
2 - AUDITORIUM STALLS LEVEL
3 - FOYER
4 - CAFE BAR
5 - KITCHEN
6 - MAIN ENTRANCE
7 - CHILDRENS' LIBRARY
8 - BACKSTAGE AREA
9 - GET IN AREA

# Reference Project 07 The Hullabaloo (Children's Theatre), Darlington, United Kingdom

### Brief building description

A new purpose-built children's theatre created within an original Edwardian fire station, and the space between these and the 1907 Grade II listed historic Darlington Hippodrome. (Note: the Darlington Hippodrome was also redesigned, refurbished, remodelled and extended by Space Architects working with the same team at the same time.)

Figure RP.07.01a Photo © Kristen McCluskie.

Figure RP.07.01b Photo © Kristen McCluskie.

### Auditorium type/types

Studio theatre space that can accommodate 150 end-on, and up to 177 with seating at the side of the flat floor stage (allowing for a cabaret layout or what is effectively a thrust arrangement).

The auditorium has been designed to provide excellent sightlines wherever you sit. The seats are built on rostra tiers that can be removed or

**Key facts**

**Client**
Darlington Borough Council
Mike Crawshaw,
Head of Heritage and Culture,
Darlington Borough Council
Darlington Hippodrome

**End user**
Theatre Hullabaloo
Laura Case, Executive Director
Miranda Thain, Artistic Producer

**Site address/web reference**
The Hullabaloo, Borough Road,
Darlington, County Durham.
DL1 1SG
www.theatrehullabaloo.org.uk

**Opening date**
11 December 2017

**Auditorium type and seating capacity**
Studio theatre space: 150 end-on; up to 177 with seating at the side of the flat floor stage.

**Stage/performance space size**
The stage in an end-on arrangement is 10m by 6m deep (and can be deeper when seating is removed).

**Other facilities**
Auditorium, get-in/scene dock, dressing rooms, technical access deck, green room, rehearsal space, café and foyer (excluding circulation space and stairs to auditorium), box office, circulation (general, lifts, stairs and fire escape stairs), creative play, office, plant, WCs × 2, store

**Overall area**
712m²

**Design team**
**Architect:** Space Architects.
**Theatre consultant:** Charcoalblue
**Acoustic consultant:** Cundall
**Conservation specialists:** Space Architects
**Interior design:** Space Architects

**Structural engineer**: Billinghurst George Partnership
**M&E consultant:** Cundall (MEP)
**Stage engineering systems contractor:** Centre Stage Engineering
Stagelighting and Audiovisual systems contractor: Hawthorn
**Auditorium seating:** Kirwin & Simpson
**Main contractor:** Willmott Dixon Construction

**Construction cost at completion date** (excluding fees and VAT): £2.1 million

See *Sightline*, Winter 2017, pp. 7–13.

The **first figure** (01a) shows an external view showing the glazed foyer, café and entrance adjacent to the old fire station. The new timber-clad 'box' forming the auditorium is visible above the brick walls of the fire station. The **second figure** (01b) shows the interior of the auditorium with its bright seats in alternating colours. **The third and fourth images** (02, 03) show the space inside the internal creative play area and a view of the external creative play area, important features of the Hullabaloo concept. **The fifth** (04) shows an interior view of the curved walls of the foyer, with the café and creative play area entrances leading off it. The **final image** (05) shows a three-year-old enjoying Roma Patel's installation 'The Enchanted Forest' in the creative play space.

**Users' verdicts**

The Hullabaloo . . . was vison-led, with children at the heart of every decision made by the project team. The venue is child-centred, where children are respected as an audience. . . . As a national centre for theatre for young audiences the venue is more than a place to watch a performance. It is as inspiring place to play and learn . . . and is a focal point for creative education.

Laura Case, Executive Director, Theatre Hullabaloo

installed in other configurations, meaning the space is extremely flexible for a variety of other setups. The theatre has a tension wire grid providing a permanent technical level and a safe environment for training without harnesses.

### Design intent

The original Hullabaloo vison and brief was to create a child-centred theatre for young audiences in the north of England. The Hullaballoo was built on the belief that the opportunities to learn, play and create through the arts should be a central part of everybody's childhood.

The following key objectives were established for the Hullabaloo:

- provision of a separate theatre specifically for children
- but one where grown-ups would not feel out of place
- provision of an identifiable children's theatre entrance, foyer, café and box office
- creation of play areas inside and out (see Figures RP.07.02 and RP.07.03)
- creation of education and activity space for all ages.

Figure RP.07.02 Photo © Kristen McCluskie.

Figure RP.07.03 Photo © Kristen McCluskie.

Central to the design and contextual response was the relationship between the historic Darlington Hippodrome theatre with its 1980's extension and the original fire station. (See site map.)

A new single-storey, lightweight, glazed structure, housing the foyer, café and box office, sits between the Hippodrome and the former fire station. Visible within this glazed link is the timber-clad drum of the creative play area. (See Figure RP.07.04.)

The seating was laid out with a single diagonal aisle, avoiding both a 'dead spot' downstage centre and the asymmetry of a single side aisle. Fixing points for technical equipment are incorporated into the wall linings. A technical control position is provided at the technical level.

Figure RP.07.04 Photo © Kristen McCluskie.

Another key aspect of the Hullabaloo design concept is the expression of the auditorium as a contemporary timber-clad 'box' sitting within the brick walls of the original fire station (see Figure RP.07.01), which is simply articulated and unambiguously contemporary (to avoid any confusion between it and the original historic fabric) and is visible both above the original walls and through the original doors and windows of the former building.

Children and young people were central to development of the design, and the architects worked with two local school groups to help define what a place for them should be. Seats were designed without arms, to be comfortable for children to sprawl over a parent's lap yet with clear demarcation showing the extent of one seat place, for grown-up audiences.

Figure RP.07.05 Photo © Alex Wardle.

**Specific features/strengths**

- A 150-seat flexible studio theatre space
- A performing area/stage of 10.0m by 6.0m with a minimum clearance of 4.5m over it
- A foyer space with child-centred 'pop up' café and snack bar facilities
- A creative play installation space with access to external creative play space
- A rehearsal space equal to the main performance space
- Dressing rooms, green room, backstage facilities
- Office space for Theatre Hullabaloo
- Gallery space (within the café, foyer and elsewhere) for child-focused exhibitions.

Space Architects, particularly David Coundon and Carinna Gebhard were an integral part of the design team for this immensely important and challenging project [and] . . . made an immense personal commitment to the success of the scheme from the outset . . . [they] were able to deliver . . . the new centre of excellence for young people's theatre, The Hullabaloo which . . . won the award for Family Venue for 2019 at the Fantastic for Families Awards. This shows what a great success the design scheme has been.

Lynda Winstanley, Director, Darlington Hippodrome

**KEY**

1 - STAGE
2 - AUDITORIUM
3 - FOYER/ CAFE
4 - CONTROL DECK
5 - GET IN
6 - DRESSING ROOM
7 - GREEN ROOM
8 - TOILET
9 - CREATIVE PLAY
10 - EXTERNAL PLAY
11 - CREW AREAS
12 - REHEARSAL SPACE
13 - DARLINGTON HIPPODROME

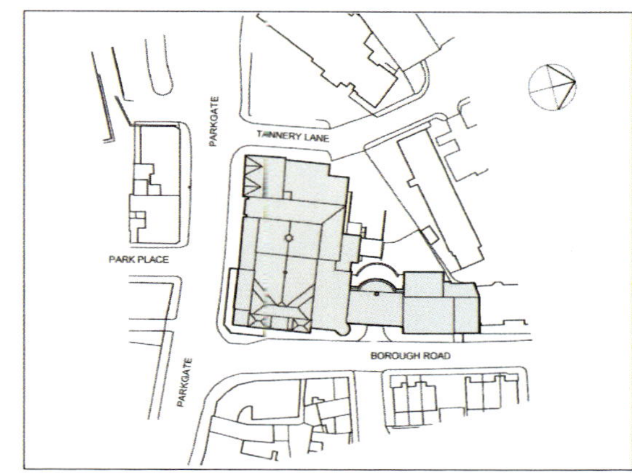


**SITE PLAN - 1:2500**

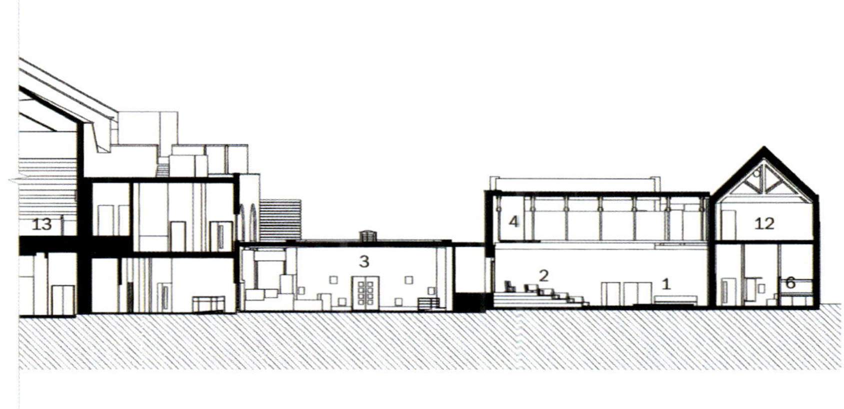


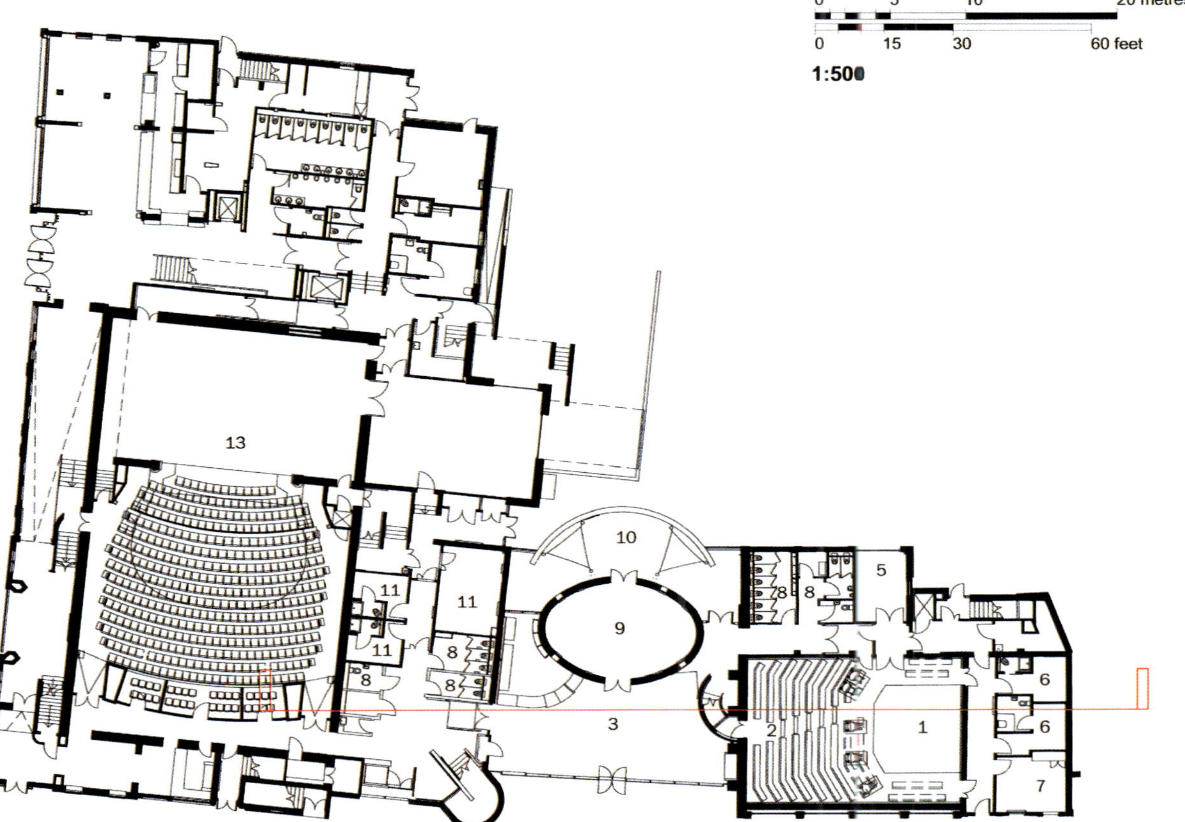

## Reference Project 08 Nevill Holt Opera House, Leicestershire, UK

### Brief building description

This project repurposes a seventeenth-century stable block as the support spaces for a new opera house and recital space built within the courtyard, on the walls of the surrounding accommodation, replacing a decade-old tent structure which previously housed the opera festival. (See Figure RP.08.01.) Located on an escarpment ridge within a rural environment (see Figure RP.08.02 and site plan), the building now provides an intimate permanent theatre for the Nevill Holt Festival Opera, which produces and stages two operas over a month-long summer festival; choral recitals at a winter festival; and a music education programme for pupils from 30 schools for the David Ross Education Trust.

Figure RP.08.01 Photo © David Grandorge.

Figure RP.08.02 Photo © Manuela Barczewski.

**Key facts**

**Clients/users**
Nevill Holt Opera,
Managing Director, Annie Lydford
and the David Ross Education Trust

**Site address and web reference**
Nevill Holt, Leicestershire.
LE16 8EG
www.nevillholtopera.co.uk

**Opening date**
June 2018

**Auditorium type and seating capacity**
Opera/recital hall: 400 seats

**Stage/performance space size**
16m wide × 8m deep

**Overall area**
816m$^2$ GIA

**Design team**
**Architect:** Witherford Watson Mann
**Theatre consultant:** Sound Space Vision
**Acoustic consultant:** Sound Space Vision
**Conservation architect:** Julian Harrap Architects
**Structural engineer:** Price & Myers
**Services & environmental consultant incl. house lighting:** Max Fordham
**Cost consultant:** Gleeds
**Access consultant:** David Bonnett
**Fire consultant:** Fire Surgery
**Approved inspector:** Oculus Building Consultancy
**Main contractor:** Messenger Construction
**Enabling works:** Northfields

**Construction cost at completion date** (excluding fees and VAT): £5.1 million.

### Auditorium type

The new auditorium is a 400-seat end stage space with a single horseshoe balcony relating to the existing openings in the stable walls. It has raked, curved stalls seating stepping down from the horizontal side aisles, a proscenium and an orchestra pit (see Section 1, Figure 1.7.1c). The embracing balcony has single side seats, all with excellent sightlines. Stage and auditorium occupy a single volume, without a flytower, and with adjustable proscenium panels to enable a wide recital space. A skylight offers rehearsal daylight and can be closed during performances.

### Design intent

The client owner brief from David Ross was to achieve an opera house to be used in the summer and as a gathering space for pupils at the David Ross Educational Trust, with excellent, intimate acoustics that support young voices, and to retain as much as possible of the distinctive character of the stone courtyard walls. The artistic brief was for an intimate opera experience for all with up to 45 orchestral players in the pit. This was actioned by judicious balance between the stage depth, orchestra pit opening and depth of audience chamber, careful exposure of the walls and choice of materials. (See Section 6, Figure 6.6.2.) The complete theatre infrastructure, including suspensions for scenery, is concealed behind ceiling and floor panelling.

### Specific features/strengths

The new upper timber walls and balcony fronts harmonise with the ironstone walls, together diffusing sound. Both rough finish board and batten upper walls and exposed original stone lower walls enhance the warmth of the acoustics. (See Figure RP.08.03)

See *Sightline*, Autumn 2019, pp. 8–11.

**The first image** (01) shows the Nevill Holt Opera during its construction process within the existing courtyard, including the rationalisation of stage levels to equal the stable floor level, the understage orchestra pit, the concrete ventilation duct and the side steps for the auditorium. **The second** (02) shows the garden space serving as a natural foyer through which the audience approach the building. **The next image** (03) shows the auditorium's stone volume extended upwards and enclosed by grit-blasted Douglas fir boards. **The final image** (04) is of a performance of *Midsummer* by the Nevill Holt Opera Company, showing the rear of the stage with doors opening out onto the garden.

Figure RP.08.03 Photo © Hélène Binet.

A silent underfloor air supply and sound attenuating air vents integrated into the upper timber walls further assist with the acoustics appropriate for musical performances. A rationalisation of floor levels allows for common audience entry, stage and backstage levels as well as connecting to the stable block wings. Stage and auditorium are united by volume, materials,

Figure RP.08.04 Photo © Ali Wright.

details and the open proscenium and the central rooflight. The complete theatre infrastructure, including suspensions for scenery, is concealed behind ceiling and floor panelling.

The room retains the atmosphere of a courtyard, ambiguously inside and out, suggestively theatrical but quietly unconventional. The environmental strategy responds economically to the festival usage while evocative architectural finishes and architectural lighting emphasise the natural ironstone walls.

**User's verdict**

Our artistic work, promoting young singers and inspiring schools, now has a home. It is an architectural gem with an amazing acoustic. A highlight for me has been hearing the audience reaction as the space transforms from a daylight court to a darkened theatre – the building working theatrically even before a note of opera has been heard.

Nicholas Chalmers, Artistic Director, Nevill Holt Opera

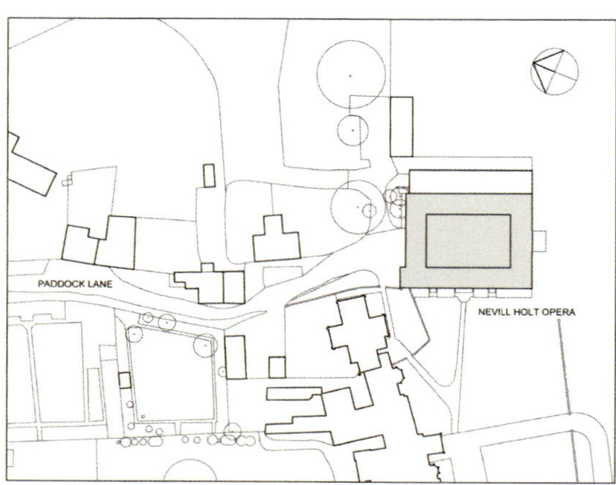


SITE PLAN - 1:2500

**KEY**
1 - STAGE
2 - AUDITORIUM
3 - ORCHESTRA PIT
4 - CONTROL ROOM
5 - STAGE STORE
6 - STAGE LAUNDRY
7 - MAIN ENTRANCE
8 - TOILET
9 - BACKSTAGE ENTRANCE
10 - HOSPITALITY/ GREEN ROOM

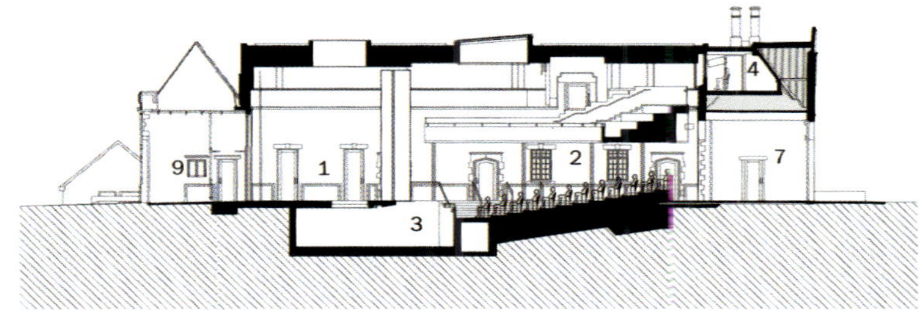


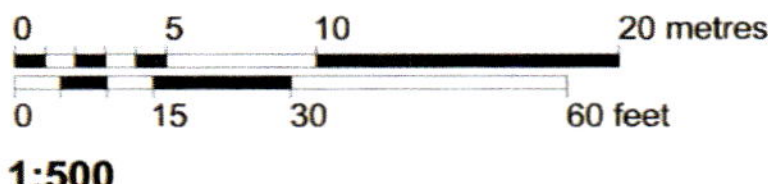


**1:500**

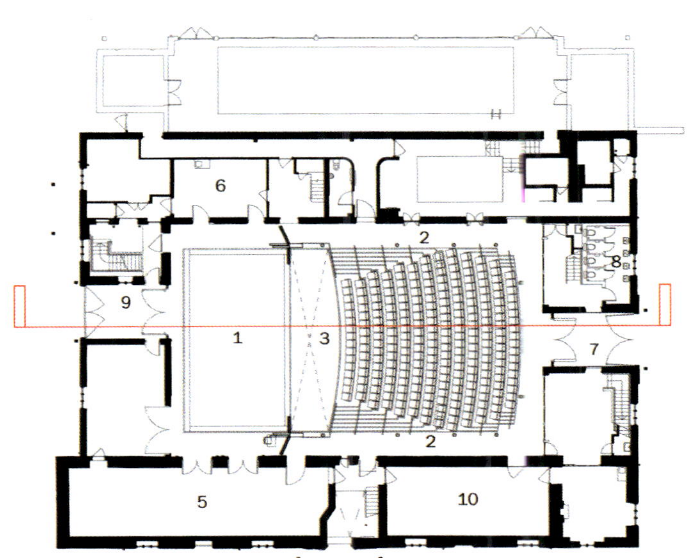

# Reference Project 09
# The Malthouse, The King's School, Canterbury, UK

### Brief building description

The building is a school theatre and drama department in a converted Victorian Malthouse that was originally built in 1898 (see Figure RP.09.01). In addition to the theatre space, it includes two studios (one dance, one drama) and two multipurpose rooms. There is generous backstage space, and school teaching and dining facilities. The theatre is used for drama teaching and exams, and for school performances. Outside term time it is hired out to touring companies.

Figure RP.09.01 Photo © Philip Vile.

### Auditorium type

A square seating area was created with a single gallery on three sides and a flexible stalls floor, comprising retractable seating and floor panels. Flexible layouts offer end stage (with option of orchestra pit for twelve), end stage with forestage (with option of orchestra pit for twenty), thrust stage or studio (flat floor). (See Figure RP.09.02.)

Above the balcony level there is a technical gallery with lighting bridges and, above the stage, two tiers of catwalks/crossovers. A loft above the stage allows for half-flying of scenery.

### Key facts

**Client**
Mark Taylor, Bursar,
The King's School.

**Site address/web reference**
The King's School.
Malthouse Rd, St Stephen's Rd,
Canterbury CT2 7JA
www.malthousetheatre.co.uk

**Opening date**
April 2019
(official opening November 2019)

**Auditorium type and seating capacity**
The auditorium is a flexible theatre space with a stalls and balcony level. It has a maximum stalls capacity of 271, and balcony seating for 63, plus 50 standing.

**Stage/performance space size**
Stage (varies depending on format):
End stage format excl. wings = 107m$^2$
Forestage format excl. wings = 130m$^2$
Thrust format excl. wings = 153m$^2$
Orchestra Pit = 29 or 44m$^2$
(depending on format)
Wings = 75m$^2$

**Other facilities**
Dance studio = 122m$^2$
Drama studio = 129m$^2$
Multipurpose room 1 = 95m$^2$
Multipurpose room 2 = 95m$^2$
Foyer (exhibition space) = 422m$^2$
Workshop = 126m$^2$

**Overall area**
4,332m$^2$ GIA

**Design team**
**Architect:** Tim Ronalds Architects
**Theatre consultant:** Charcoalblue
**Acoustic consultant:** Ramboll
**Services engineer:** Skelly and Couch
**Structural engineer:** Price & Myers
**Main contractor:** Buxton Building Contractors

**Construction cost at completion date** (excluding fees and VAT): £10.7 million

See *Sightline*, Winter 2020, pp. 14–17.

**The first figure** (01) shows the understated entrance, with three new brick openings through the thick brickwork wall. **The second** (02) shows the auditorium created within the existing structure. **Two further images** (03, 04) show the three flights of stairs connecting four levels and giving access to the foyer for use during an interval and the upper levels of the foyer in use during a school day. **The final figure** (05) is of the dance studio at The Malthouse.

Figure RP.09.02 Photo © Philip Vile.

**Design intent**

The existing building had been used since the 1960s as a car parts warehouse and was much altered since its days as a Malthouse. Nonetheless it remained intensely atmospheric. The design strategy was to make only the alterations that were essential, thereby preserving the inherent dramatic character and atmosphere, and making the Malthouse a place for creativity and experiment.

The theatre space was formed by threading five steel portal frames through the existing building structure and hanging the third-floor structure from the new frames. In the auditorium 'timber joists and steel beams roof the space' and 'bridges with tensioned-wire floors hang below' (Tim Ronalds, *Sightline*, Winter 2020, p. 17). The foyer was developed in the kiln part of the original building; the middle kiln was removed to open up a volume, in which three flights of stairs were built to connect the four levels. (See Figures RP.09.03 and RP.09.04.) The re-developed building provides a whole floor for wardrobe and prop-making studios, ample dressing rooms, a spacious backstage with workshops and scene dock as well as a studio and rehearsal rooms with charred timber trusses.

**Specific features/strengths**

- The unusual and special atmosphere of the building and the theatre within it, derived from the industrial qualities of the re-purposed Malthouse.
- The acoustic is designed to facilitate spoken/voice performances by young/less experienced performers.
- Technical equipment is specified to professional theatre standard, but also to be simple enough to allow pupils to learn on it.
- The size of the existing building means that ancillary and backstage space is more generous than would have been possible in a new-build theatre.

 Figure RP.09.03  Photo © Philip Vile.

Figure RP.09.05 Photo © Philip Vile.

Figure RP.09.04 Photo © Philip Vile

**Users' verdicts**

It's an extraordinarily inspiring space, which elevates our pupils' performances.

It has such a beautiful atmosphere.

Rebekah Beattie, Director of Drama,
The King's School

It is astonishing and exceeded expectations which were already high. It literally took my breath away; it is a very sympathetic renovation of an amazing building.

Victoria Outram, Head of Dance,
The King's School

The theatre facilities were described by the actor Joanna Lumley, who opened the building in 2019, as better than those found in professional environments.

KEY
1 - STAGE
2 - AUDITORIUM
3 - FOYER
4 - CONTROL ROOM
5 - WORKSHOP
6 - DRESSING ROOM
7 - GREEN ROOM
8 - TOILETS
9 - STUDIO
10 - DINING HALL
11 - BAR

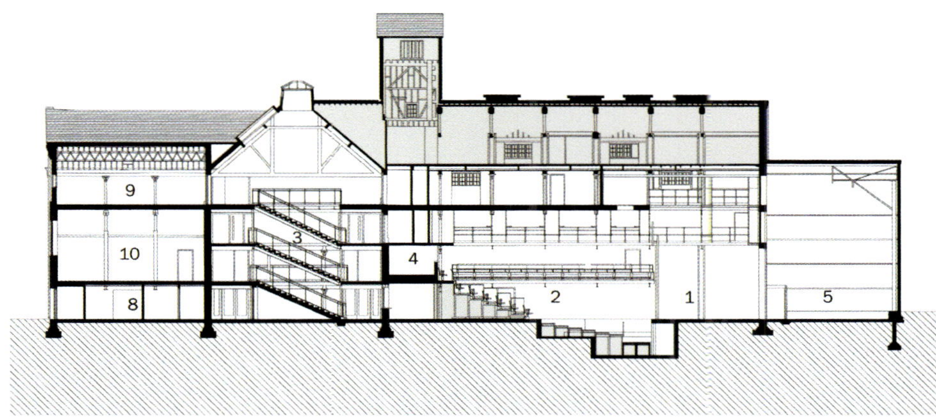


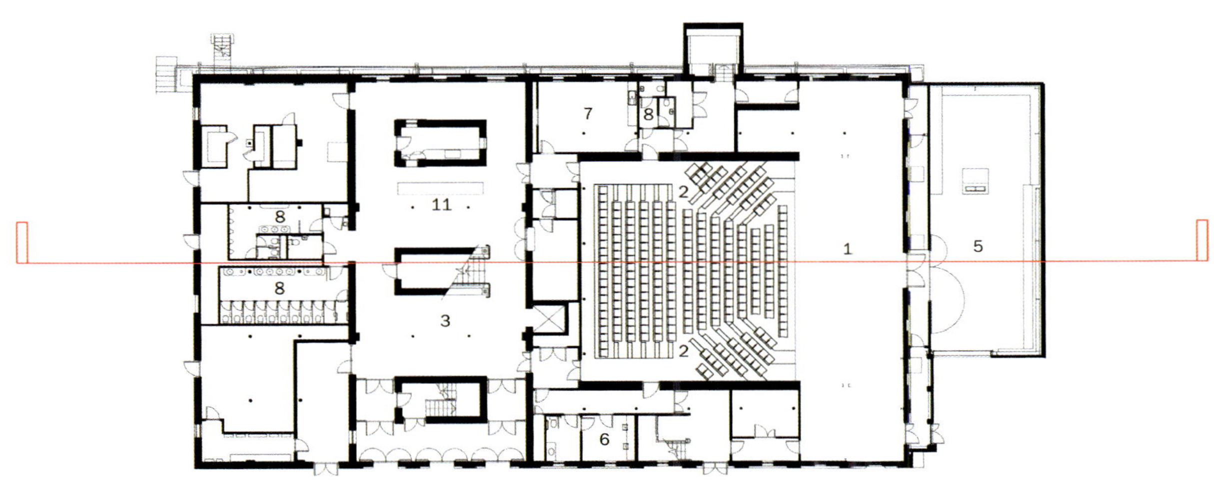


0 5 10 20 metres
0 15 30 60 feet
**1:500**

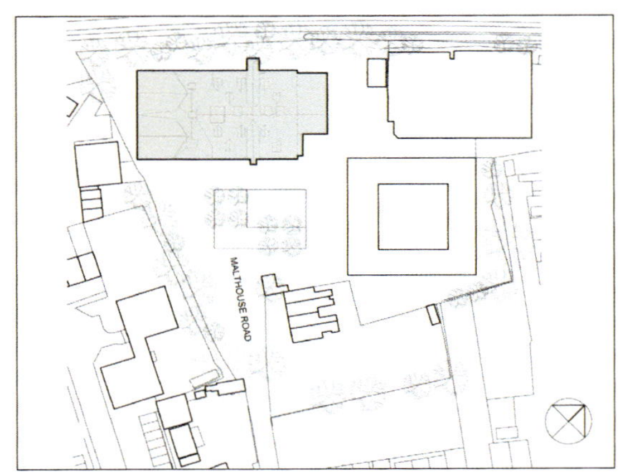


**SITE PLAN - 1:2500**

# New build theatres/small

# Reference Project 10
# Sam Wanamaker Playhouse, Shakespeare's Globe, London, UK

## Brief building description

A faithful reconstruction of a seventeenth-century Jacobean indoor playhouse, a space that Shakespeare would recognise, the auditorium has 340 seats in a compact and intimate space lit by candlelight and constructed within a pre-existing masonry envelope built twenty years previously. (See Figures RP.10.01, RP.10.02 and RP.10.03.) A part of the site that houses the rebuilt Shakespeare's Globe in Southwark (which opened in 1997), the Sam Wanamaker Playhouse hosts plays, concerts, education workshops and events throughout the year with its main theatrical season being over the winter months.

Figure RP.10.01 Photo © Pete Le May.

Figure RP.10.02 Photo © Pete Le May.

**Key facts**

**Client**
Shakespeare's Globe
Main contact: Neil Constable, Chief Executive

**Site address/web reference**
21 New Globe Walk, London, SE1 9DT
www.shakespearesglobe.com/

**Opening date**
January 2014

**Auditorium type and seating capacity**
Thrust stage, 340 seats

**Stage/performance space size**
6.35 × 4.46m

**Other facilities**
Rehearsal room in roof space above, new café, ticket office and foyer spaces

**Overall area**
1,810m$^2$

**Design team**
**Architect:** Allies and Morrison
**Reconstruction Architect:** Jon Greenfield
**Theatre consultants:** Fisher Dachs Associates; Shakespeare's Globe
**Acoustic consultant:** Paul Gillieron
**MEP:** FHP Design Consultancy
**Structural engineering:** Momentum
**Access:** David Bonnett Associates
**Fire engineering:** The Fire Surgery
**QS and project management:** Gardiner & Theobald
**Main contractor:** Virtus Contracts

**Construction cost at completion date**
(excluding fees and VAT): £5.3 million

See the Theatres Trust magazine, *Maintaining and Modernising Historic Theatres*, Issue 40, Summer 2014, pp. 7–10

See also: Andrew Nicholson, 'Devising a Fire Strategy [for the Sam Wanamaker Playhouse]', in *Sightline*, Autumn 2015, pp. 8–16.

Figure RP.10.03 Photo © Pete Le May.

**Ten figures** show the reconstruction of an indoor Jacobean playhouse linked to the Globe in Southwark, sharing foyer spaces and a glass-fronted entrance. The galleried auditorium is shown taking shape within a pre-existing masonry envelope and being decorated with authentic details including a candlelit stage with *frons scenae*; bench seating extends upwards over three floors with entrance points on each. Stage images usually include six chandeliers. Here Figure 04 shows seven, as in the first production of John Webster's *The Duchess of Malfi*. Figure 07 shows musicians in the stage gallery and audience members looking down onto the stage from a side gallery as well as from the seating facing the stage at pit and gallery levels. The final image (10) shows foyer spaces decorated for Christmas.

### Auditorium type

The thrust stage, with a decorative *frons scenae* and 'lords' rooms' either side, is deliberately very limited in scope for scenery or large props. Flexibility in the arrangement of the pit enables removable seating and an adjustable floor level. The space is primarily lit by candlelight but with a capability for production lighting discreetly integrated into the finishes. Foyers, bars and café have also been remodelled as part of project.

With excellent acoustics, the Sam Wanamaker Playhouse offers a compact and intimate experience for audience members on benches in the pit and in two horse-shoe galleries providing proximity to the stage.

### Design intent

As for the Globe project itself, the design finds a balance between creating a realistic and authentic seventeenth-century theatre and addressing the expectations and requirements of a twenty-first-century public venue. In practical terms, this means meeting modern building standards. (See Figure RP.10.05 and RP.10.06 here.)

In aesthetic and spiritual terms, this requires an understanding of the importance and value of each 'historic' element of a building and recreating those valuable attributes without compromising safety. To recreate an authentic Jacobean theatre, the intent is to ensure that both the positive and negative constraints for company leaders (directors), performers, production teams and audiences are equivalent to those of 1616. (See Figure RP.10.07.)

This has entailed accepting that the sightlines from many of the gallery seats are comparable to the expectations of Jacobean rather than today's audiences which, in turn, leads to learning to accept the importance of what can be heard as well as what can be seen.

### Specific features/strengths

A unique space in so many ways, the Sam Wanamaker Playhouse with has a hand-finished oak frame and carved decorative finishes. The hand

Figure RP.10.04 Photo © Pete Le May.

Figure RP.10.06 Photo © Pete Le May.

Figure RP.10.05 Photo © Pete Le May.

Figure RP.10.07 Photo © Pete Le May.

Figure RP.10.08 Photo © Pete Le May.

Figure RP.10.09 Photo © Pete Le May.

painted decorative scheme has gold leaf and *trompe l'oeil*. The space is lit by beeswax candles mounted in sconces, in six height-adjustable chandeliers and sometimes carried by the actors.

Rowan Moore, writing on architecture in *The Observer* (for *The Guardian* news group) on the Sunday before the opening night acknowledged that 'to have candles in a timber structure is not out of the best-practice rulebook for health and safety in modern theatres', adding

> its achievement is due both to the sophistication of smoke detectors and the patience and creativity of the fire consultant Andrew Nicholson, the fire brigade and various other relevant authorities. It is unusual to credit fire consultants in reviews of buildings, perhaps wrongly so, but here the contribution is vital: without the combination of wood and flame, which makes the interior feel like a kind of boat, floating in shadow, more than half the point of the project would be lost.
>
> (www.theguardian.com/artanddesign/2014/jan/12/sam-wanamaker-playhouse-globe-review)

**Users' verdicts**

The Sam Wanamaker Playhouse offers us a unique opportunity to explore the theatre practice of Shakespeare's day and the theatrical context within which he worked. We hope that the Wanamaker Playhouse will afford as many insights, and prove as theatrically rejuvenating, as the Globe has proved over the last 16 years.

Dominic Dromgoole, Artistic Director, speaking to Sky News, 13 January 2014

The opening play is Webster's *The Duchess of Malfi* which is a tragedy shrouded in darkness . . . ideally suited to this darkling space. . . . The success of the evening lies in the fact that Webster's play and this exciting new space make a perfect fit. There may be time in the weeks to come to raise questions about whether the candles occasionally block the sightlines of people in the upper tiers. . . . For the moment one can only rejoice that Shakespeare's Globe, about which I've not always been kind, has found a gorgeous indoor companion.

Michael Billington, on the first night of Dominic Dromgoole's production of *The Duchess of Malfi*, *The Guardian*, Thursday 16 January 2014

The Sam Wanamaker Playhouse is unlike any other theatre space I have visited – primarily because of the atmosphere created through candlelight. In a 2016 production of *The Winter's Tale*, a single hand-held candle was used to light only Antigonus's face as he arrived on the shores of Bohemia; together with the complete darkness that fell when his candle was extinguished, this use of lighting created an astonishing degree of tension. This solution to staging Antigonus's 'Exit, pursued by a bear' was followed by a startlingly long period of silence and darkness.

Ella Hawkins, Teaching Fellow in Early Modern English, University of Birmingham

The key is the relationship with the audience. The acoustics are extraordinary; the woody space creates a resonant soundbox. After our first run-through in the space, Fin (one of our boys' company) said, 'You can whisper and still be heard!' The audience is wrapped around the stage – and the performers – on different levels, it's akin to playing inside a funnel. All the time you need to keep throwing your performance up and down and round and round. And the performers share those levels and corridors with the audience; so they in turn can surround the audience. It creates a special kind of intimacy, very close and very fluid.

Perry Mills, Deputy Head of King Edward VI School, Stratford-upon-Avon and Director of Edward's Boys, who performed six little-known late-sixteenth and seventeenth-century Boy Company plays at the SWP between 2014 and 2018.

Figure RP.10.10 Photo © Pete Le May.

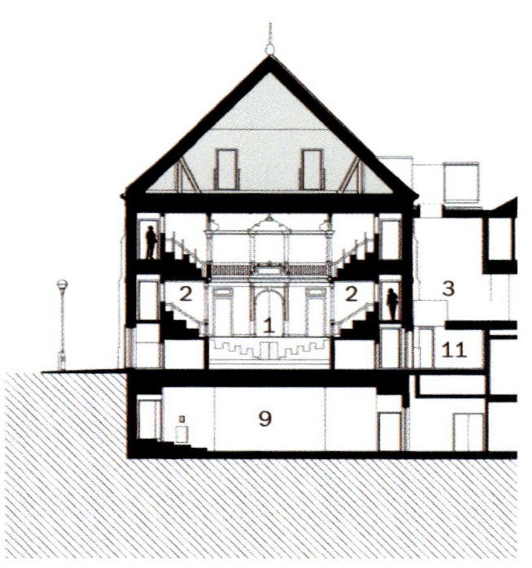

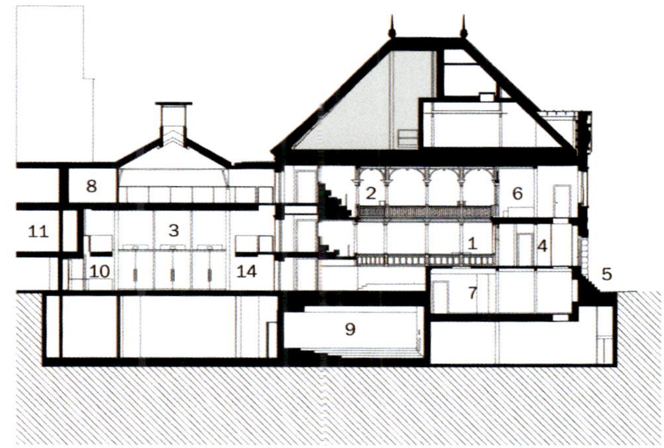

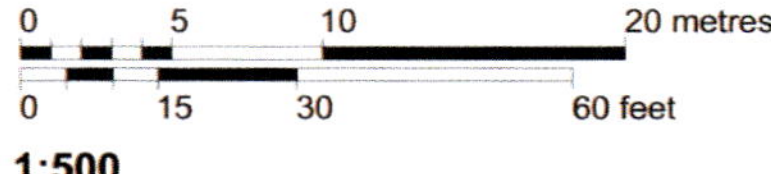


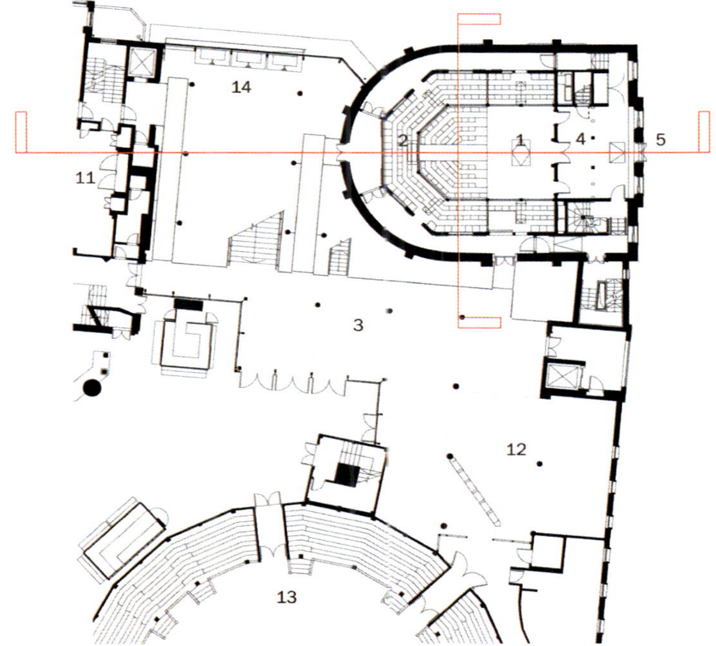

KEY

1 - STAGE
2 - AUDITORIUM
3 - FOYER
4 - TIRING HOUSE
5 - GET IN
6 - MUSICIANS' GALLERY
7 - UNDERSTAGE
8 - TOILETS
9 - LECTURE SPACE
10 - BOX OFFICE
11 - BAR/ CAFE
12 - RETAIL
13 - GLOBE THEATRE
14 - ENTRANCE FOYER

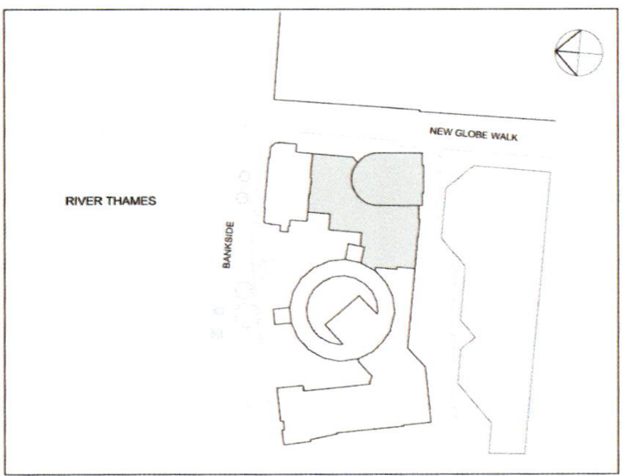


**SITE PLAN - 1:2500**

# Reference Project 11
# Elizabethan Theatre at Hardelot (Le Théâtre Elisabéthain du Château d'Hardelot, Condette, France)

### Brief building description

France's first neo-Shakespearean theatre (part of the Entente Cordial Cultural Centre near Boulogne sur Mer) was commissioned in 2013 by the Pas de Calais district council and delivered in 2016. (See Figure RP.11.01.) It is a producing and receiving house for theatre, opera and amplified music.

### Specific features/strengths

- World's first all-curved cross-laminated timber (CLT) building.
- All internal CLT left exposed and without flame spread treatment (except soffits).
- France's first naturally ventilated complex theatre designed using Gustave Eiffel's wind tunnel in Paris.

Figure RP.11.01 Photo © Martin Argyroglo.

### Auditorium type

With 388 seats in thrust/Elizabethan format, the auditorium can be reconfigured as a 270-seat baroque-scale opera house thanks to an orchestra pit lift, wings, proscenium tabs and a truckable 'tiring house' stage wall (see Figure RP.11.02). The acoustic response is set as a compromise between speech and small-format lyric music.

### Design intent

Set in lush parkland adjoining a vast nature reserve, the building's visual impact is diminished by placing technical spaces, back of house facilities and public toilets in a single basement level (necessary in any case because of the waterlogged site and poor ground conditions). (See drawing.) The superstructure is almost entirely in engineered timber, with an exterior cage in tropical bamboo (see Figure RP.11.01) which relates the building to its woodland setting (especially in winter). Front of house is kept to a strict minimum, with café facilities in another building.

### Key facts

**Client:**
Pas de Calais district council

**Site address/web reference**
Le Théâtre Elisabéthain du Château d'Hardelot,
1 rue de la Source,
62360 Condette, France
https://chateauhardelot.fr

**Opening date**
24 June 2016

**Auditorium type and seating capacity**
In thrust/Elizabethan format: 388
In baroque-scale opera house format: 270

**Stage/performance space size**
8m wide × 10.5m deep (including mobile Tiring House wall)
Orchestra pit opening 8 × 2.5m, can also be used at stall height to modulate forestage.

**Overall area m²**
1,233m²

**Design team**
**Architect:** Studio Andrew Todd
**Theatre consultant:** Charcoalblue
**Acoustic consultant:** Charcoalblue
**Structure, services and energy:** LM Ingénieur
**Fire engineering and diversity of access:** Casso
**Landscape:** L+A
**Main contractor:** Wood structure and envelope: Cruard SA

**Construction cost at completion date**
(excluding fees and VAT) 4.2 million euros

Award for the best wooden construction in the world, 2017 (*World Architecture News*, Awards).

Figure RP.11.02 Photo © Martin Argyroglo.

**Users' verdicts**

Studio Andrew Todd have a uniquely deep conviction and know-how concerning the essential links between ecological, social and creative imperatives in making space. Beauty, function and eco-footprint are conjointly benevolent in Hardelot, which is simply the most beautiful theatre in the world. My work flew there as nowhere else.

Irina Brook, Director

Studio Andrew Todd brought deep empathy to the Hardelot Elizabethan Theatre. Uniquely, they were able to provide creativity and technical know-how at equal and mutually support ve levels, consistently going far beyond the brief in the elaboration of this widely-loved building.

Sébastien Mahieuxe, Director, Midsummer Festival

**The three images** evoke the location and atmosphere of this Elizabethan-inspired playhouse in the grounds of a French château. **The first** (01) shows the exterior of the theatre with the Château d'Hardelot to the left rear of the image. **The second and third** (02, 03) show the rear stage wall with its 'tiring house' and the interior of the auditorium from the stage.

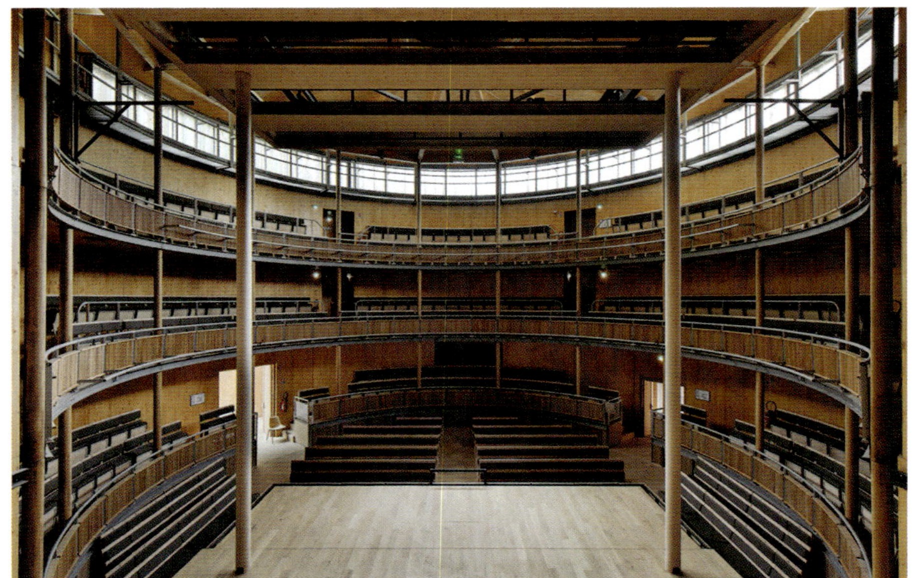

Figure RP.11.03 Photo © Martin Argyroglo.

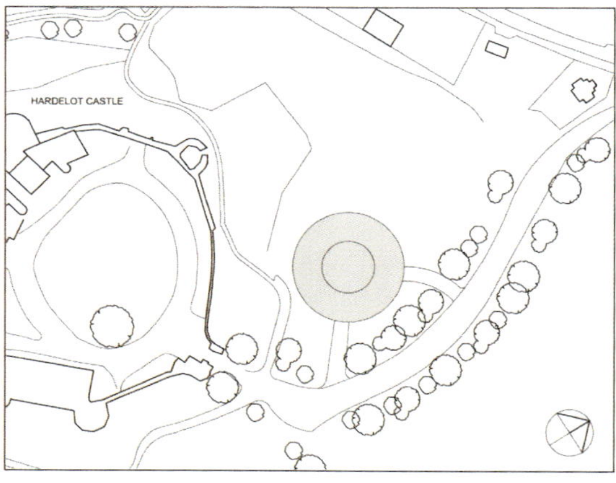

KEY
1 - STAGE
2 - AUDITORIUM
3 - ENTRANCE FOYER
4 - CONTROL ROOM
5 - GET IN
6 - DRESSING ROOMS
7 - UNDERSTAGE
8 - REAR STAGE
9 - OFFICES

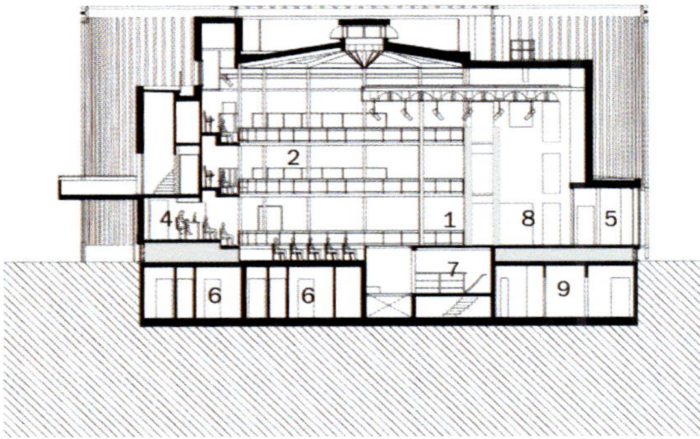


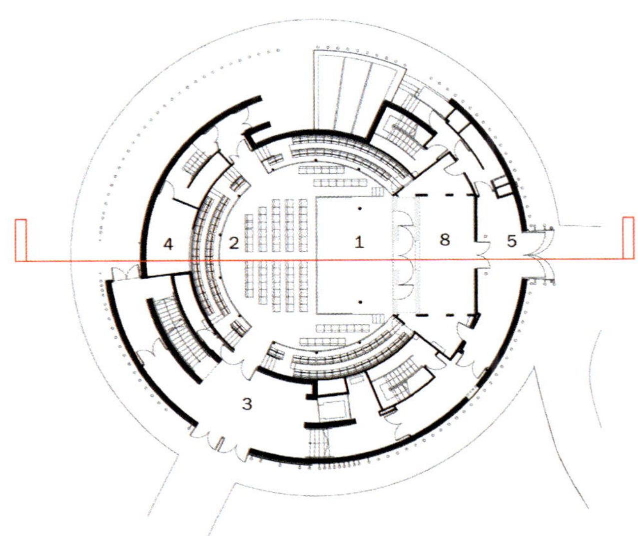


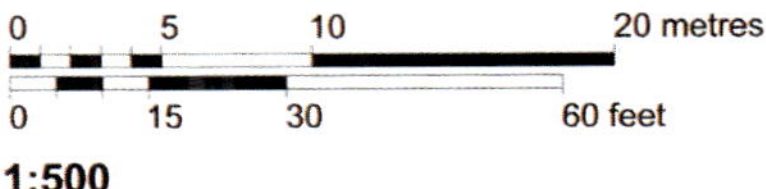

# Reference Project 12
# Tara Theatre, London, UK

### Brief building description

Tara Theatre has been the home of the UK's first Asian-led arts organisation for over forty years, launched in 1977 as a direct response to the racist murder of seventeen-year-old Gurdip Singh Chaggar. The theatre has served as a seedbed for dynamic and innovative cross-cultural arts practice for a generation of diverse arts practitioners, including directors, choreographers, musicians, writers and performers. Consistently at the forefront of BAME arts practice, the theatre has been involved in creative partnerships with theatres across the country, including the National Theatre. It has hosted theatre practitioners from around the world and has produced numerous critically acclaimed works – performing not only to its loyal South London audience but also to theatregoers around the world as part of its international touring projects.

Tara acquired its building base in 1983 – a former community church attached to a high street three-storey terrace – with a small fifty-seat studio (see article by Jatinder Verma in *Sightline*, Autumn 2016, p. 8). By the early 2000s it had become evident that the organisation's much-loved end-of terrace Victorian building had begun to place limitations on the company's artistic aspirations – with major work needed to upgrade the fabric of the building, address the train noise from the adjacent railway line and provide improved wheelchair access. Today's Tara Theatre building is the result of a major capital project completed in 2016, which rebuilt Tara's home at 356 Garratt Lane to welcome the next generation of artists and audiences.

Figure RP.12.01 Photo © Philip Vile/RHWL, Aedas Arts Team.

## Auditorium type

The rejuvenated Tara Theatre is effectively a new-build venue, set behind the rebuilt Victorian terraced frontage (see Figure RP.12.01). The aspiration was to retain the sense of history and identity of the original building; 7500 of the bricks used to construct the auditorium were salvaged from the original structure. The irregular, wedge-shaped performance space sits on the footprint of the original auditorium – a former mission hall.

### Key facts

**Client/user**
Jatinder Verma
(former Artistic Director, Tara Arts)
Abdul Shayek
(Artistic Director and Joint CEO)

**Site address/web reference**
Tara Theatre,
356 Garratt Lane,
Earlsfield, London
SW18 4ES
https://taratheatre.com

**Opening date**
September 2016 ('new' venue)

**Auditorium type and seating capacity**
101-seat flexible studio theatre with earth stage

**Stage/performance space size**
Auditorium size $85m^2$
Stage size 4.7 × 4.6m

**Other facilities**
Rehearsal room
Multi-purpose room

**Overall area**
$423m^2$ GIA (overall building)

**Design team**
**Architect:** RHWL Arts Team/Aedas Arts Team
**Theatre consultant:** Theatreplan
**Acoustic consultant:** Arup Acoustics
**Structural engineer:** Jane Wernick Associates/engineers HRW
**MEP consultant:** Atelier Ten (to Stage D)/Clearsprings ES (Stage E to completion)
**Quantity surveyor:** Davis Langdon AECOM
**Project manager:** Cragg Management
**BREEAM consultant:** Sol Environment
**Fire consultant:** Trenton Fire Ltd.
**Main contractor:** HA Marks Ltd.

Construction cost at completion date (excluding fees and VAT): £2.7 million

The intimate 101-seat studio theatre was conceived as a flexible and adaptable performance space, with seating set around an innovative 4.7 × 4.6–m earthen stage (flush with the surrounding floor). The auditorium allows for a variety of staging configurations, with a tiered bank of fixed seating (along with a small side box) to the north, and flexible seating surrounding the other sides of the stage. It is most frequently used in thrust and in-the-round formats.

Figure RP.12.02 Photo: Hélène Binet.

The generous height of the auditorium is particularly dramatic given its compact footprint. The grid level is set at 5.5m above the stage with an enclosed control room (with a sliding window) at first floor level. A window offers glimpses into the space from the main staircase, helping to create a sense of connectivity throughout the building.

Raw 'elemental' materials, reclaimed seating and the incorporation of unique Indian artefacts make for an informal and characterful studio space. (See Figure RP.12.02.) For rehearsal and daytime use, a high-level window floods the auditorium with natural light, and the ritual closing of the blackout shutter – a beautiful teak screen – creates a magical and captivating start to a performance.

## Design intent

The vision which drove the rejuvenation of Tara Theatre was to create an imaginative fusion of the global and the local in the venue's Earlsfield home. The components of the building draw inspiration from the dialogue between East and West which characterises the organisation's cross-cultural and forward-looking artistic work.

Key physical objectives of the redevelopment included the creation of a more adaptable auditorium which roughly doubled the capacity of the original performance space while providing much-upgraded technical infrastructure.

The renovation also delivered a rehearsal space for the development of new and experimental work (see Figure RP.12.03), modernised office and

See *Sightline*, Autumn 2016, pp. 8–15.

**The three figures** (01, 02, 03) show the exterior of the new Tara Theatre, its intimate, flexible studio auditorium and its rehearsal space.

Figure RP.12.03 Photo © Philip Vile/RHWL, Aedas Arts Team.

foyer spaces, enhanced WC provision, a more sustainable building fabric, a courtyard garden, better storage and support spaces, and new mechanical and electrical services throughout. A strong emphasis was placed upon optimising the audience experience and radically improving accessibility.

The building's evocative cob stage was a key element of the brief, echoing the roots of Indian theatre – sitting on the earth telling stories beneath the banyan tree (a motif which is further expressed in the building's pargeted façade). The sensory experience of performing barefoot on the earth stage is much-loved by performers.

## Specific features/strengths

The rich and tactile material palette of the auditorium strikes a sensitive balance – providing the neutrality required to let the artistic work take central focus, whilst at the same time embodying the organisation's unique identity. The building as a whole feels convivial, memorable and welcoming to all – a reflection of the open and collaborative ethos of the company who call it their home.

Situated immediately adjacent to the railway embankment, the acoustic demands of the brief were extremely stringent. The beautifully quiet auditorium is a testament to the success of the acoustic strategy – particularly impressive given the use of rustic teak doors throughout the building – with unique artefacts brought from the salvage yards of India and adapted to meet acoustic, fire and accessibility requirements.

The venue has been recognised for its sustainability credentials. Renewable, low-energy and low-flow services are integrated throughout the building. The thermal envelope was designed to be highly insulated and airtight and was constructed using responsibly sourced, healthy materials. The sedum roof and courtyard garden have enhanced the ecology of the site. The quiet, low-energy ventilation system in the auditorium works with natural ventilation flows, while the thermal mass of the exposed brickwork helps to reduce temperature fluctuations, maintaining audience comfort. The building generates energy through photovoltaic panels. The venue's heating uses a low temperature hot water (LTHW) system, fed by an air source heat pump system located at roof level. Reclaimed materials are used throughout – even down to the auditorium seating, which had formerly been used by the Royal Shakespeare Company.

**User's verdict**

Beauty and intimacy were what we hoped for – and we have been delighted by how it's been achieved. From the moment we walked into the renovated building, we were struck by the generosity of spirit it exuded – a palpable feeling of comfortable and comforting space. The elegance of solutions to audience-flow, seating and natural light, have contributed to making this unique building feel not 'precious' but rather user-friendly – a 'home' as much for artists as audiences. I am convinced Tara Theatre should become an exemplar for what any small theatre can and should be.

Jatinder Verma, Former Artistic Director, Tara Theatre

KEY
1 - STUDIO THEATRE
2 - REHEARSAL ROOM
3 - FOYER
4 - BOX OFFICE
5 - TOILETS
6 - OFFICE
7 - COURTYARD GARDEN

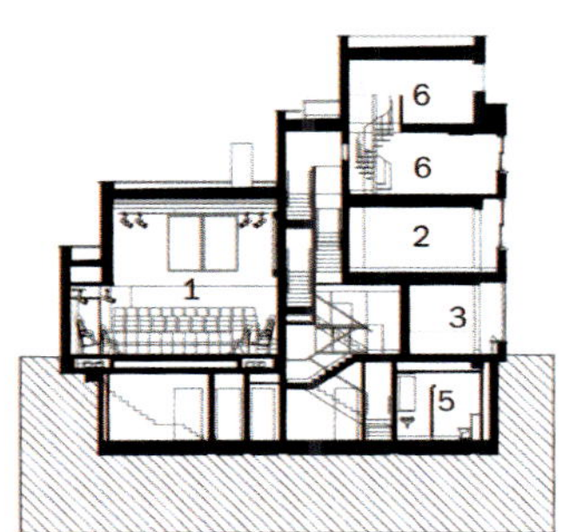


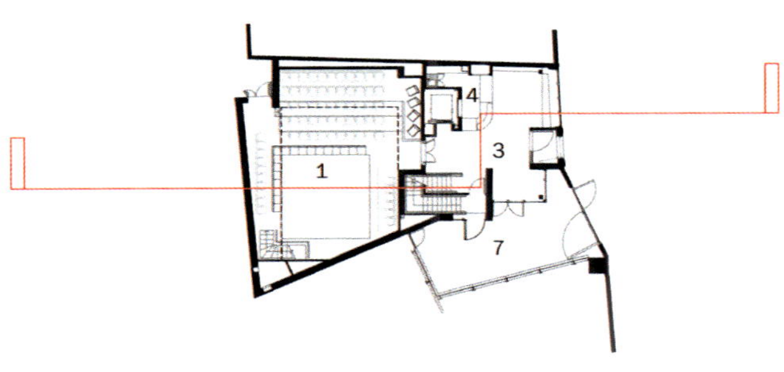


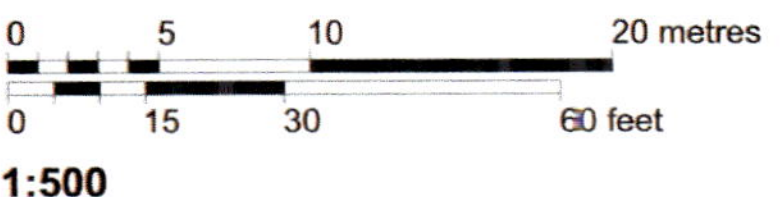


1:500

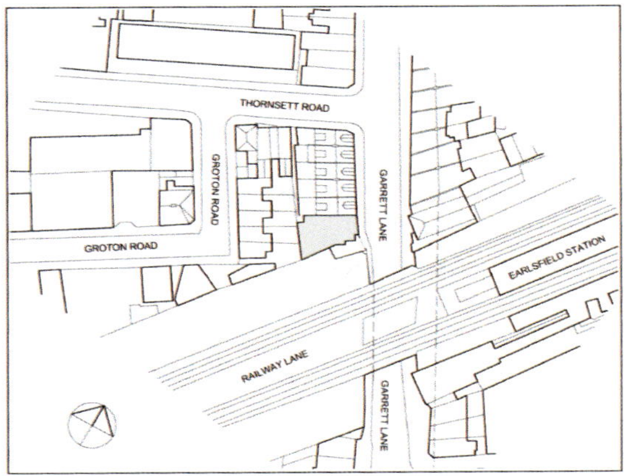


SITE PLAN - 1:2500

# Reference Project 13 Boulevard Theatre Soho, London, UK

### Brief building description

The Boulevard Theatre has replaced the iconic Raymond Revuebar in Soho with a new multifunctional performance space, featuring a revolving auditorium and mechanised floor. Contemporary brick and glass facades are topped by a remade version of the original neon sign while, inside, the theatre and restaurant interiors reflect the opulent Art Deco heritage of London's West End.

Figure RP.13.01 Photo © tomlee.gallery.

### Auditorium type/types

The cylindrical auditorium can revolve at both stalls and balcony level to provide several configurations that adapt to a diverse programme of work ranging from theatre, comedy and cabaret to fashion shows, films and dinners. It was designed using VR technology and can be reconfigured

**Key facts**

**Client**
Fawn James, Founder and Chair
Soho Estates
Artistic Director, Rachel Edwards

**Site address/web reference**
6 Walker's Court, Soho,
W1F 0BT
www.boulevardtheatre.co.uk

**Opening date:**
October 2019

**Auditorium and seating capacity**
Flexible auditorium: seating capacity up to 160, depending on configuration.
Stage/performance space size: 8.7m wide × 7.1m deep, maximum stage format.

**Design team**
**Architect:** SODA Studio
**Theatre consultant:** Charcoalblue
**Acoustic consultant:** Charcoalblue
**Seating design:** Charcoalblue, SODA Studio, Race Furniture
**Structural engineer:** Tier
**M&E consultant:** Thornton Reynolds
**Quantity surveyor:** Gleeds
**Planning consultant:** Gerald Eve
**Project manager:** Development Managers
**Main contractor:** Blenheim House Construction
**Stage engineering and revolve contractor:** TAIT
**Specialist stage lighting and audio/video contractor:** White Light

**Construction cost at completion date (excluding fees and VAT):** £40 million

Figure RP.13.02 Photo © tomlee.gallery.

See *Sightline*, Winter 2019, pp. 8–11

**Of the five images** here, **the first and final two** (01, 04, 05) show the Boulevard Theatre's street-presence in the busy Soho area of London, split across a pedestrian alleyway off Walker's Court and connected via a double-height glass bridge, with a hanging steel staircase visible on one side winding up through the building. **The second and third images** (02, 03) show two of the various configurations possible for the flexible auditorium.

Figure RP.13.03 Photo © tomlee.gallery.

within an hour, 'enabling the Boulevard to host up to four events a day' (*Sightline*, Winter 2019, p. 8).

### Design intent

As a small unsubsidised enterprise, the Boulevard Theatre planned to develop a business model which would allow it to work with theatre producers and commercial operators to generate income in a variety of ways. It was vital that the theatre would provide an important cultural anchor and help reinforce Soho's role in an area rich in entertainment. The building itself has become a beacon during the day and night, offering a multitude of different uses for locals and tourists, ranging from plays and cocktails to exhibitions and shopping.

### Specific features/strengths

The building reveals its activities to passers-by thanks to a double-height glass bridge (see Figure RP.13.04), which has been inlaid with a lace-patterned design that recalls the net curtains of the area's infamous brothels. This is joined by a glazed corner facing onto Berwick Street, featuring a dramatic hanging steel staircase (see Figure RP.13.05) that takes the audience to the auditorium above the restaurant.

Figure RP.13.04 Photo © tomlee.gallery.

'The large street-facing windows feature a triple blind system, one for blackout, another to be projected onto and a third to prevent glare during the daytime' (*Sightline*, Winter 2019, p. 11).

For a few months from its opening the Boulevard Theatre produced three acclaimed productions and was due to open a fourth while, alongside these, the Boulevard ran a programme of late night and Sunday events including comedy, jazz, podcast recordings and live poetry. The theatre was forced to close in 2020 during the COVID-19 pandemic.

Figure RP.13.05 Photo © tomlee.gallery.

**User's verdict**

I've never seen anything quite like it. It is a radical rejection both of the black box and the over-designed nightclub and is intended to accommodate a heavy and hard-working schedule from musicals and conferences to stand-up and cabaret, programmed all through the day and the night.

Edwin Heathcote, *Financial Times*

KEY
1 - REVOLVING STAGE & STALLS
2 - REVOLVING BALCONY
3 - FOYER
4 - BOH AREA
5 - ENTRANCE HALL
6 - DRESSING ROOM
7 - BAR
8 - TOILETS
9 - REHEARSAL ROOM
10 - PRODUCTION OFFICE
11 - RESTAURANT

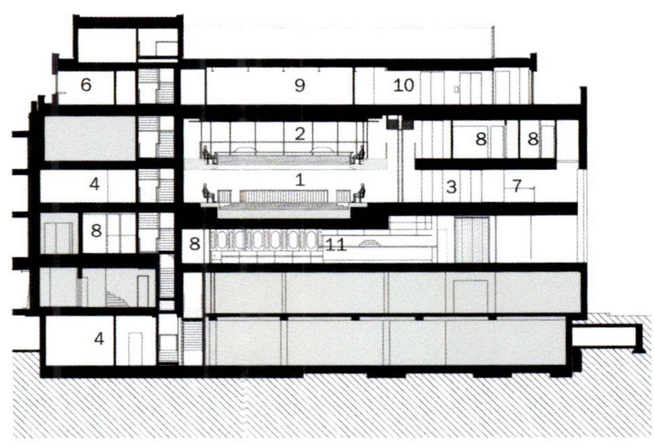


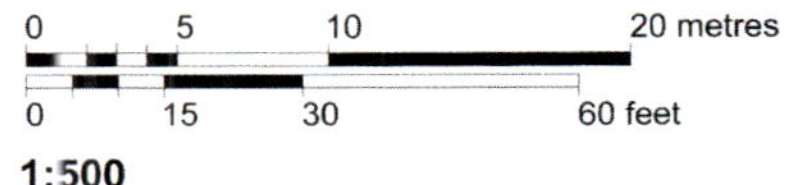


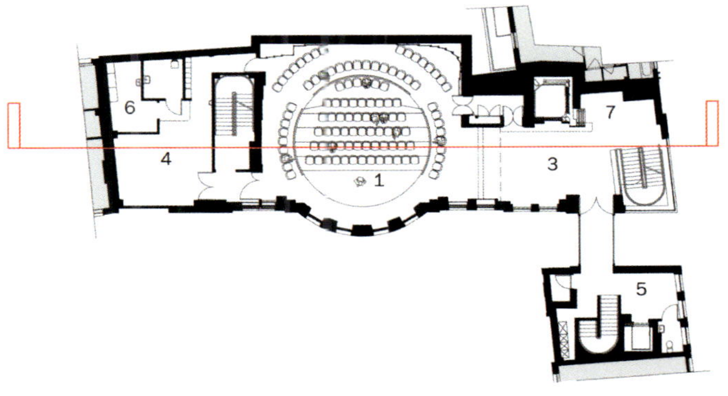

THEATRE FORMATS

SITE PLAN - 1:2500

# New build theatres/medium

# Reference Project 14
# The Lyric Theatre, Belfast, UK

### Brief building description

The development involved the demolition of the existing theatre and the construction of a new building for use by The Lyric, Northern Ireland's only full-time producing theatre. The Lyric Theatre is a complex public building providing new auditorium, rehearsal and studio theatre spaces together with an ancillary foyer, bar, education, office and technical facilities. The new building comprises of 5,026m$^2$ of gross floor area over seven levels. The three elements of theatre, studio and rehearsal room are the fundamental components of the project. Their dimensions and three-dimensional volumes are determined by the requirements of the functional operation of a contemporary producing theatre.

### Auditorium types

The 389-seat auditorium is a single steep rake, where the body of the audience is not broken by balconies and the actors are in the same room as the audience. The parabolic section of the raked seating has been developed with the assistance of a computer analysis to ensure optimum sightlines from every seat. (See Figure RP.14.01.) The seating layout is creased along one

Figure RP.14.01 Photo © Dennis Gilbert.

**Key facts**

**Client:**
The Lyric Theatre

**Site address/web reference:**
55 Ridgeway St,
Belfast BT9 5FB, UK.
https://lyrictheatre.co.uk/

**Opening date:**
1 May 2011

**Auditorium types:**
Main auditorium:
389 seats in a single rake.
Performance studio:
110–150 people.

**Stage/performance space size:**
**Main theatre:** overall stage area
19.8m (wide) × 9.9m (deep)
performance area
12.4m (wide) × 6.3m (deep)
**Studio:** end stage area
9.5m (wide) × 6.3m (deep) flat floor
area (with seats in storage)
12.2m (wide) × 14.8m (deep)

**Other facilities:**
The third space is a rehearsal room the same size as the main auditorium stage. Other facilities include an education suite, green room, dressing rooms, board room, backstage facilities, box office, café/bar and river terrace.

**Overall area:**
5,026m$^2$

**Design team**
**Architect:** O'Donnell + Tuomey
**Theatre consultant:** Theatreplan
**Acoustic consultant:** Sound Space Design
**Access consultant & CDM coordinator:** Ken Ewart Associates
**Main contractor:** Gilbert-Ash N.I. Limited

**Construction cost at completion date** (excluding fees and VAT): £13.2 million

line, folding slightly, like an open hand to hold the audience, focused on the stage but within sight of each other. The faceted acoustic lining, in the shape of three timber arches, encloses the audience.

The studio is a 6-metre-high brick warehouse-like performance space. Its flexible layout provides for end stage, traverse, thrust, in-the-round, cabaret and promenade performance possibilities. The layout provides additional staging possibilities for readings and concerts. The main seating is retractable and versatile while having a high specification.

The rehearsal room is a naturally ventilated double height space with a sprung timber floor area larger than the main stage playing area with space around for props and the production team. The acoustics of this room allow for recitals and readings.

## Design intent

The Lyric Theatre stands on a sloping site at the triangular junction between the grid pattern of Belfast's brick streetscape and the serpentine parkland of the River Lagan (see Figure RP.14.02).

Figure RP.14.02 Photo © Dennis Gilbert.

The design was developed in response to the urban and landscape conditions of the site. The building site was tightly restricted and irregular in shape. The solid sculpted brick volumes linked by transparent permeable public spaces are intended to visually connect with the surrounding landscape of street, river and Lyric woods. There are three different points of entry, one for trucks and two for people, all tied to existing street levels.

The Lyric plan is composed of three constituent elements, the auditorium, the studio and the rehearsal room. Utilising a complex cast concrete structure, each element is acoustically separated from the others and each is identifiably outlined in its own shell of 'Belfast' brick. The in-between spaces are designed to have an intimate character, providing for impromptu theatrical occasions within the flowing social space.

See *Sightline*, Spring 2011, pp. 23–24.

**The first figure** (01) shows the Lyric Theatre's main auditorium with its distinctive seating layout, while **the second figure** (02) shows the view looking out from the foyer across to the river and parkland. **The third** (03) shows an exterior approach to the theatre while **the final figure** (04) shows the internal approach to the foyer from the street, circling up to the auditoria.

Figure RP.14.03 Photo © Dennis Gilbert.

Figure RP.14.04 Photo © Dennis Gilbert.

**Specific features/strengths**

All the building materials are selected to endure and will be crafted to weather with age. Built in 'Belfast' brick, the new building holds one corner of the continuous system of brick streets, the last building on the grid marking the corner of Ridgeway Street and addressing the River Lagan. All external windows, doors and screens are hardwood timber.

The principle of the external envelope design was to utilise the benefits of thermal mass and air tightness which regulate internal temperatures. Full-fill cavity insulation was installed to maximise thermal efficiency.

Brick, timber, concrete and stone form the fabric of the internal public spaces, with bespoke furniture used throughout the building. The public approach from the street up a gently rising sandstone stair and enter a dynamic foyer space from which both performance spaces are entered. (See Figure RP.14.04) The spiralling circulation pattern empathises with the generating force of the performance spaces at the centre of the plan.

**Users' verdicts**

The Lyric team refused to compromise on its vision of building a theatre that would be both strikingly handsome and functional.

The use of Belfast brick echoes the existing south Belfast landscape. The extensive use of glass maximises the presence of natural light in the public spaces and ensures that our magnificent river aspect can be enjoyed to its full potential. Iroko, sandstone and concrete features lend warmth, sophistication and depth.

Nothing about this project has been easy. John Tuomey and his team turned our dreams into reality.

Mark Carruthers, Chairman, The Lyric Theatre

As a lighting designer, it's obvious from the start that the Lyric's architects have listened to the theatre consultants throughout the design process, which has resulted in a theatre that is both beautiful *and* practical. Much thought has clearly been put into the needs of the design and technical teams, with a raft of clever and innovative features, as well as getting the simple things right like the FOH bridges at the correct angle and distance from the stage. The Naughton Studio is probably the best designed and most versatile studio space I've ever worked in. Best of all is the large window along one wall (which can be closed behind panelling during shows) which allows you to work in daylight during the fit-up. There's no way to understate the value of sunlight to the moral of a crew who normally have to spend their entire day in a claustrophobic black box.

James C. McFetridge, Lighting Designer

KEY
1 - MAIN STAGE AREA
2 - AUDITORIUM SEATING AREA
3 - SCENE DOCK
4 - CONTROL ROOM
5 - MAIN FOYER
6 - DRESSING ROOMS
7 - BACKSTAGE OFFICES
8 - TOILETS
9 - STUDIO THEATRE
10 - FRONT OF HOUSE BAR
11 - KITCHEN
12 - LOADING DOCK

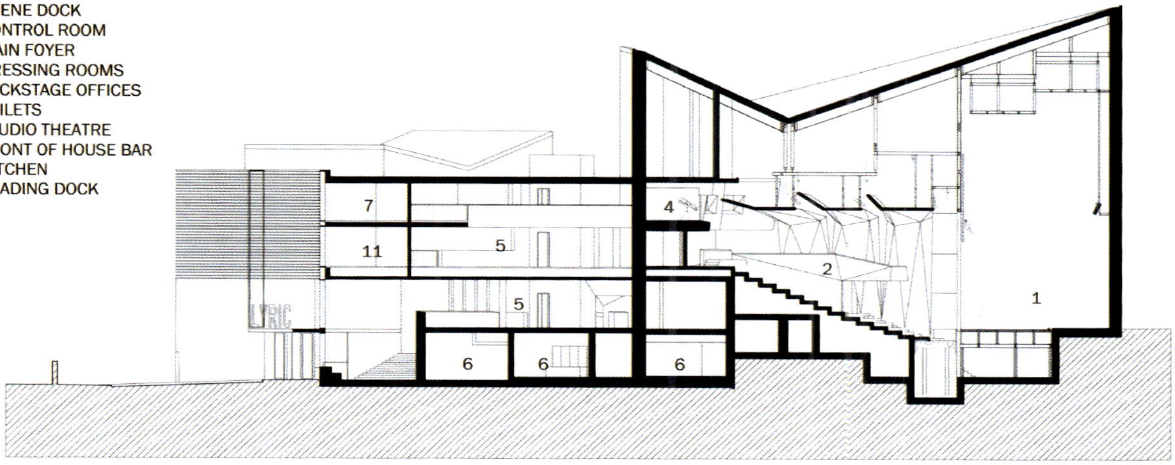

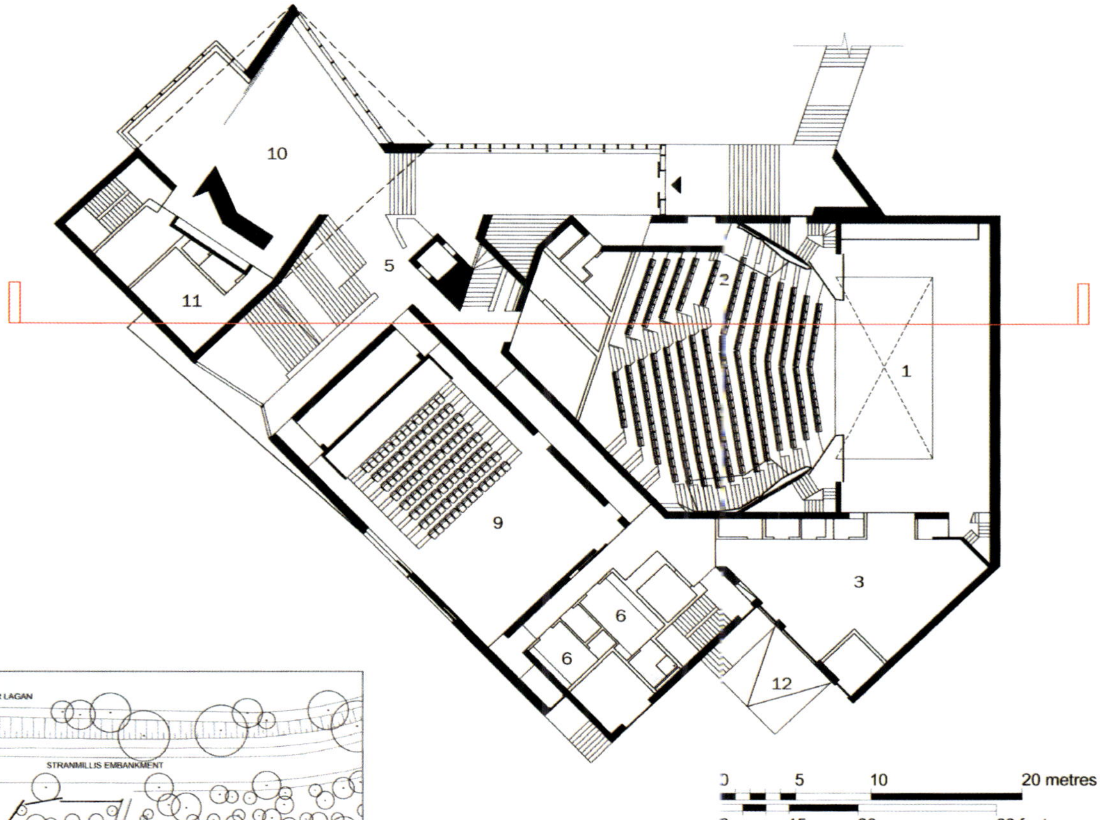

7 4 11 5 2 5 1 6 6 6

10 5 11 2 1 9 3 6 6 12

0 5 10 20 metres
0 15 30 60 feet
1:500

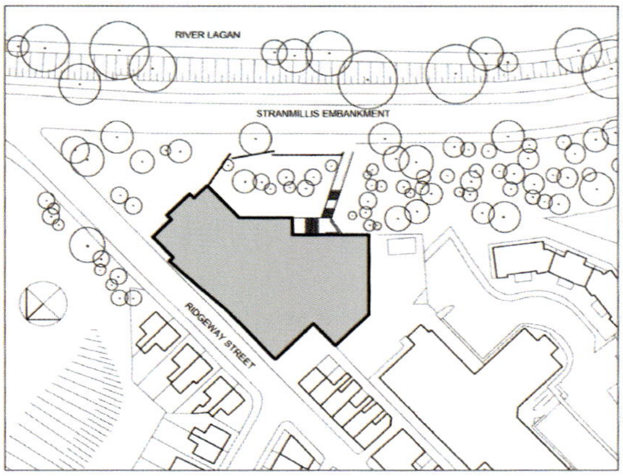

RIVER LAGAN
STRANMILLIS EMBANKMENT
RIDGEWAY STREET

SITE PLAN - 1:2500

# Reference Project 15
# CAST, Doncaster, UK

### Brief building description

Doncaster CAST opened in September 2013 – a focal point in the town's new civic and cultural quarter, which formed part of the Waterdale Masterplan. The state-of-the-art venue was conceived as a purpose-built, fully accessible toolbox for the performing arts.

Inspired by the architectural heritage of Doncaster, a simple rectilinear form faces onto Sir Nigel Greasley Square. It is glazed to the north, solid to the south in response to the urban context. (See Figure RP.15.01.) Built in local reconstituted limestone, this 'toolbox' loosely encloses the clearly defined volumes of the cultural spaces within: the main theatre, the studio theatre, dance/drama studios, an education suite, and their supporting public and back of house facilities. The foyer has an all-day café/bar with informal performance and exhibition capability.

Figure RP.15.01 Photo © Philip Vile/RHWL, Aedas Arts Team.

CAST's ethos places a strong emphasis on inclusivity and diversity, offering educational and participatory activities for those of all ages and backgrounds. The charity supports new emerging local artists and writers as well as welcoming nationally renowned companies such as the National Theatre and The Royal Ballet. CAST offers extensive outreach programmes and has a close working relationship with Doncaster College, offering students professional-level experience in a cutting-edge venue.

### Auditorium type/types

CAST's main auditorium space is a proscenium-arch theatre for drama, comedy, musicals, dance and small-scale opera. The layout is a traditional lyric theatre style, with an orchestra pit, flytower and two levels of seating, all designed for optimum sightline viewing. (See Figure RP.15.02.) The overall feel is intimate, formal and luxurious, with an emphasis on beautifully made features and locally inspired detailing, including hexagonal chandeliers that show a cross section of Doncaster-produced steel ropes in reference to the town's industrial heritage.

The venue's second performance space is a flexible studio theatre designed for everything from pop and rocks gigs to dance and drama (see Figure RP.15.03). It has an industrial 'warehouse' feel, and is a space for experimentation and creativity, with a wraparound balcony and an 'egg crate' lighting grid. The space has retractable raked seating and a cinema projection screen.

### Key facts

**Client**
Deborah Rees, Director
Clare Clarkson, Deputy Director

**Site address/web reference**
Cast
Waterdale
Doncaster
DN1 3BU
https://castindoncaster.com/

**Opening date**
September 2013

**Auditorium type and seating capacity**
Main Space: a 620-seat proscenium arch lyric theatre with a flytower and orchestra pit.
There are two levels of seating: the stalls and the dress circle.
Second space: a flexible studio theatre with semi-sprung floor.
Capacity of 200 seated or 400 standing across stalls and gallery levels.
Retractable raked seating unit.

**Stage/performance space size**
Main space: Stage 21m wide × 10m deep. 16.9m to underside of grid
Second space: 13.5m wide × 14m long × 5.8m high (to underside of lights)

**Other facilities**
Dance Studio:
11.8m wide × 11.8m long × 9m high flexible rehearsal and performance area with a seated capacity of 60.
Sprung dance floor and flown lighting trusses. Openable walls onto the foyer space.
Drama Studio:
11.8m wide × 9.5m long × 6.5m high flexible rehearsal and performance area with a seated capacity of 60.
Semi-sprung stage floor.
Technical viewing area and fixed lighting grid.

**Overall area**
5,840m² GIA

**Design team**
**Developer:** Muse Developments
**Architect:** RHWL Arts Team
**Theatre engineering:** Charcoalblue
**Structural engineer:** Arup
**MEP engineer:** Arup
**Lighting design:** Arup
**Acoustic consultant:** Arup Acoustics
**BREEAM consultant:** Arup
**Quantity surveyor:** Gardiner & Theobald
**Access consultant:** Arcadis Vectra
**Landscape architect:** Grontmij UK
**Main contractor:** Vinci Construction UK

**Construction cost at completion date** (excluding fees and VAT): £15.6 million

See *Sightline*, Winter 2013/14, pp. 7–10

**The five figures** illustrate the place of CAST in its community and its internal spaces. **The first image** (01) shows an exterior view of the theatre in the evening. This is followed by **two images**, (02, 03) one of each of the theatre's auditoria: the main auditorium seen across the stalls and dress circle and the studio theatre with its balcony, egg-crate lighting grid and flexible space. **The fourth figure** (04) looks into CAST's colourful and accessible spaces from outside showing various levels and a foyer seating area.

Figure RP.15.02 Photo © Philip Vile/RHWL, Aedas Arts Team.

Figure RP.15.03 Photo © Philip Vile/RHWL, Aedas Arts Team.

The two primary spaces are supported by a 365m² education suite containing dance and drama spaces and a meeting space, each with a capacity of sixty people. The light and spacious studios are double height, with sprung and semi-sprung floors respectively, while the single height exhibition room opens into the foyer to create an additional flexible space for events.

### Design intent

CAST is a building for everybody. The aim was to create a sustainable venue that would suit a wide range of performers – from drama, comedy, and musical theatre to live music gigs and smaller-scale experimental theatre – and host a variety of community and education projects: all within a restricted budget. The solution to this was to opt for a simple and rational form, punctuated by the three main performance spaces. The informal and 'open' design of the building also related to a key aspiration that the venue should enliven and animate the public square and be an all-day community resource. As a purpose-built theatre, CAST includes all the necessary technical infrastructure to provide the very best support for artistic expression.

### Specific features/strengths

The distinctive performance spaces and high technical specifications have given Doncaster a state-of-the-art, landmark venue that attracts performers from across the arts world to the town's cultural quarter. Since the building's completion, it has made a great impact on the local community and the regional arts infrastructure as well as providing a significant boost for the area's night-time economy.

The life inside the building is clearly visible from the square, and performances and events frequently spill out into this public space. (See Figure RP.15.04.)

The venue's architecture has enabled the organisation to fulfil its vision of a welcoming and accessible creative hub – a visible part of the daily life of the community, where patrons are equally as likely to drop into the foyer for a spontaneous coffee as to see a performance.

Figure RP.15.04 Photo © Philip Vile/RHWL, Aedas Arts Team.

### Envitonmental solutions

Environmentally conscious solutions were incorporated across the project, including naturally ventilating the foyer and using sun pipes and windcatchers in the roof to save on energy costs. The building also uses a combined heat and power (CHP) system and employs efficient water management systems. CAST was one of the first theatres in the county to achieve a BREEAM Very Good rating and the capital cost of the venue (per seat) was noticeably significantly less than other comparable new-build theatres in the United Kingdom at the time.

### User's verdict

When the Cast building arrived in Doncaster it was clear that it heralded a new start and an optimism that the town sorely needed. On the edge of a public square, it gives guests the opportunity to take in the grand glass façade from a distance and enables the curious visitor to peek inside before taking the plunge and entering. The inside/outside flooring breaks through the 'threshold fear' and we're very proud of our open and welcoming foyer which mirrors the open and welcome attitude that we try hard to promote. Our two auditoria are quite different to each other, but equally intimate, comfortable and stimulating. They draw very different audiences, and this gives a real feel of diversity rather than repetition across the two spaces. 'Meeting' and 'making' spaces add to the functionality of the venue and not only allow us to host artists and makers but also offer a revenue stream. The building has proved to be an inspiring environment for the local arts sector and has quickly become a well-loved asset within the community.

Clare Clarkson, Deputy Director, Cast

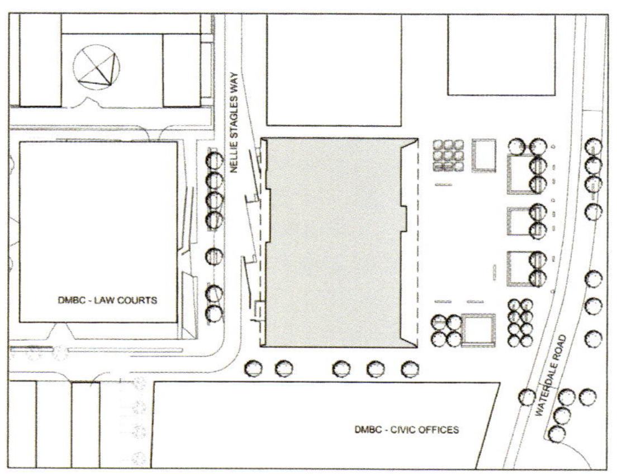


**SITE PLAN - 1:2500**

KEY

1 - STAGE
2 - AUDITORIUM
3 - FOYER
4 - CONTROL ROOM
5 - GET IN/ SCENE DOCK
6 - DRESSING ROOMS
7 - UNDERSTAGE
8 - TOILETS
9 - STUDIO - SPACE 1
10 - BOX OFFICE
11 - BAR/ CAFE
12 - EDUCATION
13 - ENTRANCE LOBBY
14 - STAGE DOOR

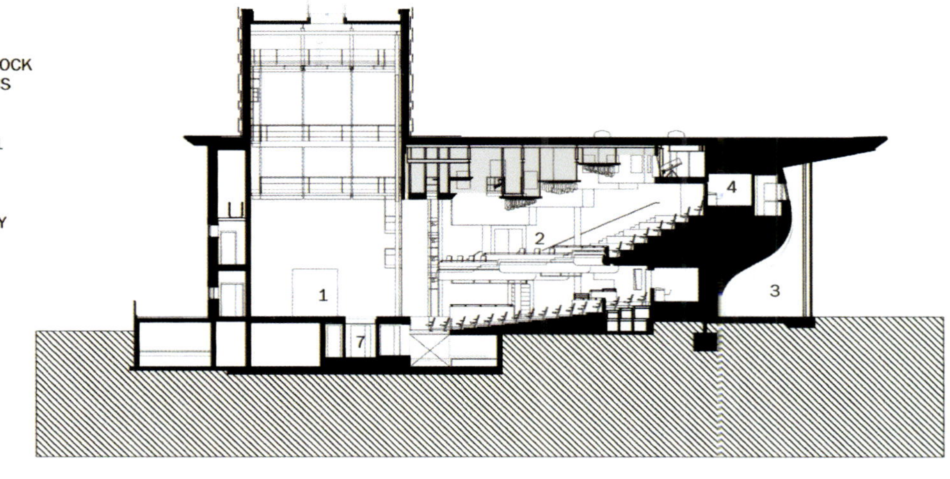

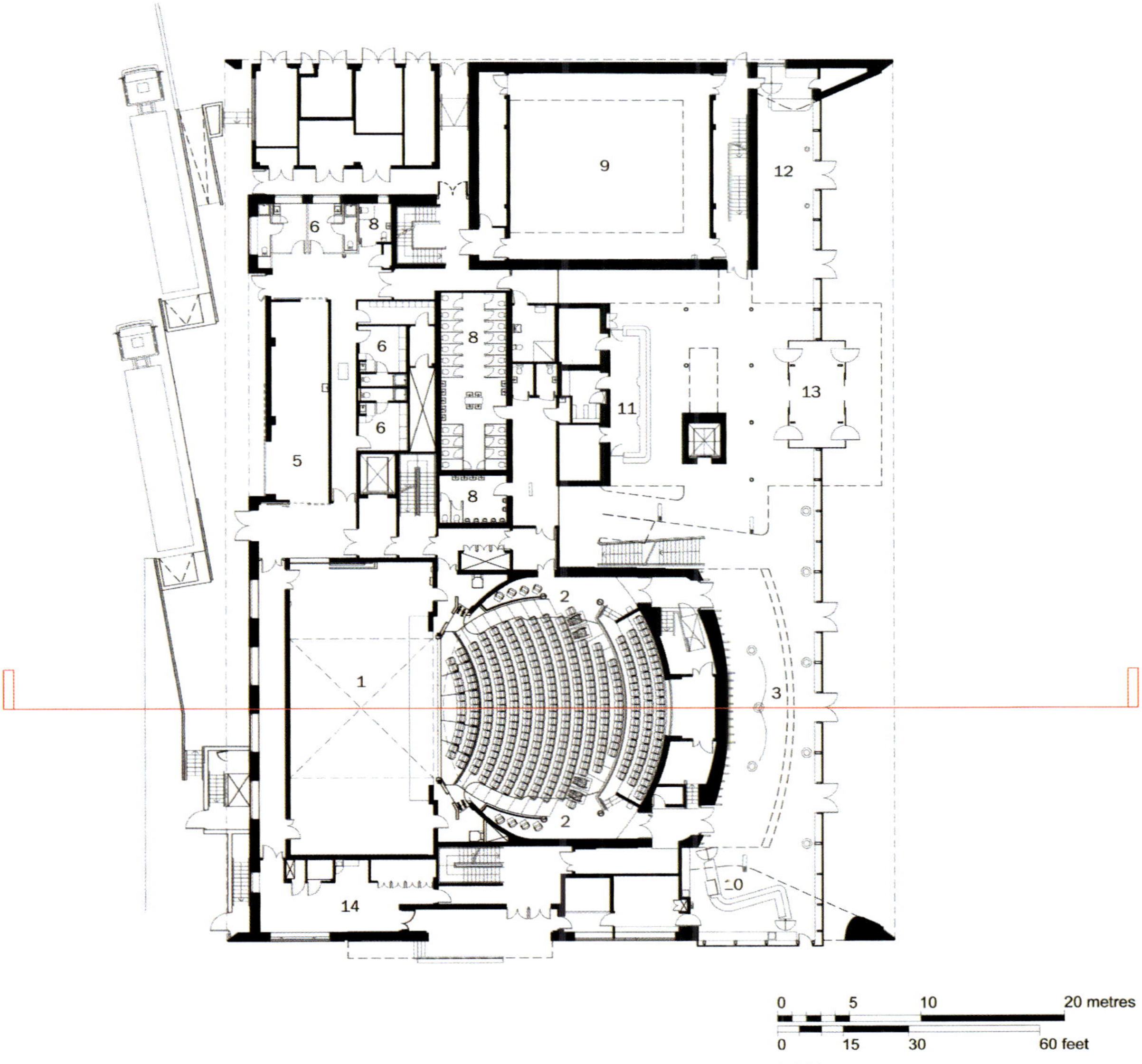

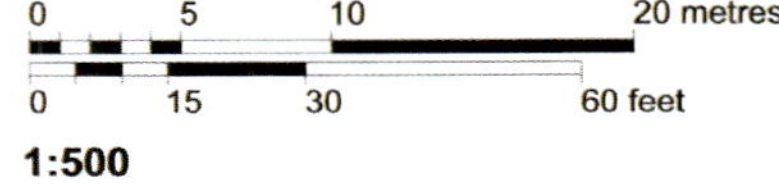


**1:500**

# Reference Project 16 The Dorfman Theatre and Max Rayne Centre at the National Theatre, London, UK

### Brief building description

The Dorfman Theatre, which formed part of the NTFuture project, included the refurbishment of the very popular Cottesloe Theatre (see Strong (ed.), *Theatre Buildings*, pp. 210–11), the remodelling of the existing foyer spaces and extension into existing workshop spaces to house improved public toilets, a cloakroom and two dedicated education spaces accessed off both levels of the foyer. The Dorfman auditorium is a rectangular room, with galleries on three sides, which can hold up to 450 people. In the central pit the new flexible seating system can be raised and lowered in minutes to create either a steep or shallow rake format, or the seats can be folded away completely to form a flat floor.

The adjoining Max Rayne Centre is a new production building which houses the relocated paint studio, which enabled the re-use of existing workshop spaces to create additional ancillary spaces forming part of the Dorfman Theatre, as well as three floors of recreation areas and designers' studios, with balconies facing towards Waterloo Bridge and new digital suites within the basement (see Figure RP.16.01).

Figure RP.16.01 Photo © Philip Vile/Haworth Tompkins.

## Auditorium type

Dorfman Theatre: extensive refurbishment of the Cottesloe Theatre retaining its primary built form with two gallery levels but increasing audience capacity with the addition of a second row of seats to the sides of both balconies and providing mechanisation of alternative formats including steep and shallow rakes for end stage, in-the-round and thrust stage layouts. (See Figure RP.16.02.)

### Key facts

**Client**
The National Theatre

**Site address/web reference**
The National Theatre
South Bank
London
SE1 9PX
www.nationaltheatre.org.uk

**Opening date**
2014

**Auditorium type and seating capacity**
End stage steep rake: 324 seats
End stage shallow rake: 394 seats
Thrust format: 480 capacity

**Stage/performance space size**
End stage: 9.9m wide × 9.2m deep
Thrust: 100m$^2$
In-the-round: 140m$^2$

**Other facilities**
Clore Learning Centre including:
Cottesloe Room (a seminar/reading room)
Duffield Studio (workshop space for teaching theatre making)

**Overall area**
Dorfman Theatre: 2,315m$^2$
Max Rayne Centre: 1,825m$^2$

**Design team**
**Architect:** Haworth Tompkins
**Theatre consultant:** Charcoalblue
**Acoustic consultant:** Arup Acoustic Consulting
**Project manager:** Buro Four
**Services engineer:** Atelier10
**Structural engineer:** Flint & Neill Ltd
**Fire engineers:** Lawrence Webster Forrest
**Quantity surveyors:** AECOM
**Access consultant:** All Clear Designs
**Construction managers:** Lendlease

**Construction cost at completion date** (excluding fees and VAT): not available: cannot be separated from the overall NTFuture project.

*Sightline*, Summer 2015, pp. 33–37

**The three images here** indicate some of the principal changes between the Cottesloe and the Dorfman when the latter replaced the former as the studio auditorium for the National Theatre. **The first image** (01) shows the exterior of the Dorfman and Max Rayne Centre accessed from the side of the National Theatre. **The second image** (02) shows the auditorium, in which audience capacity has been increased, while **the third** (03) shows the remodelled double-level foyer at the Dorfman.

Figure RP.16.02 Photo © Philip Vile/Haworth Tompkins.

## Design intent

The Cottesloe Theatre, originally conceived by Iain Mackintosh of Theatre Projects consultants, was widely regarded as the most successful of the National Theatre's three spaces but, after 35 years of continual use, it was in need of significant refurbishment. The proposals for the Dorfman Theatre addressed every aspect of the space – audience comfort, sightlines, seating capacity, ease of adaptability, technical capability, technicians' areas and accessibility – whilst preserving the inimitable personality of the theatre.

The new extension building, the Max Rayne Centre, allowed the relocation of the paint studio from within the existing building unlocking other proposals forming part of the NTFuture masterplan including the relocation of the service yard from the river frontage and enabling the creation of the new riverside cafés. The intent was for the new building to provide the National Theatre with a new workshop entrance to animate the upper ground level and to provide new facilities that it previously lacked.

## Specific features/strengths

The Dorfman provided increased capacity with the addition of a second row of seating to the sides of both balconies. Improved sightlines were made possible by modifying the design of the existing balcony fronts. Automated stage level seat decking was installed to allow quick format change between flat floor, shallow and steep rake configurations. The pit level seats fold away into bespoke floor units to form the flat floor deck across the room.

The Max Rayne Centre provides bespoke motorised paint frame platforms as well as designer studios and recreation spaces with views across the upper ground towards Waterloo Bridge.

**User's verdict**

A musical based on the life of Imelda Marcos launched the Dorfman at London's National Theatre. The show saw the former Cottesloe transformed into a disco space. Michael Billington called it 'a fine immersive spectacle', writing that 'the show's big idea is to seize on the fact that Imelda converted one of her New York townhouses into a disco. So David Korins's design turns the Dorfman into a dance palace in which the standing spectators become eager participants'.

*The Guardian*, 14 October 2014

Figure RP.16.03 Photo © Philip Vile/Haworth Tompkins.

KEY

1 - STAGE
2 - AUDITORIUM
3 - FOYER
4 - CONTROL ROOM
5 - GET IN
6 - BAR/ BOX OFFICE
7 - CLOAKROOM
8 - TOILETS
9 - ENTRANCE
10 - LEARNING SPACE/ FOYER OVERSPILL
11 - LEARNING SPACE
12 - OLIVIER SCENE DOCK
13 - CAR PARK

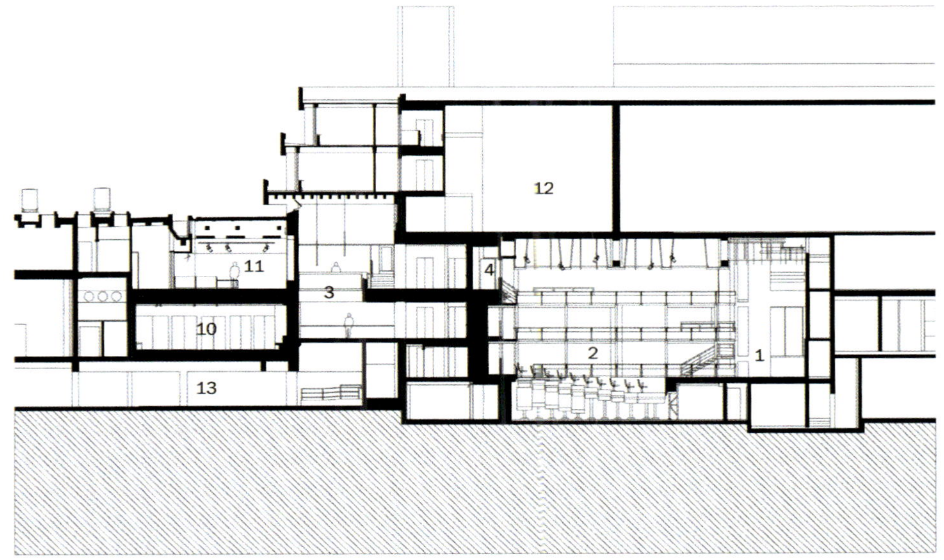

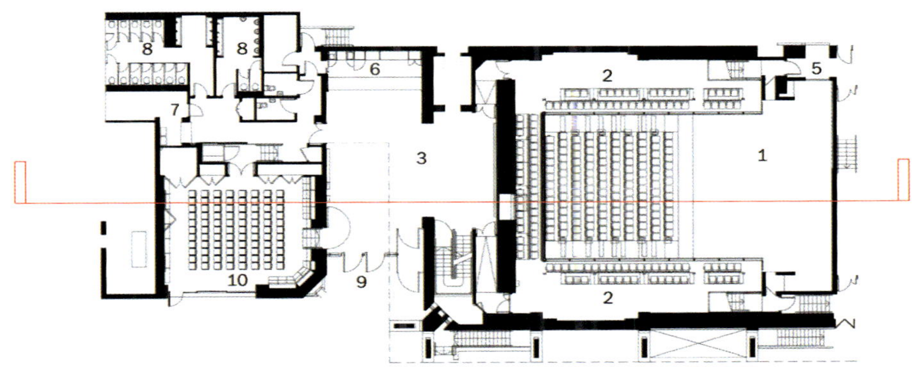

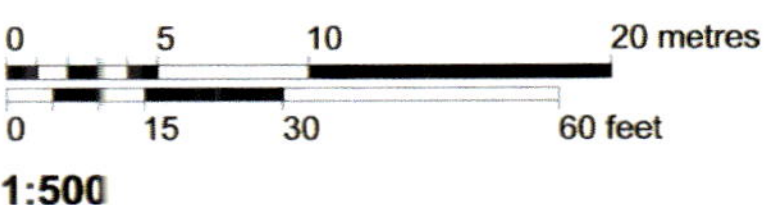


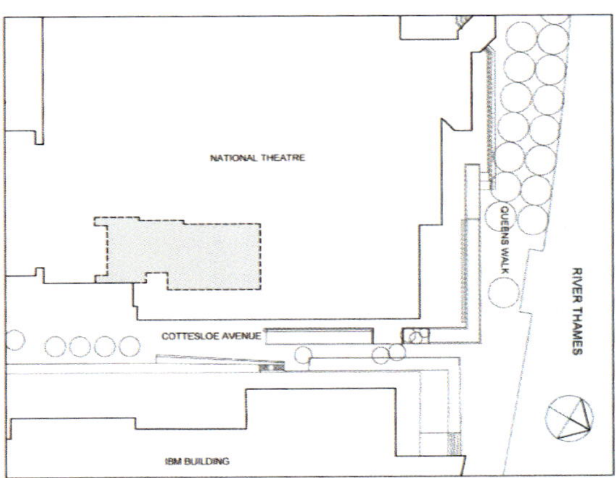


SITE PLAN - 1:2500

# Reference Project 17 Liverpool Everyman Theatre, Liverpool, UK

## Brief building description

The Everyman is a new theatre for a producing company. The building includes a four-hundred-seat adaptable auditorium, a smaller performance and development space, a large rehearsal room, public foyers, exhibition spaces, catering and bar facilities, along with supporting offices, workshops and ancillary spaces. The entire façade is a large, collaborative work of public art (see Figure RP.17.01). The Everyman holds an important place in Liverpool culture, originally converted from the nineteenth-century Hope Hall chapel. The new building occupies the same sensitive, historic city centre site in Hope Street, immediately adjacent to Liverpool's Catholic cathedral.

## Auditorium type

The auditorium is an adaptable thrust stage space of four hundred seats. (See RP.17.02.) The dimensions are close to the original auditorium formed by the chapel gallery. The stalls are formed of adaptable rostra enabling end-on and in-the-round formats as well as thrust. There is a fixed balcony level above. A sub-stage, thrust grid and flytower support the space (see Figure RP.17.03).

### Key facts

**Client:**
Liverpool and Merseyside Theatres Trust

**Site address/web reference:**
3–11 Hope Street, Liverpool
www.everymanplayhouse.com/

**Opening date:**
2014

**Auditorium type and seating capacity:**
Flexible format:
406 seats in standard thrust format

**Stage/performance space size:**
9m wide × 12m deep in standard thrust format

**Other facilities:**
Youth and community studio, rehearsals room, bistro, café and theatre bar,

Figure RP.17.01

Photo © Philip Vile/Haworth Tompkins.

assembly workshop, wardrobe workspace, dressing rooms, offices, general technical back-of-house spaces.

**Overall area:**
4,690m² (GIA)

**Design team**
**Architect:** Haworth Tompkins
**Theatre consultant:** Charcoalblue
**Acoustic consultant:** Gillieron Scott Acoustic Design
**Structural engineer:** Alan Baxter & Associates
**Service engineer:** Watermans Building Services
**Project manager:** GVA Acuity
**Quantity surveyor:** Gardiner & Theobald
**Catering consultant:** Keith Winton Design
**Access consultant:** Earnscliffe Davies Associates
**Main contractor:** Gilbert-Ash

**Construction cost at completion date (excluding fees and VAT):** £13.4 million

**Awards**
In 2014 the Liverpool Everyman Theatre was awarded the RIBA Stirling Prize, RIBA National Award, RIBA North West Building of the Year.

In 2016 the CIBSE Building Performance Awards, Building Performance Champion Project of the Year.

See *Sightline*, Spring 2015, pp. 10–18.

**The four figures** here present the new Liverpool Everyman Theatre which opened in 2014. **The first** (01) shows the front façade featuring 105 full-length portraits of Liverpool residents, while **the second** (02) shows audience members standing to applaud in the highly adaptable four-hundred-seat auditorium. **The third figure** (03) shows what may be a less familiar view of the theatre looking down through the technical grid into the brick-walled auditorium. **The final figure** (04) shows the Everyman's popular basement bistro.

Figure RP.17.02 Photo © Philip Vile/Haworth Tompkins.

Figure RP.17.03 Photo © Haworth Tompkins.

**Design intent**

Haworth Tompkins' brief was to design a technically advanced and highly adaptable new theatre that would retain the friendly, democratic accessibility of the old building; project the organisation's values of cultural inclusion, community engagement and local creativity; and encapsulate the collective identity of the people of Liverpool (see RP.17.04).

Figure RP.17.04 Photo © Philip Vile/Haworth Tompkins.

Another central aspect of the brief was to design an urban public building with exceptional energy efficiency both in construction and in use.

The building makes use of the complex and constrained site geometry by arranging the public spaces around a series of half levels, establishing a continuous winding promenade from street to auditorium.

**Specific features/strengths**

The building was designed to achieve a BREEAM Excellent rating, unusual for an urban theatre building. Natural ventilation for the theatre is achieved via four large roof chimneys and underfloor intake plenums, using thermal mass for pre-cooling. The foyers are vented via opening screens and a large lightwell. The fully exposed concrete structure (with a high percentage of cement replacement) and reclaimed brickwork walls provide excellent thermal mass, while the orientation and fenestration design optimise solar response – the entire west façade is designed as a large screen of moveable sunshades.

**Users' verdicts**

The theatre reflects the city's renegade spirit. . . . We tried very hard to create a new building that feels warm and has that earthiness, that democratic humanity that the old Everyman had . . . I felt that the first play of the new Everyman as a democratic place should not just have one star face on the poster. . . . *Twelfth Night* captured the spirit of love and naughtiness the Everyman has long embodied; and it just happened to have the perfect last lines to mark the beginning of a bright new era of theatre in Liverpool: 'But that's all one, our play is done, /And we'll strive to please you every day'.

Gemma Bodinetz, artistic director of the Everyman from 2003, interviewed by Helen Pidd for *The Guardian*, 4 March 2014.

Haworth Tompkins carried out a post occupancy evaluation [POE] in 2020 to assess the technical performance and user satisfaction. This found that the natural ventilation was working well measured by audience comfort, temperature and air quality. The feedback from the Building User Surveys, of both staff and public, was excellent.

POE report link: https://s3-eu-west-1.amazonaws.com/ht-site-assets/uploads/210726-HT_POE_Everyman-Theatre.pdf

The new Everyman feels like a found space. Here all is a new build, yet it has the ambience of an old building, in part down to the use of recycled and exposed brick in the major areas of auditorium, bars and circulation. This is a building that breathes quality in its choice of materials, in its lighting and its signage. The tour de force is the first-floor bar, a *piano nobile* stretching across the front of the building. Tucked in behind is a nook of a writer's room with the air of a gentlemen's club. The auditorium, with its burnt orange upholstery, is a clever cross between Matcham and the cosy cinema feel of the original.

www.architecture.com/awards-and-competitions-landing-page/awards/riba-stirling-prize/everyman-theatre

**KEY**

1 - STAGE
2 - AUDITORIUM
3 - FOYER/ CIRCULATION
4 - CONTROL ROOM
5 - GET IN
6 - DRESSING ROOMS
7 - UNDERSTAGE
8 - TOILETS
9 - STUDIO (VOID OVER)
10 - OFFICE
11 - BAR
12 - CAFE
13 - WARDROBE
14 - WORKSHOP
15 - BISTRO

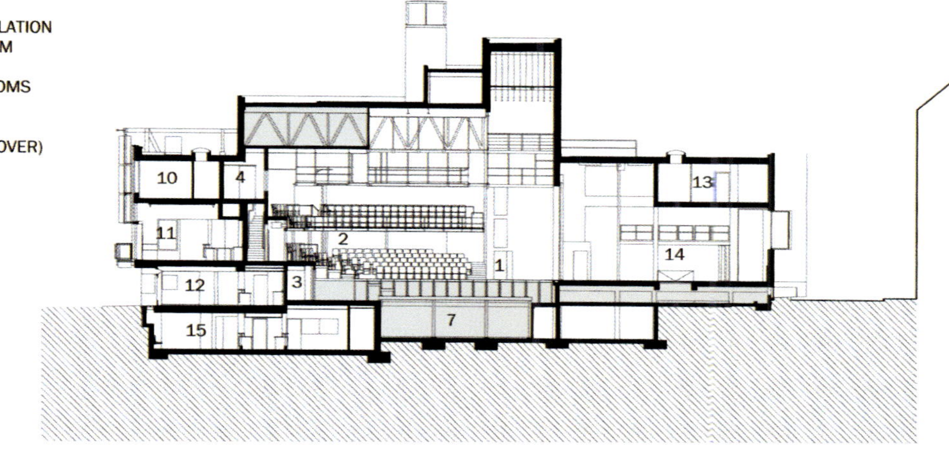


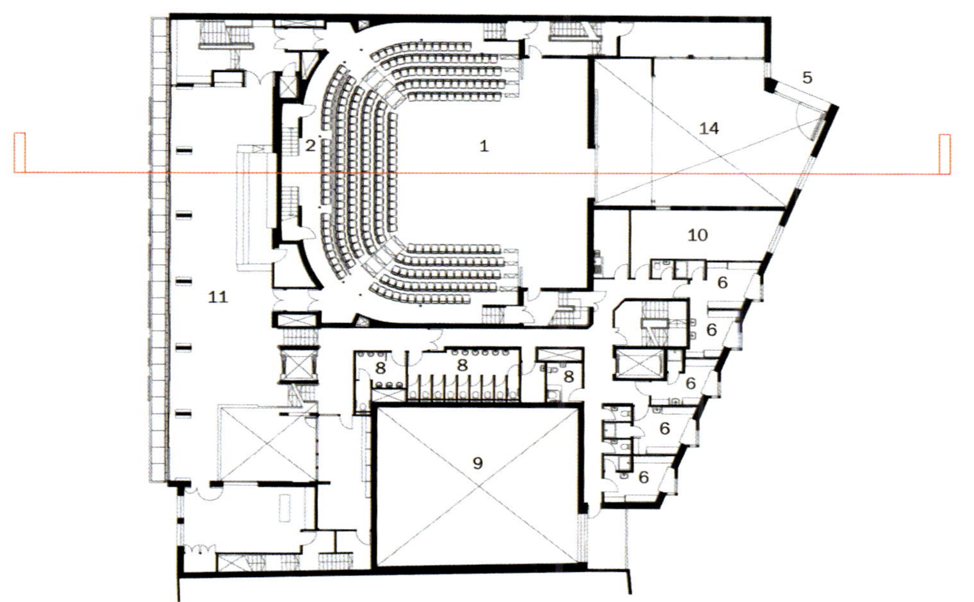


0 5 10 20 metres
0 15 30 60 feet
**1:500**

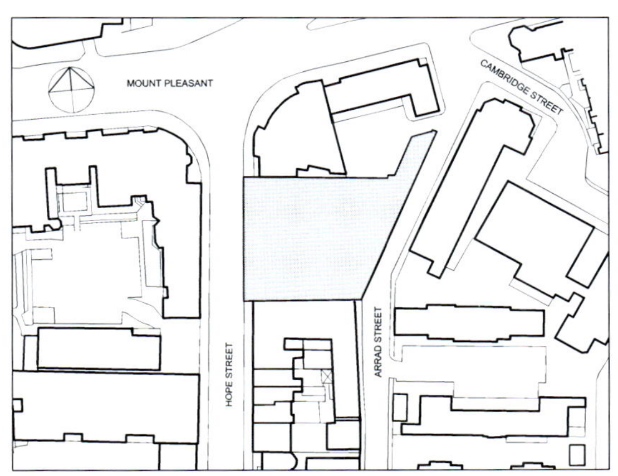


**SITE PLAN - 1:2500**

# Reference Project 18
# Cloud Gate Dance Theatre, 雲門劇場, Tamsui, New Taipei City, Taiwan

### Brief building description

The Cloud Gate Dance Theatre is the first contemporary dance company in the Chinese-speaking community. However, the members have been scattered and working separately in various rented spaces for forty years before this new theatre was built. The new theatre finally gathers people in different departments and provides various spaces for administration, shops, rehearsal and public performance.

Figure RP.18.01 Photo © Fieldoffice.

### Auditorium type

The main theatre can accommodate an audience of 450 people and was designed as a multi-functional space, which is flexible for different scales and forms of performance. The seventeen-meter-high flytower above the north side of the theatre supports the wings and drapes to create a proscenium theatre. The space can also work as a thrust theatre with audience surrounding the stage when the seats of the auditorium are retracted. The tension wire grid suspended 8.4m above the stage provides more technical possibilities for the theatre.

Figure RP.18.02 Photo © Hsin-Yin Tu.

### Key facts

**Client:**
The Cloud Gate Dance Theatre

**Site address/web reference**
No. 36, Ln. 6, Sec. 1,
Jhongjheng Rd.,
Tamsui Dist., New Taipei City
visit@cloudgate.org.tw

**Opening date**
19 April 2015

**Auditorium type and seating capacity**
Proscenium theatre/thrust theatre with retracted seating

**Stage/performance space size**
Proscenium theatre
14.7m wide × 12.7m deep

**Other facilities**
Rehearsal rooms, dressing rooms, office, background shop, costume shop

**Overall area**
8,809m²

**Design team**
**Architect:** Sheng-Yuan Huang, De-Yu Tu (Fieldoffice Architects)
**Theatre consultant:** Yi-Tai Theatre Consultant
**Acoustic consultant:** Yi-Tai Theatre Consultant
**Structural consultant:** Envision Structural Consulting
**Main contractor:** Li-Jin Engineering Co.

**Construction cost at completion date**
(excluding fees and VAT): TWD 683 million

### Design intent

The base of Cloud Gate theatre and its surroundings were once troop quarters. The military dug the original building downwards into the hillside. The existing building was adapted to become Cloud Gate theatre's joint working spaces for rehearsals, preparation and production. The main theatre is a new structure lifted above the existing military buildings and can be accessed by the public via wooden stairs which follow the contours of the landscape.

### Specific features/strengths

Natural light is introduced to the ants' nest-like back of house block through the skylight and lightwell between the existing and the new structure. When roaming around the public passage under the skylight, the audience can have a glimpse of the working spaces below without interrupting the work of the company. The stage has a full-height glass wall on two sides facing the landscape and the big trees on the slope at the north side of the site. When the curtains at the back of the stage are lifted, the surrounding nature immediately extends into the theatre, reconnecting the inner and outer spaces. The theatre has limited public spaces inside the building, but the generous overhangs of the new structure provide external gathering places for audiences, sheltered from the tropical sun and heavy rain.

**The four figures** present the new theatre, opened in 2015, as a home for a forty-year-old contemporary dance company. **The first figure** (01) demonstrates the new building's affinity with the landscape as a glass curtain wall behind the space brings nature into the theatre. **The second figure** (02) looks down through the tension wire grid, while **the third figure** (03) shows a passage with a skylight introducing natural light. **The final figure** (04) shows the theatre building emerging from its surroundings.

Figure RP.18.03 Photo © Min-Chia Chen.

Figure RP.18.04 Photo © Min-Chia Chen

**Users' verdicts**

For the members of the Cloud Gate theatre who used to work and practice in a black box space, the new theatre revealed an experience of working with controlled daylight and nature. The conventional barrier between the public and the working spaces has also been challenged and carefully rearranged. The theatre is not only a palace for performance art; it serves as a foundation which is connecting nature, art, and people's daily lives.

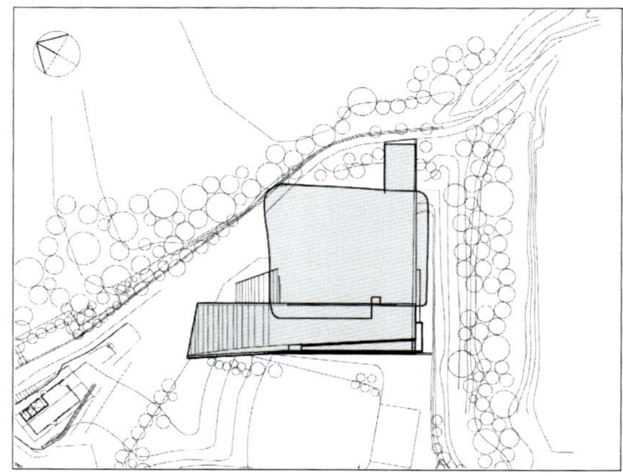

SITE PLAN - 1:2500

KEY

1 - STAGE
2 - AUDITORIUM - MEZZANINE
3 - BALCONY
4 - PROJECTION ROOM
5 - BALCONY ENTRANCE
6 - RETRACTABLE SEATING STORE
7 - VIP ROOM
8 - OFFICES
9 - TOILETS
10 - LOADING DOCK
11 - BACKSTAGE STORAGE

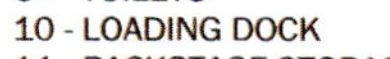

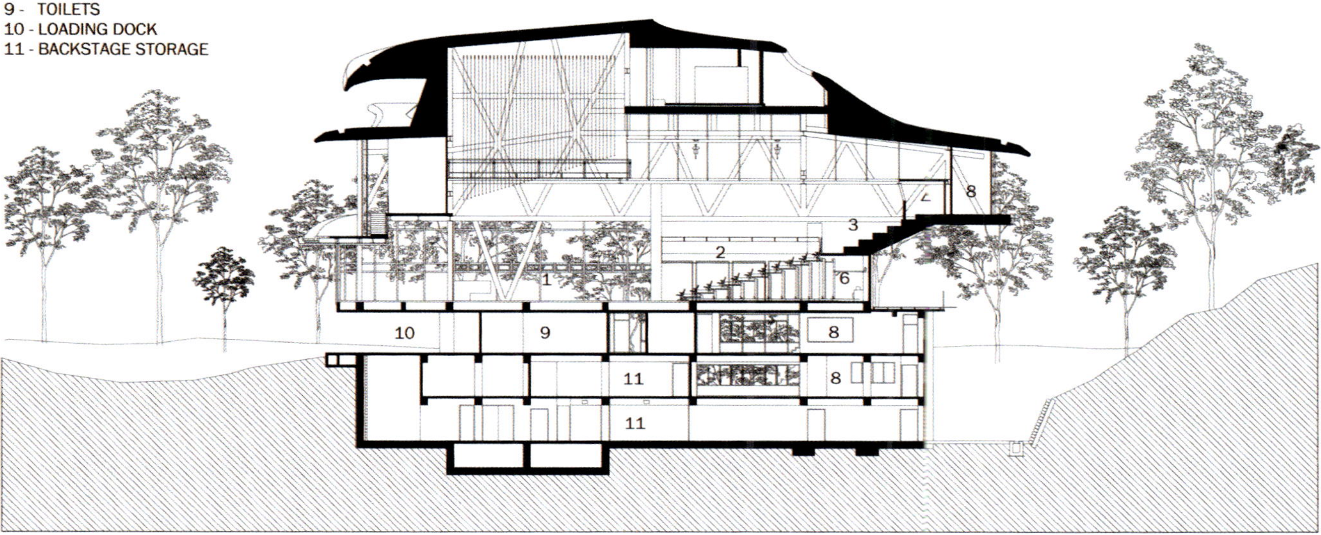


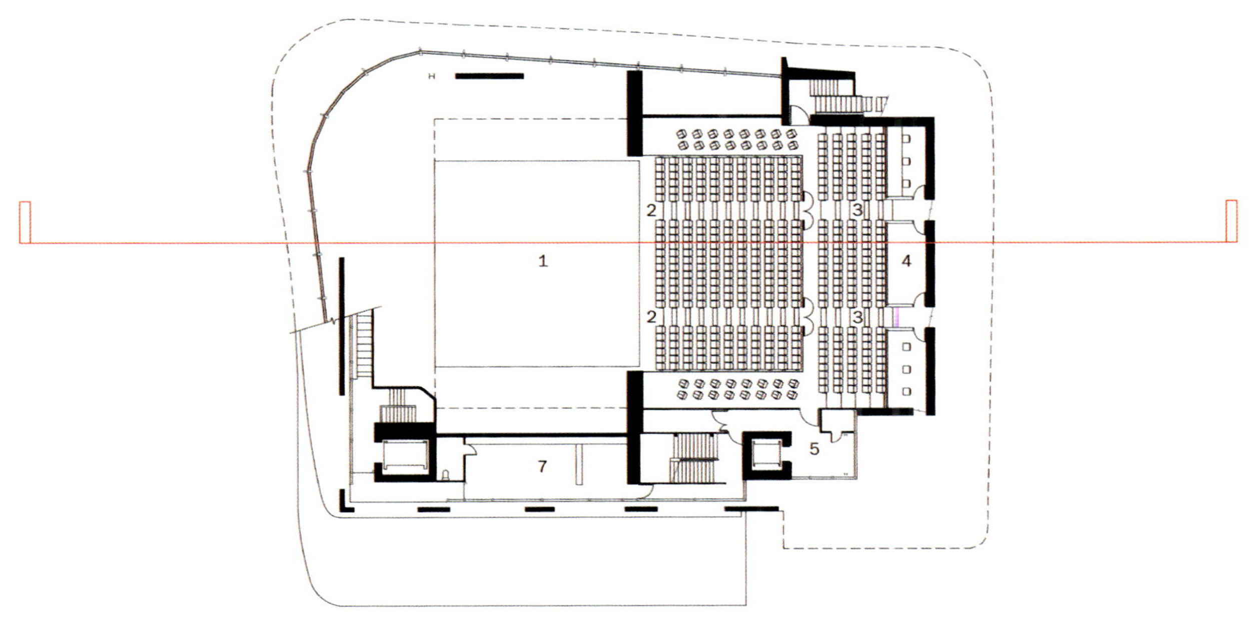


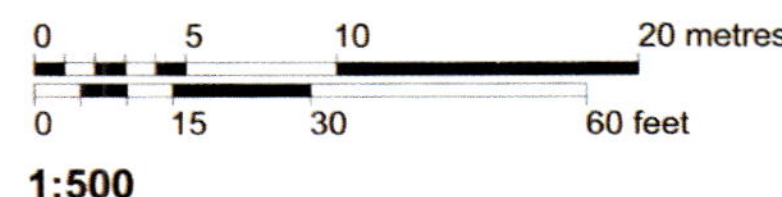

# Reference Project 19 The Yard at Chicago Shakespeare Theater

### Brief building description

The Yard at Chicago Shakespeare Theater is a next-generation performance venue that reflects Chicago Shakespeare's multi-faceted artistic vision. The project features a new flexible theatre and glazed two-storey lobby and reception space, with magnificent views of Lake Michigan, that connects to the existing theatre at Navy Pier.

Consisting of 33,000 square feet of space, the project introduces a global trend in theatre architecture that focuses on resourceful, sustainable, and adaptive design. The new theatre is tucked beneath the existing signature white tent and above the existing parking garage. The new theatre shares existing stage house and backstage support spaces.

Inside the theatre the seating towers are free standing structures that are entirely moveable with a flexible egress system that allows the seating towers to be configured into nine different arrangements, adjusting the capacity (see Figures RP.19.01 and RP.19.03).

### Auditorium type/types

The new theatre is fully enclosed beneath the existing white tent, which previously housed a seasonal, underutilised outdoor venue, known as the Skyline Stage. By working with the existing architectural design, building costs were significantly reduced. There are also plans for the white tent to prove valuable as a projection and lighting design backdrop that will animate the exterior shell in future productions.

Figure RP.19.01 Photo © James Steinkamp Photography.

With multiple configurations and multiple components, the design balances the relationship between the speed of changeover with the strong desire to achieve configurations that feel permanent. (See alternative layout drawings.) This is achieved by the air caster technology allowing the towers to be moved by a three-person team. The structures also house the theatrical technology that connects into a network of HVAC components and sprinkler systems for maximum audience comfort and safety.

### Key facts

**Client**
Chicago Shakespeare Theater
Criss Henderson
Owner/Operator; Executive Director

**Site address/web reference**
Chicago Shakespeare Theater
800 E. Grand on Navy Pier
Chicago, IL 60611
www.chicagoshakes.com/

**Opening date**
12 September 2017

**Auditorium type and seating capacity**
The auditorium features movable seating towers that can be orientated into nine different configurations, with audience capacities ranging from 150–850.

**Stage/performance space size**
Maximum: 90′ × 42′
Minimum: 23′ × 23′

**Other facilities**
Back of house, storage, reception lobby, mezzanine lobby, pre-function spaces, stage house. Connection to existing theatre.

**Overall area**
3,065m$^2$

**Design team**
**Architect:** Adrian Smith + Gordon Gill Architecture
**Theatre consultant:** Charcoalblue
**Acoustic consultant:** Charcoalblue
**Structural engineer:** Thornton Tomasetti
**MEP engineer:** Environmental Systems Design
**Lighting designer:** Gwen Grossman Lighting Design
**Civil engineer:** V3 Companies
**Fire & life safety:** Jensen Hughes, Inc
**Seating tower design build contractor:** Show Canada
**Theatre Systems:** ICL Architecture

**Main contractor**: Bulley & Andrews

**Construction cost at completion date** (excluding fees and VAT): $35 million

Figure RP.19.02 Photo © James Steinkamp Photography.

## Design intent

The Yard needed to be an imaginative, creative space for storytelling. Audience density, their focus and relationship to the stage, were crucial in designing the auditorium configurations. The nine mobile seating towers surround a modular orchestra level, and together they define the theatre. (See Figure RP.19.02.)

Linking the new performance space to the existing theatre is the lobby box with its elegant, curved curtain wall façade framing views of Lake Michigan and the Chicago cityscape to the south. The curved, south facade is the prominent elevation of the project, unobstructed from the white tent or adjacent buildings. The client requested that the lobby be as flexible as the theatre, to provide an open concept space to accommodate various events and small-scale performances. The furniture, including concierge desk, drink rails and seating are all mobile.

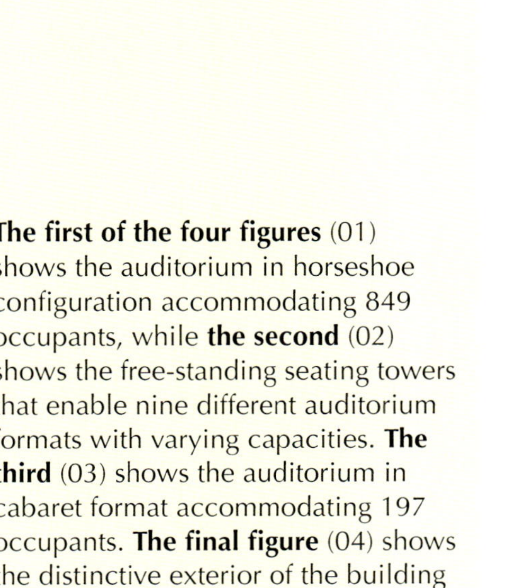

**The first of the four figures** (01) shows the auditorium in horseshoe configuration accommodating 849 occupants, while **the second** (02) shows the free-standing seating towers that enable nine different auditorium formats with varying capacities. **The third** (03) shows the auditorium in cabaret format accommodating 197 occupants. **The final figure** (04) shows the distinctive exterior of the building at night in its Chicago landscape.

## Specific features/strengths

Sustainability was paramount to the design of the Yard at Chicago Shakespeare Theater. Electrochromic glass was used as a light sensitive

Figure RP.19.03 Photo © Vito Palmisano Photography.

material that adjusts the facades level of opacity depending upon the level of sunlight. Sensors on the roof signal the glass to tint according to the positioning and intensity of the solar radiation throughout the day and over yearly seasonal variations. By using this type of glass, the theatre has approximately 11% total energy reduction, a 44% cooling demand reduction and 21% operating cost reduction.

Figure RP.19.04 Photo © Vito Palmisano Photography.

**Users' verdicts**

An extraordinary example of architectural, engineering and theatrical re-purposing, The Yard marks the transformation of a single, large, underused outdoor venue into an enclosed structure whose nine, steel 'towers' can be easily moved into dramatically different configurations, conforming to the scale and spirit of each production.

*Chicago Sun-Times*

The supple indoor edifice is both economically and environmentally sustainable. Flexibility is the new venue's calling card. More than just a malleable black box, The Yard can efficiently rearrange its contents . . . shape-shifting that can serve any show and inspire them as well.

*Stage and Cinema*

The architects balanced numerous design and constructability challenges to deliver a project that beautifully blends difficult existing conditions with a technically demanding program.

AIA Innovation Awards, Honourable Mention

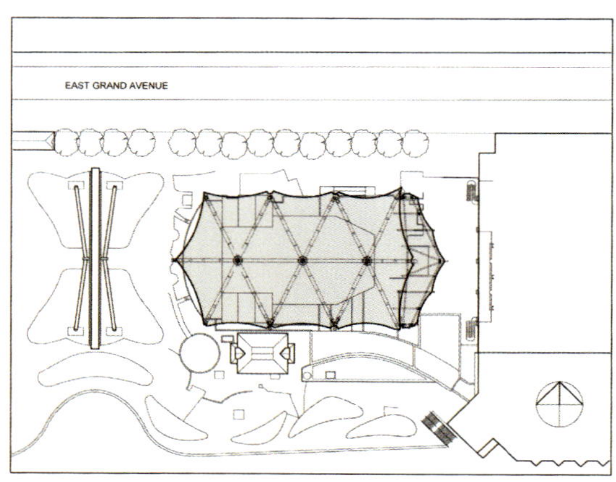


**SITE PLAN - 1:2500**

KEY
1 - STAGE
2 - AUDITORIUM
3 - FOYER
4 - SEATING TOWERS
5 - GET IN
6 - DRESSING ROOMS
7 - STORAGE
8 - TOILETS
9 - LINK TO SHAKESPEARE THEATRE

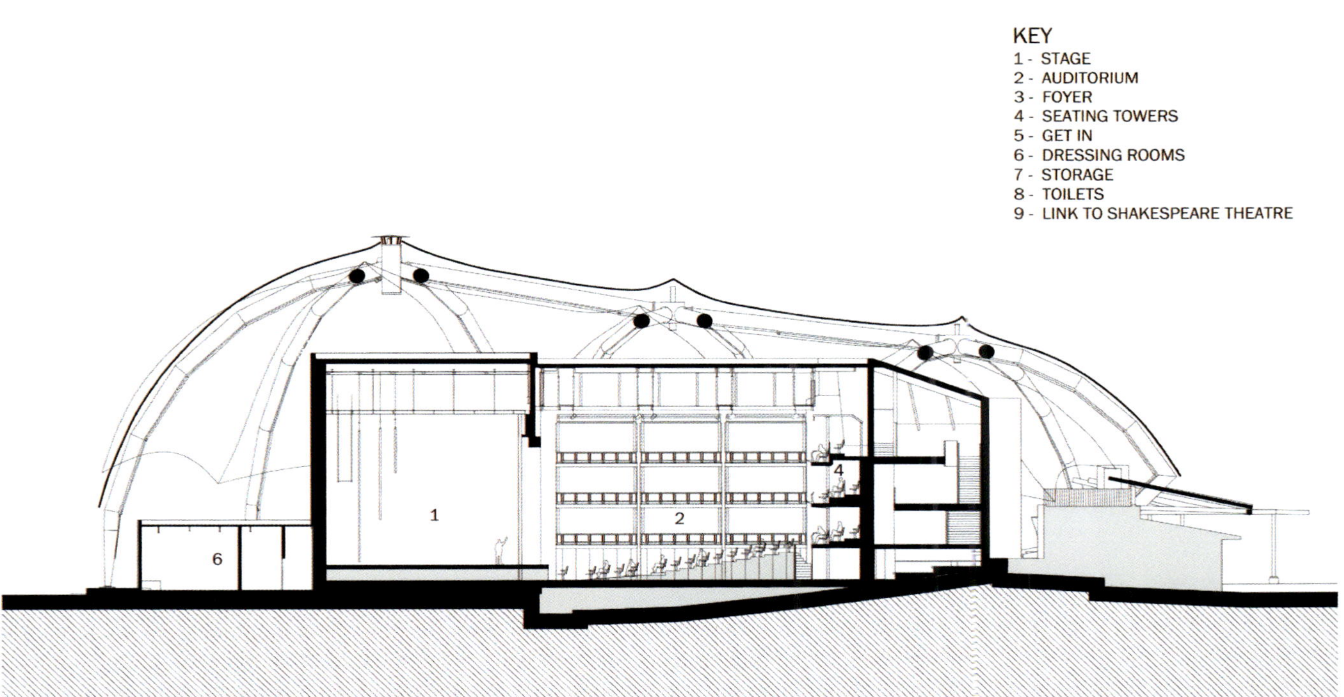

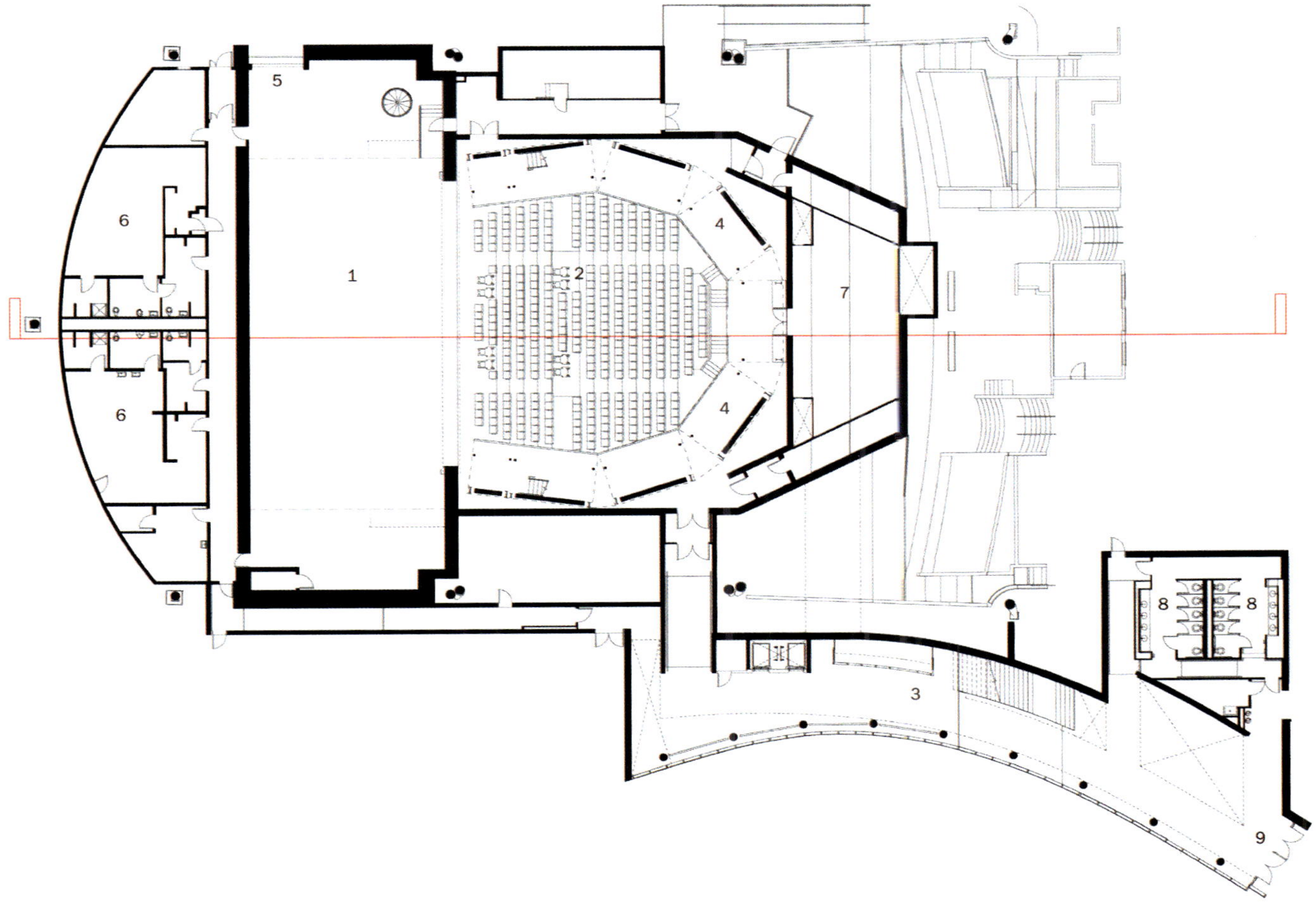

0 5 10 20 metres
0 15 30 60 feet
**1:500**

# Reference Project 20
# Bridge Theatre, London, UK

### Brief building description

The Bridge Theatre occupies an extraordinary site between City Hall and Tower Bridge, with its foyer looking out over the river to the Tower of London. (See Figures RP.20.01 and RP.20.02.) Created within the shell of a new commercial building, it was completed in just over two years from inception, using specially developed prefabrication techniques for the flexible auditorium, together with foyers, dressing rooms, stage door, company room and offices.

Figure RP.20.01 Photo © Philip Vile/Haworth Tompkins.

Figure RP.20.02 Photo © Philip Vile/Haworth Tompkins.

### Key facts

**Client**
London Theatre Company,
1 Brewery Square, Copper Row,
London, SE1 2LF

**Site address/web reference**
3 Potters Fields Park,
London, SE1 2SG
www.bridgetheatre.co.uk

**Opening date**
October 2017

**Auditorium type and seating capacity**
End stage format 950 seats
Thrust format 900 seats
In the round/promenade
1075 seated and standing

**Stage/performance space size**
End stage: 17.7m wide × 9.2m deep
Thrust stage: 286m$^2$
Promenade: 305m$^2$

**Other facilities**
Stage door and offices
Dressing rooms
Kitchen

**Overall area**
4,100m$^2$

**Design team**
**Architect:** Haworth Tompkins
**Auditorium technical design & manufacture:** TAIT Stage Technologies
**Acoustic consultant:** Gillieron Scott Acoustic Design (GSAD)
**Project director & project management:** Plann Ltd
**Quantity surveyor:** Bristow Consulting
**Services engineer:** Skelly and Couch Ltd
**Fire engineers:** Trenton Fire Limited
**Structural engineer:** Momentum Engineering
**Main contractor:** Rise Contracts

**Construction cost at completion date (excluding fees and VAT):** £12 million

### Auditorium type/types

The auditorium itself is ground-breaking both in its design, using prefabricated modular construction, and its theatrical staging flexibility. It comprises three levels of fixed galleries on three sides, with a demountable fourth side, and a flexible staging system in the central space which can be reconfigured for end stage, thrust stage, in-the-round and promenade formats, all of which have been used since its opening.

### Design intent

The design aims to provide maximum adaptability of formats without losing the intimacy and density associated with the best historic theatre spaces. (See Figure RP.20.03.) The intended 900 capacity was to be achieved within a space with numerous spatial constraints, particularly the limited height available, and was only feasible by means of a specially designed modular system which was able to achieve the very tight floor to floor dimensions required.

Figure RP.20.03 Photo © Philip Vile/Haworth Tompkins.

### Specific features/strengths

The modular auditorium was made by a single specialist manufacturer and was fully integrated in terms of electrical, ventilation and theatrical systems incorporated into the prefabricated modules. (See Figure RP.20.04.) The form of the galleries and the flexible design of the central stalls decking (also all off-site manufactured components) allows for considerable flexibility to be achieved without resorting to expensive mechanisation.

See *Sightline*, Summer 2018, pp. 14–20

**The four figures** illustrate distinctive views of the Bridge Theatre. **The first** (01) shows the exterior from Potters Fields Park. **The second** (02) shows the foyer looking up the stairs from the stalls towards the bar and entrance. **The third** (03) features the busy auditorium for the opening production of *Young Marx*, while **the final image** (04) shows a detail of the auditorium looking up through several rows of seating and gallery fronts.

### Users' verdicts

Given the abundance of theatre in London, is the opening of this new playhouse a Bridge too far? Not at all. As the first wholly commercial theatre to be built in the capital in 80 years, it makes an instantly good impression. Costing £12.5m, it occupies a prime site on the south bank of the Thames, and has a large, welcoming foyer and a flexible 900-seat auditorium with excellent sightlines.

*The Guardian*, Michael Billington

Figure RP.20.04 Photo © Philip Vile/Haworth Tompkins.

The first thing that needs to be said is that the building is a five-star triumph. If you can tear yourself away from a Thameside panorama fit to inspire a million selfies, you'll find a spacious foyer that gives plenty of milling room without (thanks to its myriad fabric-wrapped lightbulbs) sacrificing a welcoming homeliness. . . . As a means of showcasing the deluxe (but not insistently lavish) 900-seater auditorium – capacious yet intimate, with club-class seating – Young Marx can't be faulted. The acoustics are top-notch and as mid-Victorian London scenes spin into view on a revolve through the smog, it's as if technical teething troubles have become a thing of the past.

*The Telegraph*, Dominic Cavendish

An auditorium with raked stalls and stacked galleries that ideally combines the epic with the intimate.

*Independent*, Paul Taylor

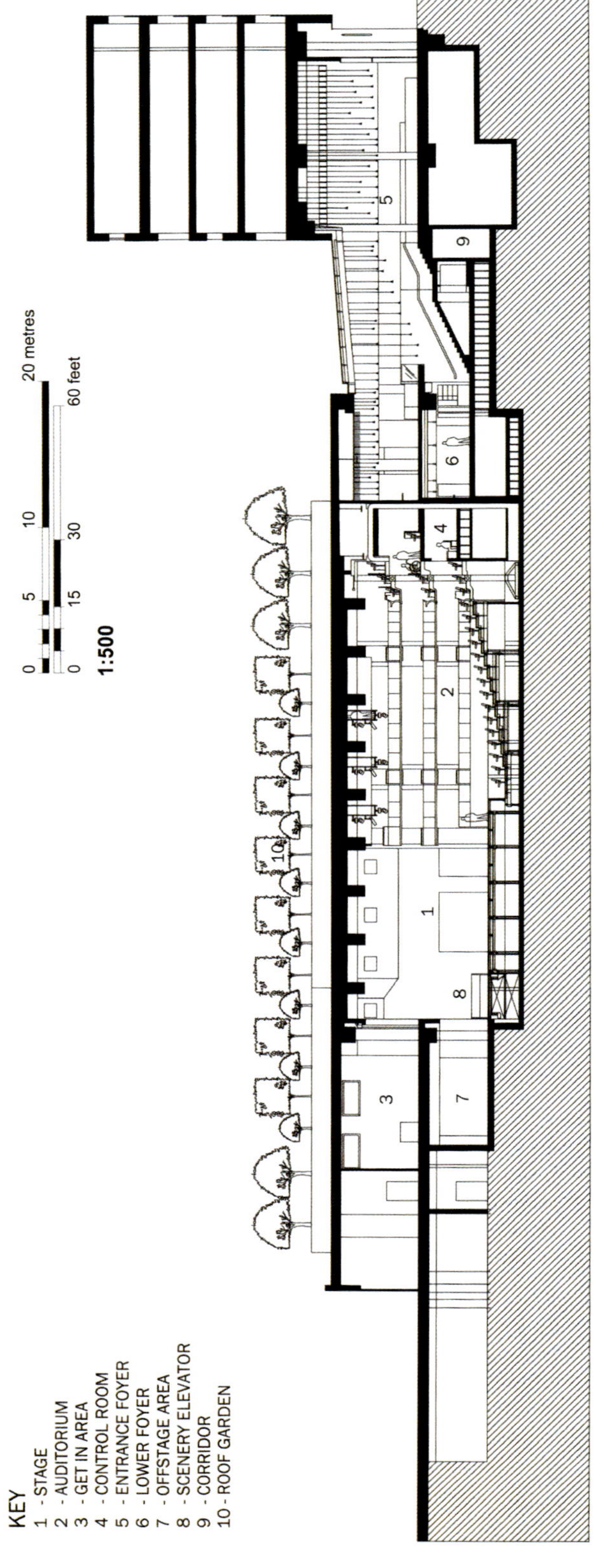

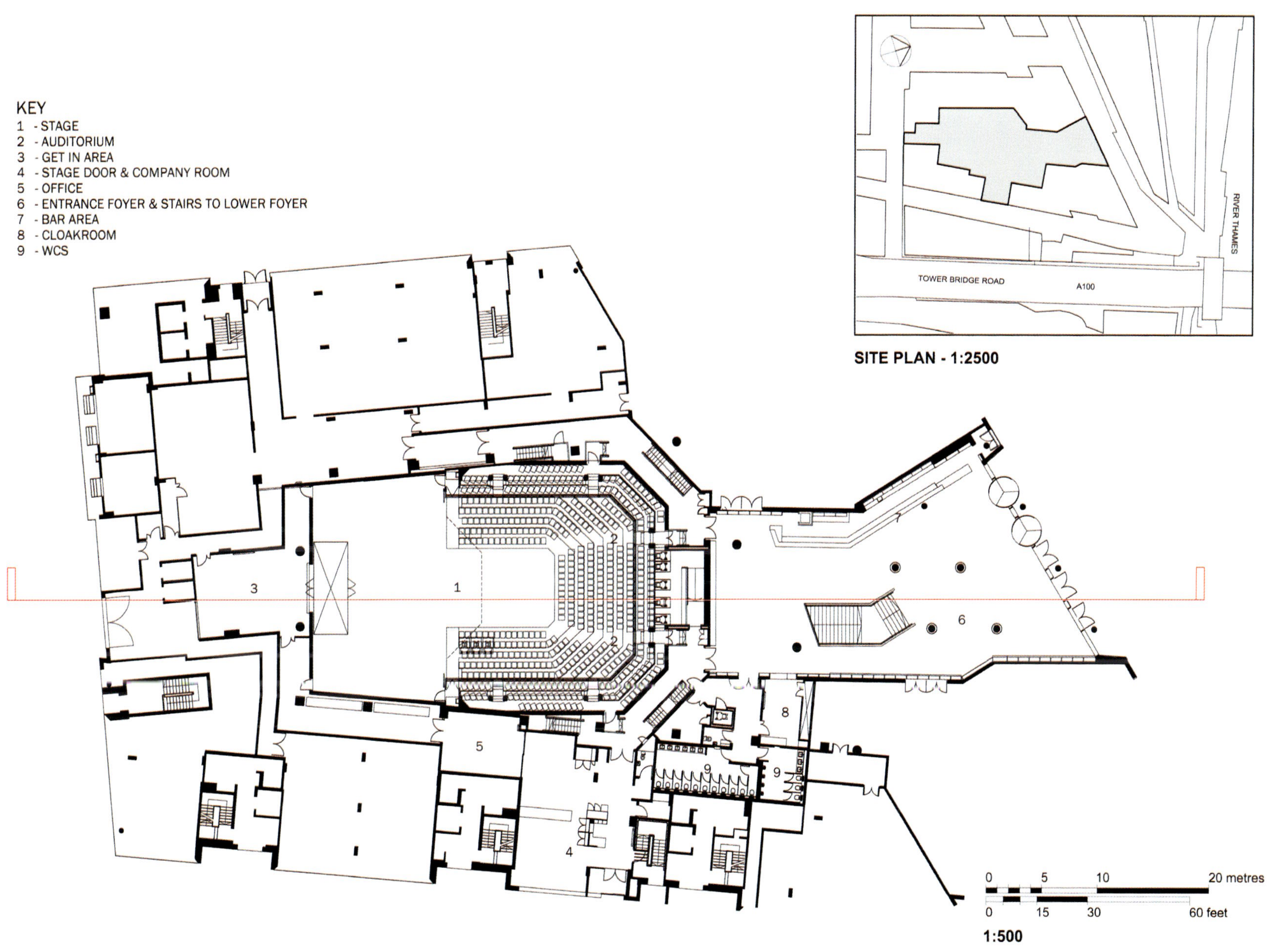

KEY
1 - STAGE
2 - AUDITORIUM
3 - GET IN AREA
4 - STAGE DOOR & COMPANY ROOM
5 - OFFICE
6 - ENTRANCE FOYER & STAIRS TO LOWER FOYER
7 - BAR AREA
8 - CLOAKROOM
9 - WCS
RIVER THAMES
TOWER BRIDGE ROAD
A100
SITE PLAN - 1:2500
0 5 10 20 metres
0 15 30 60 feet
1:500

# Reference Project 21
# Riverside Studios, Hammersmith, London, UK

### Brief building description

Riverside Studios is a charity-run arts centre in Southwest London, owned and operated by Riverside Trust. Parts of the original Riverside Studios dated back to the 1890s when it began life as a water pump factory, then a munitions factory during World War I, and then a film studio and BBC TV studio, before it became an arts centre in the 1970s.

The original Riverside Studios closed for development in 2014 and the new building opened on the same site in 2019. The site has been redeveloped as a mixed-use development with the studios in the lower part of the building and residential use on the upper floors, overlooking the river and a new river walk. The venue is used for broadcast TV applications as well as theatrical productions and cinema. There is a bar/restaurant and café on site as well as tenanted offices.

### Auditorium type/types

The complex consists of three studios, two with associated suites of control rooms and edit capability, and two cinemas. The current spaces have been remodelled on the old Riverside Studios which has had a much-celebrated history. (See Figures RP.21.01 and RP.21.02.) The old spaces defined the standard, the new build replicating and exceeding the pervious operational and acoustic performance.

Figure RP.21.01 Photo © Flanagan Lawrence.

## Design intent

The brief was highly complex and required the suite of studios to be installed within a mixed-use development. The studios had to exceed the performance of the old studios yet be wholly acoustically isolated from the flats above. This required significant effort to co-ordinate services distribution, fulfil statutory obligations and maintain operational performance. The studios are

**Key facts**

**Client**
Riverside Studios Trust and Riverside TV

**Site address/web reference**
101 Queen Caroline St,
London W6 9BN
www.riversidestudios.co.uk

**Opening date:**
November 2019

**Auditorium types and seating capacity**
**Studio 1**: Broadcast TV studio, capacity 444 people
**Studio 2**: Broadcast TV Studio and theatre space, capacity 380 people
**Studio 3**: Black box theatre space, capacity 180 people

**Stage/performance space size**
**Studio 1**/Broadcast TV studio: 25.5m wide × 23.6m deep, overall size
**Studio 2**/Broadcast TV studio and theatre space: 18.5m wide × 25.6m deep, overall size
**Studio 3**/Black box theatre space: 12.0m wide × 13.8m deep, overall size

**Other facilities**
Two cinemas, River Room Studio, rehearsal room, foyer, gallery space, restaurant and bar.

**Overall area**:
Net = 6,641m$^2$
Gross = 11,790m$^2$

**Design team**
**Architect:** Flanagan Lawrence
**Theatre consultant:** Riverside Studios
**Acoustic consultant**: Sandy Brown Associates
**Project manager:** Gardiner & Theobald
**Structural consultant:** WSP Structure

**Fire consultant:** WSP Fire
**Building services consultant:** WSP MEP
**DDA consultant:** Jayne Earnscliff
**Cost consultant:** Gardiner & Theobald
**CDM coordinator:** Gardiner & Theobald
**Main contractor:** Mount Anvil

**Construction cost at completion date** (excluding fees and VAT): £21 million

**The five figures** show the Riverside Studios, a charity-run arts centre redeveloped on its original site as a mixed-use building. **The first figure** (01) shows Studio 1, the largest and most significant space in the building. **The second** (02) features Studio 2, typically a TV studio, but here shown in theatre mode. **The third image** (03) shows the foyer, gallery space and public front of the building with its restaurant and bar looking out over the Thames. **The fourth image** (05) shows Studio 1 in television broadcast mode, ready to test.
**The final image** (05) shows the exterior approach to Riverside Studios with Hammersmith Bridge in the background.

Figure RP.21.02 Photo © Flanagan Lawrence.

all on the ground floor of the building for ease of access for large sets and OB connectivity.

The public spaces such as the restaurant and the foyer now face the river and Hammersmith Bridge to make the best use of the aspects of the site. (See Figures RP.21.06, RP.21.03 and RP.21.04.) The cinemas, cinema foyer and bar are all on the lower ground floor and are accessed off the foyer.

Figure RP.21.03 Photo © Flanagan Lawrence.

The control rooms and edit suits, changing rooms, costume and green rooms are on the basement level. The layout of the basement was developed around spatial principles that enabled core spaces to be linked with the studios above as quickly as possible. This meant that show runners and key personnel had the most efficient travel distances between the control rooms and studios. Spaces that were used less frequently were laid out beyond the core use rooms, to make an effective zoning of the basement based on use and efficiency.

**Sustainability** was a key driver in the development of the brief and, for performance buildings of this type, has a series of very specific challenges that need to be addressed and mitigated through the design and planning process. One of the strongest features of the building is its site; that the client chose not to relocate outside of London has meant that the building is in the heart of the community with limited travel distances for the users, staff and public, so that public transport and bicycles can be used to get to the building.

### Specific features/strengths

The building is a mixed-use development with a local CHP and residential properties overhead, forming an exemplar project integrating an arts venue into a residential proposal.

The studios are shielded from noise break out and break in via a robust concrete box in box construction that forms a considerable mass that insulates the building and limits the need for too much mechanical heating and cooling. The studios have switched to LED lighting to minimise heat loads in the studios and this has again affected the need for mechanical cooling. (See Figure RP.21.05.)

Riverside Studios has been built with the UK's most advanced ultra high-definition (UHD) digital capacity throughout the building. There are three UHD Studios and two UHD cinemas plus 47 UHD broadcast wall boxes located strategically in bars, restaurants, along the river walkway, on the roof, in offices and dressing rooms, green rooms, the rehearsal room, events space and under the atrium. Wherever you are in the building, or just outside of it, you can plug in UHD cameras, screens, microphones and control panels so that you can record or broadcast live.

Incoming broadcast feeds or self-generated live and recorded content can be displayed on any screen in the building with just a touch of a button.

Figure RP.21.04 Photo courtesy of Rivside Studios.

Figure RP.21.05 Photo courtesy of Riverside Studios.

**Users' verdicts**

The old building was charming and quirky, artistic and flexible and it was imperative that the new building was designed in a way that reflected the best of our heritage. We had to ensure that each of the spaces were perfectly sound proofed and had control rooms, production offices and dressing rooms that had a close adjacency to the spaces they served. The Riverside Trust Design Team spent many months working with architects Flanagan Lawrence to ensure that the layout of the building was able to cope with the broad range of activities that were going to be part of the new Riverside offering, including Theatre, Music, Dance, Comedy, Film and Television.

Flanagan Lawrence have achieved a design for Riverside Studios that is modern, spacious and engaging. The building with its eight production and event spaces, four bars and three food offerings, can accommodate over 2000 people at the same time, is environmentally sustainable and has achieved a 'very good' BREEAM rating. The use of LED lighting and low emission technology helps Riverside Trust keep running costs to a minimum.

Riverside Studios Trust

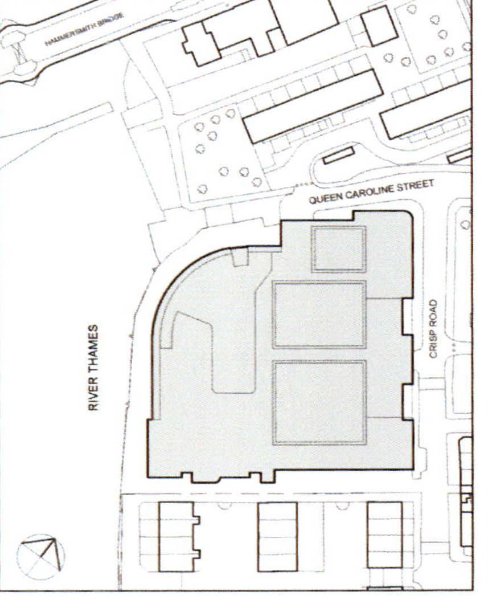


SITE PLAN - 1:2500

KEY
1 - STUDIO 1
2 - STUDIO 2
3 - STUDIO 3
4 - CINEMA
5 - FOYER
6 - DRESSING ROOMS
7 - SCENE DOCK
8 - WCS
9 - RESTAURANT/ CAFE
10 - KITCHENS
11 - CLOAKROOM
12 - BOX OFFICE
13 - OFFICE
14 - REHEARSAL ROOM
15 - SCENIC WORKSHOP
16 - SOUND & LIGHTING
0 5 10 20 metres
0 15 30 60 feet
1:500

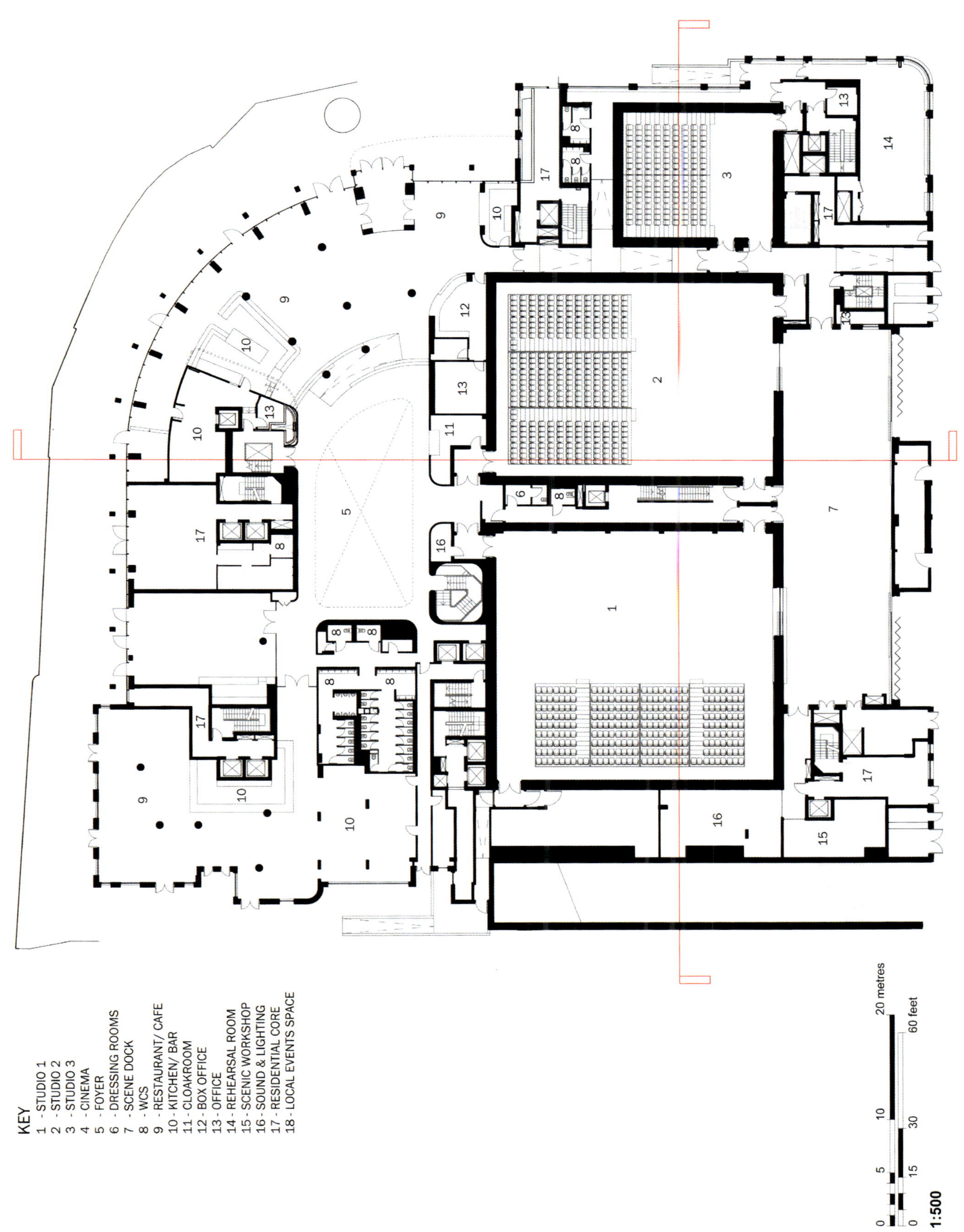
KEY
1 - STUDIO 1
2 - STUDIO 2
3 - STUDIO 3
4 - CINEMA
5 - FOYER
6 - DRESSING ROOMS
7 - SCENE DOCK
8 - WCS
9 - RESTAURANT/ CAFE
10 - KITCHEN/ BAR
11 - CLOAKROOM
12 - BOX OFFICE
13 - OFFICE
14 - REHEARSAL ROOM
15 - SCENIC WORKSHOP
16 - SOUND & LIGHTING
17 - RESIDENTIAL CORE
18 - LOCAL EVENTS SPACE
0 5 10 20 metres
0 15 30 60 feet
1:500

# Arts Centres

# Reference Project 22
# Metropolitan Arts Centre (MAC), Belfast, Northern Ireland, UK

### Brief building description

The MAC is a cultural hub set within the historic Cathedral Quarter area of Belfast. (See Figure RP.22.01.) This arts venue contains two auditoria, three art galleries, seven multi-function spaces and a café/bar all connected by a dramatic public foyer that is a welcoming and accessible public space for the city of Belfast. Open 363 days each year, MAC offers an eclectic programme including visual art, theatre, dance and family workshops. It also programmes frequent open-air events in partnership with the adjacent Saint Anne's Square.

Figure RP.22.01 Photo: Flickr/Tom Bastin.

### Auditorium type/types

The building provides two new flexible performances spaces, a 350-seat auditorium (approx. 200 of which are retractable; the remainder fixed) and a 120-seat studio space with retractable seating. (See Figures RP.22.02 and RP.22.07) The design of the two performance spaces allows for flexibility whilst retaining a strong sense of identity and character.

**Key facts**

**Client**
Anne McReynolds,
Chief Executive, MAC

**Site address/web reference**
10 Exchange St West,
Belfast, BT1 2NJ
https://themaclive.com/

**Opening date**
April 2012

**Auditorium type and seating capacity**
350-seat flexible courtyard theatre/auditorium
120-seat flexible studio theatre/auditorium

**Stage/performance space size**
350-seat flexible theatre:
14.2m wide × 10.8m deep (approximately 90m$^2$)
120-seat flexible theatre:
approximately 50m$^2$

**Other facilities**
Public foyer, café/bar/restaurant, 1,000m$^2$ of art gallery space, dance and rehearsal studios, artist in residence studio, two workshops, offices and board room

**Overall area**
6,226m$^2$

**Design team**
**Architect:** Hackett Hall McKnight (now Hall McKnight)
**Theatre consultant:** Carr & Angier
**Acoustic consultant:** Buro Happold
**Consultants on other aspects of building services, environmental sustainability, cultural and economic sustainability, inclusivity, diversity of access, placemaking and health, safety and wellbeing:** Buro Happold
**Main contractor:** Bowen Mascott Joint Venture

**Construction cost at completion date (excluding fees and VAT):**
£13.3 million

Figure RP.22.02 Photo © Alan Jones.

## Design intent

The MAC is the centrepiece of the socially driven, culture-led regeneration of the Cathedral Quarter, an important place-making initiative to encourage further development.

See *Sightline*, Summer 2012, pp. 7–12.

Figure RP.22.03 Photo © Rob Durston Photographer.

**The five images** here show the MAC as a cultural hub set within the historic Cathedral Quarter in Belfast. **The first figure** (01) shows the main entrance and campanile viewed from Saint Anne's Square. **The second image** (02) shows the auditorium of the 350-seat Downstairs Theatre. **The third** (03) is of the auditorium of the 120-seat Upstairs Theatre. **The next two images** (04, 05) are taken from inside: a view from the upper foyer overlooking Saint Anne's Cathedral and a view across the upper foyer itself, overlooking Saint Anne's Square.

The design proceeds from an idea of continuing the sense of public space from Saint Anne's Square, through the foyers and public spaces within the building where the foyers themselves function as a street or courtyard-like route within the map of the city. The primary auditoria and galleries are arranged around these foyers. The small site area necessitates an architectural language of stairs and raised floors (see Figure 4.9.3), all of which retain connection to the top-lit atrium space around which the layout of the plan is arranged.

Figure RP.22.04 Photo: Wiki/Ardfern.

Figure RP.22.05 Photo: Wiki/Ardfern.

**Users' verdicts**

I've always been impressed by the inventive way the technicians in the MAC have attempted to overcome the technical drawbacks of the venue, by continually devising new methods of solving problems and finding ways of improving the experience for the creative teams who work there. The building has a number of architectural issues which affect the design elements of a visiting show, but within the theatre there is the ambition and ability to surmount these problems and enable companies to achieve their best within a less than ideal space.

James C. McFetridge,
Lighting Designer

**Specific features/strengths**

The project provides a genuine sense of public space that has become subsumed into the map of the city. In addition to the cultural programming of the galleries and theatres, the MAC is a place to meet, eat, drink, study or simply (and literally) pass through *en route* to other destinations (see Figures RP.22.05 and RP.22.06).

The MAC's public spaces deliver a new social space for people living in and visiting Northern Ireland. The ambition and beauty of their design has provided a gift to us all and speaks to a growing sense of possibility and confidence in terms of the accessible and equitable cultural participation.

Anne McReynolds,
MAC Chief Executive Officer

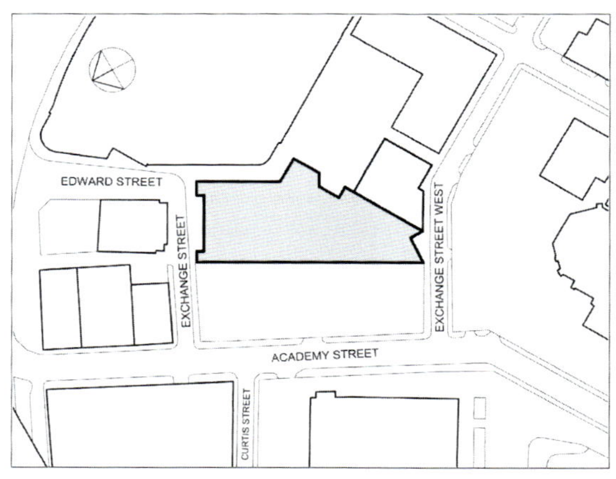


SITE PLAN - 1:2500

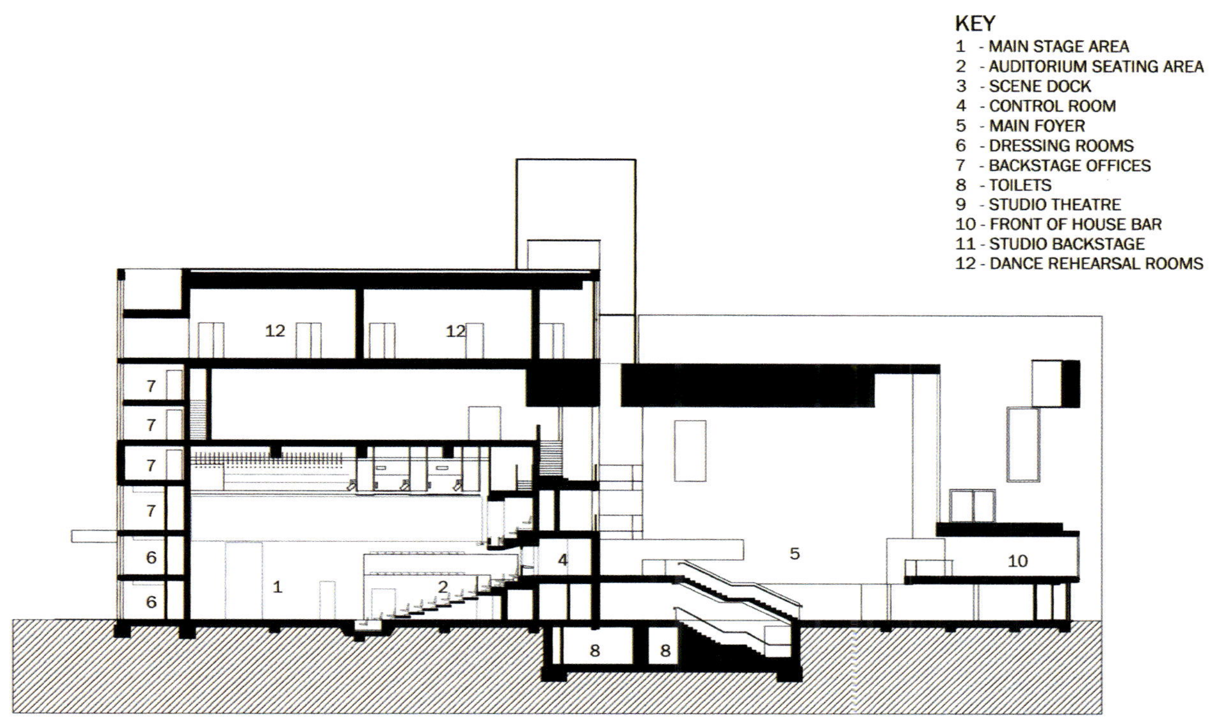
KEY
1 - MAIN STAGE AREA
2 - AUDITORIUM SEATING AREA
3 - SCENE DOCK
4 - CONTROL ROOM
5 - MAIN FOYER
6 - DRESSING ROOMS
7 - BACKSTAGE OFFICES
8 - TOILETS
9 - STUDIO THEATRE
10 - FRONT OF HOUSE BAR
11 - STUDIO BACKSTAGE
12 - DANCE REHEARSAL ROOMS

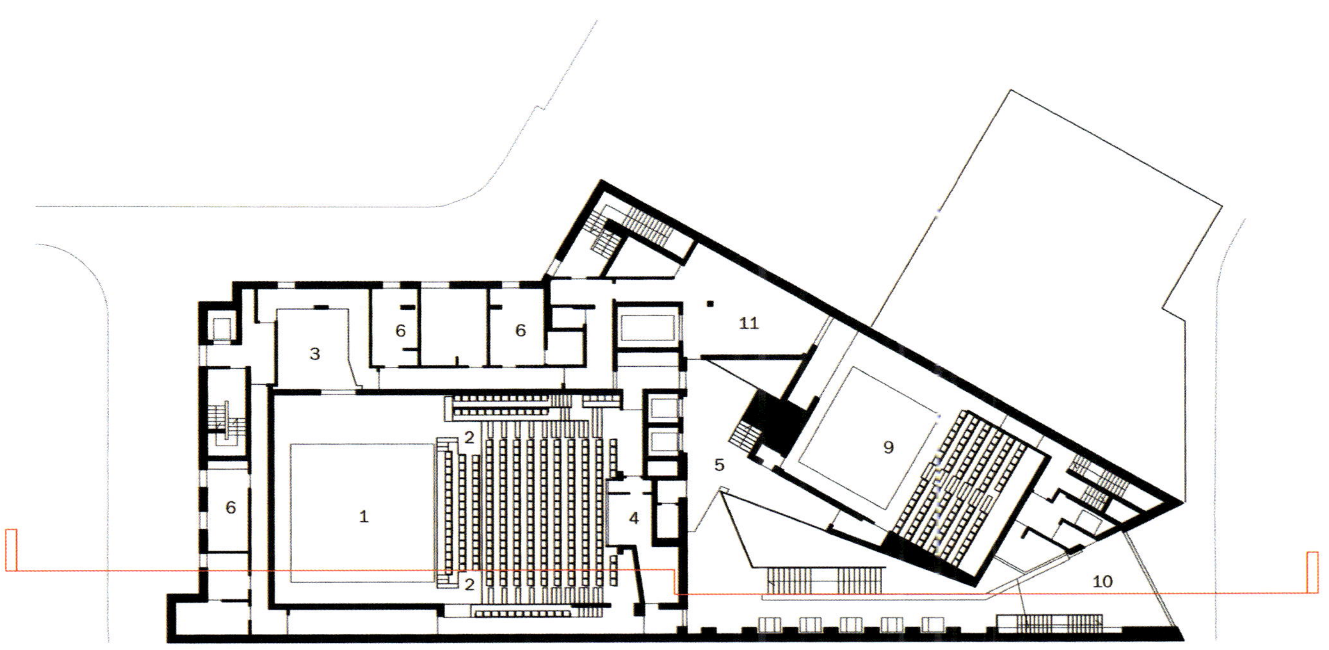

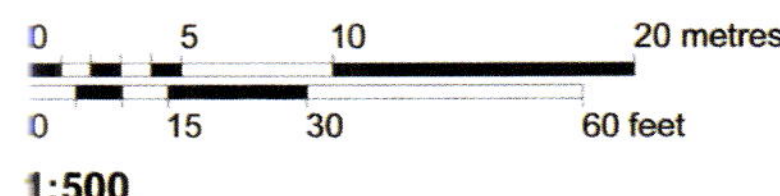
0 5 10 20 metres
0 15 30 60 feet
1:500

# Reference Project 23
# HOME, Manchester, UK

### Brief building description

Located at First Street, HOME forms the cultural heart of one of the largest areas of development in Manchester city centre. It is a flagship building that acts as a catalyst for the surrounding area. As the base for the new organisation formed by the merger of Cornerhouse and The Library Theatre Company, HOME has been designed to allow for the commissioning, production and presentation of critically engaged and technically complex artistic projects, as well as the hosting of large-scale cultural events. Its striking exterior acts like beacon, while the welcoming public spaces and social areas within are designed to be inviting to all. Designed in 2011–2012, the building was realised in 2013–2015.

Figure RP.23.01 Photo © Mecanoo.

Connecting the First Street zone with the city centre, the building is located on a triangular site in between the railway arches and a new public square. (See the site plan.) Its characteristic, triangular shape and rounded corners create a strong visual identity (see Figure RP.23.01). Inside, the triangular floorplan results in a number of unique rooms inhabited within the three corners, including the gallery, the restaurant, and one of the five cinemas which features a curved screen.

## Auditorium types

The main theatre on the first floor contains 500 colourful seats across three levels. It is designed in a way that spectators are never more than 15 metres from the stage (see Figures RP.23.02 and RP.23.03).

The smaller 150-seat flexible studio theatre space is located on the second floor.

The adjacent foyer serves as a multifunctional space that can also be used outside theatre hours. A terrace is located beneath a large overhang,

**Key facts**

**Client**
Manchester City Council

**Site address/web reference:**
2 Tony Wilson Pl,
Manchester M15 4FN
www.homemcr.org

**Opening date**
2015

**Auditorium types and seating capacity:**
Main theatre has 500 seats.
Studio theatre, a flexible space, has 150 seats.

**Stage/performance space size:**
Main theatre:
10.0m wide × 9.5m deep (including forestage)
Studio theatre, overall room size:
12.2m wide × 15.3m deep

**Other facilities**
Five cinema screens (250, 150, 60, 40 and 40 seats), a restaurant, café, roof terrace, gallery space, three foyers, bookshop, sponsor's room, offices, rehearsal room, workplaces, educational spaces, dressing rooms, expedition rooms and a public square

**Overall area:**
7,600m²

**Design team**
**Architect:** Francine Houben
**Interior architect:** Mecanoo in collaboration with Concrete, Amsterdam
**Theatre consultant:** Theateradvies, Amsterdam and Charcoalblue
**Structural, electrical and mechanical engineering, fire safety, acoustics and building physics consultant:**
Buro Happold Engineering
**Design management and cost consultant:** AECOM Design Management
**Project management:** MACE, Manchester

**Landscape architect:** Planit-IE, Manchester
**Main contractor:** Wates Construction, Manchester

**Construction cost at completion date** (excluding fees and VAT): £25 million

Figure RP.23.02 Photo © Mecanoo.

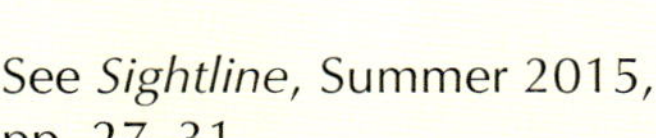

See *Sightline*, Summer 2015, pp. 27–31.

**The six images** of HOME in Manchester capture this flagship building at the heart of a large area of development. **The first figure** (01) shows the exterior of HOME on its triangular site. **The second image** (02) shows the view from the main stage looking into the five-hundred-seat auditorium, while **the third** (03) shows a rehearsal taking place on the main stage. The building serves as a busy hub: **figure four** (04) shows the foyer space and café on the ground floor, **figure five** (05) shows the restaurant and bar on the first floor with the luminous HOME sign that is visible from outside at night. **The sixth image** (06) shows this first-floor restaurant and bar with the staircase in the background.

Figure RP.23.03 Photo © Mecanoo.

connecting the café bar to the public square that can be used for outdoor cultural events.

## Design intent

The interior concept and layout are that of an urban living room, instilling a sense of warmth and intimacy. HOME was intended to have the welcoming atmosphere of a second home, a cultural home that is a place for making, meeting and socialising, alongside enjoying the very best in international contemporary visual art, theatre and film. (See Figures RP.23.04 and RP.23.05.) The rugged concrete floors and walls contrast with the warm oak of the bars, while the use of raw materials, wood, concrete, steel and glass, underline HOME's identity.

Figure RP.23.04 Photo © Mecanoo.

Figure RP.23.05 Photo © Mecanoo.

**Users' verdicts**

Since opening, HOME has continued to delight our staff team, artists, creative teams and audiences as a place to make and see work or simply hang out. This is because it meets the brief as a front room for our city by making sure that good and accessible social space inside and outside are not an added extra to our high-quality rooms for making and presenting work but integral to the building's design, programming and operation. It is a pleasure to work in as we continue to explore the many exciting and creative ways it can morph and evolve.

Dave Moutrey OBE,
Director and CEO, HOME

The wide central stairwell, designed to sit at the heart of HOME, serves as an informal social space, connecting the different uses of the venue: theatre, cinema and gallery. It encourages visitors to use the stairs instead of the lifts as the main circulation route through the building.

The bars on each floor and the restaurant are integrated into the characteristic stairwell (see Figures RP.23.06 and RP.23.07).

### Specific features/strengths

Outstanding sound insulation prevents the railway noises from disturbing the operating theatres and cinemas and allows them to be used simultaneously.

The glazed facade adorned with irregularly spaced fins reveals where the public areas are located, giving the building a varied and dynamic appearance. Depending on the weather, the colour of its iridescent facade changes from black to blue to green.

Figure RP.23.06 Photo © Mecanoo.

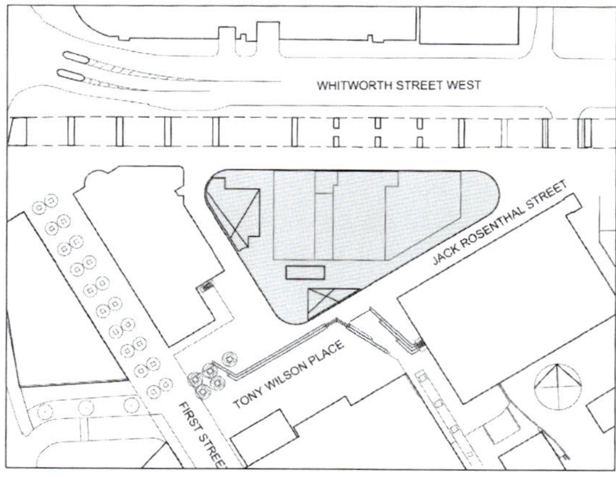


**SITE PLAN - 1:2500**

KEY
1 - STAGE
2 - AUDITORIUM
3 - FOYER
4 - CONTROL ROOM
5 - GET IN
6 - DRESSING ROOMS
7 - UNDERSTAGE
8 - TOILETS
9 - EDUCATION SPACE
10 - BOX OFFICE
11 - BAR/ CAFE
12 - EVENT SPACE
13 - ENTRANCE LOBBY
14 - STAGE DOOR
15 - GALLERY
16 - RETAIL

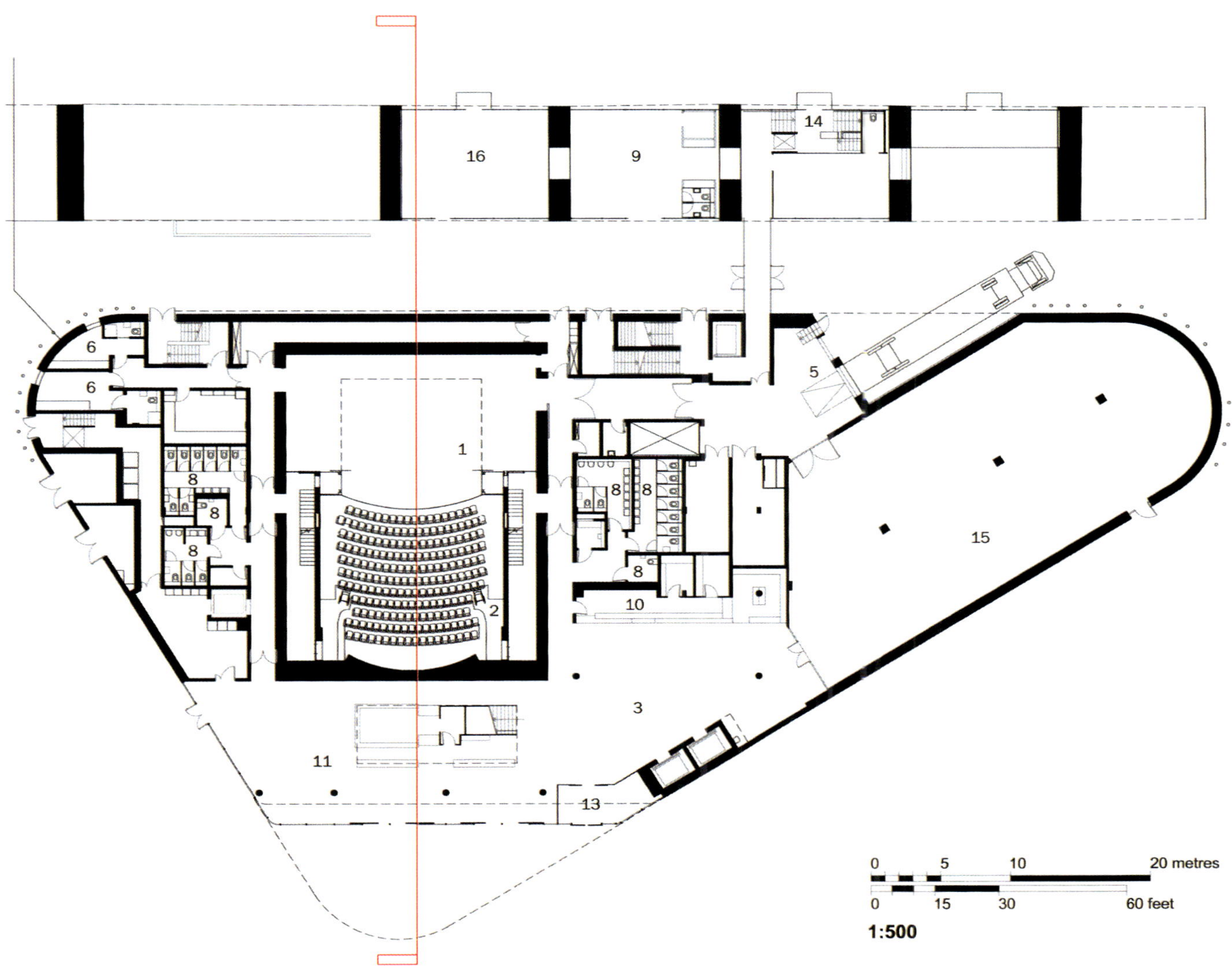

# Reference Project 24
# Pontio Arts and Innovation Centre, Bangor, Wales

### Brief building description

Bangor's Theatr Gwynedd closed in 2008; the Pontio Arts and Innovation Centre provides a new focus for arts and culture in the city. The development links the town with the university, to create a shared public space for the community that supports use by residents, students and visitors. (See Figure RP.24.01.) The facility includes a flexible theatre space (the Bryn Terfel Theatre) together with a 120-seat studio theatre and multimedia studio. This range of spaces and their adaptability allows the venue to deliver a broad programme of Welsh, English and international theatre.

Figure RP.24.01 Photo © Gyuri Szabo.

The Bryn Terfel Theatre supports a wide range of performance uses including spoken word, music and physical circus. (See Figure RP.24.02.) A series of integrated lifts and adjustable acoustic elements enable the room to transform efficiently between a number of forms. It has a capacity of up to 480 in end-on configuration, and 600 for standing events.

Figure RP.24.02 Photo © 'Sistema Cymru – Codi'r To', photographer Geraint Thomas, Panorama Cymru.

### Key facts

**Client**
Bangor University

**Site address/web reference**
Pontio, Bangor University,
Deiniol Road,
Bangor, LL57 2TQ
www.pontio.co.uk

**Opening date**
February 2016

**Auditorium type and seating capacity**
Multi-format theatre (480 seat)
Studio theatre (120 seat)
Multimedia studio (100 seat)

**Stage/performance space size**
Multi format theatre:
Stage 16m wide × 8.5m deep, or 11.5m deep with reduced seating in end-on configuration
Room 16 × 24.5m
Studio theatre: 13.5 × 13.5m

**Other facilities**
200-seat digital cinema
Teaching spaces including 500-seat lecture theatre
Student's Union social spaces and management facilities
A range of innovation workshop spaces and facilities developing the University's capability to encourage companies to develop new ideas and bring them to the market.

**Overall area:**
10,700m$^2$

**Design team**
**Architect:** Grimshaw
**Theatre consultant:** Arup
**Acoustic consultant:** Arup
**Structural engineers:** Atkins
**Environmental/M&E engineers:** Atkins
**Quantity surveyor/cost consultant:** Aecom
**Project management:** Mace
**Landscape architects:** Gillespies

**Main contractor:** Miller Construction

**Construction cost at completion date** (excluding fees and VAT): £27 million

Winner of the RIBA Regional Award, RSAW
Welsh Architecture Award 2018

**The first figure** (01) shows the Pontio Arts and Innovation Centre's location on the hillside between the town (to the left of the image) and the University of Bangor (to the right of the image). **The second figure** (02) shows the main auditorium, the Bryn Terfel Theatre, in use for a music event. **The third figure** (03) shows a staircase linking the public spaces on five levels within the building while allowing light from the outside which makes the space as a whole feel part of the landscape. These spaces can also be used for performance, as on the Centre's opening day when it welcomed the public with music, aerobatic displays and acrobats from a contemporary circus company. **The final image** (04) offers an exterior view showing details of the façade.

### Auditorium type/types

The main auditorium (Bryn Terfel Theatre: 480 seats) is fully adaptable with lifts and wagons throughout the floor area to allow rapid reformatting of the performance space.

The studio theatre (120 seats) is a space with retractable seating and a semi-sprung floor for small-scale and innovative performance as well as workshops and rehearsals.

The white box multimedia studio is an acoustically isolated flat-floor space for immersive multi-media and artistic experimentation.

### Design intent

The centre's name, Pontio (Welsh for 'to bridge'), embodies the ambition for the facility to bring together the city and university communities physically and culturally in a transformational centre for innovation where arts meet science. The building and performance spaces have been planned to link naturally to a shared public space that runs through five levels of the building (see Figure RP.24.03).

Figure RP.24.03 Photo © Gyuri Szabo.

**Users' verdicts**

I believe we can say without any doubt that this is a truly magnificent building that is a fantastic boost to the arts and culture scene in North Wales.

Ken Skates, Deputy Minister for Culture, Sport and Tourism, Welsh Government

The selection of spaces and their adaptability responds to distinctive regional arts presentation as well as to the need to be attractive to varied performance from across the country, the United Kingdom and beyond.

Figure RP.24.04 Photo © Gyuri Szabo.

### Specific features/strengths

Re-configuration of the Bryn Terfel Theatre supports a wide range of uses from in-the-round circus to touring drama to musical performance. The design uses a system of lifts, seating wagons and variable acoustic elements to enable the space to be rapidly transformed from a bare room with flat floor to a fully seated auditorium in an efficient and cost-effective way.

The project combines a wide range of normally disparate activities within flagship architecture. (See Figure RP.24.04.) The successful co-existence of public performance alongside business innovation, cinema, student activities and dining, is achieved through considered planning and careful acoustic detailing.

One of the biggest successes has been our ability to host contemporary circus, with return visits again proving that our versatility has been popular.

Gwion E. Llwyd, Technical Director

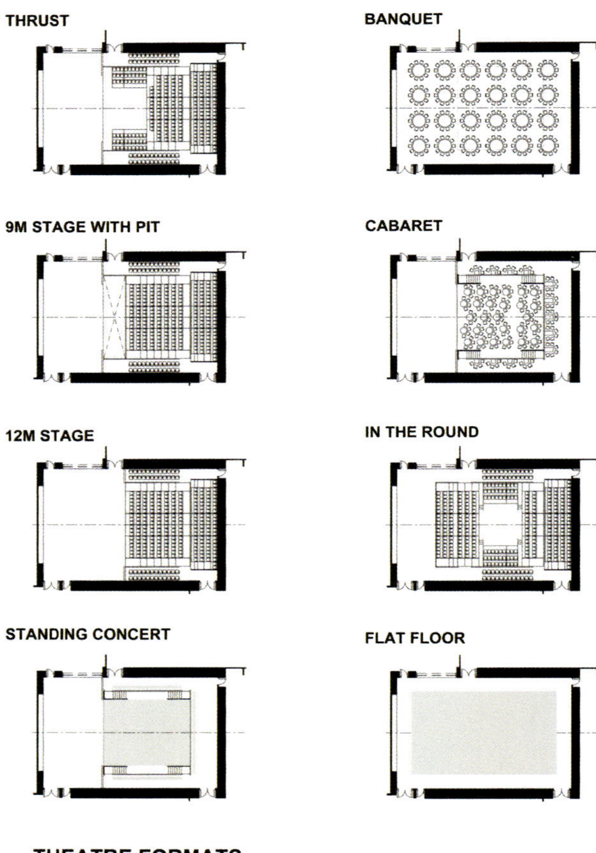


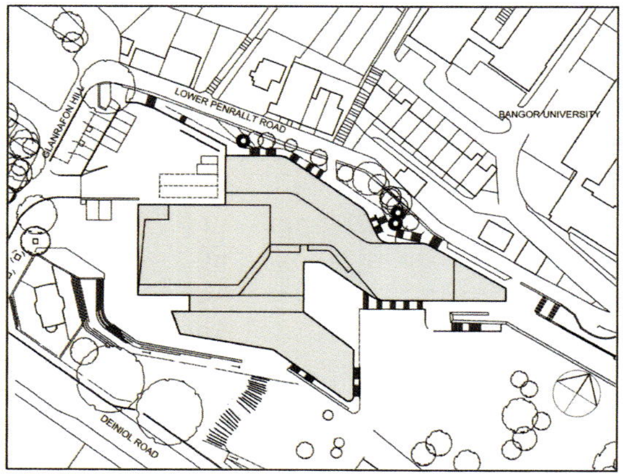


SITE PLAN - 1:2500

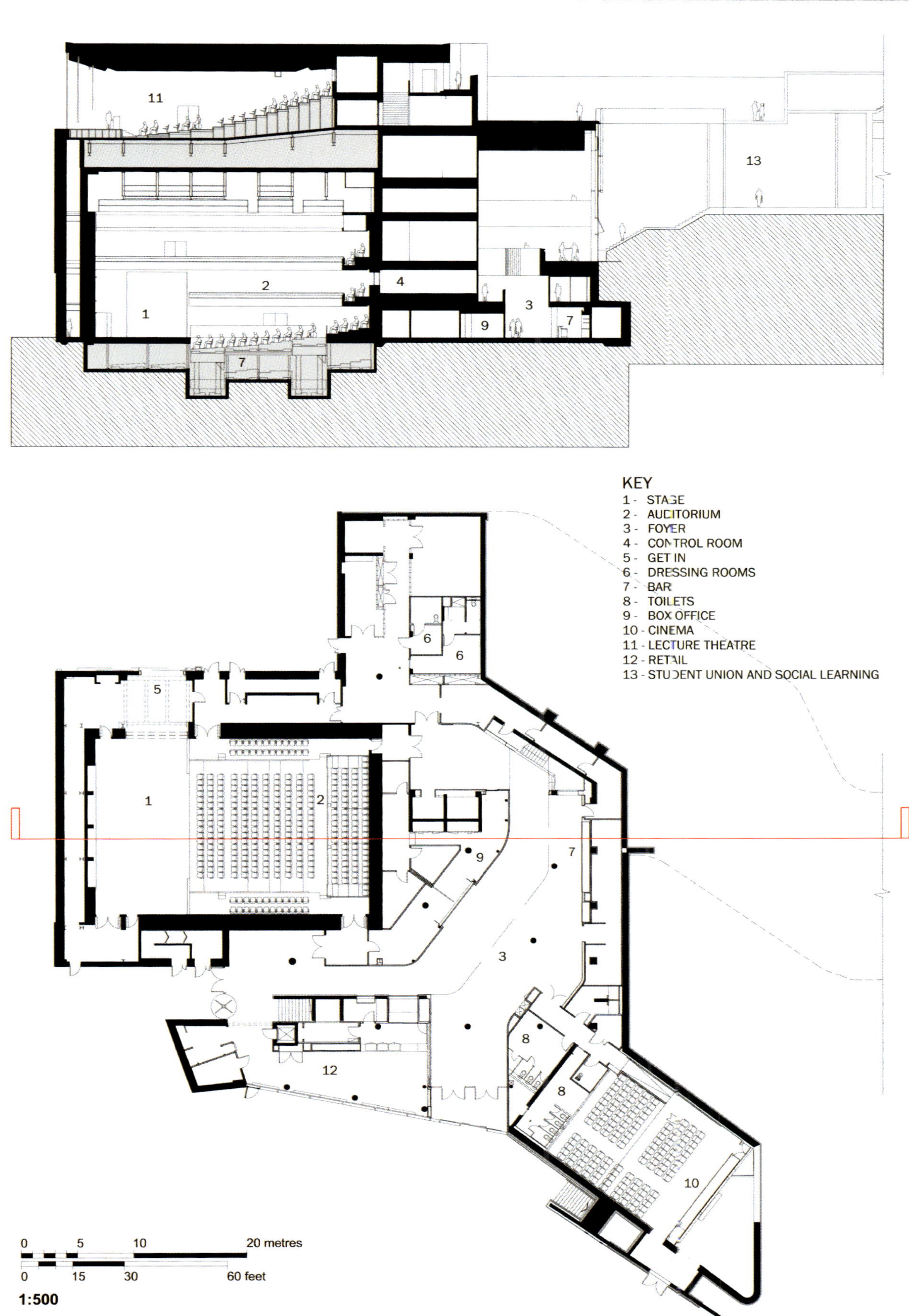
KEY
1 - STAGE
2 - AUDITORIUM
3 - FOYER
4 - CONTROL ROOM
5 - GET IN
6 - DRESSING ROOMS
7 - BAR
8 - TOILETS
9 - BOX OFFICE
10 - CINEMA
11 - LECTURE THEATRE
12 - RETAIL
13 - STUDENT UNION AND SOCIAL LEARNING
0 5 10 20 metres
0 15 30 60 feet
1:500

# Reference Project 25 Battersea Arts Centre, London, UK

### Brief building description

Battersea Town Hall is a handsome, well-crafted civic building in south-west London, designed by E. W. Mountford in 1893. It is Grade II* listed both for its architectural significance and for its important political role in the birth of the suffragette and labour movements in the early twentieth century. Since 1974 it has been home to Battersea Arts Centre (BAC), regarded as one of the most important incubators of new performance work in the United Kingdom.

Since 2006 architects Haworth Tompkins have been working alongside the BAC team, the local community and theatre artists on a series of ongoing, experimental, phased projects that have gradually transformed the entire building into a vivid, adaptive performance environment and a welcoming centre of local community life. (See Figure RP.25.01.) The task has been to reimagine a twenty-first-century public cultural building where the traditional demarcations of auditorium, foyer and back of house spaces can be dissolved and reconfigured in almost limitless combinations.

### Auditorium type/types and/or original format if repurposed, remodelled or restored

All performance spaces have been remodelled and restored. Thirty-five individual rooms in the former Town Hall building have been repurposed into flexible-use spaces for a range of live performance events (theatre shows, comedy, live music) as well as rehearsals, workshops and private event hires. These range from the large ceremonial spaces such as the Grand Hall and Council Chamber, to medium-size rooms such as the Members Bar and Recreation Room, to attic spaces and a new external courtyard performance space.

### Design intent

Architect and client worked as equal partners throughout the process, sharing design authorship and inviting creative collaborations. The project began with improvised, non-invasive alterations made alongside specific

Figure RP.25.01 Photo © Jake Tilson/Haworth Tompkins.

**Key facts**

**Client**
Battersea Arts Centre

**Site address/web reference**
Lavender Hill
London. SW11 5TN
https://bac.org.uk

**Opening date**
2018 (although the building remained open throughout)

**Auditorium type and seating capacity**
Grand Hall: up to 600 people seated depending on arrangement and stage/performance area size up to 1000 people standing
Courtyard: up to one hundred people (mixture of seated & standing)
Council Chamber: up to 200 people seated depending on the arrangement

**Stage/performance space size** (varies according to use of each space)
Grand Hall: 36m long × 17m wide × 10m high (570m$^2$ floor area)
Courtyard: 10m long × 7m wide
Council Chamber: 16m long × 10m wide

**Other facilities**
Scratch Hub co-working space, Scratch Bar Café, Bees Knees children's play space, bedroom accommodation for visiting performers & artists, workshop, offices for approximately sixty-five Battersea Arts Centre Staff, community garden on Town Hall Road

**Overall area:**
5,715m$^2$

**Design team**
*There were different design teams for the main project and the Grand Hall, so two or more for each are listed.
**Architect:** Haworth Tompkins
**Theatre consultant:** Theatreplan/Charcoalblue

**Acoustic consultant:** Gillieron Scott/ Sound Space Vision
**Quantity surveyor:** Bristow Johnson
**Structural engineer:** Price & Myers/ Heyne Tillett Steel
**Services engineer:** Skelly and Couch/ XCO2
**Collaborating artist:** Jake Tilson
**Main contractor:** 8 Build/Ashe Construction/Gilbert-Ash

**Construction cost at completion date** (excluding fees and VAT): £19.2 million for both projects

productions (such as Punchdrunk's *Masque of the Red Death* in 2007–2008), to test strategies for change and to evolve a playful but rigorous design language. Building works then progressed incrementally, beginning with alterations to the café and entrance foyer, with the building remaining open to the public throughout (see Figure RP.25.02).

Figure RP.25.02 Photo © Fred Howarth/Haworth Tompkins.

Figure RP.25.03 Photo © Alex Brenner/Haworth Tompkins.

See *Sightline*, Winter 2018, pp. 28–32.

**The four figures** here capture the remodelled and restored performance environment welcoming the local community in the Battersea Arts Centre. **The first image** (01) shows the exterior sign designed by artist Jake Tilson, while **the second** (02) shows seating booths on the main staircase. **The third figure** (03) looks down at a performance in the Courtyard Theatre of Little Bulb Theatre's *Extravaganza Macabre*. **The final image** (04) celebrates the interior of the Grand Hall, rebuilt after a fire that partially destroyed it in 2015.

To bring light deep into the building, and to help orientation, a new public courtyard performance space was created by selectively stripping back and patching a disused original lightwell in the centre of the building plan (see Figure RP.25.03).

New wall surfaces were formed in glazed white brick, increasing the luminosity of the space and reflecting natural light into the flanking circulation corridors. Circulation routes have been reopened and improved, restoring legibility to the original Mountford plan. Unused attics and rooftops have been converted and extended into offices, a staff garden and bedrooms for visiting artists. Technical improvements such as dedicated workshop and dressing room spaces, together with a new 'plug and play' sound and lighting infrastructure, allow performances to take place in spaces all over the building and in any combination.

The rebuilding of the Grand Hall, after the shocking fire that partially destroyed it in 2015, was assimilated into the project (see Figure RP.25.04). The structural brick shell that survived the fire was stabilised and repaired to support reconstructed roofs, while the pattern of the original decorative fibrous plaster barrel-vaulted ceiling, lost in the fire, has inspired a new plywood lattice ceiling which follows the same curvature as the original. New technical infrastructure concealed in the roof space above the lattice ceiling allows natural ventilation and a variable acoustic to suit a range of events.

The surfaces of the walls of the hall and its surrounding corridors have been conserved 'as-found' in their extraordinary, almost Pompeiian post-fire richness and complexity, illuminated by pendant lamps designed by Haworth Tompkins and product designer Robert McIntyre.

The Grand Hall organ has been relocated to the balcony to enable more flexible use of the hall floor. Many of the original Robert Hope-Jones designed organ components were off-site being restored at the time of the fire and will be reinstated in a new, more deconstructed arrangement to showcase the inner mechanism. Demountable audience seating and promenade galleries connect to the balcony and can be configured to suit specific events. The Grand Hall Bar has been refurbished in collaboration with the artist Jake Tilson, who meticulously recorded the damaged fabric in the weeks following the fire and has made a vibrant back bar installation with some of the resulting images.

The Lower Hall area, below the Grand Hall, has been redesigned with BAC into a new creative co-working space called the Scratch Hub. This provides a home for local businesses, start-ups, artists, creative companies, charities and social enterprises. Externally, new signage beams have been surgically inserted into the façade to pinpoint entrances to the building and hard landscaping modified to improve accessibility. Town Hall Road, running down the east elevation of the building, is being landscaped to create a shared territory with community garden planter beds and outdoor seating areas.

Figure RP.25.04 Photo © Fred Howarth/Haworth Tompkins.

**Users' verdicts**

Back in 2005, it would, I think, have been impossible to imagine what we now have in 2018, because the organisation has changed in tandem with the capital project. We now have children's play spaces, artist bedrooms, a promenade performance environment, an open-air theatre, allotments for neighbours and a hub for social entrepreneurs. Alongside all this physical change . . . our core purpose has evolved 'to inspire people to take creative risks to shape the future'.

David Jubb, Battersea Arts Centre
Artistic Director 2004–2019

**Specific features/strengths**

Refurbishment and retrofit of Grade II* listed Victorian Town Hall Building into a vibrant twenty-first-century Arts Centre, based on a radical approach to historic building conservation, to provide flexible-use performance and rehearsal spaces including an innovative reimagining of the Grand Hall after the 2015 fire.

Skilful integration of theatre technical systems (rigging systems, acoustic banners, lighting, sound & AV into pitched roof space above the Grand Hall's new vaulted plywood lattice ceiling, providing a naturally ventilated performance space (extract).

Community involvement throughout the whole design process.

Architects Haworth Tompkins were given the chance to craft one of London's most atmospheric performance spaces from the charred carcass. Along with designing a spectacular ceiling for the hall, they have worked on little interventions throughout the building creating a magical place that revels in the rich patina of its history.

Oliver Wainwright, *The Guardian*

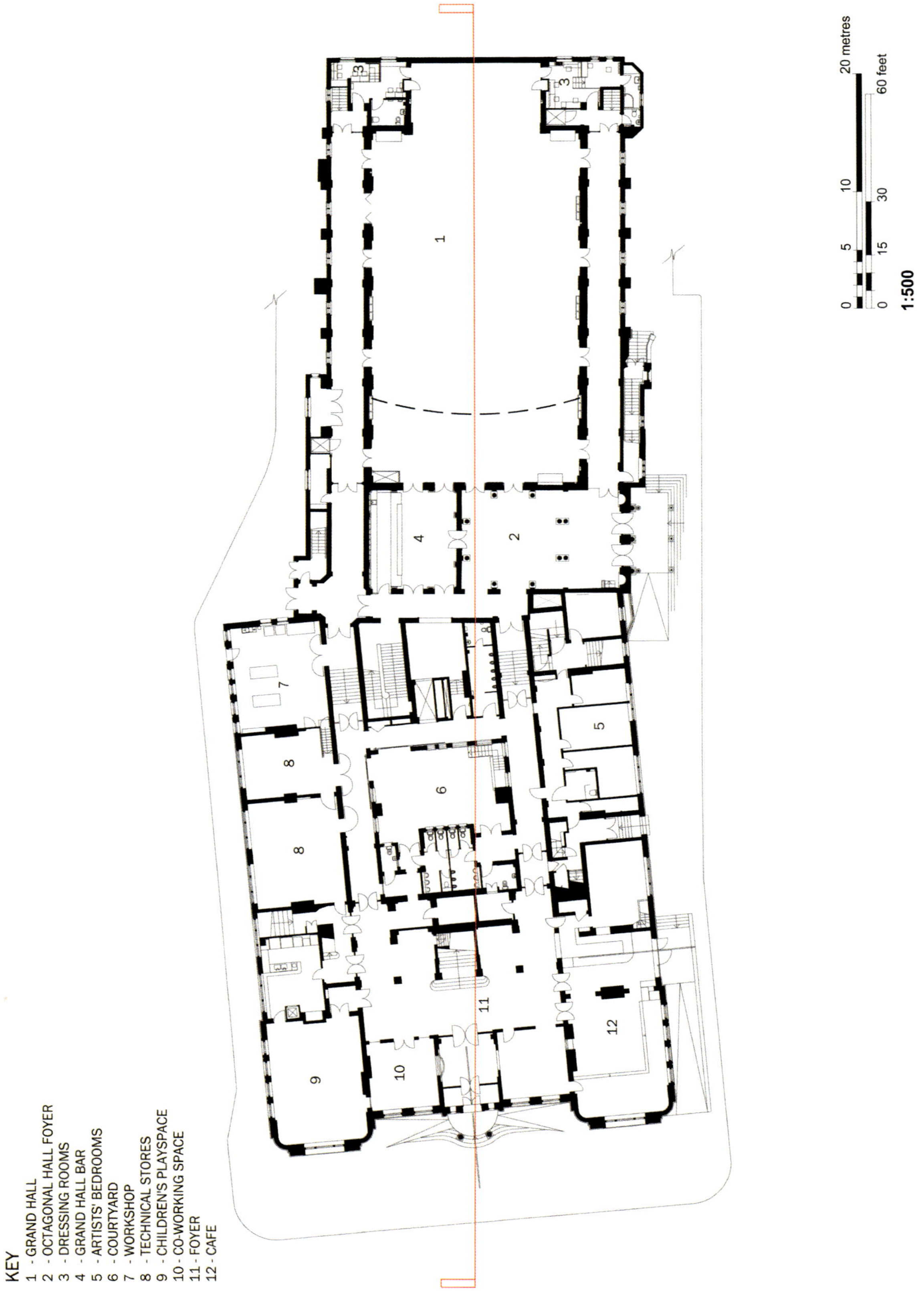

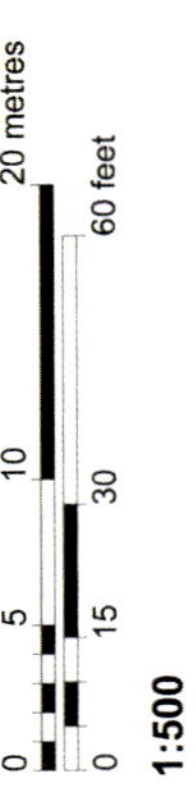

KEY
1 - GRAND HALL
2 - OCTAGONAL HALL FOYER
3 - DRESSING ROOMS
4 - GRAND HALL BAR
5 - ARTISTS' BEDROOMS
6 - COURTYARD
7 - WORKSHOP
8 - TECHNICAL STORES
9 - CHILDREN'S PLAYSPACE
10 - CO-WORKING SPACE
11 - FOYER
12 - CAFE
0 5 10 20 metres
0 15 30 60 feet
1:500

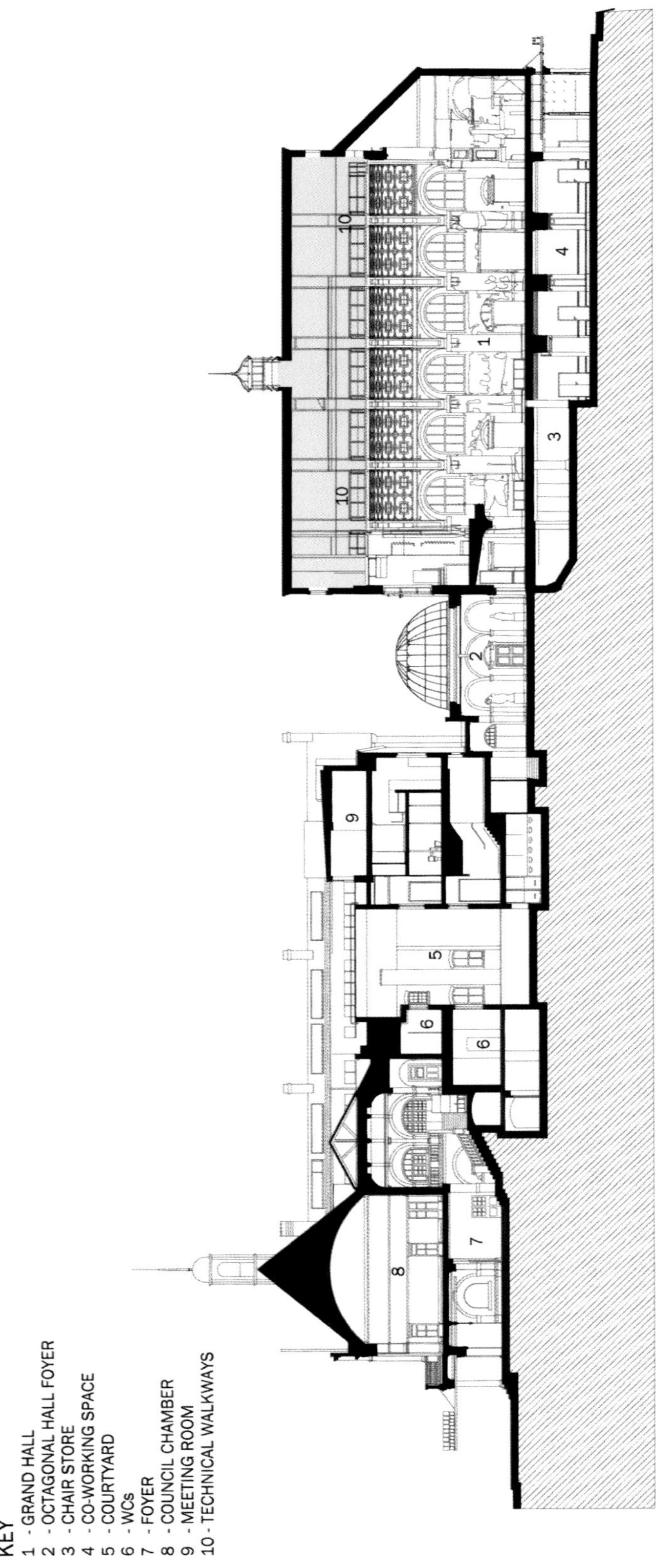


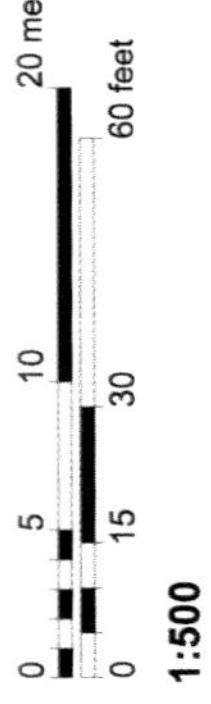


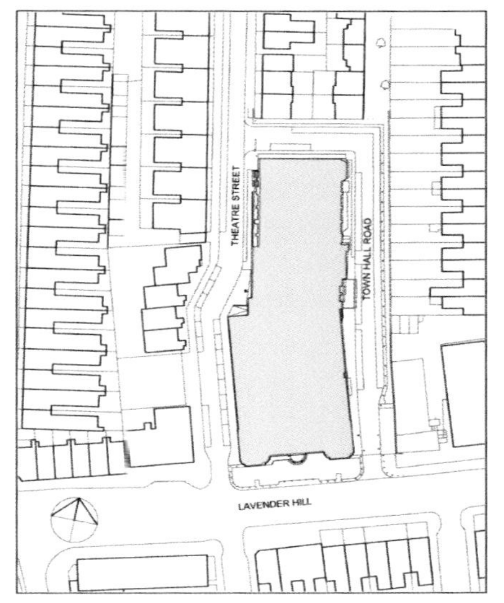


SITE PLAN - 1:2500

# Reference Project 26 Brixton House, London, UK

### Brief building description

Brixton House Theatre is a new artistic hub for Brixton and the new home for the Ovalhouse Theatre, a theatre previously located in Kennington, that has been producing exciting and challenging work for new audiences since the 1950s. The new building mixes space for the theatre together with recording studios, rehearsal rooms, university teaching spaces, small company start up and tech company workspace. (See Figure RP.26.01.) The building aims to blur boundaries between professional and community facilities, teaching and workspace, public and private use – to create space that has the ability to empower the communities in the centre of Brixton.

Figure RP.26.01 Photo © Hufton + Crow.

### Auditorium types

The two new auditoria are flexible studio spaces designed to replicate the size and scale of productions undertaken by Ovalhouse, but to offer greater creative and spatial flexibility. Theatre One (198 seats) has a fully accessible 'egg crate' technical grid and a bleacher seating system. Theatre Two (118 seats) is a smaller space that has motorised trusses that lower to ground level and a modular seating system. Additional flexibility is created by a range of entrances between the two theatres spaces that

### Key facts

**Client**
Brixton House

**Site address/web address:**
385 Coldharbour Lane,
London SW9 8GL
https://brixtonhouse.co.uk

**Opening date:**
February 2022

**Auditorium type and seating capacity:**
Theatre One is a flexible studio theatre with 198 maximum capacity. Theatre Two is a flexible studio theatre with 118 maximum capacity.

**Stage/performance space size**
Theatre One: 75m$^2$ (stage area when end on with bleacher out) total room size is 165m$^2$
Theatre Two: 14m$^2$ performance space (stage area when in-the-round) total room size is 85m$^2$

**Other facilities**
Seven flexible studio rehearsal rooms
Two floors of arts workspace, large foyer bar, basement recording studios

**Overall area:**
3,230m$^2$ arts space on three floors

**Design team**
**Architect:** Foster Wilson Size
**Theatre consultant:** Charcoalblue
**Acoustic consultant:** Gillieron Scott Acoustic Design
**Structural engineer:** Conisbee
**Service engineer:** Peter Brett Associates
**Fire consultant:** Bureau Veritas
**Planning consultant:** Tibbalds
**Site masterplanning:** Igloo Regeneration with Metropolitan Works
**Energy & sustainability consultant:** BWB Consulting
**Main contractor:** Galliford Try

**Construction cost at completion date (excluding fees and VAT):** £20 million

Figure RP.26.02 Photo © Hufton + Crow.

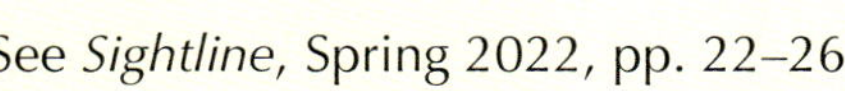
See *Sightline*, Spring 2022, pp. 22–26.

**The five figures** here show the new artistic hub in Brixton. **The first** (01) features the building's façade, composed of lightweight anodised aluminium panels that incorporate coloured LED lighting. **The second** (02) shows the carefully restored mural on the side wall of the adjacent Carlton Mansions, *Nuclear Dawn*, painted following the Brixton riot (1981). **The third figure** (03) shows one of the two new auditoria while **the fourth** (04) shows the striking pink staircase that runs through the centre of the building, with a new vertical mural by Damilola Odusote. **The final figure** (05) shows the foyer café, a light and welcoming space for the community.

Figure RP.26.03 Photo © Hufton + Crow.

allow for different performance configurations, as well as promenade and immersive theatre productions. The two main theatre spaces combine with an additional seven rehearsal studios that also have the ability to be used as performance spaces.

### Design intent

The design is intended to provide highly flexible space for new theatre productions that are small in scale but presented in a wide range of formats. The design responds to this brief by providing a robust studio environment throughout the building that is capable of constant adaptation and change. The design also aims to enhance the streetscape of Brixton by providing a large new 'living room' foyer with bar and a gallery on Coldharbour Lane, as well as a new public square for the restored *Nuclear Dawn* mural (see Figure RP.26.02), a tree-lined pavement for outdoor seating and a connection with new workspaces in the neighbouring Carlton Mansions. Outdoor terraces at each level on the south side help add amenity space for all users.

### Specific features/strengths

Specific features include a façade that mimics the appearance of the studio spaces internally and can be lit with hidden LED lighting to give a building that can change appearance for each production. Sustainability features include assisted natural ventilation to all studio and workspaces, a super insulated building envelope and an array of solar cells on the roof that produces a large portion of the power consumed on site. The interior responds to a colourful streetscape with a vibrant pink staircase that runs through the centre of the building and a new vertical mural themed on the energy of Brixton by south London artist and illustrator Damilola Odusote (see Figure RP.26.04).

Figure RP.26.04 Photo © Hufton + Crow.

A spacious foyer with bar, gallery and lounge space has similar technical facilities to the theatre spaces to enable production and performance to take place throughout the building.

Figure RP.26.05 Photo © Hufton + Crow.

**Users' verdicts**

The history of Brixton 'is proudly political and its rich blend of cultures will inspire the new theatre to be a cradle for startling stories and extraordinary art'. The idea is to be 'forward thinking, community focussed and rebelliously outspoken'.

Gbolahan Obisesan, Artistic Director and joint CEO, Brixton House Theatre, quoted by Rowan Moore, *The Guardian*, Sunday 27 February 2022

This has been a unique opportunity to make a building that gives space for the creative energy of the theatre and provide a valuable new community resource that is open to all.

Ed Wilson, partner, Foster Wilson Size, quoted by Rob Wilson in the *Architects' Journal*, 28 February 2022.

KEY
1 - STUDIO THEATRE 1
2 - STUDIO THEATRE 2
3 - TOILETS
4 - STUDIO
5 - ENTRANCE FOYER
6 - CAFE BAR
7 - GET IN AREA
8 - WORKSHOP
9 - OFFICE

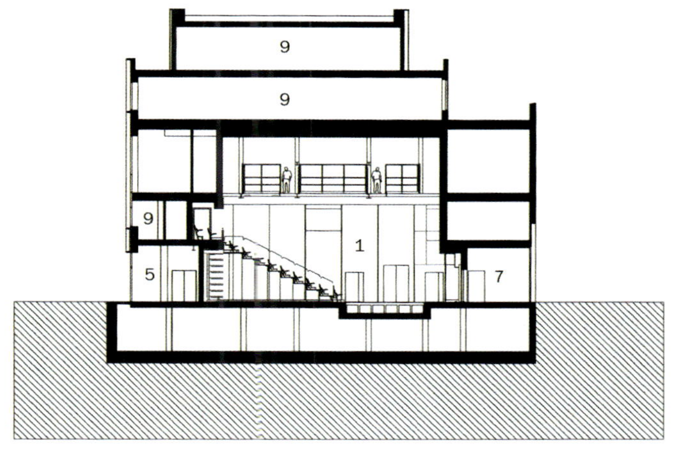


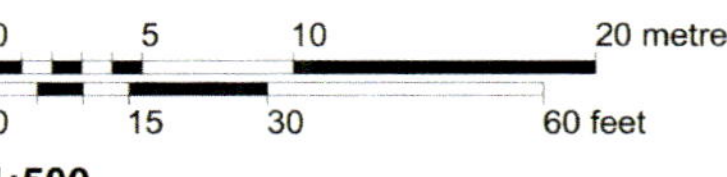


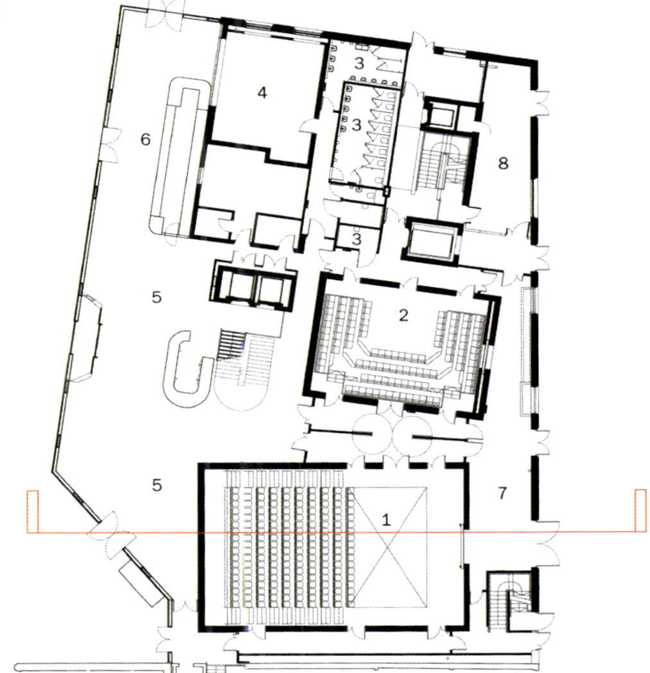


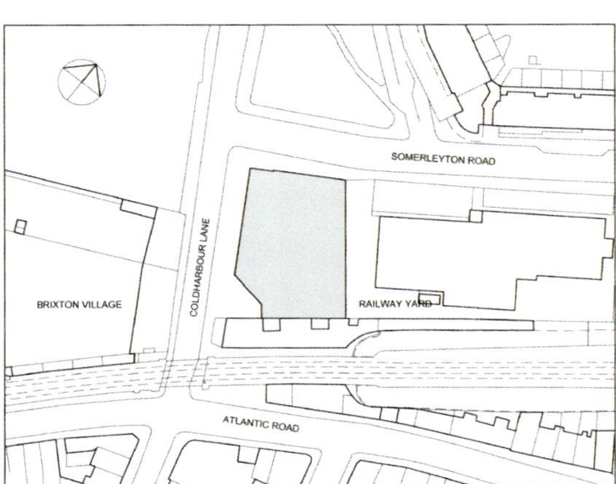


**SITE PLAN - 1:2500**

# Historic theatres remodelled/ restored

# Reference Project 27
# Royal Shakespeare Theatre, Stratford-upon-Avon, UK

### Brief building description

Situated beside the river Avon in the Warwickshire town where William Shakespeare was born this theatre is the home of the Royal Shakespeare Company and is at the main building in a campus which also includes production facilities, rehearsal studios and overnight accommodation for the resident company. The theatre was originally built in 1879, with rebuilds and extensions completed in 1932, 1986 and again as part of a major transformation project in 2011.

### Auditorium type

The Royal Shakespeare Theatre contains two auditoria; the 1000-seat thrust-stage main house which was built within the walls of the original building in 2011, and the 450-seat Swan Theatre, also a galleried thrust-stage space which was created in 1986 and refurbished and re-seated as part of the 2011 transformation project. The new main house has stalls seating and two levels of shallow galleries supported on slim steel columns which surround the thrust stage on three sides (see Figure RP.27.01). This creates an intimate space where no member of the audience is further than 15m from the stage edge.

Figure RP.27.01 Photo © Peter Cook/Bennetts Associates.

### Design intent

The previous main auditorium, dating from the 1932 rebuild was a fan-shaped cinema-like space which created a challenging environment for presenting Shakespeare's work. The main aim of the 2011 project was to create a new theatre space in a format derived from the Elizabethan courtyard forms of Shakespeare's time, but with the technical and audience capacity to present large-scale contemporary productions. The project has resulted in a completely new and intimate auditorium, built within the walls of the existing building, in a format that would be immediately recognisable to Shakespeare.

### Key facts

**Client**
Royal Shakespeare Company

**Site address/web reference**
Royal Shakespeare Theatre
Waterside
Stratford-upon-Avon
Warwickshire
CV37 6BB
www.rsc.org.uk

**Opening date:**
November 2010 following major transformation project

**Auditorium type and seating capacity**
Royal Shakespeare Theatre, thrust stage with stalls and two galleries, seating capacity 1018 Swan Theatre, thrust stage with stalls and two galleries, seating capacity 450

**Stage/performance space size/dimensions**
Royal Shakespeare Theatre thrust stage: 10m deep × 7m wide
Swan Theatre thrust stage: 10.5m deep × 5.5m wide

**Other facilities**
Theatre production facilities, rehearsal and events spaces, visitor facilities including cafes and bars, retail and viewing tower.

**Overall area:**
11,200m$^2$

**Design team**
**Architect:** Bennetts Associates
**Theatre consultant:** Charcoalblue
**Acoustic consultant:** Nicholas Edwards
**Consultants on other aspects of building services:** Buro Happold
**Main contractor:** Mace

**Construction cost at completion date** (excluding fees and VAT): £57 million

See David Ward, *Transformation. Shakespeare's New Theatre* (Stratford-upon-Avon: RSC Enterprise Ltd, 2011) and *Sightline*, Winter 2010, pp. 22–26.

## Specific features/strengths

At its heart, the Royal Shakespeare Theatre's new auditorium has revolutionised the way audiences experience live theatre in Stratford-upon-Avon, but in addition, the building's transformed and enlarged public spaces have become more accessible and welcoming. (See Figure RP.27.02.)

Figure RP.27.02 Photo © Peter Cook.

The theatre's status as a major landmark in the town and on the riverside has been reinvigorated by the creation of new outdoor spaces and routes along with a new viewing tower (see Figure RP.27.03).

**The four figures show the transformed Royal Shakespeare Theatre. The first (01) shows** a view from the thrust stage into the auditorium of the main house at the RST. **The second** (02) presents a view of the foyer between the Swan theatre and the main foyer for the Royal Shakespeare Theatre with Waterside visible through the glass on the left and the book shop forming part of the route through the building. **The third figure** (03) features the exterior of the building from across the River Avon showing the viewing tower in the background and the roof line which reveals the locations of existing spaces and extensions. **The final image** (04) shows an early example of a new technology using cross-laminated timber panels for floor slabs, a method now widely used.

Figure RP.27.03 Photo © Peter Cook/Bennetts Associates.

It is worth noting that most of the new floor slabs including the auditorium were early examples of a new technology enabling them to be made from cross-laminated timber panels, a method now in widespread use (see Figure RP.27.04).

Figure RP.27.04 Photo © Peter Cook/Bennetts Associates.

**Users' verdicts**

As someone who has played all the RSC's theatres, it seems to me that what the Company has found is a brilliant way of retaining the best of the original building while constructing a new theatre which will work wonderfully for actors and audiences alike. We are creating a theatre in Stratford that Shakespeare could walk into and recognize as a playhouse for his work. It's a spectacular idea.

Dame Judi Dench, Actor,
The Royal Shakespeare Company

It's the new auditorium that really matters – and it is superb . . . the intimacy is tremendous . . . acoustics are superb . . . infinitely more welcoming . . . a rich mixture of old and new.

Charles Spencer, Theatre Critic,
*The Daily Telegraph*

The architects have transformed Elisabeth Scott's looming, booming 1932 barn of a place into an intimate yet spacious venue. . . . Gone are the days when generations of schoolchildren, fidgeting in the far-distant punishment seats at the back of the balcony, were put off Shakespeare for life.

Fiona Mountford, Theatre Critic,
*The Evening Standard*

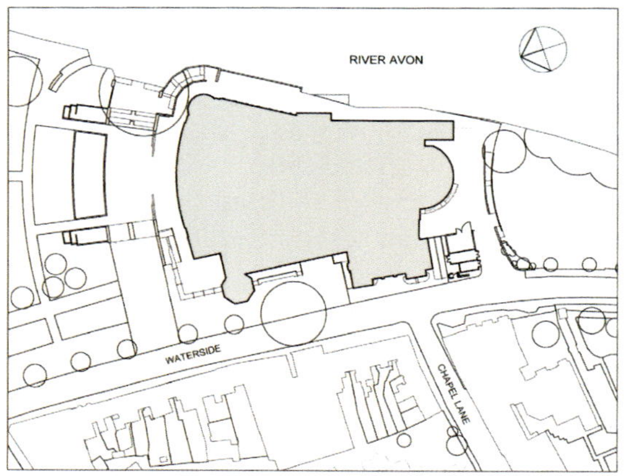


**SITE PLAN - 1:2500**

KEY
1 - RST STAGE AREA
2 - ROYAL SHAKESPEARE THEATRE AUDITORIUM
3 - SWAN THEATRE
4 - COLONNADE
5 - MAIN FOYER
6 - DRESSING ROOMS
7 - STAGE DOOR
8 - TOILETS
9 - CAFE
10 - LIBRARY AND READING ROOM
11 - REHEARSAL ROOM
12 - GET IN DOORS

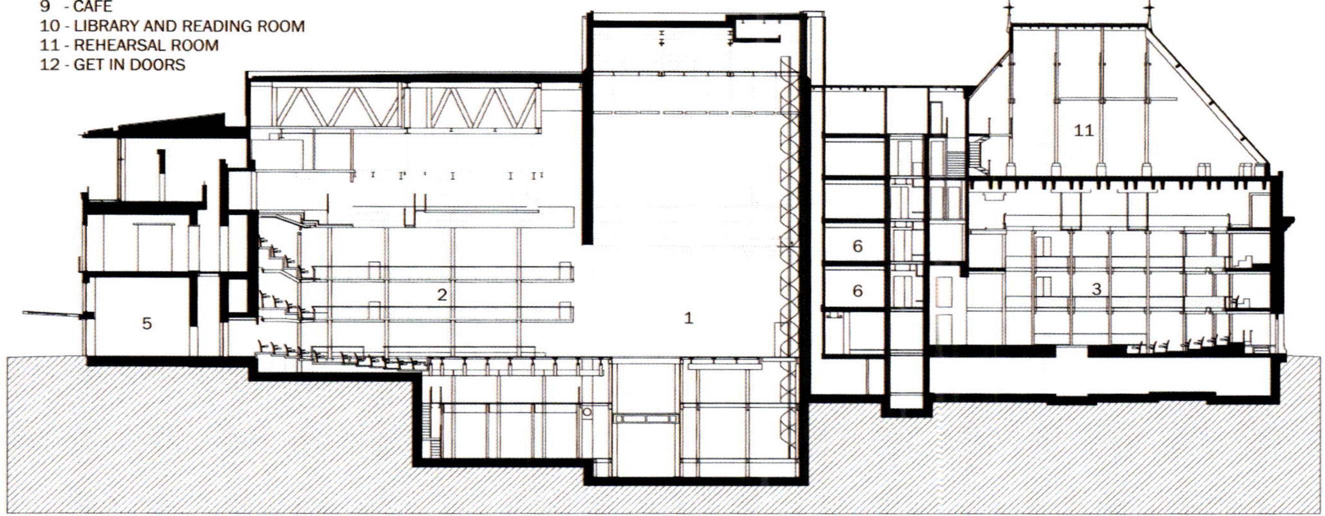

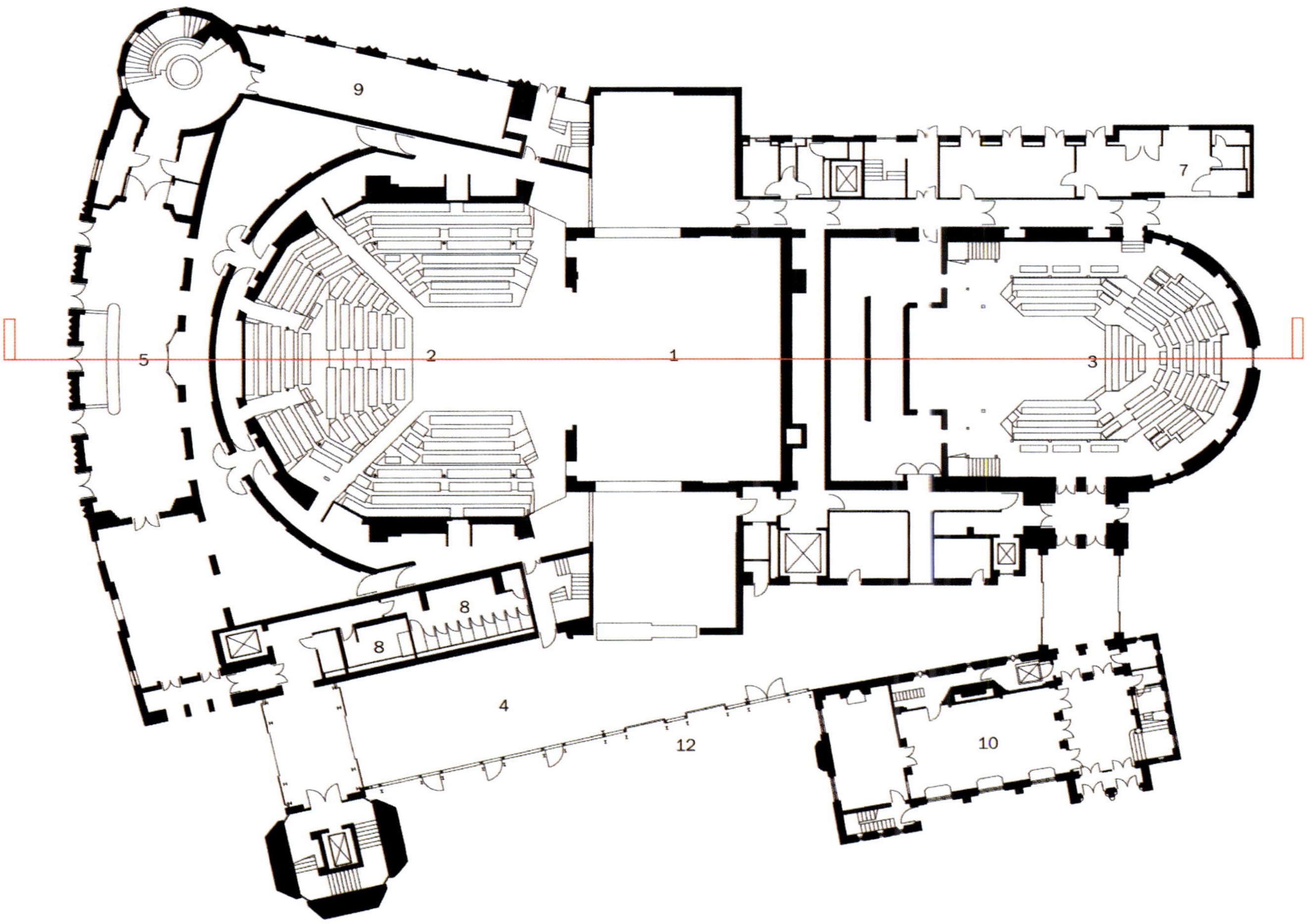

C 5 10 20 metres
C 15 30 60 feet

**1:500**

# Reference Project 28 Wilton's Music Hall, London, UK

### Brief building description

Wilton's Music Hall is unique. It is the only mid-Victorian pub music hall that survives, anywhere. It is listed Grade II*. It was in halls like this that variety entertainment was invented. For everyone who has been there, the atmosphere of this grand hall, hidden behind a row of once dilapidated houses, is unforgettable (see Figure RP.28.01).

Figure RP.28.01 Photo © Hélène Binet.

### Auditorium type

The hall is a long high room with a vaulted ceiling, a gallery on three sides, a proscenium arch on the fourth. In 1859 when it opened, the hall reputedly held a thousand people, eating and drinking, while the performers on a high stage at one end vied for attention. It is a hall made for singing.

### Design intent

The hall and its five terraced houses somehow survived the post-war, nearly complete 'slum' clearances in the area. The design intent was to preserve

**Key facts**

**Client:**
Wilton's Music Hall Trust,
Graces Alley,
London E1 8JB

**Current Executive Director:**
Holly Kendrick

**Siteddress/web reference**
Graces Alley,
London E1 8JB
www.wiltons.org.uk

**Opening date:**
Open one way or another throughout construction.
Hall reopened January 2013.
Houses reopened October 2015.

**Auditorium type and seating capacity:**
Music Hall, capacity 400.

**Stage/performance space size:**
Main stage:
10.5m wide × 5.0m deep
Demountable forestage is 6.3m wide × 3.4m deep

**Other facilities:**
Bars, exhibition room, workshop, commercial kitchen, lettable rooms, offices, learning and participation room, dressing rooms

**Overall area:**
1,300m$^2$

**Design team**
**Architect:** Tim Ronalds Architects
**Theatre consultant:** Peter Angier, Carr & Angier
**Acoustic consultant:** Raf Orlowski, Ramboll
**Environmental/M&E engineers:** Max Fordham
**Structural engineer:** Philip Cooper, Cambridge Architectural Research
**Conservation plan:** John Earl

**Access consultant:** All Clear Designs
**Main contractor:** Fullers Builders (Hall)
William Anelay (Houses)

**Construction cost at completion date** (excluding fees and VAT): £3 million

Figure RP.28.02 Photo © Hélène Binet.

Figure RP.28.03 Photo © The Theatres Trust/David San Milan Del Rio.

See *Sightline*, Winter 2015, pp. 11–17.

The **four images** included here make the painstakingly 'arrested decay' of Wilton's Music Hall and houses clear. **The first** (01) shows the street entrance to Wilton's Music Hall. **The second and third images** (02, 03) show the interior of the hall from ground level and the restored interior of the auditorium looking from the balcony towards the stage (the latter taken in September 2015 at a Theatres Trust event). **The final image** (04) shows one of the spaces in the houses that capture the atmosphere of the supporting spaces for the hall.

the hall and houses in their surviving condition (see Figures RP.28.02 and RP.28.04), making all areas safe and useable as spaces for creative performance. Our strategy was to 'do no more than essential' and this enabled us to preserve the building and its magical atmosphere.

### Specific features/strengths

It is neither restoration, nor renovation, but involved great care and ingenuity to make it look as if nothing had been done (see Figures RP.28.01 and RP.28.04). The hall gives producers great freedom (see Figure RP.28.03), each production an improvisation, while the seemingly derelict houses provide exciting support spaces. Our approach has now been labelled as 'arrested decay'. Wilton's director, Frances Mayhew, led the project for the nine years it took to raise the funds and complete the work.

Figure RP.28.04 Photo © Hélène Binet.

**Users' verdicts**

Wilton's received much attention and won many awards when it re-opened, including RIBA London Building of the Year. What was once one of London's 'Hidden Secrets' is now well-known and described as a must on any London tourist's itinerary.

The filmed performance of Britten's opera 'The Turn of the Screw' by Opera Glass Works, used the building as the set. Available online, via Marquee TV, it captures the quality of the space.

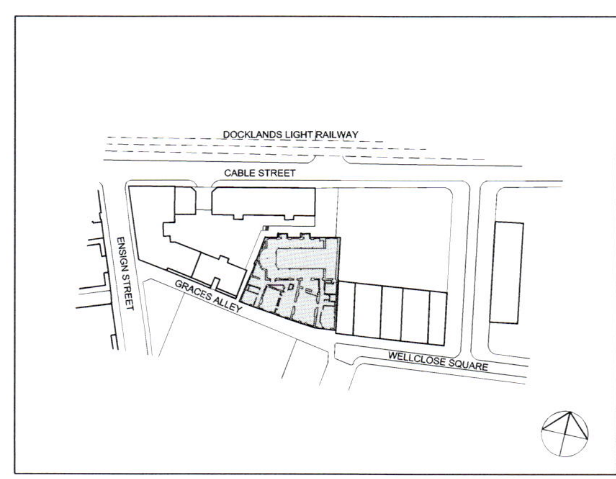


**SITE PLAN - 1:2500**

KEY
1 - STAGE
2 - AUDITORIUM
3 - FOYER
4 - FUNCTION ROOM
5 - TOILETS
6 - BAR
7 - KITCHEN
8 - UNDERSTAGE
9 - GALLERY

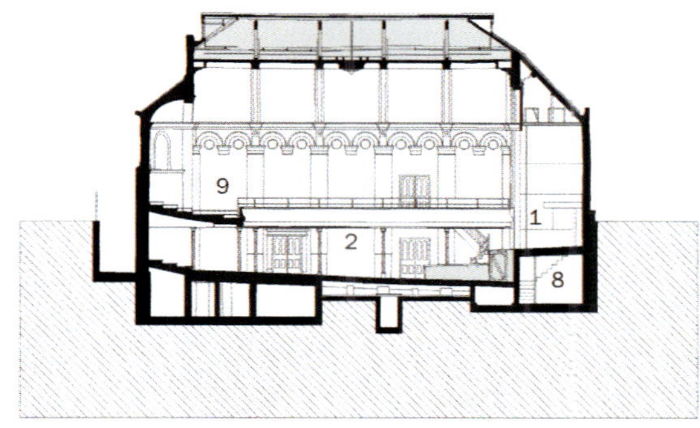


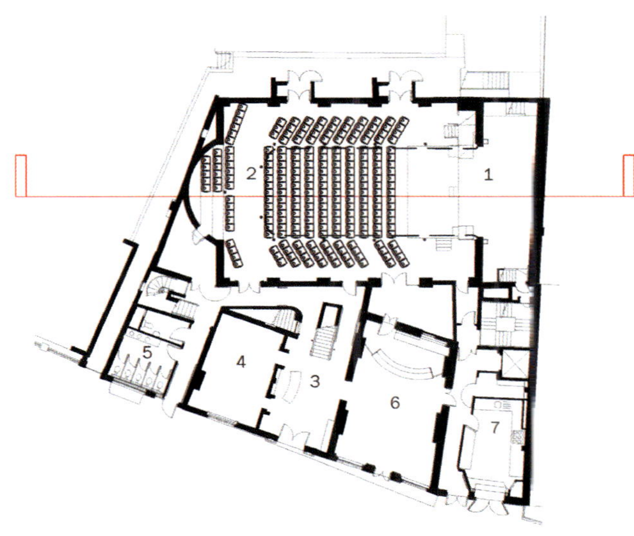


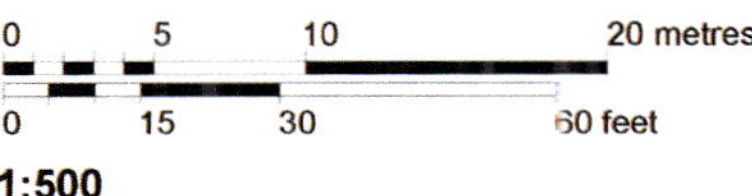

# Reference Project 29 Theatre Royal, Glasgow, Scotland

### Brief building description

The Theatre Royal Glasgow is owned by Scottish Opera and managed by the Ambassador Theatre Group. It is the home of Scottish Opera and Scottish Ballet with the remainder of the programme being touring shows. It is Category A listed; the 1867 design by George Bell underwent numerous later alterations including those by architect Charles Phipps in 1879 and 1894.

### Auditorium type

It is a traditional proscenium arch auditorium with stalls, dress circle, upper circle and balcony (see Figure RP.29.01). The entrances to the various levels were moved to align with the centre line, through new acoustic lobbies. Wheelchair positions were created at the rear of the balconies to take advantage of lift access.

Figure RP.29.01 Photo © Andrew Lee Photographer.

### Design intent

This project was about enhancing the audience journey 'from street to seat' by providing welcoming, generous foyer facilities to meet the expectations of the modern audience.

### Key facts

**Client**
Scottish Opera General Director, Alex Reedijk

**Site address/web reference**
282 Hope Street,
Glasgow G2 3QA
www.glasgowtheatreroyal.org.uk

**Opening date**
New foyers opened December 2014

**Auditorium type and seating capacity**
Traditional proscenium auditorium with seating capacity of 1540

**Stage/performance space size**
Stage: 20m wide × 12m deep (240m$^2$)

**Other facilities**
Flexible foyers, café at street level, box office, interval bars, hospitality spaces, 2 × dedicated education suite.

**Overall area:** 2,727m$^2$

**Design team**
**Architect:** Page\Park Architects
**Theatre consultant:** Charcoalblue
**Acoustic consultant:** Sandy Brown Associates
**MEP:** Max Fordham
**Structural, civil:** Arup Scotland
**CDM:** CDM Scotland
**Project manager:** tX2
**Fire engineer:** Atelier 10
**Cost consultant:** Capita
**Graphics:** Studio Arc
**Main contractor:** Sir Robert McAlpine

**Construction cost at completion date**
(excluding fees and VAT): £13 million

Figure RP.29.02 Photo © Andrew Lee Photographer.

The dramatic elliptical extension celebrates the corner plot, eases audience flow and reinterprets the Victorian auditorium in a contemporary manner in both form and materials palette.

Figure RP.29.03 Photo © Andrew Lee Photographer.

This project is an excellent example of how an imaginative modern foyer extension can provide greatly improved audience access and facilities (see Figure RP.29.04), linked to an historic and much-loved auditorium.

### Specific features/strengths

The sculptural form reflects the curved balconies of the auditorium and helps guide audience flow. (See Figure RP.29.05.) The perimeter structural concrete frame provides clear internal views of the dramatic self-supporting stair.

The foyers are naturally ventilated with air input through the attenuated metal clad fins of the elevation – a playful composition likened to musical annotation.

**The first figure** (01) shows the historic auditorium of the Theatre Royal, Glasgow, looking out from the proscenium arch stage. This provides the context for this project which has provided generous foyer facilities in a dramatic elliptical extension to this corner-plot home of Scottish Opera and Scottish Ballet as well as for touring shows. **The second figure** (02) presents an external view showing the juxtaposition of the new entrance and the historic building. The metal fins on the new extension are the attenuated ducts through which air enters the interior. **The third image** (03) focuses on the upper circle level foyer showing its double height space which is the result of the new foyer floor levels aligning with the rear of the seating balconies. **The fourth** (04) returns to the entrance level foyer showing the café at the foot of the staircase while **the final image** (05) features this sculptural stair designed to encourage exploration of the upper levels.

Figure RP.29.04 Photo © Andrew Lee Photographer.

Figure RP.29.05 Photo © Andrew Lee Photographer.

**Users' verdicts**

A wonderful transformation from very cramped nineteenth-century foyers into a welcoming, efficient and celebratory array of spaces that more than exceeded our initial vision as clients and, most importantly, absolutely delighted our customers.

Scottish Opera

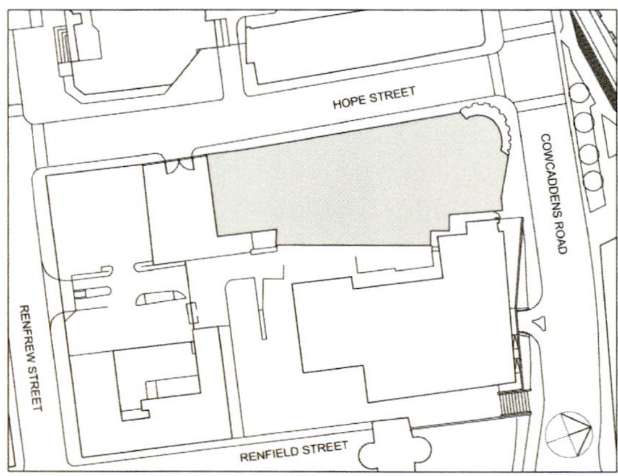


SITE PLAN - 1:2500

KEY
1 - STAGE
2 - AUDITORIUM
3 - BOX OFFICE
4 - LIGHTING BOOTH
5 - FOYER
6 - ORIGINAL ENTRANCE
7 - BAR
8 - TOILETS
9 - CLOAKROOM
10 - EDUCATION SUITE
11 - ROOF TERRACE

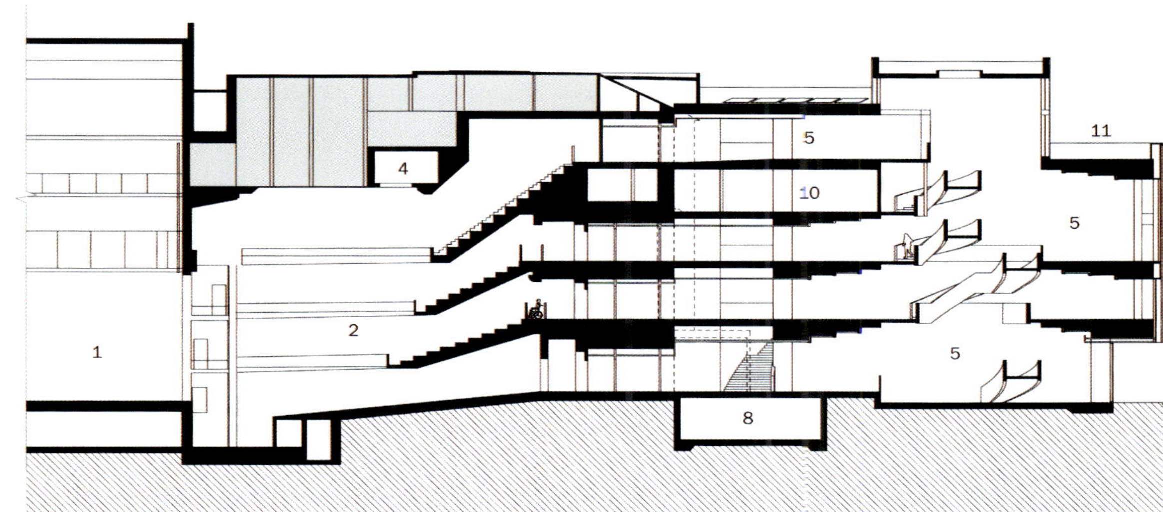


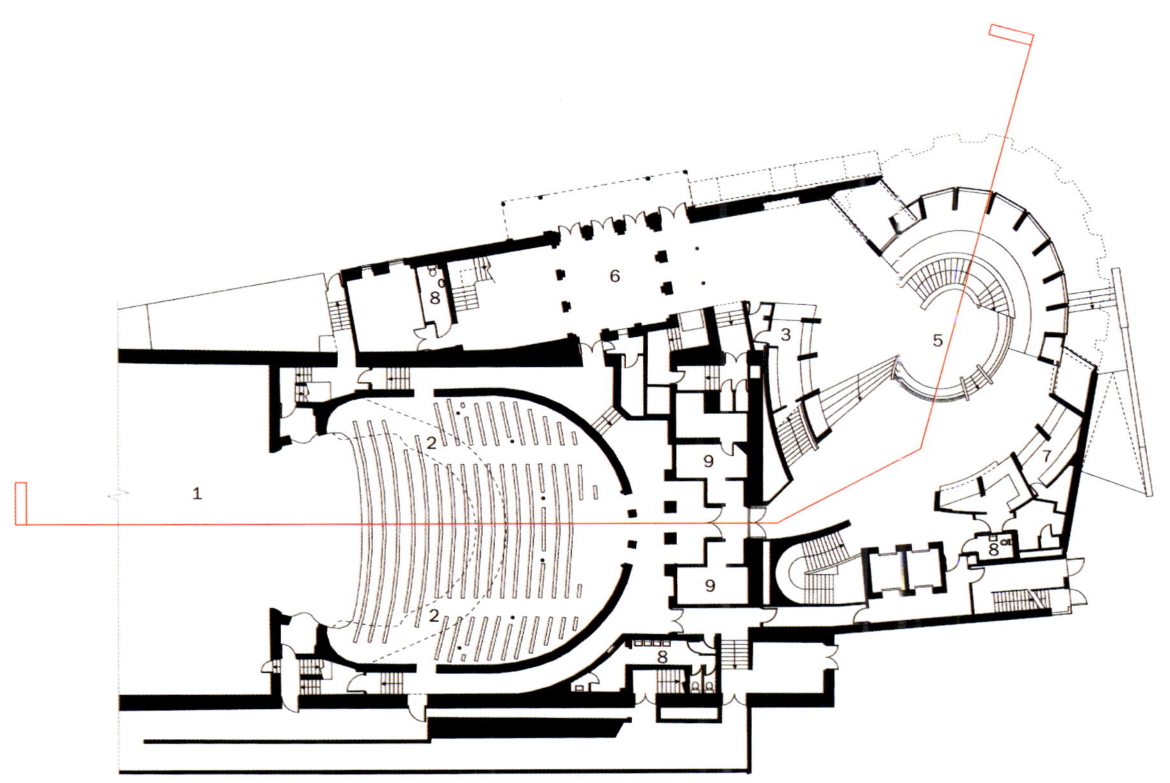


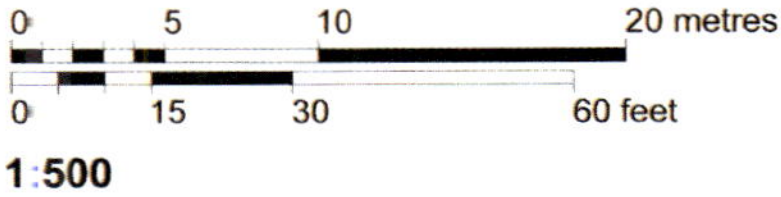

# Reference Project 30 Victoria Palace Theatre, London, UK

## Brief building description

The last major commission of the prolific theatre designer Frank Matcham in 1911, the Grade II* listed Victoria Palace Theatre features an ornate 'Edwardian-Baroque' façade and a glorious auditorium. The 1543-seat West End theatre is a receiving house which typically accommodates long-running shows, with the previous production, *Billy Elliot*, running for 11 years. It is currently the London home of *Hamilton*, the international musical-theatre phenomenon (see Figure RP.30.01).

The building is an exceptionally well-preserved example of the late Victorian/Edwardian theatre-building boom and was London's last great variety house. Purchased by Delfont Mackintosh Theatres in late 2014, the building closed for a major 20-month refurbishment in 2016. In addition to extensive works on the existing structure, this project included the construction of a new stage house and the extension of the building's east wing to create new public foyer spaces.

Figure RP.30.01 Photo © Philip Vile/Aedas Arts Team.

## Auditorium type

Victoria Palace Theatre features a grand auditorium decorated in a Baroque style and with an architraved proscenium. (See Figure RP.30.02.) There are Royal Circle and Grand Circle levels and two tiers of three boxes to either side of the proscenium. Rear stalls boxes introduced in the recent refurbishment have enhanced the intimacy of the space and reduced the length of the stalls so that the back rows have an unobscured view of the top of the proscenium.

### Key facts

**Client**
Julian Middleton
(on behalf of Delfont Mackintosh Theatres, Head of Project Design)

**Site address/web reference**
Victoria Palace Theatre
Victoria Street
London
SW1E 5EA
www.victoriapalacetheatre.co.uk

**Opening date**
December 2017
(refurbishment works).

**Auditorium type and seating capacity**
1543-seat Edwardian West End proscenium arch theatre.

**Stage/performance space size**
Current stage width: 21m (plus a raised side stage of 5.5m in addition to this)
Current stage depth: approx. 9.6m behind proscenium. Once the historic 'inner' stage house is demolished, the stage depth will increase to approx. 15.4m behind the proscenium.

**Other facilities**
Rehearsal room, extended foyer spaces and bars.

**Overall area**
5,400m$^2$ GIA

**Design team**
**Architect:** Aedas Arts Team
**Interior designer:** Clare Ferraby
**Theatre consultant:** Theatre Projects Consultants
**Acoustic consultant:** Arup Acoustics
**Structural engineer:** Conisbee
**Project manager:** Buro Four
**MEP engineer:** Buro Happold
**Cost consultant:** Bruce Shaw Partnership
**Fire consultant:** Jeremy Gardner Associates Ltd.

**Planning consultant:** Montagu Evans
**Access consultant:** People Friendly Design
**CDM coordinator:** PFB Construction Management Services Ltd.
**Main contractor:** 8Build

**Construction cost at completion date** (excluding fees and VAT): undisclosed

See *Sightline*, Summer 2019, pp. 8–13

**The five figures** here illustrate the impressive spaces of the Victoria Palace Theatre. **The first** (01) shows an exterior view of the theatre's main entrance featuring the name of the currently running musical, *Hamilton*. **The second and third images** (02, 03) show the grand Baroque auditorium following technical interventions and the rejuvenation of the interior scheme: **the second** (02) looks at the auditorium from the front of the stage, **the third** (03) looks across from the side of the auditorium. Both these images include the sky dome. **The final two images** (04, 05) show areas of the hugely enhanced, newly renovated public foyer and bar spaces.

**User's verdict**

It has been an extraordinary undertaking, both thrilling and fraught, not only because of the complexity of putting what is practically a brand-new building into the shell of a much-loved historical masterpiece, but because it was also the ideal theatre for the most eagerly awaited American musical in decades.

Cameron Mackintosh, 2017

Victoria Palace is 'an extraordinary colourful and exhilarating temple of theatrical magic and light that will certainly last for another hundred years.

Cameron Mackintosh, *The Stage*, 2018

Figure RP.30.02 Photo © Philip Vile/Aedas Arts Team.

Prior to the major 2017 renovation, the auditorium suffered key technical shortcomings, particularly in terms of the stage depth and proscenium width, which were insufficient for major musical productions. Thermal comfort was poor and the interior décor, dominated by darkly stained wall panelling and gloomy lighting, was subdued. As is commonly the case with theatres of this period, the Grand Circle level was particularly plain in terms of its décor.

The works to the building saw major structural and services interventions to resolve the venue's technical challenges and to create a more intimate space with improved sightlines. These works sat alongside a rejuvenated interior scheme, including re-seating of the auditorium, new lighting, stripping and re-polishing of the timberwork, bespoke carpets and wallpapers, restoration of the plasterwork, and complete redecoration. (See Figure RP.30.03.)

The 2017 works included the transformation of the stage house, with the proscenium widened and the raked stage made level. A new deeper and taller stagehouse was constructed around the original stage house, which will be demolished once the run of *Hamilton* ends. The enlarged stage house also has higher loading and flying capabilities. These upgrades will be key to the long-term success of the venue in continuing to attract major productions, particularly transfers from Broadway.

## Design intent

Major works to re-imagine the Victoria Palace Theatre were completed in 2017. The vision of Sir Cameron Mackintosh was for an holistic restoration,

Figure RP.30.03 Photo © Philip Vile/Aedas Arts Team.

refurbishment and extension of the building, 'finishing and enhancing' the building in the manner of its original architect. The project was extensive, rebuilding the stage house, widening the proscenium opening, reworking the auditorium boxes, fully refurbishing the auditorium and original foyers, creating new public areas and enlarging and enhancing backstage spaces.

The Front of house experience has been dramatically improved with the creation of two large salon spaces and refurbished bars and foyers throughout. (See Figures RP.30.04 and RP.30.05.) Additional audience WCs were introduced and all the existing WCs were completely refitted. Front of house circulation was improved through the creation of a rear stalls' crossover and reworking of the routes up to Grand Circle level. The reinstatement of a lightwell between the entrance lobby and Royal Circle foyer has opened up the Front of house area, making for a dramatic arrival experience and significantly improving visual connectivity between spaces so that patrons can orientate themselves within the building.

Figure RP.30.04 Photo © Philip Vile/Aedas Arts Team.

Figure RP.30.05 Photo © Philip Vile/Aedas Arts Team.

Backstage, the refurbished dressing rooms are some of the most comfortable in the West End, with a combination of star dressing room suites and chorus dressing rooms. A daylit rehearsal room has replaced the former disparate collection of offices, providing a highly desirable space available for hire in the heart of the West End.

### Specific features/strengths

Creating the required technical infrastructure within an historic auditorium was a challenge. The extensive use of unreinforced clinker concrete added a further layer of complexity when it came to 'threading in' new services. The auditorium ventilation scheme has been renewed, together with re-wiring, new LED lighting and effective zoning of the building all of which reduce energy consumption.

The quality and attention to detail in the completed venue give the sense of a seamless architectural ensemble with Matcham's original design. While Grand Circle patrons, performers and back-of-house staff previously had a lesser experience than those with 'prime' tickets, one of the most important achievements of the renovation works has been to bring parity in the quality and comfort of the facilities throughout the venue, ensuring that all building users have an equally positive experience.

KEY
1 - STAGE
2 - AUDITORIUM
3 - FOYERS
4 - FOLLOW SPOT ROOM
5 - GET IN
6 - DRESSING ROOMS
7 - BARS
8 - TOILETS
9 - STAGE DOOR
10 - UNDERSTAGE
11 - REHEARSAL ROOM
12 - EXTENDED STAGE

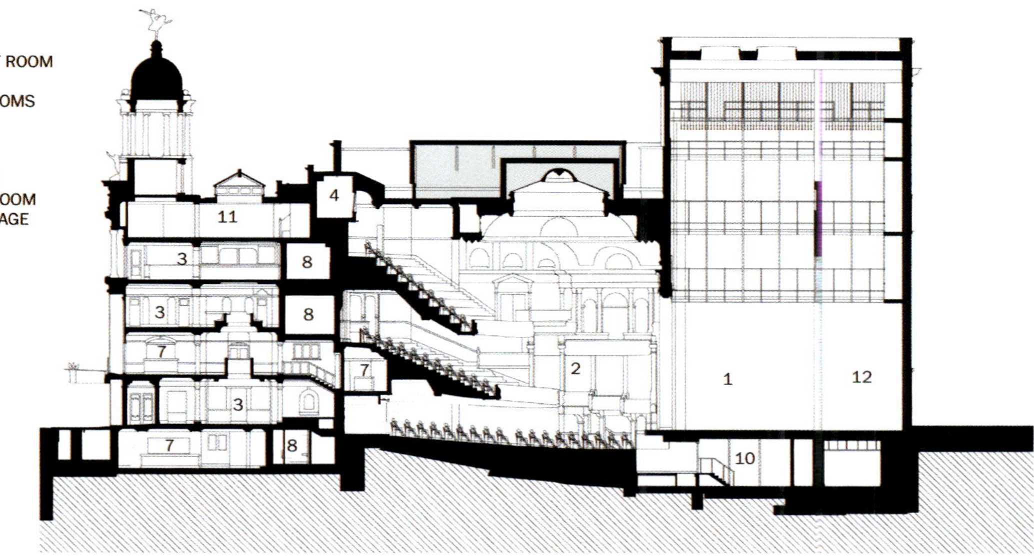

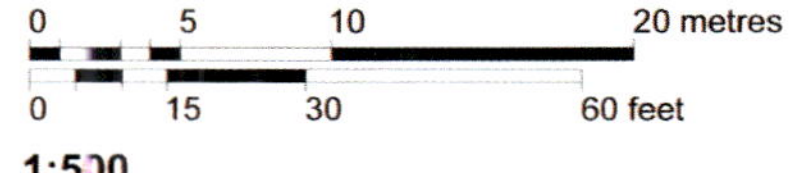

11
4
3
8
3
8
7
7
2
1
12
3
7
8
10

0 5 10 20 metres
0 15 30 60 feet
**1:500**

8
9
6
5
2
1
12
8
3
8
7
7

VICTORIA STREET
ALLINGTON STREET
ALLINGTON STREET
VICTORIA STREET
BRESSENDEN PLACE

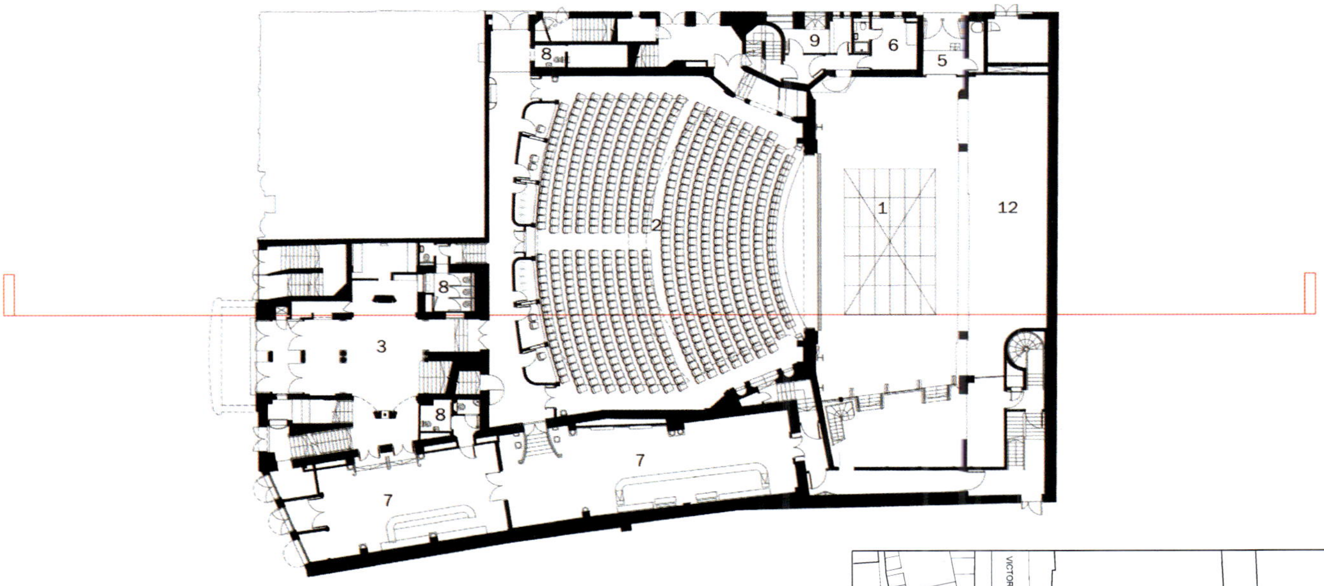

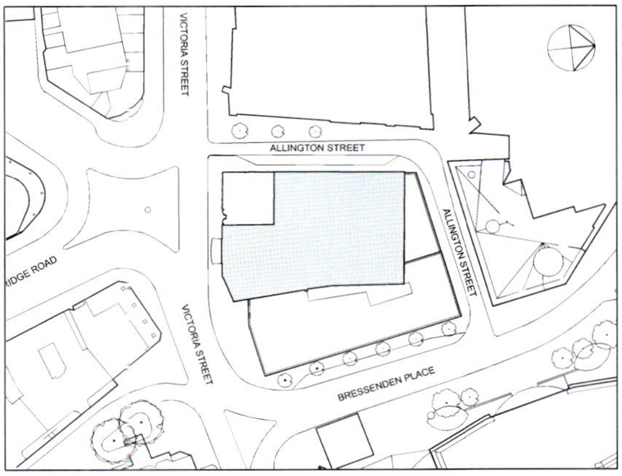

**SITE PLAN - 1:2500**

# Reference Project 31
# Bristol Old Vic,
# Bristol, UK

### Brief building description

This development created a radical new front of house and flexible foyer, with in-built technical infrastructure to host theatrical and music performance, a relocated studio theatre, and upgraded back of house facilities for the Grade I listed Bristol Old Vic, the oldest continuously working theatre in the English-speaking world.

Figure RP.31.01 Photo © Philip Vile/Haworth Tompkins.

### Auditorium type

140 to 150 seat flexible studio theatre relocated into the historic Coopers' Hall with adjacent backstage area. (See Figure RP.31.02.)

Flexible bench seating and fixed gallery (with visual connection to King Street when desired).

Figure RP.31.02 Photo © Fred Howarth/Haworth Tompkins.

### Key facts

**Building Name:**
Bristol Old Vic

**Client/user:**
Tom Morris (Artistic Director)

**Site address/web reference:**
Theatre Royal King Street,
Bristol, BS1 4ED
https://bristololdvic.org.uk/

**Opening date**
September 2018

**Auditorium type and seating capacity:**
140- to 150-seat flexible studio theatre (The existing Georgian auditorium was refurbished in a prior phase of works by a separate design team. It re-opened in 2012.)

**Stage/performance space size:**
**Studio theatre:** Stage (typically thrust): 8.7m wide × 4.2m deep (36$m^2$)
Backstage: 16.5m wide × 13.6m deep (90$m^2$)

**Other facilities:**
Rehearsal space located in original Coopers' Hall attic (acoustic separation and technical infrastructure upgraded).
Foyer equipped with plug in capability for stage lighting, speakers and raised stage area (with demountable balustrade to facilitate informal performance). Banqueting Hall/events space with catering support spaces.

**Overall area $m^2$**
Total new build: GIA 1,490$m^2$
Total refurbished existing building: 640$m^2$

**Design team**
**Architect:** Haworth Tompkins
**Theatre consultant:** Charcoalblue
**Acoustic consultant:** Charcoalblue

**Building services:** Max Fordham
**Environmental sustainability:** Max Fordham
**Cultural and economic sustainability:** Plann
**Inclusivity, diversity of access:** Jane Topliss
**Structural engineering:** Momentum
**Project management:** Plann
**Archaeology:** Avon Archaeology
**Main contractor:** Gilbert Ash Construction

**Construction cost at completion date** (excluding fees and VAT): £9 million

See *Sightline*, Winter 2018, pp. 13–20.

**The first of the three figures** (01) shows an exterior view of the front façade with the new theatre entrance and foyer forming an extension to the frontage of the original Coopers' Hall. Shutters display a poem by Miles Chamber, the city's first Poet Laureate, that pays tribute to the victims of the slave trade as well as the text of David Garrick's inaugural 1766 address. **The second figure** (02) features the new studio showing flexible bench seating and a fixed gallery as well as stage lighting infrastructure. **The final figure** (03) is of the newly built, triple-storey front of house space on a busy evening, showing the foyer café and bar, with bench-style tables on the ground floor, more seating in a second-floor gallery, circulation spaces and the auditorium wall to the rear.

Upgraded acoustic performance, stage lighting and audio-visual infrastructure.

Connection to the street (acoustic shutters enable natural daylight during get in).

### Design intent

The result of five years careful research, consultation, design and construction, the project aims to open up the front of house areas to a wider, more diverse audience and to place the theatre at the heart of Bristol's public life and public space.

### Specific features/strengths

A timber foyer structure that houses a new café and bar (along with integrated technical infrastructure to allow foyer performance).

New entrance and street announcement, including artist collaboration corten steel shutters, see Figure RP.31.01.

New events space (reinstating Coopers' Hall).

The new foyer and events space (including catering support spaces) have provided alternative revenue streams and transformed the front-of-house operations. (See Figure RP.31.03.)

Naturally ventilated foyer and studio theatre.

Upgraded back of house support spaces.

Green roof to increase biodiversity.

Original 1760's historic auditorium wall and Coopers' Hall façades revealed and conserved.

New front of house lift tying historic levels together and providing level access for the first time in the theatre's history.

Increased flexibility of studio theatre and rehearsal accommodation has supported educational and youth theatre programme.

Figure RP.31.03 Photo © Philip Vile/Haworth Tompkins.

**Users' verdicts**

This is a momentous occasion for the 252-year-old historic gem, when we finally reveal the results of knocking down the walls that have kept the theatre separate from the city for over 50 years. It represents a renewal of our commitment to be a theatre for the whole city – a founding principle when it was first imagined more than 250 years ago – and Haworth Tompkins has done a wonderful job in helping us to realise our ambitions.

Tom Morris, Bristol Old Vic Artistic Director

The theatre is undeniably a part of the slave trade legacy in Bristol. . . . The building came out of that economic boom and I don't think it is enough anymore to just assume that people then did not know the trade was wrong. So we've called this year [2018] the Year of Change [suggested as a theme for 2018 by Roger Griffin of Bristol Old Vic's Associate Company, Ujima Radio] and it has been about renewing our relationship with the city.

Tom Morris quoted by Vanessa Thorpe in *The Observer*,

Sunday, 9 September 2018

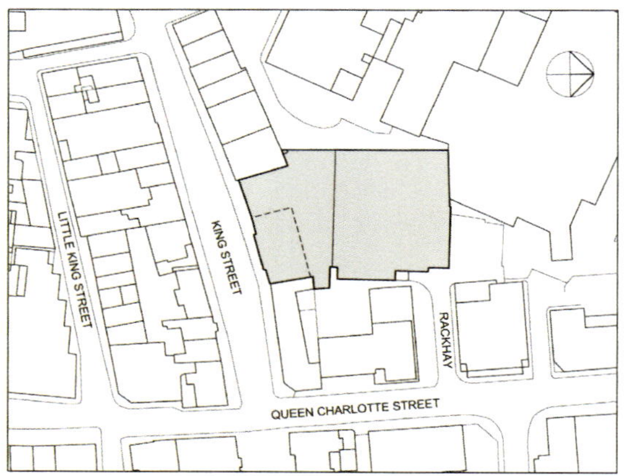


SITE PLAN - 1:2500

KEY
1 - STAGE
2 - AUDITORIUM
3 - FOYER/ BAR
4 - BOX OFFICE
5 - BACKSTAGE/ WORKSHOP
6 - DRESSING ROOMS
7 - WCs
8 - KITCHEN
9 - DIAS/ STAGE
10 - STUDIO THEATRE
11 - OFFICE
12 - VENTILATION PLENUM
13 - GREEN ROOF

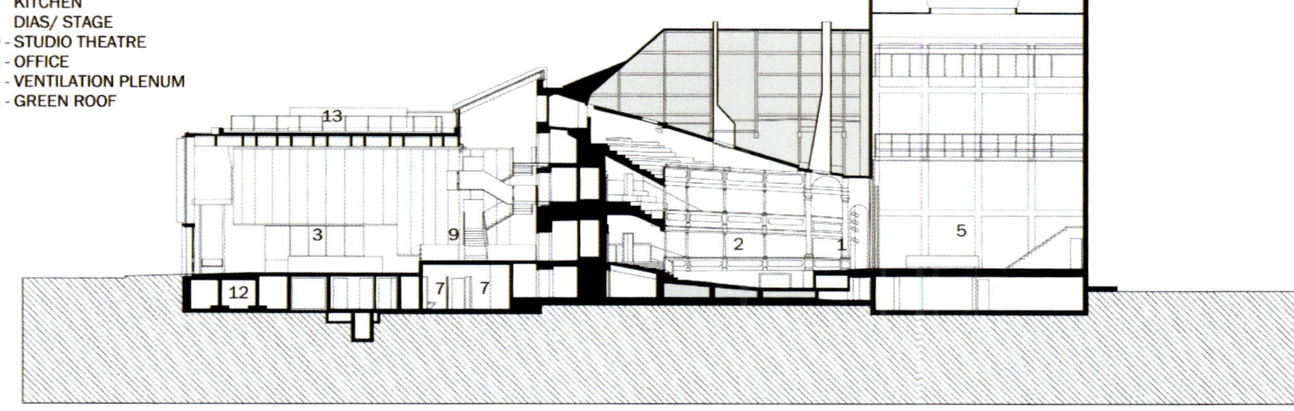


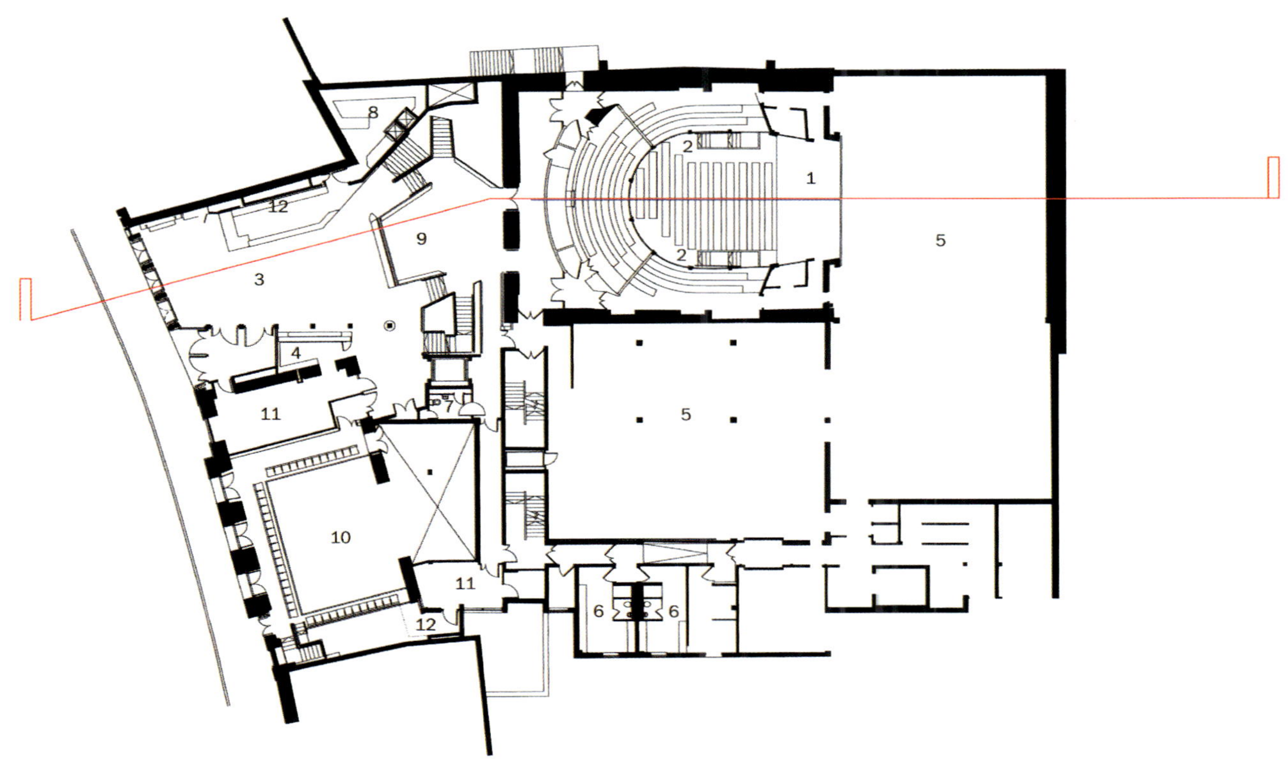


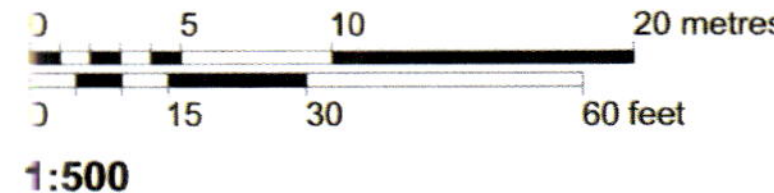

# Reference Project 32 Theatre Royal Drury Lane, London, UK

### Brief building description

The Grade 1 listed Theatre Royal Drury Lane is historically one of the most important theatres in the world. A succession of permanent theatre buildings has existed on the site since the mid-seventeenth century and the site has the longest record by far of continuous theatre use in Britain. The building is now used for large-scale West End productions.

### Auditorium type

End on proscenium format (see Figure RP.32.01).

Figure RP.32.01 Photo © Philip Vile/Haworth Tompkins.

### Design intent

The design aimed to restore the architectural quality of the building and enhance the audience experience, make the working life of the theatre more efficient and safeguard the future viability of the building by identifying additional or enhanced revenue-generating opportunities. It was intended that the proposals should promote access to this significant site for both theatre-going and non-theatre-going visitors, creating a destination venue (see Figure RP.32.02).

### Specific features achieved in the new design

The welcome and presence of entrances and approach to the building have been improved (see front of house discussion).

A major component of the technical refurbishment brief at Drury Lane was to redesign the stage floor for modern productions (see Stage House and Backstage).

### Key facts

**Client:**
LW Theatres
Dan Watkins,
TR Project Director,
65 Drury Lane,
London, WC2B 5SP

**Site address/web reference**
Catherine Street,
London, WC2B 5JF
https://lwtheatres.co.uk/

**Opening date**
Public reopening July 2021
Performances from August 2021

**Auditorium type and seating capacity**
End on proscenium format.
Seating Capacity: 1979.

**Stage/performance space size**
Main Stage 23.5m wide × 23.2m deep
+ Side stage SR 2x: 6.8 × 3m
+ Side stage SL: 6.8 × 6.6m

**Other facilities**
Grand Saloon bar, Cecil Beaton Bar and Rotunda Bar, open to the public during daytime. Offices, historic paint frame, ballet room, dressing rooms.

**Overall area:**
6,700m$^2$.

**Design team**
**Architect:** Haworth Tompkins
**Theatre consultant:** Charcoalblue
**Acoustic consultant:** Charcoalblue
**Structural engineers:** Conisbee
**Services engineers:** Skelly and Couch LLP
**Lighting consultant:** BDP
**Quantity surveyor:** Gardiner & Theobald
**Project manager:** Avison Young
**CDM adviser:** PFB Construction Management Services
**Fire Engineer:** Trenton Fire
**Access consultant:** David Bonnett Associates

**Transport consultant:** Alan Baxter
**Interior designers:** Alexander Waterworth Interiors
**Main Contractor** GTCM

**Construction cost at completion date** (excluding fees and VAT): £60 million

See *Sightline*, Autumn 2021, pp. 26–31 and Winter 2021, pp. 12–13.

**The nine figures** show the grand scale of the project. From **an initial image** (01) across the auditorium from the Grand Circle, **figures 02–06** focus on the public spaces of the café/bar off the foyer, the exterior portico from Catherine Street, the foyer restoration and the staircase. **The last three figures** (07, 08, 09) focus on technical aspects: the stage structure looking down from the Grand Circle towards the proscenium and stage, showing bars flown in for rigging stage lighting; technical staff dismantling elements of the demountable stage decks and supporting structure, using overhead hoists to assist with lifting; and looking through the stage structure, out over the Stalls, Royal Circle and Grand Circle.

Figure RP.32.02 Photo © Philip Vile/Haworth Tompkins.

Figure RP.32.03 Photo © Philip Vile/Haworth Tompkins.

**Front of house**

The foyer restoration (see Figure RP.32.04) is based on the work of Benjamin Dean Wyatt, the architect of the rebuild of the Theatre Royal in 1812, and it uses the full extent of the Wyatt footprint so that all audience members

Figure RP.32.04 Photo © Philip Vile/Haworth Tompkins.

Figure RP.32.05 Staircase. Photo © Philip Vile/Haworth Tompkins.

enter the auditorium through the Wyatt Rotunda and staircases – rather than a separate entrance for the balcony as previously. The original Wyatt design intentions, where feasible, were reinstated within the Rotunda, Staircases and Grand Saloon (see Figure RP.32.05). The foyer is now connected to a new enclosed space in Vinegar Yard, which leads to a new restaurant created on the ground floor of No.6 Catherine Street.

### Circulation and accessibility

Circulation routes into and around the building have been rationalised and the connection between foyer spaces and auditorium as well as accessibility for audiences into the auditorium have been improved and a new lift has been installed to provide step free access to all levels. Accessibility has also been improved within the auditorium, with wheelchair positions now on three levels.

### Auditorium

The decorative appearance of the auditorium has been improved while the shortcomings of the flat and cinematic 1920s auditorium have been addressed through modifications to the balcony fronts of the Royal and Grand circles, creating greater intimacy between audience and actor (see Figure RP.32.06).

The sightlines throughout the auditorium have been improved through adjustments at each level, including a re-raking of the seat tiering. Comfort of audience members has been increased by new wider seats with greater legroom than previously. Lighting, rigging points and power and data within the auditorium have been upgraded and better disguised while the overall technical facilities have been improved, including the creation of a new and extensive network of temporary cables routes, hidden from the view of the audience.

Figure RP.32.06 Photo © Philip Vile/Haworth Tompkins.

New, removable sections of the Royal Circle front allow access from the Royal Circle onto a raised deck which can be installed over the stalls area and stage to create other playing formats, including thrust and in the round.

### Stage house and backstage

With the existing stage rake removed and the historic substage machinery relocated, the stage has been levelled, a modular stage floor system has been installed and a demountable core substage area created out of demountable decks, beams and columns. (See Figures RP.32.07, RP.32.08 and RP.32.09.) The new stage system is installed within a large, re-levelled substage trap room approximately 5.8m below stage, extending almost the full width (14.8m) and depth (13.1m) of the normal performance area.

It is possible to create small and large openings of any size at either lower or upper deck levels for show machinery and set, including stage lifts and trap doors. The system incorporates unique features which allow the installation to provide Drury Lane with a high capacity, highly flexible flooring system that can be adapted to suit the various designs of prospective shows with relative ease.

Figure RP.32.07 Photo © Philip Vile/Haworth Tompkins.

Figure RP.32.08 Photo © Chris Dales.

Figure RP.32.09 Photo © Chris Dales.

New grid and gallery systems have improved access along with a new counterweight flying system. The backstage areas have been refurbished as have the building services.

**Users' verdicts**

I believe that the Lane is now one of London's most warm and beautiful auditoriums, and the most versatile historic theatrical space anywhere in the world.

Lord Andrew Lloyd Webber

For over five years, we have worked very closely with Haworth Tompkins to define, interrogate and perfect Andrew and Madeleine's extraordinary vision for the total restoration and reimagination of Theatre Royal Drury Lane. This has been a complicated project and HT have consistently risen to meet every challenge and, together, we have created something very special and peerless in British theatre.

Dan Watkins,
Theatre Royal Project Director

The changes made to the auditorium, stage house and backstage, alongside the new provisions to facilitate other auditorium formats and temporary productions, have enabled the theatre to accommodate the significant demands of the modern large-scale musical, to concurrently host weekly and one-off events and attract shows that match the scale of its stage and secure its future viability as the largest musical stage in London.

Chris Dales, Senior Theatre Consultant,
Charcoalblue

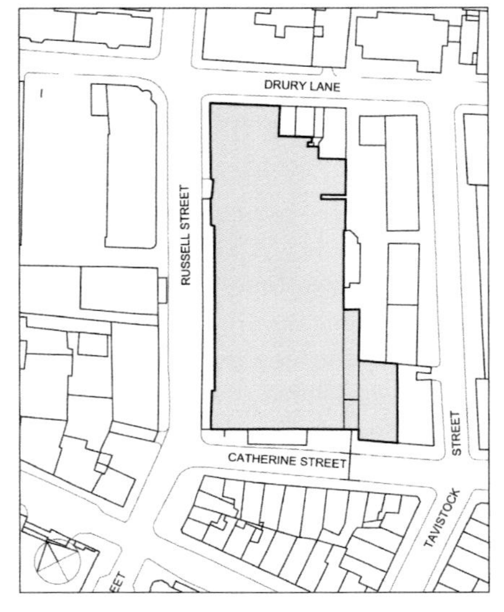


SITE PLAN - 1:2500

KEY
1 - MAIN STAGE AREA
2 - AUDITORIUM
3 - MAIN ENTRANCE FOYER
4 - GRAND SALOON
5 - TERRACE
6 - ROTUNDA
7 - ORCHESTRA PIT
8 - UNDER STAGE AREA
9 - BACK STAGE RUN
10 - PAINT FRAME
11 - BALLET ROOM

0 5 10 20 metres
0 15 30 60 feet
1:500

KEY
1 - MAIN STAGE AREA
2 - STALLS SEATING AREA
3 - MAIN ENTRANCE FOYER
4 - BAR
5 - STALLS EXIT
6 - ROTUNDA
7 - PRODUCTION ROOM & STAGE SUPPORT
8 - BACKSTAGE RUN
9 - PAINT FRAME
10 - LONG DOCK
11 - OFFICES
12 - WORKSHOPS
13 - DRESSING ROOMS

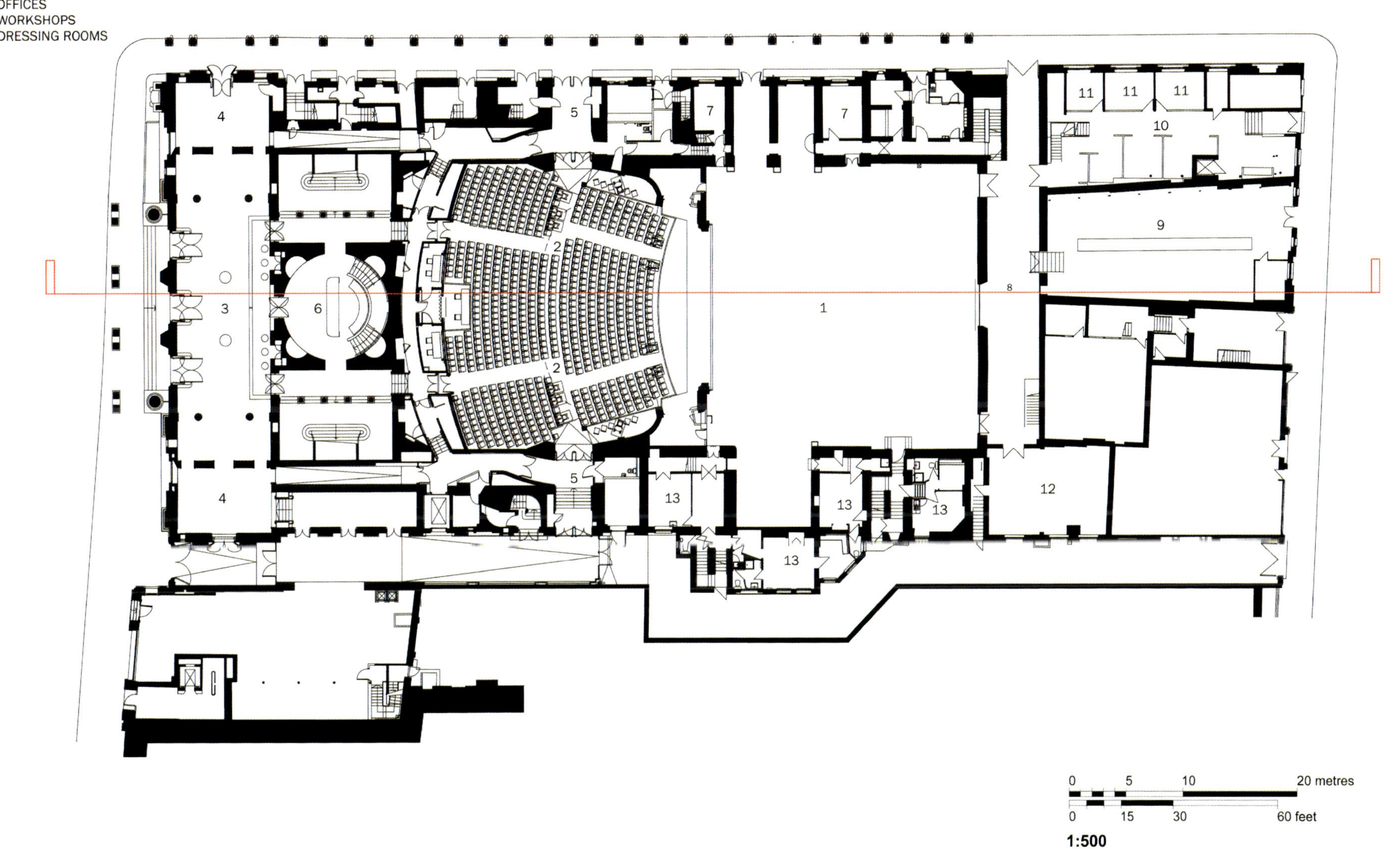

# Suggested further reading and helpful organisations

## Books

Ager, Mark & John Hastie, *Automation in the Entertainment Industry* (Cambridge: Entertainment Technology Press, 2009)
Appleton, Ian, *Buildings for the Performing Arts: A Design and Development Guide*, 2nd edition (Amsterdam, London, New York, Oxford: Architectural Press, 2008)
Coveney, Michael, *Master of the House: The Theatres of Cameron Mackintosh* (Lewes, East Sussex: Unicorn, 2022)
Fair, Alistair, *Modern Playhouses: An Architectural History of Britain's New Theatres 1945–1985* (Oxford: Oxford University Press, 2018)
Fair, Alistair, *Play On: Contemporary Theatre Architecture in Britain* (London: Lund Humphries, 2019)
Fielding, Eric & Peter McKinnon (eds), *World Scenography 1990–2005* (Taiwan: OISTAT [International Organisation of Scenographers, Theatre Architects and Technicians], co-published in London: Nick Hern Books Ltd, 2014)
Ham, Roderick (ed.), *Theatre Planning* (London: Architectural Press, 1972)
Ham, Roderick, *Theatres: Planning Guidance for Design and Adaptation* (London: Architectural Press, 1988)
Hannah, Dorita, *Event-Space: Theatre Architecture and the Historical Avant-Garde* (New York: Routledge, 2018)
Hardy, Hugh, *Building Type Basics for Performing Arts Facilities* (New York: John Wiley & Sons, 2006)
Holden, Michael (ed.), *Completed 2014–2018* (London: Institute of Theatre Consultants, 2018)
Holden, Michael (ed.), *Theatres Completed 2018–2022* (London: Institute of Theatre Consultants, 2022)
Joseph, Stephen, *Theatre in the Round* (London: Barrie and Rockcliff, 1967)
Leitermann, Gene, *Theater Planning: Facilities for Performing Arts and Live Entertainment* (New York: Routledge, 2017)
Mackintosh, Iain, *Architecture, Actor & Audience* (London and New York: Routledge, 1993)
Mackintosh, Iain (ed.), *The Guthrie Thrust Stage: A Living Legacy*. Published by the ABTT on the occasion of the 2011 Prague Quadrennial of Scenography and Theatre Architecture (London: ABTT, 2011)
Mackintosh, Iain, *Theatre Spaces 1920–2020: Putting the Fun Back into Functionalism: A Memoir by Iain Mackintosh* (London: Bloomsbury/Methuen Drama and the Society for Theatre Research, 2023)
Mackintosh, Iain & Michael Sell (eds), *Curtains!!! Or a New Life for Old Theatres* (Eastbourne: John Offord Publications in association with the *Curtains!!!* Committee of the Theatres Trust, 1982)
McCarthy, Bob, *Sound Systems and Optimization*, 3rd edition (New York and London: Focal Press, Taylor and Francis Group, 2016)
McKinnon, Peter & Eric Fielding (eds), *World Scenography 1975–1990* (Taiwan: OISTAT [International Organisation of Scenographers, Theatre Architects and Technicians], 2012)
Meadows, Donella H., *Leverage Points: Places to Intervene in a System* (Hartland: The Sustainability Institute, 1999)
Mulryne, J. R. & Margaret Shewring (eds), advisory editor Andrew Gurr, *Shakespeare's Globe Rebuilt* (Cambridge: Cambridge University Press in association with Mulryne and Shewring Ltd, 1997)
Mulryne, Ronnie & Margaret Shewring (eds), consultant editors Iain Mackintosh & Michael Reardon, *Making Space for Theatre: British Architecture and Theatre since 1958* (Stratford-upon-Avon: Mulryne and Shewring Ltd in collaboration with the British Council, 1995)
Ogawa, Toshiro, *Theatre Engineering and Stage Machinery* (Cambridge: Entertainment Technology Press, 2001)
Pilbrow, Richard, *A Sense of Theatre: The Untold Story of the National Theatre* (London and Barcelona: Wordville, 2022)
Pilbrow, Richard, *Stage Lighting Design* (London: Nick Hern Books, 1997)
Pilbrow, Richard & David Collison, *A Theatre Project: An Autobiographical Story*, published in association with Richard Pilbrow Design and the Theatre Projects Trust (New York: Aberystwyth, Wales and Plasa Media Inc., 2012; second edition 2015)
Raworth, Kate, *Doughnut Economics: Seven Ways to Think Like a 21st Century Economist* (VT: Cornerstone, 2017; new edition, New York: Penguin Random House, 2022)

Skene, Prue, *Capital Gains: How the National Lottery Transformed England's Arts* (London: Franchise Press, 2017)
Staines, Jackie, *Lighting Techniques for Theatre-in-the-Round* (Cambridge: Entertainment Technology Press, 2000)
Staples, David (ed.), with drawings by David Hamer, *Modern Theatres 1950–2020* (New York and Abingdon, Oxon: Routledge, 2021)
Strong, Judith (ed.), *Theatre Buildings: A Design Guide* (London: ABTT, 2010)
Todd, Andrew & Jean-Guy Lecat, *The Open Circle: Peter Brook's Theatre Environments* (London: Faber & Faber, 2003)

## Conference proceedings and articles

Collison, David, *The Sound of Theatre: From the Ancient Greeks to the Modern Digital Age* (London: PLASA, 2008)
Erridge, Simon, 'Up-front Carbon and Theatre Buildings', *Theatres Magazine*, Winter, 2022 (The Theatres Trust), pp. 24–26
Halliday, Rob, 'A Potted History of Solid State Lighting in Theatre (or, How We Learned to Love the LED . . .)', *Sightline*, Spring 2018, pp. 10–15
Hares, Tom, 'A Technician's Primer to Audio Description', *Sightline*, Spring 2015, pp. 34–37
Harper, Tom, 'The Theatre Industry and the Circular Economy', *Sightline*, Autumn 2019, pp. 39–41
Mehta, Prema, 'Stage Sight', *Sightline*, Autumn 2018, pp. 31–32
Morland, Rebecca, 'Theatres and Placemaking: A Report om the Theatres Trust Conference, October 2017', *Sightline*, Winter 2017, pp. 14–17
Pilbrow, Richard, 'Corona and Theatre: A New Journey', *Sightline*, Autumn 2020, pp. 8–16
Pottinger, Ali, 'Technical Theatre BSL [British Sign Language]: Putting Theatre into Good Hands', *Sightline*, Spring 2018, pp. 40–41
Ruthven-Hall, Peter, 'Designing for the Designer', *Sightline*, Summer 2016, pp. 27–35
Sharpe, Melanie, 'Technology and Accessibility for d/Deaf Audiences', *Sightline*, Summer 2019, pp. 20–21
Theatre Engineering and Architecture, Volume 1 – *Engineering and Technology*, Theatre Engineering and Architecture Conference 2002, ed. by Richard Brett (London: ABTT, 2004)
Theatre Engineering and Architecture, Volume 2 – *Architecture and Planning*, Theatre Engineering and Architecture Conference 2002, ed. by Richard Brett (London: ABTT, 2004)
Theatre Engineering and Architecture, Volume 3 – *Operations, Safety, Cost and Risk*, Theatre Engineering and Architecture Conference 2002, ed. by Richard Brett (London: ABTT, 2004)
Theatre Engineering and Architecture, Volume 4 – *Stage Engineering and Technology*, Theatre Engineering and Architecture Conference 2006, ed. by Richard Brett (London: ABTT, 2007)
Theatre Engineering and Architecture, Volume 5 – *Planning and Architecture*, Theatre Engineering and Architecture Conference 2006, ed. by Richard Brett (London: ABTT, 2007)
Theatre Engineering and Architecture, Volume 6 – *General and Management*, Theatre Engineering and Architecture Conference 2006, ed. by Richard Brett (London: ABTT, 2007)
Theatre Engineering and Architecture, Volume 7 (DVD) – *Theatre Engineering and Architecture*, International Theatre Engineering and Architecture Conference 2010, ed. by Richard Brett (London: ABTT, 2010)

## Technical standards

ABTT, et al., *Technical Standards for Places of Entertainment* (London: ABTT, 2015; updated 2020)
ASHRAE 55 'Thermal Environmental Conditions for Human Occupancy'
BS 9999 'Code of Practice for Fire Safety in the Design, Management and Use of Buildings'
BS EN ISO 7730 'Ergonomics of the Thermal Environment'
Chartered Institution of Building Services Engineers (CIBSE) Guidance, *TM54: The Limits of Thermal Comfort: Avoiding Overheating in European Buildings*
HM Treasury Green Book, www.gov.uk/government/publications/the-green-book-appraisal-and-evaluation-in-central-govenrnent
RIBA Resources, www.architecture.com/knowledge-and-resources/resources-landing-page#
Royal Institute of Chartered Surveyors (RICS) Professional Standards and Guidance UK, *Whole Life Carbon Assessment for the Built Environment* (1st edition, November 2017)

## Climate emergency and sustainability

https://drive.google.com/file/d/1aXwiPcavsUKVYqw8kaS6Hok82GcM9k4K/view
https://juliesbicycle.com/
https://living-future.org/lbc/
https://theatregreenbook.com/
https://wearealbert.org/
www.passivhaustrust.org.uk/what_is_passivhaus.php
www.rics.org/globalassets/rics-website/media/news/whole-life-carbon-assessment-for-the-built-environment-november-2017.pdf
www.sustainablepractice.org.uk/wp-content/uploads/2012/12/Green-Guide.pdf
www.theatrestrust.org.uk/how-we-help/sustainability

## Disability inclusion

http://universaldesign.ie/What-is-Universal-Design/The-7-Principles/
https://assets.publishing.service.gov.uk/government/uploads/system/uploads/attachment_data/file/874507/family-resources-survey-2018-19.pdf
https://wearepurple.org.uk/the-purple-pound-infographic/
www.artscouncil.org.uk/publication/equality-diversity-and-creative-case-data-report-2018–19
www.attitudeiseverything.org.uk/resources/seven-inclusive-principles-for-arts-and-cultural-organisations
www.gchq.gov.uk/speech/director-gchq-makes-speech-in-tribute-to-alan-turing
www.rampsonthemoon.co.uk
www.scope.org.uk/about-us/social-model-of-disability/

## Social belonging

https://bac.org.uk/scratch-hub/
https://le.ac.uk/rcmg/research-archive/museums-and-social-inclusion
https://macbirmingham.co.uk/courses
www.theatrestrust.org.uk/latest/news/1058-conference-19-blog-stepping-over-the-threshold

## Designing for health

www.legislation.gov.uk/uksi/2010/2214/contents/made

## Fire safety

www.abtt.org.uk/product/technical-standards-for-places-of-entertainment/
www.fia.uk.com/resources/british-standards/bs-5839-series.html
www.legislation.gov.uk/uksi/2010/2214/schedule/1/made

## Helpful organisations

Association of British Theatre Technicians (ABTT)
Department for Digital, Culture, Media and Sport (gov.uk: DCMS)
Institute of Theatre Consultants (IoTC)
Royal Institute of British Architecture (RIBA)
The Theatres Trust (TT)

# Index

Note: This index includes the key issues related to the design, construction and operation of a theatre that appear in the text sections of this book, as well as special features highlighted in the individual reference projects. All theatres mentioned in the text, captions and reference projects are listed along with cited actors, architects, directors, designers, technicians and others. The design teams behind each of the thirty-two reference projects are credited within the 'key facts' columns, text and users' verdicts within the relevant project. All the editors, section editors and key themes editors and contributors are listed in the preliminary pages of the book and at the end of the sections to which they have contributed.

## A

# B

# C

# D

# E

# F

# I



# J



# K



# L

# M

# N

# S

# T

# U

# V



# W

# Y



# Z